EUROPEAN IDEOLOGIES

A Survey of
20th Century Political Ideas

Edited by

Feliks Gross
Brooklyn College
New York University

WITH AN INTRODUCTION

by

Robert M. MacIver
Columbia University

PHILOSOPHICAL LIBRARY

NEW YORK

Printed in the United States of America
By F. Hubner & Co., Inc., New York, N. Y.

Authors

GIUSEPPE ANTONIO BORGESE: formerly, University of Rome and University of Milan; at present, University of Chicago.

LEWIS COREY: Antioch College.

GEORGE M. DIMITROV: Secretary-General of the International Peasant Union; former editor of "Pladne," a daily published in Sofia; former deputy of the Bulgarian Parliament.

NICHOLAS DOMAN: formerly, College of William and Mary and Asst. Prosecutor before the International Military Tribunal at Nuremberg.

FRIEDRICH W. FOERSTER: formerly, University of Vienna and University of Munich; former Editor of "Die Menscheit."

RUBIN GOTESKY: Tulane University.

FELIKS GROSS: New York University; Brooklyn College.

SIDNEY HOOK: New York University.

HORACE M. KALLEN: New School for Social Research.

THORSTEN V. KALIJARVI: formerly, University of New Hampshire; at present, Library of Congress.

REGINALD D. LANG: Carleton College.

WACLAW LEDNICKI: formerly, University of Cracow, University of Brussels, Harvard University; at present, University of California.

ALGERNON LEE: President, The Rand School of Social Science, New York.

JACOB LESTCHINSKI: Institute of Jewish Affairs.

ALFREDO MENDIZABAL: formerly, University of Oviedo; at present, New School for Social Research, Ecole Libre des Hautes Etudes.

STEPHEN NAFT: formerly, Head of the Reasearch Dept. of the Office of Inter-American Affairs, New York.

MAX NOMAD: New York University; New School for Social Research.

GUNTHER REIMAN: author of *Vampire Economics* and *The Myth of A Total State.*

RUDOLF ROCKER: author of *Nationalism and Culture.*

JOSEPH S. ROUCEK: University of Bridgeport.

FRIEDRICH STAMPFER: former member of the Reichstag and former Editor of "Vorwarts," Berlin Social-Democratic daily.

PHILIP TAFT: Brown University.

ELIAS TARTAK: formerly, Cornell University and McGill University; at present, New School for Social Research.

VLADIMIR ZENZINOV: former Member of the Russian Constituent Assembly and Member of Russian Provisional Government; at present, Editor of "Za Svobodu," Russian weekly published in New York.

Preface

Great European conflicts are not purely economic, but are conflicts of ideas, as well. They have brought that continent to a point wherein statesmen and political scientists cogitate whether a sharp decline is inevitable or—as I deeply hope—Europe has sufficient strength to rise again.

Europe is the fatherland of great political ideas, just as Asia and the eastern Mediterranean are the fatherlands of religion. Ideologies born in Europe soon spread throughout the world.

The scope of this book is the presentation, in a synthetic-survey manner, of these European political ideologies; it is not intended to serve as an introductory textbook, but rather as a synthesis for those who are interested in, and familiar with, the rudimentary principles. This explains, therefore, why some of the well-known elements of these ideologies are sometimes either merely mentioned or completely omitted.

There are a great many books dealing with important European ideologies, mostly in an introductory manner. What is the specific difference between these books and ours? Firstly, as previously mentioned, this book is intended for the reader who already has some knowledge of the principles of the various ideologies; secondly, in most of the books, only outstanding ideologies are treated. Therefore, they generally discuss the same ideologies, and those which are regarded as being inadequately developed are omitted. We feel that such ideologies, although limited to certain groups or to certain countries, are still significant enough for attention. Thus, this book devotes a considerable amount of space to those ideologies which have not been given much consideration in other symposiums or anthologies. For instance, Communism and Fascism can be found in every textbook on European ideologies, but it is difficult to uncover condensed information upon European Pacifism, Agrarianism, Peasant Movements, Russian Libertarian Movements, Falangism Hispanidad, Panslavism, Pangermanism, and Peneuropeanism. Our hope is that this volume will fill this need. Obviously, there is a mountain of literature upon all these topics, all of which is well-known to specialists, but the need for a survey-approach to these ideologies was apparent from the start.

However, limitations of space forced us to select certain representative movements only. For example, Fascism and Nazism gave birth—or, at least, invigorated—numerous native ultra-nationalist and fascist movements. From the Baltic to the Mediterranean, from the Black Sea to Gibraltar, there were scores of Fascist fellow-travelers and barbarians. But we lacked sufficient space to deal with all of them, and therefore we chose only the Falangist movement as representative of the less significant movements of this type. This was the case, too, with other problems; i.e., relations between political ideology and religion forms an important chapter in political sociology. Unable to treat all of them, we chose Catholicism as an example.

It is apparent that a book of this type must, of necessity, have a good many shortcomings and, most certainly, those which are inherent in all anthologies.

Some authors utilized more space for their contributions than was originally intended. Mere editorial cutting was insufficient to adjust the technical problem of lineage to the importance of the topic. Since further shearing would have utterly destroyed the entire structure of the article, in some cases, we were forced to let it remain.

Every author, it should be noted, represents his own personal point of view which is not necessarily shared by either his co-author or the editor. Moreover, the reader will discover conflicting views emanating from two or more contributors. It should be remembered that it was not the intention of the editor to standardize the authors' viewpoints, especially as he shares, with Lindeman,[1] the conviction that social research cannot be entirely divorced from a subjective system of values. The editor has merely attempted to give fair representation to various and vary-

[1] Edward C. Lindeman, John J. Hader, *Dynamic Social Research*, Harcourt Brace, N. Y., 1932, pp. 93 et seq.

ing views of social scientists, all of whom have a democratic background. This explains, e.g., the different viewpoints expressed by Professor Borgese and Mr. Naft, on the one hand, and by Professor Mendizabal, on the other, in their treatments of Catholicism and politics; the differences between Mr. Rocker's and Mr. Nomad's articles on the problems of Anarchism; between Professor Foerster's and Mr. Stampfer's on German problems. Despite the democratic and libertarian views of all the authors, still differences exist between them, and, through Editorial Notes, we have tried to make the reader aware of these discrepancies.

The editor wishes to thank National Cooperatives, Inc., for its assistance in securing the excellent chapter by Dean Horace Kallen; also, Harper and Bros. for its permission to reprint Professor G. A. Borgese's essay "The Origins of Fascism," from *Democracy is Different;* "Commentary" for its permission to reprint Lewis Corey's "Economic Planning Without Statism"; Professor Hook's chapter "Humanism and the Labor Movement" was published in "New Europe!"

The editor wishes, too, to express his gratitude to Mr. Max Nomad for his editorial advice; his thorough, penetrating knowledge of European politics and his unfailing kindness was an invaluable aid in the preparation of this volume. Mr. Earl Mittleman and Mr. Haig Babian also provided very helpful editorial assistance, as did Mrs. Virginia Fane who had to cope with both the editorial and technical problems inherent in a volume of this type. We were almost drowning in galley proofs, page-proofs, index-cards and letters from our contributors when Miss Roslyn Ashman, and Mrs. Jerome L. Stein, Robert Grossman, Stanley Berger and Stanley Graber, enthusiastic students of Social Science from Brooklyn College came to our rescue. Their kind and friendly editorial cooperation permitted to complete our work on time. I wish to express my whole-hearted appreciation to all of them for their cooperation.

FELIKS GROSS

New York, February, 1948.

Contents

CONTENTS—Continued

Introduction

When Emerson wrote,

> Things are in the saddle
> And ride mankind

he had no prophetic intimations of the twentieth century. In our day it has surely become clear to every thinking person that mankind is now, whatever it was before, governed by ideas, activated by ideologies, and ridden by myths. And there is no such world-shaking ideology as that conceived by those who scornfully applied the term to all other doctrines except their own, and who themselves claim that ideas are nothing but the reflections of the "material," the "real," the economic forces. In our day, ideas have become the great instruments of power. Our proliferating idea-systems work on two levels. They are the springs of collective behavior, giving purpose and direction to groups and peoples and dividing them one from another. On the other level they are used by the men of power, who to win their ends must possess one art above all others, the manipulative art of the propagandist. Thus myths are converted into the techniques of control, as the editor amply reveals in the introductory chapter.

Accordingly, no area of knowledge has greater significance today than that which explores the idea-systems of our age. What we shall do with this whole apparatus we call civilization, what goals it shall serve, whether it shall be a means of liberation or of tyranny, even whether this civilization shall survive at all, depends on our changing responses to the appeals these idea-systems have for us. Yet there is no area of available knowledge so little explored, so little subjected to scientific analysis. We know relatively little of the development of these idea-systems, of their relation to changing conditions, of the validity of their compelling claims, of their consequences on our lives when they are put into operation. Idea-systems have been treated as a mere fringe of human history, whereas they are, or have become, its core.

This book is a contribution to that knowledge. It deals with European ideologies, but Americans have to realize, as again the editor points out, that Europe is the breeding ground of the economic and political ideologies of the whole world and not least of those that have most hold in this country. Moreover, the United States in its world orientation can no longer fulfil its responsibilities without a clear perception of the idea-forces that are moving or controlling other peoples. We are introduced in this volume to aspects of modern movements that are little understood by Western readers, such as the evolution of anarchism or the liberal tradition in Russia. The author in each instance is a serious student of his subject, who has lived as well as thought within the orbit of the idea-system he assesses for us.

There are differences of viewpoint in the volume; there are inevitably, since the editor is happily no censor of opinions, conflicts of Interpretation. Many readers, like the present writer, will have some reservations on the treatment of one or another topic. Honest differences of opinion are salutary, so long as it is the truth we are seeking. For then we shall respect opinions that differ from ours, and weigh whatever evidences are presented on their behalf. The sharp intolerance of conflicting ideologies is the curse of our modern world, ideologies that divide men into angels and devils, those who share our political gospel and those who reject it. It is the return of primitiveness, the primitiveness of persecution, in an age where we must live together and where this primitive mentality works deadly ruin. These ruthless ideologies deny in the name of the group all that humanity has in common, all the universal values apart from the recognition of which our differences become wrathful prejudices.

Back of all these movements lie surging human needs, human values, human aspirations. Some are more concerned with the liberation of the body, from privation, from penury, from exploitation. Some are more concerned, but usually where primary wants are already in degree provided for, with the liberation of the spirit, from the gross tyrannies of power or from the limits of cramping conditions. Back of all the Machiavellian manipulation of these movements by selfish interests and opportunist leaders there lies the eternal quest, however ill directed, for a better life in a better world. It would be the worst of ironies if that quest, because of the conflicts of ideologies through which it seeks expression, should be self-destroying.

No one can read this book without a widened understanding of the forces that are stirring and changing this distracted age. Not only will he gain a new perspective of the movements that impinge on us from without, he will also be in a better position to face the issues that confront us at home—in short, if he reads attentively he will be a better citizen.

ROBERT M. MACIVER

I.

The Mechanics of European Politics

I.

THE MECHANICS OF EUROPEAN POLITICS

by

FELIKS GROSS

Promise and Reality

THE GREAT TRAGEDY of European idealism lies in the discord between promise and reality. For one hundred years European idealists, radicals, democrats, socialists, anarchists, and communists, as well as writers, visionaries, and statesmen have reiterated the promise of a millenium of social justice, international brotherhood, and peace. The great dream of mass happiness was followed by a rude awakening: first, in a totalitarian, barbarian, cruel world and then in a world of poverty, destruction, and misery.

The Spring of Nations of 1848 has not yet been succeeded by a Summer of Peoples. Revolutions bred counter-revolutions; more and more blood was demanded by partisans and adversaries. What emerged from the struggle was, often, as different from the great promise as was the Inquisition from the teachings of the Apostles. Such was the case in the Soviet Union.

In 1918, seventy years after the Spring of Nations, European democrats and socialists gained control over most sections of Europe, and it appeared that at last the millenium was at hand. Then, an unexpected factor arose: a mass movement of unique savagery and cruelty barred the evolutionary road. A portion and, in some cases, a large number of people joined this movement. It resulted in Nazism in Germany and Fascism in Italy, both of which were disquietingly successful in advocating evil and anti-moral goals. Unhappily, evil is often easier to accomplish than good. Millions were slain and tortured, entire nations were destroyed—everything transpired exactly as had been promised. In this case, tragic facts reveal there was no discord between promise and reality. Nevertheless, the defeat of Nazism and Fascism was mankind's moral victory over evil.

Mankind moves toward a better and more just world, but the road of progress seldom possesses the even march of a military parade. Sometimes it is aggressive, quick to advance; on other occasions it is on the defensive and suffers setbacks. But sweeping changes and revolutions cheat neither history nor time. They often bring improvement after a long lapse of time, but rarely do they grant immediate relief. The road of progress is painful, and victories are usually gained at a heavy price.

Never defeated, mankind moves through tragedies, disappointments, hopes, and dreams, in its plodding advance to improve human relations. For millions of people a life which lacked the great ideal of happy, perfect, and just society would have little value; it would mean a life of vegetation only.

The true road toward progress, freedom, and social justice cannot be found in the elaborate charts of philosophers and ideologists. The deviation of ideology from the real route of life, from real social and political progress, is a phenomenon which accompanies human destiny as closely as the deviation between the compass and the magnetic North accompanies a traveler. This social and political deviation differs with each country, just as the deviation of the compass varies with the location. Sometimes, when the obstacles are great, it changes as suddenly as a compass hand when it faces a tremendous range of mountains.

The analysis of the structure of a political ideology reveals the significance of great visions and Utopias. There is a correlation between ideology, the social classes and their interests, and a strong interdependence between economics and politics. Nevertheless, political ideologies have influences of their own, as "idées forces," and contain, particularly, certain emotional qualities.

Political ideologies are often influenced by religion in various forms; certain rites and types of symbolism penetrate into politics, adding further to its emotional character and contributing to unification and cohesion of the political movement, just as they do to religion. Irrational and emotional elements form important factors in contemporary politics.

But despite these factors, and despite the fact that the lust for power often converts politics into a powerful implement for ambitious schemes, politics is not merely a cynical game. In the dark mist of human emotions and ambitions, a real struggle for human progress is fought.

Anatomy of a Political Ideology—Strategy and Tactics

A political and social ideology as a basis of man's *Weltanschaung*, employing Webster's definition of that term—man's attitude to the surrounding world and explanation of the purpose of the world as a whole—is a typically European phenomenon.

A political ideology is a system of political, economic, and social values and ideas from which objectives are derived. These objectives form the nucleus of a political program.

Political ideologies, although more or less elaborate, are more or less consistent as well. Some are only outlined, such as peasant ideologies of eastern Europe (with the exception of Russia); others, such as Socialism, Communism, and Anarchism are thoroughly elaborated down to the most subtle details. Often they form a complete, harmonious, and consistent system of explanation of the purpose of society and of the surrounding social, economic, and political phenomena. Setting forth dynamic and practical objectives to influence future social and political developments, they try—with a most ambitious design—to decide mankind's destiny.

A system of values and philosophy form an underlying part of ideology, but economic, social, and political systems are an essential part, as well. Derived from the system of values, they are closely connected with the underlying philosophy. Such well-developed methods as Marxism aid in analyzing a current, concrete historical situation, and build a logical political program as a consequence of this broad analysis. A political program, then, is merely the outgrowth of a wide, detailed ideology, such as socialism or communism, or a less elaborate one, such as nationalist or peasant movements. The program is a formulation of immediate and practical political propositions for the attainment of concrete objectives: social, economic, or political which, in turn, are derived from the entire ideology.

We shall call ideology with a program, an ideological system. The reader may find it advisable to follow the analysis of the structure of European ideology by comparing this text with the chart of the structure shown on page 7.

An ideology contains many objectives which could be placed in a particular order to assume a hierarchy of importance. The final economic or political objectives may envisage a complete change in society: a change in economy from capitalist into collectivist, as in socialism, or a change from a state into a federation of communes, as in the anarchistic ideal. Practical objectives, or reform objectives (termed simply "reforms" in continental Europe), deal with immediate changes and improvements, such as social security, eight-hour working days, protection of minorities, etc. Some movements lack any great final objectives or solutions, but their essence forms the practical goal or objective—the reform. Final objectives are a kind of social myth; reforms are closer to life.

Reforms often pave the way to the final objectives. The attainment of a higher standard of living, the limitation of working-hours—all these restrain economic exploitation more and more, and they form a portion of the final solution. The complete abolition of exploitation is the goal of social progress; it is the final objective of a democratic ideology.

The leading European ideologies have unfolded great visions —social myths—and attainable, final solutions in the form of in-

Table 1

STRUCTURE OF A EUROPEAN IDEOLOGICAL SYSTEM

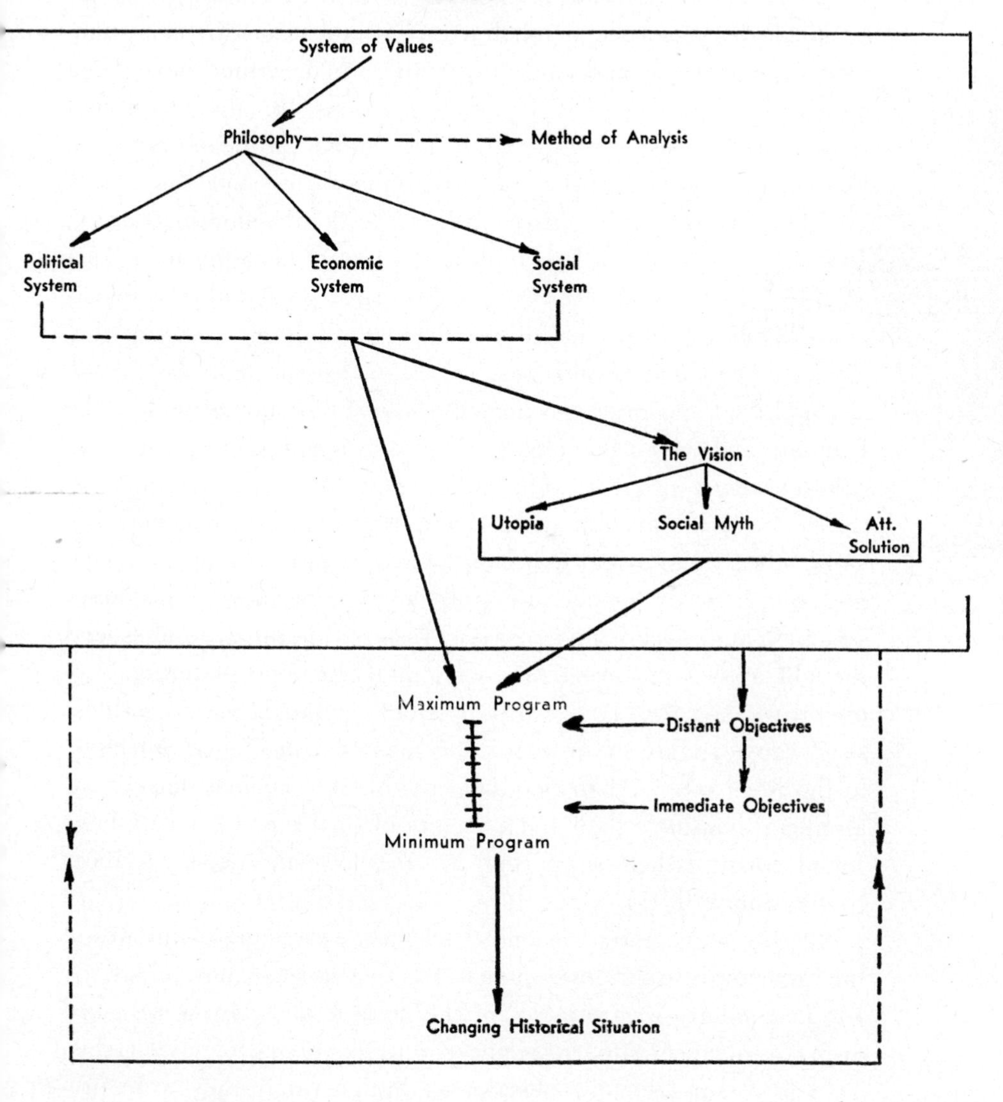

tegrated plans of social and political change.

Great political ideologies, political visions, and social myths, which effectively move masses of people are a European, urban phenomenon. None of the predominant political ideologies and social myths have been formulated outside of Europe. Great political ideologies are as much a European characteristic as symphonic music; no high-ranking composers of either have been born elsewhere.

Democracy, socialism, anarchism, communism, nationalism, French Jacobinism, radical agrarian ideologies and Zionism—all these originated in Europe. Just as Buddhism, Christianity, Judaism, Islam, and all great world religions were born in Asia and the eastern Mediterranean, so were all great political ideologies born in Europe out of that continent's misery, oppression, distress, wars, and revolutions.

From the viewpoint of a democratic and libertarian policy, the Utopian and visionary character of an ideology plays both a positive and a negative role, simultaneously.

The positive function of a social myth lies in its potentiality as an ideological stimulus. Utopianism contributed to the dynamic qualities of democracy and labor movements; visionary schemes and social myths have fostered political and social thought as well as practical social and economic planning. Cooperative, Socialist and similar visions contained moral values; they were capable of inspiring the masses to a higher objective, to the ideal of social justice and equality. Visionary schemes of an ideal, socialistic state and a society of justice and equality have found many ardent supporters willing to make high sacrifices for an ethical ideal.

But Utopianism and visionary schemes were equally important instruments in the development of totalitarian movements. A Utopian picture was painted for the masses, and they were asked to make sacrifices for it: sacrifices of freedom and of civil rights. They were brought to a peak of exaltation where they were prepared temporarily to renounce their rights for the sake of a remote idea which could be attained, their persuaders assured them, within a short time if they were willing to pay the price—a temporary sacrifice of liberty. Hitler asked for greater power for himself and his gang. He dangled the prize of a Utopia, a perfect German state. Each German resident would be a member of a privileged race (*Herrenrasse*) riding in a *Volksauto!* Hitler demanded that Germany's entire energy should be concentrated upon the attainment of this goal. In the Soviet Union, a temporary dictatorship of the proletariat—in fact, of an individual—was considered merely a transitory step towards a Soviet Utopia. "Wait five years—we shall accomplish that!"

Utopias, visions, and social myths formed an important stimulus for democratic movements, but they were equally successful in enlisting the support of the masses for totalitarian leaders.

However, the distant vision, the final solution or social myth must not necessarily always be a Utopia; a number of solutions which appeared to be Utopias were operated with varying degrees of success as practical propositions. A free association of nations was an age-old Utopia, and an unattainable dream, but the League of Nations and the United Nations organization became a reality. Today, world government is still a perfectionist dream, but its reality some time in the future can be safely predicted. A state without private industry was once regarded as a social myth, but this Utopia has been put into operation, as have states with combined socialized and private industries.

The social myth envisions the perfect society, a plan which may be removed from immediate reality and appears unattainable to the present generation; often, it is an attractive picture of a distant future.

There is little difference between *Utopia* and *social myth*: a difference rather in quantity than quality. Utopia contains more phantasy; it seems to be still more unreal and visionary than social myth.

Let us call a *practical, final solution* an attainable plan such as the transformation of a landowner's feudal state into a cooperative peasant state through radical land reform: this was a practical plan for Hungary. Or, let us use this term for the conversion of a Kingdom into a democratic Republic: this was an attainable plan for Greece. Thus, we can divide all political visions into Utopias, social myths, and practical, final solutions. However, it is extremely difficult to draw a sharp line between Utopias and practical, final solutions. A Utopia, put into operation, may prove to be thoroughly practical and attainable, while a final solution, on the other hand, may prove impractical and Utopian!

An architect before drawing up definite plans for, let us say, a Rockefeller Center, envisions this beautiful monument of twentieth century architecture. Then, after having conceived a general picture in his mind, he makes blueprints which are later translated into the reality of stone and concrete and organized into a harmonious entity.

Similarly, an economic or political planner first conceives a visionary plan such as, for instance, the first Five Year Plan. From it he prepares a practical blueprint with figures, statistics, and concrete proposals. Such a blueprint is later placed into operation. Even the cautious planner cannot definitely ascertain the outcome. Just as the paper-beautiful plans of an architect may produce, against his volition, an ugly edifice which will be outmoded within a few years, so a social and economic plan which appears logical, consistent, and harmonious may display glaring defects when translated into reality. Thus, a visionary, perfect plan—a practical, final solution may show serious deficiencies and emerge a failure instead of a success. More practical, less impressive, and less inspired plans sometimes prove more workable when attempted. In brief, practicability is the only true test of a beautiful vision.

Partisans of such well-developed ideologies as socialism or communism have developed essential and subtle distinctions between broad ideologies and programs. In European politics particularly, since they have been deeply influenced by great, well-developed ideologies for more than a century, this distinction is of real significance.

A political program is often a minimum, actual proposition—a practical outline of demands for change, for immediate action, or for the maintenance of a status quo. A political program determines political tactics; the sum total of an ideology determines the great political strategy.

Klausevitz[1] defines tactics as the use of armed forces in engagement, and strategy as the use of engagements to attain the object of the war. Hence, political tactics denote the use of political forces in a current, actual, historical, concrete situation for cooperation with, or struggle against, other political forces; political strategy is the use of tactical moves to approach the great ideological objectives, determined by the whole ideology.

Political strategy and tactics correspond to "policy-making" and practical politics. Programs and tactics change more frequently than ideology and great political strategy. The former are constantly being adjusted to the ever-changing social and political situation; tactics, especially, must be speedily revised and arranged to fit the current change and distribution of political power. Political ideology, on the other hand, evolves more slowly; it constitutes the constant element, unlike the program, which constitutes the changing and adjustable portion of the policy. Political strategy, similarly, is relatively constant because of its long-range aims, while tactics are altered continuously. Strategical moves, even in an aggressive policy, may employ tactical retreats which do not necessarily denote a change in ideology or strategy. In political, as in military strategy, a tactical retreat is sometimes an essential part of the strategy of attack. Hitler and his Nazi party accepted these tactics on the Polish issue; when Germany signed a non-aggression treaty with Poland in 1934, it was obviously only a tactical move. The agreement did not in the least signify that the great strategy of conquest of eastern Europe had

[1] Karl von Klausevitz, *On War*, Chapter I, "Branches of the Art of War," p. 62, Modern Library Ed.

been abandoned, nor that Nazi ideology concerning eastern European problems had been altered. The political objective remained unchanged: first, the conquest of eastern Europe, and then of the world. Detailed strategy was outlined. The road to domination of Eastern Europe led through the conquest of Austria and Czechoslovakia. Then, there would be time to capture Poland.

Therefore, the agreement with Poland was merely a tactical move devised to secure peace at the eastern border while conquests in the south continued. Many Poles who considered this an ideological change were proved wrong; Hitler merely enhanced his position for an attack upon Poland and Russia; political strategy and tactics, thus, were closely interwoven with military strategy. Modern history reveals that political strategy and conquest tactics are often combined with military strategy.

Inexperienced people often regard tactical moves as ideological changes. However, it is often very difficult to distinguish a tactical or strategical change from an ideological one.

When the United States and Canadian Communist Parties proclaimed their support of the free enterprise system, during World War II, it was actually only a tactical change. After the Allies took the lead and the enemy was finally defeated, Earl Browder was expelled from the Communist Party and its tactics changed again. But its ideology remained wholly unchanged, despite the dozens of books written by naïve observers who happily asserted that it had been transformed.

The Communist Party in the United States expelled Mr. Browder with a barrage of publicity; the actual signal for this step was given in Paris by Duclos, the French Communist leader. This fact alone constitutes evidence that the Comintern's discipline and huge network remained intact, even though, for tactical reasons, the Comintern itself was declared dissolved. It is too difficult to discover—especially in Communist movements—whether a change in program has resulted in a basic change in ideology, or whether this programmatic change is solely a tactical move in the great strategy of attack. A politician, like a chess player, must abandon an important piece, sometimes, to eventually win the game.

In all totalitarian movements, the distinction between strategy and tactics plays a vital role. The correct analysis of any policy change (ideological and essential, or merely a tactical move), is of primary importance to the victims of the attack. Totalitarian movements usually employ Machiavellian political methods of treachery, false propaganda, and deceit. Their leaders often display exceptional ability in utilizing the four essential elements: ideology and program—strategy and tactics. When they revise their programs and tactics, publicizing this as a change in ideology, they usually find a highly receptive audience, since their victims, desiring peace, fall into wishful thinking. Machiavelli wrote, over four centuries ago: "Alexander VI did nothing else but deceive men, he thought of nothing else, and found occasion for it; no man was ever more able to give assurances, or affirmed things with stronger oaths, and no man observed them less; however, he always succeeded in deceptions, as he well knew this aspect of things."[2]

Modern totalitarian tacticians utilize this identical Machiavellian device and are often successful for a long period of time, before final defeat overtakes them. They deceive with oaths and promise that, due to a complete change of heart and mind, they have abandoned their objectives and revised their ideology. Shortly after, what the naïve hailed and the propagandists publicized as a permanent, ideological change, proves to be merely a transient tactical retreat in preparation for a stronger attack.

It should be noted that programs and tactics may change, too, as a consequence of ideological development; such changes are of a more durable character and may represent a decisive change in the entire policy. In democratic parties the true nature of such changes is not a matter for secrecy and deceit.

When either a political party or a nation is forced to adjust her

[2] *The Prince,* Chapter XVIII, "In What Way Princes Must Keep Faith," p. 65, Modern Library Ed.

policy to an attack by a totalitarian movement, the analysis of tactics and program, of ideology or strategy is of foremost importance. Only a change in ideology indicates a lasting change in policy; programmatic and tactical changes mainly denote a struggle for a more strategic position for the final attack.

As previously mentioned, ideology is the most constant element; after it comes strategy which influences program and tactics. Tactics is the most variable element.

Table 2

POLITICAL STRATEGY AND TACTICS

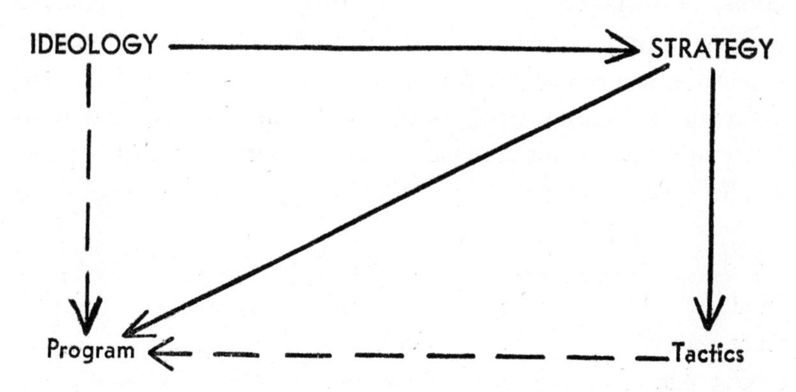

In ideology, again, the system of values forms the most constant element. Often, movements which have a certain degree of similarity in tactics, and even in deeds, vary completely in their systems of values. This fact may be of vital importance from the historical point of view.

Both Fascist and Communist movements are totalitarian and anti-democratic; both employ extreme terrorism as governmental instruments. Yet, an essential difference exists between the systems of values. In the Communist movement, the system of values is ethical, in a judeo-christian sense, while in Nazism the system of values is anti-ethical. The Communists base their system of values on the equality of man and universalism; good means help the weaker and bad means exploit the weaker. Perversely, Nazism, beside being anti-ethical, is anti-universalist and anti-equalitarian. The Nazi system of values extols the virtues of exploiting and eliminating the weaker.

The Communist system of values differs from the democratic in that it lacks the essential elements of freedom and recognition of this freedom for any political minority. As the Catholic church retained its system of values during the inquisitions of Torquemada, so has the modern Communist retained his. Communism follows the principle that the ends justify the means. Accordingly, in order to attain the objectives it has derived from this system, it has chosen strategy and tactics entirely contrary to its set of values: its means are often unethical. The conflicts between the ends and the means, and between the system of values and the practical policy which repudiates it, defeats the entire ideology. Instead of becoming increasingly libertarian, Communism is steadily growing more and more despotic. Ferdinand Lasalle wrote in "Franz von Sickingen":

> Das Ziel nicht zeige, zeige auch den Weg
> Denn so verwachsen sind hienieden Weg und Ziel
> Dass eines sich stets ändert mit dem andern,
> Und anderer Weg anderes Ziel erzeugt.
>
> Do not show the end—show me also the road.
> The road and the end are so imbedded
> That one always changes with the other,
> And a different road produces a different end.

The Psycho-Political Mechanism of Mass Movements—Peasants and Workers

Some European political movements had well-developed ideologies, while the systems of others were less elaborate. Socialist, Communist, Catholic, and nationalist movements had their theories, histories, and detailed analyses presented in books, dailies, weeklies, monthlies, and quarterlies. Political theorizing flourished in Europe for a century, and often assumed a dogmatic, semi-religious character. This is particularly true of Germany, as well as of those countries which she influenced.

Eastern European peasant movements—excepting Russia's—had a simple, concrete ideology. In fact, they had more program than they did ideology and philosophy. City ideologies, those of the urban masses, always had certain elements of Utopianism in Europe. To win over these people it was always necessary to depict a Utopian picture—a kind of practical vision—of a happy, perfect society in the future. Utopian Socialists painted a roseate picture, and Marx gave it a scientific, analytic background.

The European labor movement attracted hundreds of writers, economists, sociologists, and philosophers of an extremely high academic and scholarly caliber. Thus, the labor movement has brought forth notable scientific and artistic literature.

The peasant movements lacked a general *Weltanschaung,* a background philosophy of their own, as the Socialist and Catholic movements possessed. There were efforts to formulate a general philosophy of the peasant movement, particularly in Bulgaria and Czechoslovakia, which emphasized agrarianism; but these never attained international significance.

Russia was the sole country in which, due to the *Narodnaya Volya* and, later, the Social Revolutionaries, philosophical and theoretical backgrounds of the peasant movement reached their heights. The Russian radical peasant movement had a rich, well-developed humanistic ideology which influenced eastern Europe, especially the Balkans, but never attained the international significance among the peasants that socialism did among the workers. Eastern European peasant movements were not Utopian, and they never developed any social myth of a perfect state as did the urban movements.

The program of eastern European peasant movements was very simple and pragmatic. The partitioning of large estates and land reform, combined with a cooperative system, formed the nucleus of their economic program. Cooperatives in dairies, in ownership of machinery, consumer cooperatives, and then electrification, tariff problems, and road construction were all clear, utilitarian objectives. Their political problem, too, was concrete and completely devoid of phantasy and imagination. It was a practical proposal of a democratic self-government and a democratic, parliamentary rule—a government controlled by elected representatives of the people.

The peasant population is and was the natural sphere of agrarianism. Although urban communities are an equally essential element of the state, the peasant movements did not concern themselves with this portion of the population, and limited their interests to rural districts. The radical peasant movement developed its own theory of class society presenting the peasants—and justifiably—as a distinct social class. The conflict between city and country was often over-emphasized and overshadowed the real issues.

It is true that such conflicts sometimes existed, but there were methods of solution. Most important, perhaps, was the problem of "economic scissors," the low price of food and the high price of industrial products. The ideology of urban and rural conflict was not limited to Bulgaria or to Stambuliski and his party; in eastern European peasant movements this concept also had its followers. Most of the leaders, however, recognized the necessity of cooperation and harmony between the peasants and the townspeople. In fact, during the thirties the peasant and labor movements in eastern Europe collaborated closely in their struggle for political democracy, as well as in their resistance against domestic dictators and foreign invaders.

After 1930, the town-versus-country theory assumed less importance than ever among the peasants; the concept of a lasting political alliance between peasants and workers became more and more an axiom of the democratic policy of both movements. On occasions, this idea has been converted into a reality. Being the sole chance for a lasting democratic system, it is the contemporary trend in labor and peasant politics in eastern Europe.

At times, some of the peasants turned to such fascist or reactionary movements as Lappo's in Finland, Dolfuss' in Austria, and others in Slovakia. However, these were exceptional cases; most of the peasants clung to their peasant parties which supported democracy in eastern Europe. This was equally true in Poland, Roumania, Yugoslavia, Hungary, Lithuania, and Bulgaria.

No philosophical background, masterly technique, refined social and economic analysis, or glowing picture of a perfect future in a Utopian state was contained in the eastern European, non-Russian agrarian movements. Peasant programs were clear, simple, concrete, and practical. They touched, above all, upon the most vital part of peasant life: the land. The land and freedom were shaping the destiny of the peasants, and agrarian programs were down-to-earth political and economic plans, perfectly attuned to the peasants' minds.

Peasant leaders were realistic and practical, not dreamers; often shrewd, they possessed strong personal ambitions. Nor did they have the time and desire to read and write long theoretical treatises on various ideological problems. The peasant weekly paper lacked political and philosophical theories; it was a paper for the peasants, not for analytical intellectuals or visionary workers. It was a practical feet-on-the-ground movement which disdained ivory towers.

Unlike the peasant parties, the workers, urban, Socialist, and Communist movements all combined a fully-developed political philosophy of their own; a philosophy which determined their entire attitude toward the world, toward social, economic, political, and moral problems and toward cultural problems as well. Both movements developed sociological and economic methods of analyses. Elaborate plans for a new and better social and economic order were drafted.

The Socialist movement in Europe is rather an old phenomenon; its roots touch the French Revolution and Babeuf. Before 1848 a labor-Socialist theory and a strong and militant working class were already in existence. Even then, a Socialist plan for a perfect society was well-developed, presenting an idealistic picture of a rosy world of social justice and happiness; this was their important *idée force,* as Fouillé would have termed it. Such great scholars and philosophers, economists and social scientists as Marx, Engels, Owen, Fourier, Saint-Simon, Proudhon, Blanc, Blanqui, Robertus, Bakunin, and Kropotkin, whose writings changed whole ways of thinking, devoted their entire lives to the cause of the oppressed and exploited working classes. The workers by then were a young and dynamic force, while the peasants in eastern Europe were, in the main, awaiting their liberation. Powerful as they were and still are, at present, no peasant movement has produced a Marx, an Engels, or a Saint-Simon.

Eastern European peasantry was emancipated in the middle of the nineteenth century; in Russia, this event took place in the second half of that century, at the same time as the abolition of slavery in the United States. The European version of slavery, century-long servitude, had reduced the peasants to a passive mass. At the latter half of the nineteenth century the Socialist labor movement was full-grown and making forcible strides. In Russia, Poland, and Hungary, at this period, the peasant was still bowing low, cap in hand, when the landlord's carriage passed him on the highway. He still addressed him as "Excellent Lord," and the latter condescendingly used "Thou" to him.

But the peasants were not liberated by their own efforts. Industrial development—the rise of capitalism, in particular—and the need for more factory workers all favored emancipation. The real pressure came from radical circles in the cities. True, peasant uprisings occurred, but they did not breed and foster permanent, political peasant movements for liberation. The insurgents were cruelly punished, and the movements died abortively. Only misty traditions and beautiful peasant songs remained to perpetuate the memory of these hero-martyrs. Eastern European serfs did not gain freedom from their own struggles for liberty. Even after their emancipation, a socially feudal relationship between the peasantry and the gentry existed for decades. However, when the younger generation came of age in the twentieth century, peasantry became more aggressively dynamic in its battle for political rights.

The industrial workers, although a new, young class, were influenced by the older patterns and traditions of the artisans, guilds, and crafts. European craftsmen were free men, and they knew how to fight and defend their cherished freedom in the streets of the medieval cities. Some industries, such as masonry and salt mining, remained almost unchanged after the industrial revolution; new inventions did not make as substantial a change in production conditions in these industries as they did in textiles or steel. In the former, the workers preserved their old organization and old traditions, and their memories of freedom and independence, thus influencing other industrial workers.

These are some of the differences between the peasants and the workers in Europe; another essential variation was in their social psychology. Although renouncing their former passive role, after World War I, eastern European peasants were still slower to act than the workers, who frequently struck for political, as well as economic, reasons. The peasants, never "trigger-happy," were slow, difficult to move and, through the experience of long centuries, politically suspicious of chicanery and exploitation. But, once roused, it was difficult to stop the avalanche. (This was demonstrated by the peasant strikes and resistance in eastern Europe.) The deeply religious peasants hoped for paradise in Heaven, but never dreamed of attaining it on earth. Disinterested in social Utopias and perfectionist plans, they searched for an essential political freedom. In the village community that signified, above all, freedom from annoyance by the village policeman and his superiors, as well as by the tax office; it also signified freedom to elect their own representatives who would control the state and pass legislature to benefit the common man and improve the peasant's lot. The importance of control to the peasant cannot be over-emphasized. As previously mentioned, they were justifiably suspicious. When their suspicions turned to those "officials in the capitals who were probably stealing money," they were often not correct in their assumptions. But the peasant was completely correct in his judgment that the lot of the common man, unfortunately, was seldom the primary interest of the "higher ups," particularly in times of dictatorial rule. Still, he remained patient, and this very patience of the peasant became as proverbial as his stubbornness.

European workers, on the other hand, had imagination and alertness. Although concrete and practical in their struggle for an eight-hour working day, higher wages, and social security, they still dreamed of an entirely new world free from economic exploitation and inequality—a world of political freedom and happiness. Purely economic demands were, and still are, necessary, since workers in Europe have always suffered economic hardship; but they sought more than this. The workers longed for a great phantasy of a better world, a plan for a perfect society, for a new order, for—paradoxical as it appears—a practical Utopia, some of whose elements would be attainable. Great Utopias have always inspired the workers and the urban population in Europe, unlike the peasants who moved slowly and patiently until the stifling hunger for land and bread gave them the indomitable will to fight oppression and terrorism.

Some mention of the comparative lives of the worker and the peasant should be made: a peasant is independent, self-employed, not threatened by unemployment; no manager or employer wields power over him, and he belongs to no elaborate hierarchy in personal economy similar to the industrial hierarchy in every European factory which starts with the foreman and finishes with the "general-director." Necessarily, the factory system limits the freedom of a worker since for most of his working-day he is dependent upon his superiors and, constantly, he is threatened by unemployment. The life of a worker has all the gloom of a factory district, over-crowded city, or slum. The pressure of his environment is so unbearable that the European worker seeks liberation from all its drab unhappiness in a perfect, shining world. As much as he desires immediate improvement, he would also appreciate a complete change in living conditions; this was and, for the main, still is the European worker's hope.

The Intelligentsia and the Middle Class

Nationalism developed a "social myth" and a philosophy of its own.

The struggle against national oppression and foreign yokes is a struggle for liberation. It is closely connected with a democratic political and social program. But exaggerated nationalism in Europe always was, and still is, an anti-ethical, anti-democratic phenomenon. European nationalism is a kind of exaggerated national egotism and narcissism linked with brutal intolerance toward other nations, particularly toward national minorities.

The Nazi or Fascist state was a nationalist Utopia which promised paradise for the favored nationals and hell for their neighbors and other nationals. Nazism developed an intricate, unscientific, and anti-ethical ideology expressed in pseudo-scientific terminology. However, all the elements of this ideology were thoroughly developed: a system of values, a philosophical background, an economic, social and political system and, finally, a concrete program. The distinction between tactics and ideology, and tactics and strategy was an important element in the aggressive Nazi and Fascist policies, both domestic and foreign.

The political system of hierarchy and of dictatorial, despotic rule was particularly well-developed in the Fascist and Nazi systems. Fascism evolved a brutal concept of power which became an integral part of both parties' ideology.

Socialist and Communist movements in Europe were labor movements, basically; they were movements of industrial workers. Peasant movements, obviously, were movements of the peasant population. But Fascism and Nazism were more complicated phenomena. Orthodox Marxists treat them as huge capitalistic plots, but this is disproved by the fact that although capitalists and big business gave strong support to these movements throughout Europe, both movements were essentially of the masses. Capitalistic support alone is not to blame. Both movements had considerable historical background and were actually political movements of the middle classes. They were supported by thousands of petty public officials, army officers, professional men, teachers, the bureaucracy, a great many members of the liberal professions, and the European social stratum called the "intelligentsia," which, on that continent, embraces a goodly number of white-collar workers. It would be unjust to accuse all the "intelligentsia" of having supported Nazism and Fascism; many outstanding examples exist of their struggle for democracy against barbarian totalitarianism. On the other hand, large groups of professional people—teachers in Germany; students in Germany, Italy, Poland, and Roumania; the bureaucracy, officers, often even the clergy in Spain—extended mass support to Fascist movements.

Many ideologists prefer party division to coincide neatly and simply with social and economic division. Social reality, however, differs somewhat. In labor movements we often find many members of the "intelligentsia." But we can discuss *majorities* in political movements. Assuredly, Socialist and Communist movements always contained large groups of the "intelligentsia," but the masses—the great majority were workers. Those who watched Hitler's troops marching through the streets of German cities are aware that part of the workers joined the Nazi movement, too. This fact is often discarded in favor of pure theory and simplification. However, although Fascism and Nazism had a limited following among the working classes, the middle class and the "intelligentsia" formed a majority or, at the least, a significant, leading, large group of its membership.

In a certain sense, Nazism and Fascism were counter-revolutions of the middle class and the "intelligentsia," still employing the European meaning of this word. Fascist movements, too, attracted large numbers of dissatisfied war veterans. All over Europe the *frontsoldaten* flocked to Fascist and Nazi movements, as former officers and non-commissioned officers have always played an important role in all totalitarian movements. Soldiers who spent their youth fighting were often unable to complete their studies; those who remained civilians often were in a more advantageous position in commercial and business competition, since they had had the benefits of longer education and training. Demobilized officers and petty officers, particularly, were embittered and disappointed with civilian life and their relatively unimportant roles as civilians. They lacked any G. I. Bill of Rights to secure a fair chance for them and, simultaneously, to alleviate the dangerous social tension. These men had grown accustomed to power during the war; they had command of troops and made daily life and death decisions; they were hailed as heroes.

Mussolini promised to replace them in their former glorious positions. Glamorous uniforms—military discipline—these were familiar and dear to their hearts. Mussolini and Hitler cleverly knew how to play upon their imaginations. And, beside this, it must be recalled that historical background was ample and played a significant role in both cases.

In eastern Europe, university students were an important factor. Universities there, formerly centers of democracy and liberalism, became hotbeds of reaction, nationalism, and Fascism, after World War I. Reactionary tendencies were strong among university professors and, with only a few exceptions, equally prevalent among the students. This was the situation in Germany, Roumania, Poland, and Lithuania. After World War I, liberal student organizations were in the minority, and at student meetings, liberal and leftist students were frequently brutally beaten by reactionary students.

Most social scientists seem to have overlooked the fact that at the end of the nineteenth and, especially, during the twentieth century, a new social class was rising in Europe: the "intelligentsia," comprising public officials, professional men and women, teachers, trained technicians, journalists, etc.

In 1889, in *Bernstein und das Sozialdemokratische,* Karl Kautsky noted the sudden growth of the intellectual classes. Between 1882 and 1885 the number of workers grew 62% in Germany, while the number of intellectuals increased by 118.9%. Lewis Corey discovered a similar trend in his penetrating studies of the United States. Between 1870 and 1940, the working class was augmented almost eight times its former size in the United States, while the middle class multiplied itself sixteen times, L. Corey states in his article, "Middle Class," [published in the Spring, 1945, issue of *Antioch Review*]. These "new functional groups," as he terms them, comprised technicians, managerial employees, salaried professionals, and a great portion of white-collar workers. This new middle class, the "intelligentsia" of Europe, was not only influential but numerically important, as well. In Poland, for example—a country where only about 30% of the population was employed outside the field of agriculture before the war—"the intelligentsia," without including the officers corps and the clergy, embraced over 700,000 people in the thirties, while the industrial workers numbered about 800,000 out of a total of 4,217,000 workers.[3] The "intelligentsia," it is apparent, is not only a numerically great group in Europe, but it controls the most crucial elements in her social life: the government, the courts, schools, economic life, industry, and public opinion.

At the end of the nineteenth century, the political and social potentialities of this new class were pointed out by the Polish revolutionist, Waclaw Machajski, who wrote mainly in Russian. In *Umstevyenni Rabochi* (The Intellectual Worker), illegally published in Siberia in 1899, he attributed the conciliatory, "reformist" policies of the Socialist movement to the middle-class character of its leadership. That leadership consisted of either the college-bred offspring of the middle and lower middle classes, or of self-educated ex-workers; it constituted part of a new middle class with higher education as its specific "capital"—the source of its income that was actually or potentially higher than that of the manual workers. According to Machajski, that leadership util-

[3] Feliks Gross, *The Polish Worker*, Roy Publishers, N. Y., 1945, pp. 250-256.

ized the labor movement in the interests of its own class, for which it was attempting to find a place in the capitalist sun through the extension of democratic institutions. Democratic socialism, attainable by the gradual introduction of a system of government ownership was, in his opinion, merely the final step in the emancipation of this new social group which was slated to become the new ruling class, after the elimination of the private capitalist owner. Thus, he prophetically anticipated the new class rule which was to be established in Russia nearly two decades later, although he did not foresee its subsequent totalitarian character. (It is beside the point a little to note that Machajski was either unable or unwilling to draw the final consequence from his own theory; he assumed that only a *gradual* transition from capitalism to collectivism would lead to this new class rule, while the violent anticapitalist rebellion, which he advocated, would, by its own momentum, lead to the equalization of incomes and, thus, to the establishment of a classless society with equal higher educational opportunities available to all. Once he enlisted in Machajski's elite of conspirators, the professional revolutionist was thus endowed with a virtue of self-abnegation that was denied the professional labor politician).

The experience of the Bolshevik revolution and the conversion of erstwhile "proletarian" revolutionists into a new, privileged stratum of bureaucrats led Max Nomad, formerly a follower of Machajski, to draw his own conclusions from his friend's concept about the class character of the intellectual workers. These conclusions were largely inspired by Robert Michels' thesis on the inherently oligarchic character of all social systems. However, while admitting the inevitably aristocratic nature of any form of collectivism, whether "democratic" or totalitarian, Nomad receives an inherent revolutionary, disrupting element in the very tendency towards an oligarchic concentration of power in the hands of a restricted circle of super office-holders and managers. For various reasons, he feels, some groups of individual members of the educated strata are doomed to minor roles in the new collectivist-bureaucratic arrangement. Driven by ambition, lust for power, or resentment, these "stepchildren" are likely, sooner or later, to become rebels against their brethren, the controlling "white-haired boys." They will attempt to gain mass support by assisting the manual workers and lower salaried white-collar workers in their struggle for a fuller share of the benefits of life. Thus, Nomad applies Pareto's theory of the "circulation of elites" to the collectivist, "managerial" system, ruled by the possessors of a higher education; this system is characterized, on one hand, by class antagonism between the well-paid "knows" and the under-privileged "know-nots," and, on the other, by the permanent struggle for power between the "ins" and the "outs" within the ruling educated upper crust. In the course of this struggle each successive group of rebellious "outs" promises the masses, in one form or another, the realization of their dreams of equality of incomes and true democracy.

Ideas similar to some of those advanced by Machajski and Nomad were presented considerably later in the writings of James Burnham, author of the *Managerial Revolution.*

Some of those writers, however, overlook an important problem: the role of "individuals" from this class. Many political leaders from the intelligentsia could easily become "ins" at the price of sacrificing their ideals and convictions. But many of them choose to remain "outs," because they prefer adherence to their convictions—they would rather keep their ideals rather than surrender to the dominant ideology. Tens of thousands of those executed in Germany, and in the totalitarian countries — thousands executed in the Soviet Union — are mute testimony to the fact that moral values, ideals, and principles have played a tremendous role among those representatives of the "new middle class" of the intelligentsia. They prove that struggle for social and economic position and lust for power was not always the sole—and often not even the main—stimulus. Max Nomad, himself, belongs to that group who would not surrender to any form of totalitarianism for the reward of power and privileges, simply because he is against totalitarianism and considers it irreconcilably opposed to his democratic and ethical principles. Some of the authors who contributed to this volume preferred to remain exiles—"outs" rather than "ins," using Mr. Nomad's terminology. They preferred not belonging to the "elite," despite the fact that they might have easily climbed to the top during the process of "circulation of the elite," and there enjoy all the heady wine of power. That intelligentsia, the new middle class, was—and is—a new class in Europe today, it is true; but that this class struggled for power alone is only partially true. It is equally true that, right or wrong, members of this social stratum have always provided large number of those who, above all, were guided by their ideals and principles; and very often these were intensely high ethical principles and values which inspired them in their political struggles, encouraged them to sacrifice their personal happiness, liberty, and sometimes even their lives for what they believed was social or political justice or truth.

Machajski has obviously forgotten that thousands from this class devoted their entire lives to the cause of justice; they were guided by great ideals, rather than by personal greed and interest.

We are unable to avoid social stratification; division into social strata is determined simply by a divison of labor. Peasants, workers, and intelligentsia form definite social strata. The problem of democracy is not to permit any one class to establish a privileged, despotic position over the other classes; to the contrary, it must make certain that a peaceful cooperation between them is secured.

It is obvious that neither Machajski's nor Pareto's analysis offers any constructive solution. Even Nomad's brilliant and penetrating studies and observations were not intended to set forth any practical remedy for the problem. Lewis Corey, however, in his daring book, *The Unfinished Task,*[4] sets forth his solution: a staunch opponent of statism, the author proposes a democratic

[4] Published by Viking Press, N. Y., 1942, pp. 202 and 205.

organization of our modern economy which could challenge the workers and the "new middle class" with a project of cooperation by useful, functional social groups "in a constitutional set-up in which each of them gets definite but limited rights and powers over production in a democratic balance that prevents an absolute centralization of power in the state." In other words, he proposes "a constitutional economic order in large-scale industry in which managements, labor unions, and state are assigned definite but limited rights and powers that check and balance one another in democratic functional cooperation."

Successful cooperation between industrial labor, peasantry and the "managerial class," technicians and "intelligentsia" forms the crucial problem of our future economic and political democratic order. It is one of the essential conditions of democratic progress.

Economic Background of Political Ideas

There is an interdependence among the division into social classes in Europe, their economic interests, and their political ideologies. The Marxian materialistic school attempts to prove that ideology derives from the economic system as a sort of superstructure of it, and that ideological development is a consequence of economic changes. Changes in systems of production necessarily affect the social and ideological superstructure and, thus, political ideologies.

One of the most penetrating Marxian materialistic analysis of ideological development was written by George Plechanov, the leading Russian Marxist in his essay, *The Materialist Concept of History,*[5] based largely on Antonio Labriola's, *Socialism and Philosophy.*[6]

Plechanov agrees that economic materialism does not necessarily preclude historical idealism, and even admits that the for-

[5] George Plechanov, *Essays in Historical Materialism,* Eng. Ed., International Publishers, New York, N. Y., 1940.

[6] Antonio Labriola, *Socialism and Philosophy,* Eng. Ed., Chicago, Charles H. Kerr & Co., 1934.

mer is merely a variety of idealism. He grants the influence of economic changes over ideological trends, but states, in turn, that the economics of society are the fruit of human knowledge. In this sense only, the materialistic view appears idealistic. The economic system, however, that great robot fashioned by human ingenuity, decisively influences the history, ideology, and political ideas of society.

Plechanov rejects a pluralistic concept of "factors," a concept of many elements — ideological, psychological, and economic. Only the economic, the materialistic, is the great primary factor which shapes our history and ideology. He discredits any independent ideological factor which might affect the course of our social development, and with bitterness and uncompromisingness, he argues with the Russian "Populists" (*Narodniks*), who would recognize ideological elements as factors influencing our social development.

Briefly, changes in economics, production, and techniques are responsible for social changes, and division into social classes is a direct consequence of economic development, meaning division of different economic interests into different classes—often, this represents contradictory and sometimes irreconciliable economic interests. This variety of interests leads us to various social and political ideologies which correspond to various classes and various, differing economic interests. In short, this is the essence of the materialistic interpretation of our political ideologies.

Logical though it is, this interpretation is not wholly accurate. Despite Plechanov's bitter criticism of *Narodniki,* the economic factor is not the only one; Max Weber, too, brilliantly proves his point—the importance of ideology in our social and economic development — just as Plechanov has proven his materialistic view.

It is most assuredly true that the industrial revolution has created many of our industrial problems and originated, as well, a great many political ideas. Factories were erected, engines replaced much manual labor, new production methods replaced old artisanship, and the modern working class was born out of the new economic change. Modern, radical ideas have been evolved which coincide with their interests, and great visionary plans have been outlined to solve their problems. Socialist, anarchist, and communist ideology, as well as syndicalist systems and trade unions are closely related to the birth of the modern working class.

After the abolition of serfdom, eastern Europe's modern peasantry also developed a political movement and a general ideological background which corresponded to their economic realities and interests. A definite correlation between economic changes and political ideologies existed.

Ideas, however, possess powerful forces of their own which are capable of stirring masses and inspiring individuals to highest sacrifices; thus, ideas captured human imagination and crossed the classical Marxian class division. Workers transferred to Fascist movements; students and intellectuals joined various labor movements. By the end of the 19th and start of the twentieth century, the numerous revolutionary labor groups were largely staffed by students, intellectuals, and members of the "intelligentsia," all earnestly struggling for the ideals of the working class as professional revolutionaries.

Great ideological systems have strongly penetrated and influenced our economic life. Fustel de Coulanges, author of *Cité Antique,*[7] saw the entire economic and social life of an ancient city permeated by religious elements; de Coulanges strove to demonstrate that laws, social, family, and other institutions of Greek and Roman society emanated from religious beliefs.

Max Weber became the great master of the "ideological" school. In his brilliant writings[8] he has proved how strong an

[7] Fustel de Coulanges, *The Ancient City*, Eng. transl., Boston, 1900.

[8] Max Weber, *Die Wirtshaftsgetschichte*, München, Leipzig, 1924; Eng. transl., *General Economic History*, N. Y., 1927.

Gesammelte Aufsatze zur Religionsoziologie, Tubingen, 1922-23. A recapitulation of Weber's ideas, see—R. H. Tawney, *Religion and Rise of Capitalism*, N. Y., 1926. Also Penguin Ed.

Pitrim Sorokin, *Contemporary Sociological Theories*, Harper Bros., 1928, pp. 673-700.

influence religion has wielded over economic life (especially modern capitalism), and how legal institutions and other new ideas have contributed to a change of economic systems in more primitive groups. Weber did not sustain an anti-economic attitude, however. He was fully cognizant of the powerful role of the economic factor and the mutual interdependence of religions and economic phenomena. In his study of religion he tried to prove that western capitalism was moulded by Protestant religion and its ethics.

Economic change influences our social structure and ideology, but ideas do exert influences upon our social and economic changes; they are a potent political weapon. Man is stirred by strong emotion, and these very emotional and irrational elements are among the qualities of great, strong ideologies. Logic derived only from economics and purely rationalistic elements was never the sole creator of our history. In ancient Greek tragedies man was moved by uncontrollable forces beyond him; so, great historical changes caused by new technical discoveries and forms of production actuate modern man. Nor do our lives lack Shakespearian qualities: our historical dramas are motivated by such basic human emotions as love, hate, lust for power. Human ambitions and desires shape our history, just as they do Shakespeare's dramas. Macbeths and Henrys are always among us with their human ambitions, desires, hates, and loves, with their private lives a part of history; they change the courses of states and societies against the laws of human logic and reason.

Ideas as instruments of politics in the hands of men—above all, ideas as an integrative factor aiding in the welding of social classes, social groups into parties, defending their interests and contributing to the great emotional phenomena of contemporary life — who can deny that ideas are tremendously forceful elements? We who lived through the whole tragic experiment of Nazism and Fascism, who saw the imagination of the people captivated by posturing scoundrels, experts in treachery, jugglers of distorted concept—if we should forget the importance of ideologies as social factors we would be abandoning common sense and sanity.

However, as much as we recognize the influence of ideas upon our life, we must not underestimate the significance of economic change upon social structures and ideologies.

Religious Influences Upon European Political Ideologies

Great systems of ideas and visions have always penetrated deeply among European masses. During medieval times, religion was an all-embracing system of ideas which influenced spiritual life, art, politics, and all spheres of human interests and relations. Religious loyalty was a principal social loyalty. In the eighteenth century, national loyalty reached new heights; nationalism became the general creed, and a nationalistic ideology was developed which robbed the religious sphere of certain loyalties, as well as certain ideological functions. Various social ideologies arose and gained support. A new loyalty to the social class, to the proletariat, to a social creed, and to the socialist ideology became apparent. Ideologies based on religious and national loyalties clashed with those based on social loyalties; various spheres of human activity, although not always in direct contact with this new influence, were touched by it. Eventually, religion entered politics. Powerful Catholic parties were organized, social and political programs were formulated, and even Nationalist parties concerned themselves with "social problems" and devised Fascist ideologies.

The influences all crossed each other: religion influenced politics; nationalism and social ideologies influenced religion.

Religion had always played some part in European politics. Even one-time atheistic political movements such as communism, or religiously-indifferent ones such as socialism adopted, at their inception, many technical features which originated in the church. Techniques to influence masses—even the actual terminology—were borrowed from the church.

"Socialist Missions," patterned after "Catholic Missions," were special booklets designed to propagate the basic principles of socialism. Another example of religion's influence in politics may be noted in the phrase, "converted to Socialism," a term obviously borrowed from the church.

Religion infiltrated deeply into other ideologies. Nationalist ideologies tried to identify themselves with certain religious groups, and even used the power of the church for their own purposes. This was true of Russian nationalism (which identified itself with the Orthodox Church), and of Polish nationalism (which recognized Catholicism as an essential "quality" of a true Pole).

Like Judaism, European political ideologies often had a messianic character; this messiahship formed an element of all great European ideologies. Communism and Socialism promised to deliver the suffering masses from the evils of capitalism and economic exploitation, while national movements swore to preserve them from any foreign yoke.

Even European imperialism, to be truly effective in capturing public opinion, was forced to produce a messianic background. Rudolf Kjellen, European imperialist philosopher and ideologist of German reaction, wrote, prior to World War I: "Not merely a struggle for material profit nor the will to power, but a feeling of responsibility for a mission in the interest of Mankind forms the inner secret of modern imperialism."[9] Americans, however, unlike Europeans, are neither messianistic nor Utopian-minded; they are firm, feet-on-the-ground people. This is doubtless the reason why Kjellen was more prophetic in his European political chiromancy than in his American.

We mentioned certain religious practices and terminology which were appropriated by modern political movements. This influence of religious forms upon modern European political symbolism and ritualistic formulae has sometimes been overlooked.

[9] Rudolf Kjellen, *Die Grossmachte der Gegenwart,* Berlin, 1914.

Rituals and Symbolism

The beautiful Church of the Virgin of Guadeloupe (where a festival to her glory is celebrated each December 12th) is not far from Mexico City, at the end of the boulevard, Calzada de Guadeloupe; it is also near a great modern highway, a tribute to our motorized age. Only a few years ago Indians in full regalia danced their traditional dances for the Holy Virgin on this very day, offering her homage in this manner.

Before Archbishop Zumaraga ordered the destruction of the old Aztec shrines and temples, Mexican Indians danced here, too. (This, of course, was before the arrival of the conquerors). At that time, on the peak of Tepeyac Hill, just behind the present shrine of the Holy Virgin of Guadeloupe the temple of the beloved Aztec goddess, Tonantzin, stood. She was the Mexican Demeter, goddess of the earth and fertility, and the Indians danced homage to her. After the *Conquista* and the overthrowing of the shrine of Tonantzin, the hearts of the faithful were heavy with grief.

And then a dark-skinned Holy Virgin appeared to an Indian on Tepeyac Hill where Tonantzin's shrine had once stood. A beautiful cathedral was built on the identical site of the former temple of the good Mexican goddess; the ancient, cruel Mexican religion was supplanted by a new Christian faith. Tonantzin retired to the dim past, and Santa Maria de Guadeloupe now became the patroness of the Aztec's descendants. The old Aztec religion disappeared, but some of its rituals remained and filtered into the new religion. The Indians now danced for the Holy Virgin; their descendants have forgotten the old goddess, but the dance remains.

About 1531, when Juan Diego, the simple Indian first saw the Holy Virgin on Tepeyac Hill and listened to the celestial music, Mexico undoubtedly had some wise and intelligent Catholic clergy. They understood the attachment of the Indians to Tonantzin, and realized the social functions of the rituals were deeply-rooted in the Mexicans' souls. Rituals are an essential part of every culture; it is difficult to perpetuate religion in a somewhat primitive group without the aid of rituals and cults. They serve to remind the faithful of the significant elements of beliefs and morals. A nation composed of philosophers and intellectuals alone, could perpetuate a religion solely as an abstract system of beliefs, without any rituals or ceremonies. Durkheim[10] pointed out, in his analysis of religion, that one of the social functions of any religion is to unite and strengthen into cohesion to the religious system, the group belonging to the church. The rites and practices associated with this system are actually the "common representations" which aid in molding the religious group into a unified social group.

Primitive religion is strongly ritualistic. Sumner[11] wrote that the process by which folk-ways and mores are developed is ritualistic. Complete ritualistic submission to tradition, and extreme religious cooperation is strictly enforced.

Some of the intelligent, educated men who held important positions in the Catholic hierarchy doubtless appreciated the importance of rituals and the strength of primitive religions, long before their real significance had been recognized by modern social science. They hoped probably, that once Christianity was accepted, the old pagan beliefs could no longer harm the great teachings of the Old and New Testament, that the ritual was only a matter of form which helped to express religious feelings, while the content had already changed.

Former sites of heathen worship were chosen for Catholic shrines; pagan holidays were replaced by Catholic holidays; native gods gave way to Catholic Saints; and pagan rituals, if they survived despite the interdictions and repressions of the church —or if they survived because they were tolerated—perpetuated

[10] E. Durkheim, *Les Formes Elementaires de la Vie Religieuse*, Paris, Alcan, 1912, pp. 60-65.

[11] William G. Sumner, *Folkways*, Ginn Co., Boston, 1940, p. 60 and seq.

the new Catholic faith. Intelligent religious tactics utilized the vehicle of pagan rituals to foster Christian faith. There is substantial evidence that the early strategists of Christian conversion were aware of ritualism's important properties. The Midsummer Eve (23rd of June), or Midsummer Day (24th of June) were celebrated in Europe, long before the Christian era, by fire festivals.

"A faint tinge of Christianity," says Sir James Frazer,[12] was granted it by naming the midsummer day after St. John the Baptist, although the celebration existed long before. The attempt of the early Christian synod in the eighth century to halt these pagan fire rites were fruitless; they remained, but were now connected with Christian Saints.

This phenomenon is common and can be observed in many European countries such as Lithuania, in eastern Europe, which was not evangelized until the end of the fourteenth century.

This interesting technique, which we may term "ritualistic substitution," was, and still is the integration of an old ritual into a new, different system of ideas which has completely replaced the former one, to which the ritual originally belonged. New systems of ideas were exchanged for old ones, and the rituals of strongest vitality were integrated into the new religion or ideology. Means which were used for the advancement of mankind and accomplishment of good have been used also in history for the perpetration of evil.

The technique of "ritualistic substitution" is not limited solely to the history of religion; it has played a similar role in European politics, where certain rituals have been developed which contribute to organizational cohesion and strength of European mass movements. For example, May first is the Labor movement's great holiday, and throughout continental Europe minor labor holidays exist in individual countries. They celebrate the anniversaries of revolutions, uprisings, deaths of labor heroes, etc. Labor holidays have usually been celebrated after an established

[12] Sir James G. Frazer, *The Golden Bough, A Study in Magic and Religion*, 1-vol. Ed., N. Y., MacMillian Co., 1941, p. 609 and seq; p. 622 and seq.

pattern: mass manifestations and parades linked with mass meetings, the carrying of flags and party symbols, and singing. Many of these celebrations are detailed and rather elaborate.

May first was particularly popular among European workers. Established as an industrial workingman's holiday at the International Socialist Congress in Paris (1889), Mayday became a truly international European labor holiday. Originated as a general, revolutionary strike which would alert civil officers throughout Europe, it finally evolved into a festive holiday celebrated by workers in their best Sunday clothes. This gala Spring day celebration was, at the same time, an important reminder of the influence of labor in Europe; it was a method of refreshing and revitalizing the spirit of general proletarian solidarity. For the European worker, Mayday assumed the same importance on his calendar as Christmas.

When Mussolini and Hitler came to power they shrewdly realized Mayday's significance as a ritualistic holiday which had become part of the culture and common heritage of the European workingman. As such, it appeared the probable day for anti-Fascist and anti-Nazi manifestations, and declarations from democratic, socialist, or communist opposition.

Mayday, therefore, was a potentially dangerous day for the totalitarian dictators. Even if it were prohibited by them, its tradition would serve to recall the solidarity of the workers, their common interests and, undoubtedly, the need for a united struggle against Fascist oppression.

Therefore, both dictators prohibited Socialist and Communist parties and suppressed labor movements but—what is most significant—they kidnapped Mayday and made it an official, national holiday for Fascism and Nazism in Italy and Germany. They rushed the labor leaders into concentration camps and utilized Mayday, rituals and glamorous trappings included, as a manifestation of the new ideologies, Fascism and Nazism. In this way they hoped the old, glorious labor holiday and its accompanying rituals would become a useful vehicle for their new, barbarious system of ideas.

Like other labor celebrations, Mayday had its definite function. Labor holidays have always contributed to the unification of the labor movement and, as a common representation, they contributed an integrating force which welded the various categories of workers and organizations into a strong, harmonious, dynamic political bloc. Attempts by the Fascist and Nazi leaders to steal the working-man's institutions are typical examples of "ritualistic substitution."

An interesting phenomenon of direct ritualistic infiltration is that of the Orthodox churches into the Communist movement. This is indeed striking to the observer of Communist manifestations and Party holidays in the Soviet Union.

I witnessed the celebration of the October Revolution under the Soviet regime. A lengthy procession of people brought to mind a Catholic or Orthodox religious procession rather than a revolutionary march or a labor manifestation. Women marchers sang their revolutionary songs in the same dedicatory manner in which, formerly, they had sung religious songs; they carried the likenesses of members of the Soviet government and the revolutionary leaders. There was a precise, established order in which these pictures had to be carried: first, Stalin and Lenin, then Marx and Engels, and then the commisars of various departments, Molotov, Kaganovich, Berija, Zdanow, and others. Large pictures of Stalin, Lenin, Marx and Engels were adorned with ribbons, garlands, and wreaths; smaller ones were garnished with a few flowers or leaves. It was strikingly reminiscent of the manner in which the holy icons in the Orthodox church had formerly been adorned.

The October Revolution is celebrated in the Soviet Union just as Christmas or Easter is celebrated in eastern European countries. In 1940, several large Moscow department stores advertised chocolate and candies for the Revolutionary Holidays, just as this merchandise is offered at Christmas and Easter in Europe and in this country.

Liturgic rules, somewhat similar to those of the holy icons, even invaded the realm of art. A system of rules was outlined for painting portraits of Stalin, and were discussed in such articles as J. W. Kravchenko's "Stalin,"[13] J. Rabinowicz's "Pictures of Stalin,"[14] and many others. Kravchenko, for instance, discusses the proper method of painting the leader of the Communist Party in a composition wherein Stalin is one of the members of the group: Stalin must be placed in the direct center of such a picture.

Most of the inexpensive, popular pictures sold in the Soviet Union are portraits of Stalin and Lenin; seldom does one find the usual cheap prints of landscapes or typical scenes representing common events in the country's rural and urban life as, for instance, reproductions in this country of Currier and Ives prints. The themes of Russian paintings are reduced to the great leaders and to revolutionary history, just as in medieval times when the Catholic church was all-powerful, all painting was reduced, almost exclusively, to presentations of the Saints and other evangelical themes. Then, as in the Soviet Union today, there was a hierarchy in subject-matter; and, similarly—as Kravchenko recommends that Stalin be centered in any group picture, so, in medieval art, religious pictures observed the same "sanctissimum."

Symbolism was strongly developed in European mass movements. Extreme rightists and leftists parties both used it; probably the moderates were the only exception. The Fascists had their axes and bundle of rods, the Nazis the "hackenkreuz," the Spanish Falange a yoke and a bundle of arrows, the Hungarian Fascists a fiery cross, the Polish Fascists "Chrobry's sword," etc. The Fascists evolved an entire hierarchy of symbols, using various distinctions and signs to denote Party ranks. (Under Nazi rule,

[13] Soviet Painting and Sculpture, *Architecture, USSR* (in Russian), Moscow, Jan., 1938.

[14] Ibid, 1939.

some German calendars printed several pages of different Party symbols as a practical guide to enable the populace to pay adequate respect to each rank). Labor and peasant movements developed types of symbolism related to their social character and work. The Peasant Party used a four-leaf clover, a peaceful symbol of good luck for the peasantry—the Communists, a hammer and sickle, symbols of the workers in the factories and fields—the Socialists, in many countries, the hammer—The Cooperativists, a rainbow, symbol of cooperation, peace and conciliation. When the Fascist offensive against the labor movement became increasingly violent in the late twenties and early thirties, the latter tended toward a united democratic front and a militant defense of democratic institutions. This democratic iron front, "Die Eiserne Front," was born in Germany; its symbols were three parallel arrows representing discipline, solidarity, and unity in the struggle for democracy.

This symbol grew quite popular and began to be accepted generally as representing militant labor organizations and democratic fronts. Peaceful symbols of man's labor, such as the hammer, have often been used parallelly with the militant symbols of democratic struggle, but they never achieved the popularity of the three arrows. When Nazism gave rise to the underground, new symbols were born for these heroic organizations. The Polish labor organization, Polish Socialist Party, devised an arrangement of a factory wheel, two corn spikes, and a hammer, and the letters WRN. This symbolized Freedom, Equality, Independence (Wolnosc Rownosc Niepodleglosc).

Colors, too, were symbolic. The Communists and Socialists used red, the Peasant Parties green, the Cooperatives a multicolored rainbow, the anarchists and the Fascists black, and the Nazis brown.

Hitler fully realized the emotional values and significance of a flag and party insignia as a unifying factor. Playing with the most bestial emotions of the masses, the Nazis often used skillful techniques of mass psychology. Hitler devotes pages in his *Mein*

Kampf to the flag and insignia, describing why and how the symbols were chosen.

Space prevents further enumeration and discussion of European political symbols, of which a multitude exist. Both in Europe and Asia, however, they played a vital role as common representations of religion, especially in times of religious conflict.

Their social functions are similar to those of rituals. A unifying factor, they help to strengthen the cohesion of a social group, of a church, or of a political party based on a mass movement. The man wearing a symbol is continually conscious of his connection with the movement or institution it represents; he is constantly reminded of his affiliation with a larger group. Symbols have an emotional aspect, since they revive feelings of unity by means of psychological association. By corresponding to certain ideological stereotypes, they are expressions of emotions and, as such, play upon the sentimentality of the human soul.

Sometimes even books of a serious, scholarly nature may eventually play symbolic roles, although their primary purpose was an appeal to reason. The Romans said: "Habent sua fata libelli" (Writings have their fate). Karl Marx's *Das Kapital* was intended to be a scientific book but, after a long and dramatic history it became a symbol of ideas. Marx is often quoted, but relatively few people read his book. Millions who voted for the Marxian solution have never read Marx. Many were unable to comprehend his rather technical, ponderous writing; intellectuals and more able labor leaders interpreted, simplified, and clarified it. Many of Marx's ideas, even after interpretation by the labor leaders, were still not clear and could not be fully understood by all. But they wielded a strong emotional influence; they were a unifying factor as the symbols of a happier, better future devoid of human exploitation or oppression and replete with social justice and happiness. The common man, then, believed even more than he actually understood.

Uncomprehended words are still influential if they possess symbolic or emotional qualities. They tend to unify, just as symbols and rituals strengthen cohesion. The very utterance of such words which are not understood and yet can wield influence impart a ritualistic character to them.

Irrationalism in Politics: Terror and Power

Irrationalistic elements play a tremendous role in politics, since political phenomena are not only economic and social, but strongly emotional, as well. However, political movements may be controlled by reason and moral principles, to a greater or lesser degree. For example, the striking, pretentious emotionalism of symbolism and ritualism did not appeal to the Englishman's imagination. English political movements were sober and far more rationalistic than continental. Though an efficient democratic system requires that politics be controlled by moral principles and reason rather than be subject to sudden rushes of human emotion, it would be unfair to entirely exclude emotions as a useful political factor. Imagination is an element of moral feeling; strong imagination is often justified and causes, in turn, great emotional tension. Therefore, although emotions must never be permitted to dominate politics, they constitute a valuable factor when soundly based on moral feelings.

This is simple and logical to express, but it must be remembered that continental European politics represented an emotional labyrinth of irrationalism, almost hysterical emotionalism, inveterate prejudices, and seething hatreds. In this psychological maze, overambitious men ruthlessly plotted for power, toyed with ideas, and employed chicanery and treachery to gain their ends.

In our century, terrorism and intimidation have become important elements in control and government; tyrants and dictators have replaced the old despots, but like the latter, the modern tyrant in a totalitarian state which combines political control with economic, is empowered to deprive his subjects of work, punish them without a fair trial, starve them (by such contemporary methods as confiscating their ration cards).

The dreadful threat of hunger and misery produces the same effect as the menace of terror. In a contemporary dictatorial state, the dictator possesses the ultimate power to decide a man's right to work and to eat.

There are means of forcing the populace into a passive herd. Misery and terror can transform an active, vigorous nation into a submissive mass; vicious techniques are available for the destruction of their basic moral and ethical values. Nazi terrorism has produced thousands of collaborationists and traitors who, to save their miserable lives and earn a little money, were willing to abandon all the fundamental human loyalties. Most of the countries in Europe suffered a deep, catastrophic moral decline under this terrorism.

The average man is capable of enduring only a certain amount of terror. When terror becomes enormously ruthless, general, and seemingly permanent — when quantity changes into quality — few can resist. This fact is realized only too well by those who advocate terrorism in government. M. Piade, the Yugoslav Communist leader, said: "The altar-lamp of terror must never be extinguished. The people must have fear."[15] In this respect, at least, Mr. Piade is closer to Hitler than he probably realizes. Adolf Hitler said in *Mein Kampf*: "Weak natures have to be told that it simply means 'to be or not to be.'

The importance of physical terror against the individual and the masses also became clear to me.

The terror in the workshops, in the factory, in the assembly hall, on the occasion of mass demonstrations, will always be accompanied by success as long as it is not met by an equally great force of terror." . . .[16]

An amazing similarity in their viewpoints is obvious, although Hitler's ideas were further elaborated upon than Mr. Piade's!

Terror as an instrument of government deserves careful study. However, at least one conclusion may be drawn from our twentieth century experience: Montesquieu regarded the separation of

[15] Report on Yugoslavia by C. L. Sulzberger, 'The New York Times,' Nov. 11, 1946.
[16] Adolph Hitler, *Mein Kampf*, New York, 1939, p. 58.

powers as an essential condition of democracy. The analysis of the mechanism of a terroristic system of government will bring us to a similar conclusion; an essential condition of modern democracy, as the state gains more and more economic power, is the separation of economic power and economic control from political control. The wielding of economic and political power by the same hands is the road to totalitarianism and oppression.

The Fate of Ideas

Great idealists, proponents of perfect, visionary plans, seldom took into consideration the perversities of human nature which, paradoxically, the poets seemed to have realized. Those noble authors of lofty views were unable to foresee the effect of their ideas; ideas, at times, meet an unexpected fate. They produce effects which are often completely contrary to the intentions of their originators.

It is as difficult to prophecy the precise form in which our ideas will materialize as it is for parents to sketch a likeness of their future progeny. Even the loftiest and most ethical idea is capable of producing a nightmare against its producer's will. Would either Jesus Christ or St. Paul accept Torquemada the Great Inquisitor as his spiritual son? But just as it would be unfair to judge the whole of Christianity by some vicious disciples, so would it be to judge the inspiring plans and ideas of social justice by its failures, alone, or by those individuals who abused them.

Only an intolerant judgment of history would arrive at exclusively pessimistic conclusions from the difficulties and defeats experienced. These very experiences have taught us that a strong will and indomitable desire to continue is required. And we have learned, too, that in order to advance further we shall have to conquer and re-conquer our liberties; our goal is no Utopian paradise which, once attained, remains passively ours throughout long, hedonistic years. The constant struggles and unceasing efforts to better our world are the essential qualities of a progressive mankind.

II.

Communism

COMMUNISM

Editorial Note

In his chapter on Communism, Mr. Nomad follows the pragmatic method and attempts to analyze the relationship between ideas and reality. Social stratification into such functional groups as workers, peasants, intelligentsia, and bureaucracy is the natural outcome of any division of labor in our industrial society. It is difficult to imagine a society without such a division. The problem of democratic social adjustment consists of whether so-called useful functional classes will establish their relations on the basis of cooperation and — above all — whether all useful classes will have equal chances for political control and democratic rule in a state-controlled economy, or whether one class will establish a despotic rule over all the others.

Mr. Nomad shows, in the second portion of his article, that a new elite has developed in the Soviet Union (the bureaucracy), and it is dominating the other useful classes (workers, peasants, and a part of intellectuals) after having deprived them of all democratic control.

Other social scientists have argued that the Soviet rule has given wide recognition to the popular masses, and has given them social security at the price of temporary surrender of their civil rights. Mr. Nomad disagrees with this point of view.

The reader is also referred to Chapter I, "Mechanics of European Politics"; Chapter VII, "Liberal Tradition in Russia"; Chapter XI, "The Destinies of Russian Peasantry," and Chapter XXII, on "Pan-Slavism."

F. G.

II.

COMMUNISM

by

MAX NOMAD

COMMUNISM, IN THE sense of economic equality, and communism as a term designating the social philosophy professed by those in power in the Soviet Union, are two altogether different things.

Even before it became identified with the policies symbolized by the names of Lenin and Stalin, the term Communism had begun to assume a variety of meanings. In the early part of the past century it was associated with revolutionary equalitarian groups, such as the "Babouvists" in France and the followers of Wilhelm Weitling in Germany, who believed in the immediate violent overthrow of the existing capitalist system. It also covered the ideas represented by Karl Marx, with his frankly sceptical attitude toward economic equalitarianism. And it was likewise applied to radical-democratic tendencies within the malcontent sections of the German middle classes during the 1840's. According to Marx's closest associate Friedrich Engels, the concepts of "democracy" and "communism" were in those years practically interchangeable. Curiously enough the manual workers were the only group that did *not* take part in the "communist" movement. (See Marx-Engels correspondence).

During the second half of the nineteenth century, with the Socialist (or "Social-Democratic") parties in control of the labor movement on the European continent, the word "communism" was relegated to the museum of historico-linguistic antiquities, if we disregard the revival of its use by the followers of Peter Kropotkin, who applied the adjective "communist" to their brand of anarchism. Marx and Engels alone insisted upon calling themselves "Communists"—apparently as a gesture of radical anticapitalist defiance.

In modern times the term "Communist" has been connected almost exclusively with the party that has been ruling Russia ever since the Revolution of 1917, and with the movements in other countries which either sprung up spontaneously under the inspiration of that historical event, or were organized with the active support of the Soviet regime.

The breakdown of the Tsarist system in March 1917 was the culmination of a century-old struggle of Russia's educated middle classes for the westernization of their country. After a short interlude of democracy, the specific conditions of a vast empire in complete disintegration as a result of a disastrous war, enabled a revolutionary group professing a heretical brand of Marxism to seize power and to establish its own dictatorship.

The party created by Lenin, which has been in power in Russia since November 7, 1917, had originally been a branch of the Russian Social-Democratic Workers Party which was founded in 1898.

The R.S.D.W.P. had been a "workers party" only in a Pickwickian sense, for most of its members were college-bred intellectual workers in search of a working-class following. Taking its inspiration from Marx, that party was distinguished from the other revolutionary groups in that it saw in the industrial workers the force which eventually would break the backbone of the hated Tsarist system. Other opponents of Russian absolutism expected the accomplishment of that task from the dissatisfied peasant masses.

At first all sections of the Russian Social-Democratic Workers Party were in full agreement as to the character the hoped-for Revolution was to assume. It was to give power to the middle class parties, including the representatives of the peasantry; the Social-Democratic leaders of the working class were to constitute the law-abiding opposition, following the example of the Social-Democratic, Socialist or Labor parties of the democratic Western European countries.

Soon after the turn of the century, however, the harmony among the Russian Marxists was disturbed by the ideas put forward by the dynamic personality of Lenin. These ideas concerned primarily the organizational nature of the party and only later came to be applied to the very character of the Revolution itself.

In his book *What Is To Be Done?* (1902) Lenin laid down his specific conception of the methods of revolutionary activity. The crucial point of his argument was insistence upon the paramount importance of a body of professional revolutionists for conducting the whole movement in an efficient manner. With this insistence was coupled a belief in the necessity of recognizing as party members only those who were also active members of secret organizations in Russia. This would leave out all those middle-of-the-road sympathizers from among the educated middle class—professional men, students and high-school boys and girls alike—who had not the courage to burn the bridges behind them. In Lenin's opinion this course would avert the danger of swamping the party with weak-kneed adherents who might dampen its combative spirit.

With this object in view Lenin insisted upon the greatest possible extension of the powers given to the Central Committee of the party, which was to direct all the revolutionary activities. These powers were to include that of confirming the personnel of the local committees and even of nominating their members. These proposals met with the strongest opposition on the part of most of the old-time militants of Russian Marxism. Instead of a movement based on mass support, they asserted, Lenin wanted an organization of conspirators—his attitude implying a belief that revolutions could be planned in advance—as opposed to the genuine Marxist viewpoint that revolutions occurred but were not made. Some of Lenin's opponents, indeed, went so far as to call his postulates Bonapartist, because, if carried out, his scheme would have concentrated all the power in his hands. Among his opponents at that time was also Leon Trotsky, who admitted no necessity for such a centralization of power. Behind it Trotsky was inclined to suspect Lenin's ambition for personal dictatorship. Denouncing this ambition, he wrote in 1904 that for the dictatorship of the proletariat Lenin wanted to substitute the dictatorship of the party over the proletariat; for the dictatorship of the party—the dictatorship of the Central Committee over the party; and for the dictatorship of the Central Committee—the dictatorship of Lenin over the Central Committee.

Lenin's *What Is To Be Done?*

Lenin's position was based upon two fundamental concepts: his very realistic understanding of the mentality of the working masses who, in his opinion, could think only in terms of wages and hours, but not in terms of social systems; and his quite unrealistic faith in the infallibility, good intentions and messianic role of revolutionary leadership, as personified by himself and those intellectuals who accepted his views. (To be sure, among these intellectuals were also to be included those exceptional, self-taught ex-workers who had succeeded in absorbing certain elements of education enabling them to assume leadership).

This skepticism with regard to the ability of the masses to evolve socialist concepts out of their own midst, found its expression in a famous passage contained in the afore-mentioned *What is to be done?:* "The history of all countries shows that, by its own efforts, the working class can develop only a trade-union consciousness—that is, the realization of the need of getting together in unions in order to fight employers and to demand from the government the passing of laws necessary for the workers."

As against this inability of the masses to overcome, by their own efforts, their subordination to "bourgeois ideology" (i.e., the acceptance of the legitimity of the existing system), Lenin emphasizes the fact that "the theory of socialism grew out of the philosophic, historical and economic theories that were elaborated by the educated representatives of the propertied classes, the intellectuals. The founders of modern scientific socialism, Marx and Engels, belonged to the bourgeois intelligentsia . . ." (ibid.).

To a large extent this view of Lenin's was derived from an opinion expressed in 1901—a year before the appearance of Lenin's book—by Karl Kautsky, chief exponent of Marxian orthodoxy in Germany. In an article published in the theoretical organ of the German Social-Democratic party (*Neue Zeit*, 1901-1902, XX, I. No. 3, p. 79) Kautsky wrote: "Socialism and the class struggle [Kautsky has in mind the wage struggles of the manual workers] arise side by side and not one out of the other; each arises out of different premises. Modern socialist consciousness can arise only on the basis of profound scientific knowledge. . . . The vehicles of science are not the proletariat but the *bourgeois intelligentsia* [italics in the original]: It was out of the heads of the members of this stratum that modern socialism originated, and it was they who communicated it to the more intellectually developed proletarians who, in their turn, introduced it into the proletarian class struggle where conditions allow that to be done. Thus socialist consciousness is something introduced into the proletarian class struggle from without and not something that arose within it spontaneously."

It is beside the point here whether this view of the non-working-class origin of socialism was in keeping with the original concepts of Marxism; or whether Kautsky advanced this view merely in order to put in their place those trade union leaders within the social-democratic movement who, in their rivalry with the college-bred leaders, occasionally tried to prejudice the masses against the lawyers, journalists and professors holding top positions within the socialist movement. The fact remains that Kautsky and Lenin, two of the most outstanding thinkers of modern Socialism (including Communism), took it for granted that a set of ideas introduced into the labor movement from a non-working-class stratum, was nevertheless the true expression of the interests of the manual workers. To be sure, there were individual heretics within the radical intelligentsia, who, turning against their own group, suspected that the gift of socialism was a Trojan horse of the underprivileged, declassed lower middle class intelligentsia; and that at bottom, the idea of socialization was nothing but the substitution of a new privileged class of managerial and political office-holders for the individual entrepreneurs and stock-holders of private capitalism. But naturally enough, their logical arguments were powerless to overcome the interested rationalizations of those who were out to "emancipate" the working class by taking their historical turn as a ruling elite.

Lenin's insistence upon a strictly centralized, near-military form of organization led in 1903 to the historical split within the ranks of the Russian Marxists. The followers of Lenin, known as "Bolsheviks," were henceforth arrayed against the "Mensheviks" whose views were more or less identical with those of the traditional European Socialist parties. Eventually the rift between the two groups was to go beyond the mere organizational concept of the movement. It became a conflict between democratic "gradualism" aiming at peaceful transition from capitalism to collectivism, and dictatorial revolutionism employing the methods of conspiracies and armed uprisings. At the time the Bolsheviks ceased to call themselves Social-Democrats and assumed the name of "Communists" (1918), the difference between the Communists and Socialists had become a real class conflict between the more impecunious and hence more adventurous section of the intellectual and white collar workers (with a sprinkling of well-to-do neurotics in search of a new religion) on the one hand, and the more sedate labor politicians with a "proletarian" vocabulary, whose ambitions did not go beyond the laurels of a parliamentary career or of a cabinet post within the capitalist system, on the other.

The unsuccessful Russian Revolution of 1905 deepened the original split by extending it from the field of mere organization to that of tactical methods. As the upheaval approached—the disastrous war with Japan had brought the downfall of the hated regime within the sphere of imminent probabilities—the Mensheviks began to get ready, so to speak, for the modest role they had expected to play in the future parliament of a democratic Russia. They saw themselves as a party of parliamentary opposition to a regime headed by middle-class Liberals. A government of this kind was in their opinion the only solution under the prevailing economic conditions.

Lenin's solution was different. He believed that the Liberal bourgeoisie was too pusillanimous, too cowardly, to take the energetic measures needed to hold what had been won. The forces of reaction in his opinion, were bound to come back—as they had done in Western Europe in 1848—if the government were to be left in the hands of the Liberals. His way out was a "democratic dictatorship of the proletariat and the peasantry." These two classes would have to assume power and by ruthless measures destroy all vestiges of Tsarism and render its return impossible. This, however, was not to be a social revolution. The "proletariat and the peasantry" were to exert their dictatorship only for the purpose of establishing an honest-to-goodness bourgeois-democratic system on the Western-European model. The big landowners, the mainstay of absolutism, were to be dispossessed and their land was to be distributed among the peasants. Some concessions with respect to wages, hours and other conditions of labor would be made to the workers. Stripped of its specific terminology ("dictatorship of the proletariat and of the peasantry"), what the Bolshevik program of that period called for was the establishment of a coalition government composed of representatives of the Bolshevik professional revolutionists active among the industrial workers, on the one hand, and of those non-Marxian socialist intellectuals, lawyers, journalists, politicians and ex-conspirators, known under the name of "Social-Revolutionaries," who were influential among the peasant masses, on the other.

Trotsky's "Permanent Revolution"

At about the same time that Lenin advanced his theory of a "democratic dictatorship," Leon Trotsky, then a sort of lone Marxist not connected with either of the two sections of the Russian Social-Democrats, came forward with his theory of the "permanent revolution."

This theory held that the Russian revolution could not remain merely democratic in scope. The revolutionary government, Trotsky believed, would be obliged to make substantial concessions to the workers, such as providing for the unemployed and taking over those industries whose owners refused to satisfy the demands of the workers. He assumed that the capitalistically minded peasants would not agree to these reforms and thus come into conflict with the workers. Should the workers win in that conflict, the economic backwardness of the country would make it impossible to carry out all the necessary socialist measures. The only way out of the impasse would be a revolution in Western Europe which would join hands with the Russian proletariat in establishing socialism.

Thus, several years before the Revolution of 1917, Leon Trotsky envisaged the idea of a sort of international socialist revolution starting in Russia in the wake of a democratic anti-Tsarist upheaval, and from there spreading over Western Europe. This was something new in the European socialism of that time—when "social revolution" had become a mere liturgical phrase and the realization of the "final aim" was visualized as a gradual transition to a democratic system of government ownership.

Lenin's views on the character of the Russian Revolution to come, as recorded in his writings since 1905, underwent many changes and eventually became practically identical with those of Trotsky. In his *Permanent Revolution,* a pamphlet written after his fall from power in the late twenties, Trotsky boils down the difference between his opinion and Lenin's to the question whether "the participation of the representatives of the proletariat as a *minority* (my italics. M. N.) in the democratic government" (expected to be established as a result of the Revolution of 1905) was "theoretically permissible." This question was answered in the affirmative by Lenin, who was ready for a peasant (i.e. "Social-Revolutionary") predominance in the government, while Trotsky insisted upon a "proletarian" majority—that is, a majority composed of Marxian intellectuals, politicians and ex-conspirators. The historical test of the Revolution of 1917 actually settled the controversy. "In November 1917," Trotsky wrote in his *Permanent Revolution,* "a struggle raged in the summits of the party around the question of the coalition government with the Social-Revolutionaries and the Mensheviks. Lenin was not opposed in principle to a coalition on the basis of the Soviets, but he categorically demanded a firm safeguarding of the Bolshevik majority. I went along with him hand in hand." It was therefore Trotsky's point of view which actually became the basis of Bolshevik policy in the crucial months of the Revolution of 1917.

The Bolsheviks Take Over

By the end of February 1917 the Tsarist system broke down under the blows of the German military machine. The war-weary soldiers stationed in Petrograd made common cause with the hungry protesting masses. No revolutionary party could claim exclusive credit for bringing about the liquidation of the hated regime. During eight months—between March and November 1917—the country was ruled by a provisional government. It was a coalition of progressive middle class and moderate socialist parties among which the Social-Revolutionaries, the representatives of the Russian peasantry, were the most influential element.

In November of the same year, the followers of Lenin, who had been joined by Trotsky, taking advantage of the war-weariness of the soldiers and of the land-hunger of the peasants, staged a successful coup against the Provisional Government. The Communists have been in power ever since.

It was not the intention of the victorious Bolsheviks—they began to call themselves Communists only about a year later — to carry out an immediate socialization of Russia's economic fabric. The land was "nationalized," to be sure. But this meant only that the peasants, having seized the land of the big owners, had no right to sell their individual holdings. Beyond that the Bolsheviks proposed merely to nationalize the banking system and to establish government control—not ownership—of the industries.

Under normal conditions the process of transition from that system to full government ownership might have taken decades. Conditions in 1917 were, however, not normal, and it took only ten months to bring about a complete nationalization of all industries. A multiplicity of causes led to this development. In many cases the workers were infuriated by the refusal of the manufacturers to comply with their demands. As a result, they simply drove out the owners and occupied the factories. The Soviet Government, dependent as it was upon the support of the laboring masses, could not afford to lose face as a "proletarian regime" by restoring these plants to their legal owners. It therefore had no choice but to take them over. (Particularly as the workers themselves were not in a position to run those enterprises by their own efforts). In other cases factories were taken over to protect them against sabotage by their owners while the country was in the throes of civil war. There were also numerous instances where the plants were seized by the Government in order to prevent their being sold to German capital after the German-Soviet peace treaty of 1918. Thus the Bolsheviks did not seize power in order to establish a system of government ownership. Rather they consented to the dispossession of the capitalists and to the establishment of government ownership in order to keep power.

The nationalization of industries was accompanied by a system of forcible seizures of foodstuffs from the peasantry. The cities produced exclusively for the needs of the army engaged in civil war and so had nothing to offer the peasants in exchange. This resulted in what is usually termed "war-time communism"—a condition which lasted from the middle of 1919 to the end of the civil war, or more exactly, to the spring of 1921.

In reality it was not communism at all, if under communism one is to understand a system guaranteeing an equal share of the good things of life to every member of the community. It was a system of military bureaucratic plundering of the peasantry for the purpose of feeding the army and providing starvation rations for the workers engaged in the war industries, while securing a fairly decent livelihood for the privileged members of the administrative machine—party leaders, bureaucrats, army officers and the higher technical and managerial personnel.

The general dissatisfaction of the population, which manifested itself in numerous strikes, peasant uprisings and the sailors' revolt at Kronstadt (March, 1921), eventually led to the adoption of the so-called New Economic Policy (NEP). It was a sort of compromise between private capitalism and government ownership—with the State owning all key industries, while private enterprise was permitted in agriculture, trade and the manufacture of consumers goods. That system was maintained for about seven years—until 1928. At that time Stalin and his faction, having won in the struggle for power against the party elements opposing his personal ascendancy, adopted the program of his defeated opponents. The result was a policy of large-scale industrialization and agricultural collectivization. It was a policy which eventually did away with all vestiges of private enterprise. The entire country was converted into one great economic unit managed hierarchically by a bureaucratic apparatus that covers all aspects of industrial and agricultural production and distribution.

The New Freedom

The seizure of power by the Bolshevik party was followed by the gradual disappearance of all political liberties, not only of those established during the short interval between the downfall of Tsarism and the Bolshevik coup d'etat, but also of those, restricted though they were, which had existed under the old regime since 1905, when both liberal-democratic and socialist publications, including those of the Leninist brand, were tolerated. Shortly after the inauguration of the new regime the Communist Party established a monopoly over all public activities—political and otherwise. There was to be only one political party, one editorial policy in all newspapers, one trade union organization which thus became a company union of the Employer State, one association in every field of human endeavor—with all of these bodies becoming mere subsidiaries of the ruling party.

To be sure, there were representative assemblies, called Soviets, composed of delegates of workers and peasants; but it did not take long before these bodies were reduced to mere decorative institutions, bossed completely by the Communists. Elections to these bodies were effected by a show of hands, and the list of candidates was always submitted by the Communist caucus. No attempts at submitting other lists were made, for they meant a conflict with the "unsheathed sword of the Revolution," the dreaded secret police, known at different times as "Cheka," "G.P.U." (or O.G.P.U.), "N.K.V.D." and M.V.D.

In the early thirties this totalitarian conception of politics found cynical expression in the notorious words of Michael Tomsky, then head of the Soviet trade unions: "Any number of political parties may exist in Russia, provided one of them is in power and the others in prison." (It is a grim commentary upon that system that Tomsky was one of the first to pay with his life when Stalin decided to extend that lofty principle to all those who within the party disagreed with him on one point or another).

Russia's new "democracy" took its final shape in the Soviet Constitution of 1936. (For the benefit of those potential sympathizers who had as yet been unable to overcome their sentimental attachment to the concept of democracy, Lenin evolved the famous formula that "proletarian democracy is a million times more democratic than any bourgeois democracy and the Soviet regime is a million times more democratic than the most democratic regime in a bourgeois republic") . The new Constitution, which is officially known as the "Stalin Constitution," gives the franchise to all persons of both sexes, eighteen years or over. Nothing could be more democratic than that. Now "franchise" is granted for the purpose of elections. But there are no elections. The very word "election" presupposes a choice among various candidates. But there is no such choice because the Constitution maintains the totalitarian one-party system. There is only one candidate or one set of candidates in each district. The selection of the candidates is effected by the Communist party machine, and confirmed by an *open* vote of party members, which renders impossible the putting up of a slate of candidates who are not agreeable to the party machine. For any one who would openly vote against the officially proposed set of candidates, would automatically set himself down as an "enemy of the people."

Despite the one hundred and forty-six articles of the Constitution there is no personal liberty in the Soviet Union in the sense in which it exists in all civilized countries. A Russian physicist, Professor Peter Kapitza, had made his home in England where he had become director of the Royal Society's Mond Laboratory at Cambridge. When in 1935 he came to Russia on a visit he suddenly saw himself deprived of his passport and forced to remain in a country from which he had expatriated himself many years ago. He had never engaged in politics. But the Soviet authorities simply declared that they preferred him to do his scientific work in Russia rather than in England. It was as if Henry James, on a visit to his native country, had been told by the American authorities that he could not go back to England and that henceforth he would have to write his novels in the United States.[1]

Passports, though nominally in existence in Russia, are actually beyond the reach of the ordinary inhabitant. Applications for a passport are always rejected. That coveted document is given only to trusted members of the bureaucracy sent abroad on an official mission. The actual reason for that refusal, though never admitted, is the same as that which had prompted the governments of Fascist Italy and Nazi Germany to take the same attitude. Neither of these regimes, in the opinion of a Paris correspondent of the *N. Y. Times,* wanted its nationals to see for themselves the political and social conditions abroad.

On the other hand there is a compulsory document in Russia which has the unassuming name of "work-book." That book lists every job its holder ever had, and the exact reason why he left it in every case. This is to make it impossible for industrial workers to leave an establishment to seek better accommodations elsewhere. Such a "selfish" attitude is considered highly dishonorable and disqualifies the holder of the book from obtaining another job. In its editorial on the "work-book" the Moscow *Pravda* of December 22, 1938, stated with commendable frankness that *"the work-book will be one of the effective weapons in the struggle against the labor turn-over."* The italics were in the Russian original.

Such is the status of Russia's "free" workers. Yet it is enviable as compared with the situation of *millions* of recalcitrant "individualist" peasants and political dissenters enrolled in those branches of Soviet economy which employ forced labor, such as timber cutting and the building of canals, roads and fortifications. These branches of plain slave economy are under the direct management of the secret police. For obvious reasons there are no statistical figures about these slave workers whose number has been vaguely estimated at between fourteen and twenty million. For disloyalty during World War II entire tribes of non-Slavic races,

[1] It is in line with this attitude towards personal freedom that Russian women who married foreigners are forbidden to leave the country with their husbands, and that in 1947 a law was passed—unheard of in the annals of any civilized country—forbidding marriage between Russians and foreign citizens.

such as the Kalmucks, the Crimean Tartars, the Volga-Germans and various nationalities on both slopes of the Caucasus range, where they had lived since time immemorial, have been transplanted to regions where forced labor and an unaccustomed climate doom them to extinction. The same fate is now being meted out to the bulk of the Latvian and Estonian population for the purpose of settling the formerly independent Baltic republics with Russians proper.

Restrictions upon travel in the regions affected and absolute inability of getting in touch with any of the persons undergoing penalties on account of their political non-conformity, as well as the definite refusal of the Soviet regime to accept the inspection feature of the Baruch atom plan — all tend to confirm the most horrifying reports on that subject. Wendell Willkie, a man by no means unfriendly to the Soviet regime—his *One World* has been widely circulated by the Communist book stores in the U. S. A.—had given the readers of his articles about his Russian trip a glimpse of this aspect of Soviet Russia's economy (*Readers Digest,* Vol. 42, No. 251). But the passage in question was omitted from the book edition of his *One World.* Fear lest this feature of our Eastern ally's social system dampen the war enthusiasm of the readers induced the publishers and particularly the pro-Soviet editor of the book to suppress the suggestive sentence.

The "purges" and the "trials" of the late thirties are still generally remembered. They were devices by which Stalin—aside from getting rid of some of his opponents—was trying to placate the masses and thus to consolidate his own power. For to the man in the street the liquidated Old Guard of the Communist Party, including practically all the top figures in the various central and autonomous administrations, was the symbol of all his sufferings and privations during the first two decades of the Soviet Republic. The "confessions," extorted under threat of torture or of extermination of the victims' families—those who refused to "confess" were shot without trial—have been justly compared with medieval witch trials at which the unfortunate women gave minute accounts of their traffic with the Devil.

A state wielding such power over its subjects has also the authority of prescribing to them what they are to read or rather what they are not to read. The younger generation of office-holders cannot even conceive the idea that a newspaper should criticize the government. In 1930 the writer made a visit to the Soviet Union. In one of the museums the secretary of the institution, a young university graduate, asked him about the chances for Russia's recognition by the United States, particularly in view of the violent attacks by Hamilton Fish, then prominently reported in the Russian press. The reply that such attacks meant very little, and that the President, if he intended to extend recognition, would completely ignore them, puzzled the young man to the extreme. "Do you mean to say that the Government permits the printing of opinions which are opposed to its own? In that case it could not possibly be a stable, strong government."

At about the same time Oswald Garrison Villard had a similar experience which he reported in *The Nation.* He quoted the remarks of the head of the Ukrainian Communist Literary Society to the effect that the regime "could not allow a handful of dissenters, who are not five per cent of the Ukrainian population, to disturb the progress of the country." Villard also gathered from the remarks of that representative of Soviet literature that "the idea of the liberty of the press included only those editors who favored the communist doctrine, precisely as Mussolini permitted editorial freedom in Italy only to those who wholeheartedly support fascism."

The same restrictions that hold for the press are applied to all other aspects of the country's cultural life. The theater, the cinema, the radio, book publishing—they are all coordinated according to the most rigid totalitarian principles. Authors who for years had enjoyed the greatest reputations, such as Pilniak, Panteleymon Romanov, Zoschenko, Akhmatova, are suddenly silenced, or altogether liquidated, if in their novels, short stories, satires or poems they give expression to moods at variance with the official optimism and compulsory sycophancy required by the regime from its "artists in uniform"—to use an apt phrase coined by Max Eastman.

Science, no less than literature has been feeling the heavy hand of official inquisition. Certain branches of learning are lavishly subventioned if they promise to further the process of industrialization and thus aid the country's military preparedness. But whenever a scientific theory may lend itself to interpretations however remotely conflicting with the political theology of the regime, official intolerance is even more outspoken than with the Tennessee fundamentalists who prohibited the teaching of evolution.

Thus the ideas of Russia's foremost geneticists, particularly those of Vavilov, have been declared taboo because of their adherence to the Mendelian laws. For in the opinion of the champions of orthodox Leninist Marxism these principles may give encouragement to certain reactionary political philosophies. New discoveries in anthropology were rejected on the ground that Engels, the friend of Karl Marx, had once, in the eighties, expressed a different opinion on that subject. For quite a while even the theory of Einstein was frowned upon because there was a suspicion in the minds of Russia's official Marxists that there was an element of mysticism in that theory which could be prejudicial to the official dogma of materialism.

Occasionally entire branches of study are suppressed, if the results threaten to be distasteful to the beneficiaries of the present socio-economic setup. This was the case of "pedology," a new science which examined the extent to which success in study depended either upon inherited physical constitution or upon the social environment of individual school children. The reason for the suppression of that science is obvious. It might have established—or most likely did already establish—that the children of the new ruling class, i.e., of the office-holders and technical experts, had better chances for scholastic advancement, because of better housing accommodations; that is, because of the higher incomes commanded by their parents. This would be tantamount to the scientific establishment of the fact that a hereditary intellectual aristocracy was being formed in Russia, not on the basis of biological heredity which is rejected by the Communists, but as a result of environment, i.e. economic causes. Which of course would be a complete refutation of the Communists' claim that they aimed at the emancipation of the working class, that is, at the establishment of economic equality. The scholars engaged in these investigations were duly arrested and forced to "confess" their "hostility to the working class."

The "Classless Society"

From the outset it was the official policy of the Soviet Government to treat all opponents—even those of the various democratic socialist schools—as a sort of fifth column. Witness Lenin's note dated May 15, 1922, addressed to the then Commissar of Justice, D. I. Kursky, which stated that "a formula must be found that would place these activities [of the Mensheviks and Social-Revolutionaries] in connection with the international bourgeoisie and its struggle against us (bribery of the press and agents, war preparations and the like)."

More than a decade later, when the civil war and its after-effects could no longer serve as an excuse for the banning of all political activity outside the Communist party, another argument was advanced. In an interview given in 1936 to Roy Howard, the co-publisher of the Scripps-Howard chain of papers in the United States, Stalin ventured a theoretical explanation as to why not more than one party was permitted to exist despite the pretended democracy of the new Constitution. "As soon as there are no more classes," he said, "as soon as boundaries between classes are effaced . . . there can no longer be any nourishing ground for the formation of parties struggling among themselves. *Where there are not in existence several classes there cannot be several parties because a party is a part of a class.*"[2] In the report about the new Constitution which he made later in the same year to the Eighth Special All-Union Congress of Soviets,[3] Stalin returned to the same question: "In the U.S.S.R. there are only two classes, workers and peasants, whose interests not only are not antagonistic but, on the contrary, amicable. Consequently, there are no grounds for the existence of several parties, and therefore for the existence of freedom of such parties in the U.S.S.R. There are grounds for only one party, the Communist Party, in the U.S.S.R." Earlier in the same paragraph, he stated that: "I must admit, the draft of the new constitution really does leave in force the regime of the dictatorship of the working class, and also leaves unchanged the present leading position of the Communist Party of the U.S.S.R."

Thus, in addressing an American newspaperman he rejected the idea of a multiplicity of parties because "there are no more classes"; in speaking to a Soviet Congress a few months later, he discovered that there were in Russia "two classes" whose interests were "amicable," and that for this reason there could be only one party representing their interests. The obvious inconsistency and insincerity of Stalin's arguments was nailed immediately by many critics outside of Russia. The idea that a class could be represented by only one party was rank nonsense. Every class has its subdivisions which are often represented by different political groups. Such is the case in practically all capitalist countries with a multi-party system.[4] In the second place, one

[2] The italicized passage was omitted in the "full text" printed by the Communist *Daily Worker* of New York, of March 6, 1936. Apparently it seemed to the editor too incongruous to be swallowed by the more intelligent readers. But the missing words were contained in the full text printed in the Moscow *Izvestia* of March 5, 1936, and in the Basel *Rundschau* (organ of the Communist International) of the same date, p. 412.

[3] *Daily Worker*, New York, November 27, 1936.

[4] The Communists have always designated the Republicans and the Democrats in the U.S.A. or the Conservatives and Liberals in Great Britain, as parties of the capitalist class. And they have repeatedly offered a united front to the Socialists, Laborites, or other organizations which they recognized on those occasions as parties of the working class like themselves. On other occasions they simply lumped the Socialists with the "capitalist parties."

could not say that there was only one "class" or two "amicable classes" in Russia, if one insisted, as Stalin and his assistants do, that the Soviet Republic had already reached the phase of a "classless society."

Still more priceless was Stalin's "admission" that the Constitution left in force "the regime of the dictatorship" and the "leading position of the Communist Party." In a "classless" society, which Russia purports to be, the population no longer has any "class enemies" to fight; for the capitalists, the landlords, as well as their successors, the "nepmen" and the "kulaks," had been liquidated with a thoroughness worthy of a Genghis Khan. As a result, there would seem to be no need for a political party which in the Bolshevik terminology, was the "vanguard" of the class whose interests it defended. A political "vanguard" in a population "without classes" was a logical incongruity. Apparently something was wrong with the idea that Russia was a "classless" society.

The idea that with the elimination of the propertied classes Russia has become a "classless" society is not only part of the official "folklore" of Stalinist "communism": it is a logical sequence of the Marxist doctrine which determines a person's class status not according to his income, but according to his "relation to the process of production"; a deceptive half-truth which by stressing merely the question of "owner or employee" places the high-class executive in the category of "workers" alongside the laborer who may earn less than one-fiftieth or even one-hundredth of his income. It is this Marxist fallacy which has furnished the ideological cloak for the unmitigated class rule of Russia's new aristocracy—or new bourgeoisie, if you will—over the enormous mass of workers and peasants. It is as the most militant "part" of this new nobility that the Communist Party maintains its political domination. A domination which Stalin, in that speech, cautiously enough, called "the regime of the dictatorship of the *working class*" instead of using the liturgical Marxist term "*pro-*

letariat." For, according to the folklore of present-day Russia, there are no longer any proletarians in that country. Stalin particularly emphasized that idea in his aforementioned speech on the Constitution. The workers, he insisted, "possessed the industries in conjunction with the whole people."[5] Just as the American sailors and letter-carriers own the Navy and the Post Office Department, respectively. . . .

Curious situations sometimes arose out of this article of faith of present-day Russia. Here are the workers, "owning" their industries, yet as a rule dissatisfied with the collective agreements which they conclude with . . . themselves concerning wages and hours. Sometimes they even run away from "their own" factories, and all kinds of methods of persuasion and compulsion have to be applied to keep them at their jobs, or more correctly, at "their" property. The confusion is even greater than that. The workers as the "owners" of the factories, are thus logically the real "employers." The technicians, the engineers, the managers, are their "employees." No wonder that the Bolsheviks, as the defenders of the oppressed, take all the possible care of the "hired men," that is, the technicians, and pay them much more than they do the "owners."

But there is a hitch somewhere. The ballyhoo is too crude—it could be believed only by the college graduate American liberals who are four thousand miles away, but not by the uneducated workers who are on the spot. As a result it sometimes happens that the unsophisticated editor of a provincial paper complains that "labor discipline is deteriorating in the Irkutsk district, and the workers do not consider the industries as their own."[6] Even Lazar Kaganovich, a man of steel second only to Stalin, occasionally makes a slip in the presence of that mystery. In a speech reported by the Moscow *Izvestia* of June 8, 1930, he mentioned that the "proletariat begins to realize the fact that it is the owner of the production, the owner of industry." So it took the pro-

[5] *Daily Worker*, New York, November 27, 1936.

[6] *Vlast Truda* (The Power of Labor), Irkutsk, January 26, 1930.

letariat thirteen years to "begin to realize" that it is the master of the country. . . .

The Theory of Dictatorship

In *State and Revolution,* a pamphlet written a few months before the seizure of power by his party, Lenin laid down the theoretical justification for his policy. His argument is largely based upon a famous passage from Karl Marx's *Critique of the Gotha Program.*

That passage reads as follows: "Between the capitalist and the communist society lies the period of revolutionary transformation of the former into the latter. To this also corresponds a political transition period in which the state can be no other than the revolutionary dictatorship of the proletariat."

Lenin in his *State and Revolution,* and after him, Stalin, in his *Foundations of Leninism* interpreted this "revolutionary dictatorship of the proletariat" as a "state that is . . . democratic for the proletariat and the poor in general" (Lenin), or as a "proletarian democracy—the democracy of the exploited majority based upon the limitation of the rights of an exploiting minority and directed against this minority" (Stalin).

It would seem that with the complete elimination of all vestiges of capitalism in Russia there was no longer in existence any "exploiting minority" in the Marxist-Leninist-Stalinist sense, against which that "limitation of rights" would have to be exercised. Yet as time went on those "limitations" grew to fantastic proportions both qualitatively and quantitatively. Witness the mass executions with and without trial. Witness also the complete elimination of all vestiges of democratic procedure within the new setup, as testified by the well-known "evolution" of the dictatorship from the initial rule of the Soviets (a period of a few months only) to the rule of the Communist party; and finally from the rule of the Communist party to that of its Secretary General and the police apparatus controlled by him. (During the mid-twenties when telling of political jokes was not yet a form of suicide, they spoke of the substitution of the "dictatorship of the secretariat for the dictatorship of the proletariat.") Witness finally the fact that the victims of those "limitations" ever since the late twenties were no longer capitalists but workers, peasants or intellectuals holding non-conformist socialist or communist views, whose only "anti-proletarian" crime was opposition to the autocratic methods of the regime.

In extolling the democratic character of the coming "dictatorship of the proletariat" Lenin insisted that after the seizure of power the regime would be a "state of *armed workers*" (emphasis in the original) and not a "state of bureaucrats." (*State and Revolution*). The main attributes of that state would be the election of all officials without exception, their recall at any time, and their remuneration at salaries that have been reduced to the level of "workingmen's wages." Under modern capitalism, according to this classic of Lenin's (chapter 3, subdivision 2), "the great majority of functions of the old 'state power' have become so simplified and can be reduced to such simple operations of registration, filing and checking that they will be quite within the reach of every literate person and it will be possible to perform them for 'workingmen's wages,' which circumstance can and must strip those functions of every shadow of privilege." In other words, there would be no bureaucracy, as everybody who can read and write can become a bureaucrat.

That regime, however, according to Lenin was not meant to be the definitive form of a socialist society. With the development of the technical resources, society would gradually be enabled to dispense with compulsory measures necessary for maintaining certain inequalities inherent in the "first phase of communism." That process of gradual dispensing with governmental compulsion is called by Lenin "the withering away of the state," an expression coined by the founders of Marxism. Thus the "dictatorship of the proletariat" would eventually evolve into that ideal system which the theorists of anarchism choose to call "anarchy"

—an expression by which they understand a system of libertarian communism functioning on the basis of voluntary agreements.

It is beside the point whether Lenin had his tongue in his cheek when he argued that the main functions of government could be reduced to checking, filing and registering. The fact is that as time went on, with all the power in the hands of the "proletariat," all the main attributes of "proletarian dictatorship," as specified by Lenin, went the way of all promises made by political parties. Soviet government officials are not elected, but appointed from above; they are not subject to recall by their constituents, but are simply demoted, with or without lethal sequels; and their renumeration is as much above "workingmen's wages," as are the emoluments of a judge or factory manager above those of a mechanic or filing clerk in any capitalist country. And last, but not least, the development of the technical resources of the Soviet Union has brought in its wake not a relaxation, but on the contrary a sharpening of the compulsory measures necessary for maintaining the ever *growing* inequalities in the standard of living of the various groups of Russia's "classless" society. The "withering away of the state" was fated to become a mere liturgical phrase devoid of any practical significance.

For the interim period preceding the complete "withering away of the state" Lenin had launched the slogan that soon "every cook" would be able to attend to the affairs of the state. A new generation of those humble little ladies has grown up since that time, but they keep on cooking for the commissars.

There are unorthodox partisans of the Bolshevik revolution who believe that the dictatorship of the Communist Party, culminating in the personal dictatorship of its top leader, are deviations from the original concept of the proletarian dictatorship, as advocated by Lenin. Unfortunately for them, there are "slips" by the founder of Bolshevism himself indicating that they are sadly mistaken. When during the months preceding the November uprising of 1917 the Soviets, at that time still controlled by the Mensheviks and Social-Revolutionists, showed no inclination to join the Bolsheviks, Lenin dropped the pretense of "all power to the Soviets" declaring openly that from then on the slogan was to be the dictatorship of the Bolshevik party. On another occasion he stated that "Soviet socialist democracy is not inconsistent with personal rule and dictatorship, for the will of a class is at times best carried out by a dictator who alone will accomplish more and who is often more needed." (Vol. 17, page 89, Russian edition of 1925.)

Communism and Equality

In *State and Revolution* the founder of Bolshevism remarks that "the question of control and accounting must not be confused with the question of the scientifically educated staff of engineers, agronomists and so on. These gentlemen work today obeying the capitalists; they will work even better tomorrow, obeying the armed workers." Needless to emphasize that now, thirty years after the appearance of Lenin's classic, "these gentlemen" "obey the armed workers" only in so far, as under "armed workers" we are to understand the new elite of political administrators and their uniformed and non-uniformed pretorian guard going by the name of G.P.U. or N.K.V.D.

Lenin's reference to the "scientifically educated staff of engineers etc." and to the "armed workers" whom they are supposed to obey, brings up the question of distribution under the system of "proletarian dictatorship," the political aspect of the "first phase of communism." The father of Bolshevism knew very well that he found himself on very dangerous ground. He had to appear as an equalitarian in order not to step on the toes of the party's working class element which at that time was exposed to a barrage of anarchist propaganda. And he had to take care not to be too explicit about his equalitarianism, lest his utopianism or plain demagogy became too apparent as soon as the realization of that "first phase" was to be attempted. So he followed in the footsteps of his teacher, Karl Marx who dealt with that subject in a way that lent itself to the most contradictory interpretations. In a document called *Critique of the Gotha Program* Marx had written that "the first phase of communism" represented a system that was still "in every respect tainted economically, morally and intellectually with the birthmarks of the old society from whose womb it is emerging." Hence the "equal right" of the new system was "still handicapped by bourgeois limitations. The right of the producers is proportional to the amount of labor they contribute; the equality consists in the fact that everything is measured by an equal measure, labor. But one man excels another physically or intellectually, and so contributes, in the same time, more labor, or can labor for a longer time; and the labor, to serve as a measure, must be defined by its duration or intensity, otherwise it ceases to be a standard of measure. This equal right is an unequal right for unequal work. It recognizes no class differences because every worker ranks as a worker like his fellows: but it tacitly recognizes unequal individual endowment, and thus capacities for production, as natural privileges."[7] In other words, there is "equality"—even though an engineer or manager, because of his intellectual superiority, is paid ten or fifty times as much as an unskilled worker. For, as Lenin—in commenting upon Marx's views expressed in the *Critique*—says in Chapter 5, subdivision 3, "every worker receives from society as much as he has given it."

In expanding upon these ideas of Marx Lenin glosses over the unequalitarian aspects of this passage which, as a matter of fact, he does not quote. Instead, he uses such expressions as "equality of labor and equality in the distribution of products," "for an equal quantity of labor an equal quantity of products," "equality of labor and equality of wages," "the whole of society will have become one office and one factory, with equal work and equal pay."

[7] Did Marx deliberately use obscure and unintelligible verbiage in presenting his views on the subject? The well-known Marxist historian, Franz Mehring, in his biography of Marx, frankly admits that the *Critique* went over the heads of the delegates to the Socialist convention to whom it was addressed.

In the minds of practically every reader these phrases create the impression that in the "first phase of communism" equality of incomes was going to be established. The only drawback in this equality, as Lenin puts it, would seem to be merely the fact that "different people are not alike: one is strong, another is weak; one is married, the other is not; one has more children, another has less, and so on." "With equal labor" Lenin quotes Marx to this effect "and therefore an equal share in the social consumption fund, one man in fact receives more than the other, one is richer than the other, and so forth. In order to avoid all these defects, right, instead of equal, must be unequal." And he further paraphrases Marx's argument in the *Critique* by saying: " 'For an equal quantity of labor, an equal quantity of products'—this Socialist principle is also *already* [italicized by Lenin] realized. However, this is not yet communism, and this does not abolish 'bourgeois right' which gives to unequal individuals, in return for an unequal (in reality unequal) amount of work, an equal quantity of products." Which, for all its obscurity, or because of its obscurity, again creates the *impression* that there is to be equality of incomes, affected only by the size of the family, etc., and marred by the necessity of "distributing the articles of consumption 'according to work performed' (and not according to need)."

Thus it would *seem* that the only difference between the "first phase of communism" and the "higher phase" was the circumstance that under the former there was equality of incomes enforced by the authority of the state, while under the "higher phase," to use Marx's words, quoted by Lenin, "it will be possible to pass completely beyond the narrow horizon of bourgeois rights, and for society to inscribe on its banners: from each according to his ability; to each according to his needs!"

It is hard to say whether Lenin misunderstood Marx's obvious plea for inequality of rewards for intellectual and skilled, as against manual and unskilled labor (which is hard to assume in a man of Lenin's genius); or whether he thought it more expedient to disregard this fundamental aspect of Marx's views. At any rate, both in his "April theses" of 1917, and in *State and Revolution* published a few months later, Lenin demanded that government office holders be paid not more than manual workers. This was an open advocacy of equalitarianism, for it is hard to conceive that in speaking of government officials he should have meant only letter-carriers and garbage removers.

The actual practice of the Soviet regime has made hash of all the equalitarian or near-equalitarian ideas — regardless of the question of whether Lenin's phrases were or were not deliberately concealing the very opposite they seemed to convey. To be sure, Lenin himself—who was hungry only for power but not for material comforts—personally never claimed for himself a share that could have placed him in any privileged category. But, to paraphrase the remark of a disgruntled ex-official of the Soviet regime, the important thing was not how Lenin lived, but how the good things of life were distributed among the various sections of the Russian people.

Russia's top stratum, after the victorious Bolshevik revolution, consisted of the former revolutionists and conspirators who had been the driving force of the great upheaval. Though calling themselves Communists, they took it for granted that they were to take the cream of all the good things that were still left after all the turmoil of war and revolution. The idea that it behooved men claiming to be the saviors of the downtrodden to live on the same rations as their charges did not occur to them. As in the proverbial case of the Spanish monks and the American Indians, the Communists worked for the future salvation of the masses and the masses were compelled to work for the present comforts of the Communist office-holders. (True, for many years the salary of a Communist was supposed not to exceed the maximum of 300 rubles monthly; but in practice this salary constituted mere "pin money"; for all the real expenditures, such as automobiles, country houses, etc. were supplied by the state over and above the nominal salary.[8] This restriction, by the way, has been rescinded many years ago).

The necessities of an efficient production made the Soviet leaders realize that it would be very practical to raise the managerial technical personnel to the status of the best paid stratum of the population. Politically they had nothing to say, of course, but neither did anybody else.

In the early thirties the principle of preferential treatment was established in favor of another stratum as well. Skilled labor had always been at a premium in Russia; so in order to keep that element loyal and satisfied the Stalin regime engaged upon a policy of such a differentiation between the wages of skilled and unskilled workers as is altogether unthinkable in the capitalist countries. In a speech delivered on June 23, 1931, Stalin solemnly proclaimed inequality as the guiding principle of a better world in the making. "It is unbearable," he said, "to see the locomotive driver receiving the same wages as a copyist." That sentence meant that from now on not only the unskilled manual workers, mostly raw peasants from the countryside, but also the lower clerical employees whose education did not go beyond spelling and figuring, would stay in the lowest income brackets. And that everything would be done to give satisfaction not only to the technical experts but also to the highly skilled workers. The same principle of extreme inequality was applied to the army as well. It was widely reported during World War II that the discrepancy between the pay of a private soldier and that of an army lieutenant was in the proportion of one to one hundred (ten rubles as against 1000 per month.) In the United States army the discrepancy was at the ratio of one to three.

At the Seventeenth Convention of the Communist Party held in 1934 Stalin expanded theoretically on the subject of inequality.

[8] In a moment of impish non-restraint Walter Duranty, a journalist generally considered as very friendly to the Soviet regime, expressed his wonderment in the *New York Times*, as to how the Kremlin crowd could afford keeping French and English governesses for their children—all on a salary of 300 rubles [for the commissars, not for the governesses who, as foreigners, certainly got more.]

In his speech—published in pamphlet form in most foreign languages as well—he paraphrased that passage from Marx's *Critique of the Gotha Program* which was quoted above. The head of the Soviet regime chose to apply the designation "socialism" to that period following the overthrow of capitalism which Marx called the "first phase of communism"; and he called "communism" that phase which in the *Critique* was referred to as "the higher phase of communism." Under the former, everybody was to be paid according to his services, while under the latter the principle of "to everybody according to his needs" was to reign supreme. Marx had not been very specific about that "higher phase of communism." In fact, that "higher phase" was a mere pipe dream penned with his tongue in the cheek for the benefit of those emotionally in need of an Utopia. And Lenin frankly stated (*State and Revolution,* chapter V, subdivision 4) that "it has never entered the head of any socialist to 'promise' that the highest phase of Communism will arrive."[9] Stalin, however, whose realm is now apparently approaching that "higher phase," had to be more explicit; for officially Russia has already become a "classless society," all capitalists—the only real exploiters and parasites, according to Marx—having been thoroughly eliminated. He was therefore eager to emphasize the fact that "Marxism proceeds from the point of view that the tastes and the needs of human beings with regard to quality and quantity are not equal and cannot be equal, either in the period of socialism or in the period of communism." If words have any meaning at all, then the remark about "quality" and "quantity" meant that the weaker or less educated worker apparently "needs" no more than let us say, twenty-five dollars a week, while the select ones need twice, or ten or a hundred times as much. For just as everything is decided by the government, the "needs" will no doubt likewise be established by the same agency.

[9] In his *Critique of the Gotha Program* Marx did not use the expression "*highest* phase of Communism"; he spoke of the *higher* phase. Such "alterations" of the text (there is also another word for it) are not accidental. They serve the purpose of obscuring the issue.

Apparently conscious of the ugly implications of his words, Stalin immediately proceeded to mitigate them—at least for the great majority of the unsophisticated underdogs who might not be cheered by this prospect of being always on the bottom rung in matters of "quality" and "quantity." So he added that it was tantamount to "slandering Marxism" if one were to assume "that according to Marxism all humans had to wear the same clothes and to eat the same foodstuffs in the same quantities."

That expression about "wearing the same clothes and eating the same foodstuffs in the same quantities" has become one of Stalin's stock phrases on that subject; he had used it almost word for word in 1932 during his interview with Emil Ludwig. It was of course a conscious distortion of the idea of the equality of incomes which he was attacking. For that idea meant merely that a laborer, if he put in a whole day's work, was entitled to the same amount of money as the office-holder or technician for the same time, and that for this money he could buy any quantity or quality of goods or services he chose. Leaving aside the question of practicability, the very fact that Stalin had to attack so often the "equalitarian idiocy" indicates that to the workers at large, and particularly to the lowest paid, that "idiocy" must have a great appeal, and that they see in it the essence of communism.

Even before Stalin's speech, Michael Kalinin, Russia's late "worker-peasant" President, from time to time tried to allay the workers' dissatisfaction over the prevailing inequalities. "We are still very far from real equality" he said in one of his speeches; "until we have attained complete communism there can be no real equality." But as communism, in its true economic connotation means nothing else than equality of incomes, Kalinin's consolation amounts to the promise that there would be no equality, as long as there was—no equality. Which was certainly as unassailable as the remark made—not in jest—by Napoleon III, that "a nation's welfare depends upon its general prosperity"; or as the celebrated *bon mot* of the German writer Fritz Reuter, that "poverty came from destitution."

In proportion as these inequalities increased, simultaneously with the greater consolidation of the army and the secret police, the Communist rulers began gradually to dispense with the "proletarian" masquerades in which they had been indulging. Formerly the champions of the working class had been flirting with an outward show of poverty, wearing caps and shabby clothing so as not to arouse the envy of the workers. (It was in accordance with the same principle that during the first years after the seizure of power by Hitler the active Nazis were instructed to shun sumptuous banquets and similar affairs.)

Stalin's proclamation of inequality as the basic tenet of socialism was the signal for a speedy abandonment of all the aforementioned masquerades of the initial phase of the Revolution. The Russian cities eventually returned to the normal aspect of the Western capitalist world with their external manifestations of wealth and poverty. In the December 22, 1935 issue of the New York Times, Walter Duranty, who has been consistently friendly to the Soviet regime, remarked that the "differentiation of wages....must lead to a new class differentiation in what claims to be a classless society, a new class of bureaucrats and directors of state enterprises, a new class of high paid upper workers all of whom together will form, or are forming a new bourgeoisie." Since Duranty wrote these lines the introduction of comparatively high tuition fees for secondary schools and universities has rendered the acquisition of higher education a monopoly of the new bureaucratic and managerial aristocracy. Inequalities of social and economic status have thus become hereditary institutions.

The Soviet regime is of course very careful not to give any exact income statistics. Critics of the regime—particularly Trotsky and Burnham—who studied what figures were available, came to the conclusion that "the upper 11 or 12 per cent of the Soviet population now receives approximately 50 per cent of the national income", while a similar fraction of the population of the

United States—to be more exact, the upper 10 per cent—"receives approximately 35 per cent of the national income."

The New Élite Drops Its Radical Mask

The frank admission that an increasing inequality of incomes was henceforth to be the chief feature of a system that claimed to represent socialism on its way towards "full communism" was the unheralded landmark of a new departure in the history of "new Russia." That new departure implied the now *conscious* realization by the Communist party of the accomplished consolidation of a new privileged class of political and administrative office-holders, technical experts, managers, and army officers. A new privileged class which had risen from the ranks of the lower middle class professionals, declassed intellectuals, and self-taught white collar and ex-manual workers. At last it no longer had to pay its obeisance to the workers and peasants whose struggles and privations had raised it to power and affluence. For the masses were now thoroughly cowed and disoriented. They had been gradually deprived of their most intelligent and militant elements who had either been absorbed by the new bureaucratic apparatus, or liquidated by a most efficient secret police that was not hampered by any legal squeamishness.

Slowly, but steadily the Communist top layer of the new ruling class began to shed all those modern ideas which in the course of the nineteenth century had become a sort of common property of all liberals and radicals. Traditional bourgeois concepts on all aspects of life began to come back with a vengeance. True, there was no reversion to the racial and religious intolerance of the Tsarist system. In a country consisting of nearly two hundred different races and tribes, and in which the Russians proper constituted hardly more than half of the population, this would not be practical, particularly as Stalin himself and his Chief of Police, Beria, were both of non-Slavic origin, and since such a policy would have hurt the regime's expansionist designs in Asia.

But aside from racialism, the official propaganda agencies shelved once and for all the original cosmopolitanism of the bohemian days of the Bolshevik conspirators, which was coupled with a deep contempt for Russia's despotic past. The new ruling class began to wallow in an orgy of nationalist vanity. Russia's history was no longer a horrid nightmare of barbarism, feudalism and serfdom. Its glorious aspects, as represented by the country's victorious struggles against all her neighbors, whether invaders or invaded, were again presented as an inspiration to old and young. Peter the Great was no longer the sadistic brute he had been in the descriptions of the early Soviet historians, when it was still necessary to combat all the vestiges of Tsarist ideology. Now that the Tsarist peril was laid to rest, he became a symbol of Russia's grandeur, glorified in novels and heroic cinema serials. In the eyes of Russia's new nobility Peter's military conquests, as well as those of Ivan the Terrible and Catherine the Great, outweigh all the crimes they committed against Russia's peasant masses whose burden became even heavier under their glorious rule. No wonder then that those early historical works were condemned and withdrawn from circulation, particularly those written by Professor M. Pokrovsky. Yet for decades he had been considered the foremost Marxist-Leninist historian, and when he died in 1932 Stalin personally attended his funeral. It was in line with this reversion to bourgeois type that during Russia's war with the Nazis the highest reward for military prowess was named after Suvorov, a great warrior, to be sure, but one who had won his laurels in the struggle of reactionary Europe against the French Revolution and who had earned the bitter hatred of all liberals and progressives by the suppression of Pugachev's peasant uprising, and by the Warsaw massacre perpetrated in the campaign in which he was instrumental in destroying Poland's independence.

Hand in hand with this reversion to fierce nationalism, went a retreat in all other fields as well. Easy divorce and voluntary parenthood—birth control and abortion—extolled during the first decade as great achievements towards individual freedom in personal relations, are now a matter of the past. At present divorce is connected with such expenses as to put it within the reach only of those in the highest income brackets; abortion has been prohibited, contraceptives have become practically unavailable; and child-bearing has been declared the chief duty of woman. The daily paper of the Communist Youth began to expound Victorian notions with regard to chastity and woman's honor.

Having come to appreciate the conservative value of the once derided shibboleths of patriotism, family, marriage, chastity and so on, Russia's new ruling class of office-holders, technical experts, and army officers quite naturally reconsidered its previous iconoclastic attitude with regard to religion. Old Russia's conversion to Christianity was extolled as a great civilizing feat, and a musical comedy by the hitherto popular official poet, Demian Byedny, was taken off the stage because it had burlesqued that event. Anti-religious propaganda was suspended and the Russian Orthodox hierarchy was accepted as part of the Soviet system—provided it says its prayers on behalf of the regime. And after the annexation of Eastern Poland, as a result of World War II, the Ukrainian peasants inhabiting that region, who had hitherto professed an Oriental version of Roman Catholicism, were compelled to give up their allegiance to the Vatican and to join the Orthodox Church to which the Ukrainians of the Soviet Union belong. (It was in line with the same opportunist policy dictated by the desire to win the Catholic electorate, that in April 1947, the Italian Communists voted with the Rightist parties for the recognition of Catholicism as the country's state religion, a decision which implied the obligation of all non-Catholics to pay taxes for the support of the Church. That the Italian Communist vote was no "deviation" is evidenced by the fact that at about the same time Roman Catholic services preceded the Warsaw funeral of General Karol Swierczewski, a Polish Communist, who, under the name of "Walter" was one of the leaders of the "International Brigade" during the civil war in Spain. A decade ago such services for a prominent Communist would have been unthinkable. These two facts were admitted in the New York Communist Daily Worker of April 5, and April 12, 1947, respectively).

The same retrogression has marked the attitude of Russia's present rulers towards art as well. During the first years of the Revolution the Soviet authorities encouraged all sorts of modernistic trends in art, thus rallying to their cause all the younger elements which struggled against academism. But the years of "storm and stress" were over in the middle of the thirties and since that time the Government began to cater to the simple tastes of the country's none too cultured new nobility of office-holders. Artists blazing new paths fell into disfavor. Modern currents in art were officially condemned as "decadent modernistic influence" —to borrow a phrase used by the Moscow *Izvestia,* official organ of the Soviet Government, in its issue of September 2, 1938. The condemnation likewise included "French impressionism", "post-impressionism" and "bourgeois romanticism". As the Austrian Marxist Otto Bauer put it, in matters of art and literature "Bolshevist Russia of today combats exactly the same thing that Fascism in the West is fighting as 'Kultur-Bolschewismus' ". It goes without saying that only artists following the official government art "line" can expect to have their works presented to the public.

The Ethics of Power

Soviet Russia's backsliding to bourgeois respectability was accompanied by the abandonment of all ethical values which throughout the nineteenth century were cherished by liberals and radicals of all denominations.

True, their moral standard was not always very high when an intra-party and inter-party struggle for power would arouse all the evil passions such conflicts have been known to call forth since the beginning of time. Slander, for instance, was as natural in those controversies as it had been in the previous centuries, when Cromwell could accuse his democratic opponents of being in the pay of the Stuarts, or when Robespierre was able to send his Jacobin rivals to their doom as British, Austrian and Prussian spies. Hence it is not astonishing that Karl Marx could accuse Michael Bakunin, the founder of modern revolutionary anarchism, of being a crook and a Tsarist agent, or that Marx's followers bandied similar accusations against their Leftist opponents and that the latter often resorted to similar arguments among themselves. With the Communists in power, the gentle art of character assassination became one of the main weapons of propaganda and politics in general. It assumed proportions comparable only to those attained by the Nazis whose Fuehrer acted on the principle proclaimed by himself that the bigger the lie the greater the probability that it would be believed. With the maintenance of power over one-sixth of the globe at stake the Communists let go of all moral restraint, even as—according to a famous saying by Marx—a capitalist would not refrain from any crime if a profit of 200 per cent would beckon to him. Leon Trotsky, in his heyday, had no compunctions in slandering the Leftist opponents of his dictatorship as agents of the monarchists, the capitalists and the "kulaks." When he lost to another faction of his own party, he and his followers were eventually branded as "Nazi agents"; and after his assassination by a G.P.U. agent, the *Pravda* (August 24, 1940), the largest newspaper of the Soviet Union, announced the news in a story headlined: "Death of an international spy." This was in line with the persistent application of the term "social-fascist" to all Socialist leaders — at the time when Soviet diplomacy was exerting itself to come to a friendly understanding with Hitler and Mussolini.

The assassination of Trotsky on foreign soil — in the Communist press the murderer was presented as a disgruntled follower of the victim—was only one link in a series of similar assassinations committed with impunity in Switzerland, France, Spain, Mexico and the United States and, after the termination of World War II, in the various countries and "zones" occupied by the Russian army. These murders were not acts of protest by self-sacrificing fanatics against their respective governments or ruling classes, acts which, in the opinion of radicals and liberals, were often surrounded with a halo of heroism and martyrdom. They were perpetrated in cold blood by professional killers entrusted by the Soviet Government with the extermination of ex-Communists or members of Leftist groups for whose sake the governments of the foreign territories concerned did not care to raise a diplomatic issue.

In still another respect did the Communists recede behind the standards commonly observed by all progressive organizations. Nineteenth century radicalism was republican and democratic at heart and as such vigorously opposed to excessive leader worship. Cheering of leaders on all occasions or, what the Germans called "Personen-Kultus" (cult of leading personalities), was condemned as one of the vestiges of reactionary, monarchist mentality. The Communists resuscitated this ultra-reactionary, authoritarian vice to an extent almost unthinkable in the bourgeois world. Lenin's body was embalmed and preserved as a sort of deity for the veneration of the masses. Stalin has been celebrated in songs and stories in several scores of languages of the Soviet Union. Postal stamps, during World War II bore the legend *Za Rodinu—za Stalina* (For Fatherland—for Stalin). For nearly two decades every speech, every article, every treatise published in Russia had to be studded with quotations from the *Vozhd,* the Russian equivalent of the *Fuehrer,* a title which was invariably applied to him. The top leaders of the Communist parties outside of Russia, Thaelmann in Germany, Thorez in France, Browder in the U.S.A., Tito in Yugoslavia, Dimitrov in Bulgaria, became the object of a similar servile veneration cleverly organized by the party and willingly submitted to by the membership.

However, more telling still than the retrogression behind the generally accepted standards of radical and liberal conduct, more telling than the "framing" and the extermination of political dissenters, are certain stipulations of the criminal code referring to non-political offences. Soviet Russia has the distinction of being the only country in which the capital penalty was applied for theft—thus harking back to the most barbaric periods of European history. The Communist *New Masses* of New York (May 11, 1937), in discussing this fact which had been widely publicized in the daily press, tried to minimize its monstrosity by asserting that not every theft carries this penalty, and that a worker would certainly not be condemned to death if he stole "a pair of trousers from another" worker. This was correct—only government property, that is, property of the ruling bureaucratic and managerial class, is protected by such extreme measures. Thus, according to an Associated Press dispatch from Leningrad, which had passed the Soviet censor and was printed in the New York Times of September 24, 1935, "a woman worker in the Leningrad chocolate factory was sentenced to death today for stealing chocolate to sell in the open market." According to the Act of April 7, 1935 (printed in *Pravda* of April 8, 1935) "Minors, twelve years of age and older, apprehended stealing, committing violence" etc. are to be "brought before the criminal court where all measures of criminal punishment may be applied to them." This obviously included the capital penalty—for twelve-year olds!—even though the Communist weekly mentioned above, which gave the text of that law, argued that the text of the law did not mention the death penalty. (But neither did it mention imprisonment; it merely spoke of "all measures of criminal punishment.")

Russia is likewise the only country in which a peace-time deserter, if apprehended, is condemned to death (Law of June 8, 1934), and where in case of his escape or failure to return from a journey abroad, all close relatives of the offender are subject to imprisonment.

The Communist International

At its outset the movement centering around the person of Lenin was specifically Russian in character, concerned, as it were, exclusively with the Russian Revolution. To be sure, during World War I Lenin had launched the slogan that the carnage could be stopped only by converting the imperialist conflict into a civil war throughout the world. But considering the absence of any really revolutionary elements outside of Russia, this slogan was more in the nature of a propaganda phrase rather than a serious attempt at any action for achieving a definite social change in the direction of a communist society.

It was only after the Bolshevik Revolution of 1917 that the task of survival in a hostile capitalist world brought to the fore the idea, originally launched by Trotsky in 1905, of carrying the revolution to the countries of the West. What only a few years before had been considered a fantastic pipe-dream of a lone Marxist free-lance journalist, now became a concrete task. The Communist International, an organization destined to further the cause of the "proletarian revolution" in the West, was launched in 1919 and Leon Trotsky, between 1917 and 1923 second only to Lenin in the councils of the Communist Party and of the Soviet Government, wrote during that period all the official appeals of that organization.

At first the parties of the Communist International outside the U.S.S.R. were comparatively small sects of enthusiasts or fanatics. In this respect the affiliated organizations were not different from other revolutionary bodies that had sprung up in the course of the nineteenth and twentieth centuries. Soon enough, however, a very important difference became quite apparent. The Communist organizations abroad were organized along the same lines as the parent body: as a strictly disciplined army of professional revolutionists following instructions given from above. That "above" was the Soviet Government which supplied all the funds necessary for the functioning of those organizations. Thus, for all practical purposes the German, the Hungarian, the French, the Chinese and all other Communist party leaders became paid functionaries of a foreign government. This was something new in the history of revolutionary movements and it was bound to have disastrous effects upon the moral integrity of the Communist leadership the world over. From bodies of revolutionary enthusiasts interested in the seizure of power in their respective countries, the Communist parties gradually became what was at first called "frontier guards" and later "fifth columns" of the Moscow regime—in utter disregard of the interests of the working masses of their own countries. The preservation of the Soviet Government, and later the strengthening of its position on the chessboard of international diplomacy, became the only criterion for the activities of all Communist parties. As a leader of one of the factions opposing Stalin during the intra-party struggles of 1926 put it, the Communist International had become a "band of lower middle class flunkeys living at the expense of Russia's gold." Flunkeys, that is, of the faction in charge of the Soviet Union's bureaucratic apparatus.

The political and theoretical acrobatics performed by the Communist parties between 1919 and 1943 would be utterly incomprehensible if one were to disregard the fact that behind all those kaleidoscopic changes were hidden the momentary interests of the domestic and particularly of the foreign policies of Soviet Russia.[10]

Between 1919 and 1923, during the period of civil war and post-civil war dangers, the Communist International was encouraging uprisings all over Europe, even if they were altogether hopeless either because of the weakness of the Communists, or because of the passivity of the bulk of the working masses. Characteristic in this respect were the 1921 uprisings in Germany which amounted to mere wanton bloodshed. These adventures were undertaken, upon orders from Moscow, for the only reason that the wavering and exhausted Russian masses needed bolstering up by some practical sign that the European revolution against capitalism was stirring, and that the wealth of the West would soon come to their rescue.

By 1923 the situation in Germany was approaching the breaking point, with the masses ready to follow the lead of the Com-

[10] In the May 28, 1945 issue of *PM* (New York), a daily extremely friendly to the Stalin regime and staunchly opposed to what it calls "Red-baiting," its chief editorial writer Max Lerner admitted that "the fact is that American Communist policy has all along been shaped by the interests of Russian foreign policy."

munists, but to the Communist International this was not a propitious moment, because by that time the economic situation in Russia had improved and the regime hoped to come to an understanding with the Western powers.

As Hitlerism was rising in Germany the Communists went through the motions of fighting the Nazis. Yet their hostility was directed mainly against the still powerful Socialist (Social-Democratic) Party with which they refused to cooperate against the National-Socialist peril. On many occasions they went so far as to form a united front with the Nazis, as when in 1931 they voted with the Nazis in a referendum directed against the Prussian Government then controlled by the Socialists, and again, when a year later the Nazis joined the Communists in supporting a strike of the transport workers directed against the Socialist municipal administration of Berlin. Throughout these years they never ceased hurling insults at the Socialists, such as calling them "Social-Fascists" and "main supporters of capitalist dictatorship." It was not sheer suicidal insanity, prompted by factional hostility towards their moderate-leftist "step-brothers." It was a deliberate policy of the Moscow Foreign Office which at that time was afraid of a possible Western bloc directed against Russia. For this reason it preferred a Nazi regime in Germany from which it expected a militant opposition to the Western powers.[11] These, however, were reasons which could not be publicly admitted; hence the argumentation that the Socialists were the main enemies of the working class, that their destruction as a party by the Nazis was not to be regretted, that the rule of the Nazis would be a short-lived one, and that the Communists were bound to take over as soon as the Nazis had their brief fling.

[11] In the *New York Times* of March 2, 1933, Walter Duranty, a correspondent friendly to the Soviet regime, inadvertently (or cynically) spilled the beans by stating at the time of Hitler's assumption of power: "It is beyond question that Moscow would welcome even a one hundred percent Hitler regime on the grounds that it would conjure away the nightmare that has harrassed the sleep of Soviet statesmen for the past five years: namely, an anti-Bolshevik European coalition or a 'holy war against the Red Peril'."

When a few years later it began to look as if the Nazis might turn against Russia rather than against the Western powers, the Communist International dropped its previous hostility to the Socialists and began to advocate a united front with the former "Social-Fascists" (that insulting epithet was dropped, of course) and even a popular front with all middle class parties of the Western countries, provided they were opposed to the Nazis. The French Communists, who until that time had been staunch anti-patriots, suddenly became most vociferous in professing their devotion to their country, going even so far as to top their posters with the legend "France for the French!"—a slogan by the way which, a few decades previous, had been coined by Edouard Drumont, leader of the French anti-Semites.

And when shortly before the outbreak of the second World War Soviet Russia concluded that fateful alliance with Hitler, the Communists the world over repeated Molotov's famous phrase about fascism being "a matter of taste," and kept echoing the assertions of the Moscow press that it was the Allies who were the aggressors, since after the partition of Poland between Nazi Germany and Soviet Russia in 1939, France and England insisted upon continuing their war against Germany. And they maintained their opposition to the Allied war efforts against the Berlin-Rome Axis until the moment when Russia was attacked by the Nazis.

Not all Communists outside of Russia were ready to accept without questioning all those changes of policy dictated by the interests of Russia's ruling bureaucracy. Many of them bolted, either to withdraw completely from all political activity, or to join various groups of the moderate or ultra-radical Left.

The Great Fascination

The fascination which the Stalin regime has had for a great number of the foremost intellectuals of our day is one of the greatest spiritual tragi-comedies of history. No doubt it has its deep-seated reasons. Early in the past century dissatisfaction with feudal reaction induced most European liberals outside of France to hail the new tyranny of the Corsican usurper. Similarly the growing insecurity under a system of recurrent depressions in our days has reconciled many progressive intellectuals outside of Russia to the new despotism of the Georgian upstart. They behold the abolition of unemployment and are willing to suspend judgment on the undemocratic features of a regime which, in their opinion, has done away with exploitation. They forget that unemployment had been abolished in Nazi Germany as well, and they apparently assume that the Russian workers are no longer despoiled since the high incomes formerly pocketed by the now dispossessed capitalists, are distributed among the new bourgeoisie of office-holders, technical experts, writers and scholars defending the new regime.

The inability to see in their true shape things that are a few thousand miles away, particularly if cherished hopes and illusions attach to them, may serve as an excuse to some of those to whom the Russian version of totalitarianism still seems to hold out the promise of a better world. Honest and self-deluded malcontents, or tormented souls in quest of a noble "cause," they are unable to understand that the concept of a "higher" form of production is devoid of any progressive meaning, if it is coupled with the sacrifice of personal and cultural freedom which has been the great achievement of the modern age. They are on a level with those who turn their indignation only against the Roman emperors who persecuted the Christians, but close both eyes to the autodafes of Torquemada or Calvin. And they naively believe in the necessity of a dictatorial super-tyranny as a precondition for the realization of the Kingdom of Freedom, just as the pious Omar ben Abdalaziz, we are told, believed that it was necessary to make a hell of this world in order to enjoy paradise in the next.

There are also admirers of the Stalin regime whose attitude has nothing to do with honest delusion or sincere passion. These are the professional Communists and some of their not quite disinterested hangers-on. During the last few years they have won a considerable following by coupling a spurious enthusiasm for American institutions with an unconditional apology for Russian absolutism which they contrive to present as genuine democracy. Thus Earl Browder, until 1945 the uncontested leader of the party, came out "unequivocally in defense of the full maintenance of the Constitution and Bill of Rights for Communists as well as all others" (*Daily Worker*, Oct. 15, 1939). Yet only three years earlier, when asked whether "the one per cent [of the population that holds dissenting views] is entitled to the freedom of the press in Soviet Russia,"? he answered: "It is not. We believe in majority rule." (*Daily Worker*, September 1, 1936).

Communism and Fascism

The defenders of the Russian regime violently object to the inclusion of the so-called Soviet system among those forms of government which are labelled totalitarian. Their objection is mainly on the ground that totalitarianism is a form of capitalist oppression and exploitation, while the dictatorial methods of the Communists have helped to destroy capitalism and to abolish exploitation. It has been shown in the preceding pages that the Communist "abolition of exploitation" consisted merely in the substitution of a new bureaucratic aristocracy for a capitalist aristocracy, just as the latter had in its day replaced the old feudal aristocracy. The Communists and their friends are equally wrong in their contention that the fascist regimes represent a capitalist form of oppression. Wherever the Fascists were or have been in power long enough, they left no doubt that they were, or are, bent upon the elimination of private enterprise, first through government control and later by means of government ownership. In contradistinction to the Russian experiment, theirs has been a gradual process, carried out in the form of restrictions, levies, assessments and heavy taxation. That process is now going on in Argentina; for, having learned his lesson from the Russian Revolution, the gifted disciple of Mussolini and Hitler wants to avoid the chaotic confusion that would follow a sudden and simultaneous expropriation of all property owners. Perón and his following of army officers and office-holders, prefer to get their "roast pig"—that is, all the wealth of the capitalists and big land-owners—without burning the barn.

Historically the real difference between the two totalitarian camps was in the strategic approach. The Communists used as stepping stones to power the war weariness of a defeated country, anxious for peace at any price, and the land-hunger of an exhausted peasant soldiery; while the Fascists were in a position to exploit the post-war depression and the Bolshevik bogey in order to get the support of large sections of the impoverished middle classes and of the frightened capitalists at home and abroad. As a result of the different circumstances under which they were operating, the Communists suddenly dispossessed the rich and gradually enslaved the poor, while the Fascists reversed the process, by first destroying all independent labor organizations and only gradually proceeding with the dispossession of the capitalists.

Thus the first large-scale experiment in authoritarian collectivism, as conducted in Russia, which is erroneously called "communism," has revealed itself as the original form of modern totalitarianism carried to its final conclusion both in the political and economic field. The democratic, libertarian and internationalist coloring of its ideological superstructure need not deceive anybody—for it has no counterpart in reality.

The thinking man of today has been placed before a cruel choice: either the preservation of the status quo guaranteeing a certain amount of personal and cultural freedom at the exorbitant price of insecurity and unemployment, or a plunge into the dark ages of a "security" which has, once and for all, substituted unquestioning obedience and martial law for the right of criticism and for civilized democratic procedure.

To find a way out of this double impasse, to combine the advantages of a planned economy with the blessings of liberty, will be a challenge to the best minds and a task which will require the collective effort of all those who are not willing to accept either of those alternatives.

The Fourth International

Factional strife within the Soviet Union's ruling body was bound, sooner or later, to result in the creation of a party of dissident Communists. It was primarily a struggle for power, directed against the predominance of Stalin, the "boss" of the party machine. The character of that struggle is illustrated by the fact that during the 1926 campaign against the Stalin-controlled majority, the Opposition was unwilling to publish its platform prior to the Party convention, lest Stalin steal their thunder. The leadership of the Opposition, though headed by Leon Trotsky, consisted of many elements who prior to 1926 had vigorously attacked all the views the great tribune had held before and after the Revolution of 1917. And Trotsky himself, to placate many of his new allies, publicly renounced those views of his which in the past had been in contradiction to those of Lenin.

The "Opposition" was expelled from the party in 1927, and its leaders were arrested, forced to recant, and eventually exterminated as "traitors" and "Nazi agents." Destroyed in Russia, opposition to the official party policy remained alive abroad. The monolithic character of the parties affiliated with the Communist International outside of Russia resulted in frequent schisms, due either to differences of opinion or to personal rivalries. Those dissenting "outs" who were more radically inclined usually rallied around the glamorous name of Trotsky and eventually formed their own international organization, called "The Fourth International."

International Trotskyism views itself as representing the gospel of undiluted Marxist-Leninist intransigency towards the capitalist system the world over. (It was one of Trotsky's personal tragi-comedies that for reasons of propaganda he had to bow to

Lenin's prestige, even though in reality it was the founder of Bolshevism who had accepted Trotsky's idea of an anti-capitalist revolution "in our time," as it were, which the latter had advanced as far back as 1905). It is equally intransigent with regard to the Socialist and Communist parties, attacking the former as the flunkeys of capitalism, and the latter as the mercenaries of the treacherous, parasitic Soviet bureaucracy. It hopes some day to displace official Communism in the leadership of the labor movement.

However, the hostility of the Trotskyists towards the Communist parties and the ruling bureaucracy of the U.S.S.R. does not extend to the social system established in Russia by the November Revolution of 1917. In their opinion, the Soviet Union is still a "workers' state," a system which has abolished capitalist exploitation and therefore in case of war should be defended as the "workers' fatherland."

The Trotskyists do not ignore the glaring economic inequalities existing in the Soviet Union. They admit that the ruling stratum of office-holders, experts and managers enjoys a privileged status and consumes an enormous and disproportionate share of the national income. However, in their opinion, Russia's new masters do not constitute a new class of exploiters; for, according to the Marxian concept, only land-owners and capitalists could be included in that category. Once these two groups had been eliminated, the Russian masses—according to all Communists, including the Trotskyists—have actually become the owners of their country's national wealth. If, in spite of it, the enormous majority remains as miserable as prior to the Revolution, it is in their view due to the low productive level of the Soviet Union and to the consequent backwardness of the masses which is taken cruel advantage of by the Soviet bureaucracy. However, the latter is merely *swindling* the masses, but *not exploiting* them. A revolution and civil war will eventually dethrone those cheats and parasites and put in their stead a new administration of honest men who would have the interests of the masses at heart.

"Un-Marxian," as this "good-man" theory may seem, Trotsky was on good Marxian ground when he took this naïve position. For Marx could never visualize the simple fact pointed out to him by his confused, yet sometimes inspired, heretical disciple and rival, Michael Bakunin, that an upper stratum of educated men, whether they be college-bred professionals or upstart ex-workers, could constitute themselves as a new ruling class. The admission of that fact would have broken the edge of Marx's contention that the elimination of the capitalists was equivalent to the emancipation of the working class.

Shortly before his death Trotsky made a statement which amounted to a reversal of his dearly cherished position. In an article published in *The New International* (November, 1939) two months after the beginning of World War II, he expressed his "firm belief" that this war would "provoke a proletarian revolution" which would "inevitably lead to the overthrow of the bureaucracy in the U.S.S.R. and to the regeneration of Soviet democracy." "If, however," he added, "it is conceded that the present war will provoke not revolution, but a decline of the proletariat . . ." and "in the event that the proletariat of advanced capitalist countries, having conquered power, should prove incapable of holding it and surrender it, as in the U.S.S.R., to a privileged bureaucracy," and again, "if the world proletariat should actually prove incapable of fulfilling the mission placed upon it by the course of development, nothing else would remain except openly to recognize that the socialist program based on the internal contradictions of capitalist society, ended as a Utopia." In that case it would have to be admitted, in Trotsky's opinion, that "the Stalin regime is the first stage of a new exploiting society" and "then, of course, the bureaucracy will become a new exploiting class." And he concludes that paragraph with the words that if this should happen "it is self-evident that a new 'minimum' program would be required—for the defense of the interests of the slaves of the totalitarian bureaucratic society."

Trotsky thus hypothetically accepted the views of those who see in totalitarian collectivism nothing but another link in the endless chain of human exploitation systems, the office-holders and managers merely stepping into the shoes of the capitalists, just as these, in their time, had supplanted the feudal lords. Had he lived long enough, the great tribune might have possibly approached the point of view of those progressives who, though having no illusions about any sort of a classless millennium, believe that a mixed economy under a system of political democracy offers the greatest guaranties for the protection of the underdog and for human progress in general.

By having his old rival assassinated, Stalin relieved Trotsky of the melancholy necessity of revising his Marxian principles, considering that World War II did not bring about the "proletarian revolution" in whose coming Trotsky so "firmly believed." Most of Trotsky's followers, however, who still cherish the hope of succeeding the Communist Party in the leadership of the working class, have chosen to ignore Trotsky's admission by the ingenious device of declaring that the World War is not over yet. For the myth of the working class character of the Soviet system (for all its temporary counter-revolutionary deviations, as the Trotskyists would put it), and the fascination it exerts upon all malcontents who never had any direct contact with it, is too valuable a propaganda asset to be given up wantonly for the sole reason that it is . . . a myth.

There are groups of heretical Trotskyists—they had fallen out with their teacher when he defended the invasion of Finland by the Red Army—who have accepted as definitely valid Trotsky's hypothetical admission that the Soviet bureaucracy may be a new exploiting class and that the Soviet system may not be a workers' state. By maintaining their revolutionary Bolshevist position, they apparently take the view that once *they* would be in charge of a "proletarian dictatorship" things would develop in a perfectly satisfactory way. To them one might apply Israel Zangwill's famous quip directed against Bernard Shaw, that "the way he believes in himself is very refreshing in these atheistic days, when so many men believe in no God at all."

P.S. This chapter was already set up when a confirmation of the reports about Russia's slave labor was supplied in a volume by David J. Dallin and Boris I. Nicolaevsky, entitled *Forced Labor in Soviet Russia.* It has been pointed out in this connection that by inviting foreign correspondents to inspect the localities mentioned in that book the Soviet Government could easily refute those charges if they were not true.

BIBLIOGRAPHY

ADLER, FRIEDRICH: *Das Stalinsche Experiment und der Sozialismus,* Vienna, 1932.

CHAMBERLIN, WM. H.: *Soviet Russia,* Boston, 1931.—*Russia's Iron Age,* Boston, 1934.

CHERNOV, VICTOR: *The Great Russian Revolution,* New Haven, 1936.

DALLIN, DAVID J.: *The Real Soviet Russia,* New Haven, 1944.

EASTMAN, MAX: *The End of Socialism in Russia,* Boston, 1937.

GORDON, MANYA: *Workers Before and After Lenin,* New York, 1941.

HOOK, SIDNEY: *Reason, Social Myths and Democracy,* New York, 1940.

BIENSTOCK, G., SCHWARTZ, S. M., and YUGOV, A.: *Management in Russian Industry and Agriculture,* New York, 1944.

KAUTSKY, KARL: *Bolshevism at a Deadlock,* London, 1931.

KAUTSKY, KARL: *Terrorism and Communism,* London, 1920.

KOESTLER, ARTHUR: *The Yogi and the Commissar,* New York, 1945.

LAURAT, LUCIEN: *L'Economie Soviétique,* Paris, 1931.

LENIN, V.: *Collected Works.*

LENIN, V.: *State and Revolution,* New York, 1932.

LUXEMBURG, ROSA: *The Russian Revolution,* New York, 1940.

MASARYK, TH. G.: *The Spirit of Russia,* 2 Vols., London, 1919.

NOMAD, MAX: *Rebels and Renegades,* New York, 1932.

NOMAD, MAX: *Apostles of Revolution,* Boston, 1939.

ROSENBERG, ARTHUR: *A History of Bolshevism,* London, 1934.

SERGE, VICTOR: *Russia Twenty Years After,* New York, 1937.

SOUVARINE, BORIS: *Stalin,* New York, 1939.

STALIN, JOSEPH: *Leninism,* 2 Vols., New York, 1933.

TIMASHEV, N. S.: *The Great Retreat,* New York, 1946.

TROTSKY, LEON: *The Real Situation in Russia,* New York, 1928.

TROTSKY, LEON: *The Revolution Betrayed,* Garden City, 1937.

UTLEY, FREDA: *The Dream We Lost,* New York, 1940.

YVON, M.: *What Has Become of the Russian Revolution,* New York, 1937.

III.
Socialism

III.

SOCIALISM

by

Algernon Lee

The beginnings of centuries by which we measure past time bear no definite relation to the dates of historically memorable events. It happens, however, that for the purpose of this paper the starting point which for practical reasons has been chosen for the symposium to which it belongs is appropriate. Within a few years before and after 1901 the Socialist movement did actually undergo a notable change in its ways of thinking and acting..

At the advent of the twentieth century this movement could look back with pride upon a continuous, though checkered, existence of a little more than fifty years. Its path had not been an easy one. Many thousands of its adherents had lost their lives on the scaffold, in the violent dispersal of public meetings and demonstrations, on the barricades, or in the summary shooting of unarmed prisoners after the fighting was over, or by private assassination; and perhaps still larger numbers had died in prison or in the penal colonies of Siberia and New Caledonia. The terms of imprisonment and transportation had aggregated tens of thousands of years; and hardly less dreadful had been the "cold guillotine" of blacklisting by employers and hounding from pillar to post by the police. The organized movement had repeatedly suffered crushing defeats, each followed by a more or less prolonged period of weakness; and from time to time it had been torn by sharp internal conflicts. Its funeral obsequies had been celebrated over and again, but had always been disturbed by the too lively behavior of the supposed corpse. It is no mere paradox to say that it had drawn fresh vigor from each reverse and had become solidified through its schisms.

Such had been the half-century of Socialist history, conforming to the pattern which Karl Marx had foreseen in the dismal winter of 1851-'52, when he wrote *The Eighteenth Brumaire of Louis Bonaparte.* If he erred in that forecast it was in underestimating the duration of the period of alternating advance and repulse which must precede the consummation of "*the proletarian revolution of the nineteenth century.*" As that century neared its end, however, many Socialists believed that he had not been very much too sanguine in his timing and that "demain l'internationale sera le genre humain."

The Duel with Bismarck

In 1891 the German Socialist movement emerged victorious from its thirteen-year duel with Prince Bismarck. In 1874 the two Socialist parties (Lassallean and Marxian) had polled altogether 340,000 votes, in 1875 they united, and in 1877 the vote rose to almost 500,000. The next year the government procured the enactment of the drastic "exceptional laws," under which, although the Socialists retained the use of the ballot and eligibility to office, their organizations were outlawed, all their propaganda activities were penalized, and what their author called "the pig-sticking" began. Party funds, equipment, and printed matter were confiscated, records and name lists were seized, some prominent Socialists were formally banished, editors, writers, speakers, organizers, and distributors of party literature were fined and imprisoned. Prison sentences totaled 2,000 years, not including short terms in jail for such an offense as wearing a red flower in one's lapel. At the first election under these laws, in 1881, the Socialist vote fell to 312,000, but in 1884 it reached a new high mark of 550,000. The next year, thinking the velvet glove as needful as the iron hand, the Chancellor proposed a system of social insurance and got his parliamentary majority to support it by cynically explaining that its purpose was "to take the wind out of the sails of the Social Democrats." It failed of this purpose, for the Socialist vote grew to 763,000 in 1887 and to 1,427,000 (19.3% of the total) in 1890. A few months later Bismarck was dismissed, the exceptional laws expired, and the initiative in matters of social and labor legislation passed to the Social Democratic parliamentary group, which before the end of the century comprised one-seventh of the Reichstag members and was backed by more than one-fourth of the voters.

For a full generation after Bismarck's fall no responsible public man in Germany dreamed of repeating his attempt at suppression. If Frederick Engels, collaborator with Karl Marx in the authorship of the *Communist Manifesto*, who had never believed that Socialism would succeed anywhere on the Continent without a violent revolution, could at the age of seventy openly express his pleasure as well as his astonishment at seeing "how well we go forward by legal methods," it is no wonder that the vision of an ultimate Armageddon tended to give way to a growing hope among Socialists, not only in Germany, but in other lands as well, that the lion might sooner or later lie down with the lamb. As we now look back to those days, with the successive triumphs of Bolshevism in Russia, of Fascism in Italy, and of Nazism in Central Europe, the overthrow of the Spanish Republic by military traitors in 1936-'37, and the Berlin-Moscow Pact of 1939, occupying the foreground of the picture, that hope may seem to have been almost incredibly naive. It was, however, at the time, an understandable fact. The German experience which we have been summarizing was perhaps its chief objective cause, but it was not the only one. We must turn our eyes also to France and to Great Britain.

France's Long Fight for Democracy

The French have never shown as much capacity for disciplined organization as have the Germans and the British, and accordingly their struggles for liberty and progress have been more spasmodic and more violent. As to violence, it must be noted that the monarchist, aristocratic, clerical, and capitalistic elements, when in power, have far outdone the revolutionaries in bloodshed and other cruelties—and this not only in moments of passion or of panic, but with cold deliberation, as in the White Terror of 1795, the gigantic massacres of June, 1848, of December, 1851, and of May, 1871, and in the ensuing orgies of imprisonment and deportation. As to the spasmodic character of the political development, its chronology through the 98 years from the abolition of the old Bourbon monarchy to the date of Bismarck's fall tells the story. The First Republic lasted (nominally) for 12 years; the First Empire, the Bourbon Restoration, and the July Monarchy filled the next 44 years; the Second Republic endured (again nominally) for 4 years; the Second Empire lived for 18 years; and through an equal span of time the Third Republic was obviously neither secure nor very genuinely republican.

Socialism is too commonly thought of as having been born in France and as being a child of the Great Revolution. This is true enough as concerns the Socialism of the first half of the nineteenth century—or rather the two separate and parallel Socialisms of that period, the Babeuvist and the Utopian, the Socialism of "les misérables" and that of the panacea mongers. Only in small measure is it true of what we distinguish as modern, proletarian, and international Socialism, which succeeded these two and almost completely displaced them, which survived and grew and is an integral part of contemporary world history. Its ancestry is indeed partly French and partly German, but most of all it stems from the Industrial Revolution of the Eighteenth Century. It is essentially the counter-product of industrial capitalism, of the economy which centers in the large-scale production of commodities by the use of huge, costly, complex, privately owned aggregates of power-driven machinery and the employment of vast numbers of wage workers. Because this mode of production played but a minor part in the French economy of a century or half a century ago (even now it is hardly dominant), because the French bourgeoisie was more largely financial, commercial, and agrarian, because the industrial wage workers were not yet numerous or self-conscious enough to lead and direct the anti-capitalist forces—because of all this the earlier development of modern Socialism in France was not quite normal in either its ideological or its organizational aspects.

Through nearly the first half of its life—say, from February, 1848, through the tragi-comic fiasco of Boulangism in 1888-'89—the French Socialist movement had again and yet again to permit its own specific aims to fall into the back-ground, in order to function as the heroic advance guard in the fight for political liberty; and in so doing it had but grudging support, alternating with cynical betrayal, by more or less sincerely republican elements among the peasantry and among the petty bourgeois, the shop-keepers, the self-employing handicraftsmen, and the intellectual *déclassés* of the cities. Having to defend the achievements of the Great Revolution against Bonapartist, Legitimist, and Orleanist champions of a pretended future which was in fact an unburied past, against a motley crew of greedy and ambitious adventurers, and above all against the unholy alliance of High Finance, Catholic Hierarchy, and General Staff, it had little opportunity to criticize its ideas or to unify its fighting forces.

There were always two, three, or more Socialist parties, which seldom waged war upon one another so fiercely as did the German Lassallean and Marxian parties in the 1860s and early '70s, which usually co-operated fairly well in critical moments, but which were never able to build one strong and stable organization. Not one of these parties ever had a dues-paying membership at all commensurate with the support which it could enlist at the polls, in street demonstrations, or occasionally on the barricades. As late as 1907 Jean Longuet, the grandson of Karl Marx, said to the present writer: "At the next election we shall have a million votes, and we may not have one more party member or one more franc in our treasury than we have today." He was not far wrong.

Socialist Unity in France

For about a decade after 1888, French republican institutions did not appear to be in grave danger, and the Socialists were therefore free to give more attention to propagating and incidentally clarifying their specially socialistic theories and ideals. There resulted an encouraging increase of their voting strength and a perhaps proportionate growth of their party membership. It did not, however, bring about solidification of the organized movement; this did not come until 1905—that is, not until there had been in France and elsewhere an exhaustive discussion of ideological as well as tactical problems, in which some old attitudes were abandoned, some new ones were developed, and a considerable degree of agreement was attained, not by diplomatic bargaining but as a genuine synthesis of opinion, which made it practicable to act unitedly on essential points, and yet permit freedom of public discussion and a wide range of tolerance for divergent views in the field of theory.

A step toward this kind of unity was taken in France not long after the election of 1893, which had seated about 50 Socialists in the chamber (nearly one-twelfth of the whole number of deputies), including representatives of all the five Socialist parties then existing, and also a number who were as yet independents. (At this point, to forestall misunderstanding, let us note that these figures do not include the "Radicaux socialistes" or Socialistic Radicals, whom American and English writers almost always convert into "Radical Socialists.") On the initiative of Alexandre Millerand, 33 members subscribed the following declaration:

"The Socialist group of the Chamber affirms its determination to continue its daily struggle against reactionary governments,

"It will introduce and support immediate reforms which, even within the capitalist system, will ameliorate the condition of the working people.

"It does not mean to restrict the liberty of its members and the development of Socialism itself by any narrow formula.

"But, in order to eliminate troublesome misconceptions, it clearly declares that, in conformity with the fundamental thinking of the Socialists in all countries and with the tradition of French Socialism ever since the Revolution, it aims to abolish the capitalist system itself and to put an end to the exploitation of man by man, through the conquest of political power by the proletariat, through the substitution of social property for capitalist property, and through international agreement (l'entente internationale) of the workers."

This became in effect the common platform of all the French Socialist parties and groups. It did not, however, and in the nature of things it could not, prevent a renewal of conflicts and even very sharp conflicts within the movement, arising out of new events which posed new problems.

For the present it is sufficient to say that in France, as in Germany, though for a shorter time, there prevailed a cheerful and optimistic mood, a relaxation of the long continued storm and stress, which favored the calm thinking-over of principles and policies. Events on the other side of the Channel, in themselves quite different, harmonized with this new mood.

British Labor Seemed Inert

From the middle of the nineteenth century almost to its close the inertness of British labor was a source of grave disappointment and misgivings to the Continental Socialists.[1] Among the British intellectuals there were a good many who sympathized with and partly understood some of the stirrings of popular un-

[1] Marx and Engels shared the regret, but they never doubted that in its own slow way, the British working class would create a native Socialist movement comparable with any other in the world; and Engels lived to see the beginning of what became in 1945 the governing party of the United Kingdom.

rest on the Continent and who at least pitied and wished well to the poorer classes in their own country, but their utterances hardly woke an echo among the masses. Had there been in Britain a labor movement, however weak, which resembled the German or the French in revolutionary aim and spirit, it could have given them invaluable aid in critical moments; and if it had been comparable with them in strength it might, by influencing British public opinion and Britain's foreign policy, have brought about the formation of a western democratic entente capable of holding its own against the reactionism of St. Petersburg, Potsdam, Vienna, and the Vatican. Nothing of the sort happened. The British working people seemed to be hopelessly immune to the ideas by which the European Socialists were guided and inspired.

The political backwardness of the British workers was not only displeasing to their European brothers; it seemed to them almost incomprehensible. From the Peasants' War and the Anabaptist risings (1524-'36) at least until the sudden awakening of national patriotism in 1812, the political history of the German people had been a blank; and in France for a yet longer time, from the days of Etienne Marcel and the *Jacquerie* (1355-'58) down to 1789, the nearest approaches to popular revolt had been the brief episode of Jeanne d'Arc in 1429 and the sectarian resistance of the Vaudois and of the Huguenots. The English and Scottish peoples, on the contrary, had revolutionary and largely democratic traditions which ran back to the fourteenth century, and these had been kept alive by poets and ballad makers, by playwrights and novelists, as well as by historians and parliamentary orators. Moreover, within comparatively recent times the lower strata, and specifically the urban and rural wage workers, had set examples that encouraged similar elements abroad.

There are faint traces of trade unionism in England as early as 1709. For a long while the unions were few, small, narrowly local, and in most cases short-lived; but by the later 1780s, when the Industrial Revolution was clearly showing its effects in mass unemployment, depression of wages, and rise of food prices, trade unionism began to take on proportions and a character which gave alarm to the propertied classes, and especially to the newly rich factory owners, who were not troubled by any sense of social responsibility or any traditional scruples about grinding the faces of the poor. Side by side with this, there appeared a type of social-political radicalism far superior to any that had been known since the days of Algernon Sidney and of John Locke. In a manner somewhat different from that of the contemporary French *philosophes*, though partly influenced by them, a number of writers began to subject all institutions, creeds, customs, and moral judgments to a critical examination which was humane in its purpose, usually moderate in its tone, but extremely bold.[2] Unschooled and even illiterate as were the mass of the wage workers, many of them were deeply affected (infected, the children of good fortune would have said) by the radical ideas which somehow filtered down to those who could not afford to buy books or even could not read them.

Echoes of French Revolution

For a few years before and after 1789 these developments had a considerable influence upon the thinking and the conduct of the pioneers of the Revolution. Conversely, the news from France, at least down to 1793, cheered and strengthened the British progressives, both intellectual and proletarian. Most of them regretted and even disapproved the more violent features of the revolution, but it was possible to palliate and even to excuse them. As Englishmen they were not really shocked by the execution of Louis XVI, for they remembered without shame that their own ancestors had beheaded a king; but the increasingly frequent

[2] Perhaps the most notable among these were William Godwin, author of *Political Justice*, published in 1793, and Mary Wollstonecraft, author of *A Vindication of the Rights of Women*, published in 1792, who afterwards became Godwin's wife. H. Noel Brailsford's *Shelley, Godwin, and Their Circle* (Henry Holt & Co., New York, undated, but probably 1914) is almost indispensable for the understanding of this period.

execution of earlier heroes of the Revolution, from Bailly to Danton and the Desmoulins, by their more ruthless successors, the avowed policy of "putting Terror on the order of the day," and the growth of sordid corruption step by step with systematic bloodshed—these things did cause among the British protagonists of liberty a moral revulsion far more sincere than the upper-class thrills of horror so theatrically expressed by Edmund Burke.

The Reign of Terror, the fall of Robespierre, and the ignoble ending of the First Republic did not, however, so much weaken the British radical and labor movement as it aroused and united the oligarchic elements. The suspension of the right of habeas corpus in 1793 marked the turning point. Most historians picture the next three decades or thereabout as an age of self-sacrificing patriotism and military glory, and grow dithyrambic when they speak the names of Pitt and Nelson and Wellington, and of course writers of text-books and romances follow their lead. In truth it was one of the blackest periods in English history—a time of economic and governmental tyranny at once cruel and calculating: for the masses it was a time of squalor, degeneration, and increasing misery. We use the word "cowardly" not as a mere angry epithet, but with a definite meaning. Besides the cold ruthlessness of greed, there was the senseless and often self-defeating excess of cruelty which is associated with panic fear. There is abundant evidence that the propertied classes—and most of all the industrial capitalists, whose rise to wealth and power had been so recent and so rapid that they had not acquired that self assured poise which long continued eminence confers—were struck with terror, first by the onrushing vigor of the French Revolution, and then by the success of its raw and often ill equipped troops in combat with the veteran forces of the old monarchies. They were haunted by the nightmare of a vast conspiracy of workingmen and peasants, planning to re-enact on British soil all the subversive acts of the French *canaille*. The existence of the nightmare was a fact, and potent for evil; but the nightmare itself was an illusion, unconnected with objective truth. There was no conspiracy, no inclination toward mass revolt. Adventurers of the type of Lord George Gordon could indeed have promoted serious riots, as had often occurred in the past; no outbreaks did occur, however, in the earlier years of the period in question. The organized workers showed no disposition to resort to violence and the radical ideologists, so far from trying to incite revolt, positively discountenanced it.

The first overt sign of desperate unrest was the naval mutiny of 1797, which involved several thousand seamen, composing the crews of twenty-five or more warships then lying in home waters. For two months they had possession of the vessels, with the cannon, small arms, and ammunition, and they were defeated only by the cutting off of their food supplies. Their conduct was amazingly self-disciplined, moderate, and humane. There was no trace of revolutionary aims. The whole affair resembled what we now call a sit-down strike, to support demands for a very slight increase of wages and payment of arrears; for full-weight rations of wholesome food instead of mouldy bread and half-putrid meat and cheese; and for discontinuance of arbitrary flogging in excess of the limit set by the regulations. After the surrender, and in violation of a general pardon signed by King George III, twenty-nine men were hanged, nine savagely flogged, and 29 sent to prison for terms ranging from one to eight years. This done, a few of the grievances were partially redressed, but the officers who had flogged men literally to death and the civil officials who had enriched themselves by grafting on food supplies went scot-free.[3]

War Upon the Unions

Two years later the government launched a vigorous assault upon the trade unionism which had been gaining strength espe-

[3] The best account of this memorable affair, ignored by many historians, is *The Floating Republic*, by C. E. Mainwaring and Bonamy Dobrée (London, 1935; American reprint, 1937, Pelican Books). *Mutiny on the Bounty*, by Charles Nordhoff and James Norman Hall (New York, 1932, Little, Brown & Co.) may well be read in this connection. It is one of the few "novelized histories" that can be heartily recommended.

cially in the rapidly expanding textile industry. In 1799 the first of the two Combination Laws was introduced, passed by both houses, and signed by the king, all within twenty-four hours; the second, enacted in 1800, rendered it more effectively severe. These acts made it a criminal offense for three or more wage workers in any trade to meet and consult with a view to obtaining higher wages or other improvement in their conditions of employment. Ostensibly they likewise prohibited combinations of employers, but no attempt was ever made to enforce this provision, though it was brazenly violated. Some of the older unions in small-shop trades were not seriously disturbed, but the full force of the law was exerted against the younger and more aggressive organizations of factory operatives. It was easy to get convictions, for nearly all the magistrates were "substantial citizens," not a few of them owners of factories, and in courts of record the judges were seldom oblivious of the biblical injunction "Servants, be obedient to your masters," while the juries were largely composed of local shopkeepers who could not safely offend wealthy customers. Year by year large numbers of workingmen were sent to prison for terms varying between three months and two years; still more were fined and, if unable to pay, had to lie in jail for weeks or months; and after punishment under the law came the factory owners' refusal to employ "jailbirds," the tramping in search of jobs, and the danger of being jailed again as vagrants.

The Combination Acts soon yielded the result at which their framers had aimed, but after some delay they produced another effect which had not been foreseen. Open and peaceably inclined unions being suppressed, secret and oath-bound organizations took their place, probably not so strong numerically, but with the new strength of desperation; and with secrecy came the resort to violence. The working people knew quite well—what professional economists of the Pollyanna school denied and still deny—that the cause of increasing unemployment was the introduction of power-driven machinery, which enabled fewer workers to produce more goods. Being forbidden to deal collectively with the owners, they directed their attack upon the machines. Sometimes this took the form of setting fire to factory buildings. Oftener, bands of desperate men, carrying heavy hammers or crowbars, broke into the factories at night, systematically smashed the machines, and dispersed as quickly as they could. Of course there were occasional clashes, with casualties on both sides but mostly among the rioters.

These outbreaks began early in 1811 and became more frequent as time went on. Before long the owners appealed to the government and squads of soldiers were detailed to guard their works. This method was not very successful, as everyone could know where the redcoats were, and attacks were made elsewhere. More effective was the use of spies; and as always occurs in such a situation, many of the spies became provocators, magnifying their own importance by inciting men to criminal acts and then betraying them. In March, 1812, parliament branded wilful breaking of machines and taking of unlawful oaths as capital offenses, and for the next two or three years men charged with such crimes were being hanged, singly or in batches; fourteen were hanged on one day in one city in January, 1813. Much greater numbers were imprisoned or transported to Australia. The attacks on factories gradually became less frequent, and by 1817 they had practically ceased.

Considered as a purposeful movement, Luddism was essentially reactionary—that is, it aimed at restoring a dead past, not at creating a practicable future. It was revolutionary only in an emotional sense, as expressing a passionate will to revolt. The same is to be said as to the burning of hayricks by impoverished peasants and agricultural laborers, of which there were repeated outbursts in this period and even later.

Class Struggle at the Top

The ending in 1815 of the twenty-two years of almost continuous war with revolutionary and Napoleonic France brought to Britain some measure of economic relief and a considerable abatement of the fear-psychosis which had prevailed so long. It also permitted the normal antagonism of material interests and of social attitudes between the agrarian oligarchy and the industrial bourgeoisie to reassert itself. The dignified and leisurely recipients of land rent had still an almost complete monopoly of the powers of legislation and government, but this monopoly (or the effective utilization of it) was now being menaced by the growing and mobile wealth and the superior energy of the less respectable scramblers for profit. This class struggle in the higher strata of society did not break out at once, but within a few years it became acute, and in the long run it deeply affected the development of the working classes.

It was too late in English history for such a conflict to be settled by an appeal to arms; it had to be fought out on the political field. Even more than a civil war, a political revolution always includes an effort to convince or to persuade the public, and the consequences of such an appeal to reason and to emotion may extend far beyond the immediate issues and beyond the intentions of those by whom it is made. The writers and speakers are not always conscious of being advocates of the material interests of this or that class, and some of them even consciously oppose the groups to which they respectively belong.[4] It is nevertheless true that the opinions and sympathies of most intellectuals are in the main shaped and colored by their economic background, even if not by their personal interests.

The radicalism which flowered in the 1790s had pretty well died out long before Waterloo. Its waning was due less to repression than to disillusionment. The repression, indeed, was not very severe. Juries were not so ready to convict men for spoken or

[4] This was notably true of Byron and Shelley. Both of these came of "good family" and were themselves at least well-to-do. Yet Byron's speech in the House of Lords, opposing the "hangman's bill" in 1812, and several of his later poems, as well as most of Shelley's, culminating in *Men of England* and *The Masque of Anarchy*, breathed ardent sympathy with the oppressed. This must be qualified, however, by the remark that they saw the sins of the bourgeoisie more vividly than those of the landlords.

written words as for overt acts. Moreover, at least some leading statesmen underestimated the danger. When Godwin's *Political Justice* was published (at an exorbitant price) in 1793 the prime minister, William Pitt, was urged by his colleagues to prosecute the author and the printer. He refused on the ground that "a three guinea book could never do much harm among those who had not three shillings to spare." He was right in thinking it unwise to prosecute, but he was wrong in thinking the book innocuous. Even before a second and cheaper edition came out in 1796, Godwin's ideas were seeping down into circles whose thinking he had probably never expected to influence.

The Early Radicals

Godwin's own basic doctrine—that which we now call philosophical or non-violent Anarchism, which carries with it the belief in human perfectibility—had no great vogue at the time and certainly had little effect on the conduct of the discontented masses, nor has it ever found wide acceptance. Within little more than a dozen years it was losing such vogue as it had enjoyed; then Percy Bysshe Shelley, a student at Eton, perhaps fifteen years of age, read *Political Justice,* which had been published when he was a year old. It became his gospel, and it runs through the succession of great poems which he poured forth from 1813 till his death in 1822. Shelley's poems are still a revolutionary force; they are such, however, not because of the philosophical theory, but because of the passion for human freedom and equality. the burning hatred of cruelty and falsehood, which they express.

Writers more prosaic than Shelley and less didactic than Godwin had awakened popular thought in the earlier period—such men, for example, as the Reverend Doctor Priestley, the Reverend Doctor Price, and the very irreverent Thomas Paine. The dark period from the passage of the Combination Acts till their repeal was bridged by the plain common sense of William Cobbett, whose *Weekly Register* struck right and left at every species of outrage and sham, with the weight of a cudgel and the incisiveness of a rapier. Cobbett combined the aggressive spirit of early radicalism with the practicability of the bourgeois liberalism that was to mark the nineteenth century. Above all, he never failed to point out the necessity of reforming the utterly misrepresentative parliament.

If we note that Thomas Robert Malthus' *Observations on the Corn Laws* and the definitive edition of his *Principles of Population*, David Ricardo's *Principles of Political Economy and Taxation*, and James Mill's *Political Economy* all appeared between 1815 and 1826, and also that this period included the early manhood of George Grote and Thomas Babington Macaulay and the youth of John Bright, Richard Cobden, and John Stuart Mill, we realize that a new era was beginning—the era of optimistic liberalism. The books of Malthus, Ricardo, and the elder Mill are not easy reading, but they were widely read and discussed, and more popular contemporary writings show that many members of the lower middle and working classes were eager to understand the relations among land rent, profits, wages, and the cost of living, and the bearing of taxation upon these and other economic phenomena. Not the least interested were the mechanics and factory operatives, in view of the fact that, while industry and commerce were expanding and becoming ever more profitable, and while the price of land (which reflects the rental that land yields to its owners) was increasing—that is, while both of the wealthy classes were growing richer—money wages were falling, their purchasing power was declining still faster, and long hours of labor coincided with widespread unemployment. Illiterate though most of the wage workers were, workingmen's clubs and even Saturday night talks in the alehouse brought the new teachings of economics within their ken and linked them with those of bitter experience.

The complete failure of the workers' attempt to bring back the relatively good old times of hand labor and small-scale production by physically destroying power-driven machinery compelled them to turn their attention to non-violent trade unionism and to political action. Some might think of using the power of their numbers to change the whole property system; more numerous were those who deemed it more practical to concentrate upon the repeal of the Combination Acts and of the Corn Laws, hoping thus to get more shillings for their labor and more bread and beer[5] for each shilling. The first of these objectives coincided with the views of the factory owners, who counted that reduction of the cost of living would enable them to push wages still further down, and was fiercely opposed by the landowners, who held that the "pegged" price of grain was the palladium of national greatness; and conversely, the landlords rather favored a rise of wages for workers in industry, since it would increase the effective demand for grain, while the capitalists regarded organization as little short of sedition and declared that increase of wages would ruin British industry. Seldom has a three-way antagonism of class interests appeared with such diagrammatic clearness.

Workers Turn to Politics

The cessation of the Luddite disorders did not appease the government's hostility to working-class activities. Combination for the purpose of raising wages was still a criminal practice, and prosecutions continued. For voteless workingmen, finding violence futile, to turn to open political activity was, the rulers felt, the height of impudence and, if not promptly and sternly checked, would be a prelude to the forcible overthrow of state, church, and property institutions. Provisions of common and statute law were invoked, spies and stool pigeons were employed, and military force was held in readiness, to break up the clubs and committees of correspond-

[5] In those days, and for decades thereafter, the British masses considered beer a form of nutriment as necessary as bread. See Frederick L. Olmstead's *An American Farmer in England* (1859), especially a passage in the fortieth chapter.

ence, and to deal with public meetings as riotous assemblages, no matter how orderly they might be. Under suspension of habeas corpus great numbers of persons were held in prison for as much as ten months without being charged with any crime or misdemeanor. Yet the agitation went on, gained strength, and spread into Scotland. To the demand for repeal of the Corn Laws and the Combination Acts was now added the cry for electoral and parliamentary reform. This gave the landed oligarchy two reasons instead of one for fearing and hating the working-class movement. The same reasons would have prompted an intelligent bourgeoisie to regard it with some favor, for it would be to the advantage of that class to obtain such changes as would give adequate representation to the industrial cities, which had grown enormously with the growth of the factory system. Some even began to see that, although the material interests of employers and wage workers were by no means identical, neither were they in all respects antagonistic, since expansion of industry would mean increase of aggregate profits for the former and fuller employment for the latter. This consideration might suggest the practicability of an armistice if not an alliance between them. As yet, however, these liberal views[6] were not widely accepted by the factory owners; in any case, the government was still in the hands of the landowners, who were willing to "do the dirty work" of the employers whenever it did not conflict with their own class interests.

The war of the rich against the poor reached a crisis at Manchester on August 16, 1819. A midday mass meeting to urge parliamentary reform had been called, to be held in St. Peter's Field, a large unbuilt space within the city, and to be addressed by Henry Hunt, commonly called "Orator Hunt". It is alleged that 60,000 persons attended. Among them were women, especially wives with their husbands, in some cases bringing their

[6] We use the word "liberal," not in the vague and almost meaningless way it is now commonly used in the United States, but in the definite sense it bears in modern British and European history, as designating the normal ideology and political tendencies of a fairly mature industrial bourgeoisie, in distinction from those of the landed aristocracy on the one hand and of the proletariat on the other.

children along, a sufficient proof that they had been given no reason to expect forcible interference. Hunt had hardly begun to speak when three bodies of cavalry, with sabres drawn, debouched from three directions out of back streets in which they had been held in readiness, and charged at a gallop upon the rear of the dense crowd. Within a few minutes nine men and two women were killed and about 440 men and 120 women injured, some of them crippled for life.

Such in bare outline is the story of what in bitter irony was called the battle of Peterloo. Many well attested details, dating from August 5 to August 19, which we have not space to relate, leave no room for reasonable doubt that the affair was an ambush with intent to kill, planned and perpetrated for the purpose of terrorizing the half starved, outraged, and disfranchised masses all over England who were asserting their right to a share in making and administering the laws. The conduct of the magistrates concerned, whatever their individual characters, vividly typifies the reactions of a propertied ruling class when it feels that its wealth, power, and privileges are in danger.

Most of the owners of lands and factories openly exulted in the defeat which had been inflicted upon those seditious and irreligious rascals who were not content with the station in life to which God had assigned them. There were, indeed, some persons of rank and wealth who openly condemned the massacre—notable among them being Sir Francis Burdett, who paid for his boldness with three months in prison and a fine of $10,000—but these were rare exceptions.

A defeat it was, for the time and through most of England, Orator Hunt was imprisoned for two and a half years and three of his associates for a year, and prosecutions followed at other places. Public meetings almost ceased. In a short autumn session parliament passed what are called the Six Acts, putting yet sharper teeth into the various repressive laws, and especially prohibiting correspondence between the political clubs and imposing a tax of fourpence (eight cents) on every copy of a political pamphlet or periodical selling for less than sixpence. As sixpence meant from a quarter to a half a day's wages for most of the workers, this practically suppressed the literature of the labor and reform movement.

A Second Era of Violence

Such stifling of open and peaceable activities of course turned many men's minds to conspirative and violent methods. This soon showed itself in Scotland, where the agitation had hitherto been less vigorous. Early in 1820 it became known that secret working people's clubs were being formed in the textile and mining districts. On April 2 placards appeared, calling for cessation of work until universal suffrage was granted, in the name of the "Committee for Organization of a Provisional Government"—a piece of folly which suggests the activity of stool-pigeons. The proposed strike was fairly extensive, and small bands of badly armed men made their appearance. One such group came into conflict with a body of soldiers and was quickly put to flight. Nineteen of the men were captured, arrests were made elsewhere, and the strike collapsed. A mass trial on charges of high treason ensued, many were imprisoned or transported, and three were hanged. In London, meanwhile, a still more spectacular event took place. The government had for several weeks been receiving from one of its hired provocators almost day-to-day information about the doings and the personnel of a group of hotheaded dupes whose plan was to assassinate all the ministers at one stroke, open the prisons, raise the London mob, and so initiate a nation-wide revolution. On February 23, a few hours before the blow was to be struck, police and soldiers raided a house in Cato Street and seized a number of the leaders, and others were soon traced and arrested. After a sensational trial, a feature of which was the exposure of the sinister part played by the secret agent, five were hanged and many others transported or sent to prison.

For the next few years the working-class movement, in both its peaceable and its violent forms, seemed to be dead and was actually quiescent. One might say that the workers were taking stock of their past and thinking what to do next. William Thompson, John Gray, Thomas Hodgskin, and other writers, whose works have long been forgotten, stimulated this process. They were largely influenced by the ideas of Bentham and the elder Mill, of Ricardo, and of Robert Owen, whose voluminous contributions on economic subjects had begun with his pamphlet on *The Effect of the Manufacturing System*, published in 1815. For the time, while the minds of the masses were stimulated, the stimulation had a divisive rather than a unifying effect, attention being distracted from the main objectives of their previous efforts—trade-union organization, repeal of the Corn Laws, and winning of the right to vote—by sectarian interest in a variety of other projects, some of them wrong-headed and others premature, such as either socialization or distribution of the land, substitution of organized barter for the use of money, co-operative production, and so forth.

Combination Laws Repealed

The repeal of the Combination Acts in 1824-'25 may be taken as an ending and a new beginning in the political history of Great Britain and in the history of the British working class.

The Webbs tell us—and their statements of fact are seldom open to question—that the repeal of the Combination Laws "was rapidly passed through both houses, without either debate or division."[7] There had, however, been patient and skilful work by Joseph Hume and a few others in privately convincing or persuading hesitant members and in managing a committee of inquiry to the point of getting a unanimous favorable report. Back

[7] The best account of this remarkable legislative act is to be found in the second chapter of *The History of Trade Unionism*, by Sidney and Beatrice Webb, first published in 1894 and most accessible in the second edition of 1902.

of this lay the tireless labor of Francis Place, not a member of parliament, in collecting documentary material, promoting petitions, and enlisting witnesses. "There was," say the Webbs, "no popular movement whatever for the repeal," mainly because experience had convinced the workers that no help was to be expected from parliament as then constituted. For the moment this was fortunate, for mass demonstrations would have stirred up opposition to the repeal. In fact, the bill went through so easily just because all concerned were completely mistaken as to the effect it would produce. Place held that, once combinations ceased to be unlawful, they would soon cease to exist; Hume and others either already held this view or accepted it from Place; and so far as the record shows, nobody questioned it at this time.[8]

They had a rude awakening. Within a few weeks new unions began to spring up, while those which had existed in secret or had been tolerated came into the open and gained new members; in a few cases, local unions merged or federated on a nation-wide scale; and strikes become more numerous than ever before. The upper classes were of course angry and frightened—the employers and other business men because they saw their profits directly threatened, the landed gentlemen because they feared that the farm laborers might follow the example set by the urban workers. For a moment in 1825 it looked as if parliament would "repeal the repeal." Well informed men, however, warned the political leaders that an attempt to do this would provoke a revolutionary uprising which the armed forces at the government's disposal could not suppress. They had to be content with an amending act which whittled down the concessions made the preceding year.

[8] That intelligent men could entertain this notion may be partly explained by the vogue which the bourgeois doctrine of *laissez faire* enjoyed at this time, creating a general tendency to disapprove prohibitory and restrictive legislation. The fact that within the four preceding years parliament had begun to soften the penal code and had repealed some of the Navigation Acts and all statutes restricting workingmen's rights to travel or change their places of residence would seem to favor this hypothesis, which is strengthened also by Burdett's speech in 1799 against the first Combination Law, in which he declared that "the wise policy is to leave trade of every kind to find its own level." (See *Sir Francis Burdett and His Times,* by M. W. Patterson, London, 1931, page 545).

The net result was that trade-union action was not in itself unlawful, though it was subject to legal attack at many points.

Even this was a substantial gain. From 1824 on, though the labor organizations have had to fight many a hard battle to defend the rights they had won, and bit by bit to win new rights, trade unionism in both great and small industry has had a continuous existence and a gradually broadened basis of legality; more slowly it has extended into the fields of agricultural and "white collar" employment.

More disastrous to the labor movement than the amending act of 1825 was the business depression which began toward the end of that year and continued till 1829. Unemployment on a large scale so weakened the unions that, instead of improving their conditions, they struggled in vain against wage reductions. After a momentary revival of machine-breaking, which was easily put down, the workers again turned to political radicalism. Parliamentary reform was their immediate objective, but they now looked beyond this to economic and social changes which, once manhood suffrage was established, they might obtain by the power of their numbers.

An Oligarchic Parliament

The struggle for reform, carried on by the bourgeoisie and the proletariat simultaneously, though not for identical purposes nor by identical means, calls for a historical background.

In the seventy years from 1690 to 1760 the population of England and Wales grew from less than 5,000,000 to 7,000,000. Had the same rate continued, the number would by 1830 have increased to 10,000,000; in fact it reached 14,000,000, and this solely by an amazing increase of the birth rate. The doubling of the population was accompanied by momentous changes in its geographical distribution and in its class structure.

From the earliest times the southern and eastern parts of the country, having soil and climate more favorable to agriculture, had been by far the most densely peopled; but with the rise of machine production the more abundant water power offered by the hilly North and West attracted industrial enterprise, and when steam power came into use the proximity of coal and iron deposits strengthened this attraction and so determined a flow of population into these hitherto backward regions. London, with its environs, as being the commercial, political, and cultural capital, continued to grow, and so did a few other seaports; but nearly all the inland cities, towns, and large villages in the South and East, which had formerly thriven as centers of handicraft and local trade, became stationary or declined.

The number of persons engaged in agriculture and grazing still increased, but at a much slower rate than did the population as a whole. Its increase, indeed, was positively retarded by improvements in methods of tillage and in the breeding of cattle and sheep which had got under way earlier in the century. From the 1760s on, the urban population gained on the rural at an accelerating rate; and, injurious as the process was to the comfort, health, and domestic morality of the masses, it did make for a livelier intellectual tempo, for the formulation of opinions and aspirations, and for their expression in united effort.

It was of course the wage-working class, and especially the factory proletariat, that grew most rapidly.[9] Next to it in speed of numerical increase came the rural proletariat, comprising agricultural laborers and petty tenant farmers, whose numbers were swelled by the ruin of small proprietors. These were almost as cruelly exploited as the workers in mine, mill, and factory, but they lagged behind in development of class consciousness and capacity for organized effort. In that miscellaneous aggregate known as the middle class, some elements become less and others more numerous; on the whole there was an increase, but less rapid than that of the working classes.

[9] Here and in some other places, for the sake of brevity, we use the term "factory workers" or "factory proletariat" to include also persons working for wages in mines, smelters, forges, potteries, shipyards, and other large enterprises.

By the end of the seventeenth century it was a settled fact that the powers of the Crown were subordinate to those of Parliament; and by the middle of the eighteenth it was clear that, if any crucial test of power should occur (which was as yet unlikely) the hereditary House of Lords would have to bow to the will of the nominally elective Commons. All this did not mean that the government had become more democratic, for the lower house was a grossly misrepresentative body.

Out of 6,000,000 adult males in the United Kingdom only 435,000 had the vote. This included practically no laborers, mechanics, factory operatives, or tenant farmers and but few small business men. As votes had to be given by voice and in public, there was ample opportunity for bribery and for intimidation of voters who could not be bribed. Furthermore, the allotment of seats bore no proportion to the number of voters or of inhabitants in the various counties and boroughs. The six northernmost counties of England had 10 per cent more inhabitants than the ten southernmost, but the latter had 235 seats and the former only 68. Young industrial cities with populations ranging from 50,000 to 100,000 were entirely unrepresented, while many decadent boroughs with only a few hundred or even a few dozen inhabitants were entitled to one or two members.[10]

The 186 members representing counties were more or less honestly elected by a very limited number of landed gentlemen. Of the 472 borough members Professor Ogg says that "not more than 137 may be regarded as having been in any proper sense elected." Each of the remaining 335 was virtually appointed by some local magnate. This gentleman or nobleman might appoint himself or

[10] At least eight members of parliament sat for constituencies which had absolutely no inhabitants, and one of which could have none, because its site had long since been completely eroded by the sea. For more detailed accounts of suffrage and representation at this period, of the fight for reform, and of the Act of 1932, see *The Governments of Europe*, by Frederic Austin Ogg, New York, 1914, pages 77-96; *Modern and Contemporary European History*, by J. Salwyn Schapiro, New York, 1918, chapters IV and V; *A History of British Socialism*, by Max Beer, London, 1919, first volume, pages 280-321; and Patterson's *Sir Francis Burdett*, second volume, pages 542-613. Beer's two-volume work, and also the later chapters of H. B. Gibbins' *Industrial History of England* (first published by Methuen in 1890, but revised and continued in 1912) may be recommended as dealing much more fully with all the British movements and events discused in this paper.

a member of his family, but he might and often did sell the seat for the term of a single parliament, at the best price he could get, which often ran up to $25,000 or more. Not a few of the purchasers considered this as an investment, counting that they could get it back with a good profit by selling their votes in parliament or by making their support of the ministry at a critical moment conditional on getting a peerage, a lucrative public office, or a pension. Some, however, who could afford the luxury, were actuated by desire for fame, social recognition, or popularity, and possibly a few by more idealistic motives.

Reform had been urged by distinguished public men as far back as the 1760s, '70s, and '80s, but no action had resulted. Rooted in the most parasitic and corrupting species of exploitative property, misrepresentation had grown in the manner of a dry-rot until, by the 1820s, the power of filling a large majority of seats in the Commons was held, not by the landlord class as a whole, but by a monopolistic minority within that class, by six or eight thousand of the large proprietors, and among them a few hundred of the very richest. The parliament reproduced in the political sphere the attitudes and practices that might be expected from its provenance—bribery, peculation, nepotism, wasteful and inefficient administration, stubborn resistance to new ideas, cynical inhumanity to the poor and servility to the rich, and—worst of all from the bourgeois point of view—maintenance of outworn institutions and policies which obstructed the development of modern industry. Logic and common sense seemed to exclude any hope that a parliament most of whose members individually profited by these abuses, would or could reform itself. The alternatives appeared to be stagnation and violent revolution. The masses had so little to lose that they were not averse to revolution; they only doubted whether parliamentary reform was worth the price. The capitalists, knowing how deeply and with what good reason they were hated by the masses, feared that revolution might ruin them as well as the agrarian oligarchy, and so they "let I dare not wait upon I would."

The Struggle for Reform

With the ending of the war in 1815 the bourgeois demand for reform became more insistent, and with the collapse of the Luddite activities soon afterward the working people raised the same demand in a sterner tone and with more far-reaching views. The fundamental antagonism between capitalists and wage workers could not easily be ignored, and for a few years the two ruling classes continued to act together in trying to stamp out the working class movement. In the early 1820s, however, an "era of good feeling" set in and after the repeal of the Combination Laws this truce developed into an informal alliance for separate but parallel assault on the stronghold of the oligarchy. Of course it fell to the bourgeois reformers to carry on the campaign in parliament, while the workers were to do the rougher fighting outdoors. Were the latter explicitly assured that if they proceeded to violent action they would find defenders in high place, and were they definitely promised that the reform would include manhood suffrage and secret voting? Possibly so, probably not; but it is certain that the bourgeois reformers wished their opponents to be frightened and were willing to let their allies hope for a share in the fruits of victory.

The election of 1826 somewhat strengthened the reform group in parliament and some rifts began to appear in the oligarchic front. During the four-year life of this parliament three proposals affecting only a few seats were introduced in order to give opportunity for debate. Of these one was passed in the Commons and defeated in the Upper House. The death of George IV in June, 1830, necessitated a new election, in which the reformers won a narrow and insecure majority. After a long deadlock parliament dissolved, and the reformers came back with a decisive majority. In September, 1831, a bill which the bourgeoisie considered very satisfactory was carried by a vote of 345 to 236. A month later the Lords rejected it, but by a margin of only 40 votes out of 357,

This seemed to indicate that the oligarchy had begun to see the handwriting on the wall, which the masses promptly underlined by widespread demonstrations, many of them marked by rioting and violence. Once more the bill was introduced in the lower house, with but slight alterations, and was passed in March, 1832. Under pressure King William let it be known that if necessary he would create enough peerages to overwhelm the opposition and in June, a majority of the members absenting themselves, the House of Lords passed the bill.

The victory was won—a victory of the capitalists over the landlords, won mainly by the courage of the proletariat.[11] By transferring 143 of the 658 parliamentary seats from small rural boroughs to populous regions and centers the act gave the bourgeoisie a dominant position, which was strengthened by further acts in 1867 and 1885. As to the franchise, the act of 1832, by slightly lowering the qualification for voting, increased the electorate from 435,000 to 656,000—that is, from 2 per cent to 3 per cent of the population. It left the working classes and a large part of the lower middle class without votes. Certain economic changes, however, brought about a perceptible extension of the franchise in practice. The right to vote depended on ownership or tenancy of premises having at least a specified rental value. Rents were of course higher in the cities than in the country, and continued migration to the cities increased the number of those who had to pay these higher rents. Thus many low-income city dwellers were pushed up into the electorate, which within thirty-five years was doubled in absolute number and grew from 3 to 4.5 per

[11] Of course there were contributing causes. The extreme concentration of political power and privilege in the uppermost section of the landowning oligarchy had alienated many in its middle and lower strata. Moreover, the exclusiveness of that class had been sapped by several processes—matrimonial alliances between rank and riches; purchase of landed estates by wealthy bourgeois; granting of many baronetcies and occasional peerages to commoners; and investment by nobles and gentlemen in business enterprises. There is no room for doubt, however, that the decisive factor was the menace of revolution which, once launched by the industrial wage workers, would probably be joined by the agricultural laborers and peasants. This danger was accentuated by revolutionary events of 1830 and '31 in France, Belgium, Poland, Italy, and Spain, and agrarian disturbances in Ireland.

cent of the population. This economically forced increase of voting strength went mostly to the lower middle class.

The legislation of 1867-'68 lowered the franchise requirement in cities enough to increase the whole number of persons entitled to vote from 1,370,000 to 2,256,000, bringing it up to 8.2 per cent of the population, and enfranchising a large fraction, perhaps a majority, of the urban wage workers. In the next seventeen years the upward movement of rents (and now also of wages) again doubled the electorate, and an act passed in 1884 brought it up to 7,000,000, or about 20 per cent of the people, chiefly by giving miners, agricultural laborers, and small tenant farmers the same franchise as had been given the city workers.

Even this third and last of the patchwork reforms did not touch the abuse of plural voting. Tens of thousands of wealthy men, mostly of the landowning class, could vote in each of the two or more—in some cases ten or a dozen—constituencies in which they maintained residences. A time came when the plural votes numbered almost half a million. This abuse survived into the present century.

A forward step, and a very important one, was taken in 1872 when, over long and violent opposition, the secret ballot was introduced, and in 1883 the opportunities for bribery were further reduced by a law regulating campaign expenditures and limiting their amount.

No further liberalization of the electoral system took place until the second decade of the twentieth century, when plural voting was abolished and women received the suffrage. Their net effect is measured by the fact that in the three most recent elections—1931, 1935, and 1945— the number of votes cast has run from 46 to 50 per cent of the total population, whereas in the United States it has never yet exceeded 37 per cent.[12]

12 The discrepancy is accounted for by our larger proportion of persons below voting age, by our larger number of unnaturalized aliens, by the virtual disfranchisement of many Negroes and poor whites in the South, by the wider dispersal of our rural population, which increases the difficulty of getting to the polls, and by the greater fluidity of our working class, which causes many to lose their residence qualifications. The second and third of these five factors are the most important.

Defeat for the Workers

When in 1932 the working people realized how they had been betrayed their reaction was one of bitter but impotent wrath. The moment for revolt was past. Whigs and Tories, manufacturers and landowners, had reached an armistice. They could now unite to crush any possible uprising, and would have the support of those middle-class elements whom they had at least partially appeased. The utter failure of this genuinely revolutionary effort of the working class was not due to lack of courage and devotion, but to their error in trusting as political allies a class whose material interests were antagonistic to their own. Many lost faith in the working-class movement and sought comfort in religion or forgetfulness in drink. Others, with more strength of character, took what was then the bold step of emigrating to the United States.[13] The rest disagreed as to what they should do next. Various utopian schemes had their day—mutual barter, co-operative workshops, communal settlements on the land—but their day was not very long nor very bright. More practical men turned to trade unionism, and that movement was considerably strengthened. The members, however, and especially the new recruits, had as yet no clear notion of the difference between the aims and methods appropriate to unionism and those of political organization. This lesson had to be learned through experience.

[13] No doubt most of these (whose whole number was not very large) were aware that within recent years manhood suffrage and free public schools had been established in several states and that along the Atlantic seaboard, from New Hampshire down to Maryland, a hopeful and vigorous labor movement was functioning on both political and trade-union lines. This movement took shape in the later 1820s and was practically extinct by 1840. Its decline was probably due to several causes—the competition of Owenite and Fourierite utopianism, growing interest in the slavery question and the land question, and the effect of the new railways in drawing off the most energetic of the workingmen from the seaboard to what we now call the Middle West.—This period in American history has not yet, we think, been adequately treated, even by such outstanding scholars as Charles A. Beard and Arthur Schlesinger. Credit is due to Frank Tracy Carlton, who pioneered in the field some forty years ago. Reference may be made to James Oneal, *The Workers in American History*, and A. M. Simons, *Social Forces in American History*, both published in 1911.—The present writer's old friend, the late Hermann Schlüter, told him that in the course of research preliminary to writing *Die Chartisten-Bewegung* (New York, 1916) he found evidence that some of the British immigrants became active in the American labor movement.

The relatively small number of well established unions in certain skilled trades, such as those of the carpenters, masons, engineers (machinists, in American parlance), shipwrights, cabinet makers, and printers, tended to limit their functions to dealing with employers in their respective fields over wages, hours, and shop conditions, and administering mutual aid among their members. The smaller and weaker unions, in worse paid trades and in factory industries, naturally thought of gaining strength by amalgamation or federation into larger bodies; this led to the bolder but not so easily realizable plan of bringing all trade unions together in one huge "trades" union; and then, by logical extension, to that of uniting in one body the whole population except the minority who live by other men's labor. In this development the trade-union idea of step-by-step improvement by direct struggle with the employers gave place for a time to that of sudden and complete, but non-violent, social revolution.

A Grand Fiasco

Vigorous agitation by the Owenites for a "General Union of the Productive Classes and Others" got under way late in 1833, and Owen himself offered "a short outline of the great changes . . . which shall come suddenly upon society like a thief in the night." In January, 1834, came the launching of the Grand National Consolidated Trades Union. Those who joined it may well have supposed that the methods to be used at the critical moment and the forms of the new social order had been worked out, but this was not the case. The only answer to such questions was that all producers are to join the Grand Consolidated, and then the employers, the landlords, and the government, seeing themselves vastly outnumbered, will not think of resisting. Such vagueness as to details, combined with rosy pictures of the new society and with confident assurances that it would be realized within a year, were well adapted to attract the enthusiastic and the reckless, who were also, of course, the most impatient and least reliable. In the first six months the organization enrolled half a million members, constituting with their dependents about one-tenth of the population, but still far short of the necessary overwhelming majority. Then the growth of membership ceased and a yet more rapid decline set in. Unfortunately, such a movement cannot operate so quietly as does a thief in the night. The propertied classes and their government were wide awake, and they took prompt and drastic action. Under those parts of the combination laws which had been re-enacted in 1825, under various other statutes, and under rules of the common law, many arrests were made, middle-class jurors were ready to convict, and upper-class judges imposed sentences out of all keeping with the generally trivial overt acts committed. The general strike, too tardily proposed, and yet proposed without any preparation, never even began. What did come and saved the Grand Consolidated from being a complete fiasco, was the energetic protest against governmental cruelty—the mass demonstrations, the monster petitions, the raising of funds for the victims and their families, in which the conservative unions and many unorganized sympathizers took part, and which continued after the Grand Consolidated itself had ceased to exist.

The fact that, while the Grand Consolidated was still in its growing phase, and when the repressive measures had already begun, parliament passed factory laws in advance of any that had previously been enacted illustrates our statement already made, that formidable activities of the working class, even though failing of their immediate aims, did wring concessions which were never made when the workers were quiet.

The fantastic episode of the Grand Consolidated had a sobering and clarifying rather than a depressing effect. From this point on the activities of the British working class ran in three parallel channels, not unfriendly one to another and all in their different ways contributing or seeking to contribute to the welfare of the working people, but with little direct collaboration or mutual support—that of conservative or at least nonrevolutionary and for a time almost completely nonpolitical trade unionism; that of independent political organization and agitation, aiming at democratization of government and through that at social and labor legislation and ultimately at socialization of the economic order; and that of consumer cooperation, aiming to improve the livelihood of the low-income elements by saving for the ultimate purchaser the "middlemen's profit," or margin between wholesale and retail price.

Consumers' Co-operation Begins

In the 1820s and '30s some hundreds of societies had been launched in Great Britain for co-operative buying as well as for co-operative production. They were formed under the influence of Fourierite, Owenite, and Saint-Simonian utopian propaganda and were motivated, not by a desire to serve the immediate material interests of the masses, but rather by the notion that they could put the capitalists out of business by underselling them. Their spans of life ranged from a few months to a very few years. In 1844, however, a handful of weavers at Rochdale in Lancashire, impoverished by low wages and irregular employment, clubbed together to purchase food and other necessaries, getting the benefit of quantity buying. Undisturbed by grandiose visions, and combining mutual good faith with plain good sense, they made a success of their modest venture, gradually expanded it, and set an example which other groups followed. One hundred and three years later, the general office of the British co-operative societies was able to report a membership of 7,976,000 and gross sales within the year to the amount of nearly a billion dollars. Besides the material benefit effected, these societies have rendered a great service by accustoming their members to organized action for the common good, training them in the art of administration, and developing social idealism through practice.

Starting about a quarter of a century later and profiting by the British experience, consumer co-operation had a similarly vast and beneficent development on the Continent, first in the Low Countries, Central Europe, and Scandinavia, then spreading to France, Italy, Poland, and Russia. Within the last three decades, however, in all the areas that came under totalitarian rule, whether red or black or brown, the co-operatives (as also the trade unions) were deprived of their autonomy, plundered, and degraded into subordinate agencies of the all-powerful, rapacious, and antidemocratic state. In those regions that have at length been liberated by the Allied arms, they are being rebuilt, but this process is hampered by the frightful ruin of the whole European economy.

Conservative Trade Unions

The conservative character—some might say the excessive caution and "stodginess"—of British trade unionism from the 1830s till the 1890s is to be attributed, not to certain alleged racial characteristics of the British people nor to the accident that certain individuals having these qualities somehow became union leaders, but to the conditions under which the unions had to operate and the experiences which influenced their decisions. Those experiences, from the grim tragedy of Luddism to the romantic adventure of the Grand Consolidated, showed that while spasmodic and tumultuous outbursts of popular discontent may sometimes achieve worth-while gains, usually of a legislative nature, they seldom or never effect an increase of wage rates or take-home pay. To comfortable folk this is a sordid concern, but working people know that "the destruction of the poor is their poverty" and that a hungry and ragged proletariat is hardly capable of constructive and sustained effort toward any more distant or less prosaic goal.

In 1834 the trade unions stood alone; there was for the time no political movement, and the idea of social revolution, to be won by general strike or any other method, was thoroughly discredited. The employers were firmly united against any attempt of the workers to interefere with the bosses' right to "hire and fire" and to fix wages, hours, and shop conditions. They were bent on crushing all labor organizations, no matter how moderate their aims or how scrupulously law-abiding their methods. Against such an attack small or loose groupings of workings could do little or nothing; their only hope was in enlisting and retaining more and more members, limiting their aims in order to avoid dangerous crises, and giving material assistance to actual or prospective members who might be individually victimized. The immediate issue was "the document"—something very like the "yellow dog contract" which the older generation of union men in the United States still vividly remember. True, by this time the law recognized the right of workingmen to belong to unions and to deal collectively with their employers; but it also upheld the employer's unrestricted right to discharge any employee and refuse employment to any person seeking a job, without even stating a reason unless he saw fit. Many employers did see fit at this time to require every applicant to sign a paper stating that he did not belong to and promising that he would not join any labor union. His refusal to sign was of course communicated to other employers; by exercising his lawful right he lost his opportunity to earn a livelihood in any place where he was known. If the union was to gain members and hold them it must give not only the right hand of fellowship but also the helping hand of financial relief to men who took this risk. Only a little less imperative was the necessity of relieving members who fell sick or were injured at their work[14] or who lost their jobs in time of business depression. Not until a union had a considerable number of members who by payment of dues had come to feel that they had a stake in its continued existence, and only when it had acquired a favorable reputation by aid given to members and friends in need, could it think of more aggressive activity. The rank and file as well as the officers knew that a lost strike or lockout, or a too long struggle, even though ending in victory, might deplete its funds, lower its morale

[14] In Great Britain for many years after the time of which we speak, and in the United States until about forty years ago, the law as to employers' liability for accident to employees gave every advantage to the defense and made it in most cases not worth while for an injured workman to sue for damages.

and its prestige, and perhaps decimate its membership. Only the manifestation of a resolute fighting spirit among the members could justify responsible leaders in proposing any bold venture, and only a grave emergency could arouse such a spirit.

While these unions for a considerable time functioned primarily as "friendly" or mutual benefit societies and avoided open conflict with their employers, they were able also to win small but cumulative improvements in the conditions of employment, especially in prosperous periods, and not altogether to lose them in hard times. This was practicable only in those relatively well paid trades in which men worked principally with hand tools or small and simple machines, individual skill was an important factor, and the number working for any one employer was not very large. Under such circumstances men personally acquainted each with each could talk things over and plan their action without formal and recorded rules and decisions, and could by various unavowed methods check the competition for jobs and tacitly impress upon the employer the wisdom of keeping on good terms with his workmen. Although they were unwilling to become involved in demonstrative political action or to commit themselves to social theories extending beyond their immediate problems, they realized the bearing of the laws, for good or for ill, upon their conditions and interests, and they showed considerable skill in quietly lobbying for favorable legislation and against such proposed acts as would make their situation worse. That their practical conservatism was not due to ignorance or stupidity is evidenced by the fact that members of what was called the Junta—an unofficial steering committee composed of several of their ablest officials—were in the early 1860s in close touch with Karl Marx and Frederick Engels and some of them were for a time members of the International Working Men's Association.

After the unions of this type had got well started, unionism gained a foothold also in the coal fields and in the textile and other factory industries. Here the larger scale of the employment units and the greater standardization of processes called for somewhat different methods. Less reliance was placed on benefit features, while strikes, even on a large scale, were much more frequent. Although they had no votes till 1868—the miners not till 1885—they became politically conscious and active much earlier, than the small-shop hand workers, and it was among them that the Chartist movement, to which we must now turn our attention, had its largest following.[15]

Although the unions, especially those in the skilled trades, held aloof from politics for more than a generation after the rise and fall of the Grand National Consolidated Trades Union in 1834, they did not impose neutrality upon their members nor actively antagonize political action when it was revived, so long as it did not interfere with their own more cautious policy. Such a revival soon took place.

The Rise of Chartism

In June, 1836, a number of skilled workmen in London, most or all of whom had participated in the activities of 1831-'32 and of 1834, formed a society for the purpose of making parliament a democratically representative body by the adoption of six points, namely,—Manhood suffrage; Electoral districts equal in population; Election by secret ballot; All qualified voters to be eligible to parliament; Payment of members; Annual elections. These demands, none of which was new, but only the first of which had in the past been sufficiently emphasized, constituted what came to be known as the People's Charter. It was essential to the plan to concentrate attention on these six points, and, pending their adoption, not to commit the organization to any particular projects of social legislation, which it would be the function of a democratized parliament itself to enact. Equal emphasis was laid on the advice to the working people to rely on themselves instead

[15] Better than from any learned treatise the reader may "get the feel" of the factory workers' movement from the novel *Mary Barton*, written by Elizabeth Gaskell, the biographer of Charlotte Bronte, and published in 1848. It is, in our judgment, decidedly superior to Dickens' *Hard Times*, which came out six years later.

of trusting to such professed friends as had betrayed them in 1832. Furthermore, it was resolved not to invite the affiliation of trade unions or other already existing bodies, but to build an association on the basis of individual membership, with branches throughout the country, for the sole purpose of carrying the Six Points and thus, it was hoped, to avoid both a frittering away of energy and a danger of schism. As we shall see, these hopes were not and probably could not have been completely fulfilled, but a sincere effort was made. The Chartists were by no means hostile to nor jealous of the trade unions, and many of the members and adherents of the movement were loyal and active union men. There was simply a recognition of the fact that the forms and methods suitable to the one movement were unsuitable to the other.

The story of Chartism, from its origin in 1836, through its three peaks in 1839, 1842, and 1848, and its lingering death-in-life from then till 1858, with its intervening schisms and aberrations, has been so fully told in books which are easily available[16] that it need not detain us long. Could the movement have been held to the original plan of concentrating all its efforts on the one object of democratizing parliament, its following might never have been so large as it was at the peaks, but it might have been more effective. Inevitably, however, as soon as it showed some strength, it was joined by groups that were especially interested in land reform, money reform, repeal of the Corn Laws, or repeal of the new Poor Law, each group striving to put its particular objective on at least an equal footing with the reform of parliament. Moreover, sharp antagonism developed between those who more or less openly favored the use of physical force and those who hoped by peaceable propaganda to build up such a strong public opinion as the antidemocratic elements could not resist. Finally, in the later 1840s the influence of Continental

[16] See Beer, *History of British Socialism*, vol. I, ch. x, and vol. II, ch. i to ix; *The Chartist Movement*, by Mark Hovell, Longmans Green, 1918; *The Chartist Movement in Its Social and Economic Aspects*, by Frank F. Rosenblatt, and *The Decline of the Chartist Movement*, Preston William Slosson, same pub., 1916; and, in our opinion the best of all, but not translated into English, *Die Chartisten-Bewegung*, by Hermann Schlüter, New York, Socialist Lit. Co., 1916.

Socialism became clearly evident, and interest in internationalism perhaps somewhat distracted attention from the immediate purpose. News of the third French Revolution, which late in February, 1848, overthrew the Orleans Monarchy, heightened the already rising wave of Chartist enthusiasm. A monster petition to parliament, calling for the enactment of five of the Six Points (the demand for the ballot was omitted) was almost ready. By the first of April it was declared that this had been signed by six million persons. Monday, April 10, was fixed as the date for its presentation, and a monster mass meeting and procession was planned.

Its Pathetic Collapse

The government had been as deeply impressed by the events in France as had the Chartists, but with quite opposite emotions, all the more as within the two months many Chartist demonstrations throughout the country had taken on a riotous aspect and there had been a great deal of loose talk about a violent revolution. Several regiments of trained soldiers were concentrated in London, more than 150,000 special constables were sworn in and armed to reinforce the police, and the Duke of Wellington was in command. Twenty thousand persons are said to have gathered for the mass meeting, which was a tame affair; there was no procession; in only a few cases did the police see occasion for using their clubs; and when the petitions, in several large bales, were carried into the House they were greeted with "Homeric laughter." The government did not however, let the drama end on the note of ridicule. Numerous prosecutions were set on foot, and two of the leaders were sentenced to two years in prison and several were transported to Australia.

These reprisals were not sufficient to have terrorized any formidable popular movement. Like "hitting a man when he's down," they inspired contempt rather than terror. Chartism died out, not because of the defeat on April 10, but because of a recognition that by its own faults and follies it had earned that defeat. By 1858 its last vestiges had disappeared, and not until the 1880s was there even the barest beginning, nor until the '90s a really visible beginning, of independent political action. For all that, the efforts of the Chartists had not been altogether wasted. By 1885 four of the Six Points had been enacted into law—manhood suffrage; secret voting; approximately equal electoral districts; and abolition of the property qualifications for election to parliament—and while other causes had contributed to these results, much of the credit belongs to the movement whose humiliating end had been forgotten, but whose somewhat romanticized traditions were cherished in tens of thousands of working-class homes.[17]

The trade unions continued through the Chartist period and for a full generation thereafter on the conservative lines already described, gaining considerably in numerical strength and solidifying their organizations, but failing—perhaps we may justly say neglecting—to extend their activities into the very numerous lower-paid strata of the British working class.

The Trade Union Congress

Taking advantage of the industrial depression of the late 1850s and later of the mass unemployment in the '60s indirectly caused by the American Civil War, the employers launched an all-out attack upon trade unionism. For several years the workers fared badly. Especially were they threatened with drastic anti-union legislation. The necessity of carrying on a defensive fight led to the formation in many industrial centers, between 1858 and 1867,

[17] It is worth while to read in this connection the preface which Frederick Engels prefixed in 1892 to the second edition of Florence Kelley Wischnewetzky's English translation of his *Condition of the Working Class in England.*—The translator was then a young woman, of American parentage and Irish descent, who is now remembered, under her maiden name, for more than a quarter of a century of brave and tireless work for the improvement of factory legislation and especially for its enforcement, and for her success in enlisting the sympathy of women of the more comfortable classes in behalf of the shamefully exploited female workers in factories, stores, and offices.

of what were called trades councils—that is, delegate bodies which linked together, without much authority, but with great effectiveness, the local unions of various trades and industries within each area. In 1864 the danger of hostile legislation became acute and the Glasgow Trades Council called for a national conference to combat it, and three years later the Sheffield Trades Council took the lead in convoking such a conference to plan defense against extensive lockouts which were then taking place. These conferences were not looked on with favor by the Junta and the unions under its leadership, but eventually they had to accept the innovation. In 1868 a conference met in Birmingham, in response to a call issued by the Manchester Trades Council, which proposed a very broad agenda. The delegates present claimed to represent 118,000 union members. They took the name of Trade Union Congress, and decided that such a gathering should be held every year to discuss whatever questions should be of interest to unions at the time. In 1869 the number of members represented was put at 250,000 and the next year at 375,000, which was probably about half of the whole number of organized workers at the time. Except for the year 1870, when by a maneuver the call was not issued, the Trade Union Congress has met annually ever since. While it does not claim for itself and its interim officers and committees any actual authority over the affiliated unions, the resolutions which the Congress adopts by substantial majorities are generally complied with. Representing more than 7,000,000 organized wage workers, it shares with the Annual Conference of the Labor Party the responsibility of formulating and uttering the thoughts and aspirations of the now dominant force in the British nation.[18]

18 The British Trade Union Congress is the oldest body of its kind in the world. The American Federation of Labor (under a different name for its first five years) dates from 1881. In Germany a corresponding body was formed in 1891, France followed in 1895, and the example was imitated in most European and Latin American countries. There came into existence also international federations of great industries, and at length an International Federation of Trade Unions. Two world wars and the Communist schism have crippled but not killed these international bodies.

"The Epoch of Reform"

It has long been the fashion to represent English history through the nineteenth century as a halcyon age, when rights and liberties were dropping as the gentle rain from heaven upon the place beneath or, to put it more prosaically, when wise Liberals and occasionally magnanimous Tories were handing out sugar plums to the people as fast as they could be digested. Perhaps belief in that bedtime story is in some measure excusable in this country, where most of us know even less about the facts of English social history than about our own. It is rather comforting (to those of us who prize comfort above truth) to be assured in these unsettled times that we "Anglo-Saxons" are essentially unlike Kelts and Teutons, Latins and Slavs, in that it is our nature to go ahead at a quiet and even pace, without jumping or jostling or otherwise disturbing the peace. Strangely enough, most Englishmen seem to be equally credulous. English workingmen at least should remember the pit whence they have been digged and the rock whence they have been hewn, and how dark was the pit and how painful the task of hewing away the rock that weighed them down. When British labor leaders shake their heads disapprovingly at the very thought of revolution and solemnly repudiate the notion of class struggle, we may suspect that this is a matter of "good form" rather than a confession of faith.[19]

It is true that in the course of that century, and even during its first and second third, when the power of making laws was still rigorously monopolized by a wealthy minority, a great many measures were enacted which, from one point of view or another, may rightly be called progressive; and it is true that a considerable number of these were either directly or incidentally, either im-

[19] Some forty years ago Dr. Anna Ingerman, a well known New York socialist, had an interview with Keir Hardie in London. At a certain point Hardie interrupted to say, "We British socialists don't believe in class struggle." "Yes, I know that," was the reply, "but we American socialists think of you, Comrade Hardie, as the finest embodiment of the idea of class struggle"—and, she afterward told us, Hardie seemed to be very well pleased.

mediately or after a time, beneficial to the working classes. But it is equally true that some of those which are called progressive measures and many outside that list which were enacted by the same parliaments were definitely injurious to the workers and were meant to be so. There is a familiar adage warning us not to look a gift horse in the mouth; but if we are called upon to give three generations of British statesmen a credential for progressive legislation it is our right and duty to examine into its motives and its effects. The motives call for our attention, not in order that we may award praise or blame to the legislators as individuals, but in order that we may learn by what means and methods an exploited and oppressed class can best advance its interests.

The outstanding measures in the honor roll of British statesmanship as usually presented are—the partial humanizing of the penal laws; the repeal of the Combination Acts; the repeal of old laws making it difficult for workingmen to travel in quest of employment; the Poor Law of 1834; the repeal of the Corn Laws; the Ten Hour Law; a long list of minor factory laws;—besides, of course, the parliamentary reform measures and those abolishing discrimination against Jews and against Catholics. These last two are laudable, but have little to do with the question before us, as they do not involve class interests. The same may be said of the penal law amendments, the most telling argument in their favor having been that diminution of the penalties would result in more convictions.

The Combination Acts, as we have seen, would not have been repealed if the upper-class legislators had not stupidly supposed that the result would be to diminish the working people's tendency to form trade unions and political clubs. When they saw how they had blundered they made haste to reenact as much of the old laws as they dared. In 1824 as in 1825 the interest of the employers was obviously the ruling motive.

As to the laws of settlement, which dated back to the sixteenth century, there had been no false pretense as to their original purpose. The landowners, then in full control of the legislative function, wished to have always at their beck and call so large a number of laborers that there should be no need for giving them extra pay in plowing and harvest time, even at the cost of doling out niggardly relief through the less busy seasons—virtually, to keep them in a state of serfage. But as factory industry grew in magnitude it was the urban capitalists who demanded an oversupply of workers, so that their competition for jobs should hold wages down to a bare subsistence level. For the immediate welfare, or illfare, of the workers it was a matter of indifference where they should be half-starved. In the long run, the shift from country to city strengthened the forces of social revolution, but the repeal of the old laws was purely a victory of bourgeois over agrarian class interest.

The new poor law was an act of cold and calculated cruelty, which served two purposes. It saved a great deal of money for the taxpayers; but at the same time it drove the aging or half invalid workers to sell their services to the employers for less than the barest living, thus dragging down the general level of wages, in order to escape the physical and moral misery of going to the workhouse, which the advocates of the law declared ought to be made "a house of terror." As Scrooge said, "If they would rather die they had better do so, and reduce the surplus population." Betty Higden did.

In the matter of the Corn Laws there would appear to be a clearly defined antagonism between the landlords, who were assured an excessively high price for their grain, and the working people, whose numbers made them the principal customers. The workers, however, showed comparatively little interest in the question because they believed, as did the employing class, that a cheapening of bread would make possible a counterbalancing reduction of wages. Such would have been the case, had not growth of England's exports of manufactured goods brought about a perceptible increase of demand for labor power by the time the laws were repealed. The benefit was consequently divided between employers and wage workers and ultimately went in the main to the latter. It was the employers who fought the battle, but for their own class interest, as they believed, not from altruistic motives.

The Ten Hour Law was unquestionably beneficial to the wage workers—more so, indeed, than either they or its capitalist opponents expected. If it did not in the long run diminish the employers' profits it did so for the time and they had then no reason to doubt that the injury would be permanent. Since the act did not apply to farm laborers nor to domestic and personal servants, the landowners welcomed the opportunity to strike back at the factory owners by giving it their support. Tardy and inadequate as this measure was, applying only to women and persons under the age of eighteen, and only to such of these as worked in factories, Karl Marx hailed its passage as "the victory of a principle." It was the first law in the world giving even limited protection to any adult workers, and in practice, unexpectedly to all concerned, it brought the shorter workday also to large numbers of men working side by side with women.

To Whom Should Credit Go?

We have yet to speak of earlier factory legislation, beginning in 1802. The act of that year fixed twelve hours, exclusive of mealtimes, as the maximum workday for boys and girls under ten who, being orphans or pauper children, were lodged with the employer. Not until 1819 was the employment of children less than nine years old prohibited and the twelve-hour rule extended to youth under sixteen, and only in 1831 was 69 hours made the maximum workweek. Comment would be superfluous.

To explain the economic and social legislation of this period by the growth of humane sentiment or of mental alertness is to ignore tangible elements. However individuals may vary in sensitiveness to human misery or in receptiveness to new ideas, the lines of action in which they exhibit these qualities are determined by quite other factors. Conservatives were surely no more likely than Liberals to be humane and open minded; yet it was usually the former who promoted labor legislation, while the latter stubbornly opposed it; the very paladin of Liberalism, the pious and philanthropic John Bright, denounced the Ten Hour Law as "one of the worst measures ever passed." The Liberals were strong for redistribution of seats, but very hesitant as to extension of the right to vote. In 1842 the Liberal historian Macaulay declared in parliament that manhood suffrage "would be fatal to all the purposes for which government exists . . . and utterly incompatible with the very existence of civilization"; and the ensuing division indicated that most of the Liberal members agreed with him. In 1867 it was a Conservative ministry that carried through an act extending the suffrage to more than twice as many men as would have been enfranchised by a bill which the Liberals had proposed a few months earlier; had the Liberals had their way, comparatively few workingmen would have got the vote. These and many other facts justify us in saying that neither party did anything for the workers at its own cost politically or at any economic cost to the propertied class which it represented. But we may safely go farther and say that no important law especially beneficial to the working people was enacted except under pressure exerted in one form or another by the working people. Toward the end of this period and thereafter, as the workers were able to exercise influence by the disposal of their votes, there was less occasion for the use or threat of violence.

The later 1860s marked an ending and cleared the way for a new beginning. The trade-union movement assumed an organizational form which enormously increased its stability and its capacity for united action. The projected anti-union legislation was thrust aside, and soon thereafter a number of repressive laws that had survived from darker times were repealed and a broad and intelligently framed Employers and Workmen Act set an example for countries on both sides of the Atlantic to follow. The passage of the Second Reform Bill enfranchised the urban wage workers and made it a certainty that before long those of the agricultural and mining districts would be added to the electorate.

The speed and comparative ease with which these great forward steps were taken made it easy to believe that a durable social peace had taken the place of the strife and turmoil of the last seventy years. It is no wonder that a mood of easy going optimism and we may almost say of intellectual indolence ensued.

British Role in World Socialism

By a striking coincidence, the first volume of Marx's *Capital,* written in England and mainly from English materials, was first published in Germany in the year 1867. In its preface we read:

> In this work I have to examine the capitalist mode of production, and the conditions of production and exchange corresponding to that mode. Up to the present time, their classic ground is England. That is why England is used as the chief illustration in the development of my theoretical ideas. If, however, the German reader shrugs his shoulders at the condition of the English industrial and agricultural laborers, or in optimistic fashion comforts himself with the thought that in Germany things are not nearly so bad, I must plainly tell him, *De te fabula narratur* . . . The country that is more developed industrially shows to the undeveloped the image of its own future.

It is a mistake to suppose that Socialism is a French or a German product, brought over to England late in the nineteenth century. In fact, both as a movement and as an ideology rooted in that movement, its English ancestry ran back to the Puritan Revolution of 1640 to 1660[20] and it passed through its childhood as a movement in Great Britain from the 1790s till the 1850s. A period of adolescent uncertainty and irresolution ensued, but by the 1890s it came to the front as a warrior armed for the fight,

[20] Much light has been thrown on this by Eduard Bernstein in his *Sozialismus und Demokratie in der Grossen Englischen Revolution*, 1908, an English translation of which is to be desired.

but somewhat contemptuous of its childish adventures. True, there had been no working-class revolution in the ordinary sense of the phrase—and indeed there still has been none and probably will be none, in that sense—but to deny that there had been a revolutionary movement of the British working class, with a history full of heroic efforts and tragic reverses, for decades before any comparable movement had begun on the Continent, or that its results and experiences have contributed to make the British labor movement what it is today, is altogether unjustified. There is something vividly symbolic in the fact that Andrew Hardie was hanged in 1819, and that in 1892 his great-nephew, James Keir Hardie, was the first avowed Socialist independently elected to the House of Commons, where his party now holds a secure majority.

It may be thought that in this monograph we have given far too large a portion of our space to the early history of the working class movement in Great Britain. Our defense is, in the first place, that we regard ideologies as growing out of movements, much more than the reverse; and in the second place that, as summarily stated in the foregoing paragraph, Great Britain was in fact the cradle and elementary school of modern Socialism and that today (we must change our figure of speech) British Socialism is the vanguard and massive center of what has become a world-wide movement. Passing over with bare mention even the high lights of its later development—such as the foundation of the Fabian Society and the Social Democratic Federation in 1883 and 1885, the rise of the New Unionism in 1889-'90, and the organization of the Labor Representation Committee in 1900, which became the British Labor Party in 1906—we must now turn our attention to the European Continent.

The Background of Marxism

In the field of social history all beginnings are relative. Back of whatever we may call the date of origin of any institution or movement lie the conditions and tendencies out of which it grew.

With this qualification, 1848 may be counted as the birth-year of international Socialism, and the issuance of the *Communist Manifesto* as the first step in the development of a new social force which, challenging all the accepted ideas, assailing all the established institutions, threatening all the vested interests of aristocratic and capitalist society, boldly set itself the task of putting an end to the exploitation of man by man and of building from the bottom up a free and classless world.[21]

Karl Marx (alone or in conjunction with Frederick Engels) is often and not without reason spoken of as the founder or creator of modern Socialism. Yet the phrase needs some reservation. To use a rough parallel, Marx was the creator of Socialism in much the same sense as Martin Luther was the creator of Protestantism. Neither of them made something out of nothing. In each case the creative worker utilized materials (especially intellectual materials) derived from the past and dealt with them under conditions not of his own making. No doubt the inner nature of the thinker and leader—his mental and emotional habits and attitudes, as inherited or as formed by childhood experiences—is an important factor. Unfortunately we can know very little about this, and can reconstruct it only by conjecture and inference.[22] Concerning materials with which and conditions under which he worked we can have objective knowledge, and we may do well to confine our attention to these—bearing in mind also that Marx was not the sole demiurge of midcentury Socialism, though clearly foremost among those who made it what it was, which is equally true of Luther and the origin of Protestantism.

[21] Here and at a few other points in the following pages the writer takes the liberty (kindly granted by the Rand School Press) of borrowing some passages from his general introduction to *Essentials of Marx,* published in 1926. It will not be necessary to identify these by quotation marks or otherwise.

[22] The best biographies are *Karl Marx: Geschichte Seines Lebens,* by Franz Mehring, and *Karl Marx: Man and Fighter,* by Boris I. Nicolaevsky and Otto Mänchen-Helfen. Otto Rühle's *Karl Marx: His Life and Work* supplements these at some points, but his attempt to psychoanalyze Marx is amateurish and inaccurate as to facts. Wilhelm Liebknecht's *Karl Marx: Biographical Memoirs,* Karl Kautsky's *Aus der Frühzeit des Marxismus,* and Gustav Mayer's *Friedrich Engels: A Biography* are invaluable.

When we speak of the origin of Socialism, its growth and its changing forms, we may have in mind a certain body of historical and economic theory or a certain social and political movement of the masses. We may think of these separately, may describe or criticize either one by itself; but really to understand either, we must take the other into account. They are indeed two interacting aspects of the same developing phenomenon. If we ask which of them is primary, which more influences the other, it seems well to give precedence to the movement—to say with Faust: *Im Anfang war die That,* "In the beginning was the Deed." For convenience's sake, however, we shall here speak first of the intellectual heritage received by the Forty-Eighters.

With even better right than Ferdinand Lassalle, who actually made the boast, Marx and Engels might have claimed that they wrote every line armed with the entire culture of their century. We need specify, however, only three of the currents of thought which were assimilated into the Marxian theoretical system.

The French Materialists

First comes the influence of the French materialists of the later eighteenth century, notably Diderot, Condillac, Helvetius, d'Alembert, Holbach, Condorçet, and Cabanis, whose overlapping periods of intellectual activity stretched from 1746 to 1798. The primary interest of these men was not in social, economic, and political problems, though they did not ignore them and though the results of their work did deeply affect later thinking in these fields. What concerned them first of all was to understand the nature of the world and of man as a feeling and thinking part thereof—a range of interest that reaches from physics to psychology and may extend thence into the social sciences. Like Berkeley and other idealists, they obtained clearness and consistency by denying the duality of things and ideas, matter and spirit, Nature and God—the one school by denying the reality of material things, the other by accepting it as the whole and sole reality. If they came to the limit of their present knowledge on any line of inquiry, they did not fly to what Spinoza had called "that last refuge of ignorance, the will of God"; instead, they set themselves to gain more knowledge. They are but little thought of today because they did so effectively their work of laying the materialistic basis of modern science; by our time the magnitude and firmness of the superstructure have become so impressive that we forget about its foundations.[23] The weakness of the *philosophes* was that their thought-method was largely static, tending to set up a codified system of supposedly eternal truths or laws of nature, which easily became an obstacle to the further advancement of knowledge. This was particularly disastrous when they came to the study of human behavior, individual and social, in which, because of the greater difficulty of using the methods of observation and experiment, there was a greater temptation to deal in abstractions, building up lists of man's faculties and his passions, and so making a stereotype of human nature, upon which might be modeled the laws of a "perfect state."

Hegelien Philosophy

The second of the intellectual influences which went to the formation of Marxism, and the one which corrected the shortcoming of French materialism, was that of the German philosopher Hegel. Born in 1770, Hegel was already nineteen when the French Revolution began, and it was in the same memorable year that Holbach died, leaving only two of the seven protagonists of materialism whose work we have discussed still alive; Condorçet died in 1794 and Cabanis' activity ended in 1798. Hegel's teaching life began in 1797, synchronizing with Napoleon's accession to dic-

[23] It is true that, especially in the English speaking countries, there are a good many reputable scientists who repudiate materialism. But it is equally true and important that the methods which they use in their respective branches of research are entirely consistent with the philosophy of materialistic monism and wholly inconsistent with philosophical dualism. In their pursuit of knowledge, as Laplace told Napoleon, they have no need for hypotheses about God, spirit, or other immaterial beings, and would be hampered and misled by their intrusion.

tatorial power. The next eighteen years saw the growth of the Hegelian philosophy to its maturity, and coincided with the Napoleonic period, the almost complete subjugation of Europe, and then the huge disaster of the Russian campaign, the German War of Liberation, the battles of Leipzig and of Waterloo, the Holy Alliance, and the restoration of the Bourbon dynasty. Hegel died in 1831, in the midst of a new turning of the political tide, marked by the second French revolution of 1830, which drove out the Bourbons and substituted the bourgeois and moderately liberal Orleans Monarchy, the independence of Belgium in the same year, the unsuccessful but inspiring Polish insurrection in 1830-'31, and the first reform of the British parliament in 1832. We think this collocation of dates worth pondering. If Heine was right in calling Immanuel Kant the Robespierre of German and European philosophy, we may regard Hegel as its Napoleon—but with the difference that in this case the empire survived its ruler.

In 1836 Karl Marx, then eighteen years old and with credit for a year's study at Bonn, transferred to Berlin, where Hegel had taught for the last thirteen years of his life. One of the younger universities (founded in 1809) Berlin was still a sanctuary of academic freedom, even under the shadow of Potsdam. The Hegelian philosophy was still dominant there, but not unchallenged. Although Hegel had been in intent and effect a German nationalist and a champion of Prussian monarchy, and had long been accepted as such, some intelligent reactionaries had by this time come to realize that in one of its aspects his philosophy had revolutionary implications, and there was an active opposition within the faculty. Simultaneously there was developing within the student body a revolt from the other direction, bringing into the light just those dangerous implications.

Hegel, in sharpest antagonism to the French materialists of the preceding era—an antagonism made yet keener by the two decades of political struggle between France, first revolutionary, then imperial, and half-subjugated Germany—had been a thorough-going and aggressive idealist. To illustrate the meaning of these philosophical terms:—For the materialists, individual *men* were substantially and objectively real, while *man* expressed only our way of recognizing that all men are sufficiently alike to be thought of collectively, leaving out of account individual differences among them; for the idealists, from Plato to Hegel, with many other thinkers in the twenty-two intervening centuries, the idea *Man* was the eternal reality, and the individual men only its more or less accurate copies, reflections, or manifestations; and the same, of course, for the idea tree or stream or table.[24]

This age-long conflict as to the reality of ideas and of things is not a sterile dispute over words. It has involved the difference between believing and knowing, between orthodoxy and freedom of thought; it has usually, if not always, had a social-political significance. Plato, the outstanding antidemocratic theorist of ancient Greece, was the first advocate of what we should now call a totalitarian state. Throughout the Middle Ages the realists (in modern phrase idealists) stood for the supreme authority of the universal Holy Church, except in some instances when they favored the supremacy of the would-be universal Holy Empire, while the growth of nominalism (an approach to modern materialism) was associated with the rising of national states and with schism within the church. Not to multiply instances, it was in the regular course of things that, the universal church having been dismembered and the notion of universal empire having, as it then seemed, lost all validity, the latest form of idealism should be accepted as the philosophic bulwark of each national state and of each state church against subversive movements for regional or local independence,

[24] We are aware that this is a very inadequate statement of the two ways of thinking, but we hope it may be comprehensible, so far as it goes.—The medieval thinkers whom we call idealists were in their own time called realists; there is no difference in meaning—to hold that *ideas* are real is the same as to hold that ideas are *real*. Their opponents, the nominalists and the conceptualists, approximated the position of our materialists. In modern times "spiritualism" is often used as a synonym for "idealism," but this is unfortunate; the two views overlap, but are not identical.—We must of course guard against attaching to these philosophical party names the meanings they convey in common parlance. A spiritualist in the philosophical sense does not necessarily believe in ghosts and patronize "mediums"; an idealist may not be more altruistic or less practical than his neighbors; the medieval realists were not particularly "hard boiled"; nor are materialistic thinkers noted as money grabbers or as gourmands.

for religious liberty, for the civil rights of individuals, for responsibility of governments to peoples—in a word, for democracy.

The democratic aspirations which had blossomed in revolutionary France did not die with the fall of the Jacobins. Though thwarted in practice under Napoleonic and Bourbon rule, they lived on as aspirations, not only in their homeland, but in all the countries where French influence was felt. Of their embodiment in obscure conspiracies and occasionally in abortive revolts we shall presently have something to say. They lived also, however, in the minds of many young intellectuals who as yet neither conspired nor rebelled, and nowhere more than in Germany, where a high and fairly widespread culture co-existed with a very effective system of repression. Cut off from action and even from open discussion of social and political subjects, they took to philosophy, not as an avenue of escape, but as possibly a way to the solution of their problems.

The Dialectic Method

Far from everyday reality as the Hegelian philosophy superficially appears, it was capable of meeting this need. In the first place, Hegel did not, like Leibnitz, hold that "Everything is for the best in the best of all possible worlds." He saw an intelligible development in the physical universe and in human society. Even though he treated this as an evolution of "the Idea" reflected in the world of things and of persons, this was in itself a potentially dangerous notion, for it made even the Prussian monarchy not a perfect state, but only "the best yet." Moreover, there were passages in his latest work, *The Philosophy of History*, which show that he did not unreservedly reject popular revolution as an element in social progress.

More significant, however, from our point of view, than Hegel's conclusions was his highly original logic, his manner of thinking and communicating his thought. Again in contrast to that of the French materialists, Hegel's thought-method was dynamic or evolutionary—or, to use terms less familiar now than they were a century ago, his method was dialectic and theirs metaphysical. He thought of everything in terms of process rather than of static existence. Instead of saying "This is and that is not," he said "This is ceasing to be what it was and becoming what it was not." Something very like this method had been independently conceived about five hundred years before Christ by the Greek Herakleitos and by the Indian Gautama, but to nineteenth century Europe it came as a startling and invigorating novelty. Its specific form and technique have since been almost forgotten, but only because in substance it has become merged into the stream of scientific thought.

Until the young Marx came to Berlin his liveliest intellectual interest had been in pure literature. Having without much enthusiasm chosen the law as a future means of livelihood, he had begun his legal studies at Bonn and had found the subject more attractive than he had expected; actually it served him only as a bridge of philosophy, to history, and later to economics. He shared his father's rationalistic and liberal views but, as befitted his age, held them in a more aggressive way. He had at this time but little knowledge of or interest in philosophy, and was somewhat prejudiced against Hegelianism. In the stimulating atmosphere of the great university, however, his interest in the subject awoke, he studied it eagerly for a year, emerged as an ardent but not uncritical follower of Hegel, and found himself among those who called themselves the Young Hegelians. The Continental universities at that time retained some traces of their medieval origin as voluntary associations of students, who engaged famous scholars to lecture to them, but whose method of learning consisted more in free discussion or formal "disputation" within more or less fluid student groups than in listening to lectures. The line of distinction between faculty and student body was therefore much less sharp than it has ever been in our American universities. If not with the more distinguished professors, it was at any rate possible and not unusual for the youthful undergraduates to associate intimately with considerably older men who held doctoral degrees and were in at least the lower ranks of the teaching body. Such was the case with Marx, and he very soon won a high standing among the Young Hegelians. The members of this group—if it can rightly be called a group—were held together by reverence for Hegel, by use of the dialectic thought method, and by open and sometimes demonstrative opposition to one or more aspects of the existing order of society. For the rest, there was wide divergence of opinion among them.

Marx as Publicist

By 1841, the twenty-third year of his life, well as Marx had earned his doctorate by intellectual attainments, it became known that, solely because of his equally well earned reputation as a "dangerous radical," government pressure would prevent the university from granting him the degree. He had no difficulty in dealing with the situation by transferring to Jena and there submitting his dissertation, whereupon that university readily made him a doctor of philosophy. This did not solve the problem of livelihood. He had long since given up the idea of entering the legal profession, but had hopefully qualified himself to become a professor of philosophy. The fact of strong Prussian government hostility, however, made it unlikely that he could obtain a professorship anywhere in Germany and extremely doubtful whether, if appointed, he could hold the place very long. The alternative was to live by his pen. In May, 1842, he became a regular contributor to the *Rheinische Zeitung*, a politically liberal paper which had recently begun publication in Cologne, and five months later he was made its chief editor. Another five months and he resigned his position in the hope that this might save the paper from threatened suppression, but within a fortnight the edict was carried into effect. It is known that in this, as in many other instances before and later, the authorities in Berlin acted under pressure from Saint Petersburg.

The importance of this "brief interlude" is that, having to deal editorially with certain current events unfavorably affecting the life of the peasants, Marx had to throw himself into the study of economics, a subject which he had hitherto neglected.

We come now to the third of the intellectual legacies that entered into the nascent ideology of Socialism—namely, the then relatively young science of economics or, as it was usually called until late in the nineteenth century, political economy.

In this field, as in that of dialectic reasoning, an ancient Greek had made a brilliant beginning. About the middle of the fourth century before Christ both Xenophon and Aristotle had written books about *oikonomia*—literally, management of a household or, by extension, of an estate or enterprise—but these were hardly more than practical handbooks for landowners. Besides his *Economics*, however, Aristotle wrote a theoretical treatise, which has somehow come down to us as the introduction to his *Politics*. In this he defines such broad concepts as production, barter, money, commerce, acquisition and accumulation of riches; distinguishes value from utility; briefly discusses usury; and hesitantly works out a defense of slavery. He barely mentions the existence of self-employing mechanics and of wage workers, and stops short of analyzing price, value, rent, interest, wages, and profit. The treatise is incomplete in scope and sketchy in form, but as a rough-hewn torso it is full of promise.

The promise, however, went unfulfilled for two thousand years. Throughout the Greco-Roman period, the Middle Ages, and the Renaissance no further contribution to economic theory was attempted.[25] Only in the sixteenth century did problems arising from the increased financial needs of the national monarchies and from the expansion of commerce and the price revolution which followed the discoveries of Da Gama and Columbus and the conquest of Mexico and Peru call forth empirical works comparable

[25] An exception may be made for the North African Arab historian Ibn Khaldún, who died in 1406. He does not seem to have had any forerunner or successor in the Moslem world, and his work was unknown in Europe until it was translated into French four hundred years after his death.

with those by Xenophon and Aristotle. In the next two centuries came efforts toward analysis of the economic process as a whole, which led up to the theoretical systems of the Mercantilist and Physiocratic schools, and these at length gave place to the masterly work of Adam Smith, whose *Wealth of Nations* was published in 1776.

Let us note that the inventions of Hargreaves, Arkwright, Smeaton, and Watt were made between 1760 and 1770; that Crompton's improvement on the earlier spinning machines came only in 1779; that the first use of steam to run a factory was in 1785; that Cartwright's power loom, patented in 1785, was but little used until 1813; and that Eli Whitney's cotton gin came into use after 1795. These dates show why, when Adam Smith gave his book to the press, he had no idea that an unprecedented revolution was getting under way. His *Wealth of Nations* closed an era in the history of economic thought and cleared the road for a new development.

Within a generation the revolution in the world of fact was visible to all who were not unwilling to see. The factory system was spreading like a green bay tree (see Psalms, 37.35)—or like the upas tree of travelers' tales. Low-born mill owners were taking precedence of the landed gentry. The old class of self-employing hand workers in homes and small shops was being exterminated by the competition of machine-made goods. In its place the relatively new class of wage workers was rapidly growing, the employment of whose women and children dragged men's wages down and swelled the profits of the factory lords. As the workers' earnings fell, the price of bread and the rentals of overcrowded lodgings rose. Undeniably, as the rich grew richer, the poor were growing poorer.

The revolution in the world of thought, as usual, lagged behind. True, there was bitter resentment at the bottom of the social pyramid, but it was an unenlightened and futile resentment. True, there were individuals in the higher strata who pitied the poor; but their pity brought no healing, for they knew not what to do. The parson told the sufferers to be content in that station of life whereto God had called them, and for his own part thanked God that his own lines were fallen to him in pleasant places. The honest business man honestly declared that he'd never stolen sixpence in his life, and least of all from a penniless starveling. And all this was not wanton cruelty nor conscious hypocrisy. They did not understand the world in which they lived and throve. They did not think in terms of an economic system. To their way of thinking the misery of the masses was in the same category as earthquakes and tornados—causeless and humanly cureless evils —and so, *laissez faire, laissez passer*—which being interpreted meant "Every man for himself and the Devil take the hindmost."

Ricardian Economics

Let us pass on to David Ricardo's *Principles of Political Economy*, which came out in 1817, and of which Thomas De Quincey wrote:

> I wondered at the book. Had this profound work really been written in England during the nineteenth century? Was it possible? I supposed [analytic] thinking had been extinct in England. Could it be that an Englishman . . . oppressed by mercantile and senatorial cares, had accomplished what all the universities of Europe . . . had failed to advance by one hair's breadth? All other writers had been crushed and overlaid by the enormous weight of facts and documents. Mr. Ricardo had deduced . . . laws which first gave a ray of light into the unwieldy chaos of materials, and had constructed what had been but a collection of tentative discussions into a science."

This tribute is not extravagant. Ricardo was the Isaac Newton of economics.

Ricardo was neither a reactionary nor a reformer, neither a praiser of past times nor the herald of a good time coming by-and-by, and surely not an advocate of drastic social change. He did not appeal to popular enthusiasm nor to the upper-class fear of innovation. Far from being in private life indifferent to ethical ideals, in his book he strictly limited himself to the scientific task he had undertaken; he passed no moral judgments, neither endorsed nor condemned what he saw about him, stirred no hopes and raised no warnings.

His book gives us the impression that he was singularly lacking in historical sense, was not interested in how the present came to be what it is nor in what it was going to become. Certainly not a cold hearted man, he was an extraordinarily cool headed and objective observer and analyst. To all appearances he accepted production for sale, private ownership of the means of production, freedom of enterprise and of competition, individualistic quest of material gain, and the relations of landlord and tenant, employer and wage worker, seller and purchaser, creditor and debtor, as things eternal for the future, though not in the past. There could and would be improvement, but it would consist of changes of detail within the existing order. Taking all this as granted, he stated and explained with marvelous acuteness the normal inner workings of the system of production and exchange as it had taken form within the forty-five years that he had lived. In the light of his demonstration, the economic laws of value, of rent, of wages, and so forth might seem to have the same kind of validity as have the laws of gravitation and of chemical affinity.

Not only because the subject is abstruse, but also because of a deficiency in literary style and artistic arrangement, the *Principles of Political Economy* is rather hard reading. Yet it was and long continued to be very widely read and diligently studied. All the conservative and reactionary elements welcomed it as an inexhaustible armory of destructive weapons to be used against "radicals" of every shade. So it was, but what the standpatters overlooked was that the doors of the armory were open to all and that the weapons could be pointed either way.[26]

Marx did not simply accept Ricardo's conclusions. He studied him critically, as he had studied Hegel, though he found less occasion for dissent. At certain points he modified the Ricardian laws—or perhaps it would be more accurate to say that he developed them to a finer precision. Above all, he recognized, as apparently Ricardo had not, that these laws were the statement of economic relations prevailing within a certain social order, that this order was not eternal, that it was undergoing change, and that economic laws must not only state relations as prevailing at a given moment, but must indicate the directions and, so far as practicable, the momenta of change. In brief, economics became dynamic in the hands of Marx, and it thereby became a revolutionary force.

Marx Vitalizes Ricardo

In the first place, Marx the economist, completing the Ricardian static analysis, exhibited the capitalist pure-and-simple as a parasite pure-and-simple—or, to put it less rudely, showed that as the growth of capital divorces the primitive capitalist's aspect as director of the productive process from his continuing aspect as owner of means of production, it renders the capitalist socially unnecessary and injurious. In the second place, treating capitalism as but the latest in a series of property systems, each of which by its own full development exhausts itself and at the same time

[26] This is no doubt the reason why bourgeois economists began, after the third quarter of the nineteenth century, to moderate their devotion to Ricardo, and why they have now got to the point of treating his work as a historical curiosity. It requires some very difficult contortions to accept Ricardo and reject Marx. The present writer can well remember the time when our high school textbooks of political economy were still based on Ricardo, but showed some effort to avoid logical inferences from his theories. A few years later, at any rate on the college level, Marshall was being exalted in his place, and then Böhm-Bawerk took front rank, with his "marginal" theories—which, by the way, are not fundamentally inconsistent with Ricardian principles. More recently still the tendency is to pay as little attention as possible to theories of value, price, rent, and wages and to substitute an empirical treatment of commercial and financial phenomena.

prepares the conditions of existence for its successor, Marx the historian brings to light the normal process by which capitalism "produces its own grave-diggers."

Such are the main intellectual roots of the theoretical system of Marx and Engels, which had taken form by 1848, though it had not yet been developed in its various details, and which, subject of course to modifications, was and is the theoretical system of modern Socialism.[27] Let us turn now to social-political tendencies which entered into the composition of the Socialist movement when it took shape in 1848.

Marx and Engels would perhaps not have worked out their theories, and even if they had done so the theories might have remained barren, had there not already existed the vague and unlinked elements of a movement of social discontent, to which they devoted themselves and which their clear thinking greatly helped to unify, to guide, and to inspire.

Neither the speculative radicalism of Rousseau and the *philosophes* of Priestley and Godwin nor the Utopian plans of Saint-Simon, Fourier, and Owen, need detain us. Each of these had rendered service by illuminating exposure of some aspects of the existing social order. Some of them had formed what may be called sects rather than movements. In so far as attempts had been made to realize their dreams of society "as it ought to be" by founding colonies or communities, not only did these fail, but they retarded the working class movement in the same way that a mirage retards the desert traveler by diverting him from his right course. Except for that, only the Saint-Simonian sect presented an obstacle in 1848.

[27] Let us here emphatically declare that the Marxian theoretical system is not a body of rigid dogmas. In its very nature it is self-critical. Those who, as followers or as antagonists, cite utterances of Marx, Engels, and their collaborators and contiuators as religious sectaries or controversialists cite scriptural texts, do not know the very elements of their way of thinking. The Marx of 1860 or 1870 sometimes disagrees with the Marx of 1848. To the honest student this presents no difficulty, but he is interested to find out how Marx came to change his mind.

Strivings for Democracy

Of the more vital tendencies that merged to form modern Socialism the most general was the striving for political democracy. Nowhere in Europe did manhood suffrage prevail at that time, but in the most advanced nations on the Continent, as well as in Great Britain it was being vigorously demanded.

When the rising bourgeoisie of France undertook to wrest power from the monarchy, the aristocracy, and the state church, it needed the help of the lower classes and made "Liberty, Equality, and Fraternity" its slogan. Democracy triumphed in 1793-'94, and then the bourgeoisie promptly kicked away the ladder by which it had climbed. Under the Directory, the Napoleonic Consulate and Empire, and the Bourbon Restoration of 1814-'30, now broader and now narrower sections of the propertied classes monopolized the powers of government. In the revolution of 1830 it was the workers and students of Paris who bore the brunt of the fighting, but once the old government had been overthrown, the propertied classes united to seize upon the fruits of victory, and as a result a large part of the lower middle class as well as the artisans and wage-workers were excluded from political power through the eighteen years of the Orleans Monarchy, while the financial bourgeois took precedence of the large landholders, the industrial bourgeoisie being as yet not highly developed, and the numerous class of peasant proprietors were inert so long as they felt secure in possession of the lands which they had obtained through the confiscations carried out under the First Republic.

Germany was still far behind France on the road toward popular self-government. Only in a few of its thirty or forty loosely connected states did any but the rich bourgeois share power with the aristocrats. It was therefore possible for the middle classes to hold democratic opinions, except—and it was an important exception—in so far as they were deterred by fear of what the lower classes might do if a revolution was to get under way. In some parts of Germany the factory system was developing, though it was still small in comparison with the British, and the not very numerous wage-working class, while bitterly discontented, was handicapped by the lack of a revolutionary tradition.

In Great Britain, the native land of industrial capitalism, the wage-working class had for half a century, as we have seen, fought bravely for democracy as well as for betterment of their economic conditions, but it was without any clear idealogy and its revolutionary fervor was almost worn out by unsuccessful struggle. The advent of Socialism in its modern form on the Continent came just too late to establish effective contact with the British proletariat.

Second among the roots of the modern Socialist movement we must name trade unionism. Only in Great Britain had this attained any great strength and maturity. In Western and Central Europe the factory system was from thirty to sixty years younger than the British. The working men felt the competition of British machine-made goods, which caused great misery among them, but only in a few localities had any considerable proletariat of the modern type come into existence. In general, too, having even less of civil rights and political liberty than had their British comrades, the lower classes and particularly the wage workers were less able to organize on the economic field. Organization of workingmen to obtain better wages had been made criminal in France by a law enacted in 1791—that is, while the Great Revolution was still in its ascending phase, and eight years before the British Combination Laws—and legislation of this type prevailed in most parts of Europe down to the 1860s or later. Naturally there were many attempts at building secret unions, but they had little success.

Underground Communism

Finally we must take note of the underground societies whose existence was a normal response to repressive governments. Many of these had in view only political purposes of a more or less democratic character, but some aimed at profound economic and social change. The most famous had been the Society of the Equals, led by François Noel Babeuf, who called himself Gracchus Babeuf, which in 1795-'96 planned to overthrow the French government, nationalize the land, and reorganize the nation on communistic lines. The plot was discovered, Babeuf and one associate were guillotined, and the society disappeared, but for more than half a century, especially in France, Germany, and Italy, such groups were being formed, dissolved, unearthed, broken up, and formed again.

This underground communism was generally of a utopian sort —that is, to use Plekhanoff's words, "starting from an abstract principle, it sought to devise a perfect society." Each group had its ready-made scheme, based on its own conception of harmony, justice, or some other moral abstraction. But whereas the followers of Saint-Simon, Owen, or Fourier expected all wise or good persons, regardless of class, to accept their ideas, these conspirative communists were free from the illusion that the propertied classes could be persuaded to abdicate. They relied, if not precisely on the working class, at any rate on that more inchoate mass, "the poor and oppressed," and they counted on these to rally to them whenever they gave the signal of revolt and to impose their system upon society by force. It must be added that their schemes were sometimes reactionary, in that they aimed to revive local small-scale production by hand labor, rather than to socialize the now strongly developing system of great machine industry. As the midcentury approached, however, some clarification of ideas took place.

This was the case with the League of the Just, a society composed mostly of German exiles, organized in 1836, with headquarters at first in Paris, but afterward in London. Primarily a conspirative group, watchfully awaiting the moment for revolt, it had formed around it an open society for education and propaganda.

In 1844-'45 Marx and his friend Frederick Engels[28] became closely associated with this group, which was now acquiring English, Dutch, French, Hungarian, Polish, Russian, and Scandinavian members and correspondents. Their influence counted for much in dispelling Utopian fantasies. By 1847 it was becoming evident that another revolutionary crisis was approaching on the Continent and, they might hope, in England as well. At two delegate meetings the society was reorganized on a broader basis, its international character was emphasized, propaganda of communistic ideas and organization of the workers for self-directed action was definitely accepted as its function, and the passing of its former Utopian and conspirative aspects was symbolized by changing its name to Communist League and by substituting for its former sentimental motto, "All men are brothers," the aggressive slogan, "Proletarians, of all countries, Unite!" Ten days were spent in considering a statement of principles to be given to the public, and by unanimous vote Marx and Engels were commissioned to give it final form. In the month of January, within a few weeks before the armed uprisings in Paris, which overthrew the Orleans Monarchy and proclaimed the Second Republic, they gave the German text of the *Communist Manifesto* to the printers and immediately afterward it was translated and published also in French.

[28] Engels' background and early experiences contrasted sharply with those of Marx, who was two years his senior. He came of a narrowly pious Protestant family, which had built up a prosperous textile manufacturing business in the Wupperthal (a hundred miles north of Marx' native Trier) with an important branch in England. A year before he had completed gymnasium he was placed in his father's business and in 1842, at the age of twenty-four, he was sent to Manchester, which, with slight interruption, was his home until he retired from business in 1870; thereafter he lived in London, where he died in 1895, having outlived Marx by twelve years. Engels knew the life of the wage workers, German and English, by direct observation, and he knew capitalist industry and commerce by twenty-eight years of active participation, from the status of clerk to that of managing partner. His intellectual development, up to the time when he met Marx as an equal in 1842-'43, had been achieved without academic aid, yet it had run in a closely parallel course. For the next forty years they shared their thinking and, although he always minimized his part, he undoubtedly made a very large contribution to the joint product.—Gustav Mayer's *Friedrich Engels: A Biography* (published in German, at the Hague, 1934; English translation by J. H. Crossman, Knopf, New York, 1936) ranks with Mehring's and Nicolaevsky's biographies of Marx. Karl Kautsky's *Aus der Frühzeit des Marxismus* (Prague, 1935) richly supplements both.

Thus modern Socialism was born, not solely out of the minds of two great theoreticians (who were also, as their whole lives thereafter showed, also great propagandists, organizers, and tacticians) but out of a combination of a number of intellectual currents and popular strivings which they, among all the participants, were best able to understand, co-ordinate, and explain.

It is neither practicable nor necessary for us even to sketch the whole history of Socialism through the last hundred years. What we have yet to do is to note the outstanding features of the Socialist or Communist[29] ideology of 1848 and then to indicate when, how, and why they have been substantially changed. In some instances the changes have come gradually or at any rate by amicable discussion and decision upon differences of opinion that have grown up within the movement. In other cases they have involved violent controversy culminating in secession or schism. In order to indicate what we regard as the continuous body or stream of the movement which has from time to time thrown off dissident elements, some of which have survived, and at other times has received affluents, we may name a dozen or more prominent men,

[29] We shall henceforth speak of the Socialist movement, except when there is particular occasion to do otherwise. When the League of the Just resolved to change its name it had to decide whether to call itself the Communist or the Socialist League. Both adjectives were already in use. Both were applied to the followers of Saint-Simon and of Fourier. The Marxians wished to distinguish themselves from these and also from certain German "would-be philosophers," as Marx dubbed them, who professed to represent "True Socialism," and they felt closer to the underground societies which from the time of Babeuf had been known as Communists, indicating their relation to the extreme revolutionary party of 1791 to '94—the party of Danton, Chaumette, Hebert, Billaud-Varennes, and Collot d'Herbois, which had its stronghold in the "commune" or municipality of Paris. Within a few years after 1850 the True Socialists had disappeared, the Utopian sects had lost their vogue, the secret societies died out, and the name of Communist gradually gave way to that of Socialist. In the latter part of the nineteenth century the followers of Bakunin called themselves Communist Anarchists. Finally, after the Russian counterrevolution in the autumn of 1917, when the triumphant Bolshevist faction found that it could split and weaken the Socialist parties in other countries, but could neither conquer nor destroy them, it picked up the long unused Communist name and claimed to be the only true successor of the party which bore that title in 1848.—Socialist parties in various countries have for one reason or another used different names—Socialist Labor, Social Democratic, Social Democratic Labor, or simply Labor Party, as in Great Britain. These do not, as a rule, imply difference of principles or aims.—It is worth while to note that in at least two cases the name Socialist has been brazenly stolen and used for infamous purposes—by the Antisemitic Clericals in Austria, who called themselves Christian Socialists, and later by Hitler's totalitarian organization in Germany, which took the name National Socialist.

whose overlapping lives within the movement have bridged the whole century. The list might be made much fuller without including any unimportant men, but these may suffice:—Karl Marx, Frederick Engels, August Bebel, Eduard Bernstein, Jules Guesde, Karl Kautsky, George Plekhanoff, Victor Adler, Filippo Turati, Emile Vandervelde, Ignacy Daszynsky, Pieter Jelles Troelstra, Keir Hardie, Rudolph Hilferding, Sidney Webb, Jean Jaurès, and Leon Blum.

There are five adjectives which Socialists have commonly used when they had occasion briefly to define the movement or distinguish it from any of the other movements which are frequently confused with it. They are—*scientific, proletarian, revolutionary, international* and *democratic*. We put them in this order because the first of the five is basic and because there has been more frequent occasion to use the fifth since the rise of Bolshevist totalitarianism than in earlier times.

Marxian Economics

The phrase "scientific Socialism" has not been used as a mere boast, but as a descriptive epithet. Marxian theory may be divided into two parts—the analysis of capitalism as a developing system of economic relations and what we may for the moment call the philosophy of history. As we have already noted, Marx turned seriously to the study of economics in 1843 and before 1848 he had evolved a body of theory consistent with that of Ricardo but carrying it to novel conclusions. His studies in this field were repeatedly interrupted, while the need for study broadened before him. Not until 1859 did he feel justified in giving to the public a substantial volume entitled *A Contribution to the Critique of Political Economy*, which he intended as the first volume of a larger and more comprehensive work. By this time, however, he had altered his plan and resolved on a new start. The first volume of *Capital* came out in 1867. Because of demands upon his time by various exigencies of the movement, and because also of gradually failing health, the second and third volumes were not yet in form for publication when he died in 1883. The laborious task of editing was undertaken by Engels and the volumes were published in 1893 and '94 respectively.[30] Many persons—by no means all—find even the first volume difficult reading. To them it may suffice to say what Joseph Schumpeter says to those who make the same complaint about his own work on *Business Cycles*—"Did they expect to find it easy?" As for those who think that *Capital* is dry or dull, it is their misfortune to have no sense of wit or humor. It is of course quite outside our scope to attempt a summary of Marx' economic theories. What we have to say is that after eighty years *Capital* is still very much alive. Enormous numbers of books on economics have been written since 1867, many of them of real importance. Marx has come in for a great deal of hostile criticism, but no writer competent to judge has denied the scientific character of his work or its rank as one of the few epoch-making contributions to general economic theory from Smith's *Wealth of Nations* on.

It would be childish to claim that Marx the economist was infallible or that he said the last word in economic science. But it is not less childish to find fault with him, as some do, for not having written about phenomena which did not exist while he was living or to distort his meaning by quoting single sentences out of their context.[31] Worst of all is to forget that in *Capital* he was analyzing the capitalist made of production as it existed in his lifetime, not writing cook books for the future.

Of at least equal importance is Marx' work in the field of social history. At about the same time when he set himself to an

[30] The authoritative English translation of the first volume of *Capital*, by Samuel Moore and Edward Aveling, appeared in 1886, and those of the second and third volumes, by Ernest Unterman, in 1907 and 1909. The *Critique* was translated by N. I. Stone and published in 1904. As to the various popularizations, the two which we deem valuable are *Karl Marx's Oekonomische Lehren*, by Karl Kautsky, 1887, English translation bv H. J. Stenning, 1925, and *Karl Marx's Capital: An Introductory Essay*, by A. D. Lindsay, 1925.

[31] Marxian economics did not become a closed canon with the publication of the third volume of *Capital*. Rudolf Hilferding's *Das Finanzkapital* (1910) and Rosa Luxemburg's *Die Akkumulation des Kapitals* (1921) are but two of the important works of his disciples,

exhaustive study of economics he felt the necessity of mastering what was then called the "philosophy of law," and this soon led him "to the conclusion that legal relations as well as forms of the state could neither be understood by themselves nor explained by the so-called general progress of the human mind, but that they are rooted in the material conditions of life." He soon found, to his great satisfaction, that Engels "had come by another road to the same conclusion."

Historical Materialism

The first formal statement of this materialistic conception of history, and that a very brief one, but admirably precise, appeared about fifteen years later in the preface to his *Critique of Political Economy*, but it is clearly visible to the thoughtful reader in his and Engels' intervening works, such as the *Communist Manifesto*, the *Class Struggles in France*, the *Eighteenth Brumaire*, the *Revolution and Counter-Revolution*, and the *Peasants' War*. Since then, and increasingly through the last six decades, it has been used in a very large number of theoretical and historical works by outstanding Socialists, has been ardently attacked and defended, and has deeply influenced, directly or at second or third hand, much of the best historical writing of our times.[32]

British and American writers have not facilitated the right understanding of the materialistic conception of history by re-christening it the economic interpretation of history. They tend to ignore the influence directly exercised upon habits, customs, attitudes, beliefs, and ideals by material conditions which are not themselves economic; to underestimate the effect of tradition in causing ethical, religious, and political development to lag be-

[32] The fullest and best exposition and development of Marxian historical theory is to be found in the two large volumes of *Die Materialistische Geschichtsauffassung*, by Karl Kautsky, published in 1929 and unfortunately not yet translated into English. Edwin R. A. Seligman's *Economic Interpretation of History* (1902) is erudite, conscientious, and very well written, and comes as near to an understanding of the Marxian theory as seems to be attainable by any academic scholar who has had no personal contact with the Socialist movement,

hind the development of productive technique and of economic relations; and to overemphasize the role played by the motive of gain—or, if they do not themselves commit these errors, to accuse Marx of having committed them, which he did not.

The respect which has been paid to the historical as well as the economic portions of the Marxian theoretical system by many qualified persons who do not accept his conclusions or accept them only in part justifies us in calling it a scientific system, and in so doing we sharply distinguish it from a body of theological doctrine.[33] Usually through sheer ignorance, but sometimes not without malice, opponents of Socialism speak of "the Gospel According to Saint Marx"—and then they too often misquote or garble the so-called gospel. In fact, it is of the essence of Marxism that it should be subject to discussion, to criticism, to correction, to development. No one has been disciplined or denounced for questioning or frankly rejecting Marxian "doctrines." An outstanding example is Jean Jaurès, who was very far from being an orthodox Marxian and made no secret of his dissent, but who remained one of the most trusted and honored leaders, in the French Socialist party and in the Socialist International, till the day of his untimely death. Eduard Bernstein is another striking example.

Because it was not a creed, but a body of scientific thought, Marxian theory has contributed immensely to the vitality and endurance of the Socialist movement. It has led the rank and file as well as the leaders to think, to gain knowledge, to weigh arguments, to pass sound judgment. It has made the movement a school as well as a party, a body of intelligent collaborators, not of docile followers, a democratic fellowship, not a mob. It has given its members good reason to respect themselves as active par-

[33] It is true that the English word *doctrine*, like the Latin *doctrina*, from which it is derived, originally meant a thing that is taught, a teaching; but in English usage it almost always means something taught on authority, to be believed without proof or question. The use is almost limited to the fields of religion and of law; we do not speak of the Newtonian doctrine of gravitation, the Darwinian doctrine of the origin of species, or the economic doctrine of diminishing returns. The present writer therefore regrets that the English translation of Kautsky's excellent *Karl Marx's Oekonomische Lehren* has been entitled *The Economic Doctrines of Karl Marx*. In this case *Lehren* might better have been translated *Teachings*.

ticipants in a great historic effort which they hold to be sure of success, even though they may not live to see its triumph. Their persistence through periods of defeat and often under bitter persecution may appear fanatical to those who look at it from outside; those who have a more intimate acquaintance call it brave and thoughtful patience, all the more admirable and more formidable because it is not sustained by any hope of personal reward either here or in a life to come. This alone would be enough to make Marx' arduous intellectual labors worth while, but they had also another and more tangible effect. While the Marxian theoretical system did not create the Socialist movement and while it did not give that movement a ready-made program of action nor a blueprint of the future society, it did provide certain broad concepts for its practical guidance. Foremost among these we note the concepts of class, of class consciousness, of class interest, and of class struggle.[34]

Class Struggles

When Socialists speak of classes they have in mind very definite economic categories, and the distinctions they draw are based not so much on differences in the amount of income as in its form —that is, the manner in which it is obtained. To illustrate:— The average American farmer may not have a larger real income than the average American wage worker; but the fact that the farmer possesses his material means of production and gets his income by selling the commodities he has produced, while the wage worker holds no productive wealth and lives by the sale of his labor power, results in a marked difference between the immediate interests of the two classes and between their respective

[34] The term used by responsible Socialists has been in English "class struggle," in German *die Klassenkampf*, in French *la lutte des classes*, and so forth. Within the last thirty or forty years certain so-called "intellectuals" have found it more thrilling to talk of *class war*, and this has had a dangerously misleading effect, especially upon juvenile and otherwise susceptible elements. Of course every war is a struggle, but not every struggle is a war, and Socialists worthy of the name are most unwilling to have the struggle for a classless society take the specific form of war.

ways of thinking and feeling; furthermore, although most American farmers are owners of productive wealth and to some extent employers of wage-labor, their interests and their social attitudes distinguish them from even the small capitalists as sharply as from the wage workers. We thus have three important classes—one the richest and least numerous, the other two not very unequal in economic status, but one of them much the largest and still growing while the other is diminishing in numbers—with three antagonisms of interest[35] and three widely different ideologies. In other economically advanced countries the class system may be somewhat different, but is similar in its main lines. In countries of backward or deflected economic evolution very dissimilar class relations prevail, and in these there has been no normal development of Socialism.

The class struggles of the past had been of two types—those in which a new and growing middle class had risen against an old and often decadent ruling class, as the plebeians against the patricians in ancient Rome or the young bourgeoisie against aristocracy in modern Europe, and had in many cases won equality or even supremacy; and risings of slaves against their masters or of serfs against their lords, which had rarely been successful. Until the sixteenth century there had nowhere been a body of wage workers sufficiently large and cohesive to carry on a serious class struggle, and until the end of the eighteenth, if they acted as a class they had made common cause with the bourgeoisie, helped it to win its battles, and then found that they had won less than nothing for themselves.

Proletarian Consciousness

But now the coming of power-driven machinery, of the factory, of large-scale production for an ever expanding market, had brought a new class upon the stage of history—as Marx described it, "a class always increasing in numbers, and disciplined, united, organized by the very mechanism of the process of capitalist pro-

[35] This is not to deny the existence of community of interest between any two or among all three.

duction itself." It is, we think, not unreasonable to say that this proletariat—as Marx called it, giving a precise new meaning to an almost forgotten word—would in time merely out of its own experience, have become conscious, not only of its own common interests and of the antagonism between these and the interests of both the propertied classes, nor only of the power of its numbers, but also of its own indispensability and of its latent capacity to take over the functions of direction and management which the owners of capital were already delegating to salaried employees; they would have seen, moreover, that their right course was not to destroy the capitalist mode of production nor even to hamper its development, but to socialize the ownership and control of the means of production and transform them from instruments of exploitation into instruments for lightening the burdens and enriching the lives of all the people; and finally, they would have recognized this as involving a political revolution—that is, a transfer of power from the bourgeoisie and the aristocracy to the proletariat and through it to the people as a whole. It is no accident, however, that there were exceptionally keen thinkers who were able to see all this and explain it, thus saving the time that might otherwise have been lost in groping.

To call Socialism a proletarian movement is not to say that it confines its appeal to the working class, and certainly not that it wishes to repel adherents who personally belong to other classes. In the *Communist Manifesto* itself, indeed, Marx points out that members of the bourgeoisie may be expected to rise intellectually and morally above their class interests and in all good faith array themselves with the proletariat, and such recruits have actually come to the movement in much larger numbers than he probably expected. The Socialist program does include support of the wage workers' immediate interests in conflicts with their employers, but it includes much more than this, taking account of broad social interests which transcend those of the wage workers as employees.

The word "revolution" calls for more comment. Perhaps there is no other word which bears so many and such diverse meanings.

To many persons it means overthrow of a government by armed force. Did Marx and other Socialists of his time approve of revolution in this sense? They did not incite such revolutions nor approve of reckless attempts, but when revolutionary risings took place, as in France and Central Europe in 1848, and later in Poland, Italy, Spain, and Ireland, they heartily approved them and many Socialists participated in them even though the risings had no Socialist objective, but only the overthrow of despotic governments or independence for subject nationalities. In this democratic and liberal elements generally took the same stand. No one who knows the history of that period can condemn the revolts against the Romanoff, Hohenzollern, and Habsburg governments at that time, or the Austrian, Papal, and Bourbon rule in Italy, or that of Louis Bonaparte in France. If in any case Socialism had been an issue Marx and his comrades would have supported the effort yet more strongly, for there seemed no possibility that Socialism could ever prevail in those countries by peaceful means. In countries where some fair measure of civil rights and self government prevailed their views as to violence were different. In 1871 an American newspaper correspondent asked Marx whether the British Socialists contemplated civil war. "We do not want civil war and we shall not start one," Marx replied; "but if the capitalists start a civil war when the people declare for Socialism, we shall know how to fight." And the next year, speaking at the Hague, he said that in the United States and Great Britain, and perhaps in Holland, Socialism might come by peaceful means.

In brief, Socialism has never been a pacifist movement. In certain cases—notably with regard to the Crimean War against Russia and to the American Civil War, which he regarded as a war against slavery, Marx and Engels frankly supported the "capitalist" governments. They thought freedom was worth fighting for.

When we say that Socialism was and is a revolutionary movement, what we mean above all is to distinguish it from mere reform movements, which seek to remedy certain evils in the capitalist system, but not to change its basic character.

Socialist Internationalism

Socialist internationalism has often been misunderstood as meaning a negation of love of country, appreciation of national culture, and attention to national interests. Such misunderstanding has sometimes occurred within the movement, reaching its extreme form some thirty years ago in the aggressive antipatriotism of Gustave Hervé, who proposed to "plant the tricolor in a dunghill." Marxian internationalism was a protest against jingism, national vanity, and xenophobia, and a warning to the workers against the danger which these involved.

The value which Socialism puts upon national independence is illustrated by two little known phases of Marx' intense and many sided activity. For many years he, a German and a Jew, was a frequent speaker at the public meetings and patriotic demonstrations of the Polish "colony" in London, largely composed of refugees. It may be said that his passionate desire for Polish liberation was motivated by the fact that an independent Poland would be a bulwark against Russian aggression. This is in large part true, but it is not the whole truth. He was deeply moved by admiration for the steady courage of a people who had resisted the partitions of 1772, 1792, and 1795 and who, under the most drastic repression, had preserved their national consciousness and their will to be free. In an address delivered in 1862, the manuscript of which was not published till twenty years after his death, he called Poland *l'immortel chevalier de l'Europe* and bitterly reproached the Western Powers for their folly as well as their ingratitude in failing at each repeated opportunity to come to Poland's aid and so place a frontier guard of "fifteen million heroes" between the Tsarism and themselves . To the end of Marx' life there was no strong Socialist movement in Poland. In Ireland there was none, but this did not prevent him from being an ardent champion of Irish freedom and sharply condemning the working class of Great Britain for its failure to support that cause.

"The people that helps to oppress another people," he told them, "is forging chains for itself."

It is hardly necessary to repudiate the accusation that Socialism aims to destroy the home and the family. The Socialist attitude toward religion and the state, however, cannot be overlooked.

There is, indeed, no room for the supernatural in the Marxian philosophy, but atheism has never been a Socialist article of faith. If many and perhaps most Continental Socialists are unreligious, it is because they have had to combat clericalism, whether Catholic, Orthodox, or Protestant, for its servility to the rich, its opposition to science and secular education, and its efforts to make the workers endure all hardships and humbly trust for happiness in heaven. The German Social Democratic Party long ago disposed of the religious question as such in three words: *Religion ist Privatsache*, and consistently with this called for complete separation of church from state and exclusion of clerical influence from the schools.

Space does not permit us to do more than mention some disputed points of Marxian economic theory—among them the theory of crises, which was barely sketched in the lifetime of the two "patriarchs" and to which both Socialist and bourgeois economists (notably Rudolf Hilferding among the former) have devoted much study, but without reaching unanimity and, we think, without seriously discrediting the basic Marxian formula; the theory of concentration, which Bernstein, depending largely on American data, thought he had almost demolished, but which such economists as Berle and Means[36] have rehabilitated; and the theory of increasing misery, now so often apologized for by Socialists, but which seems to us completely defensible if we think of it in terms of the world market and take into account the countervailing force of trade unionism and of social and labor legislation which have grown so enormously in recent times.

[36] See *The Modern Corporation and Private Property*, by Adolf A. Berle, Jr., and Gardiner C. Means, New York, 1933.

Socialist Ideology Today

Socialist ideology is not the same now as it was in 1848—if it were it would lack the essential quality of Marxian thought. It has grown by the elaboration of its original elements through the critical labors of many Socialist scholars. It has grown by adaptation to the changes in economic and other conditions, which were so largely foreseen by the great Socialist thinkers a century ago and to which three generations of Socialist combatants have contributed so much. And it has grown also through intelligent criticism (mingled with much misconstruction and unintelligent abuse) from outside the Socialist ranks.

The process of ideological development has been marked by a series of internal struggles. First came the intellectual conflict between the newborn Marxian thought method and the Utopian wishful thinking of Saint-Simon, Fourier, and Owen. Next, in the 1850s, came the settling of accounts with another form of Utopianism, the curious petty bourgeois Anarchism of Pierre J. Proudhon. This was followed by three distinct but overlapping conflicts, begining in the 1860s, all of which concerned the conception of the state and the Socialist attitude toward it.

In so far as the Socialist attitude toward the state has changed, this is partly due to the necessity which the Marxians faced in the 1860s and '70s of defining their views on this subject and distinguishing them from those of the followers of Ferdinand Lassalle, of Auguste Blanqui, and of Michael Bakunin respectively. In a deeper sense, however, at least from the 1870s on, it resulted from the change which has taken place in the nature of the state itself—a change which was largely, though not wholly, brought about by the growing pressure of the Socialist and Trade Union movements upon public opinion and, at first indirectly and then more and more directly, upon the legislative, the executive, and even the judicial agencies of the state.

At the middle of the nineteenth century Marx and Engels were only slightly exaggerating for the sake of emphasis when they said (in the *Communist Manifesto*) that political power is merely the organized power of one class for oppressing another. And they continued: "When, in the course of development, class distinctions have disappeared and all production has been concentrated in a vast association of the whole nation, the public power will lose its political character." The oft quoted passage in Engels' *Socialism, Utopian and Scientific* (written in 1880) differs from this in somewhat fuller and more precise verbal expression. Particularly it indicates the state as the agency by means of which the ownership of productive property is to be socialized, whereby the state terminates its own existence as state—that is, as an instrument of class rule—and "the government of persons is replaced by the administration of things; the state is not abolished, it dies out." It is not worth while, we believe, to speculate as to whether Engels thought that with the ending of class rule and exploitation all kinds of crime would cease and penal law become unnecessary. If so—well, Engels was no doubt wrong on that point; but the error, or the failure to note that qualification of his epigrammatic statement, is not very important. More serious is the fact that he did not foresee that within forty years a state set up by a dissident faction of the Socialist movement would "take possession of the means of production in the name of society" but would combine with this an extraordinarily tyrannical "government of persons" and develop a new ruling and exploiting class. But if he did not foresee the rise of totalitarianism, first in its Bolshevist or Communist form, and then in the form of Fascism or Nazism, neither did anyone else in 1880 or even two decades later.

Even in England and yet more on the Continent at the time when the *Communist Manifesto* was written the state in its contacts with the working classes and even with the lower middle class, was represented chiefly by the tax collector, the drill sergeant, and the policeman. Universal education, promotion of scientific research, care for the public health, legal limitation of the workday, social security laws, provision of improved housing for the low-income elements—these are among the additions to the functions of the state which have been made almost wholly within the last hundred years and mainly within the last sixty. In all European countries west of the Soviet Empire, and with the exception of Spain and Portugal, the state combines its old character as an instrument of class rule with its newer character as an agency for promoting the welfare of the whole population; and if we think of it in terms of process, we must say that its old character is waning and its new character is gaining ground.

Already before Engels' death Socialists were becoming conscious of this tendency, and the increasing representation of Socialist parties in most of the parliaments and in vast numbers of municipalities made the attitude of intransigeant opposition untenable and called for a modus vivendi. The theoretical and practical problems which this raised formed the subject matter of the Revisionist and Ministerialist controversies which occupied several years at the turn of the century. By the eve of World War I this conflict was practically settled on a basis nearer to the Revisionist position than to that of the "Orthodox" elements. There were, however, extremist minorities on both sides, and the strains of the war itself and its sequels revived the controversy in new forms and with increased bitterness, culminating in the Communist schism. At this point we must turn back to the 1860s and 70s in order to make a new approach.

Conflict with Lassalleans

In the early 1860s, at a moment of extreme weakness of the Socialist movement in France under the Second Empire and in Great Britain after the last trace of Chartism had disappeared, there came a great new wave of Socialism in Germany. Under the audacious leadership of Ferdinand Lassalle the *Allgemeine Deutsche Arbeiter Verein* (General German Labor Union) far outstripped the older Marxian organization. Lassalle was a phenomenally brilliant propagandist and organizer, but not a patient and accurate theorist. For the sake of present success he tended to oversimplify those principles and general rules of policy which in the long run are of determining weight. Wishing for quick results, he perhaps laid too little stress on political democracy and was certainly too ready to establish an entente with the Prussian state which dominated German political life; and Prince Bismarck, a much less brilliant man, but more farsighted and surer of his long-range objectives, was not unwilling to "play ball" with him. The question of attitude toward the state was the central point of the conflict between Marxians and Lassalleans, which was diplomatically adjusted in the Gotha Program of 1875, when the two German parties were merged, but was not clearly settled in the Marxian sense until the Erfurt Program of 1891.

Conflict with Bakunists

Next came the far sharper struggle with the Anarchists. Of all Revolutionists Michael Bakunin[37] best deserves the title which Mephistopheles gives himself—"the spirit that denies." Not until the later 'sixties, however, when he was past his fiftieth year and had become a legendary figure, did he fully define his own brand of revolutionary theory and practice. On its theoretical side it was thoroughly Utopian and unhistorical. According to him religion and government are the twin causes of all economic and social evils, and they have their own origin in usurpation by the few and the docility of the many. In its practical aspect, accordingly, Bakunism is completely negative. The task of the revolution is not to build, but to destroy. Extirpate belief in the supernatural and respect for human authority, excite and incite the masses to violent revolt, wipe out state and church and all property institutions, and then there will remain a classless society. Bakunin

[37] Born in Russia in 1814, Bakunin went abroad in 1841 and never voluntarily returned. After a few years in Germany and Switzerland, spent in studying philosophy and dreaming of rather than planning the liberation of Poland and the overthrow of the Tsarism, he became an active revolutionist in 1847, first in France, then in Germany. Arrested in 1849, he passed eleven years in German, Austrian, and Russian prisons and in Siberian exile, from which he escaped in 1860. He then agitated and conspired for several years in England, France, and Italy. At this point the story is taken up in our text.—He died at Bern in 1876.

gave little thought to the form and nature of the resultant society; freed from fear and the habit of obedience, men will arrange their social relations by mutual consent. It was his disciples, notably Peter Kropotkin and Elisée Reclus, who thought it worth while to picture a Communist-Anarchist world, and thereby to incur the task of answering all the questions that the unconverted may ask. But to discuss this would be to go quite beyond our limits.

In 1868 Bakunin organized his followers into a body which (with what purpose it is hard to say) took the very misleading name of Social Democratic Alliance, and a year later this was merged into the International Working Men's Association. Ostensibly the Alliance gave up its separate existence, but in fact it continued as a secret society inside the International and devoted itself to intrigue against the Marxian leadership, which it branded as authoritarian and also as German. The International Congress held at the Hague in 1872 brought this internal dissension into the open. Bakunism in theory and practice was hotly debated, as well as certain specific acts committed within the International. The outcome was the expulsion of Bakunin and his lieutenant, James Guillaume, and the adoption of a resolution which repudiated the Anarchists' theory and declared that the workers must be organized on the political as well as the industrial field and must aim not at destroying the state, but of taking it out of the hands of the propertied classes and using it as an instrument for socializing the means of production and thus putting an end to exploitation and class rule.

In spite of this decisive action (which left no excuse for publicists to confuse Socialism with Anarchism) and in spite of Bakunin's announced withdrawal from revolutionary activity, the Anarchist movement showed considerable vitality, manifested chiefly in political assassinations. It got no foothold in Central or Northern Europe or in Britain. How far, if at all, it contributed to the systematic terrorism of the People's Will party and later the Revolutionary Socialist party in Russia is doubtful; it seems more likely that this was a product of special conditions in that country, including the activity of provocators in the service of the secret police. In France it found adherents chiefly in two minor social elements—the intellectual *déclassés* and the decadent class of skilled hand workers. Its greatest popular strength was in Italy and Spain.

The First International practically died with the Hague Congress. The black reaction which prevailed in France until the forced resignation of MacMahon in 1879, together with the *revanche* psychology which naturally prevailed for a much longer time, and the antagonism between Marxians and Blanquists, and in Germany the schism between Eisenachers (the Marxian group) and Lassalleans which began to be healed in 1875 and the Bismarckian repression which started three years later—these facts made renewal of international organization impossible until 1889, when the Second International was launched at a congress in Paris, which endured until the First World War. Under these circumstances there was more or less infiltration of Anarchistic or at any rate antipolitical elements into some of the Socialist parties, but full discussion and an unambiguous resolution adopted by the London Congress in 1896 ended this danger.

Conflict with Blanquism

At the Hague Congress the partisans of Auguste Blanqui[38] stood with the Marxians as against the Bakunists, but as soon as that struggle was over a new struggle began between Marxists and Blanquists, again over the question of the state and of political action. The Blanquists stood for an all-powerful state, which of course must be a democratic and socialistic state; the state could be taken out of the hands of the propertied classes only by armed

[38] Louis Auguste Blanqui was born in 1805. His father had been a member of the Convention, but risked his life opposing the Terror. The son joined the Carbonari while still a youth and was influenced by Buonarroti, the close associate of Babeuf. In 1827 he took part in demonstrations against the Bourbon Restoration, receiving two saber cuts and a bullet wound, and he fought on the barricades in 1830. With equal courage he opposed the Orleans Monarchy, the Second Empire, and the governments of Thiers and MacMahon in the 1870s. Dying in 1881, he had passed almost exactly half of his seventy six years in prison under some twenty convictions for revolutionary activity.

revolt; until victory was won on the the barricades, political action in the usual sense of those words had in their opinion no value except as a method of propaganda; and as trade unions began to develop in France they too were looked on with favor only so long as they were fighting for existence; as soon as they became strong enough to strive for higher wages and a shorter workday they were deemed to have lost their value for the social revolution. On all these points Marxism and Blanquism were clearly opposed.

The struggle was not so fierce as that which had culminated at the Hague—probably because both factions paid regard to what the Bakunists and forty years later the Bolshevists called the "bourgeois virtues" of truth, honor, and humanity—nor was it carried to a definite issue. Blanquism did not gain ground in Central and Northern Europe nor in Great Britain. In France the Blanquists gradually modified their position, especially after the fall of MacMahon, the collapse of Boulangism, and the reconstitution of the International, but organizational unity was not achieved until 1905. Blanquism, like Bakunism—which agreed in their reliance on violent methods, though in nothing else—found its most favorable soil in the economically undeveloped countries of the South and East, and especially in Spain and in Russia.

We have remarked in the early pages of this paper that the period from the middle 1890s until the beginning of World War I in 1914 was for the Socialist movement a time of numerical and organizational growth and optimistic outlook. The year 1900 brought the formation of the Labor Representation Committee in Great Britain, which six years later became the Labor Party. The year 1905 brought the unification of the various Socialist parties in France. The German Social Democratic Labor Party had continued the steady growth which had begun even in the last years of Bismarckian repression and could reasonably expect to gain an absolute majority at the polls and in the Reichstag and to proceed with a peaceful socialization of the German economy. In Austria,

Italy, and several of the smaller countries, though victory was not so near, it seemed assured. The hopes aroused by the great revolutionary wave of 1905-'06 in Russia were disappointed in 1907, but by 1912 a new forward movement seemed to be impending, which might be less violent but more successful. It is significant that the Stuttgart Congress of the Second International in 1907 adopted a resolution clearly defining the fields of action of the Socialist parties and the trade unions and the manner in which they should collaborate as parallel and autonomous movements with a common aim; and that the Copenhagen Congress in 1910 recognized the co-operatives as a third force, with a field of its own, working in harmony with the other two.

It was in this period that a brilliant young American, registering at a Swiss hotel, had signed "Yours for the Revolution, Jack London," and the next registrant had written "There ain't going to be no revolution, H. G. Wells." The Englishman lived to see his prediction contradicted by current history all over the Continent; but had London lived as long he would hardly have rejoiced over the verification of his own forecast. On the very eve of what we were soon calling "the war to end war" there was a very general belief that there would never again be an armed conflict among the great powers of Europe nor a violent revolution anywhere west of Russia and the Balkan states. Most of us who were then adults feel that the first of August, 1914, cut our lives in two.

Yet the period in question was not without conflicts within the Socialist movement—conflicts, however, less fierce than those of the preceding fifty years.

Anarcho-Syndicalism

We must first briefly note that, just as Bakunist Anarchism was ceasing to be formidable even in Italy and Spain, and as the French Blanquists were ceasing to foment insurrections and beginning to take political and parliamentary action seriously, a new antipolitical movement came into the picture — the movement known as Revolutionary Syndicalism or, more accurately, as Anarcho-Syndicalism.[39] Trade unionism had hardly existed on the Continent before the 1860s and it was then practically begotten and nurtured by the Socialists. By the 1890s it had passed its infancy and developed aims and methods of its own. It was acquiring a membership which, while including most Socialist workingmen, had no place for any who were not actual wage workers, and its membership included large and growing numbers of wage workers who were not Socialists; and it concerned itself increasingly with the direct relations between employers as such and their respective employees, rather than with the broader and more far-reaching antagonism between bourgeoisie and proletariat. Under these circumstances the parent-and-child relation between the political and the industrial movement became embarrassing to the unions if not to the party. This was especially true in France, where there were two or three and at times four or five Socialist parties, whose diverse tendencies, however legitimate on the political field, were often irrelevant to the employer-employee conflicts and tended to weaken the solidarity of the unions.

Chiefly for this reason the then young French General Confederation of Labor in 1895 adopted the rule of political neutrality, which was not meant to restrain members from political activity, but only to exclude political questions from the agenda of the Confederation and affiliated unions. This example was followed in several Continental countries.[40] Under normal conditions such neutrality is a sound policy, since it is essential to the success of a union that it should, so far as possible, enlist all the wage workers qualified for employment in its particular craft or industry,

[39] It may be well to explain to American readers that the French words *syndicat* and *syndicalisme* (and similar words in Italian and Spanish) mean "trade union" and "trade unionism" respectively, neither more nor less.

[40] It was not followed in Belgium, where the working class party—known there as the Labor Party, *le Parti Ouvrier*—had been built as a federation of trade unions, co-operative societies, and political groups. Nor was it followed in Germany, where side by side with the Social Democratic Party and the federation of "free" (that is, non-sectarian) unions, there existed a Catholic clerical party, having its strength chiefly among the wage workers, and a federation of Catholic unions, and these organizations were working out a *modus vivendi.*

regardless of their religious beliefs or political opinions. In face of existing weakness or schism on both the political and the industrial field, however, the practical result may be to produce, not a politically neutral unionism, but one that is aggressively antipolitical. Such was the case in France and still more in Italy and Spain, and to a lesser extent in some other countries.

Unionism of this sort does not distinguish between the struggle of wage workers and employers over wages, working hours, and other terms of employment and the broader class struggle for a basic change in the whole economic system—indeed, it rather gives precedence to the latter, but totally rejects the use of the ballot and of parliamentary action as means to this end, as involving continual compromise and paralyzing the revolutionary spirit of the proletariat. Thus far, it agrees with both the Blanquist and the Bakunist concept of social revolution. It differs from Blanquism, however, in that it aims at the complete destruction of the state; and it differs from Bakunist Anarchism in that it would substitute for the state, not independent local communities, with freedom for individuals to shift from one community to another, and with such *ad hoc* federations as any communities may see fit to set up or to dissolve, but instead of these, it would substitute regional or worldwide organizations of the workers in various industries—mining, metal working, production of textiles, transportation, and so forth—each organization owning its means of production and each exchanging products with other organizations on such terms as may be agreed upon.[41] For the struggle within the shop its characteristic methods were striking without notice, "striking on the job"—that is, systematic loafing—and sabotage, and it rather welcomed than avoided conflicts with the authorities;

[41] In 1905 an Anarcho-Syndicalist organization was launched in the United States under the name of Industrial Workers of the World, or I.W.W. for short. It was hostile both to the existing unions and to the Socialist Party. It was strongest among the migratory workers then numerous in the Far West—not the "Arkies and Okies" of the 1930s, but men who were continually moving from place and shifting from one industry to another, now following the harvest from Texas and Southern California up to Western Canada, now working in the lumber woods, the mines, or the fisheries, or employed in railway building, as opportunity offered at different seasons. It has had but little strength in any part of the country for the last twenty-five years. See Paul F. Brissenden, *The I. W. W.*, New York, 1919.

in the larger social struggle it relied on riotous disturbances, barricade fighting, and more or less extensive general strikes, which might be the prelude to armed insurrection. All these were valued, not mainly for immediate gains that might be made, but as cultivating the spirit of revolt and preparing the workers for the time when they would forcibly "seize and hold" the means of production. In fairness it ought to be noted that the Anarcho-Syndicalists did not follow the Anarchists in practicing assassination, and that they have firmly opposed Bolshevism.

The Bolshevist Schism

At the turn of the century there were two Russian Socialist parties, both with headquarters abroad and operating underground in Russian territory. The Revolutionary Socialist Party appealed especially to the peasants and at this time was concentrating its efforts on a war of assassination against the Tsarism—which, as was proved a few years later, was being directed by one Eugene Azeff, a paid agent of the secret police. We are concerned rather with the Social Democratic Labor Party, which was strictly Marxian, was ready to co-operate with liberal bourgeois elements in democratizing the government, and felt that socialization must await a further development of capitalist industry and of the wage-working class. At this time there appeared within it a dissident element, headed by Nikolai Lenin, a recent recruit, who held that European Socialism had lost its revolutionary character and cried out for aggressive action in Russia. By 1905 there was a clear schism in the party, so deep that no reconciliation was possible. On the basis of a vote taken in a party congress held abroad, Lenin's group called themselves Bolsheviki, a word derived from *bolshestvo*, meaning majority.

The heroic revolutionary effort of 1905-'06, in which the two Socialist parties and the democratic liberal groups joined hands, ended in an almost complete defeat, to which the schismatic activity of the Bolsheviks contributed. A black reaction followed, under which the one thing gained, the *Duma* (parliament) conceded by the Tsar, was almost a nullity. In 1913 and '14 the democratic and socialist forces were regaining strength, but then came World War I and a wave of national patriotism.

By the spring of 1917 autocratic inefficiency and corruption had brought complete military collapse, profound disorganization of the national economy, and desperate discontent, strongest in the armed forces, but extending to almost all classes of the population. The Tsarism fell like a house of cards, a group composed of leaders of the two Socialist and two Liberal parties proclaimed the democratic republic and called for election of a Constituent Assembly.

The elections gave the Socialists a majority, with a Constitutional Democratic fraction ready to co-operate, and a negligibly small antidemocratic opposition, but the new provisional government, headed by Alexander Kerensky, faced an almost impossible situation. Yet it might have succeeded, if the Western Allies had given prompt assistance. Their failure to do so—no doubt largely motivated by hostility to any Socialist government—gave the Bolshevists their opportunity. In November, having at their disposal a force of mutinous soldiery, they dispersed the Constitutional Assembly, arrested opponents right and left, proclaimed peace with Germany, land for the peasants, and bread for everybody, and set up a so-called "dictatorship of the proletariat" which meant in fact dictatorship by a single minority party which was in turn dictated to by a ruthless minority in its own ranks.

Such was the origin of the Bolshevist or Communist regime in Russia, whose whole subsequent history has followed logically from the nature of its initial triumph and which in that first step corresponds perfectly with Lenin's theory. It set the pattern of the totalitarian state—a type of state altogether new in history, differing widely from the old autocratic and aristocratic states and the mere military dictatorships; a type which was imperfectly imitated in Italy, but very successfully (with minor adaptations) in Germany, and which apparently, once it has held power for a few years, cannot be overthrown from within; a type, however, which by its very nature must pursue aggressive policies and thereby risks overthrow from without.

Leninist theory is Blanquism carried to its extreme, with an infusion of Bakunism, all camouflaged with early Marxian phraseology. Its principal Bakunist element is the negation of all the moral standards which modern civilization had for centuries been developing and with which Marxian and also Blanquist Socialism has complied. For the rest it is Blanquist in that it aims at conquering the state and then exalting it at the expense of all individual and group rights; that as means to this it rejects political action and prefers insurrection—in other words, it does not count on convincing a majority, but on organizing a "resolute minority" strong enough to subjugate the masses; and that it regards trade unions, co-operative societies, and other voluntary groupings as instruments to be manipulated for its own purposes during the period of struggle and then to be destroyed or absorbed into the centralized and omnipotent state.

Blanqui would have been horrified could he have foreseen the concrete working-out of his theory. It is probable, too, that Lenin was sincere in declaring that the dictatorship which he and his associates had set up would within a few years transform itself into a democracy. A dozen years after his death the surviving "Old Bolsheviks" were being branded as traitors and put to death. Frankenstein's monster destroyed Frankenstein and then created other monsters as atrocious as itself.

Socialism Since 1917

World War I did not in itself seriously injure the Socialist movement in Europe. In some countries it emerged stronger than ever before. Within a year after the armistice, however, it began to feel the effects of the Bolshevist counterrevolution in Russia —schism, confusion, and for many of its adherents paralyzing disappointment. Then came the rise of Fascism in Italy, of military dictatorship in Poland and later in Spain, of Clerical Fascism in Austria, and of Nazism in Germany, the first and the last of these five being definitely totalitarian. Many, though not all, of the great capitalists and landowners backed these abnormal revolutions, at first because they expected them to destroy the Socialist and Labor movements, afterward because they did not dare to withdraw their support. The Great Depression, which began in Europe somewhat earlier than in the United States, caused many peasants and petty business men, many unorganized workingmen, and especially great numbers of the youth, who had never known a normal existence, to flock to whatever leadership would make the wildest promises—in which vicious practice the Communists and the Fascists and Nazis tried to outbid each other. The fairly large Communist Party in Germany, taking its orders from Moscow, devoted its energies mostly to attacking the Social Democratic Party and the Free Trade Unions and at a critical moment brazenly joined forces with the Nazis against the Social Democrats.[42]

The injury was not only in the field of ideas. In Russia—to state it very moderately—tens of thousands of the active Social Democrats and Revolutionary Socialists were killed outright and hundreds of thousands were worked to death as slaves of the state in the mines, forests, and fisheries of the Far North. In Germany, Poland, Austria, Italy, Spain, and more recently in the Baltic and the Balkan countries, though no one of these countries has matched the death toll in "the workers' fatherland," the aggregate has probably far exceeded it.

Despite all this, since the ending of World War II, the Socialist parties are stronger at this moment (January, 1948) are stronger than they were in 1918 or at any time since. In regional and local elections held in the American, British, and French zones of Germany in the postwar period the Social Democratic vote has been about equal to that of the Christian Democrats and much

42 The official organ of the Russian Communist Party, the daily *Pravda*, justified this conduct on the theory that by some made-to-order law of history, the triumph of Nazism was a necessary preliminary to the Communist revolution.

larger than that of any other party. In all other countries west of the Russian sphere of domniation they are strongly represented in the parliaments and ministries. Most important of all, the British general election in the summer of 1945 gave the Labor Party (which frankly avows its Social Democratic character) a clear majority at the polls and a decisive majority in parliament. With the same dogged resolution that they showed in the war, the British are proceeding, under extremely hard conditions, with the socialization of their economic system.

It remains to be seen, however, and it may be seen within months rather than years, whether Western Europe is to be Socialist or Communist, democratic or totalitarian. The answer must come from this side of the Atlantic. It may take the form of rehabilitation of the European economy—including the British—in which case World War III may be averted. If it does not take that form, the choice will soon be submission to Moscow or a war whose issue it would be rash to predict and whose cost in human life and in all less precious things can hardly be imagined.

On Socialism since 1917 *see also "Epilogue"* (*The Balance Sheet*).

BIBLIOGRAPHY

For extensive bibliography see: Laidler, Harry W.: *Social-Economic Movements,* Thomas Y. Crowell, New York, 1944.

* * *

Beer, Max A.: *History of British Socialism,* London, 1921.

Beer, Max A.: *Fifty Years of International Socialism,* New York, 1935.

Braatoy, Bjarne: *Labor and War,* London, 1934.

Blum, Leon: *A L'Échelle Humaine,* Paris, 1945.

Cole, G. D. H.: *British Working Class Politics, 1832-1914,* London, 1941.

Engels, Frederick: *Socialism Utopian and Scientific.*

Gross, Feliks: *The Polish Worker,* New York, 1945.

Hillquit, Morris: *Socialism in Theory and Practice,* New York, 1909.

Hyndman, H. M.: *Historical Basis of Socialism in England,* 1883.

Jaurès, Jean Leon: *Oeuvres,* Paris, 1931-39.

Kautsky, Karl: *Parlamentarismus und Demokratie,* Stuttgart, 1911.

Laidler, Harry W.: *Social-Economic Movements,* New York, 1944.

Macdonald, James Ramsay: *The Socialist Movement,* New York, 1911.

Marx, Karl: *Capital.*

Marx, Karl and Engels, Frederick: *The Communist Manifesto.*

Nomad, Max: *Rebels and Renegades,* Macmillan, 1932.

Nomad, Max: *Apostles of Revolution,* Boston, 1939.

Owen, Robert: *A New View of Society,* New York, 1825.

Russell, Bertrand: *Proposed Roads to Freedom; Socialism, Anarchism and Syndicalism,* New York, 1919.

Saposs, David J.: *The Labor Movement in Postwar France,* New York, 1931.

Sturmthal, Adolf: *The Tragedy of European Labor,* New York, 1943.

Thomas, Norman: *America's Way Out; A Program for Democracy,* New York, 1931.

Vandervelde, E.: *Jaurès,* Paris, 1929.

Webb, Sidney: *Socialism in England,* 1889.

Webb, Sidney and Beatrice: *The History of Trade Unionism,* New York, 1920.

IV.

European Trade Unionism

IV.

EUROPEAN TRADE UNIONISM

by

PHILIP TAFT

THE ACTIVITIES AND objectives of European trade unionism have militated against the elaboration of an involved doctrinal edifice. Essentially organs for the defense and improvement of the conditions of labor, they have been more successful in formulating their immediate demands than in elaborating involved theories. Sometimes European trade unions have actively espoused political Socialism, but as they became more secure in their position, their Socialist ideology has been pushed into the background, and in their daily operations they became largely bargainers over wages and other conditions of employment. Yet their ideologies have frequently exercised an open or subtle influence upon their long-run policies.

The ideologies accepted by European trade unionism have responded to outside influences and internal pressure and consequently, the unions of some countries have changed their attitudes on politics, government and other social issues. Ideologies influence conduct subtly and indirectly, and while there may be no visible change in the relations between the union and the employer, a shift from one ideological position to another may in time show itself in the willingness or unwillingness of the unions to support Socialism, increased political activity or other reforms. The ideologies of the trade unions in some countries—Germany and Belgium—showed a high level of stability, while in other countries ideologies changed, as in France; as a result of the more competent leadership of a militant minority, which converted trade unionism into revolutionary Syndicalism. Later the exhaustion of revolutionary elan led to a return to trade unionism more conservative and politically minded than the one supported prior to World War I. In contrast, the change in ideology in Sweden was due to the growing influence of political Socialism among the workers; and in England a change in ideology came as a result of the entrance of large masses of workers holding neither the philosophical prejudices nor the favorable economic positions of the earlier unionists.

In contrast to the political movement of labor, the trade unions have never strongly emphasized ideas or ultimate objectives.[1] Thus, for a student of German labor, trade unionism was an attempt to equalize bargaining power between labor and capital.[2] Professor Selig Perlman has held bargaining power and the consciousness of scarcity of opportunity to be the basic drives of all trade unions even when they professed revolutionary doctrines.[3] It would be difficult to find a mature trade union in which the drives described by Professor Perlman did not play a major role. Not only defense against the employer and the sharing of jobs, but a system of mutual benefits for members was the frequent goal of unionism. Yet ideology, in contrast to practical policy, is not without significance in influencing the attitudes of trade unions, for while a trade union must establish a rapport between itself and the employer, as open and continual warfare is neither to the interests of its members nor practically feasible, its ideology will determine its attitude towards politics and economics and will influence its support or rejection of subsidiary and peripheral activities which in the long run may exercise a decisive influence over government and society.

[1] Karl Zwing, *Sociologie der Gewerkschaftbewegung*, Verlagsbuchhandlung, Jena, Erster Teil, p. 17.

[2] *Ibid.*, pp. 124-134.

[3] Selig Perlman, *A Theory of the Labor Movement*, Macmillan, New York, 1928, p. 308.

England

European trade unionism did not follow a common pattern of development; nor were the unions of the several countries inspired a common fund of ideas. The earliest unionism — the English — passed through a period of vigorous militancy accompanied by severe repression ending with the collapse of Chartism. The ideology and activity of the unions showed strong traces of protest against the ruthless industrialism then moving like a dark cloud over England. The end of the Chartist agitation closed this phase, and the quasi-Socialistic unions were replaced in the 1850's by the "New Model" trade union based upon a combination of trade—protective—friendly benefits. The typical "New Model" union, the Amalgamated Society of Engineers, provided both strike benefits and insured its members against unemployment, sickness and old age. In contrast to the earlier unions, the Engineers, as did the unions in other trades, relied on their own economic power which was based on a monopoly of the labor supply. The skilled English trade unions, which dominated the trade union movement for several decades, were unconcerned with welfare or labor legislation which the leaders opposed on philosophic grounds. Highly centralized, the skilled union of the 1850's depended on monopoly and restriction of labor supply and concentrated upon a combination of protective and friendly activities. Nor were they hospitable to any type of Socialist ideal. In common with the employer and the prevailing Victorian temper, the skilled unions accepted the dogmas of classical economics and their restrictionist and exclusive policies were based upon the principle that limiting supply would tend to raise the price of labor.

The leaders of the "New Model" located at London came into frequent contact with each other. Robert Applegarth, William Allan, Daniel Guile, and George Odger, the chiefs of the more important "New Model" organizations, have been called the "Junta" by the Webbs. It was the policy of the Junta to steer a course that would not arouse unduly the British community, nor involve the unions in risky political or social experiments. Their conduct was in part opportunistic and was influenced by their desire to placate a public opinion suspicious of workers' combinations. Nevertheless it was in harmony with the economic doctrines the leaders accepted.[4]

The ideology of the "New Model" was undermined by the influx of semi-skilled and unskilled workers in the 1880's. These workers could not assemble the large resources nor were they able to exert monopoly power in the labor market. Not as well placed economically as their skilled fellow workers, they could not look with disdain upon improvements through legislation. The infusion of "new blood" into English trade unionism gradually led to the breaking down of the older "laissez-faire" ideology, and its replacement by an ethical Socialist outlook which increasingly became the creed of British trade unionism. It has, however, not led to a rejection of the older organizational forms and institutions—such as collective agreements and concentration upon improvements of job conditions—for these activities are inherent in the very definition of trade unionism. It has, however, led to the change in ideology which has in turn exercised a significant influence upon the long-run objectives of British unionism. The shift from a "laissez-faire" to a Socialist ideology brought with it a greater emphasis upon political action and led to the eventual formation of the Labor Party. Despite the recognition by the trade unions that collaboration with the employer in every day affairs was necessary the trade unions never surrendered the long-run ideals of Socialism. The Socialism of the English trade unions had none of the harsh rigidity of the Marxist system, but the unions nevertheless looked forward to the day when a new cooperative society would be established. It was this hope in the eventual achievement of a better and juster social system that induced the trade unions to support morally and financially the La-

[4] Sidney and Beatrice Webb, *The History of Trade Unionism*, Workers' Educational Association, London, 1919, pp. 233-242.

bor Party. Other English political parties have been ready to make broad concessions to labor and have, in fact, initiated many social reforms, but the sponsoring of an independent political party was increasingly, although not initially, due to the belief in the desirability of a Socialist society. Nor can one argue that the acceptance of a specific view with regard to political action or the future form of society has made no essential difference in the history of British labor, for the unions not only gave financial support but also became the propagandists for the Socialist ideal. Without the huge reserves drawn from the British trade unions, the Labor Party could not have achieved political power. The English trade unions have not, because of their espousal of Socialism, avoided the day-to-day compromises and they have been ready to retreat whenever conditions made such a step necessary. Yet these compromises forced upon the unions by conditions, has not affected their hope of attaining by slow and gradual steps a Socialist Commonwealth.

Germany

German trade unionism at its beginning in the 1860's was closely tied to the emerging Socialism. Despite the low value the followers of Ferdinand Lassalle placed upon trade unions, it was members of their group, Friedrich Wilhelm Fritsche, the founder of the tobacco workers' union, and Johann Baptiste von Schweitzer who organized and directed the first modern trade union congress in 1868. However, it was the followers of Marx and not of Lassalle who were most favorable to trade unionism. The unions that arose in this period were under Socialist influence, although the liberals were unsuccessfully aspiring for leadership. The anti-Socialist laws first introduced in 1878 struck a sharp blow at the trade unions and they recovered more slowly than the Social Democratic Party after these laws had been repealed. Trade unionism revived slowly and the relations of trade unions to the Party required definition. After the setting-up of the General

Commission at the Berlin trade union Congress in 1890, the unions became virtually independent of direct political domination. In their practical activities they pursued a limited policy of concentrating upon economic improvements, and their relations to the Social-Democratic Party became a source of debate.

To succeed in its major objective—the improvement in the conditions of work—the trade unions had to evolve a permanent apparatus and, as the unions grew in strength and numbers, their management became more complicated and difficult. Moreover, the trade unions always had to prepare for the next step forward or brace themselves for a possible attack upon them by the employer. There thus developed a cautious attitude in the German trade union movement, and a desire to avoid legal and employer attack.[5]

At the outset, a close tie-up between political Socialism and unionism was natural, for both movements drew their inspiration from the same intellectual and spiritual reservoir. However, the expansion in the power and number of trade unions gave them an independent appeal, one based on immediate advantages that could be gained from an effective organization of labor.

Organizing workers in a plant or industry as effectively as possible, irrespective of the individual's political or social philosophy, forced upon the free German labor unions the need for adopting a neutral position toward political parties. But while the ideal was pushed into the background due to the need for collaborating with the employer, the German trade unions never surrendered their Socialist views. The Socialism of the trade unions was the moderate, evolutionary type and when a faction of more revolutionary Socialists led by Rosa Luxembourg attempted, in 1905, to gain approval of the mass strike, the trade unions objected. They regarded the strike as an economic weapon whose exercise should be directed by the trade unions and not by a political party. What the trade unions sought and accomplished was exclusive control over the economic movement of labor, and,

[5] Richard Seidel, *Die Gewerkschaften Nach dem Kriege, Dietz,* Berlin, 1925, pp. 19-21.

despite the criticism of some Party leaders, the German trade unions insisted upon their political neutrality. However, neutrality did not mean opposition on practical or theoretical grounds to political action, but only to domination by a political party. The free trade unions cooperated closely with the Social Democratic Party to advance their social and legal position, but they recognized that in their pursuit of immediate aims their independence must be assured even though the ultimate ideal of the political and economic wings of labor were the same.

Actually the free trade unions not only accepted a Socialist philosophy, but cooperated closely with the Social Democratic Party and during World War I the unions supported the majority pro-war views. After World War I, German trade unions raised the banner of industrial democracy. The desirability of Socialism was still affirmed and central planning, an increasing voice of labor in industry was held to be the means of approaching Socialism. As one examines the ideology of trade unionism, it is clear that the acceptance of the ideal of Socialism colored the trade union attitude toward government intervention, welfare legislation and the position of labor in industry. A Socialist-indoctrinated membership could accept with equanimity resolutions that non-Socialists would reject.

Italy

Italian trade unionism goes back to the 1840's and the organized resistance of the Torino printers against a wage reduction in 1848 is one of the first manifestations of organized economic action. Attempts—successful and unsuccessful—to establish unions were made in the 1860's and 1870's. Under French influence, "Camere del Lavro" (Chambers of Labor) were organized beginning in the late 1880's. The spread of unionism met the opposition of the government, and a wave of repression was instituted by Prime Minister Crispi. With a change of the government, a different and a more lenient attitude toward trade unionism was introduced. With the spread of organization, the "Centrale della Resistenza" (Central Committee of Resistance) was set up in 1902 which was transferred four years later into the "Confederazione Generale del Lavoro" (Central Federation of Labor). The Federation emphasized immediate gains, but in ideology it urged a moderate Socialist philosophy. Italian unionism was, however, not as completely dominated by political Socialism as was German labor, for a significant Syndicalist current also existed. This was, in part, due to the influence of the followers of Bakunin. Despite the existence of the more militant minorities, the trade union movement of Italy looked for inspiration to, and cooperated with the reformist wing of Italian Socialism. Thus, when in 1918 the Italian Socialist Party endorsed the dictatorship of the proletariat, the endorsement was rejected and a more conservative position taken. Italian trade unionism feared that the leftist Socialists would arouse the hopes of the masses, and thereby push the labor movement into dangerous ventures. Instead of a radical program, the Italian unions demanded a greater voice for labor in industry, disarmament, self-determination of nations, and equal suffrage. During the occupation of the factories in 1922 the trade union leaders took a moderate view and they sought to avert a crisis. Italian trade unions unsuccessfully attempted to evolve a practical policy of collaborating with the employer, but in ideology they were Socialistic with emphasis upon its gradual character.

Belgium

As in Germany, the link between the moderate Socialistic Belgian Labor Party and the trade unions was very close. In fact, the Party aided in the formation of many trade unions, and actually set up the Trade Union Commission in 1898. The latter, while essentially a statistical and information agency, helped to cement close relations between trade unions. At the outset it was completely dominated by the Belgian Labor Party, but in time the Trade Union Commission became autonomous. It has, however, recognized the Belgian Labor Party as the representative of labor's political interests.

Those trade unions not under religious influence, recognize the existence of a class struggle and hope for the eventual socialization of the means of production. The relations between the Labor Party and the trade unions have continued close, and each group is represented on the other's national executive. In sum, the ideology of Belgian trade unionism has been based upon reform and moderate Socialism, and with the recognition of the class struggle as a sociological law. Such recognition has not prevented the unions from day-to-day cooperation with the employer.

Sweden

In many respects the ideology of the Swedish trade unions went through an evolution similar to that of English labor. The earliest labor unions—founded in the 1840's—were dominated by liberal philanthropists who emphasized piety and uplift. The beginning and the increase in the political Socialist movement had an effect upon the outlook of the trade unions. Yet one of the early trade documents, published in 1882, does not show a direct Socialist influence. Improvement in working conditions, establishment of old age benefit funds, and more rigid regulation of working conditions are requested.

With the growth of Socialist influence, the position of liberalism upon Swedish labor was undermined. The growth in the importance of Swedish Socialism manifested itself in a requirement that local unions affiliated with the General Federation of Swedish Trade Unions must affiliate with the Social-Democratic Party. This rule was rescinded in 1900, but the close ties between the trade unions and Swedish political Socialism have never been severed. In 1909 the congress of the Federation declared the Social-Democratic Party to be "the natural and self-evident bearer of the political aims of the Swedish working class." Local unions can and often do affiliate with the Social-Democratic Party, although it is no longer required. A majority vote of the members is required, and members can "reserve" themselves against such a decision and thereby be exempt from payment of Party dues.

Conclusion

European trade unionism, regardless of differences in initial origin and inspiration, has tended, in time, to develop a cooperative attitude in its relations with the employer and a basically Socialistic ideology. As practical organizations, the trade unions have not given as much attention to theoretical and philosophical problems as political parties. Moreover their character has imposed upon them the need for more drastic compromises. Yet their acceptance of gradualistic and essentially ethical Socialism has made them ready to support governmental reforms in economic relations, and has given them the hope of an eventual Socialist society.

BIBLIOGRAPHY

BERTRAND, LOUIS, *Histoire de la Democratie et du Socialisme,* Dechene, Paris, 1906.

GUALTIERE, HUMBERT, *The Labor Movement in Italy,* S. E. Vanni, New York, 1946.

HANSSON, SIGFRID, *The Trade Union Movement of Sweden,* International Federation of Trade Unions, Amsterdam, 1927.

HEBERLE, RUDLOF, *Zur Geschichte der Arbeiter Bewegung in Schweden,* Fisher, Jena, 1925.

MICHELS, ROBERTO, *Storia Critica de Movimento Socialista Italiano,* "La Voce" Firenza, 1921.

PERLMAN, SELIG, *A Theory of the Labor Movement,* Macmillan, 1928.

SEIDEL, RICHARD, *Die Gewerkschaften Nach dem Kriege,* Dietz, Berlin, 1925.

VANDERVELDE, EMILE, *Le Patri Ouvrier Belge, L'Eglantine,* Brussels, 1925.

WEBB, SIDNEY and BEATRICE, *History of Trade Unionism,* Workers Educational Association, London, 1920.

ZWING, KARL, *Soziologie der Gewerkschat Bewegung,* Verlagsbuchhandlung, Jena, 1927.

V.

Consumer Cooperation and the Freedom of Man

CONSUMER COOPERATION AND THE FREEDOM OF MAN

Editorial Note

The Cooperative Movement is above all, a social and economic movement. A political party based solely on cooperative ideology could scarcely be found in Europe. Nevertheless, cooperative ideas exerted a strong influence upon such movements as the Peasant Movement and the Trade Union and Socialist movement, as well as other political labor movements. Further discussion of Cooperativism may be found also in George Dimitrov's chapter on "Agrarianism."

Prof. Horace M. Kallen treats some of the philosophical aspects of cooperativism, rather than general background or trend.

Since this book is intended to deal mainly with political ideologies, this aspect of Cooperativism appeared more important than a general presentation of the subject.

F. G.

V.

CONSUMER COOPERATION AND THE FREEDOM OF MAN

by

HORACE M. KALLEN

AS THE FIRST century of the Consumer Cooperative Movement comes to its close, we may speculate a little about what was in the minds of Charles Howarth and his twenty-seven mates when they chose to call themselves The Society of Equitable Pioneers. During wars, pioneers are the advance guard of an army, the soldiers who build the roads and clear the way, making it as smooth and safe as possible for those who follow after. In times of peace, the pioneer is the explorer and experimenter, the forerunner who spies out the wilderness and prepares the ground—be it in religion or politics or science or art or in the economy of life—for the generations that come after. The men who called themselves Equitable Pioneers—that is pioneers who undertook to share their labor and its fruits according to their several abilities and needs—could not have given themselves such a name unless they had a feeling of mission and a sense of destiny.

What, if they were alive this day, would the twenty-eight weavers of Rochdale think had come of their mission and destiny as they looked upon the world-wide company of the more than hundred million men and women who had formed consumer societies according to the Rochdale pattern and conduct their affairs upon the Rochdale rules? They would, I fancy, be as surprised as Columbus, who trying out only an untried road to the Indies, found he had broken a new way to a new continent. For fundamentally, the members of the Toad Lane Society had not liberated themselves from the ways of thinking and feeling of the producer economy that they had grown up in and were the victims of. It had not occurred to them that by nature they were consumers, consumers first, last and all the time, and that they were producers by nurture only, and intermittently. The need they felt was for what we today call "security," and they identified security with "employment" just as their descendants do. Of course they knew that there were more fortunately placed people who could eat and love and live without working, but it never occurred to them that they themselves could be thus fortunate; that it is those who do not eat that must die, not those who do not work. Only if those who do not work are prevented from eating, leisure is a road to disaster and death, instead of what it has always been considered, the way to freedom, the way to the good life. The Rochdale Pioneers had no thought of leisure or freedom. They organized their Society in order to provide themselves with employment and food and clothing and shelter; in order to set up "self-supporting colonies of united interests" whose inhabitants might, by working them, earn and share "profits . . . in proportion to purchases." "Profits," "employment," were focal in the aspirations of the men of Rochdale.

Nor could it have been otherwise. The English world in which they lived and moved and had their being was a producer-minded world where they figured not as men but as workmen, not as masters of themselves but as employees and servants of their employers. And so they also considered themselves. It was in the hope that they might relieve this condition that they organized their Society of Equitable Pioneers.

But as this Society of theirs grew and budded and bourgeoned in Branches and a Wholesale Department, and as it was joined by new societies, inspired by their example, the Pioneers, remaining all the while employees of the businesses for which they worked, became in their turn employers in the businesses that they owned. Early in their history they had been befriended by a number of gentlemen who were also Christian Socialists—gentlemen moved by a deep pity for the state of the workingmen of Britain. These humanitarians, gentlemen though they were, were as producer-minded as the workingmen they sought to aid. The latter, these gentlemen believed, could help themselves best by organizing cooperative societies of producers and sharing the profits of their labors on equal terms. They and their companions had set up several such producers' cooperatives; and they insisted that in equity the rule of the primacy of the producer should govern also the association of the Rochdale consumers.

Had they prevailed, the employees of the consumer societies would have been set up as a privileged caste of workers and the societies which employed them would have been put at a serious disadvantage in the competitive field. One of the many contributions of J. T. W. Mitchell to the theory and practice of consumer organizations was to drive that point home, and in driving it home to uncover the new meaning which consumer enterprise was giving the term "profit." By training and experience as producer-minded as his opponents, Mitchell for a long time thought of "profit" in the usual way. He long regarded consumer organization as but a combination of "purchasing power," and cooperation as but a means of securing the "profits of trade to all the people." In the course of his defense of the interest of the consumer members of the cooperative societies against inequitable demands by their employees and against the justification of those demands by the Christian Socialists, he came, however, to realize *the primacy of the consumer*. Profit, he declared, is made by the consumption of the people, and the consumers ought to have the profit. "The Pioneers," he advised the Cooperative Congress of 1892, "did not start with capital or labor but with consumption." All economic values—costs, profits, taxes, interest, wages, rent,—are rooted in consumption and the burden of those values falls heaviest on the poorest who have least to consume. If, consequently, there really is a class-war, it consists not in the so-called struggle of labor with capital over "surplus value" but in the struggle of the people as consumers with joint organizations of capital and labor into industries as producers. The meaning of the principle of the primacy of the consumer for the social economy of a free people is, then, inevitably—consumer organization and consumer control; and Mitchell brought the meaning out. Let the worker receive a generous wage for his work, he told the Royal Commission on labor that year of 1892. But whatever accrues to him beyond his wage should accrue to him as consumer through his membership in a consumer society. In the nation's economy it is the citizen as consumer and not as producer who should own the capital and get limited interest on capital.

In the United States, about the same time, Ira Steward, three years younger than Mitchell, arrived at this principle of the primacy of the consumer by a very different route. Steward was the inspirer and founder of the Eight Hour League that agitated all over the United States for a shorter working day. By vocation a machinist, like Mitchell unschooled and self-taught, a devoted trades-unionist, Steward found that the one sure justification for short hours and high wages lies in the fact that consumption and not production comes first. When men worked with their hands only they often could not produce enough to consume. But now that they use machinery, the case is altered. Machinery enables mass production and mass production is a blessing "provided the wealth more rapidly produced is *consumed* as fast as days' work is destroyed. But if this blessing is to continue to bless, wages must continue to rise. If wage stops rising, machinery stops blessing." The wages must rise to absorb the abundance of goods and services whose production they pay for. We produce, Steward urged, in order to consume. First come our habits and wants that make up our standards of living, then our labors to satisfy and sustain them. The money-wages we receive must be realized in the real wages of goods and services which our habits and wants require and which our money-wages should pay for.

First and last, then, man is a consumer. Upon this only can a free people build itself a strong and healthy economy. This is the lesson John Mitchell learned as he defended the the organized consumers of England. This is the conclusion Ira Steward's reasoning led to as he championed the unorganized producers of the United States.

II.

Then what does it mean, in a world such as ours - where a minority are privileged to live without working while the great multitudes seem destined to work without living - to regard each and every human being as first and last a consumer?

Essentially it means the universal freedom of man. It means that the laboring man is equal in dignity and worth with the man of leisure. It means such an organization of a nation's economy that every one of the people will in some sort be enabled to work for himself and not for another, and will know that he is his own employee and not another's. Thus he will have power over his own support. A man whose power over his own support is in his own will is a free man. A man whose support is in the power of another's will is not a free man. As *The Federalist* pointed out long ago, "power over a man's support is power over his will." Experience has shown that an economy based on the primacy of the consumer, in the form of consumer cooperation, brings power over a man's support to the man's own will.

In the long history of the human struggle for freedom, the plain people rarely had this power. They were not free men. In the classical civilization from which both the literary and the theological "humanists" of our own time draw their tradition, labor was not held to be worthy of free men. "The dignity of labor" would have been a contradictory phrase to Plato and Aristotle, the thinkers who are taken as the spokesmen for what is best and noblest in that tradition, and whose views and judgments are so powerfully a part of our own living past. In the society for which they spoke, as in every society until our own, the entirely free men were the gentlemen, the men of birth and station, and they were free because they could live their lives without earning their livings. They were free because they were at leisure, and were very busy in their leisure. But their business was not the business of the farmer, the artisan, and the mechanic, earning his living. It was the business of the man who does not need to earn his living—and who is therefore free to perform all functions public and private whereby he could diversify and ennoble his life; free to live more abundantly. Their business was the business of the soldier and the ruler, of the sportsman, the connoiseur, the athlete, the orator and the philosopher. It consisted —Aristotle said it—in the enjoyment of leisure which is better than occupation and is the end, being the practice of the "liberal arts," the achievement of "pleasure, happiness and the delight of living." By contrast, labor, useful or not, is painful, ignoble, inimical to the virtue proper to free men. By contrast, labor is the activity appropriate to slaves; it is a means only, never an end, and its nature is, ever to serve leisure. The laborer is a slave by nature, by nature incapable of freedom. The laborer is a tool with life in it, even as a tool is a lifeless slave. The laborer is to be trained in his useful function as an animal is trained or a tool is modelled, and no more. Contrariwise, the education of the free man should not equip him with the servile skills of the artisan, the farmer or the mechanic; it should equip him with the liberal and noble arts. These are arts of consumption, not of production, and the free man is consumer, not producer.

Religion confirmed philosophy in this judgment of the relative values of labor and leisure, of production and consumption. The pagan gods, being free, were at leisure, and their existence was an immortality of free activity with its "pleasure, happiness, and delight in living." Aristotle gave this general appreciation of divine existence as consumer existence, a philosophical formulation. "God's life in eternity," he wrote, "is that which we enjoy in our best moments, but are unable to possess permanently: its very being is delight." The men who imparted its characteristic shape to the Christian view of human nature and human destiny combined the judgments of classical thought with the implications of certain narratives of the Hebrew Scriptures regarding labor and leisure, consumption and production. It was not, they noted, the six work-days of the creation that the Creator blessed; it was the seventh, the Sabbath, that God blessed and sanctified, "because in it he rested from all his work which God created and made." And Heaven, consequently, is one eternal Sabbath. In the life of man, again, it was not in the Garden of Eden that Adam ate his bread in sorrow and earned it in the sweat of his face. God had created Eden to be the happy habitation of the first man and the first woman. The economy of Eden was an economy of abundance, and life in Eden was life without labor, a consumer life, all free activity bringing pleasure, happiness and delight in living. But God had forbidden Adam and Eve to eat of the fruit of the tree of knowledge. Eve, persuaded by the serpent, had eaten, and Adam had followed suit. This disobedience was the original sin. It altered the inward nature of Adam and Eve. And this corrupted nature of theirs is transmitted to their descendants. And all the generations of man are tainted with it. Because of it, God expelled Adam from the abundance and leisure of Eden "to till the ground whence he was taken." Because of it, God laid a curse upon Eve to bring forth her children in sorrow. Because of it, God laid a curse upon Adam, to eat his bread in the sweat of his face, to win his bread from a now condemned earth that would bring forth for him "thorns also and thistles." In sum, labor is a curse, leisure is a blessing. Labor is a sentence for sin which we work out on an earth whose abundance has by that sin been corrupted to scarcity. Labor is a consequence of evil, itself an evil, made necessary by sin; labor is the price which most of us pay for survival in a world where we must work or perish. By contrast, leisure is a state of innocence, of the free and joyous functions of all our powers whereof consists the life more abundant. The good life is not the laborious life, but the contemplative life, wherein we may see God and enjoy him forever. The state of labor, thus again, is a state of bondage; the state of leisure is a state of freedom. Production is servility, consumption liberty. Society condemns its criminals to hard labor.

The modern mind tries hard not to think of labor and leisure in this way. When we moralize, we are disposed to deprecate, even to condemn, leisure, and to commend, even to exalt, labor. We speak boldly and often about "the dignity of labor;" we have even invented a "right to work." We have come to use the word "worker" with much the same feeling of appreciation and approval that still attaches to the word "gentleman." This change has grown out of the democratic revolution, whose fighting faith is contained in the seven propositions of the Declaration of Independence, which proclaim that individual human beings, each different from the others, are by nature equal in their inalienable right to life, liberty and the pursuit of happiness, and that governments are merely changeable means devised to secure these rights. The principles that the workingman must be a free man, that labor has dignity—even a nobler dignity than leisure—follow from the articles of faith in this American-born charter of equal liberty for all the billions of different men and women who people the earth.

These principles, however, do not contradict the traditional religious and humanist conception of the relation of leisure to labor, of consumer to producer. They confirm the conception, but they reject its traditional application. They refuse to confine it to the small numbers of men and women who from the beginning of civilization were, because of birth or station or other forms of privilege, free to live their lives without needing to earn their livings. They purposefully extend it to the great multitudes of human beings who are cut off from living any life because nothing of their lifetime is spared from earning a living. They affirm that the workingman, no less than the gentleman, is a consumer by nature; that his natural goal is leisure, not labor, freedom, not bondage; that he becomes a producer by necessity and that he strives all his life to unshackle himself from this necessity. Else, why the struggle to devise "labor-saving" devices? Why the honor and gratitude to inventors of such devices? Why the efforts of labor-unions ever to raise wages and reduce hours, that is, to increase leisure and the possibility of consumption? Indeed, whatever may be a modern man's professions regarding "the dignity of labor," his practices confirm the judgment passed upon it by both the humanities and the religion of our civilization. John Mitchell and Ira Steward, speaking for the liberation of the unfree multitudes from want and from fear regarding things and thoughts, simply harmonized, each in his own way, profession with practice. They reaffirmed the primacy of the consumer.

The principle of the primacy of the consumer expresses the innermost nature of the human creature. It embodies the truth about all the freedoms he gropes after and labors for to the end of his days. We are born consumers and consumers we remain all our lives. But in most of us, the society we live in overlays the consumer we are born as by the producer it compels us to become. By original nature consumers, and producers only by nurture, nevertheless we must, most of us, produce or perish. Not many may all their lives consume without producing, while too many must all their lives produce without consuming, produce consuming only enough to keep them producing. And every soul of those unfree multitudes dreams of the day when he may be purely a consumer again; every soul struggles to be freed of the chain gang of production in which survival shackles him.

Imagine the years of any such man who must earn his living, as he spends it from the cradle to the grave. As a babe in arms he produces nothing. He is absolutely a consumer. He is fed, clothed, sheltered, amused and defended. His needs are served, his wishes gratified, his activities encouraged and praised. He is protected from the consequences of his mistakes. His life is the life of Riley. He grows into childhood living his life without needing to earn his living. As his powers develop, his environment is enlarged, his opportunities are multiplied. He goes to school, to the ball game, the church, the dance, and so on. Then, perhaps at the age of fourteen or fifteen this carefree consummatory daily life of his stops. The fourteen year old must now earn his living. He gets a job on a farm, in a factory, in a shop. He spends his day repeating a few single, simple actions in which his work consists. If he wishes to continue doing the things he had been doing before he was required to earn his living, he must do them at night. His existence, which had been one and whole is now split in two. He has a daylife in which he earns his living; he has a nightlife in which he lives his life.

This boy is, almost, Everybody. There are a more fortunately placed few who do not need to become workingmen at fourteen. They are not called upon to earn their livings. In high school, in college, they continue to live their lives. Tradition allows them certain privileges, certain liberties, which constitute "college life." They are liberties and privileges analogous to those enjoyed by gentlemen of leisure everywhere in the world. They are the liberties and privileges of infancy, not to be held accountable for violations of the adult social code; to consume without producing, food, clothing, shelter, to engage in sports and play and every sort of free activity, without any splitting into daylife and nightlife. But if, when they are graduated, they also must devote their days to earning a living, then they, too, can have only a few hours of night for the free activities to which, in school and college, they give their days. For them, too, night becomes the time for living, day for only earning a living. During the day they are but producers, working for money. At night they are consumers, converting the price of their labor into goods and services which nourish and please the body, which exercise and delight the mind.

Daylife is the means, nightlife is the end.

The farmer, for example, is often envied on the ground that he lives a more natural life than the factory hand. A man's life is natural when what he does to earn his living and what he does to live his life are not separate, but flow together in such a way that the freedom and the pleasure of nightlife are felt in the labors of daylife, and the satisfactions of consumption are enjoyed in the activities of production. A life is natural when its means and its ends flow together in such a way that even though they are distinct, they are not different. A life is natural when work yields the same feeling as play, and play is as productive as work. A life is natural when production and consumption flow together and are not to be separated.

Thus, it is not natural, for example, either to eat to live or to live to eat. It is natural to enjoy living as eating, and to take delight in eating as living. Rightly or wrongly, the farmer's existence is supposed to possess this naturalness. Yet his life, too, divides into daylife and nightlife. By his work on the farm he is engaged in earning his living. Most of what he produces—let it be grain, or cotton, or milk, or fruit, or vegetables—he produces, not to consume for himself, but to sell to others for money. With this money he buys, of course, the tools and materials which he has used up as producer and which he must replace if he is to continue producing. But if those were all his money could buy, he would indeed be no more than a tool with life in it. To be a free man, he must be able to exchange his money, not for producer goods only, but for consumer goods, material and spiritual: not only for work-clothes, but leisure clothes—clothes for church, for parties, for political meetings; not only for a farm truck but a passenger car; not only for manuals on farming, but for newspapers, magazines, books, radio, an occasional motion picture, a play or concert; for something to risk on the races, at checkers or at bridge; or a baseball game; for hunting and fishing in the season; not only for good barns, but for a good school and good teachers for his children; for a well-built, well-appointed house with adequate plumbing and heating and good furniture to be his home. Obviously, his interests as a consumer are many and varied in kind and quality, his interests as a producer are of one kind and few. Yet, as a rule, his mind and heart are concentrated on the narrow arts of production. From sunrise to sunset, and beyond, he performs his back-breaking labors for money to spend; and he joins with other farmers in order to buy his producers' goods as cheaply and to sell his product as dearly as possible. Then, when he has his money, he, for the most part, continues to leave the art of spending and using, which is the art of consumption, to shift for itself. Through his working day, from morning till noon, from noon to night, our farmer burns his energies in his hard labor. When he stops for lunch, the food he eats is merely so many calories of fuel which his working oxidized into fatigue products and which his meal replaces. He bolts his bread and meat and pie; he gulps his coffee; he snatches his smoke. He is scarcely aware how his food has tasted. He has no effective interest in how it was served. The food only stokes the labor-expending animal engine, restoring its "horsepower." It does not feed the human being.

For the human being cares about exactly those qualities which the animal engine, the labor-expending organism, the wage-earning or profit-seeking producer must needs disregard. But the laborer, the producer, is not freed to be a man again until the day is done and the day's work is over. In this respect, the factory worker is far worse off than the farmer. His life is far more unnatural. On the job he is not a man with a proper name, but a "hand" with a number. His work is not varied like the farmer's, nor does he have the mobility of the farmer. His tools are not moveable like the awl of the shoemaker or the needle of the tailor, which those craftsmen take up or put down at will. It is the "hand" which is moveable, and attached to a stationary machine like any other attachable and detachable gadget. If that man is a tailor who makes a whole suit of clothes, and that man is a shoemaker who makes a whole pair of shoes, the factory worker is neither a tailor nor a shoemaker. The act of making suits or shoes is divided into twenty or thirty separate operations, with one worker to repeat each operation endlessly throughout the working day. In terms of a whole suit or a whole pair of shoes, it is the factory that is the tailor, the shop that is the shoemaker.

In terms of the whole product, the operative is only 1/20 or 1/30 of a shoemaker or tailor. The operative's lunch, even more than the farmer's, is a replacemnt of burnt up calories, not the gratification of a human being's hunger. It stokes the animal engine, it does not feed a man with a heart and a mind.

But finally, like the farmer's, the factory hand's workday ends. Here they are now, farmer and factory worker, released from being producers earning their livings, free to be the consumers they were born as, living their lives. They clean up. They wash away, so far as they can, the marks of their producer day. They put off their labor clothes and put on their leisure clothes. By contrast, they now move without haste and speak without strain. The supper they sit down to may consist of exactly the same dishes they ate at noon. But their food is not just so many hundreds of calories to be swallowed but not savored. It is now an exciting and delightful combination of sights and flavors and scents and textures. The cloth it is laid on, garnished perhaps, with flowers, the dishes it is served on, the knives and forks and spoons it is taken with, feed the eye and the hand with sight and touch as much as the fragrance, the taste, the chewing and digesting please the palate and comfort the body. Communion with others, table talk, music or news on the radio, may accompany the meal. Compared with the noonday event, this meal is eaten without haste, lingeringly, and the qualities of each dish may be discussed like the contents of a good book, or the events of an exciting game or movie or play.

This is how we take our meals as human beings, that is, as consumers. And significantly, both the physiologist and the psychologist advise us that in taking our meals thus, we not only do not diminish, we heighten the caloric or producer value of our nourishment. But we are free to eat thus only at night and perhaps on Sundays, when we are at leisure. The waking hours that remain are taken up similarly by actions which farmer and worker perform for the fun of it, freely because they want to, not necessarily because they have to. They may read, or sing or play cards or play billiards, or go bowling or attend a movie or a concert or a lodge meeting or a church social or a political rally, or they may go shopping for clothes or baseballs or shotguns or boxing gloves. Whatever they do, they will be spending the money they earned as producers, and in spending they will be doing those many different things for the sake of which they labor monotonously to produce one thing; they will be living their lives.

IV.

Obviously, if it is good for people to come together in joint stock companies, in trades-unions, in buying and sales cooperatives, it is a far, far better thing for them to come together in consumer cooperatives. It is as much better, as the multiplicity, the variety, the range and the meaning of each man's interests as consumer inevitably outnumber and outweigh his interests as a producer. That which human beings can offer to exchange for money, in order to earn their livings, is valuable to them only in terms of things that they can exchange their money for in order to live their lives. All that the farmer wins through his cooperative, in reducing the costs and increasing the profits of the products he sells, is often entirely lost in the prices he pays for the things he buys with those profits. It is not earning that measures income, it is spending. It is not production that governs the standard of a standard of living—President Roosevelt called the standard of living "that primary weapon of our defense"—it is consumption. It is not power over production that gives a man the power over his own support, it is power over consumption, and power over production through power over consumption. It is not by producer-organization that a man achieves his freedom, it is by consumer-organization.

This is the truth that wise men of Greece and Rome saw and taught, that the Christian Church transmitted and interpreted, that John Mitchell and Ira Steward rediscovered and restated with fresh meanings. This is the principle that the consumer cooperatives of the world have tested and verified. Their rules of association, which the twenty-eight weavers of Rochdale put together and first applied, define the economic organization of liberty. Addressing themselves to freedom from want, the rules cannot, however, work effectively unless the other three freedoms of Mr. Roosevelt's four freedoms are also in force—especially freedom of thought and freedom of conscience. On the record, it is where these have been in force, alike in England, on the continent, and elsewhere in the world, that Rochdale cooperatives worked their way through the business cycles of peace-time, the distortions and scarcities of wartimes, more stably, more evenly, than any other form of economic organization. During the First World War they served as a check on inflation and at some points as a preventive. Governments, parties, churches everywhere are aware of the cooperatives' potential. In some instances they solicit their voluntary collaboration, in others they divert the cooperatives from their true functions and degrade them into tools of policy. When this happened—it did happen in Austria, in Poland, and other Slavic countries, in Italy and in Germany — the faith in the primacy of the consumer, which is the soul of cooperation, is dissipated, its morale destroyed. With its organization based on open membership, democratic government, limited interest on capital, and a return to the purchaser of the difference between cost and price, the cooperative is allergic to alien uses. It cannot be harmonized with authoritarian government of any sort. It is irreconcilable with totalitarianism.

When allowed to survive or perish on its merits, consumer cooperation is the one form of collective liberty which can serve as the "grass-roots" implementation of the free man's peace. It is alone capable of turning a "good neighbor policy" from a policy into a way of life. When the United Nations have won the victory there will be millions of uprooted, homeless human beings to care for, to settle, to rehabilitate in health, in hope, in self-dependence, and self-respect. On its record, the consumer cooperative technique is the simplest, the surest way to attempt this. Whatever survives of cooperative skill and cooperative power can be mobilized and set to work; where none survives, men and women trained elsewhere can be sent in. Rehabilitation can be thus initiated and carried through at a minimum of economic cost and a maximum of profit in terms of human life and liberty. The same would hold for demobilized soldiers, for farmers, for craftsmen, for wage-earners employed on the inevitable public works of restoration. For all of them, the conversion of money-wages into real wages in terms of food, clothing, shelter, education, protection against disease and crime, and all the other goods of life, by means of the credit union, of the cooperative store, of the cooperative wholesale and marketing-society would serve as a counter alike to the profiteering monopolistic private trader and to debilitating government management.

But far more important is the fact that consumer cooperation alone can provide a discipline in the democratic way of life, labor, and thought for both war and peace. The neighborhood units could be confederated into regional wholesales and unions, the regional into national, and the national into world-wide alliances, through which they could pool their financial resources and keep up a continuous free trade of skills, knowledges, goods, and services.

The cadres of such a world-wide economic collaboration of free men existed and were growing in the free countries before the war. One of the tasks of the cooperative movement entering upon its second hundred years is to think out in detail how they may be filled and employed to win the war, and adapted to assure the peace. Its other task is to communicate this knowledge as a fighting faith to the peoples and the governments of the United Nations—the faith that the economy of consumer cooperation, based upon management by, of, and for the forgotten men of the world, can channel all the liberties of man into the structure of lasting peace.

Should this be fulfilled, even in part, future historians might well regard the rules of Rochdale a more momentous forwarding of freedom than Magna Charta.

VI.

Liberalism in Crisis

VI.

LIBERALISM IN CRISIS

by

RUBIN GOTESKY

WHEN THE TWENTIETH century arrived, the material and ideological conditions already existed for making the inevitable diagnosis that classical liberalism is dead and liberalism, in general, dying. Yet the vast majority of intelligent, cultured adults nurtured on these principles, did not believe this. To them until the first world war, liberalism seemed only to have begun its triumphant conquest of the world. Capitalism, free enterprise, was only beginning to dominate the globe and to bring the glories of machine civilization to the barbarians outside of western Europe and America. Kings were being overthrown or abdicating with great dignity. Republics were springing up everywhere. Churches were apparently beginning to accept their separation from the state and interesting themselves more and more with the spiritual life of the people. Reason and science, properly seasoned with Christian morality, were everywhere becoming more and more influential in school, in politics and diplomacy. Even the most primitive people of Africa and the Pacific were sending their noble sons to western schools and colleges. Everyone, except a small minority of socialists and radicals, believed that the millenium was at hand. Nearly everyone and particularly the poor believed he was ultimately to become rich. Nearly everyone believed he would receive his just due and reward, given time. Special privilege was coming to an end. No one was to be denied the opportunity of reaching for the highest honors possible. Terror, brutality, exploitation, cruelty, unreason and war were no longer to be the prime instruments of government. Morley, at the pinnacle of this optimism, wrote eloquently of compromise as the golden rule of liberalism and reason. Others wrote of the new golden age and the final reign of peace, international justice and democracy. The Christian ideal of the brotherhood of man, after 1900 years of struggle, had been achieved not by the Man on the Cross but by John Locke, Adam Smith, Newton and Darwin.

However firmly convinced the generations at the turn of the 19th century may have been of the final triumph of liberalism or of liberal capitalism, it is now as evident as such matters can ever be that classical liberalism is dead and its liberal inheritors are falling before the onslaught of totalitarian communism. More than one-fifth of the world is already in the hands of Stalin. Europe seems to be next; then the world. The trend toward some form of totalitarian statism, even among the most anti-statist capitalist countries is obvious to all who want to see. For example, the number of democracies which increased considerably after the Versailles Treaty of 1919, has drastically fallen since the end of World War II. Important democracies like France teeter at the edge of Totalitarianism. Western Germany and Italy are being artificially preserved as Democracies by the Western Allies. This trend is not offset by the fact that there is evidence occasionally of a movement in the opposite direction. These offset changes are mere oscillations in the general graph of movement towards totalitarianism.

The hope that certain fundamental liberal rights—political freedom; freedom of press, of thought, of speech and of writing; freedom of organization—will be preserved in the new social orders appearing in the world is evaporating in the face of what is actually taking place. The inability of the vast majority — partly due to social conditions, partly to lag in education and partly through natural incapacity—to understand the complexities of modern life is a decisive fact in the trend towards establishing totalitarian social orders.

Nothing in history is inexorable; and conditions may exist or arise, unknown to an objective observer, which can upset the most perfect of calculations. Thus, it is not excluded that man may acquire sufficient sagacity to exercise proper control over his social life before a long, black period of totalitarianism sets in. But it is important to remember that "not excluded," does not mean the same thing as "probable."

Even if it seems improbable that totalitarianism will suffer any serious setbacks in the foreseeable future, it is intellectually cathartic to understand how liberalism, which once upon a time seemed the white hope of mankind, should have fallen into so desperate a decline. Even though it seems as if it may vanish, for an indefinite period, from the face of the earth, it will be good to realize that it is still, after analysis, the most hopeful and the most rational interpretation of the life of man which was ever developed by man. And even if its demise is certain, it may give hope to those who think not in terms of the narrow limits of a single lifetime, but from the broader horizons of social epochs, that it may yet arise again in a form suitable to new conditions a few centuries from now.

I

THE ORIGINS OF LIBERALISM

The ideas which together go by the name of Liberalism, classical and modern, were not produced in a day. Unlike Anarchism or Marxism, they are not largely the work of single individuals, nor do they possess the same systematic logic or ambiguity. It is easier and perhaps more accurate to talk of *Liberalisms,* each kind of liberalism being associated with the life and theories of a particular man, than to talk of the liberal movement. As a result, the theory of liberalism is often in violent contradiction with the practice of those who profess it; and what is liberalism to one man is anathema to another.

These ideas, in their earlier forms, are not always like their latest. It is difficult to determine exactly how the idea of a Marsilio or an Ockham who said, "the voice of the people is the voice of God" — meaning by "people" only the well-born, the well-placed — should finally have evolved into the modern idea of the people as all the members of a society or state. By what manner of means did the doctrine of natural rights on which feudal society so solidly rested become the foundation-stone on which was built the superiority of capitalism over feudalism?

Most writers usually go back to the seventeenth century for the origins of liberalism, but they are found in primitive flower-form in the ancient maritime commercial cities of Greece and its colonies. As Gilbert Murray points out, the Greeks were the first to establish the first two great principles of classical liberalism:—freedom of thought and political freedom. Admittedly these great liberal principles were available in practice only to Greek citizens and the leisure classes; and they were never extended even in principle—there is no question of social practice—vertically to include all men or horizontally to include all nations and states. Yet the establishment of these principles as recognized rights of the ruling classes produced during a period of six centuries a radical transformation in the understanding of the world and of man whose effects continue to be felt even to the present day.

Judo-Christianity, even though it began as an otherworldly, anti-rationalistic, anti-naturalistic movement of the oppressed classes, contributed its share directly and indirectly to the tenets of liberalism. Indirectly as a lower class movement antagonistic to pagan civilization, it helped to undermine slavery. Directly, through the dogmas of the spiritual brotherhood and equality of man before God and of the Universal Church, it provided the ideological seeds for the extension of political and religious freedoms horizontally and vertically. Yet the universalization of political and religious liberty were not so much the product of the feudal Church as of the struggle against it.

The geniuses of many countries contributed to the clarification and final statements of these liberal ideas. It was Spinoza who most thoroughly expounded the idea of the complete separation of Church and State in a form so extreme that his books have remained, ever since their publication, on the Catholic Index. It was he, too, who defended in its most extreme form freedom of thought and expression. The struggle of the Protestants in France, Germany, and particularly in England against Romanism and a state-dominated religion led to the formulation of a concrete doctrine of religious freedom classically expressed in the Tracts of John Lilburne, Leibniz, Locke, Spinoza, Hobbes, Newton,. Harvey, Gassendi, Gallileo—to name a few—influenced by and influencing the new mathematics and science—developed a new rationalism and empiricism which ultimately undermined the long-established doctrines of feudal economics, politics, science, philosophy and religion. Another line of thinkers from Legnano to Grotius prepared the way for liberal conceptions of war, economic and diplomatic relations between states and, in particular, for the modern notion of the equal sovereignty of states. Recognition of the terrible consequences of the religious wars of the 16th and 17th centuries led many like Henri II to work actively, if fruitlessly, for a world federation of states to guarantee universal peace.

Liberal ideas however, did not germinate merely from ideas. They were equally as often the products of social experience and class conflict. Beginning with the ninth century, cities began to dot in ever increasing numbers the continent and coasts of Europe. These cities were commercial, industrial and maritime; and their existence involved the existence, growth and increasing importance of social classes which previously had played only a minor role in feudal society. These new classes were not static. Some became prominent for a short time, only to disappear forever. Others like the commercial, financial and artisan classes rose and fell in importance, as the economic and technological typography of the cities altered. New kinds of problems arose for which

Greek and Roman culture had already found some sort of solution as, for example, in disease, sanitation, economic exchange, military protection, etc. Newly awakened acquisitive drives led men to seek to understand the nature of metals, to invent new instruments of production and new kinds of commodities, and to investigate the heavens, the earth and the sea.

But besides these problems for which some sort of answer was discoverable among the ancient writers, all sorts of new problems arose which were unknown to the ancients. Thus, in the course of ten centuries, beginning from the ninth, a bewildering variety of political institutions from military autocracies through ecclesiastical oligarchies to direct democracies made their appearance, each contributing in one way or another to a clearer understanding of the nature of political institutions, their origin and development. Between cities, too, an equally astonishing number and variety of leagues, alliances, federations were created in order to solve problems of monetary standards, commercial exchange, credit, inter-city disputes, piracy, war, pillage and robbery.

Ultimately as capitalist, economic relations dominated and came more and more in conflict with feudal or transitional economic forms, as the transitional classes vanished or were reduced to impotence by the capitalist third estate, more and more clearly visible became the first primitive set of ideas which compose classical liberalism and furnished the ideological fuel for reducing feudalism to ashes.

II

THE BASIC TENETS OF LIBERALISM

Perhaps nowhere have the essential ideas of classical liberalism been better stated than in Hobhouse's little book on "Liberalism." Hobhouse is profoundly aware that these ideas were born of the struggle of the middle classes against feudalism. Thus he feels they are not so much a positive contribution towards a social philosophy appropriate to our times (we must remember he published his little book in 1911), as a negation of the evils of feudal and proto-capitalist society. These principles, in other words, are statements of what *ought not to be* rather than principles of a constructive social philosophy. Yet he thinks that adequate criticism, in the perspective of contemporary experience, can show them to be the basis of sure progress in resolving the total evils of a world consisting of huge urban populations, national states and mass-machine production. But Hobhouse wrote before two world wars and totalitarianism made clear the kind of social order such a world portended.

Hobhouse orders liberal principles under nine headings, each of which represents to his mind, the quintessential fruit of the experience of the middle classes in their effort to free themselves from feudal rule. The first he calls "civil liberty." This is the principle that people should not be governed by men, but by laws. Feudal and proto-capitalist societies had operated under another principle: that laws were made by kings, princes, feudal lords and churchmen who did not need to apply them equally and impartially to all. It was admitted in principle that those who made the laws had the right to use, abuse, change or administer them as they pleased. Thus no one ever knew exactly how they would be administered in any given instance, since the application depended upon the caprice or whim of the law-maker or his executor. Property and profits, therefore, could be taken away without justification; people could be imprisoned or sentenced to death without charge; houses searched and belongings seized without warrant or warning; for the king, the church and their henchmen could do no wrong.

Closely allied with this principle is the one Hobhouse calls "fiscal liberty." In rebellious colonial America as in England, "fiscal liberty" meant "no taxation without representation." Hobhouse does not indicate that fiscal liberty, as a tenet of early liberalism, did not apply to all, but only to the propertied, middle classes who felt themselves the producers of all wealth. Those who had no property, even though they paid direct and indirect taxes, were considered not to need representation or legislative protection.

Since the middle classes considered themselves the producers of all the new, enormous wealth of the community, they felt it was only reasonable that they decide on what and on whom their wealth was to be spent. And certainly they could find little reason for supporting the king, his army and clergy who were so often used against them.

Hobhouse remarks that fiscal liberty is obviously inseparable from political liberty and its corollary, the sovereignty of the people. But we shall find that all the liberties which become the substance of liberalism are indissolubly related to political liberty and popular sovereignty.

Both fiscal and civil liberty, as first developed in the anti-feudal struggle, were specifically related to property and the rights of their owners. The middle classes wanted no discrimination against their property and persons; they wanted laws concerning property and persons of property which would apply equally and impartially to all; and they wanted above all to determine how much, how, where and on whom their money were to be spent. In essence, the struggle for these rights was the struggle for their actual existence. They realized that without them, their years and days were numbered and at the disposal of those who wanted to exploit and despoil them. It was inevitable, therefore, that the rights of property should be exalted above all other rights and that their legal establishment as inalienable should be the hub around which all society had to revolve.

The third principle, Hobhouse calls "personal liberty." Under this heading, he includes a number of rights or liberties which are nowadays distinguished from others and considered for themselves. One is liberty of thought *without* governmental or ecclesiastical inquisition. No government or church has a right to invade the privacy of a man's thought as of his home and demand that he make his thoughts known. Concretely, this principle meant opposition to such procedures and institutions as third degree, torture, spying, star chamber proceedings, inquisitions and public retractions of ideas considered inacceptable by the authorities. Another is liberty to exchange thoughts—the well-known liberties of speech, writing, printing and discussion. It avails a man and society nothing, if he is not permitted, except at personal peril and risk, to make his thoughts public to those who want or may want to know them. Lastly, there is liberty of religious belief and worship. Hobhouse does not state that this tenet meant and still means to many, not the right to believe in any religion or to worship in any way, but the right to believe in only those religions which are approved by the majority of the populace.

The fourth he calls social liberty. This means that hereditary advantages or disadvantages like birth, wealth, color, race or sex, should not bar men or women from the enjoyment of social rights, privileges and opportunities. In principle, this is not social liberty but rather *social equality*. Hobhouse is concerned with saying that liberty for some is impossible without equality; that the right to an education, for example is without meaning if one is debarred from enjoying that right only because one is a Negro, a woman or a Jew.

It is unfortunate that Hobhouse seems to confuse so unequivocally the concept of liberty with one of the *possible conditions* of liberty—equality. Not all liberty means equality nor all equality liberty. All men may be equal in that they all have the right to vote; but none of them may be free in that they have the right to vote for whom they please. All men may be equal in that they all must work eight hours a day, but no man may be free in the sense that he has the right *not* to work or to choose the kind of work he finds most congenial to him.

When he wrote his book, the difference between freedom and equality was not of moment, for it seemed to most thinking men that the two were indissoluble. Freedom meant equality and equality freedom. The falsity of this identity has been made manifest in the totalitarian countries, yet many who profess liberalism are still under the nineteenth century illusion that the two are identical. The increasing emphasis upon equality today has resulted and is resulting in greater and greater losses of libertarian rights only because so many who seek equality are under the irremovable illusion that equality necessarily involves freedom. These totalitarian liberals do not see that to make all men equal, for example, with respect to work, does not mean to make all men *free* with respect to work; that the one does not necessarily imply the other. These people have been so impressed with the fact that *inequality* with respect to work has prevented men from enjoying or exercising their liberties that they think the *bare removal* of inequality is *sufficient* to guarantee men the enjoyment and exercise of their liberties.

Economic Liberty is the fifth tenet. Hobhouse makes specific reference here to the rights of property as incorporated in the idea of freedom to make contracts and in the doctrine of Laissez-faire (non-interference in the economic process by the state). He includes here, too, the idea of freedom of association which he limits exclusively to the right to form economic associations like corporations or partnerships. He does not seem to have in mind its larger meaning of the right to form associations of any kind: political, religious, cultural, social like social clubs, as well as economic.

As indicated before, the selection of these subordinate principles under the heading of economic liberty is not done in the interests of logic but of history. The middle classes specifically struggled for these principles as part of their struggle against feudalism. It was not a question for them of logical classification, but of existence. The feudal state placed all kinds of restraint upon buying and selling of land, commodities and real property; hiring and firing of labor; money-lending and borrowing. These restraints had to be removed; the state had to be reduced to a minor economic role so that it would interfere as little as possible in the business of capitalist accumulation. Thus for the early bourgeois this kind of liberty had to be distinguished from civil and fiscal liberty, even though these latter were just as intimately related to the economic process as buying and selling or money-lending and borrowing. The right of association, too, was intimately connected with economic liberty in the sense of Laissez-faire. Under feudal and proto-capitalist societies, the kings, princes, or economic guilds and associations controlling cities, would limit the rights of individuals to engage in particular occupations. They would grant monopolies to particular individuals or groups, thus excluding all other individuals and groups from engaging in those fields of commerce, finance and industry. They would limit the number of economic associations possible within a given industry or for all economic enterprises. Such associations would be completely closed, limited in membership and enjoying a monopoly in their particular field. These restraints and monopolies had to be broken and ultimately were. But in the early development of capitalism, the right of free association was strictly limited to capitalist associations. The attempt of labor to associate was at first punishable by death. The capitalists wanted to remain free not only to associate for profit but also to exploit labor without restraint by labor associations.

The doctrine of Laissez-faire which is largely the product of the thinking of Adam Smith, has had like all such similar doctrines a strange history. It is based on the paradoxical moral principle that the ravagings of wolves will produce a variety of good things for the ravaged sheep. Since the wolves were the ones who benefited, they did not mind the cloud of moral benevolence which hid their handiwork from the sheep. Nevertheless, the doctrine was never consistently applied. It depended upon circumstances, the specific economic needs of the middle classes or of some of its more powerful sectors. If an industry felt itself losing out in free competition, it invariably demanded state protection; if an infant industry felt it had not sufficient capital, it would demand state loans or even gifts; but if labor or agriculture demanded the same rights under Laissez-faire, capital would scream for military and legal protection. Laissez-faire was fine as long as it yielded them big profits, but as soon as other classes or groups began encroaching on their territory, the middle classes would begin crying for the most rigid forms of state protectionism or divide among themselves as to what was to be done.

The sixth area of freedom is the domestic. Hobhouse points out that liberalism began early to demand the same rights for women as for men, particularly with reference to property and marriage. Demands began soon to be made that marriage be looked upon as a contractual relation like any business relation between individuals. Logically, of course, this involved that women should have the same rights as men with regard to property. Children, too, were gradually assumed to have rights against their parents rights to be protected against mistreatment, cruelty, exploitation. They were also assumed to have rights for themselves and in the interests of society. Children had a right to an education; to proper care and protection against parental as well as non-parental exploiters.

But the attitude of liberalism to children came in direct conflict with the attitude towards Laissez-faire, for the protection of children against parents and economic exploitation involved a considerable degree of state protectionism, thus a denial of the freedom of parents and adults to do as they pleased with children.

Properly speaking, Hobhouse ought not to speak here of domestic freedom, but of domestic rights, some of which were freedoms and some of which were restraints upon freedom. It is obvious that the insistence on marriage as a contract conferred freedom upon both men and women in a variety of respects. Their consent, without coercion, would now be required; in theory, they could enter a marriage contract upon the basis of consideration or break it on the failure of one or the other to abide by the terms of the agreement. The right of a child to protection against exploitation by the parent is not a freedom; it is a restraint upon the parent. The child does not have a choice nor is it assumed that the child should be put in the position of having to make a choice between being protected and not protected. The right to an education again is not a case of freedom but a coercion upon the child, imposed upon it for its own good, on the assumption that it will ultimately increase its area of total freedom. The fact that children may not want to go to school has as much to do with this right as the fact that they may dislike taking disagreeably tasting medicines when they are sick.

The seventh area of liberty is both administrative, geographical and racial. As the middle classes grew in power, they found themselves in conflict with different social orders in areas where they wanted to establish themselves. Thus they early became one of the most intrepid, if inconsistent defenders of the rights of nations to self-determination, as long as the self-determination was in a direction which they approved. They also became defenders of relative local, administrative autonomy. They used this as a means of combating the tendency of states whose economic and social interests protected other classes than their own, to interfere with the growth and expansion of capitalist economic relations. They also became the defenders of racial equality where the exploitation of an alien race like the Negro involved the destruction of their own economic order. If the middle classes, at times, raised racial equality to a high principle, in practice, they acted according to circumstance and their particular interests, defending an inferior status for the blacks of Africa or the Hindus of India or the blacks and Indians in America, because they were easier to exploit in this way.

But again it must be observed that racial equality is not the same thing as racial freedom, not that the one has not been interfused with the other. Still it ought to be clear that the equality of all races to be slaves is not identical with the freedom of all races. The freedom of races involves such questions as the right to intermarry, to choice careers, to determine their political fate, to develop different cultures, etc.

International liberty is the eighth tenet of liberalism. In essence, Hobhouse insists that liberalism is opposed to the use of force as an instrument of national policy or to militarism (armaments). Undoubtedly, the expansion of capitalism over wider and wider areas of the globe has intensified the medieval realization of the futility and destructiveness of war. In one sense, capitalist expansion—the development of a world market and an international division of labor—has led many leading members of the middle classes to a realization of the need for international organization, a world federation of states. To keep goods flowing uninterruptedly from one part of the world to another; to remove the political and other barriers in the way of an efficient development of world resources, capitalism needs peace and international co-operation. On the other hand, its drive after profits, its indifference to the welfare of the peoples it exploits; the rivalry of capitalists for control of the world; and lastly, its inability to control the productive process nationally and internationally, are conditions which produce war in spite of every effort to prevent it.

Since capitalism itself contains and produces the conditions which make war inevitable, it is compelled, in spite of the cost and its horror of the military, to support militarism on a larger and larger scale. Thus the movement for international peace and federation, which developed early among the middle classes, has continually been wrecked upon the economic rocks of world economic rivalries and the non-rational organization of production.

The last group of tenets, political liberty and popular sovereignty, are to Hobhouse as well as to others, the crown and glory of liberalism. These two, according to Hobhouse, involve and support each other. The first involves a wide system of subordinate liberties which we have already discussed. Only in terms of it can this system of liberties be maintained, enforced and controlled. But it would be meaningless or rather it would be necessarily limited in its range to a small section of the total human population, if it did not rest on the notion of popular sovereignty—the theory that the people are the end and be—all of government; that government and society exist solely for their benefit. The theory of popular sovereignty rests on the assumption of the essential equality of all men, socially speaking; that the rights of one man can not be different from that of another, in so far as they are considered human units of the community.

The middle classes, in supporting both notions, did not do so consistently, but with an eye primarily on their own interests. At the time Hobhouse wrote, both tenets were far from realization among the most advanced capitalist countries—the United States, France and Great Britain. As for Asia, Africa, Latin and South America, and the greater part of Europe, they did not exist at all, except as ideals among a tiny minority. In England, France and the United States, women did not vote; many races were denied the right to exercise political freedom. Many colonies were held in complete tyrannical subjection and the attempt of colonies to demand such rights was met with imprisonment for long terms and sometimes even with death. In some states of the United States, direct and indirect property qualifications were required in order to exercise the franchise. In certain sections of the populations of all these countries, there even existed a movement, both theoretical and practical, against what was considered the farce of Democracy. Extreme conservatives, like Mallock, with considerable insight into the follies of Democracy, wrote devastating criticisms of the manner in which Democracy worked.

Moreover the pressure for the realization of these two tenets did not come from the middle classes among whom they originated. It came from the lower classes, in particular, the proletariat, who had begun to be active and independent social forces after 1830.

III

THE LIBERALISM OF MILL

Even the above cursory statement of basic liberal ideas shows clearly certain facts. First, these ideas are not systematic or consistent. They are loosely conjoined, being rather the effect of social pressures and social changes upon the middle classes. Secondly, for the majority of the middle classes, economic interests soon stopped their struggle to realize many of these ideas; and by 1860 or thereabouts, most were satisfied with only two; (a) non-interference by the state with the economic process, except when such interference was in their interest and (b) political liberty limited to and controlled by themselves.

There were, of course, exceptions. Andrew Carnegie and Ivan Bliokh, for example, continued each in their own way to develop particular strands of liberal thought. Andrew Carnegie, for example, emphasized the role of the capitalist as a trustee of the wealth of society and attacked the principle of the inheritance of wealth. Wealth, he maintained, should be entrusted only to those who are capable of using it in the interests of society. Scions and heirs have no legitimate rights to the fruits of their parents' labor. He believed in universal education and dedicated a vast part of his huge fortune to building libraries for the education of the poor. He also became tremendously interested in the problem of universal peace; and again he used a large part of his huge fortune to aiding and abetting the struggle against war.

Ivan Bliokh, a poor boy like Carnegie, who ultimately became one of the most powerful bankers and railroaders in the Russian Empire, devoted a large part of his life, intellect and fortune to the establishment of a federation of nations for peace. In the interests of peace, he devoted a large part of his time to the study of war. As the final fruit of this labor, he wrote a six-volume work on ancient and modern warfare in which he showed the social cost of war for all concerned. He anticipated in essential outlines the character of the first world war. He was far in advance of the military experts of his time. Long before the bitter experience of the first world war taught them, he outlined the military strategy and tactics involved. He also proved that the war would necessarily be world-wide in the number of its participants and in its effects and that the total cost in property and lives would be prohibitive. His fear of its effects upon the middle classes was so great that he used all his power and wide influence among the governments of the world to build an international movement for peace. He failed, but it was not for lack of effort.

If after the 1860's, the middle classes as a whole lost interest in the realization of ideals developed during the period of their struggle for power, they were certainly even less interested in the further clarification and systematization of their original ideas. The further development of these ideas,—ridding them of inconsistencies, organizing them into systematic form, revising them so that they would be better applicable to existing conditions and evils in society—became the task of isolated thinkers without a mass following and of thinkers who had lost all faith in capitalism and wanted, by one means or another, a radical transformation of society as a whole.

The latter thinkers thought in organizational terms, in terms of building international movements for the destruction and overthrow of capitalism. They did not think like many liberal thinkers merely in terms of general principles. Among the former were men like Bentham, James Mill, John Stuart Mill, T. H. Green, L. T. Hobhouse, and John Dewey; among the latter, men like Fourier, Proudhon, Bakunin, Lassalle, Marx, Engels, Kautsky, Lenin and Trotsky. But whether they felt themselves continuators and inheritors of the liberal tradition or repudiated it, they each, in their own way, helped to clarify, systematize or modify some facet of that tradition. Out of the emphases—over and under—, the errors and blunders they all made, has been born a doctrine which today composes a liberal social philosophy as adequate as can be formulated, yet paradoxically enough the masses and their dominant leaders the world over are more indifferent and hostile to it than ever.

Before capitalism in the 19th century came to dominate Europe and the world, it had seemed to many the answer to all men's dreams. They thought it would bring a world into existence in which men would be free to think their own thoughts and live their own lives. Poverty would disappear along with tyrants. Men would learn how to control nature and their own evil dispositions in accordance with God's original intention. These dreams were dreamed by men who knew the worst of the feudal system; who had suffered from its disease, ignorance, brutality, lechery and exploitation; who, impressed with the enlightenment of the Greeks and the progress of the new natural sciences, thought that this new knowledge could be used to destroy these institutionalized, tradition-sanctified evils.

The long struggle for victory from the 15th to the 18th century brought new evils into existence—almost continual warfare; universal impoverishment; epidemic starvation; social chaos. For some like Hobbes, these new evils brought disillusionment with the new world and so they sought to find some satisfactory compromise between the old and the new, although unknowingly, their efforts led them to undermine the intellectual and moral foundations of the old. Others lived only in the fond hope that the evils of their day would disappear in the blessings of the future.

The final victory of capitalism in the latter part of the 18th century, however, revealed that many of these new evils in a new form, had come to stay. Poverty was not to come to an end; it was made more glaring by the greater wealth which capitalism was able to produce and by the removal of even the few social protections which feudalism, in the long course of its history, had established for the poor. Under feudalism, at least, the chasm between noble and serf was not anywhere near as great as that between capitalist and worker. Poverty was after all, the obvious work of drought, exhaustion of soil and fire. When the crops were good, all had something to eat. When the crops failed, the failure could not be blamed on king or priest or noble. But poverty, under capitalism was obviously man-made. In a world of plenty, the poor died of starvation. The rapacity and greed of the middle classes, therefore, stood revealed in all their gouty nakedness. Neither drought nor frost nor fire could be used as excuses for hunger nor ignorance of medical science and the will of God for disease. The law and the state, stripped by 18th century middle-class criticism of their religious sanctity, could be clearly seen as instruments of class domination and social injustice. Religious institutions—their priest and ministers unmasked as instruments of the divine among men—could be also seen as psychological and ideological instruments for keeping the vast majority—the poor—in obedient subjection to their exploiting rulers.

The reaction to these disillusioning discoveries followed various directions, depending upon class interest, knowledge, character and experience. Among those who continued to live in the traditions of radical capitalism, these evils were looked upon as temporary; leftovers, in part, of a previous world; consequences, in the main, of a failure to clarify the essential ideas upon which capitalism stood. They therefore, concerned themselves with clarifying principles, writing and agitating for reforms in the existing order of society.

The work done by men like James Mill, Bentham and John Stuart Mill was enormous. Their attacks upon established religions and upon religion, in general, their attempts to establish an ethics, a law, a politics, a psychology, and an economics devoid of divine sanctions and based on social utility, their analyses of specific problems like political liberty, liberty of thought and expression, the relation of economics to politics and political aims, in short, their attempt to find a coherent philosophy of the social life, had revolutionary consequences. It definitely turned the upper middle classes, the big bourgeoisie, against liberalism, except in those tenets which were practically useful to them. They were even led to repudiate those like Cobden and Bright, who were considered their ideological leaders. The Manchester school, of which Cobden was the most luminous star, expressed in practical terms the objectives of the upper middle classes. It wanted complete freedom of contract which meant the doing away with all forms of state protectionism, particularly for the landlord class; the removal of restraints like entail upon the buying and selling of land; the doing away with all state interference in the hiring and distribution of labor, and of tariffs which interfered with the free exchange of goods in foreign trade.

The most consistent exponent of this point of view was William Cobden. A man of high morality with a well-developed logical sense and a profound respect for facts which he studied earnestly, he tried strenuously for more than thirty years to convince the middle classes that their best advantage was served by following a policy of Laissez-faire in every department of economic and political life.

Cobden was not an opportunist. He did not seek his own immediate gain. He was concerned only with the welfare of society, and he sought to bring peace and prosperity to the farthest corners of the world. Blinded by his own uncritical faith in the middle classes he saw them as the means by which his world vision would be achieved. The middle class and particularly the upper bourgeoisie ultimately repudiated him, or rather pushed him aside as an impractical idealist who wanted unattainable things. The big industrialists, merchants, financiers of England felt they knew better what was in the interest of the middle class.

If Cobden toward the end of his life was pushed aside as a visionary, this was certainly true of a liberal like John Stuart Mill, who had unremittingly continued to develop and systematize his ideas in terms of the actual conditions of his time. The big bourgeoisie wanted to have nothing to do with the sort of liberalism which was so consistent that it hit at their profits and so visionary that it seemed to involve the radical transformation of society and their overthrow as its natural rules.

Moreover, the gulf between liberal ideals, now relatively clearly developed both in theory and apparent in effect, helped to advance those European movements—the anarchist and marxist—which looked upon liberalism as a fraud and folly. Because liberalism, in its classical vein, seemed to associate itself with capitalism, even when it was most critical of it, it was possible for anarchists and socialists of all varieties to identify the philosophy of liberalism with capitalism. This false identification—which was true in the case of many individuals who professed faith in liberalism—played an important part in disillusioning the masses with Democracy and provided the psychological basis for the lower middle and working classes to accept totalitarianism in the twentieth century as the only way out.

Back of all the thinking of classical liberalism was an indestructible faith in science and its methods. Thinkers like Stewart, Reid, Bentham, Mill were raised on the doctrine that reason, when applied experimentally to the sensible world, was the only way human problems could be solved. If the universe presented problems too deep for man, then the answer could not be found in religious superstition. The history of human error and stupidity stood always before their eyes; and they shuddered at the bloody consequences which the dogmatic acceptance of ideas as eternally true had provoked. Had men been intelligent enough to look upon theory as testable hypotheses, then persecution, the dark ages, the religious wars, poverty, disease, intolerance would never have plagued the conscience of man. They would have certainly known what they did know and experimentally tried to find out what they did not. They would have had a proper respect for differences of opinion and known how to get about determining which opinions were right. They would have known how to withhold judgment until adequate evidence was forthcoming and how to change their judgment when accumulated evidence showed the wisdom of doing so.

Thus the belief in science meant that knowledge was not something attained once and for all by thought or by intuition or by revelation, but a process in which ideas were rectified by testing them in terms of experience. It also meant that knowledge was only attained in the process of testing conflicting opinions or ideas. Thus the custom of previous centuries of censuring or prohibiting opinion was intolerable. It could only mean that men would be prevented from learning the truth as soon as they might.

The liberal belief in science also meant that truth was not something open only to a chosen few, an elite. It was open to all who took the trouble to think. A true idea might be thought up by the most ignorant peasant in the Balkans. Thus no one could be, in principle, denied the right to have ideas, since anyone, in the nature of things, might hit upon an important truth or truths.

These liberals recognized, of course, that those who were specially trained were more likely to discover truths. In any case, they were more capable, because of their training, of testing the truths of ideas. But here again, in principle, it was not excluded that any human being, except the completely idiotic, might be able to learn how to test the truth of the ideas he hit upon. Moreover, since truth has no special preference for any individual—whatever his status in society, color or religion—it seemed important to permit all who wanted to learn to acquire the necessary training.

If the widest freedom was necessary in the natural sciences, how much more so was it necessary in the practical sphere of the social life? The theoretical problems of natural science might be considered remote from those of the average man; and it might be argued that the average man did not need to know enough to dispute the conclusions of natural science. But no one could reasonably deny the right of the average man to decide whether or not he wanted to suffer or enjoy the practical effects of scientific discovery. Here then, was a sphere where the greatest freedom of discussion would aid the average man to determine for himself the rightness or wrongness of opinions, since he could discover this in their effects upon himself.

This consideration was even more important in the spheres of economics and politics, in the determination of policies to be followed by any government. How could man rectify his errors and see the truth, unless he were made aware of the arguments, pro and con, by means of which he could interpret the effects of policies upon himself?

Thus the belief in liberty for all man capable of reason and learning from experience, inevitably had to be one of the cardinal tenets of liberalism. But what this really meant in social practice and how it is to be practically effectuated was the most crucial problem of the nineteenth century and is of the twentieth.

In John Stuart Mill, we have the first complete formulation and practical working out of this problem from the liberal standpoint. Mill did not immediately see the necessity of developing a completely formulated theory of liberty. He did exactly the thing which most people do. He fought for the application of principles which he had been taught as a child by his father, James Mill, and his father's friend, Jeremy Bentham. As these men had carefully systematized their ideas and, in principle, seemed to be far ahead of their time, the possible inadequacies of their ideas which experience later revealed, were not immediately perceptible. As experience and circumstances dictated, Mill fought for the extension of civil rights to all social classes including women. In the sphere of economics, he at first fought for the most extreme forms of Laissez-faire in order to destroy all forms of feudal-protectionism. Yet later when he saw that Laissez-faire did not lead in the direction of freeing the individual, he became an exponent of economic socialism. No matter what may have been his attitude on any question, he always was attentive to the fruits of his theories in practice. Did experience agree with his anticipations? If they did not, why not? Thus experience constantly led him to new and more general formulations of his principles. Mere consistency, however important, as a logical ideal, was subordinate to the principle of conformity or agreement with experience.

Mill, like those before him, began with the assumption that the way of attaining truth was through science; that science involved the widest freedom of thought and expression; and without this unfettered freedom, truth would be suborned. When this principle was first grasped, its enemy seemed to be the state and the feudal classes which supported it. Thus it was believed that unlimited freedom could only be obtained by limiting the activities of the state as much as possible. The less there was of state interference, the more free the individual man. But as democracy was extended to new classes; as the principle that government of and by the people became a dominating ideal and actuality, the defects of this point of view became more and more obvious.

The people through the state could bind the actions and thinking of minorities, but not only through the state. They could bind their actions and prohibit the free expression of their ideas through social pressure. The majority, through ignorance and prejudice, could be as tyrannous as a church and its clergy or as a king and his counselors. Thus the problem of freedom became not merely one of extending certain civil rights to all members of society who had previously been deprived of such rights, but the more difficult one of freeing dissident individuals and minorities from the tyranny of the majority. If it was true that the majority had the right to decide what was good or bad for all in those matters which concerned the community good, it was also true that dissident minorities and individuals ought to have the right to express their disagreement with the majority in such forms and through such channels as would make possible a reconsideration by the majority of their opinions or the change of minorities into majorities. Mill, as much as anyone, insisted that the *majority conception* of the community good was not necessarily *identical with* the community good; and it often happened that a dissident individual or minority was proven right by experience.

Practically speaking, the liberties which Mill thought were most important from the point of view of the community good, are (1) freedom of thought; (2) freedom of speech, writing and publishing; and (3) freedom of organization. These rights interpenetrated and supported each other. They were as essential to the life of a community as bread and air and water. Where they were not recognized and implemented, there the community suffered from the trinity of error, ignorance and superstition,—the trinitarian destroyers of civilization.

Freedom of thought was a right that must be guaranteed every man. Every man must feel easy in his mind about his right to think and disagree. He must not fear that his neighbors or the authorities created by his neighbors would interfere with his right. Practically speaking, this meant the doing away with the legal prescriptions and agencies which medieval society had established in order to control men's thoughts. No man could be questioned by state authorities or by his neighbors. His private papers could not be seized and examined. In Mill's time, many of these rights of the privacy of a man's thoughts had been established in the law, but it had not yet been accepted as a *mores* of the populace. Thus in his effort to defend this privacy, Mill began to move away from the Manchesterian doctrine of no state interference. He began to see the necessity of using the state authority to protect the individual against the multitude. He also began to see the necessity of educating the populace to accept differences in the behavior and thought of other men, as long as they involved no harm to themselves.

Freedom of speech, writing and publishing inevitably followed from the freedom to think for oneself. Thinking, however original and true, was obviously of no particular utility either to a man or his neighbors unless it were expressed; and no man could possibly feel free in his thoughts who did not dare express them to his neighbors or publish them without jeopardy to himself. Yet such was the tyranny of custom and majority intolerance of difference of opinion that any one who exercised his theoretical right to express his differences from the majority placed himself in a position of considerable jeopardy. Loss of job; unjustified and illegal imprisonment; social ostracization; even brutal treatment like tar-and-feathering and lynching; were often the consequences to honest men who spoke their minds or published their views.

This tyranny was further bolstered by the doctrine that the majority belief was the voice of the people as a whole and the voice of the people must be the voice of God. The justice which resides in this idea was distorted by two serious errors. As first stated by English and American thinkers, it meant essentially that the majority of the people were better judgers of the acts and effects of their governors than the governors themselves; that government, in other words, should be in the interest of the people. But later, it was taken to mean that the majority of the people are identical with the people as a whole. Thus the majority opinion

of what is good is identical with the community good. This was the first error. The second was that anyone who disagreed with majority opinion disagreed with the people as a whole. Since this notion was enmailed in the sanctity of religious dogma, it was interpreted to mean that anyone who disagreed with the majority disagreed with God. The dissenter was doubly guilty. He violated not only the commandments of his natural sovereign, the people, but his divine sovereign, God.

There was no mechanical solution to this problem. The establishment of a legal right to publish and express was not sufficient protection in itself. However necessary, it offered little protection against an intolerant, viciously aggressive majority. The majority had to be educated; their illusions as to the sanctity of their opinions and the foolishness of holding such opinions sacrosanct made clear to them. But this was a slow, laborious process and involved a thoroughgoing change in the educational system and the attitudes and pedagogic techniques of educators.

Freedom of organization was inevitably involved in the rights to think and express one's thought. Mill himself, in *Liberty*, spent little time discussing this problem, but in *Representative Government,* he concerned himself with the kind of social or rather political organization necessary in order for it to be possible. Mill felt that Representative Democracy was the natural political vehicle for the expression of the will of the people. But he wanted to be sure that the will and the interest of the people were actually expressed. He was, as always, deeply troubled with the way in which majorities tyrannized over minorities and individuals. He saw that representation no more expressed the will of the people or gave it the chance to express itself adequately than political tyranny. A people only expressed themselves adequately where the representatives of minorities and majorities had equal chances to discuss the pros and cons of political action; and where it was possible for a political minority to obtain easily the status of a majority. There was also the question of the people controlling those representatives who failed to comply with the mandate given them. Often representatives once elected, were untouchable by their electors. There was also the related problem of the independence of the representatives themselves. Often enough, further consideration of a policy could justifiably involve a change of opinion. To what extent, could representatives act independently of their mandate, if they felt it was in the interest of the people to do so? Mill, too, was afraid of the disciple of political parties. He saw them overriding the interests of the people for their own partisan interests and for the interests of their supporters. The power of political parties was such that they could prevent independents from speaking and being elected by the people: and because they had the organization and experience, they could easily rid themselves of political figures who refused to obey them. Mill made many concrete proposals for reforming the existing systems of representatives governments so that they could more easily express the will of the people and give heed to their needs.

At first, Mill did not concern himself with the broad social conditions in which these liberties were embedded, but in his autobiography, the last edition of his *Political Economy*, and the posthumous work *Socialism*, he admitted that there was considerable justification for socialist criticism. Mill, who from 1832 until almost the sixties had supported the basic economic and legal reforms demanded by the Manchester school of Cobden, Bright, and of his father James Mill, and Jeremy Bentham, had finally come to see that these reforms did not basically alter the conditions of life for the vast majority. Already in *Utilitarianism* he had recognized that society was technically capable of providing the essential elements of a happy life which he considered were found in a proper combination of variety and security. In his early years when associated with English radicalism, he was largely concerned with the clarification of the principles of political democracy; he did not feel the need to analyze in detail the conditions which made political democracy an actuality in the lives of men. Later on he became aware of socialist criticisms, particularly those of Fourier, Considérant and Louis-Blanc (the writings of Marx apparently were unknown to him.) They made him realize that the question of property and its control was the pivot around which the political liberty of the masses revolved.

Thus, he set himself shortly before his death the important task of writing a critique of socialism in order to determine the extent to which the arguments of socialism were justified. He never completed this work but even in its incomplete form, there can be no doubt about his essential conclusions. He considered the basic arguments of socialist critics of capitalism to be essentially true. Capitalism, he agreed, had no moral and intellectual justification for its widespread poverty; its system of rewarding individuals; the incredible waste of human beings, adulteration of goods and general inefficiency of operation. Secondly, he admitted that economic enterprises in which competition had ceased to be an important factor for improving efficiency of production and the quality of goods and for lowering prices are to be managed and controlled by the state. Thirdly, he admitted that it was high time that something was done to establish adequate wages and universal education, and to remove by law the inequities of birth and wealth and to provide adequate means for the proper utilization of society's productive machinery and human material.

He did not think, however, that the absolute faith of socialists in the efficacy of a planned socialist economy was justified by the available facts. (He was referring specifically to the blueprints of a socialist economy of a revolutionary socialist like Louis Blanc.) He pointed out that human beings, as now constituted, need more than the incentives of conscience, public spirit and reputation to do what is needed or expected of them. He did not deny that such motives were influential, but he pointed out that they usually operated in a negative sense only. People in general would do nothing *against* their conscience, reputation or the general welfare, but it was rare that they would do anything more without additional and more selfish incentives. He pointed out that most individuals would have to be motivated through advantages to be gained for themselves as a result of the work they did. That Mill's judgment was prophetic is proved by the fact that the Soviet Union today not only uses such incentives as differentials in wages and payment on the basis of piecework but also coercion in order to attain the planned indices of production; and even with such added incentives as gain and fear Soviet production is still after thirty years of existence among the lowest, per unit person, among those countries which base themselves on mass and machine production.

Mill also pointed out that a planned economy on a national scale requires a very high level of industrial development which means therefore that the planners must have at their disposal a huge accumulation of both fixed and circulating capital. He thought it doubtful that such a huge accumulation of capital could be obtained without demanding extraordinary sacrifices of the populace: and he wondered whether the nationalization of economies which had not yet developed a sufficient accumulation of capital would be worth the public cost. Not only would it mean unnecessary and extraordinary sacrifices on the part of the populace but it was likely that the level of socialist efficiency might be much lower than in an economy in which production was not entirely controlled by the state. Here he advanced two arguments in substantiation: the first was that the managers of state enterprises would be deprived of the necessary independence of judgment and initiative needed to operate such large enterprises. The second was that total planning would place unnecessary handicaps and restrictions in the way of the advancement of any particular sector of production. Mill here spoke as a prophet. Although his arguments of 1869 were impatiently swept aside by socialist dogmatists, they have been verified to the hilt in the twentieth century.

It must be understood that Mill did not argue against the establishment of national socialist economies. He thought whatever might be the difficulties in the way of making them work effectively, future developments might require that they be attempted, but he wanted men to enter upon such endeavors with clear heads and the utmost caution in order to prevent the populace paying heavily in lives and in wealth. He even recommended that governments and groups of individuals should attempt to build small communities as facsimilies of the larger experiment in order to evaluate properly the difficulties to be met with if the same thing were attempted on a national scale.

For many years after his death, Mill lost an enormous part of his prestige and influence among the new generations of political thinkers and radicals. The twin influences of imperialism and revolutionary socialism took hold of various classes in whose interests these doctrines were formulated. But Mill ought no longer to be looked upon with contempt or indifference by most individuals who have been taking to heart the lessons of the twentieth century.

Mill did not provide answers to all the problems which mankind has had to face since his death; but his mode of analysis, his anxiety to study the facts and the perserverance with which he studied them, and his search after principles and concrete techniques by which to implement his principles—the many recommendations he made—should serve as examples to liberals of the way they should proceed in investigating the weighty problems which burden men today.

IV

THE MARXIST CRITIQUE OF LIBERALISM

If one phase of modern liberalism:-the broad political principles of social freedom, was developed by the radical thinkers of the middle classes, the economic basis for making these principles effective was developed by those who often spoke in the name of the lower middle classes—the small farmer, merchant and artisan—and the proletariat. Those who, like the Utopians and the Marxists, concerned themselves with developing the theory of an economic order based on egalitarian principles were at first opposed to liberalism and justifiably considered it the ideological defense of capitalism. But as time went on, and far-reaching changes occurred in economics, politics and technology and particularly in the status and character of classes—some classes disappearing or losing importance; other classes coming into existence and classes which continued to exist being affected adversely by economic changes—a rapproachement began between political liberalism and socialism, a rapproachement which was completed in the twentieth century. We observed this rapproachement in John Stuart Mill who found in the early socialist thinkers— Fourier, Saint Simon, Considérant—some of the necessary economic foundation-stones for his political beliefs. John Stuart Mill was one of the first in whom this rapproachement occurred. We turn therefore to an examination of these movements and certain of their economic doctrines from which are derived the economic principles of modern liberalism.

As capitalism began to spread after the middle of the eighteenth century over all the seven continents and to reveal more and more its characteristic structure and defects, there arose a small group of thinkers who vividly brought these defects to the attention of the world. These thinkers did not believe that the capitalist class was interested in equality and freedom. They therefore tried to build among the lower classes a powerful anticapitalist movement. From these small, intelligent groups which met in cafes or conspiratorally in houses in Paris, Berlin or London there grew slowly but with gathering momentum after 1800 powerful nationalistic and international lower class movements drawing to them large numbers of the disinherited and exploited peoples of the feudal and capitalist countries.

When these movements were first organized they were often negative or filled with high but illusory hopes of what could be done immediately to reform society. The negative movements were simply opposed to change and wanted back the good old days. Peasants wanted to be relieved of their excessive taxes and heavy debts; the artisans wanted their old markets; and the workers wanted the times when work was plentiful and wages were good. The workers and artisans in the cities were particularly aroused over the use of machinery and the factory system. And often enough they hated this new overwhelming phenomenon, capitalism, with a hatred that only men who had once been free could hate those who had deprived them of their freedom.

The more positive movements like Fourierism, Owenism, Saint-Simonism, were not only anti-capitalist and anti-monarchist but offered wonderful blueprints of a new social order. Some hoped that by building little communist islands in the vast ocean of exploiting capitalism, they would ultimately convince sceptics and non-believers in the preferability and practicability of their blueprints. Others did not think such communities were effective of themselves and expended all their efforts in trying to arouse the lower classes to overthrow capitalism and establish socialism. Both movements—those who believed in communist islands and those who wanted the immediate overthrow of capitalism—were later dubbed by Marx "utopian."

In the earlier half of the nineteenth century, these Utopian movements existed in all countries where capitalism had established itself or exercised considerable influence; and their members came from every social class. But these movements were merely temporary social eruptions which appeared as a consequence of the discovery that capitalism was not all men had once imagined it to be. By the 60's and 70's these groups had already lost their not inconsiderable influence and were beginning to disappear permanently. One cause was the unanticipated success of capitalism in raising the standard of living of the lowest classes above that of anything ever known before. Another was their failure to achieve their goal. Still another was the increasing humanity of government as expressed in protective social legislation and the extension of political rights to other classes than the propertied. Judging from the persistent direction in which capitalism was going, it seemed as if it were seeking to erase all distinctions between classes and all privileges in favor of the upper classes. This conclusion was strengthened by the fact that many of these changes were brought about by the Liberal Party of Gladstone, the Republican Party of Jefferson and the new Republican Party of Lincoln.

The failure of Utopianism and the broader freedom and the greater prosperity which capitalism introduced gave a new lease of life to a decadent liberalism. Many of those who at first had been anti-capitalist became reconciled with capitalism, and many of those who in the 30's and 40's might have been anti-capitalist or utopian believed with Cobden and Bright that the middle classes could create a just and free social order. In other words, liberalism after the 1870's gained a popularity with the masses in the most advanced capitalist countries which it had never known before. The average man no longer believed it to be the social ideology only of the middle classes. He accepted it as the basic principles of a progressive society. In those countries of Europe which had not yet successfully overthrown feudalism, the masses accepted it as their philosophy even more enthusiastically than did the masses in the capitalist countries.

Yet, ironically enough, liberalism after the 1870's was not any longer what it had been. There was no certainty any longer that a party calling itself liberal was actually, liberal, in the sense in which the philosophical radicals Cobden, Bright and Mill were liberal. Liberalism had become a catch-all word with which to attract the masses; and its meaning depended upon the country in which it was used and by whom it was used. For example, within the Liberal Party of England after the 70's there came into existence outspoken tendencies defending Britain's far-flung imperialism. The national Liberal Party of Germany after the 80's was not even democratic. It supported the Hohenzollerns and opposed any progressive constitutional reforms.

Ironically enough, political parties which ardently supported basic liberal ideas often denied their liberalism. The socialist parties, for example, insisted they had nothing in common with liberal ideology; they were the parties of the exploited masses of the world dedicated to one task only: the revolutionary establishment of socialism. So strong was this opposition to liberal ideas that the question of defending Dreyfus against the trumped-up charges of treason was hotly debated by leaders of different currents in the socialist parties. It was argued by revolutionary socialists that socialist parties could have no interest in defending members of the upper classes against their own class injustice. Let the upper classes take care of their own, they cried, and we, the working class, take care of ours. Abstract justice does not exist: there is only class justice—the justice of the working man and the justice of the capitalist; between them there is no identity except in name. Yet in spite of themselves they felt compelled to deny their Marxian logic and to defend a justice above class—the justice of humanity.

In any case, liberalism was no longer to be found where it was customary to find it. Those parties which might profess it did not act upon it; and those which might act upon it often denied kinship.

If liberalism was no longer clearly identifiable with any one political movement; if politically it was beginning to stand for a thousand, different things, this was even more true of the growing numbers of non-party individuals who after 1870 began calling themselves "liberal." Their liberalism was highly individualized, so highly individualized in fact that no one could know what any man professed from the mere fact that he called himself a liberal. He might mean that he preferred reason to sentiment or the very opposite. He might mean he was a thorough-going follower of Cobden and Bright or a partisan of Marx. In short, a "liberal" could mean anything from an arch conservative to an arch radical.

The failure of Utopianism, however, did not mean the death of the socialist ideal or the end of the socialist movement. It meant only that socialism had to find a new theory and a more practical direction. Despite the considerable improvement in the living conditions of the vast majority in the capitalist countries, utopian criticism was still as applicable after 1870 as before. In some respects it was even more to the point. There had been a number of sharp crises which had produced starvation, unemployment, bankruptcy and war. Productive resources both human and material were still being wasted as shamefully as ever. The upper classes were as insatiably greedy as ever. The working classes were being exploited and believed themselves to be as much exploited as ever. Thus the vision of human equality, the brotherhood of man and of liberty, still lived in the hearts of men. But it demanded theoretical expression and support, without the fantasy, unrealism and purely imaginative projections of wishes which characterized the thinking of the utopians. What was now needed was a socialism apparently realistic, practical, a logical development from the conditions of living society.

This demand was theoretically satisfied by Marx, aided by his friend and life-partner, Friedrich Engels. Realizing that the utopians had not studied capitalism scientifically, he set himself the great task of discovering what he called the fundamental laws of motion of capitalism. Every society for him was a constantly changing, organismic-like thing, and like all organisms its life depended upon its ability to feed and reproduce itself. He did not mean by reproduction the purely biological process of the reproduction of the species, but the reproduction of the species to perform the wide and various tasks required to keep capitalist society going. Thus if capitalism was to be understood, it must be examined from the point of view of the capitalist mode of production and reproduction. Without doing this, nothing could be understood—neither the formation of its great cities, nor its great social classes nor its wars nor its emphasis upon technology nor its social and political ideas.

And this was particularly true of ideas. Ideas could not be understood in and of themselves without understanding their connection with the material basis of the social life. Just as most people imagine themselves to be one thing and are in reality something else, so Marx pointed out that a society's ideas of itself were one thing and what that society is in actuality, was another. Only when the laws of its behavior and development are revealed can its ideas be understood in all their truth, falsity, motivation, imaginative scope and fantasy. If in one sense Marx insisted that ideas were purely a reflection of the conditions of society and the interests of men, in another, he recognized that they were not true reflections or even reflections at all, for they often expressed what men wished or imagined or believed to be true rather than the actual conditions of things. Were ideas merely reflections of the world in which men lived, then an examination of them alone would have been sufficient to reveal the nature of the society in which men lived. Nor would it have been necessary for Marx to study capitalist society so earnestly for more than forty years.

The avowed aim of Marx, as he declared repeatedly, was to determine whether socialism was possible or not. He denounced the utopians for imagining all kinds of grandiose plans for the emancipation of mankind without ever trying to discover whether they were realizable. Utopians, he scolded, were people who took dreams for realities, and continued to dream forever in a real world full of dangers; and they were all the more dangerous in that their visions contained all the things which the exploited masses wanted and would, if properly aroused, risk their lives for. What was the sense, he asked, in believing in unrealizable dreams? Everyone would be better off, if they knew there was nothing to them. Therefore he searched to find a realizable socialism, a socialism rooted in the conditions of modern society and which the masses, if properly organized and educated, could bring into existence.

It is not our purpose here to discuss whether Marx ever intended more than this; whether he wanted to show that socialism was inevitable or merely a scientifically realizable hope for mankind. There is certainly plenty of evidence proving that Marx believed in the inevitability of socialism, that he thought it would come about as a natural consequence of capitalist development whether men wanted it or not. But that is not the essential issue here. One fact, however, remains indisputable:—Marx wanted a socialism that was scientifically realizable and provable as such.

With Marx, therefore, it can be said that a new period in the history of man began. Unlike most thinkers before him, he studied society from the point of view of trying to discover those techniques, means or instruments by which it could be altered to suit the heart's desires. He established in all probability for the first time the principles that the instrument of social revolution is not the individual but the class or mass; that the techniques for the realization of the ideal of socialism are to be found in knowledge of the laws of social change and not in high ideals or fervent convictions. Thus Marx united the two elements so widely separated in the doctrines of the utopians: a devastating critique of capitalism with an ideal of a new social order apparently based not in wish fulfillment but in science. Since no other doctrine could be compared to it in practicality and in the fusion of science with social idealism, it very soon became the outstanding influence among the working class and the lower middle classes of the world. Its nearest competitor was anarchism which had a large following among the proletariat and peasantry of the least economically developed countries—Russia, Spain and Italy. In the highly advanced countries like England, Germany, France, Austria and the United States, wherever there was any kind of labor movement it almost invariably based itself upon the ideas of Marx.

Since Marx's prime problem was to prove that socialism was realizable and justified in terms of the material conditions of capitalist society, he examined all ideas from the point of view of their relation to material social conditions and class interests. Thus he often felt it was sufficient to show that certain ideas were beneficial to classes whose interests were alien to those of the working class in order to reject them. He did not pursue the same method towards ideas which appealed directly to the working class. These he attacked directly by their authors, as, for example, in the cases of Proudhon, Lassalle, Bakunin, Dühring.

Until 1870 liberalism was generally recognized as the social philosophy of the industrial and commercial classes. Many of the lower class movements, particularly in England, often opposed liberalism and even united with the landed aristocracy to oppose specific measures which the liberals proposed, like free trade. Thus Marx never felt it necessary to criticize liberalism as a doctrine distinct from that of capitalist ideology as a whole. Such criticism became necessary at a much later time and after his death. For him, therefore, to expose capitalism was sufficient to expose liberalism.

However much Marx might prefer capitalism to feudalism, it was still a class society, exclusively concerned with promoting the rights of capital. It had no concern, except for the purpose of deluding the vast majority, with humanity. It had no desire to allow the rest of mankind to participate in the advantages and rights which it had won for itself and enjoyed. It was dominated by one motive and one ideal only—the making of profit. For the sake of profit, it would sell Heaven to Hell or Hell to Heaven; it recognized no morality, no justice other than the morality and justice of profit.

Thus Marx considered liberalism primarily a theory of the justification of the absolute rights of capital over labor, of capitalist exploitation over social justice. Even the best representative of liberalism, John Stuart Mill, for example, he described as a superficial thinker who looked like a mountain among his countrymen because the best among them were of the size of molehills. He could not see liberalism as a doctrine which contained within itself the seeds of a development beyond its class origins, which might incorporate the best ideas of socialism. It was necessarily limited by its class origins and class interests.

Nevertheless Marx did not reject outright all liberal ideas—for example, those concerned with political liberty. In fact he felt that their development had gone about as far in principle as they could go, for they were being extended to include all classes. Under socialism, they might need only a reworking or modification in technique effectively to express the ends of socialist society. This conclusion, however, he did not reach until nearly the end of his life when he recognized that socialism might be possible in England and the United States by political action alone without the forceful overthrow of the capitalist class. More frequently, he considered such political liberties merely abstractions without any other purpose than to keep masses submissive to their rulers. He seemed often to forget that the political liberty of modern times was profoundly different from that of ancient Rome or Greece or the cities of the French, Italian and German Renaissances. Whatever its imperfections, modern liberty, as Bryce pointed out in his *Modern Democracies,* transcends classes. Marx, often enough, forgot this in his insistence, reiterated in new forms by his followers, that the masses were often thwarted in the proper use of their political liberties by ignorance, backwardness or the machinations of the political machines controlled by the capitalists. Nevertheless he was often enough right in saying that the liberal emphasis upon political liberty was often too abstract and unrelated to actual conditions. The liberal seemed to be satisfied merely with the legal existence of political liberty and not at all with determining and creating the social conditions which would make it a living reality. Not to understand this was not to know whether political liberty was possible or whether the means existed by which it could be realized. Thus his first criticism of liberalism was its abstractness.

His second criticism was its unhistoricity. The liberal, in Marx's time, seemed to develop his ideas without any sense of the historically determining conditions which made him believe in them. He seemed to think his ideas were original with God or inherent in the natural conditions of men. He did not and could not conceive of them as ever having been false or wrong even though for thousands of years they had not even been known or were considered as treasonable or heretical.

In making these criticisms Marx did not concern himself with the isolated thinker exercising little or no influence upon the capitalist class. His criticisms were directed at popular attitudes to be found among the supporters of capitalism. These certainly believed that their ideas rested in natural rights or were of divine ordination. Marx never seemed to have heard of Bentham's criticism of the natural rights' theory or Mill's insistence upon the historicity of all economic and political institutions.

His third criticism was that liberalism excluded all considerations of the role of class and class interests in the making of fundamental changes in society. Even though the liberal often urged important reforms he nevertheless failed to ask who would be interested in bringing about these reforms. He acted as if all men were rational and actuated only by rational consideration. But man is not completely rational nor is he decisively influenced by rational conclusions. Marx agreed with Hobbes who two centuries before had pointed out that economic or personal advantage would override in most instances a man's reason.

If this was true for the individual, it was even more so for a class. A class is almost entirely motivated by its class interests. If it enjoys decided material advantages over other classes, or if it is content with its status, it will do nothing to alter its situation or the situation of society no matter how cogent may be the arguments offered. The fact is that a well-situated class will often fight to the death to retain its advantages. It will often prefer civil war, anarchy or even death to give up even one of its vested interests. A class not well-situated or even horribly exploited will often senselessly attack an impregnable ruling class even though it may have been warned in advance that such an attack is futile or that there may be better, more effective ways of achieving its ends. The slowness with which a class can be educated to social reality, the ease with which it accepts false theories pandering to its desires and the necessity for it to act through leaders and organized groups are irreducible obstructions to intelligent adjustment to difficult social situations. In addition, prejudice, ignorance and tradition play their part in perpetuating a distorted picture of social reality.

Yet despite these difficulties, Marx believed that some classes could act more intelligently than others. This depended, of course, upon the character of the society and the available knowledge. These were the classes whose objective situation cried for all sorts of radical changes; and these were the only classes which could be appealed to to support any change, since they were the only ones who were ready to make the necessary sacrifices. To Marx, history had assigned this role in capitalist society to the proletariat; and if any ideologue was sincere in his desire for social improvement, it was to them that he had to appeal.

Marx's criticism of liberalism, therefore—insofar as he did on occasion distinguish it from capitalist ideology—was that it did not appeal to any particular class. It spoke in the name of humanity or in the interests of the majority. It disregarded the patent fact that the upper classes—the landlords and capitalists—were not interested in the welfare of the majority. In so far as the liberal was honest, he was merely a victim of his own blindness, but in so far as he knowingly refused to consider class interest, he was covertly supporting capitalism.

A fourth criticism was that the liberal looked upon the state not as an instrument of a class but as the means by which the interests of all men were expressed. But state and ruling class were inseparable; the state was the instrument by which one class ruled over others. Thus no state could act in such a way as to serve the interests of all; and no class would grant other classes the legal means by which it could be destroyed.

Before 1870, this criticism was, in the main, justified since the political rights by which given classes ruled had not yet been extended to all classes. Even though in America, all political rights, in principle, were granted to all the citizenry,—thus to all individuals whatever their social class—yet property requirements often restricted their use to a relatively small section of the populace. Marx, therefore, could legitimately speak of the state as being entirely the instrument of the propertied classes. They were the only ones who had the legal right to form political parties and elect political representatives. The parties of the peasantry and the proletariat—and in the semi-feudal countries—even the parties of the bourgeoisie were usually illegal and acted illegally. Actually until events proved otherwise, Marx and Engels believed that if ever parties of the working class were granted the same political rights as the bourgeois parties, this would mean the end of capitalism and the establishment of socialism.

These criticisms—it must be repeated—were not directed so much against liberalism as against capitalism with which he identified it. And it is true that liberalism, for a long time, was inseparable from the struggle of capitalism against feudalism and the feudal classes. It was also difficult to imagine that political power would take a form so diffuse that the proletariat would obtain the same political rights as the propertied classes. Thus the struggle for general suffrage, for protective social legislation, like the eight-hour day, for the right of non-bourgeois parties to exist legally—all of these struggles were tied in Marx's mind to the victory for socialism. If such rights became universal, it meant the bourgeoisie had signed their own death warrant.

V

THE LIBERAL CURRENT IN MARXISM

After 1870, Marx's criticisms of capitalism as a corollary of liberalism did not appear so convincing to many radical intellectuals and working men. First, the capitalist state no longer appeared to be the exclusive possession of the upper classes. Suffrage was being extended to all classes. After 1900, general suffrage existed in most of the advanced states. After 1890, Proletarian parties existed legally in England, Austria, France, Germany, Italy and the United States; and as they grew in size and influence among the masses, they created a vast network of trade unions, co-operatives, and cultural institutions. Their influence was felt everywhere—in the type of laws being passed; in the legislature where their representatives sat; in the general acceptance among all classes of more and more of their ideas of social reform. Secondly, liberalism as a doctrine had changed significantly. Not only had its original meaning been forgotten, but it was no longer identified exclusively with the capitalist class. As capitalism spread to the hinterland of the world, the capitalist class became more and more imperialist and less and less liberal. Liberalism was more and more identified even by its enemies with the enlightened lower middle classes or with intellectuals in or outside the labor movements. But this shift in the allegiance of classes was also due to radical modifications in the ideas of liberalism. Without having given up its basic faith in reason and democracy, it had adopted many of the basic economic doctrines of Marxian socialism; even in its less radical forms, it admitted the necessity of equalizing economic disparities by various types of protective legislation like ownership or control of monopolies and social security legislation for the poorer classes. Lastly within the labor movement itself, there arose an important current which ultimately led to a world-wide schism of the labor movement and came to represent, in essentials, the doctrine of twentieth century liberalism.

The current which now is called *reformist socialism* or *reformism* and after the formation of the Third International has been politically associated with the now nearly defunct Second International, did not represent itself as anti-Marxist. In its early stages, through its leaders, Bernstein, the German theoretician, and Jaurès, the French Socialist philosopher and historian, it considered itself simply revisionist; it sought to correct the theoretical errors and doctrinaire excesses of Marxism.

The revisionists were intent upon proving that a revolutionary struggle was not necessary in order to achieve socialism. That the socialist society would be a political democracy along liberal lines was not disputed by anybody. In fact, it was expected that all the restrictions which capitalist society imposed upon political democracy would be removed. Age limits would be lowered; women would be given the vote; recall and referendum would be established for all offices; some system of proportional representation would be used; dual legislatures would be abolished; all political offices would be elective and not appointive; no restrictions of any kind would be imposed upon free speech or free press or the right of organization other than those required to protect reputations or maintain a high level of social decency. But was it necessary to prepare the proletariat for the forceful conquest of power? Was the modern state still purely an instrument of the ruling class? Was the attainment of political power by the proletariat by peaceful means out of the question? This was the issue which divided the labor movement into factions until the First World War, and after resulted in a world-wide, mortal schism.

The debate on this question was not limited simply to the relation of political power to the modern state but involved, for reasons not purely logical, the question of the soundness of Marx's law of the accumulation of capital.

That Marx's law of accumulation of capital was not logically involved can be seen from the various consequences which were derived from it by different thinkers. Daniel De Leon, for example, concluded that capitalism must inevitably turn into socialism. The working class therefore must not fight for a betterment of their economic conditions, for if they won concessions, they would lose interest in socialism. They would be content to live in the swamp of capitalism rather than in the paradise of socialism. But betterment of the workers' conditions under capitalism, of course, is impossible. The law of accumulation of capital denies this. Therefore the task of the workers is to create their own mass organizations and to prepare themselves for the time when capitalist economy is ripe for socialism. Then the workers will seize power by force. Why force is necessary, De Leon did not explain. If the law was true, then, at this stage, the capitalists would be so few and the working class so enormous and powerful, there would be no need of force at all.

Others like Lenin argued that the law was a tendency alterable in its effect by the action of various economic forces. Thus the proletariat must struggle for reforms in order to improve its living conditions. The struggle for reforms is one of the means by which the proletariat organizes and educates itself for the conquest of power. At first, of course, the concessions it wins deludes it into believing that the law of accumulation of capital can be overcome, but as the struggle continues, it becomes clearer and clearer that the law can only be modified; it can not be overcome. When the proletariat realizes there is no escape from the iron law of accumulation, it will turn revolutionary and establish the dictatorship of the proletariat. Like DeLeon, Lenin considered the law as ultimately unalterable in its effect, but, unlike DeLeon, he considered the struggle for reforms an essential element in the realization of the inevitability of the law. Kautsky considered the law of accumulation of capital inevitable in its workings, but considered that the socialist society would come about peacefully where democracy exists. Still others believed that the law was only a tendency and therefore modifiable or even transformable and concluded that the establishment of socialism was possible only through the political action of the proletariat. They believed socialism was not the inevitable result of the workings of the law of accumulation, but the united action of an educated proletariat *could* make it inevitable.

These various interpretations of the possible consequences of the law of accumulation of capital—each maintained with a considerable show of logic—show that the law had no logical connection with the question whether socialism could be achieved by revolution or by evolution. Yet so high was the authority of Marx that no arguments for or against either point of view could be made without relating it to the question of the truth or falsity of the law of accumulation of capital. Influenced by this high authority, Bernstein tried to show that the predictions which Marx had derived from the law were not verified in experience. The number of capitalists were not becoming smaller; the misery of the working class was not decreasing; the capitalists were willing to make concessions both economic and political to the working class; and the working class, through its political parties and other organizations, was gradually approaching the point where it could take political power by means of the ballot. As for the capitalist class, it was not a unified, single-minded group of individuals. They differed in their social vision and understanding and in their willingness to compromise; it was the task of the socialist leadership to recognize and to utilize these differences between the different sections of the capitalist class to the advantage of the working class.

If the question of the peaceful transformation into society had only involved the queston of the truth or falsity of the law of accumulation of capital, it might very well have happened that Bernstein would have been victorious. But after the beginning of the twentieth century, other questions arose which took precedence over it. Blackening the horizon of successful socialist struggle was the issue of the coming imperialist war. Those who believed in the peaceful transformation of society were inclined to de-emphasize the possibility of a future world war, since they thought recognition of its possibility might also involve recognition of the necessity of armed insurrection, a dismal prospect for those who expected the millenium to come by means of slogans, ballot boxes, parliamentary speeches and caucuses.

Also without cognizance of its power, a new force was insidiously working in the ranks of socialism—patriotism or national sentiment. Socialists, before World War I, did not believe that any among them could believe in anything less than a world society. Patriotism was for the capitalists and middle classes. They did not realize that the lower classes, particularly the proletariat, had become so profoundly attached to their national homeland. Thus when World War I began, the various socialist parties which boasted at that time a world membership of some seven millions and a controlling voice in organizations whose numbers totalled above twenty million, found themselves unable to act to stop the war. With few exceptions, the socialist parties were as patriotic as everyone else. However, they found their own excuses for their patriotism. It is tragically true that the First World War would never have occurred had the socialist parties stood firm in their opposition to it.

The revolutionists in the Second International fiercely criticised the reformists. In the period before the First World War, they followed Kautsky, who was the main defense for the law of accumulation of capital. He was the most orthodox and learned disciple of Karl Marx and his heir. Kautsky's answer to the fact that the predictions of the law of accumulation of capital had not been verified was that Marx had not meant his law to be understood in terms of absolute numbers but of percentages. He had not meant that the absolute number of capitalists was decreasing, but that the percentage of capitalists in relation to the percentage of proletariat is decreasing. This was obviously so. While it is true that the standard of living of the working class as a whole had been raised, this did not mean that the misery of the working class had not increased, for misery is not an economic but a psycho-sociological concept. The misery of the proletariat was increasing simply because they were receiving less relatively to what society could give them and were conscious of this fact. Thus even though they received absolutely more, their consciousness of the fact that they received less, relatively speaking, than they ought to receive meant that their misery was increasing.

Interesting enough, no one attempted a popular poll of working class sentiment on this question and so far as the orthodox Marxists were concerned, they would not have accepted its results. They would have said contradictorally enough, that the masses did not know their own feelings or interests. To use Freudian terms, they would have insisted that the masses were not aware consciously of what they felt unconsciously. Thus, the law of accumulation of capital must have the results which Marx predicted; the conflict between capital and labor must reach a critical point when the proletariat will try by force to seize political power and capital will act to prevent it. In preparation for this inevitability, the capitalists must maintain permanent control of the armed forces and the state apparatus. Thus the revolutionists maintained that the facade of popular elections, parliamentary government and civil liberties camouflages and is intended to camouflage the fact that political power is at all times in the hands of the capitalist class.

Revolutionists defended this conclusion all the more violently because the proletariat, in 1870, had not been able to seize power and the capitalist class was found to be much stronger than had formerly been realized. The proletariat had disappointed them and their disappointment was deepened by the fact that the proletariat was so slow in taking advantage of its power. It had been hopefully and rightly anticipated that the working class would compel the new ruling class to establish genuine suffrage and other civil rights. But it was thought that the struggle for these rights would lead the working class to make the socialist revolution. They had felt, (in agreement with the attitude of the middle classes) that if the working class was granted these rights, it would act to end capitalism. But when these rights were granted, nothing of the sort happened. The working class parties and other working class organizations concerned themselves with wresting this or that concession from capitalism. Even though they might preach revolution, they acted reform.

The Marxist revolutionists before 1870, had concluded, on the basis of previous political history, that the extension of political rights to other classes inevitably involved the political triumph of these previously disenfranchised classes. This had been again and again illustrated in the struggle of the various classes of Greece and Rome and even of modern times. Political power is always exercised by the rulers and the right to exercise it is limited exclusively to them. If it is extended to other classes, it means the social triumph and rule of these classes.

But matters seemed to work differently under capitalism. The extension of democratic rights to all classes did not seem to involve the immediate political victory of the exploited or a new social order. The revolutionists, therefore, tried to find another explanation, one which involved a radical alteration in their original conception of the state as an instrument of a class. There was no longer any necessity to confine all political rights to the ruling class or classes. It was now only essential that the ruling class should control the armed forces and the state apparatus. Thus it made no difference in the essentials of class rule whether political rights were widespread or limited solely to a class so long as control of the armed forces and the state apparatus, i.e., the bureaucracy, remained in the hands of the ruling class.

This new theory prepared the ground for the complete disillusionment of the masses with democracy which characterizes the twentieth century. What difference does it make whether the masses have political rights or not, since having them means nothing from the point of view of political power! The masses can not use these rights to place themselves in power, and if they should establish themselves in power, they can not use it, since the armed forces and the state apparatus would still remain entirely in the hands of the ruling class. Moreover, if they tried to use their power legally to replace individuals in the state apparatus or the armed forces, they would find themselves blocked at every turn.

Actually modern political democracy is not different in these respects from the ancient. In the ancient democracies, the armed forces and the state apparatus were always controlled by and dominated by the ruling class. Nevertheless when a particular ruling class, such as the landed aristocracy of ancient Greece, was compelled by revolt or alien class pressure to extend political rights to other classes—the commercial and the artisan—that action invariably resulted in the state administration and armed forces falling predominantly into the hands of these new and more numerous classes. There is no doubt that the struggle for control of these agencies was at times violent but ultimately their control fell into the hands of that class or classes which gained the political right to govern. This fact was recognized by all ancient students of politics.

The conception, originally accepted by Marx and revolutionists before 1870, is right: The extension of democratic rights to all classes means in the end all power to the masses. But the anxiety of revolutionists for the socialist Utopia in their time and their fear that the proletariat would never learn to use their power politically led them to develop the false theory that modern democracy is *class* democracy. Thus they failed to utilize to the full, the significant fact that the exploited classes today had rights which were never before granted to any exploited class in the history of man—rights which if properly used, might have created a really free society of men all over the world. Instead they taught the masses to be cynical of democracy, to become indifferent to the great power which democracy for the first time has really placed in their hands; and they provided the basis for developing the theory that democracy and totalitarianism are not opposing political principles but identical forms of class exploitation, a theory which found its terrible realization in National Socialism and Soviet Communism; that is, in extreme exploitation of the masses by the Nazi and the Communist Parties. And today, after fighting a world war against Nazism, it means a new world struggle in which the deluded masses will probably follow totalitarianism either to world enslavement or destruction.

Co-incidental with these disagreements over revolutionary action and the nature of the state occurred another in 1900 in the Russian Social Democracy, over the organization of the political party which has had repercussions all over the world. In *What's To Be Done*, Lenin developed the theory of a party completely subordinate to its leadership, militaristically organized and consisting of a professional "class" of revolutionists wholly devoted to the goal of revolutionary socialism. These revolutionists were not to be namby-pamby moralists. Revolution required men without squeamish stomachs and with iron wills who wanted power desperately and were not afraid to use it to the utmost. Revolutionists like Trotsky, who afterwards changed his mind, and Rosa Luxembourg, criticized Lenin's conception of the party as involving ultimately a totalitarian or autocratic state, dominated by an authoritarian leader; and they denounced it as contrary in principle to the spirit and letter of socialism. The discussion at that time seemed like a tempest in a teapot but it was brewed in a teapot of world dimensions.

The first World War brought each of these theoretical issues, at different times, to the boiling point. It was no longer a question of theory but a matter of life and death for the working class. Unfortunately what was to be done had little or nothing to do with the disagreements which had agitated the labor movement since 1870. In the first place, these different issues had been so emotionally fused with one another that to take sides on any one of these complex questions involved being identified with the camp of revolutionists or reformists, even though revolutionists and reformists took different sides on every issue which agitated the international labor movement of that time. This tendency to lump all individuals into a particular camp, whatever may have been their actual opinions, became a settled policy of the revolutionists after the Bolshevik Revolution of October 1917; and after 1921, it hardened into a principle for abusing and excommunicating all who disagreed with any policy of the majority in the Third International. After 1928, it became a fixed principle that no disagreements of any kind are permissible among members of the Communist Party or the Third International and anyone who differs in the slightest from the program, strategic or tactical, of the Third International is an agent of capitalist reaction.

As the war continued, the practical issue of for or against the war more and more sharply divided labor into camps—those who agreed with Lenin that capitalism had entered into a period of final decay, the "last stage of capitalism," from which the only way out is revolution, and those who, whether or not they agreed with Lenin, still continued to believe that socialism might be brought about by peaceful means.

Those who supported Lenin or were more or less close to his point of view insisted that the law of accumulation of capital had now been verified to the hilt, that the revisionists had been proven completely in the wrong. Where previously revolutionists had followed Kautsky in his reinterpretation of the law of accumulation, they now defended its literal interpretation. They were now certain that the capitalist class is becoming not merely relatively but absolutely smaller and the misery of the proletariat is not relatively but absolutely worse. The less firm among the literal interpreters of the law of accumulation tried to explain the period after 1870 as a temporary drift away from the main direction of the law but were now certain the drift was ended permanently. Hereafter events would occur in strict agreement with the predictions of Marx. But certain final consequences were now evident which meant that capitalism is ripe for socialism. The cyclical crisis of capitalism will no longer be national but international in geographic breadth and effect. Such international crisis can be overcome only in one of two ways—world war or world revolution. This proved also that capitalism had reached the highest stage of the centralization and concentration of world economy under international finance capital. The world stage, therefore, was now set for socialism. The essential historical task for revolutionists is the creation of a new international of revolutionary parties to make the world revolution and introduce world socialism.

If the war seemed to the revolutionists a vindication of Marx's law of accumulation of capital, the victory of the Bolsheviks in October 1917 seemed a further vindication of the same law but in terms of politics. Socialism in Russia had not come about peacefully. It had required two revolutions: First, a revolution of the Russian bourgeoisie against czarism and secondly, a revolution of the proletariat against the bourgeoisie. Only by seizing the government by force were the Bolsheviks successful in establishing for the second time in history "a dictatorship of the proletariat." The revolutionists not many months afterwards pointed out that their view of the necessity of revolution by force had been vindicated a second time in the case of the German Revolution of 1918. This revolution, they pointed out, could have been successful if the social democracy of Germany had had courage enough to seize power. But the social democracy failed to do exactly that and as a result the capitalist class retained possession of Germany.

The revolutionists also felt vindicated in their contention that modern democracy is a sham and purely the class instrument of capitalism. They thought the October Revolution had conclusively shown that socialist society cannot live or pretend to live in a democracy organized along bourgeois lines. The rights of free speech, free press, of peaceful meeting and the right of political parties to exist and to seek election to political power for a given number of years are bourgeois rights, which are inimical to the socialist society. Democratic capitalism can allow all kinds of political parties to exist including anti-capitalist parties, because their democracy is a sham. Power always remains firmly in the hands of the capitalist. But socialism cannot afford this kind of democracy and no socialist society would want to afford it. The people and socialism must be protected against their enemies. The true form, therefore, of democracy under socialism is the democratic dictatorship of a single party. Any socialist who would argue for the right to exist of any other party but the revolutionary party is an enemy and a traitor to socialism. He is secretly conniving to provide a wedge by which capitalism can return and reconquer what it has lost. It is a false argument to say that conflict can arise between the party of the proletariat and the proletariat:—The party and the proletariat are one and the same and no division between them in interest or in aim can possibly arise.

Why a socialist society which presumptively expresses the interests and has the support of the vast majority should be afraid of losing this support to parties not expressing the interests of the vast majority is and has remained an unsolved political mystery. This is all the more perplexing when one considers that capitalism, which expresses the interests of a minority of the populace and has wide differences of policy, allows anti-capitalist parties to exist.

Lastly the revolutionists felt that the October Revolution had vindicated their contention that the party of socialism must be a military machine trained and prepared for every kind of illegal and legal work from that of running a political campaign to the organization of a revolutionary uprising. They now contend that this conception of the political party must be realized on a world scale, for without a world political organization the proletariat could not accomplish the task which history had set for it and for which capitalism was now ripe: the revolutionary establishment of socialism.

VI

THE TOTALITARIAN CURRENT IN MARXISM AND TOTALITARIAN LIBERALISM

As one studies the disagreements which arose between the reformists and revolutionists from 1870 to the Bolshevik Revolution of 1917, one cannot help observing how easily the revolutionary strands were woven together into an ideology of socialist totalitarianism. Had the October Revolution been defeated shortly after the Bolsheviks took power, this totalitarian ideology might never have become a decisive force in the twentieth century or had the liberal socialist elements been successful in defeating the totalitarians the same result might have been accomplished. Unfortunately, the Bolsheviks defeated all oppositions and maintained themselves in power; and their success has helped considerably in strengthening totalitarian philosophies at the expense of the liberal everywhere. In saying this it is necessary to remember that the success of the dictatorship in Russia is not the only factor responsible for the spread of totalitarian ideas. There are others of even greater importance of whose long-term effects we shall have occasion to speak further along.

The period following the end of World War I is full of epoch-making events that enormously weakened the liberal trend in all areas of human activity and unbelievably strengthened the totalitarian principles defended by the leaders of the Bolshevik Revolution. One immediate consequence of the end of World War I was the widespread disillusionment with capitalist liberalism. The masses including most liberals had believed that the war was fought to make the world safe for democracy. Instead they found it had been maneuvered by militarists, diplomats and economic imperialists for their own selfish benefit. Even though the signing of the Versailles peace treaty brought into existence a large number of democracies, these democracies were looked upon by increasing numbers as snares and delusions intended to defraud the vast majority of their rights. Thus any liberal party which hoped to influence the masses had to include elements of socialism previously unconsidered or even rejected. But as old-style liberalism included more and more of socialist doctrine, so more and more did it become identified with labor. During this period the reformist current in labor which had formerly repudiated any connection with liberalism now joined forces with all the remnants of old-style liberalism. Reformists began to call themselves liberals and liberals began to call themselves reformists. This joining of left-ward moving liberalism, which had previously kept apart, with reformist socialism was accelerated by Bolshevik criticism. The Bolsheviks denounced the reformists as the supporters of capitalism in the ranks of labor, as pseudo-socialists and later as Fascists in socialist disguise; and the liberals as disguised reformists.

The union of liberalism and reformism indicated that striking changes had occurred in the attitudes of the middle classes. During Marx's time liberalism had been identified exclusively with the rising middle classes and its support came almost exclusively from them. In the period after Marx's death it came to be identified with the more progressive elements of industrial and commercial capital and with the lower middle classes who wanted to be protected from the rapacity of the upper middle classes. At this point liberalism was not yet joined to the reformist socialists and the reformist socialists still repudiated any connection with liberalism. This was true even though leading liberal thinkers like T. H. Greene, L. T. Hobhouse and Emil Faguet had begun to preach a type of liberalism which was reformist socialism. After the first world war disillusion with capitalism followed; and large numbers of the urban lower middle classes began voting for the reformist socialist parties and increasing numbers continued to flock to their banners.

Unfortunately the reformists were either unable or incapable of doing anything to solve their economic plight. Thus almost as rapidly as the middle classes gained faith in reformist socialism, they lost it. In the meantime, the intense barrage of criticism by the Bolsheviks against reformism and political democracy plus the failure of reformism to solve their economic difficulties disillusioned them with democracy. And so the middle classes very quickly concluded that capitalism was no good, reformist socialism was no good, and political democracy was no good. They might have turned to Bolshevism, if Bolshevism had not followed the policy of rule or ruin in the 20's and 30's until the triumph of Hitlerism in 1933.

A similar process took place among the workers. Long before World War I large numbers of workers became disillusioned with capitalism, but the war accelerated this disillusionment and they turned in enormous numbers to socialism, both reformist and Bolshevik, as the way out. The failure of reformist socialism to solve the postwar problems of World War I and the inability of Bolshevism to make the wonderful revolution it promised turned them away in increasing numbers from both reformism and Bolshevism. This recoil from Bolshevism in particular was strongest among the unemployed and unskilled workers who formed the mass base of the Bolshevik following in countries outside the Soviet Union.

The upper classes too were seriously affected by World War I. Large numbers of them lost faith in old-style capitalism and in the pre-war ways of doing things. They saw nothing useful to them in reformism and they feared Bolshevism.

Of course, these changes did not occur at the same rate among these classes. The rate of change was most rapid among the European countries particularly among those which were most seriously affected by the war. It was slower in those countries which were least affected. In some countries like the United States, there was little or no perceptibly important change in the social attitudes of classes, or there occurred a remarkable mixing or blending of all kinds of political ideologies as in the case of the New Deal. In the main Italy and Germany became the crucial centers of these rapid changes in ideologies among the various classes.

In a situation as precarious as this in which capitalism, reformist socialism and Bolshevism were found sadly lacking, a vacuum was created which needed to be filled in. The filler-in was Fascism. It spawned an ideology that was all things to all men. It was anti-capitalist, anti-democratic, anti-reformist and anti-Bolshevik. It promised security against capitalist crisis and mass unemployment. It promised an end to unending discussion, indecision, corruption and graft with which democracy was uniquely identified by all classes; and it promised a leadership which knew how to plan as well as to act. To the middle and upper classes it promised inviolability of property which meant protection against reformist socialism and Bolshevism; to the workers, jobs; and to the peasants, markets and good prices.

Fascism and Bolshevism look upon political power in much the same way. Mussolini and Hitler both declared that they learned much from the Bolsheviks. But Fascism differed, by and large, from Bolshevism in one important respect. It knew how to unite classes instead of dividing them. It knew where and when to use violence. The Bolsheviks knew how to use violence; but they did not learn the technique of uniting classes until after Hitler came into power. Then with wonderful success, Bolshevism became like Fascism all things to all people. During the period between 1934 and 1939 when World War II began, the Bolsheviks gathered about themselves through the Democratic Front more people from all classes in the Western world than they had been able to gather in the years between 1917 and 1934. But they ruined their chances of conquering the Western world by entering suddenly into a pact with Hitler that started World War II.

Despite Bolshevism's rule or ruin policy it continued to become more and more important in world affairs as a result of the continued existence of the U.S.S.R. From the very beginning the U.S.S.R. was the criterion, the touchstone of progress. Bolshevik propaganda was consciously directed in such a way that people would consciously or unconsciously judge each other in terms of the crude criterion for or against the Soviet Union. The great historic struggle between the democratic and totalitarian elements in Russia were given the kind of interpretation most suitable for employing this criterion. Few ever learned or tried to understand the true meaning of the anti-Lenin and later anti-Stalin oppositions which appeared at different times between the years 1918 and 1939. Everywhere Bolshevik propaganda lumped together these opposition elements with reactionary, semi-Fascist or Fascist attempts to overthrow by violence the most "progressive," most "democratic" society in the world. Tirelessly the Bolshevik leaders propagated the myth of Russian democracy and equality through their international network of organizations. Not knowing any better, people who considered themselves enlightened universally accepted this myth as true, even though facts were piling sky-high showing the rapid growth of stratified inequality between classes and the complete absence of any democracy in the Soviet Union, even the kind of *class* democracy which existed in England in the early eighteenth century or under Czarism in 1900.

The distinction of "for or against the Soviet Union" has become one of the prize weapons by which Bolshevism blackjacks and intimidates liberals everywhere. Because the liberal was more and more accepting the ideology of reformist socialism, anyone, therefore, who was called a liberal was called so because he favored in particular the cause of labor and in general democracy, equality, progress and peace. Many liberals joined reformist organizations, but a large number of them preferred to remain independent of any particular political party. These liberals on one hand prided themselves upon their independence and on the other upon their readiness to do whatever they could for the cause of labor. The most important segment among them is, of course, the intellectuals whose articulateness makes them particularly influential. It was upon these liberals that the Bolsheviks used most effectively their distinction between pro- and anti-Sovietism.

By 1930 so effective was the propagandistic work of Bolshevism that liberalism was now interpreted in terms of being either for or against the Soviet dictatorship. If any liberal was critical of the Soviets then he was immediately accused everywhere of being a crypto-Fascist—that is a Fascist who wore the disguise of liberalism. But if he approved of the Soviet Union then he was praised everywhere as a true liberal. Thus beginning with the late twenties, Bolshevism created a new type of "liberal" utterly unknown before World War I; one who is a contradiction in terms; who speaks in the name of liberty only in order to deny it; who calls the Soviet Union a democracy and a democracy a capitalist dictatorship. This "liberal" denies the very things for which his ancestral namesakes fought—free speech, multiple political parties, free press, free religion, etc. Under present circumstances, the best name by which to describe and clearly understand him is "totalitarian liberal." A totalitarian liberal is a supporter of Soviet communism, although he is not a member of any of the parties affiliated to the Soviet Union. Wearing the mask of liberalism, he defends the new totalitarianism of the twentieth century: totalitarian communism.

The usefulness of the totalitarian liberal to Bolshevism is not merely in terms of his articulateness, however useful that may be. His importance lies in that he helps to organize and administer all kinds of communist-front organizations which the communist party wants to employ for varying purposes and with which it tries to reach different strata of the population. The totalitarian liberal is the front behind which totalitarian communism works. Without him the totalitarian communist would never be able to reach so effectively large numbers of people who want nothing to do with totalitarian communism.

VII

TWILIGHT OF LIBERALISM

The twentieth century shows the transformation of liberalism from the status of an ideology of the rising middle class to that of an ideology *speaking not for a particular class but for the broad masses of mankind.* Two currents merged more or less completely into one during the 20's and 30's to form modern liberalism:—the current of political democracy which had been the battle cry of the philosophical radicals, the utilitarians and those who specifically called themselves liberals and the reformist socialist current in the labor movement which had its origins in Utopianism and Marxism and stood for a radical transformation of the capitalist order. Thus modern liberalism is the final logical culmination of the drive of our liberal and socialist ancestors for a world free of tyranny and exploitation. It is therefore a far cry from the liberalism and socialism of the nineteenth century.

Yet at its peak of abstract perfection, modern liberalism is being defeated by a new kind of totalitarianism, Soviet totalitarianism, which also has its origin in Marxism and also speaks in the name of equality, liberty and the exploited majority. Paradoxically even though it speaks in the name of the highest ideals, Soviet totalitarianism is introducing on a world scale a new kind of inequality between men and a new kind of absolute tyranny over man. Why, then, is modern liberalism being defeated?

The minor reasons ought to be mentioned first before turning to the major. One reason is that modern liberalism even though largely identified as a political movement with labor parties of various kinds and the labor movement in general, is rather amorphous both as movement and as doctrine. It is not only not completely consistent but its concrete program is not accepted by all liberals.

In principle, liberalism, as interpreted by contemporary expositors like John Dewey or Morris Raphael Cohen, involves both an attitude and a program. The attitude is one in which reason and scientific method are made the guides to social action. Thus it is an attitude undogmatic with reference to any solution which may be offered. It commends itself upon its open-mindedness. It allows for the possibility not only of error but of a variety of different solutions.

As a program it insists upon three basic principles: First, the social channels of communication should be kept always open and as wide and deep as possible so that people can be adequately informed on all issues. As an integral part of the same idea, it insists that the people should have the right to form political parties and elect those representatives who support programs of action with which they are in agreement. Moreover, it denies the right of any group, no matter how large, to suppress any other group which may be in disagreement. Secondly, it accepts the Marxian contention that the economic problems of society will be solved only when the major industries, which are today either monopolies or oligopolies, are owned and run by the state. It also agrees that all the economic resources of the world should be integrated and operated on a scale of world planning. Thirdly, it believes that this can be achieved by education and the orderly action of the enfranchised majority in those countries where political freedom exists in sufficient proportion to permit the process of popular education in economic realities to be completed. But apart from this rather abstract program, there is no agreement among liberals on how to achieve their ends. Thus, opposed by organized minorities with a concrete program, a military organization and an iron discipline, liberalism is helpless to act.

It is essential to observe that political parties today are divisible into two kinds: the old-style, which are relatively loose, allow for considerable difference of opinion, and accept the traditional conception of political democracy; the other, the totalitarian, which are tightly knit, organized on military lines, and completely opposed to political democracy in the traditional meaning of these words. Each of these types are again divisible into subordinate types: Among those who accept traditional political democracy are the capitalist parties and the reformist parties. The capitalist parties have no clearly formulated program concerning society; since they accept capitalism, they are primarily concerned with offering such policies as will win enough votes to get control of the gravy trains. The socialist or reformist parties have a program for the social transformation of society, but they want the right to make such changes through the reeducation and winning of the majority to their point of view. The totalitarian parties are either affiliates of the Soviet party or home-grown Fascist parties. The non-totalitarian liberal whether affiliated or not with the traditionally democratic parties, still does not as a whole sharply differentiate between the type of party to which he may belong and the totalitarian party. Many non-totalitarian liberals both in Europe and America, and particularly the American, think they can oppose totalitarian parties with the same methods they use against traditional democratic parties. They still do not seem to realize that totalitarian parties act on principles completely opposed to their own and against which their conceptions of below-the-belt opposition are helpless.

A second minor reason for the inability of liberalism to influence decisively the political life of modern times is that large numbers of liberals are afraid to join any political party. Liberals deeply prize their right to think and act without restrictions, that is, in essence, their right to disagree, but they are afraid with justification of having this liberty restricted by the demands of organizational loyalty. Since so many liberals are without any organizational affiliations they are easily put to flight or utilized for non-liberal purposes by any determined minority militaristically organized and disciplined. Their anxiety to help some worthy cause often results in making them allies of totalitarian front organizations.

A third minor reason is the open-mindedness of the liberal to ideas. His ability to act with firmness and decision is thereby retarded. He is much too ready to give the other fellow the benefit of his own uncertainty. The other fellow may be right after all. A last minor reason is the tendency of the liberal to remain on the level of general principles when what is needed are concrete plans or techniques of action.

These minor reasons, important though they are, are insignificant in comparison with certain larger factors affecting the world today. A major factor is the character of contemporary economic development. In analyzing capitalism, Marx made a profound observation which he never developed to its logical conclusion. He made the ironical observation that the individual capitalist who has established controlled planning in his own factory is opposed to its establishment for society as a whole. Derisive in making this observation, Marx did not reflect upon the character of the planning which existed in the factory of the individual capitalist. He did not observe that this planning is totalitarian, that the individual capitalist completely controls all living and material resources within his factory as completely as Stalin controls the material and living resources of the national Soviet factory. Marx himself did not envision that his planned society would assume a totalitarian character. Despite his recognition that capitalist development went in the direction of greater and greater concentration and centralization of capital, he did not recognize these as indicators of the possible nature of the kind of society which he was anxious for the proletariat to introduce.

Now Marx meant by concentration of capital: that capital is operated more and more on a mechanized basis, that more and more industries become interdependent and incapable of production without each other. The highest stage of concentration is reached at that point where all the economic resources of the world are as interdependent as the different units of a gasoline engine. The other side of this picture is described by the term "centralization," which means that the reins of control, largly due to the process of concentration and in part to other factors, come into the hands of a smaller and smaller number of individuals. The final culmination of this process is the control of the total economic machine by a tiny oligarchy of men topped by an infallible leader. To Marx this oligarchy was entirely the result of the capitalist process. If the proletariat should have their way they will remove this oligarchy and operate the economic system on a completely democratic basis in the manner of the phalansteries of Fourier. His hatred of utopian blueprints seems to have held him back from envisioning what a highly mechanized society, in which the process of concentration and centralization has reached its peak point, would really look like. Had he followed through, he would have foreseen the nature and structure of present day Soviet economy.

Elsewhere Marx remarks that in a mechanized and planned society there will necessarily have to exist for a long time to come a functional differentiation between brain and hand. This differentiation will also involve an important difference in the social status of each. The brain worker will necessarily dominate the hand worker. Now this functional differentiation is a consequence of mechanized mass production which requires a majority of workers reduced to robot-like attendants of machines, a minority of technicians who have mechanical skill and an even smaller minority of specialists who stand at the apex of this cone because they have the theoretical knowledge and specialized skill needed to run the economic system. Marx apparently did not see the connection between the increasing concentration and centralization of capital which leads to an oligarchy of leaders and this process of functional differentiation between brain worker and hand worker. He apparently did not see that the brain workers—the experts or specialists—would become the leaders of the new totalitarian socialist order.

This, then is a primary factor which seems to lead to the defeat of liberalism on a world scale:—The concentration and centralization of industries and the specialization of knowledge, both seem to involve totalitarian planning. There are good reasons why this type of planning connot permit the vast majority to express their will. First they are too ignorant to understand the complex problems of modern planning. Secondly, modern planning, since it involves complete interdependence of the parts of the economic order, precludes any action by a majority or minority opposed to the carrying out of the plan. Thirdly, equality between brain workers and hand workers is impossible since the hand worker is incapable of understanding what the brain worker is trying to do. Lastly, as long as the economy is incapable of producing all commodities in sufficient numbers to make them as free as air, there must be a differentiation of rewards according to skill and social function which means of course that the brain workers in control will distribute to themselves the maximum rewards.

If the picture drawn above of the general broad tendencies of economic development is correct, then modern liberalism finds itself in an intellectual impasse. The new economic order which seems to be evolving out of present economic conditions is incompatible with political liberty. This new order requires, or seems to require, a totalitarian political system in order to achieve its objectives. It is not necessarily true that those who are at the apex of the planned society desire a totalitarian system: it is simply that the economic needs of society cannot be satisfied without a highly centralized autocratic system. But political liberty is one of the central tenets of liberalism. How can it then favor political liberty on the one hand and some sort of economic system in which large-scale planning is an essential element?

The liberal has given little attention to this problem even from the point of view of how concretely it can be solved in an already operating planned economy like the U.S.S.R. Nor has the liberal taken seriously the problem of showing that the form of political organization which exists in the Soviet Union is not inevitable. He has usually attacked those who assert that a socialist economy involves totalitarianism or where he has been ashamed to use terms of moral condemnation he has glibly pointed out that totalitarianism is after all not logically necessary in a socialist society. However, he has failed to see that the issue is not one of pure logic, that is, whether socialism in the abstract logically implies totalitarianism in the abstract—but whether socialism as it manifests itself concretely in the working of its institutions involves totalitarianism for all practical purposes. To argue that socialism in the abstract does not involve totalitarianism in the abstract is like arguing that capitalism in the abstract does not involve exploitation or poverty or monopoly in the abstract. While liberals are generally inclined to repudiate the latter as a valid argument on the ground that it does not concern itself with the actual institutions of capitalism, they are not willing to apply the same logic to their own arguments for the existence of a free or democratic socialist society.

A second major factor responsible for the persistent defeats of modern liberalism is the extreme state of tension in which contemporary man lives. Everywhere about him he faces economic and social insecurity. This economic insecurity is of various kinds. One kind is that of not having enough income or of frequent loss of job, or the fear of unemployment or of sudden loss of economic status, as for example, in loss of fortune due to economic crisis, war or revolution. As part of this, often enough is the insecurity which derives from a status of social inferiority because of race or religion. The hatred of those who are in an inferior position is intensified by the absence of any economic security or hope of security. Where they do not face, in the ordinary sense, economic insecurity, they suffer either from social inferiority or from the general insecurity of a world subject to monstrous social crisis like war and revolution. This general insecurity reaches beyond the economic and social into the psychological and cultural. Men feel inwardly insecure because they no longer have faith in themselves and in society. They no longer accept the values which they were taught to value. Often enough they feel themselves without values of any kind.

When such are the conditions for enormous numbers of individuals in all classes, society lives in a state of panic. There is a hysterical search for some way of ending this unendurable state of psychological and social tension. People want violent action. They want to ally themselves with anything which will give them, even for the moment, the high feeling of psychological security. They do not want to reason. Reason is insecurity; it bares difficulties and perplexities. They want a faith in which they can believe fanatically. Thus they tend to join those political groups which offer them a faith with an immediate out from all their tensions. Against mass hysteria of this type, any rationalistic social philosophy is helpless; and modern liberalism, being highly rationalistic, is not equipped to meet the psychological problem of peoples in a state of extreme tension.

Another major factor is the stage of economic development to which the world has come. It was already obvious at the beginning of World War I that the world could work on a high level of economic efficiency only on a world scale. Nations as isolated economic units had outlived their economic usefulness. The high development of the world division of labor was symptomatic of the necessity for an economic order based on international principles of economic organization.

The period after World War I made this fact even more apparent by the appearance of opposing economic tendencies:—one which involved regression to a simpler and costlier economic stage: national economies; the other which involved the establishment of a world empire or a world federation of nations. Indications of the regressive were the breakdown of international trade; the tendency of more and more nations to become self-sufficient economically even though this cost their people dearly; the tendency of more and more nations to break away from the doctrines of free trade and to make unilateral economic agreements; and finally in the tendency, which reached a high stage of development in Germany and was a technique also employed by the Soviet Union, to involve other economies unilaterally in a creditor relationship to themselves. In the interim period between World Wars I and II, it was obvious to most economists that the world economy implicit in the expansion of capitalist forms of production to the rest of the world was breaking down. Countries were trying to attain economic security for themselves at the cost of other nations and to separate themselves economically from the rest of the world.

On the other hand, the very needs of modern machine production led those nations which were leaders in production and dependent upon other nations for essential raw materials and agricultural goods to tie these nations to themselves by whatever means—economic, political or military—were available. Since the end of World War II, or rather the cessation of hostilities between the Allies and the Axis powers, it has become even more obvious than before that economic isolationism or autarchy is impossible. The world can live today only under some form of international economy.

The necessity for establishing an order in which the national states are made subordinate to international economic needs is the cause for increasing tensions or antagonisms between the Soviet Power and the Western Powers. Whether the political leaders of the United States, England or France are aware of this or not, they are being forced to move in the direction of some form of international economic cooperation. This is illustrated in the move, largely unplanned, to organize as much of Europe as can be included into a single economic unit; in the tendency of the United States to seek some form of international implementation of free trade relations between itself and the rest of the world. It is also indicated by the compulsion of the Soviet Union, forced by the requirements of its planned economy, to extend its economic borders as far as it can without coming into open conflict with the Western Powers.

The world today, economically speaking, exists in a vacuum. If the Western powers are unable to fill it by establishing some form of world economic order, then it is extremely likely that the Soviet Union will do so. The European Western powers, however, are compelled to follow the United States whose leaders are dominated by Big Busines; and Big Business is hog-tied to an obsolete economic and political philosophy. It still feels it can act upon economic principles which are, in the main, no longer applicable to the present world. Thus it thinks in terms of ideas from which a successful plan for a world order can never be evolved —even if it could enlarge its vision sufficiently to think in terms of a world order. But it does not think in terms of a world order; it still thinks mainly in terms of continental United States. Modern Liberalism, therefore, even if it had a thoroughly worked out and practical plan for a democratic world order, would find Big Business a powerful opponent of any such plan. And not only Big Business; it would find provincial minded, isolationist lower-class America an even more powerful foe. The typical American —particularly he who has been overseas—wants to think American and nothing else.

On the other hand, even if liberalism were able to convince the American people of the value and practicability of its plan, it would still have to face an intransigeant enemy in Soviet totalitarianism. Soviet totalitarianism does not want a world order which is not completely controlled by itself. A world democratic order would mean only one thing: the end of Soviet totalitarianism.

Thus no matter where liberalism turns, it finds itself opposed by overpowering enemies. Its ideas are not acceptable to Big Business or the American People; and its ideas are equally unacceptable to the Soviet leaders. The prejudices perhaps of Big Business and the American people might be overcome by an intense educational campaign, but such a campaign could not overcome the opposition of Soviet leaders. Objective arguments can not convince them; they have different aims and objectives; and they know what they want. Perhaps then one might try an intense campaign of educating the Soviet people? Unfortunately, they can not be reached; they are permitted no other educators than their leaders.

The worst element in the situation is the insufficiency of time. There is not sufficient time to educate the people in those countries where freedom of speech still exists to the necessity of a world order. The urgent necessity of creating a world order of some kind and the irreconcilable differences between the Soviet Empire and the West are bringing closer and closer the time of the beginning of World War III. If such a war did not destroy the world, there might emerge at its conclusion some sort of world order. Unfortunately, this war will not be fought with ordinary weapons such as were mainly used in World Wars I and II. Such weapons, however destructive, do not involve the annihilation of modern civilization. Assuming the war were fought with ordinary weapons, such as were used prior to the invention of the atomic bomb, it might be reluctantly welcomed only because it might finish both Soviet totalitarianism and nineteenth century capitalism. One might look forward to a new age in which economic and political liberty might actually be achieved to an extent never known before. Unfortunately, the weapon which is now at the disposal or will be at the disposal of the warring parties is not an ordinary weapon. It is the basic energy of the universe and it is annihilatory; its employment means the end of civilized life on earth and the return of man in all probability to the kind of primitive life he lived thirty or forty thousand years ago.

Obviously modern liberalism sits on the horns of a dilemma invented in inferno. To oppose the coming conflict means to strengthen the grip of Soviet totalitarianism on the world and it means in all probability the ultimate triumph of Soviet totalitarianism as a world system—thus the enslavement of the majority of men to an hierarchy of despotic administrators. On the other hand, the struggle against the Soviet tyranny involves a world war in which the atomic bomb will be used to destroy modern civilization. The dilemma of liberalism is made all the more tragic by the fact that as the war comes nearer, atomic defense or offense will require the establishment in all countries of some kind of despotism. To prevent sabotage and the possible explosion of hundreds of atomic bombs by enemy agents, a system of internal espionage and restrictions upon traditional liberties of movement and expression will be necessary. All persons and private homes will be subject to search and seizure at any time. People will have to carry passports at all times and will be required to explain their presence in one place or another or their reasons for travelling.

A last major factor working to defeat modern liberalism is the international totalitarian communist movement with its base in the Soviet Union. In what respects does this totalitarian movement differ from all other totalitarianism previously known? The first thing to note is the base itself of this movement: the Soviet Union is a huge empire sprawling over the greater part of Europe and Asia. At its disposal are an enormous military organization and enormous economic resources which are rapidly being transformed from potentiality into actuality. The second thing to notice is that the Soviet Union stands upon a philosophy which makes no distinction between men as to race, religious creed or color although it does distinguish sharply between men according to their political creed and sometimes class origin. (The latter nowadays is relatively unimportant as long as those of alien class are willing to serve as tools of the Soviet leadership.) Again it promises economic security for all or to paraphrase a slogan of the Hoover era, "a chicken in every pot and a Moscovich in every garage."

In other words, it promises all the exploited masses of the world the two things which they want most: equality and economic security. Nearly three-quarters of the world's population is colored and nearly all of the colored peoples are exploited by the white man. The vast majority of them are also considered inferior to the white man in intelligence, general ability and culture. Even though the colored peoples are, in turn, subject to exploitation by members of their own races who consider them inferior to themselves, nevertheless there is a bond between colored exploiter and exploited in that both want to be free of the white man's burden. Sovietism promises them not only this freedom from the yoke of the white man but equality with him. Secondly, most members of the human race, whatever their color, live a life of wretched poverty subject to epidemics of starvation or disease, driven hither and yon by their war lords, conquerors or exploiters, knowing little of any outward security or peace. To them, the Soviet Union promises the kind of economic security which they hunger for but have never known. The promise of these two things, security and racial equality, alone makes Soviet totalitarianism a mighty power to be reckoned with in the affairs of the world.

Modern liberals who have lived their entire lives in an intellectual atmosphere and in countries with a long-established tradition of political freedom fail to realize how unimportant to the people of this world is political freedom. These people have never known freedom, they have lived all of their lives under some form of absolute dictatorship and they consider no state different from any other state except with respect to what it offers them economically. To the peasants of China, the pariahs of India or the fellahin of Arabia and Mesopotamia, it is more important not to be under the heels of the white man and to be sure of their rice or bread than to be offered the finest democratic constitution in the world. They have not culturally reached the point where the relation of political democracy to economic security and racial equality can be appreciated. It might be observed that even in the so-called civilized countries of England, France, Germany, Italy and the United States, great numbers, including the intelligentsia, are not yet awakened to the import and significance of political liberty for maintaining and establishing wider and wider equality among men. If this is true of civilized nations, what can one expect of peasants and primitive peoples living millenia under the yoke of absolute monarchs and human gods?

A third thing to notice is that Soviet totalitarianism is not a national phenomenon. It is the base of a world society and the instrument for creating it. To achieve this objective, the Soviet Union has helped and helps in the establishment and maintenance of political parties, trade unions, cultural institutions and a vast variety of front organizations in every foreign country to spread and popularize the idea of a Soviet world society. These foreign political parties whose membership numbers in the tens of millions are closely knit together and firmly controlled from Moscow. They operate with military precision, doing exactly as they are told without question. Their leaders are supported directly or indirectly by Moscow. Moreover their allegience is not entirely bought with money; many believe fanatically in the Soviet cause and are ready to die as martyrs. These Soviet organizations have not only a toehold but often a stranglehold on the important political, economic and cultural institutions of a country; they can and do exert enormous pressure direct and indirect in favor of Soviet interests. By shouting the battle cry "racial equality and economic security," in a million different forms, they can and often do win the allegiance of millions to whom existing society can offer nothing better.

A fifth thing to notice is that the communist leadership are highly trained and highly specialized in the arts of propaganda, agitation, trade union work, insurrection, conspiracy and sabotage. Before they are placed in any position of importance they are tried and tested over a considerable period of time. They are secretly schooled in the propaganda and agitation schools in Moscow. Thus they represent a trained personnel on a world scale for the establishment of world Soviet totalitarianism with only one parallel in history: the Roman Catholic Church.

The last thing to notice is that these men and the organizations they control have at their disposal the enormous resources of the Soviet Union as and when needed.

It is with this world-wide army of organizations, skilled, disciplined and united by a monolithic ideology that liberalism has to contend. Is it any wonder that liberalism, divided into so many factions, is invariably helpless before it?

The final picture which emerges from our analysis of the present situation of liberalism is hopelessly tragic. It is the struggle of Prometheus against the Totalitarian Gods. Liberalism offers the basic principles of a philosophy by which man can become conscious of himself and his needs and learn how to make maximum use of his capacity to think, to feel and to do. Yet it can not be made available to him; he has not time enough to become acquainted with it, let alone to live by it. The confluence of forces is overwhelming. There are the United States, most powerful of nations, dominated by Big Business with nineteenth century ideas and a people, unpolitical and provincial; a world of human beings who care nothing about liberty and everything about equality and economic security which are unobtainable without liberty; an economic technology which seems to involve a centralized hierarchy of administrators pedestalled upon a vast horde of state serfs; a totalitarian order, with its base in the Soviet Union, organized internationally for the conquest of the world; and finally an atomic war in the offing between totalitarian Soviet Union and the rest of the world. Were there sufficient time, these forces might not seem so overwhelming; each could be conquered in turn, and even the worst enemy of liberalism, Soviet totalitarianism, might suffer from an internal collapse, aided by liberal forces from the outside. But time is exactly the one thing lacking.

Nonetheless, liberalism must continue its struggle against stupidity, prejudice, ignorance and tyranny. And it must concentrate on finding the techniques by which a world can be made permanently free. These techniques may not be used for a long period of time; they may remain hidden in the ruins of libraries or covered with earth, and man may need to suffer through the new Dark Ages before he will again seek the lost light. But if he survives and seeks again like Renaissance men before him, to regain the arts and sciences of the Neo-atomic Age, then the ideals of liberalism and the techniques of social freedom should be ready for him, buried in the crypts of an ancient civilization. If there is nothing else that can be done, then this should be the final Promethean gift. *Amen!*

BIBLIOGRAPHY

BLIOKH, IVAN: *The War of the Future,* Eng., New York, 1899.

BONAR, JAMES: *Philosophy and Political Thought,* 3rd ed., London, 1931.

CARNEGIE, ANDREW: *The Gospel of Wealth,* New York, 1900.

HALEVY, ELI: *Growth of Philosophical Radicalism,* Eng., London, 1928.

HOBHOUSE, L. T.: *Liberalism,* London, 1911.

MILL, JOHN STUART: *Principle of Political Economy,* 1909.

MILL, JOHN STUART: *On Liberty,* 3rd ed., 1864.

MILL, JOHN STUART: *Considerations on Representative Government,* 1865.

RUGGIERO, GUIDO DE: *History of Liberalism,* Eng., London, 1927.

VII.
The Liberal Tradition in Russia:
A. Herzen and V. Soloviev

Editorial Note

The liberal Russian tradition is not very widely known among the general public nor among a good many political scientists. Despite the fact that Herzen was a nineteenth century writer, his influence extended deep into the twentieth century. With rare perceptive intelligence, Herzen predicted the dangers of totalitarianism in social change and in socialistic plans. Mr. Tartak devotes his chapter mainly to Herzen and Soloviev, and merely mentions other liberal thinkers.

The reader is also referred to Vladimir Zenzinov's chapter, "The Destinies of the Russian Peasantry."

F. G.

VII.

THE LIBERAL TRADITION IN RUSSIA: A. HERZEN AND V. SOLOVIEV

by

ELIAS L. TARTAK

THE ESSENTIALS OF the libertarian doctrine are so well known that a definition of the term is hardly required. It is a doctrine which, since the time of Herodotus and even before him, has been advancing, both in political practice and rational argument, the proposition that a *polis* of *isonomoi*, i.e., a state, with its citizens equal before the law, is both possible and desirable; and, hence, that the law itself could and should be the deliberate expression of the sense and will of the persuaded citizenry of the *polis*.

The term *isonomoi* implies much that, since the Greeks, has become familiar to us as the contents of the general liberal doctrine. It implies free discussion of political problems by the citizenry—hence, freedom of speech and opinion. It also implies "untramelled", uncoerced decisions by the citizenry on policies and laws—hence, the hostility of the libertarian to all entrenched and excessive power, both political and economic, and his opposition to special privileges, whether to monarchy by divine right, or to aristocracy and dictatorship. The *pathos* of the liberal's ideas seems to have originated in his historical experience with "oppressive" and "arbitrary" government, resulting in an intense fear of anything approaching slavery or tyranny.

On the positive and apologetical side of his doctrine, the liberal seems to be guided by his knowledge and interpretation of history. He notes the small self-governing Greek republics which have produced, under conditions of *isonomia* and political freedom, a pattern of life and a culture of singular splendor, variety and richness; he sees similar conditions and results, with modifications, in the Medieval and Renaissance city-republics (Florence); later, in Holland and England. The citizens of these small states were capable of successfully resisting the vast armies of Persian and Spanish despotic empires. From these, the liberal concludes that the very atmosphere of political freedom or *isonomia,* breeds a more self-reliant and versatile citizen, a richer culture, a "better" man.

The ideas and doctrines of liberalism came to Russia, for the greater part, from the West. They were, however, given a hospitable reception by the Russian minds; for, as will be shown later, there already existed a native tradition and a soil prepared to assimilate these visitors from the West.

The first important expressions of libertarian thought in Russia appeared in the second half of the eighteenth century. A national literature, in the modern sense of the term, began to emerge soon after Peter the Great. By the second half of the eighteenth century, this new literature had turned to portrayal and discussion of the national scene. Denis Fonvizin (1782) wrote *The Minor* a famous comedy satirizing the brutalizing effects of serfdom on the serf-owners.

More startling in context and consequences was *A Voyage from Petersburg to Moscow,* written and published by Radishtchev in 1790, a political work of primary importance. Under the thin disguise of travelling notes, observations and impressions, Radishtchev boldly exposed such contemporary evils as serfdom, savage Army discipline, and the corruption and venality of officialdom and the courts. He threatened the authorities and the nobility with a justified people's rebellion. He dared to portray the hatred of the peasantry for their oppressors, and wrote: "The peasant today is dead in law, but some day he will be very much alive."

Catherine II read Radishtchev's book and was horrified. She wrote about the author that "he is more dangerous than Mr. Franklin." Radishtchev was imprisoned and sentenced to death; the sentence was later changed to banishment to Siberia. Radishtchev's book was burned by the hangman, but it has since become one of the classics of Russian liberal thought, and its author one of its martyrs.

It is interesting to note at this point that in his youth Radishtchev studied in German universities and, therefore, was thoroughly familiar with contemporary German and French literature and philosophy. His teachers were Spinoza and Rousseau rather than Voltaire and other "encyclopedists." Thus, there is, on the one hand, the unmistakable influence of older Western thought on new Russian liberalism. However, early in Radishtchev's writings, there is also an indication of the native historical strain—the recollection of freer and more democratic institutions of ancient, pre-Muscovite Russia (tenth to fifteenth centuries). During that era, ancient Russia had powerful self-governing city-republics (Novgorod, Pskov), broad local self-government by town-meetings and elected magistrates, and princes whose power was limited by oath and by the pressure of local self-government. With the rise and expansion of the centralized Muscovite monarchy, these liberties and autonomies were gradually destroyed by the Czars and emperors, although not without a lengthy and stubborn struggle. This struggle was renewed in the seventeenth and eighteenth centuries by the semi-independent frontier republics; where, the Cossacks fought against the encroachment of central despotism upon their autonomies. The last great rebellion, part-Cossack and part-peasant, under the leadership of Pugachev, took place in 1773-75 when Radishtchev was already a young scholar with a liberal philosophy.

Thus, not only the memory, but the actual reality of battles for "ancient freedoms" survived well into the eighteenth century and found expression in a body of moving songs, historical, peasant, and Cossack. In taking up the cause of the defeated people, such writers as Radishtchev and his successors imported Western liberal ideas to the aid of a genuine native aspiration. Like Peter the Great who modernized the ancient Russian state, these writers were "westernizing" the people's struggle for their ancient liberties. The fusion of these two trends, native and Western, proved to be an arduous and complicated task. It was taken up by such nineteenth century successors of Radishtchev as the "Decembrists" and, later, by Bielinsky, Herzen, and Bakunin—the first Socialist writers; later still, Mikhailovsky, Plekhanov, and Soloviev took up the struggle.

Russian participation in the Napoleonic Wars gave a powerful impulsion to literature and political ideology. Many of the younger members of the intelligentsia fought in the campaigns, observed Western Europe, and were familiar with Western political thought. The result of those stirring events was not only the beginning of the Golden Age of Russian literature (Pushkin, etc.), but also the rise of the first Russian revolutionary movement, that of the "Decembrists." Their revolt came to a bloody end in December, 1825; some of its leaders were executed, the remainder were imprisoned or sentenced to exile. The revolt, however, left a deep imprint on the minds of the Russian people; neither did they forget the discussions of political and social problems of contemporary and future Russia expounded by such talented writers and Decembrist leaders as Pestel, Rylieyev, A. Bestuzhev, and others. Two trends in their writings are of interest: first, a cleavage began to form between the more liberal, decentralizing and federalist wing, represented by Rylieyev, and the more Jacobinist, centralizing group, represented by Pestel. Some of the Decembrists actually feared Pestel as a "future Robespierre." Secondly, the majority of the leaders agreed that the liberation of the peasants from serfdom should be accompanied by granting them land. The prospect of a vast, landless proletariat in Russia was abhorrent to them.

Thus, the problem of *economic justice*, together with the problem of political freedom, was firmly grasped by the Decembrists and incorporated in their ideology. The defeat of their movement, the execution, imprisonment, or exile of its members, prevented them from further elaboration upon their ideas. This was accomplished later by their spiritual heirs in the next generation: Herzen, Bakunin, and, to a lesser extent, Bielinsky, the critic; but, above all, by Herzen (1812-1870) of whom Tolstoy said, "He is both brilliant and profound."

If Herzen's predecessors applied Western ideas to the interpretation of Russian problems, Herzen may be considered to have presented the problem of Russia to the West. In a sense, he himself was the living incarnation of the problem: Russia *versus* the West, or Russia *with* the West. Herzen's father was a Russian nobleman, and his mother a poor German girl: Herzen was the illegitimate son of the wealthy I. Yakovlev who adopted the boy and gave him an excellent education. Having completed his studies at Moscow University, Herzen was about to become an astronomy instructor, when the young scholar's troubles with the police began. Herzen was suspected of being a radical and—even worse—a Socialist. He was several times arrested, banished to, and recalled from, various remote Russian towns.

At the age of 35, Herzen was a Hegelian and an established writer; he decided to leave his native country and spent the remaining twenty-five years of his life in France, Switzerland, and England, continuing his Socialist writings in political exile. He wrote in Russian, German, and French, and was equally at home in the fields of philosophy and politics, as well as being an accomplished novelist; as a publicist, he was justly called the "Voltaire of Russian literature." *The Past and Thoughts,* a book of his memoirs, is generally recognized as a masterpiece.

The central problem to which Herzen devoted much mature thought and writing was a twofold one: 1) Russia and Europe; and 2) the destiny of Socialism in Russia and in Europe. If we consider that Herzen applied himself to this problem almost a century ago (1848), he demonstrated unusual penetration in the very positing of it.

Herzen's versatility and range of intellectual pursuits were only part of the "larger man." His intellectual courage and deep feeling for the individual human being are highly significant to the reader and analyst. He frequently speaks of the individual in society and, at times uses the Russian word, *leetzo,* meaning both face and personality.

It has been said that Nicholas I brought the young astronomer down to earth. Herzen had displayed an early interest in history and in the writings of the early French Socialists. His experiences with censorship and banishments only served to strengthen those interests. Searching for a larger synthesis, in the late 1830's he turned to the study of philosophy and, by 1840, was a Hegelian. (His friends, Bakunin and Bielinsky, had been converted to Hegelianism a few years before). But this triumvirate of young writers did not remain "orthodox" Hegelians for long. Whatever may be the interpretation of Hegel's famous dictum, "Everything real is rational," it required special exegesis in the Russia of 1840. Herzen and his friends soon became "left Hegelians" and confirmed Socialists, thus paralleling the almost contemporary evolution of Marx and Engels. As Herzen tells us, they soon perceived that Hegel's dialectical philosophy of history (strife and evolution) could become "the algebra of the revolution," instead of merely a textbook of conservatism. Above all, it was necessary to remove the contradiction between "reality" and "the rational." "It is necessary to make reality rational." To Herzen and his colleagues, the "rational" meant the "rights of the personality," awakened and clamoring for such rights. "Thought" was to become "action," for "man is not only a thinking but"—above all—"an acting being."

Applied specifically to Russia, this meant the abolition of serfdom, the removal or overthrow of autocracy, the granting of land to the peasants, the freedom of women and the family from medieval laws, freedom of the press, freedom of thought, political freedom, and economic justice. No wonder, then, that both Bakunin and Herzen had to leave Russia; once abroad, Bakunin was destined to become one of the fathers of Anarchist theory, and Herzen—the founder of the Russian Socialist school. Author of *From The Other Shore,* and *Russia and the Old World,* Herzen also founded and edited "The Bell," the first Russian political periodical published abroad, and, hence, entirely free of censorship.

But how was Socialism and "the liberation of the person" to come to backward Russia? And how could the Western "rational" idea become a "reality" in Russia? To answer these questions, Herzen had to take up the problem of Russia and the West, as well as the general destiny of Socialism. In the subsequent development of his theories, his experience in and observations of political life in western Europe were of no less importance than his philosophical studies. He participated in the victories and the defeats of the revolution of 1848, was expelled from France, and, finally, went to England to live. There, together with Marx, he watched the triumphant monarchies stamp out both liberalism and Socialism on the European continent. Although deeply saddened, Herzen did not despair of the future of Socialism; to him, economic justice for "the person" was the problem of the nineteenth century, posited both by "thought" and "reality."

Herzen wrote: "The French Revolution and German science have opened a series of revolutions." Here, by this brief formula, Herzen meant (as he, himself, explained) both the effects of the advance of science in technology and production—as well as the stirring of minds under the impact of French and German thought of the eighteenth and nineteenth centuries. He meant, also, the series of revolutions from the Reformation to the nineteenth century: Dutch, English, American, and French. Capitalism and parliamentary institutions were no longer sufficient. Under capitalism, "human beings are discontented with the economic conditions of labor, with the slavish drudgery of work, but they *do not want:* (a) to be removed to labor-barracks; (b) to be driven to servitude-tasks by a government; (c) to relinquish their right to possess property." *(Letters to a Traveler).*

Here we note how early Herzen became critical of both capitalism and "phalansterian" and "statist" Socialism. The problem of "the rights of the person" was always a preeminent concern to him.

But, if the above is accepted, Western Europe, industrialized and literate, should be the country of "future" Socialism. After the defeats of 1848, Herzen began having doubts, and turned his attention more and more to the young and rising countries, Russia and America (U. S.) He may have been influenced here by de Tocqueville, but in his Russian theories he was certainly influenced by the tradition of "ancient liberties" of Russia, referred to previously.

Thus, Herzen had a larger political and cultural vision of "Western" civilization—a vision which included the rising role of Russia and America and the originality of their potential contribution. He speaks of America with caution due, no doubt, to his lack of data concerning that country; he spoke with assurance, however, of the advent of the Russian revolution. He foresaw that it would not be a mere political, bourgeois parliamentary revolution, but would be a Socialist revolution. "Russia," he wrote, "will not be satisfied with a mere parliamentary-political revolution." A note of apprehension may be detected in Herzen's forecast that "perhaps we demand too much and shall achieve nothing." But, he continued, "Russia will not be protestant; Russia will not be a country of *juste-mileu* (the golden mean)." Startling as these "prophecies" were when Herzen first wrote them (around 1850), he did not consider them to be "insights" or political crystal gazing, but prognostications based upon thought and study; they were drawn from his interpretation of Russian history and from the potentialities of certain surviving institutions, such as the *mir* and the *artel*, themselves remnants (*although* frequently distorted) of "ancient freedoms." The *mir* was the peasant self-governing commune with a joint communal ownership of land which was periodically realloted among its members. The *artel* was a type of workers' cooperative organization, popular with the peasants. Given such factors as the generally violent character of Russian history, the severity of the state, and the *mir*, Herzen felt justified in his forecast.

Herzen summarized the problem of Russia's future in one concise formula: "To preserve the commune and to give freedom to the person is the future problem of Russia;" i.e., the coordination of Socialism with individual rights and political freedom. And, even today, is this not still the unsolved problem not only of Russia, but of the entire modern world?

It should be understood that Herzen never entertained the idea of a "Russian mission" or of a "chosen people." He utterly rejected such ideas and, scoffed at the Slavophiles for their acceptance of the "chosen people" concept. Herzen possessed a mind of singular range, intuition, and ironic sobriety; he maintained few illusions, if any at all. Weighing each probability, he accepted the most likely one for the proper generation either to use or abuse. Nor did he underestimate the residual importance of Western Europe. Like de Tocqueville, however, he considered the thinkers and publicists of Western Europe somewhat too self-centered and provincial; hence, they should be reminded of Russian and American potentialities. Although Herzen dealt, primarily, with Russia, he still firmly held to the vision of a larger, unified and varied Western civilization. He may be considered a libertarian universalist.

It was in the 1850's that Herzen began to formulate his views concerning the probable nature of the Russian revolution. As he saw it, Western Socialist ideas, entering Russia and merging there with an old tradition of primitive Socialism in the villages, would further serve to give this revolution of the future a definite Socialistic character. Thus, he linked the Russian revolutionary movement with Western Socialism to form a synthesis of Russia and Europe. Here, however, he was confronted—both in theory and in propagandist practice—with the next problem: what type of Socialism would it be, and by what methods could it best be achieved? (Here he was dealing with another modern problem, that of *ends* and *means* of Socialism). His advice and warnings upon this point are singularly far-sighted, since they anticipated the arguments of G. Plekhanov, Rosa Luxemburg, and Jaurès—as well as contemporary conflicts—by almost fifty years.

Herzen's views upon the relationship between political freedom and Socialism are no doubt clear to the reader, at this point. If parliamentary-political democracy without economic justice for the individual was insufficient, Socialism without "liberty of the person" was even less satisfactory; it might bring, in its wake, "labor-barracks" and "tasks of servitude" imposed by the state. To Herzen, the libertarian and personalist, there could be no compromise with the despotism of the State.

Freedom and Socialism were not for the state, "class," or party, but for the "person." "The freedom of the person is the greatest thing. Only out of this freedom can there grow the true liberty of the people." He also speaks of "the person with his incurably human dignity." Hence all forms of Jacobinism, "statism," and dictatorship found a resolute opponent in Herzen. He would not just change masters. His dislike of Robespierre was almost personal.

After 1860, both the Russian radical movement and the Western Socialist movement expanded, although on different scales. The more impatient and aggressive elements in Russia pressed for an immediate social revolution, "abolition of the state," and, generally, for Bakunin's "irresistible conflagration." They called for a permanent peasant revolution. Some of these groups, like that of Nechayev, were dictatorial and terroristic even within their own organizations. Eventually, a definite Jacobinist wing (part Bakunist, part Blanquist) developed, inspired by the capable Tkachev. It was to be expected that such groups would view Herzen and his followers in Russia (Lavrov) as timid liberals and mere "gradualists" in Socialism; but even the followers of the more influential and erudite Chernyshevsky found Herzen too moderate for their tastes.

Herzen was temperamentally and philosophically opposed to all "root and branch" upheavals or a "permanent revolution." Above all, he rejected dictatorial and Jacobinistic theories and practices. He did not overestimate the immediate importance and strength of the "extremists" and "nihilists" in either Russia or the West; but, with amazing prescience and penetration, he foresaw and even traced the future lines of battle between the libertarian and dictatorialist camps. Herzen took a firm stand against "permanent revolution" and conspiratorial Jacobinism (one-party dictatorship) in *Letters To a Traveler*, published in 1865, and in his literary testament, *Letters To an Old Comrade*, written in 1869, but published posthumously (1872).

It is sufficient here to outline Herzen's essential theses. For him, as before: "There are only two important problems: the social and the Russian problem." But the apostle of "the free person" is opposed to professional revolutionarism, revolution for revolution's sake. He declared that revolution may be a painful necessity, but it is "the least desirable form of progress." In this light, a one-group revolutionary dictatorship appears even less desirable—in fact, an unmitigated evil. The aim of Socialism is to achieve "a world of freedom in reason" (rational freedom). Our society cannot be converted into "a Sparta or a Benedictine monastery" or "Araktcheyev's[1] military-economic Utopias." "Where," he continues, "shall we find so many executioners and informers?" Here, for once, Herzen appears to have been overly-optimistic. But his thought is summarized in a formula, remarkable for both its precision and depth: "By the methods of Peter the Great, a social revolution will go not further than *galley slave equality* and communist servitude in the style of Babeuf and Cabet."

[1] Araktcheyev, reactionary Russian general, famous for his cruel "military settlements."

Herzen might be considered the Pushkin of Russian political and libertarian thought. He founded the "Russian Socialist School," the Populists. All later Russian liberals and Socialists with democratic leanings were indebted to him; the Populists were directly obligated to Herzen, while the Social-Democrats, whose main inspiration, of course, was derived from Marx, were indebted only in part—and, at times, through their very effort to "overcome" him! Plekhanov, the father of Russian Marxism, wrote several scholarly and highly appreciative articles on Herzen's work.

Such Populists as Chernyshevsky (1828 - 1889), Lavrov (1823-1900), and Mikhailovsky (1842-1904), may be considered direct disciples of Herzen. Each, however, made further original contributions: Lavrov, to the study of general problems of Socialism; Chernyshevsky, to economic and aesthetic theory; and Mikhailovsky, to sociological theory and literary criticism. Today, Victor Chernov is an outstanding, vigorous representative of the Herzen school of thought.

This article would be incomplete without brief mention, at least, of the other school of Russian libertarian thought represented by the gifted philosopher and poet, Vladimir Soloviev (1853-1900). Herzen was one of the foremost Russian positivists and realists; Soloviev was a Christian mystic and, at the start of his career, a political Slavophile. As a Christian philosopher, however, he aspired towards a free reunion of the Catholic, Protestant, and Eastern-Orthodox (Russian) churches. This soon alienated him from the Slavophiles, to whom church orthodoxy included hostility to Catholicism.

The rift grew wider. To Soloviev, religious tolerance and freedom were the very foundations of enlightened Christianity. The last quarter of the nineteenth century, however, witnessed the ascendancy of Pobédonostsev ("Procurator of the Holy Synod"), who developed a veritable theory and pratice of reaction. His policies included persecution of the Russian "sectarians," repressive measures against the Catholics (Poles),—and anti-Jewish discrimination,— all this, of course, in the name of religion and nationalism ("Russia for the Russians"). Soloviev was aroused to frank and bold denunciation which, since he expressed himself in a courteous tone and conducted his argument on the highest level of Christian ethics, was particularly irksome to the government and to the nationalist Slavophiles. It was unpleasant for them to be called "Christians in speech and heathens in behavior and deed," since their critic was a fellow-Christian and a faithful son of the Russian church.

Soloviev finally concluded that nationalism, whether German, Russian, or any other, exemplified self-glorification, smugness, and imperialism; and was, therefore, "heathen." His book, *The National Problem,* appeared in 1888; its thorough analysis and condemnation of nationalism and Slavophile theories caused a sensation.

Soloviev was not a Utopian internationalist. He fully recognized the importance and value of the nation and the state, but he foresaw the dangers of militant nationalism, as well: "I am a patriot, but not a nationalist," he declared. He considered patriotism as devotion to one's nation and country, and respect for it; hence, respect was due other nations as participators in the universal, "ecumenical truth." In the evolution of nationalism, Soloviev discerned a sort of idolatry in its ultimate stage: "the worship of one's nation combined with a negation of the universal truth"—hence, oppression of national minorities and imperialistic wars which inevitably lead to a catastrophe for the nationalist's "chosen" nation. He pleaded for the utmost national and religious tolerance in multi-national and multi-religious Russia. "The task of our fathers was the liberation of the peasants from serfdom; our task is to prepare for the spiritual liberation of Russia."

Soloviev regarded the humiliating laws against the Jews as even more humiliating to men like himself, Christian human beings. He studied Hebrew and the Talmud, and wrote a series of profound and sympathetic essays upon Jewish religious thought.

Soloviev's writings made him the intellectual leader of what might be termed the "Libertarian-Christian School" of Russia. Here we have a libertarian philosophy arising from the Christian and - by protest and negation - from the Slavophile tradition of Russia. Different as Soloviev's point of departure had been from Herzen's positivist and realist philosophy, their political theories soon converged. Ultimately, they arrived at the same libertarian conclusion. Speaking different philosophical languages, the two schools arrive at an affirmation of the same truth: the right of man to be a member of "isonomoi," a free man in a free society.

BIBLIOGRAPHY

HERZEN, A., *Past and Thoughts* (Eng. transl.); *Polnoye Sobraniye Sochineniy* (Complete Works, in Russian; 21 vols.).

LABRY, RAOUL, *A. I. Herzen* (in French), Paris, 1928.

CARR, *Romantic Exiles* (factual biography of Herzen).

PLEKHANOV, G. V., *N. Tschernyschewsky* (in German), Stuttgart, 1894.

SOLOVIEV, VLADIMIR, *The Meaning of Love*, New York, 1948.

SOLOVIEV, VLADIMIR, *Lectures on God-Manhood*, with an Introduction by Peter P. Zouboff, New York, 1947.

SOLOVIFV, VLADIMIR, *War and Christianity*, New York, 1915.

VIII.

The Evolution of Anarchism and Syndicalism: A Critical View

ANARCHISM AND ANARCHO-SYNDICALISM

Editorial Note

The following chapters dealing with Anarchism and Anarcho-Syndicalism discuss the problem from two different angles. Mr. Max Nomad, author of "Rebels and Renegades" and "Apostles of the Revolution," critically analyzes the impact of anarchist ideology upon reality; Mr. Rudolf Rocker, in his chapter, presents the elements of anarchist and anarcho-syndicalist philosophy. Max Nomad, to use the terminology of William James, attempts to find the "cash value" of anarchist ideas, and how they functioned in practical politics. Rudolf Rocker unfolds the vision of anarchist philosophy.

Mr. Rocker, prominent in Europe as a libertarian socialist philosopher, belongs to the few survivors who exchanged views with Kropotkin. Bertrand Russell described Rocker's book, "Nationalism and Culture," as a "penetrating analysis . . . and a brilliant criticism of state worship, the prevailing and most noxious superstition of our time."

F. G.

VIII.

THE EVOLUTION OF ANARCHISM AND SYNDICALISM: A CRITICAL VIEW

by
MAX NOMAD

IT IS A truism that in all political movements a distinction must be made between what their participants profess and believe, on the one hand, and what subconsciously they are actually striving for, on the other.

This distinction is rendered somewhat complicated with regard to anarchism. For there are various schools of anarchism differing from each other on many essential points. Some of them accept the principle of private property, (the "mutualist" and the "individualist" anarchists), while others reject it. Among the latter there are those who believe in renumeration according to performance (the "collectivist" anarchists), and those who advocate the right of unrestricted enjoyment of all good things without compulsion to work (the "communist" anarchists). The latter believe in the essential goodness of man, while their "collectivist" predecessors took a more realistic view. And there are also differences of opinion as to the methods to be used for the attainment of the goal: the believers in peaceful persuasion were opposed by the advocates of violent revolution; and even among the latter there were those who, like the followers of Bakunin, believed in methods of conspiracy, and those who saw, or see, in the revolution a spontaneous process. And last but not least, there were and are those who believe in the class struggle, and those who reject it.

They all agree on one point only: the negation of the state, i.e., the rejection of all forms of government. But even on this point there is no uniformity in the concepts of the various anarchist thinkers. Proudhon's "anarchist" rejection of the state was at bottom merely an advocacy of a "federalist", or decentralized form of state administration; his concept of an "anarchist" France did not go beyond the idea of breaking up his country into twelve small administrative entities. Bakunin's "collectivist anarchism" was compatible with the idea of a revolutionary dictatorship by his own group, which apparently was to constitute the first phase of his classless and stateless ideal. On the other hand, there is no such dictatorial or governmental transition period in the "communist-anarchist" concept of Kropotkin. The realization of his ideal consequently recedes into the mists of a distant future. In a still later variant of anarchism, known as anarcho-syndicalism, the various local and regional federations of trade unions are to assume the tasks entrusted to the state under the systems of democratic collectivism.

At the time of their vogue each of these variants of anarchism represented the current interests or aspirations of certain social groups. Proudhon's "mutualist anarchism", with its panacea of a "People's Bank" granting free credit to all in need of it, championed the cause of the small producers and skilled workers anxious to attain economic independence at a period when modern large scale industrialism was still in its infant stage. His "anarchism" or "anti-statism" was at bottom only an Utopian or paradoxical formulation of the small producer's hostility to a voracious, ubiquitous and all-powerful bureaucracy swallowing up a substantial part of the national income. It was also in line with Proudhon's championship of this social group that he was opposed to labor unions and to the class struggle. For these had no meaning to a group of aspiring independent producers. With the growth of large-scale industrialism which demonstrated the futility of the skilled workers' hopes for economic independence, the followers of Proudhon gradually turned either to Bakuninism, or to Marxism or to plain trade-unionism. (The individualist anarchism of Max Stirner, the fame of his *Ego and His Own,* notwithstanding, never gave rise to a movement properly speaking. His complete rejection of all ethical obligations, coupled with a few sympathetic remarks about the underdogs' violent resistance to their masters, occasionally served as a theoretical justification to stray groups of marauders who had chosen a life of outlaw parasitism and banditism.)

Bakunin—A Precursor of Lenin

It was different with the anarchism of Bakunin. His collectivism—at that time the panacea of nearly all radical schools—coupled with the conspiratorial and insurrectionist tactics of Blanqui and invigorated and embellished by the class struggle concept of Marx and the "anti-statist" verbiage of Proudhon, expressed the aspirations of a stratum then very numerous in all economically and politically backward countries. These were the declassed professionals, intellectuals and semi-intellectuals, the then proverbial lawyers without clients, physicians without patients, newspapermen without jobs and college students without a future. At that time these elements were anxious for an immediate revolution leading to the seizure of all power by their own respective group. Unconsciously, their profession of anarchism served both as a blind for concealing their ambitions and for outdoing in revolutionary radicalism their competitors on the Left: the Blanquists whose open championship of a revolutionary dictatorship had discredited them, as mere office-seekers, in the eyes of many radical workers, and the Marxists whose "proletarian" radicalism was drifting towards parliamentary and trade-unionist gradualism, particularly in the economically more advanced countries.

Bakuninism which, for almost a decade, from the late sixties to the late seventies of the past century, was attracting the same elements which Leninist communism attracts at present, eventually receded. Its decline was due to the economic upswing which during the last two decades of the past century gradually began to bring industrialism even to the backward countries. It is as a result of this upswing that those educated malcontents, who usually assume the leadership of the labor movement, eventually deserted Bakunin's insurrectionary anarchism for the gradualist socialism of Marx whose revolutionary professions had in time become a mere lip-service. It is only in Spain that anarchism (though not in its undiluted original Bakuninist version) has retained its hold upon a large section of the labor movement. This is due largely to the fact that in that country the followers of Bakunin had laid the foundations of the labor movement, thus securing for the anarchists a lasting reputation as champions of the workers' cause. It may be added that the anarchists of that country, whether they were conscious of it or not, to a certain extent represented the extreme left wing of the democratic-liberal opposition to clerical semi-absolutism.

Bakuninism, for all its anarchist verbiage, had been at bottom merely a sort of ultra-leftist variant of Marxism. (It must not be forgotten that Marx, too, accepted the idea of a stateless society, i.e. of anarchism, in a higher phase of socialism). A well-known Bolshevik historian, Y. Steklov, in a monumental four-volume biography of Bakunin, written during the early period of the Soviet regime, established beyond any doubt, on the basis of Bakunin's less known writings, particularly his correspondence, that the founder of revolutionary anarchism was in reality a forerunner of Lenin, and that his concept of revolutionary activity and post-revolutionary reconstruction really did not differ much from those of the Communist International and of the Soviet system, as established immediately after the November Revolution of 1917.

Communist Anarchism

The failure of Bakuninism to give rise to a successful revolutionary mass movement resulted in the conversion of many of its followers into a sect of millennial, if sometimes violent, dreamers.

The outstanding theorist of this school, Peter Kropotkin, postulated the pure ideal of "communist anarchism" based on the principle of "to each according to his needs", as against Bakunin's collectivist anarchism based on the idea of "to each according to his works." For a certain period the outstanding feature of the Kropotkin school was its advocacy of terrorist acts of protest ("propaganda by the deed") which were intended to arouse the masses against existing injustices. Some outstanding representatives of this movement, such as the Italian Errico Malatesta, visualized the role of the anarchists in the revolutionary process as that of a sort of extreme-left wing of the anti-capitalist army, helping the Socialists in the task of overthrowing the capitalist system and, once democratic socialism was established, engaging in the task of winning over the majority by means of propaganda and experimentation. This was a recognition of the impossibility of establishing the anarchist ideal by the methods of revolution. The anarchists of that period can therefore be characterized as a group of intransigeant "nay-sayers" among the intellectual and self-educated manual workers who were dissatisfied with the slow progress of the anti-capitalist struggle and wanted to hasten the coming clash between democratic socialism and capitalism. They did not foresee that the violent clash they hoped for would lead to the victory of a totalitarian form of collectivism which would give the anarchists no chance to win over the majority through "propaganda and experimentation".

Anarcho-Syndicalism and Revolutionary Syndicalism, Pure and Simple

The futility of their propaganda, by "deed" and otherwise, caused many followers of the Kropotkin school of anarchism to revert to some of the concepts of Bakuninism and to seek a closer contact with the labor movement. The result was the emergence of what is known as "anarcho-syndicalism" with its emphasis upon such methods of the class struggle as direct action, sabotage and the general strike, and its substitution of the trade union to the "free group" as the basis of a free, state-less society. The class basis of this new departure was the antagonism of many French trade union militants to the influence exerted by socialist politicians over the labor movement. During a certain period the undeveloped rudimentary state of the French trade unions, coupled with the discredit into which socialist political leadership had fallen among many workers, enabled the anarcho-syndicalists and the syndicalists without the anarchist prefix, to achieve ascendancy over the French trade unions and to inspire the emergence of similar movements in other countries as well. However, the very growth of the French trade union movement in which the anarcho-syndicalists held the upper hand, spelled the eventual decline of anarcho-syndicalism. For that growth brought in its wake the formation of a self-satisfied trade union bureaucracy which eventually went the way of all trade-unionist flesh. The anarcho-syndicalist revolutionists became gradually trade-union bureaucrats, dabbling at the same time in politics, either of the gradualist socialist or of the radical "communist" brand. The French General Confederation of Labor (CGT), once the stronghold of anarcho-syndicalism, was until 1947 entirely under the control of the Communist Party. In those countries in which syndicalism was a minority group within the trade union movement, the revolutionary slogans and promises of Bolshevism easily won over many of the more temperamental anarchist and anarcho-syndicalist elements, both among the leaders and the following.

In this connection it may be also mentioned that the theory of revolutionary syndicalism, pure and simple, of those syndicalists who prefer not to attach the label of anarchism to their syndicalism, though otherwise they differed very little from the anarcho-syndicalists, has undergone a certain modification since the Bolshevik revolution. Previously they completely ignored the question of power, assigning in their concept, to the local and regional trade union federations, the function of production and distribution. After 1917 they coined the slogan of "(Political)

Power to the Trade Union" *(Au syndicat le pouvoir.)*[1] Which implies the acceptance of state power—rejected by the original syndicalist theory—provided that power is wielded by syndicalist trade-union leaders, and not by Communist politicians.

The Sorel Interlude

The vogue enjoyed for a long time by Georges Sorel's *Reflections on Violence* has had the effect that, to the uninitiated, the idea of syndicalism has become inextricably connected with his name. As a result many of his personal inconsistencies and theoretical vagaries have often been erroneously attributed to the movement of which he had become the self-appointed philosophical champion.

Now, in justice to Sorel it must be said that he himself never claimed to be the originator of revolutionary syndicalism. He frankly admitted his indebtedness to Fernand Pelloutier, an erstwhile Marxist who later became an anarchist, and who, still later, formulated the basic concept of revolutionary syndicalism. A concept which can be condensed in two simple propositions: 1. The general strike is the method of the working class uprising that will overthrow the capitalist system. 2. The labor union (in French, *syndicat*) with its local and national federations, is the basis for building up a cooperative, non-exploitative commonwealth.

Sorel himself made no essential contributions to syndicalist theory. The "violence" which he glorified, was at bottom merely a sensational synonym for the "direct action" advocated and practiced during a certain period by the French syndicalist militants who ignored Sorel and his writings. And as for the general strike to which Sorel devoted so many pages, that idea had been in vogue in the French labor movement since the early nineties of the

[1] The anarcho-syndicalists too changed their attitude towards government power. During the period following World War I, the French anarcho-syndicalists in their organ, *Le Combat Syndicaliste,* carried on the front page the motto *Toute l'Economie aux Syndicats! Toute Administration Sociale aux Communes!* (All economic activity to the trade unions! All social administration to the municipalities) which actually implies the acceptance of a decentralized form of state administration.

past century. And it is one of those curious twists of history that one of its first and most glamorous propagandists at that time was a man who in time was to become the embodiment of that democratic opportunism which Sorel so hated: it was a rising young socialist politician by the name of Aristide Briand who had borrowed the idea from Pelloutier, used it as a stepping stone in his career, and eventually, as Prime Minister, crushed the first general strike attempted by the French labor unions.

However, both concepts—that of violence and that of the general strike—assume under Sorel's pen a significance which they did not have in the minds of the militants and of the rank and file of the syndicalist movement. Sorel was at bottom a moralist. He saw in working class violence a means of disturbing the "social peace" which in his opinion was a corrupting influence both upon the workers and their capitalist masters; an influence which was bound to lead the world to decadence and barbarism. Application of violence would, in his view, reduce and discredit the influence of the parliamentary socialists who were trying to reconcile the working masses with the existing social order. It would also arouse the enthusiasm of the masses and thus lift the individual worker above the level of a purely animal existence. It would bring the element of beauty and heroism into his life. And, last but not least, it would serve as a healthy stimulus for the bourgeoisie. Under the impact of proletarian violence the employers themselves would become "class-conscious", they would abandon philanthropy and resort to an aggressive attitude both in repelling the attacks of the workers and in attempting to do their utmost in developing their own productive and organizational potentialities. The purely economic, or bread-and-butter, aspect of direct-action violence, aiming at immediate results in terms of wages and hours, was in the eyes of Sorel not particularly important. Moral uplift of both workers and employers thus becomes the chief purpose of revolutionary violence as Sorel sees it.

The general strike became the victim of a similar distortion under the pen of the revolutionary moralist. To him the *grève gén-*

érale is not the hoped-for reality of the future, envisioned by the dissatisfied workers eager for security, a fuller dinner-pail, shorter hours and more liberty. It is merely a social "myth" whose function it is to inspire the workers in their struggles. This concept was in keeping with Sorel's pessimistic disbelief in what is called the final emancipation of the working class, and with his approval of violence for the sake of moral uplift, so to speak. Critics were not slow in pointing out that nothing short of religious fanaticism could induce the masses to risk life or limb if no prospects of immediate benefits were beckoning to them.[2] Sorel was, no doubt, cognizant of this fact; and it was out of this realization that he advocated the "myth" of the general strike as a substitute for traditional religious fervor which no longer animated the modern industrial worker of France. Sorel's critics have very pertinently pointed out the fact that once the general strike was openly declared to be a "myth", the myth itself would lose all its religious, stimulating force; for mass enthusiasm could be aroused only by actual faith in the possibility of achieving their salvation by a practical method.

Sorel's later pro-medievalist and finally pro-Bolshevist enthusiasms can be explained by the basic psychological attitude on which his original pro-syndicalist position was based. It was his disgust with the corruption of bourgeois political democracy or democratic politics of France—as manifested in the orgy of profiteering indulged in by the victorious liberal "Dreyfusards"—which had turned his sympathies from democratic socialism to the revolutionary "a-political" labor movement, as expressed by syndicalism. In that movement Sorel saw a force openly at war with bourgeois democracy. In due time, however, he discovered that this movement was not measuring up to his expectations. The labor union militants were not exactly like the romantic heroes who, he felt, should be worthy of the name of a

[2] Race riots—also one of the forms of "proletarian violence"—have always an unavowed, subconscious economic motive, directed as they are against those who, rightly or wrongly, are hated as exploiters or job competitors.

"proletarian elite". They were thinking in terms of material results; and they also believed in birth control and sex freedom. All these things were abominations to Sorel who, to quote a friendly Catholic critic, the Jesuit Father Victor Sartre, was "a tormented moralist, a non-believer in search of God". Yes, a moralist in the most vulgar sense of the word; for he could actually write that "there will be no justice until the world becomes more chaste" (in Sorel's volume entitled *Matériaux d'une Théorie du Prolétariat, p.* 199).

As a result, Sorel turned to another group of men who, he felt, were fighting with real fervor against the corruption and the decadence of the bourgeois democratic republic. These men happened to be the pro-monarchist nationalists of the *Action Française* movement, who were the closest approach to what a decade later was to appear as Fascism.[3]

But they too failed to come up to his expectations, for they proved quite ineffectual in eliminating the corrupt politicians of the bourgeois republic. So in the end, a few years before his death, he turned to Lenin, though in the past he had nothing but scorn for those French revolutionists—they were called Blanquists during the Second Empire—who, in the name of socialism, advocated dictatorial rule by their party. For in Bolshevism he saw, at last, a force heroically and successfully opposing bourgeois democracy, and he gave vent to his new enthusiasm in his since famous "Plea for Lenin," a chapter added to a later edition of his *Reflections on Violence.*

Paradoxical as it may seem, Sorel's adherence to Bolshevism was not a mere whim of a wayward philosopher of violence. For at about the same time that he hailed Lenin as the embodiment of the proletarian revolution, most of the prominent old-time revolutionary syndicalist militants, such as Pierre Monatte, Robert Louzon and others, joined the French Communist Party whose ap-

[3] It was this short phase of his spiritual wanderings, coupled with his "myth" theory and his glorification of violence, which gave the Italian Fascists—many of whom had come from the syndicalist camp—the pretext for claiming Sorel as one of the teachers of Mussolini.

peal to the radical section of the French working class was proving irresistible in the early twenties—just as in the later forties, for that matter. Apparently both Sorel and the syndicalist militants who ignored him, saw in Communism the potentialities for a triumph of what they called the "proletarian elite", composed largely, if not exclusively, of ex-horny handed trade union leaders. They were all headed for a bitter disappointment; for, after a short honeymoon—Sorel had died in the meantime—the syndicalists realized that they were slated to play second fiddle to political adventurers in tow or in the pay of the Moscow oligarchy. Those who were not satisfied to play that role struck out for themselves by elaborating a sort of combination of syndicalism and communism, claiming, as mentioned before, all power for the syndicalist trade union leadership.

A curious feature of both "Sorelism" and plain revolutionary syndicalism (without the anarchist prefix or adjective) was a mild —and not always very mild—sort of anti-Semitism pervading the utterances of some of their outstanding representatives, such as Sorel and his friends and followers Berth and Delesalle, as well as the top leader of the electrical workers' union, Pataud, and the editor and "angel" of the theoretical magazine, *Revolution Proletarienne,* Robert Louzon. It was a sort of throwback to the middle of the past century, when men like Marx, Proudhon and Bakunin—and the syndicalists as a rule were inspired by all three of them—found it possible to identify Jewry with capitalism and to indulge in generalizing, sweeping statements which made their followers of a few decades later blush with shame. That attitude of Sorel and of other syndicalists—not all of them to be sure—could be attributed to the fact that *French* Jewry was largely an upper middle class group with many financiers among them, and that French radicals, like many other Frenchmen, were, as a rule, altogether ignorant of political and social conditions outside their own country.

"Anarcho-Bolshevism"

For a while, during the early twenties, those among the "bolshevizing" anarchists in Russia who were either unable or unwilling to throw overboard all their anarchist past at one stroke, found a sort of ideological refuge in a theory called "anarcho-bolshevism" which openly advocated a revolutionary dictatorship by anarchists during the transitional period from capitalism to anarchist communism. It was a frank reversion to that aspect of Bakuninism which as a rule was ignored or denied by the later anarchists. In most cases, however, "anarcho-bolshevism" proved merely a short "transitional period" between anarchism and complete acceptance of official Russian "Communism."

In Spain both the Russian Bolshevik revolution of 1917 and the Spanish revolution and civil war of 1931-1939, had a marked effect upon the anarchist movement. The bloodless revolution of 1931 which ushered in an era of political democracy, resulted in the breaking away of a powerful wing of anarcho-syndicalist trade-unionists who decided to abandon the old revolutionary tradition and to pursue gradualist tactics of typical trade-unionism while retaining the old slogans of syndicalism, very much as the gradualist socialists retained the old slogans of revolutionary Marxism. On the other hand, the same event, and the example of the Bolsheviks of 1917 led to the formation of a strong organization of insurrectionist anarchists called FAI (*Federacion Anarquista Iberica*) which was frankly out for an immediate anticapitalist revolution headed by anarchists, with a thinly veiled program of anarchist dictatorship, Bakunin style. These were the younger, more impulsive elements among the self-educated manual and "white collar" workers who were just as hungry for power as the corresponding elements which in other countries embrace the Communist "line". The subsequent events in Spain (1936-1938) led to the further abandonment by the Spanish anarchists of some of the traditional concepts of anarchist tactics:

they voted for the democratic parties during the elections of 1936 (hitherto, voting was taboo with all anarchists); and, after the Falangist military uprising, they actively participated as cabinet members in the Loyalist Government. Anarchists in theory, the Spanish followers of the "anti-state" gospel became hardly distinguishable from democratic socialists.

Waclaw Machajski or the Rebel's Dilemma

In conclusion, it may not be amiss to mention the curious story of a Russian revolutionary group which was usually classified as "anarchist" even though it did not use that label. That group made its appearance about the turn of the century, at a time when Leninism as a distinctive theory was as yet non-existent. It centered around the person of the Polish-Russian revolutionist Waclaw Machajski (Makhaysky) who became known by his criticism of nineteenth century socialism as the ideology of the impecunious, malcontent, lower middle class intellectual workers. These, according to Machajski, were out to remove the capitalists, not for the purpose of emancipating the working class, but with a view to establishing a new system of exploitation: a system of government ownership under which well-paid office-holders, managers and technicians would take the place of the private owners. In short, he predicted what is now called the "managerial revolution" more than forty years before the appearance of the book of that title.

Writing in the peaceful days of capitalism's upward trend, Machajski saw this change coming as a result of the gradualist policy of the Social-Democratic (Socialist) parties whose leadership in the Western democratic countries had become quite a respectable group of Leftist politicians averse to any revolutionary adventures. At that time the rebellious, declassed professional (or "intellectual") of the decades preceding and following 1848 was no longer a mass phenomenon outside of such politically backward countries as Russia (including Russian-Poland) and Spain. That phenomenon was to recur in the wake of the first world war when the hordes of unemployed or underpaid professional or white collar workers began to embrace, en masse, the Bolshevist gospel of immediate anti-capitalist revolution. Long before Lenin, Machajski, a conspirator by temperament, hoped to initiate an international, anti-capitalist revolution with the help of those then not very numerous, déclassés who, in Russia, were not satisfied with a mere democratic, bourgeois revolution, and who, in the democratic West, wasted their anti-capitalist intransigency in the Utopian protest of various post-Bakuninist anarchist sects. His criticism of the intellectual workers, as a growing middle class stratum whose more active members were heading the gradualist socialist movements, was the theoretical drawing card with which he was trying to attract those radical elements who were dissatisfied with the tempo of the anti-capitalist struggle.

Machajski's criticism of socialist leadership as the champions of a new rising middle class of would-be organizers and managers of a collectivist form of economic inequality, might have been inspired by a remark made by Bakunin in his *Statism and Anarchy* (in Russian) in which he accused the Marxists of aiming at such a new form of exploitation. The similarity of Machajski's views to those of Bakunin shows up in another respect as well. Bakunin operated with two contradictory theories, as it were: one, for the general public, which advocated the complete destruction of the state immediately after the victorious revolution, and another which was expressed in letters to members of his inner circle (and in other documents as well), in which he favored a revolutionary dictatorship by his own leading elite. Machajski, who may or may not have been aware of this dualism of Bakunin's, likewise had two theories: one was somewhat related to syndicalism, in which he advocated an exclusively non-political mass struggle for higher wages and for jobs for the unemployed—a sort of direct action movement against private employers and against the state; a struggle which in its further development would lead to the expropriation of the capitalists and to the complete equalization of incomes of manual and intellectual workers—thus bringing about the liquidation of the state by the process of the disappearance of economic inequalities. The other theory postulated the seizure of power in the form of a "revolutionary dictatorship." It was hidden away in some passages of his earlier writings; in the opinion of most of his followers it was considered abandoned by the teacher himself. But Machajski never explicitly repudiated that "outdated" view of his. And, thus, his non-political, direct-action, equalitarian semi-syndicalism, as it were,[4] was allowed to exist side by side with a pre-Leninist form of Bolshevism, i.e. advocating a "world conspiracy and dictatorship of the proletariat," and seizure of power by his own group. This view was in contradiction to his basic sociological thesis about the exploitative, unequalitarian tendencies animating the owners of higher education with regard to the manual workers. For it implied that those members of the new middle class of intellectual workers who were to constitute the bureaucratic setup of a Machajski-controlled revolutionary government would be exempt from those tendencies. Thus the thinker's logic and consistency—because of their pessimistic, nonrevolutionary implications—were sacrificed on the altar of the revolutionist's will to power.

The post-war period has seen the revival of traditional anarchism of the Kropotkin school, and of anarcho-syndicalism in some of the countries in which they had been in vogue before, such as France and Italy. But they seem doomed to remain small groups of "irreconcilables" unable, so far, to break the spell which the revolutionary anti-capitalist halo of official Russian Communism is still exerting upon most malcontent elements among white-collar and manual workers.

[4] Machajski himself did not apply any label to his views. His group which aspired to become an international secret organization of professional revolutionists, was called the "Workers Conspiracy." The idea of seizure of power in the wake of a revolutionary mass struggle for the workers' bread-and-butter demands was a carefully guarded "top secret"—lest the group lose its appeal as a genuinely working class organization.

IX.

Anarchism and Anarcho-Syndicalism

IX.

ANARCHISM AND ANARCHO-SYNDICALISM

by

RUDOLF ROCKER

Ideology of Anarchism

ANARCHISM IS A definite intellectual current of social thought, whose adherents advocate the abolition of economic monopolies and of all political and social coercive institutions within society. In place of the capitalist economic order, Anarchists would have a free association of all productive forces based upon co-operative labor, which would have for its sole purpose the satisfying of the necessary requirements of every member of society. In place of the present national states with their lifeless machinery of political and bureaucratic institutions, Anarchists desire a federation of free communities which shall be bound to one another by their common economic and social interests and arrange their affairs by mutual agreement and free contract.

Anyone who studies profoundly the economic and political development of the present social system will recognize that these objectives do not spring from the utopian ideas of a few imaginative innovators, but that they are the logical outcome of a thorough examination of existing social maladjustments, which, with every new phase of the present social conditions, manifest themselves more plainly and more unwholesomely. Modern monopoly-capitalism and the totalitarian state are merely the last stages in a development which could culminate in no other end.

The portentous development of our present economic system, leading to a mighty accumulation of social wealth in the hands of privileged minorities and to a continuous repression of the great masses of the people, prepared the way for the present political and social reaction and befriended it in every way. It sacrificed the general interests of human society to the private interests of individuals, and thus systematically undermined a true relationship between men. People forgot that industry is not an end in itself, but should be only a means to insure to man his material subsistence and to make accessible to him the blessings of a higher intellectual culture. Where industry is everything, where labor loses its ethical importance and man is nothing, there begins the realm of ruthless economic despotism, whose workings are no less disastrous than those of any political despotism. The two mutually augment one another; they are fed from the same source.

Our modern social system has internally split the social organism of every country into hostile classes, and externally it has broken up the common cultural circle into hostile nations; both classes and nations confront one another with open antagonism, and by their ceaseless warfare keep the communal social life in continual convulsions. Two world wars within half a century and their terrible after-effects, and the constant danger of new wars, which today dominates all peoples, are only the logical consequences of this unendurable condition which can only lead to further universal catastrophies. The mere fact that most states are obliged today to spend the better part of their annual income for so-called national defense and the liquidation of old war debts is proof of the untenability of the present status; it should make clear to everybody that the alleged protection which the state affords the individual is certainly purchased too dearly.

The ever-growing power of a soulless political bureaucracy which supervises and safeguards the life of man from the cradle to the grave is putting ever-greater obstacles in the way of cooperation among human beings. A system which in every act of its life sacrifices the welfare of large sections of the people, of whole nations, to the selfish lust for power and the economic interests of small minorities must necessarily dissolve the social ties and lead to a constant war of each against all. This system has merely been the pacemaker for the great intellectual and social reaction which finds its expression today in modern Fascism and the idea of the totalitarian state, far surpassing the obsession for power of the absolute monarchy of past centuries and seeking to bring every sphere of human activity under the control of the state. "All for the state; all through the state; nothing without the state!" became the *leitmotive* of a new political theology which has its open or concealed adherents in every country. Just as for the various systems of ecclesiastical theology God is everything and man nothing, so for this modern political creed the state is everything and the citizen nothing. And just as the words the "*will of God*" were used to justify the will of privileged castes, so today there hides behind the *will of the state* only the selfish interests of those who feel called to interpret this will in their own sense and to force it upon the people.

In modern Anarchism we have the confluence of the two great currents which before and since the French Revolution have found such characteristic expression in the intellectual life of Europe: Socialism and Liberalism. Modern Socialism developed when profound observers of social life came to see more and more clearly that political constitutions and changes in the form of government could never get to the root of the great problem that we call the *social question*. Its supporters recognized that an equalizing of social and economic conditions for the benefit of all, despite the loveliest of theoretical assumptions, is not possible as long as people are separated into classes on the basis of their owning or not owning property, classes whose mere existence excludes in advance any thought of a genuine community. And so there developed the conviction that only by the elimination of economic monopolies and by common ownership of the means of production does a condition of social justice become feasible, a condition in which society shall become a real community, and human labor shall no longer serve the ends of exploitation but assure the well-being of everyone. But as soon as Socialism began to assemble its forces and became a movement, there at once came to light certain differences of opinion due to the influence of the social environment in different countries. It is a fact that every political concept from theocracy to Caesarism and dictatorship have affected certain factions of the socialist movement.

Meanwhile, two other great currents in political thought had a decisive significance on the development of socialist ideas: Liberalism, which had powerfully stimulated advanced minds in the Anglo-Saxon countries, Holland and Spain in particular, and Democracy in the sense, to which Rousseau gave expression in his *Social Contract,* and which found its most influential representatives in the leaders of French Jacobinism. While Liberalism in its social theories started off from the individual and wished to limit the state's activities to a minimum, Democracy took its stand on an abstract collective concept, Rousseau's *general will,* which it sought to fix in the national state. Liberalism and Democracy were preeminently political concepts, and, since most of the original adherents of both did scarcely consider the economic conditions of society, the further development of these conditions could not be practically reconciled with the original principles of Democracy, and still less with those of Liberalism. Democracy with its motto of *equality of all citizens before the law,* and Liberalism with its *right of man over his own person,* both were wrecked on the realities of capitalist economy. As long as millions of human beings in every country have to sell their labor to a small minority of owners, and sink into the most wretched misery if they can find no buyers, the so-called equality before the law remains merely a pious fraud, since the laws are made by those who find themselves in possession of the social wealth. But in the same way there can also be no talk of a right over one's own person, for that right ends when one is compelled to submit to the economic dictation of another if one does not want to starve.

In common with Liberalism, Anarchism represents the idea that the happiness and prosperity of the individual must be the standard in all social matters. And, in common with the great representatives of liberal thought, it has also the idea of limiting the functions of government to a minimum. Its adherents have followed this thought to its ultimate consequences, and wish to eliminate every institution of political power from the life of society. When Jefferson clothes the basic concept of Liberalism in the words: "That government is best which governs least," then Anarchists say with Thoreau: "That government is best which governs not at all."

In common with the founders of Socialism, Anarchists demand the abolition of economic monopoly in every form and shape and uphold common ownership of the soil and all other means of production, the use of which must be available to all without distinction; for personal and social freedom is conceivable only on the basis of equal economic conditions for everybody. Within the socialist movement itself the Anarchists represent the viewpoint that the struggle against capitalism must be at the same time a struggle against all coercive institutions of political power, for in history economic exploitation has always gone hand in hand with political and social oppression. The exploitation of man by man and the dominion of man over man are inseparable, and each is the condition of the other.

As long as a possessing and a non-possessing group of human beings face one another in enemity within society, the state will be indispensable to the possessing minority for the protection of its privileges. When this condition of social injustice vanishes to give place to a higher order of things, which shall recognize no special rights and shall have as its basic assumption the community of social interests, government over men must yield the field to the administration of economic and social affairs, or, to speak with Saint Simon: "The time will come when the art of governing men will disappear. A new art will take its place, the art of administering things." In this respect Anarchism has to be regarded as a kind of voluntary Socialism.

This disposes also of the theory maintained by Marx and his followers that the state, in the form of a proletarian dictatorship, is a necessary transitional stage to a classless society, in which the state, after the elimination of all class conflicts and then the classes themselves, will dissolve itself and vanish from the canvas. For this concept, which completely mistakes the real nature of the state and the significance in history of the factor of political power, is only the logical outcome of so-called economic materialism, which sees in all the phenomena of history merely the inevitable effects of the methods of production of the time. Under the influence of this theory people came to regard the different forms of the state and all other social institutions as a "juridical and political superstructure on the economic edifice" of society, and thought that they had found in it the key to every historic process. In reality every section of history affords us thousands of examples of the way in which the economic development of countries was set back for centuries by the state and its power policy.

Before the rise of the ecclesiastical monarchy, Spain, industrially was the most advanced country in Europe and held the first place in economic production in almost every field. But a century after the triumph of the Christian monarchy most of its industries had disappeared; what was left of them survived only in the most wretched condition. Most industries they had reverted to the most primitive methods of production. Agriculture collapsed, canals and waterways fell into ruin, and vast stretches of the country were transformed into deserts.—Princely absolutism in Europe, with its silly "economic ordinances" and "Industrial Legislation," which severely punished any deviation from the prescribed methods of production and permitted no new inventions, blocked industrial progress in European countries for centuries, and prevented its natural development.—And even now, after the horrible experiences of two world wars, the power policy of the larger national states proves to be the greatest obstacle to the reconstruction of European economy.

In Russia, however, where the so-called dictatorship of the proletariat has ripened into reality, the aspirations of a particular party for political power have prevented any truly socialistic reorganization of economic life and have forced the country into the slavery of a grinding state-capitalism. The proletarian dictatorship, which naive souls believe is an inevitable transition stage to real Socialism, has today grown into a frightful despotism and a new imperialism, which lags behind the tyranny of Fascist states in nothing. The assertion that the state must continue to exist until society no longer divided into hostile classes almost sounds, in the light of all historical experience, like a bad joke.

Every type of political power presupposes some particular form of human slavery, for the maintainance of which it is called into being. Just as outwardly, that is, in relation to other states, the state has to create certain artificial antagonisms in order to justify its existence, so also internally the cleavage of society into castes, ranks and classes is an essentual condition of its continuance. The development of the Bolshevist bureaucracy in Russia under the alleged dictatorship of the proletariat—which has never been anything but the dictatorship of a small clique *over* the proletariat and the whole Russian people—is merely a new instance of an old historical experience which has repeated itself countless times. This new ruling class, which today is rapidly growing into a new aristocracy, is set apart from the great masses of the Russian peasants and workers just as clearly as are the privileged castes and classes in other countries from the mass of the people. And this situation becomes still more unbearable when a despotic state denies to the lower classes the right to complain of existing conditions, so that any protest is made at the risk of their lives.

But even a far greater degree of economic equality than that which exists in Russia would be no guarantee against political and social oppression. Economic equality alone is not social liberation. It is precisely this which all the schools of authoritarian Socialism have never understood. In the prison, in the cloister, or in the barracks one finds a fairly high degree of economic equality, as all the inmates are provided with the same dwelling, the same food, the same uniform, and the same tasks. The ancient Inca state in Peru and the Jesuit state in Paraguay had brought equal economic provision for every inhabitant to a fixed system, but in spite of this the vilest despotism prevailed there, and the human being was merely the automaton of a higher will on whose descisions he had not the slightest influence. It was not without reason that Proudhon saw in a "Socialism" without freedom the worst form of slavery. The urge for social justice can only develop properly and be effective when it grows out of man's sense of freedom and responsibility, and is based on it. In other words, *Socialism will be free or it will not be at all.* In its recognition of this fact lies the genuine and profound justification of Anarchism.

Institutions serve the same purpose in the life of society as physical organs do in plants and animals; they are the organs of the social body. Organs do not develop arbitrarily, but owe their origin to definite necessities of the physical and social environment. Changed conditions of life produce changed organs. But an organ always performs the function it was evolved to perform, or a related one. And it gradually disappears or becomes rudimentary as soon as its function is no longer necessary to the organism.

The same is true of social institutions. They, too, do not arise arbitrarily, but are called into being by special social needs to serve definite purposes. In this way the modern state was evolved, after economic privileges and class divisions associated with them had begun to make themselves more and more conspicuous in the framework of the old social order. The newly-arisen possessing classes had need of a political instrument of power to maintain their economic and social privileges over the masses of their own people, and to impose them from without on other groups of human beings. Thus arose the appropriate social conditions for the evolution of the modern state as the organ of political power for the forcible subjugation and oppression of the non-possessing classes. This task is the essential reason for its existence. Its external forms have altered in the course of its historical development, but its functions have always remained the same. They have even constantly broadened in just the measure in which its supporters have succeeded in making further fields of social activities subservient to their ends. And, just as the functions of a physical organ cannot be arbitrarily altered so that, for example, one cannot, at will, hear with one's eyes or see with one's ears, so also one cannot, at pleasure, transform an organ of social oppression into an instrument for the liberation of the oppressed.

Anarchism is no patent solution for all human problems, no Utopia of a perfect social order (as it has so often been called), since, on principle, it rejects all absolute schemes and concepts. It does not believe in any absolute truth, or in any definite final goals for human development, but in an unlimited perfectibility of social patterns and human living conditions, which are always straining after higher forms of expression, and to which, for this reason, one cannot assign any definite terminus nor set any fixed goal. The greatest evil of any form of power is just that it always tries to force the rich diversity of social life into definite forms and adjust it to particular norms. The stronger its supporters feel themselves, the more completely they succeed in bringing every field of social life into their service, the more crippling is their influence on the operation of all creative cultural forces, the more unwholesomely does it affect the intellectual and social development of any particular epoch. The so-called totalitarian state is only the last expression of this development of power and a dire omen for our times, for it shows with frightful clarity to what a monstrosity Hobbes' *Leviathan* can be developed. It is the perfect triumph of the political machine over mind and body, the rationalization of human thought, feeling and behavior according to the established rules of the officials and, consequently, the end of all true intellectual culture.

Anarchism recognizes only the relative significance of ideas, institutions, and social conditions. It is, therefore not a fixed, self-enclosed social system, but rather a definite trend in the historical development of mankind, which, in contrast with the intellectual guardianship of all clerical and governmental institutions, strives for the free unhindered unfolding of all the individual and social forces in life. Even freedom is only a relative, not an absolute concept, since it tends constantly to broaden its scope and to affect wider circles in manifold ways. For the Anarchist, freedom is not an abstract philosophical concept, but the vital concrete possibility for every human being to bring to full development all capacities and talents with which nature has endowed him, and turn them to social account. The less this natural development of man is interfered with by ecclesiastical or political guardianship, the more efficient and harmonious will human personality become, the more will it become the measure of the intellectual culture of the society in which it has grown. This is the reason why all great culture periods in history have been periods of political weakness, for political systems are always set upon the mechanizing and not the organic development of social forces. State and Culture are irreconcilable opposites. Nietzsche, who was not an anarchist, recognized this very clearly when he wrote:

"No one can finally spend more than he has. That holds good for individuals; it holds good for peoples. If one spends oneself for power, for higher politics, for husbandry, for commerce, parliamentarism, military interests—if one gives away that amount of reason, earnestness, will, self-mastery which constitutes one's real self for one thing, he will not have it for the other. Culture and the state—let no one be deceived about this—are antagonists: the *Culture State* is merely a modern idea. The one lives on the other, the one prospers at the expense of the other. All great periods of culture are periods of political decline. Whatever is great in a cultured sense is non-political, is even antipolitical."

Where the influence of political power on the creative forces in society is reduced to a minimum, there culture thrives the best, for political rulership always strives for uniformity and tends to subject every aspect of social life to its guardianship. And, in this, it finds itself in unescapable contradiction to the creative aspirations of cultural development, which is always on the quest for new forms and fields of social activity, and for which freedom of expression, the many-sidedness and the continual changing of things, are just as vitally necessary as rigid forms, dead rules, and the forcible suppression of ideas are for the conservation of political power. Every successful piece of work stirs the desire for greater perfection and deeper inspiration; each new form becomes the herald of new possibilities of development. But power always tries to keep things as they are, safely anchored to stereotypes. That has been the reason for all revolutions in history. Power operates only destructively, bent always on forcing every manifestation of social life into the straitjacket of its rules. Its intellectual expression is dead dogma, its physical form brute force. And this unintelligence of its objectives sets its stamp on its representatives also, and renders them often stupid and brutal, even when they were originally endowed with the best talents. One who is constantly striving to force everything into a mechanical order at last becomes a machine himself and loses all human feelings.

It was from this understanding that modern Anarchism was born and draws its moral force. Only freedom can inspire men to great things and bring about intellectual and social transformations. The art of ruling men has never been the art of educating and inspiring them to a new shaping of their lives. Dreary compulsion has at its command only lifeless drill, which smothers any vital initiative at its birth and brings forth only subjects, not free men. Freedom is the very essence of life, the impelling force in all intellectual and social development, the creator of every new outlook for the future of mankind. The liberation of man from economic exploitation and from intellectual, social and political oppression, which finds its highest expression in the philosophy of Anarchism, is the first prerequisite for the evolution of a higher social culture and a new humanity.

History of Anarchist Philosophy From Lao-Tse to Kropotkin

Anarchist ideas are to be found in almost every period of known history. We encounter them in the Chinese sage, Lao-tse, (*The*

Course and The Right Way) and the later Greek philosophers, the Hedonists and Cynics and other advocates of so-called *natural right,* and, particularly, in Zeno, the founder of the Stoic school and opposer of Plato. They found expression in the teachings of the Gnostic Carpocrates in Alexandria, and had an unmistakable influence on certain Christian sects of the Middle Ages in France, Germany, Italy, Holland and England, most of which fell victims to the most savage persecutions. In the history of the Bohemian Reformation they found a powerful champion in Peter Chelcicky, who in his work, *The Net of Faith,* passed the same judgment on the Church and the State as Tolstoi did centuries later . Among the great Humanists there was Rabelais, who in his description of the happy Abbey of Thélème (*Gargantua*) presented a picture of life freed from all authoritative restraints. Of other pioneers of libertarian thinking we will mention here only La Boétie, Sylvain Maréchal, and, above all, Diderot, in whose voluminous writings one finds thickly strewn the utterances of a really great mind which had rid itself of every authoritarian prejudice.

Meanwhile, it was reserved for more recent history to give a clear form to the Anarchist conception of life and to connect it with the immediate process of social evolution. This was done for the first time by William Godwin (1756-1836) in his splendidly conceived work, *Concerning Political Justice and its Influence upon General Virtue and Happiness,* London 1793. Godwin's work was, we might say, the ripened fruit of that long evolution of the concepts of political and social radicalism in England which proceeds from George Buchanan through Richard Hooker, Gerard Winstanley, Algeron Sidney, John Locke, Robert Wallace and John Bellers to Jeremy Bentham, Joseph Priestley, Richard Price and Thomas Paine.

Godwin recognized very clearly that the cause of social evils is to be sought, not in the form of the state, but in its very existence. But he also recognized that human beings can only live together naturally and freely when the proper economic conditions for this are given, and the individual is no longer subject to exploitation by others, a consideration which most of the representatives of mere political radicalism almost wholely overlooked. Hence they were later compelled to make constantly greater concessions to the state which they had wished to restrict to a minimum. Godwin's idea of a stateless society assumed the social ownership of the land and the instruments of labor and the carrying on of economic life by free cooperatives of producers. Godwin's work had a strong influence on advanced circles of the English workers and the more enlightened sections of the liberal intelligentsia. Most important of all, he contributed to the young socialist movement in England, which found its maturest exponents in Robert Owen, John Gray and William Thompson, that unmistakably libertarian character which it had for a long time, and which it never assumed in Germany and many other countries.

Also the French Socialist Charles Fourier (1772-1832) with his theory of attractive labor must be mentioned here as one of the pioneers of libertarian ideas.

But a far greater influence on the development of Anarchist theory was that of Pierre Joseph Proudhon (1809-1865), one of the most gifted and certainly the most many-sided writer of modern Socialism. Proudhon was completely rooted in the intellectual and social life of his period, and these influenced his attitude upon every question with which he dealt. Therefore he is not to be judged, as he has been even by many of his later followers, by his special practical proposals, which were born of the needs of the hour. Among the numerous socialist thinkers of his time he was the one who understood most profoundly the cause of social maladjustment, and possessed, besides, the greatest breath of vision. He was the outspoken opponent of all artificial social systems, and saw in social evolution the eternal urge to new and higher forms of intellectual and social life; it was his conviction that this evolution could not be bound by any definite abstract formulas.

Proudhon opposed the influence of the Jacobin tradition, which dominated the thinking of the French democrats and most of the Socialists of that period, with the same determination as the interference of the central state and economic monopoly in the natural progress of social advance. To him ridding society of those two cancerous growths was the great task of the nineteenth century revolution. Proudhon was not a Communist. He condemned property as merely the privilege of exploitation, but he recognized the ownership of the instruments of labor for all, made effective through industrial groups bound to one another by free contract, so long as this right was not made to serve the exploitation of others and as long as the full product of his individual labor was assured to every member of society. This association based on reciprocity (mutuality) guarantees the enjoyment of equal rights by each in exchange for social services. The average working time required for the completion of any product becomes the measure of its value and is the basis of mutual exchange by labor notes. In this way capital is deprived of its usurial power and is completely bound up with the performance of work. Being made available to all it ceases to be an instrument for exploitation. Such a form of economy makes any political coercive apparatus superfluous. Society becomes a league of free communities which arrange their affairs according to need, by themselves or in association with others, and in which man's freedom is the equal freedom of others not its limitation, but its security and confirmation.—"The freer, the more independent and enterprising the individual is the better for society."

This organization of Federalism in which Proudhon saw the immediate future of mankind sets no definite limitations on future possibilities of development and offers the widest scope to every individual and social activity. Starting out from the point of Federation, Proudhon combated likewise the aspiration for political and national unity of the awakening nationalism of the time which found such strong advocates in Mazzini, Garibaldi, Lelewel and others. In this respect he recognized more clearly the real nature of nationalism than most of his contemporaries. Proudhon exerted a strong influence on the development of Socialism, which made itself felt especially in the Latin countries.

Ideas similar to the economic and political conceptions of Proudhon were propagated by the followers of so-called Individualist Anarchism in America which found able exponents in such men as Josiah Warren, Stephen Pearl Andrews, William B. Greene, Lysander Spooner, Benjamin R. Tucker, Ezra Heywood, D. Tandy and many others, though none of them could approach Proudhon's breath of view. Characteristic of this school of libertarian thought is the fact that most of its representatives took their political ideas not from Proudhon but from the traditions of American Liberalism, so that Tucker could assert that "Anarchists are merely consistent Jeffersonian democrats."

A unique expression of libertarian ideas is to be found in Max Stirner's (Johann Kasper Schmidt 1806-1856) book, *Der Einzige und sein Eigentum,* which, it is true, passed quickly into oblivion and had no influence on the development of the Anarchist movement as such. Stirner's book is predominantly a philosophic work which traces man's dependence on so-called higher powers through all its devious ways, and is not timid about drawing inferences from the knowledge gained by the survey. It is the book of a conscious and deliberate insurgent, which reveals no reverence for any authority, however exalted, and, therefore, appeals powerfully to independent thinking.

Anarchism found a virile champion of vigorous revolutionary energy in Michael A. Bakunin (1814-1876), who based his ideas upon the teachings of Proudhon, but extended them on the economic side when he, along with the federalist wing of the First International, advocated collective ownership of the land and all other means of production, and wished to restrict the right of private property only to the product of individual labor. Bakunin also was an opponent of Communism, which in his time had a thoroughly authoritarian character, like that which it has again assumed today in Bolshevism.—"I am not a Communist, because Communism unites all the forces of society in the state and becomes absorbed in it; because it inevitably leads to the concentration of all property in the hands of the state, while I seek the complete elimination of the principles of authority and governmental guardianship, which under the pretence of making men moral and civilizing them, has up to now always enslaved, oppressed, exploited and ruined them."

Bakunin was a determined revolutionary and did not believe in an amicable adjustment of the existing conflicts within society. He recognized that the ruling classes blindly and stubbornly opposed every possibility for larger social reforms, and accordingly saw the only salvation in an international social revolution, which would abolish all institutions of political power and economic exploitation and introduce in their stead a Federation of free Associations of producers and consumers to provide for the requirements of their daily life. Since he, like so many of his contemporaries, believed in the close proximity of the revolution, he directed all his vast energy to combining all the genuinely revolutionary and libertarian elements within and outside the International to safeguard the coming revolution against any dictatorship or any retrogression to the old conditions. Thus he became in a very special sense the creator of the modern Anarchist movement.

Anarchism found a valuable exponent in Peter Kropotkin (1842-1921), who set himself the task of making the achievements of modern natural science available for the development of the sociological concept of Anarchism. In his ingenious book, *Mutual Aid—a Factor of Evolution*, he entered the lists against so-called *Social Darwinism*, whose exponents tried to prove the inevitability of the existing social conditions from the Darwinian theory of the *Struggle for Existence* by raising the struggle of the strong against the weak to the status of an iron law of nature, to which man is also subject. In reality this conception was strongly influenced by the Malthusian doctrine that life's table is not spread for all, and that the unneeded will just have to reconcile themselves to this fact. Kropotkin showed that this conception of nature as a field of unrestricted warfare is only a caricature of real life, and that along with the brutal struggle for existence, which is fought out with tooth and claw, there exists in nature also another tendency which is expressed in the social combination of the weaker species and the maintenance of races by the evolution of social instincts and mutual aid. In this sense man is not the creator of society, but society the creator of man, for he inherited from the species that preceded him the social instinct which alone enabled him to maintain himself in his first environment against the physical superiority ot other species, and to make sure of an undreamed-of height of development. This second as is shown by the steady retrogression of those species whose tendency in the struggle for existence is far superior to the first, have no social life and are dependent merely upon their physical strength. This view, which today is meeting with constantly wider acceptance in the natural sciences and in social research, opened wholly new vistas to the prospects concerning human evolution.

According to Kropotkin the fact remains that even under the worst despotism most of man's personal relations with his fellows are arranged by social habits, free agreement and mutual co-operation, without which social life would not be possible at all. If this were not the case, even the strongest coercive machinery of the state would not be able to maintain the social order for any length of time. However, these natural forms of behaviour, which arise from man's innermost nature, are today constantly interfered with and crippled by the effects of economic exploitation and governmental tutelage, representing the brutal form of the struggle for existence in human society which has to be overcome by the other form of mutual aid and free co-operation. The consciousness of personal responsibility and the capacity for sympathy with others, which make all social ethics and all ideas of social justice, develop best in freedom.

Like Bakunin, Kropotkin too was a revolutionary. But he, like Elisée Reclue and others, saw in revolution only a special phase of the evolutionary process, which appears when new social aspirations are so restricted in their natural development by authority that they have to shatter the old shell by violence before they can function as new factors in human life.

In contrast to Proudhon's Mutualism and Bakunin's Collectivism, Kropotkin advocated common ownership not only of the means of production but of the products of labor as well, as it was his opinion that in the present state of technology no exact measure of the value of individual labor is possible, but that, on the other hand, by rational direction of our modern methods of labor it will be possible to assure comparative abundance to every human being. Communist Anarchism, which before Kropotkin had already been urged by Joseph Déjacque, Elisée Reclus, Carlo Cafiero and others, and which is recognized by the great majority of Anarchists today, found in him its most brilliant exponent.

Mention must also be made here of Leo Tolstoi (1828-1910), who, from primitive Christianity and on the basis of the ethical principles laid down in the gospels, arrived at the idea of a society without rulership.

Common to all Anarchists is the desire to free society of all political and social coercive institutions which stand in the way of the development of a free humanity. In this sense Mutualism, Collectivism and Communism are not to be regarded as closed economic systems, permitting no further development, but merely as economic assumptions as to the means of safeguarding a free community. There will even probably be in every form of a free society of the future different forms of economic co-operation existing side by side, since any social progress must be associated with free experimentation and practical testing-out of new methods for which in society of free communities there will be every opportunity.

The same holds true for the various methods of Anarchism. The work of its adherents is pre-eminently a work of education to prepare the people intellectually and psychologically for the tasks of their social liberation. Every attempt to limit the influence of economic monopolism and the power of the state is a step nearer to the realization of this goal. Every development of voluntary organization in the various fields of social activity towards the direction of personal freedom and social justice deepens the awareness of the people and strengthens their social responsibility, without which no changes in social life can be accomplished. Most Anarchists of our time are convinced that such a transformation of society will take years of constructive work and education and cannot be brought about without revolutionary convulsions which till now have always accomplished every progress in social life. The character of these convulsions, of course, depends entirely on the strength of resistance with which the ruling classes will be able to oppose the realization of the new ideas. The wider the circles which are inspired with the idea of a reorganization of society in the spirit of freedom and Socialism, the easier will be the birth pains of new social changes in the future. For even revolutions can only develop and mature the ideas which already exist and have made their way into the consciousness of men: but they cannot themselves create ideas or generate new worlds out of nothing.

Before the appearance of totalitarian states in Russia, Italy, Germany and later in Portugal and Spain, and the outbreak of the second world war, Anarchist organizations and movements existed almost in every country. But like all other socialist movements of that period, they became the victims of Fascist tyranny and the invasions of the German armies, and could only lead an underground existence. Since the end of the war a resurrection of Anarchist movements in all Western European countries is to be noticed. The Federations of the French and Italian Anarchists already held their first conventions, and so did the Spanish Anarchists of whom many thousands are still living in exile, mostly in France, Belgium and North Africa. Anarchist papers and magazines are published again in many European countries and in North and South America.

Anarcho-Syndicalism—The Origins

Many Anarchists spent a great part of their activities in the labor movement, especially in the Latin countries, where in later years the movement of Anarcho-Syndicalism was born. Its theoretical assumptions were based on the teachings of libertarian or anarchist Socialism, while its form of organization was taken from the movement of revolutionary Syndicalism which in the years from 1895 to 1910 experienced a marked upswing, particularly in France, Italy and Spain. Its ideas and methods, however, were not new. They had already found a deep resonance in the ranks of the First International when the great association had reached the zenith of its intellectual development. This was plainly revealed in the debates at its fourth congress in Basel (1869) concerning the importance of the economic organizations of the workers. In his report upon this question which Eugène Hins laid before the congress in the name of the Belgian Federation, there was presented for the first time a wholly new point of view which had an unmistakable resemblance to certain ideas of Robert Owen and the English labor movement of the thirties.

In order to make a correct estimate of this, one must remember that at that time the various schools of state-socialism attributed no, or at best only little importance to the trade unions. The French Blanquists saw in these organizations merely a reform movement, with a socialist dictatorship as their immediate aim. Ferdinand Lassalle and his followers directed all their activities towards welding the workers into a political party and were outspoken opponents of all trade union endeavors in which they saw only a hindrance to the political evolution of the working class. Marx and his adherents of that period recognized, it is true, the necessity of trade unions for the achievement of certain betterments within the capitalist system, but they believed that their rôle would be exhausted with this, and that they would disappear along with capitalism, since the transition to Socialism could be guided only by a proletarian dictatorship.

In Basel this idea underwent for the first time a thorough critical examination. The views expressed in the Belgian report presented by Hins which were shared by the delegates from Spain, the Swiss Jura and the larger part of the French sections, were based on the premise that the present economic associations of the workers are not only a necessity within the present society, but were even more to be regarded as the social nucleus of a coming socialist economy, and it was, therefore, the duty of the International to educate the workers for this task. In accordance with this the congress adopted the following resolution:

"The congress declares that all workers should strive to establish associations for resistance in their various trades. As soon as a trade union is formed the unions in the same trade are to be notified so that the formation of national alliances in the industries may begin. These alliances shall be charged with the duty of collecting all material relating to their industry, of advising about measures to be executed in common, and of seeing that they are carried out, to the end that the present wage system may be replaced by the federation of free producers. The congress directs the General Council to provide for the alliance of the trade unions of all countries."

In his argument for the resolution proposed by the committee, Hins explained that "by this dual form of organization of local workers' associations and general alliances for each industry on the one hand and the political administration of labor councils on the other, the general representation of labor, regional, national and international, will be provided for. *The councils of the trades and industrial organizations will take the place of the present government, and this representation of labor will do away, once and forever, with the governments of the past.*"

This new idea grew out of the recognition that every new economic form of society must be accompanied by a new political form of the social organism and could only attain practical expression in this. Its followers saw in the present national state only the political agent and defender of the possessing classes, and did, therefore, not strive for the conquest of power, but for the elimination of every system of power within society, in which they saw the requisite preliminary condition for all tyranny and exploitation. They understood that along with the monopoly of property, the monopoly of power must also disappear. Proceeding from their recognition that the lordship of man over man had had its day, they sought to familiarize themselves with the administration of things. Or, as Bakunin, one of the great forerunners of modern Anarcho-syndicalism, put it:

"Since the organization of the International has as its goal, not the setting up of new states or despots, but the radical elimination of every separate sovereignty, it must have an essentially different character from the organization of the state. To just the degree that the latter is authoritarian, artificial and violent, alien and hostile to the natural development of the interests and the instincts of the people, to the same degree must the organization of the International be free, natural and in every respect in accord with those interests and instincts. But what is the natural organization of the masses? It is one based on the different occupations of their actual daily life, on their various kinds of work, organization according to their occupations, trade organizations. When all industries, including the various branches of agriculture, are represented in the International, its organization, the organization of the toiling masses of the people, will be finished."

And at another occasion: "All this practical and vital study of social science by the workers themselves in their trades sections and their chambers of labor will—and already has—engender in them the unanimous, well-considered, theoretically and practically demonstrable conviction that the *serious, final, complete liberation of the workers is possible only on one condition: that of the appropriation of capital, that is, of raw materials and all the tools of labor, including land, by the whole body of the workers.* . . . . The organization of the trade sections, their federation in the International, and their representation by the Labor Chambers, not only create a great academy in which the workers of the International, combining theory and practice, can and must study economic science, they also bear in themselves the living germs of the *new social order*, which is to replace the bourgeois world. They are creating not only the ideas but also the facts of the future itself..."

After the decline of the International and the Franco-German War, by which the focal point of the socialist labor movement was transferred to Germany, whose workers had neither revolutionary traditions nor that rich experience possessed by the Socialists in the western countries, those ideas were gradually forgotten. After the defeat of the Paris Commune and the revolutionary upheavals in Spain and Italy the sections of the International in those countries were compelled for many years to carry on only an underground existence. Only with the awakening of revolutionary Syndicalism in France were the ideas of the First International rescued from oblivion and inspired once more larger sections of the labor movement.

Socialism and Anarcho-Syndicalism in France

Modern Anarcho-Syndicalism is a direct continuation of those social aspirations which took shape in the bosom of the First International and which were best understood and most strongly held by the libertarian wing of the great worker's alliance. Its development was a direct reaction against the concepts and methods of political Socialism, a reaction which in the decade before the first world war had already manifested itself in the strong upsurge of the syndicalist labor movement in France, Italy and especially Spain, where the great majority of the organized workers had always remained faithful to the doctrines of the libertarian wing of the International.

It was in France that the opposition against the ideas and methods of the modern labor parties found a clear expression in the theories and tactics of revolutionary Syndicalism. The immediate cause for the development of these new tendencies in the French labor movement was the continual split of the various socialist parties in France. All these parties, with the exception of the Allemanists, which later gave up parliamentary activities completely, saw in the trade unions merely recruiting schools for their political objectives and had no understanding for their real functions. The constant dissensions among the various socialist factions was naturally carried over into the labor unions, and it happened quite frequently that when the unions of one faction went on strike the unions of the other factions walked in on them as strike breakers. This untenable situation gradually opened the eyes of the workers. So the trade union congress in Nantes (1894) charged a special committee with the task of devising means for bringing about an understanding among all the trade union alliances. The result was the founding in the following year of the *Confédération Générale du Travail* at the congress in Limoges, which declared itself independent of all political parties. From then on there existed in France only two large trade union groups, the C.G.T. and the *Fédération des Bourses du Travail,* and in 1902, at the congress of the Montpellier the latter joined the C.G.T.

One often encounters the widely disseminated opinion, which was fostered by Werner Sombart in particular, that revolutionary Syndicalism in France owes its origin to intellectuals like G. Sorel, E. Berth and H. Lagardelle, who in the periodical *Le Mouvement socialiste,* founded in 1899, elaborated in their way the intellectual results of the new movement. This is utterly false. None of these men belonged to the movement, nor had they any appreciable influence on its internal development. Moreover, the C.G.T. was not composed exclusively of revolutionary syndicates; certainly half of its members were of reformist tendency and had joined the C.G.T. because even they recognized that the dependence of the trade unions on political parties was a misfortune for the movement. But the revolutionary wing, which had had the most energetic and active elements of organized labor on its side as well as the most brilliant intellectual forces in the organization, gave the C.G.T. its characteristic stamp, and it was they who determined the development of the ideas of revolutionary Syndicalism. Many of them came from the Allemanists, but even more from the ranks of the Anarchists, like Fernand

Pelloutier, the highly intelligent secretary of the Federation of the Labor Exchanges, Emile Pouget, the editor of the official organ of the C.G.T. *La Voix du Peuple*, P. Delesalle, G. Yvetot and many others. It was mainly under the influence of the radical wing of the C.G.T. that the new movement developed and found its expression in the *Charter of Amiens* (1906), in which the principles and methods of the movement were laid down.

This new movement in France found a strong echo among the Latin workers and penetrated also into other countries. The influence of French Syndicalism at that time on larger and smaller sections of the international labor movement was strengthened in great degree by the internal crisis which at that period infected nearly all the socialist labor parties in Europe. The battle between the so-called Revisionists and the rigid Marxists, and particularly the fact that their very parliamentary activities forced the most violent opponents of the Revisionists of natural necessity to travel along the path of Revisionism, caused many of the more thoughtful elements to reflect seriously. They realized that participation in the politics of the nationalist states had not brought the labor movement an hair-breath nearer to socialism, but had helped greatly to destroy the belief in the necessity of constructive socialist activity, and, worst of all, had robbed the people of their initiative by giving them the ruinous delusion that salvation always comes from above.

Under these circumstances Socialism steadily lost its character of a cultural ideal, which was to prepare the workers for the dissolution of the present capitalist system and, therefore could not let itself be halted by the artificial frontiers of the national states. In the mind of the leaders of the modern labor parties the alleged aims of their movement were more and more blended with the interests of the national state, until at last they became unable to distinguish any definite boundary whatever between them. It would be a mistake to find in this strange about-face an intentional betrayal by the leaders, as has so often been asserted. The truth is that we have to do here with a gradual assimilation to the modes and thoughts of the present society which necessarily had to affect the intellectual attitude of the leaders of the various labor parties in every country. Those very parties which had once set out to conquer political power under the flag of Socialism saw themselves compelled by the iron logic of conditions to sacrifice their socialist convictions bit by bit to the national policies of the state. The political power which they had wanted to conquer had gradually conquered their Socialism until there was scarely anything left but the name.

The Role of the Trade Unions—Anarcho-Syndicalist View

These were the considerations which led to the development of revolutionary Syndicalism or, as it was later called, Anarcho-Syndicalism in France and other countries. The term *worker's syndicate* meant at first merely an organization of producers for the immediate betterment of their economic and social status. But the rise of revolutionary Syndicalism gave this original meaning a much wider and deeper import. Just as the party is, so to speak, a unified organization with definite political effort within the modern constitutional state which seeks to maintain the present order of society in one form or another, so, according to the Syndicalist's view, the trade unions are the unified organization of labor and have for their purpose the defense of the producers within the existing society and the preparing for and practical carrying out of the reconstruction of social life in the direction of Socialism. They have, therefore, a double purpose: 1. To enforce the demands of the producers for the safeguarding and raising of their standard of living; 2. To acquaint the workers with the technical management of production and economic life in general and prepare them to take the socio-economic organism into their own hands and shape it according to socialist principles.

Anarcho-Syndicalists are of the opinion that political parties are not fitted to perform either of these two tasks. According to their conceptions the trade union has to be the spearhead of the labor movement, toughened by daily combats and permeated by a socialist spirit. Only in the realm of economy are the workers able to display their full strength, for it is their activity as producers which holds together the whole social structure and guarantees the existence of society. Only as a producer and creator of social wealth does the worker become aware of his strength. In solidary union with his followers he creates the great phalanx of militant labor, aflame with the spirit of freedom and animated by the ideal of social justice. For the Anarcho-Syndicalists the labor syndicates are the most fruitful germs of a future society, the elementary school of Socialism in general. Every new social structure creates organs for itself in the body of the old organism; without this prerequisite every social evolution is unthinkable. To them Socialist education does not mean participation in the power policy of the national state, but the effort to make clear to the workers the intrinsic connections among social problems by technical instruction and the development of their administrative capacities, to prepare them for their rôle of re-shapers of economic life and give them the moral assurance required for the performance of their task. No social body is better fitted for this purpose than the economic fighting organization of the workers; it gives a definite direction to their social activities and toughens their resistance in the immediate struggle for the necessities of life and the defense of their human rights. At the same time it develops their ethical concepts without which any social transformation is impossible: vital solidarity with their fellows in destiny and moral responsibility for their actions.

Just because the educational work of Anarcho-Syndicalists is directed toward the development of independent thought and action, they are outspoken opponents of all centralizing tendencies which are so characteristic of most of the present labor parties. Centralism, that artificial scheme which operates from the top towards the bottom and turns over the affairs of administration to a small minority, is always attended by barren official routine; it crushes individual conviction, kills all personal initiative by lifeless discipline and bureaucratic ossification. For the state, centralism is the appropriate form of organization, since it aims at the greatest possible uniformity of social life for the maintenance of political and social equilibrium. But for a movement whose very existence depends on prompt action at any favorable moment and on the independent thought of its supporters, centralism is a curse which weakens its power of decision and systematically represses every spontaneous initiative.

The organization of Anarcho-Syndicalism is based on the principles of Federalism, on free combination from below upward, putting the right of self-determination of every union above everything else and recognizing only the organic agreement of all on the basis of like interests and common conviction. Their organization is accordingly constructed on the following basis: The workers in each locality join the unions of their respective trades. The trade unions of a city or a rural district combine in Labor Chambers which constitute the centers for local propaganda and education and weld the workers together as producers to prevent the rise of any narrow minded factional spirit. In times of local labor troubles they arrange for the united co-operation of the whole body of locally organized labor. All the Labor Chambers are grouped according to districts and regions to form the National Federation of Labor Chambers, which maintains the permanent connection among the local bodies, arranges free adjustment of the productive labor of the members of the various organizations on co-operative lines, provides for the necessary coordination in the work of education and supports the local groups with council and guidance.

Every trade union is, moreover, federatively allied with all the organizations of the same industry, and these in turn with all related trades, so that all are combined in general industrial and agricultural alliances. It is their task to meet the demands of the daily struggles between capital and labor and to combine all the forces of the movement for common action where the necessity arises. Thus the Federation of the Labor Chambers and the Federation of the Industrial Alliances constitute the two poles about which the whole life of the labor syndicates revolves.

Such a form of organization not only gives the workers every opportunity for direct action in the struggle for their daily bread, but it also provides them with the necessary preliminaries for the reorganization of society, their own strength, and without alien intervention in case of a revolutionary crisis. Anarcho-Syndicalists are convinced that a socialist economic order cannot be created by the decrees and statutes of any government, but only by the unqualified collaboration of the workers, technicians and peasants to carry on production and distribution by their own administration in the interest of the community and on the basis of mutual agreements. In such a situation the Labor Chambers would take over the administration of existing social capital in each community, determine the needs of the inhabitants of their districts and organize local consumption. Through the agency of the Federation of Labor Chambers it would be possible to calculate the total requirements of the whole country and adjust the work of production accordingly. On the other hand it would be the task of the Industrial and Agricultural Alliances to take control of all the instruments of production, transportation, etc. and provide the separate producing groups with what they need. In a word: 1. Organization of the total production of the country by the Federation of the Industrial Alliances and direction of work by labor councils elected by the workers themselves; 2. Organization of social contribution by the Federation of the Labor Chambers.

In this respect, also, practical experience has given the best instruction. It has shown that the many problems of a socialist reconstruction of society cannot be solved by any government, even when the famous dictatorship of the proletariat is meant. In Russia the Bolshevist dictatorship stood helpless for almost two years before the economic problems and tried to hide its incapacity behind a flood of decrees and ordinances most of which were buried at once in the various bureaus. If the world could be set free by decrees, there would long ago have been no problems left in Russia. In its fanatical zeal for power, Bolshevism has violently destroyed the most valuable organs of a socialist order, by suppressing the Co-operative Societies, bringing the trade unions under state control, and depriving the Soviets of their independence almost from the beginning. So the dictatorship of the proletariat paved the way not for a socialist society but for the most primitive type of bureaucratic state capitalism and a reversion to political absolutism which was long ago abolished in most countries by bourgeois revolutions. In his *Message to the Workers of the West European Countries* Kropotkin said, rightfully: "Russia has shown us the way in which Socialism cannot be realized, although the people, nauseated with the old regime, expressed no active resistance to the experiments of the new government. The idea of workers' councils for the control of the political and economic life of the country is, in itself, of extraordinary importance...but so long as the country is dominated by the dictatorship of a party, the workers' and peasants' councils naturally lose their significance. They are hereby degraded to the same passive rôle which the representatives of the Estates used to play in the time of the absolute Monarchy."

The Struggle in Germany and Spain

In Germany, however, where the moderate wing of political socialism had attained power, Socialism, in its long years of absorption with routine parliamentary tasks, had become so bogged down that it was no longer capable of any creative action whatever. Even a bourgeois paper like the *Frankfurter Zeitung* felt obliged to confirm that "the history of European peoples had not previously produced a revolution that has been so poor in creative ideas and so weak in revolutionary energy." The mere fact that a party with a larger membership than any other of the various labor parties in the world, which was for many years the strongest political body in Germany, had to leave to Hitler and his gang the field without any resistance speaks for itself and presents an example of helplessness and weakness which can hardly be misunderstood.

One has only to compare the German situation of those days with the attitude of the anarcho-syndicalist labor unions in Spain and especially in Catalonia, where their influence was strongest, to realize the whole difference between the labor movement of these two countries. When in July 1936 the conspiracy of the Fascist Army leaders ripened into open revolt, it was by the heroic resistance of the C.N.T. (National Federation of Labor) and the F.A.I. (Anarchist Federation of Iberia) that the Fascist uprising in Catalonia was put down within a few days, ridding this most important part of Spain of the enemy and frustrating the original plan of the conspirators to take Barcelona by surprise. The workers could then not stop half way; so there followed the collectivization of the land and the taking over of the plants by the workers' and peasants' syndicates. This movement which was released by the initiative of the C.N.T. and F.A.I. with irresistable power overran Aragon, the Levante and other sections of the country and even swept along with it a large part of the unions of the Socialist Party in the U.G.T. (General Labor Union). This event revealed that the anarcho-syndicalist workers of Spain not only knew how to fight, but that they also were filled with the constructive ideas which are so necessary in the time of a real crisis. It is to the great merit of Libertarian Socialism in Spain that since the time of the First International it has trained the workers in that spirit which treasures freedom above all else and regards the intellectual independence of its adherents as the basis of its existence).[1] It was the passive and lifeless attitude of the organ-

[1] Here are just a few opinions of foreign socialists of distinction who had no personal connection with the Anarchist movement. Thus Andres Oltmares, Professor at the University of Geneva, said in an address about his experiences in Spain:

"In the midst of the Civil War the Anarchists have proven themselves to be political organizers of the first rank. They kindled in everyone the required sense of responsibility, and knew how, by eloquent appeals, to keep alive the spirit of sacrifice for the general welfare of the people. As a Social Democrat I speak here with inner joy and sincere admiration of my experiences in Catalonia. The anti-capitalist transformation took place here without their having to resort to a dictatorship. The members of the syndicates are their own masters and carry on production and the distribution of the products of labor under their own management, with the advice of technical experts in whom they have confidence. The enthusiasm of the workers is so great that they scorn any personal advantage and are concerned only for the welfare of all."

ized workers in other countries, who put up with the policy of non-intervention of their governments that led to the defeat of the Spanish workers and peasants after a heroic struggle of more than two and one half years against the combined forces of Franco, Hitler and Mussolini, a struggle which has been justly called the prologue to the second world war.

The Political Struggle—Anarcho-Syndicalist View

It has often been charged against Anarcho-Syndicalism that its adherents had no interest in the political structure of the different countries and consequently no interest in the political struggles of the time. This idea is altogether erroneous and springs either from outright ignorance or wilful distortion of the facts. It is not the political struggle as such which distinguishes the Anarcho-Syndicalists from the modern labor parties, both in principles and tactics, but the form of this struggle and the aims which it

The well known Italian professor Carlo Rosselli, who was later assassinated in France by agents of Mussolini, expressed his judgment in the following words:

"In three months Catalonia has been able to set up a new social order on the ruins of an ancient system. This is chiefly due to the Anarchists, who have revealed a quite remarkable sense of proportion, realistic understanding, and organizing ability. . . . All the revolutionary forces of Catalonia have united in a program of Syndicalist-Socialist character. . . . Anarcho-Syndicalism, hitherto so despised, has revealed itself as a great constructive force. I am not an Anarchist, but I regard it as my duty to express here my opinion of the Anarchists of Catalonia, who have all too often been represented as a destructive if not as a criminal element. I was with them at the front, in the trenches, and I have learned to admire them. . . . A new world was born with them, and it is a joy to serve this world."

And Fenner Brockway, the secretary of the Independent Labor Party in England, gave the following opinion about his experiences in Spain at that time:

"I was impressed by the strength of the C.N.T. It was unnecessary to tell me that it is the largest and most vital of the working class organizations in Spain. That was evident on all sides. The large industries were clearly in the main in the hands of the C.N.T. — railways, road transport, shipping, engineering, textiles, electricity, building, agriculture. . . . I was immensely impressed by the constructive revolutionary work which is being done by the C.N.T. Their achievements of workers' control in industry is an inspiration. . . . There are still some Britishers and Americans who regard the Anarchists of Spain as impossible, undisciplined uncontrollables. This is poles away from truth. The Anarchists of Spain through the C.N.T. are doing one of the biggest constructive jobs ever done by the working class. At the front they are fighting Fascism. Behind the front they are actually constructing the new workers' society. They see that the war against Fascism and the carrying through the social revolution are inseparable. Those who have seen them and understood what they are doing must honor them and be grateful to them. . . . That is surely the biggest thing which has hitherto been done by the workers in any part of the world."

has in view. Anarcho-Syndicalists pursue the same tactics in their fight against political suppression as against economic exploitation. But while they are convinced that along with the system of exploitation its political protective device, the state will also disappear to give place to the administration of public affairs on the basis of free agreement, they do not at all overlook the fact that the efforts of organized labor within the existing political and social order must always be directed toward defending all achieved political and social rights against any attack of reaction, and constantly widening the scope of these rights wherever the opportunity for this presents itself. The heroic struggle of the C.N.T. in Spain against Fascism was, perhaps, the best proof that the alleged non-political attitude of the Anarcho-Syndicalists is but idle talk.

But according to their opinion the point of attack in the political struggle lies not in the legislative bodies but in the people. Political rights do not originate in parliaments; they are rather forced upon them from without. And even their enactment into law has for a long time been no guarantee of their security. They do not exist because they have been legally set down on a piece of paper, but only when they have become the ingrown habit of a people, and when any attempt to impair them will meet with the violent resistance of the populace. Where this is not the case, there is no help in any parliamentary opposition or any Platonic appeals to the constitution. One compels respect from others when one knows how to defend one's dignity as a human being. This is not only true in private life; it has always been the same in political life as well. All political rights and liberties which people enjoy today, they do not owe to the good will of their governments, but to their own strength. Governments have always employed every means in their power to prevent the attainments of these rights or render them illusory. Great mass movements and whole revolutions have been necessary to wrest them from the ruling classes, who would never have consented to them voluntarily. The whole history of the last three hundred years is proof of that. *What is important is not that governments have decided to concede certain rights to the people, but the reason why they had to do this.* Of course, if one accepts Lenin's cynical phrase and thinks of freedom merely as a "bourgeois prejudice," then, to be sure, political rights have no value at all for the workers. But then the countless struggles of the past, all the revolts and revolutions to which we owe these rights, are also without value. To proclaim this bit of wisdom it hardly was necessary to overthrow Tzarism, for even the censorship of Nicholas II would certainly have had no objection to the designation of freedom as a *bourgeois prejudice.*

If Anarcho-Syndicalism nevertheless rejects the participation in the present national parliaments, it is not because they have no sympathy with political struggles in general, but because its adherents are of opinion that this form of activity is the very weakest and most helpless form of the political struggle for the workers. For the possessing classes, parliamentary action is certainly an appropriate instrument for the settlement of such conflicts as arise, because they are all equally interested in maintaining the present economic and social order. Where there is a common interest mutual agreement is possible and serviceable to all parties. But for the workers the situation is very different. For them the existing economic order is the source of their exploitation and their social and political subjugation. Even the freest ballot cannot do away with the glaring contrast between the possessing and non-possessing classes in society. It can only give the servitude of the toiling masses the stamp of legality.

It is a fact that when socialist labor parties have wanted to achieve some decisive political reforms they could not do it by parliamentary action, but were obliged to rely wholly on the economic fighting power of the workers. The political general strikes in Belgium and Sweden for the attainment of universal suffrage are proof of this. And in Russia it was the great general strike in 1905 that forced the Tsar to sign the new constitution. It was the recognition of this which impelled the Anarcho-Syndicalists to center their activity on the socialist education of the masses and the utilization of their economic and social power. Their method is that of direct action in both the economic and political struggle of the time. By direct action they mean every method of the immediate struggle by the workers against economic and political oppression. Among these the outstanding are the strike in all its graduations, from the simple wage struggle to the general strike, organized boycott and all the other countless means which workers as producers have in their hands.

The General Strike

One of the most effective forms of direct action is the *social strike*, which was hitherto mostly used in Spain and partly in France, and which shows a remarkable and growing responsibility of the workers to society as a whole. It is less concerned with the immediate interests of the producers than with the protection of the community against the most pernicious outgrowths of the present system. The social strike seeks to force upon the employers a responsibility to the public. Primarily it has in view the protection of the consumers, of which the workers themselves constitute the great majority. Under the present circumstances the workers are frequently debased by doing a thousand things which constantly serve only to injure the whole community for the advantage of the employers. They are compelled to make use of inferior and often actually injurious materials in the fabrication of their products, to erect wretched dwellings, to put up spoiled foodstuffs and to perpetrate innumerable acts that are planned to cheat the consumer. To interfere vigorously is, in the opinion of the Anarcho-Syndicalists, the great task of the labor syndicates. An advance in this direction would at the same time enhance the position of the workers in society, and in larger measure confirm that position.

Direct action by organized labor finds its strongest expression in the general strike, in the stoppage of work in every branch of production in cases where every other means is failing. It is the most powerful weapon which the workers have at their command and gives the most comprehensive expression to their strength as a social factor. The general strike, of course is not an agency that can be invoked arbitrarily on every occasion. It needs certain, social assumptions to give it a proper moral strength and make it a proclamation of the will of the broad masses of the people. The ridiculous claim, which is so often attributed to the Anarcho-Syndicalists, that it is only necessary to proclaim a general strike in order to achieve a socialist society in a few days, is, of course, just a ludicrous invention of ignorant opponents. The general strike is the last resort of the workers in a given situation when dire necessity leaves no other way.

The general strike can serve various purposes. It can be the last stage of a sympathetic strike, as, for example, in Barcelona in 1902 or in Bilbao in 1903, which enabled the miners to get rid of the hated truck system and compelled the employers to establish sanitary conditions in the mines. It can also be a means of organized labor to enforce some general demand, as, for example, in the attempted general strike in the U.S.A. in 1886, to compel the granting of the eight hour day in all industries. The great general strike of the English workers in 1926 was the result of a planned attempt by the employers to lower the general standard of living of the workers by a cut in wages.

But the general strike can also have political objectives in view, as, for example, the fight of the Spanish workers in 1904 for the liberation of the political prisoners, or the general strike in Catalonia in July 1909, to force the government to terminate its criminal war in Morocco. Also the general strike of the German workers in 1920, which was instituted after the so-called Kapp putsch and put an end to a government that had attained power by a military uprising, belongs to this category. In such critical situations the general strike takes the place of the barricades of the political uprisings of the past. For the workers, the general strike is the logical outcome of the modern industrial system, whose victims they are today, and at the same time it offers them their strongest weapon in the struggle for their social liberation, provided they recognize their own strength and learn how to use this weapon properly.

Anarcho-Syndicalism Since the First World War

After the First World War the peoples in Europe faced a new situation. In Central Europe the old regime had collapsed. Russia found herself in the midst of a social revolution of which no one could see the end. The Russian revolution had impressed the workers of every country very deeply. They felt that Europe was in the midst of a revolutionary crisis and that if nothing decisive came out of it now their hopes would be dispelled for many years. For this reason they based the highest hopes on the Russian revolution and saw in it the inauguration of a new era in European history. In 1919 the Bolshevist party, which had attained power in Russia, issued an appeal to all the revolutionary workers' organizations of the world and invited them to a congress in the following year in Moscow to set up a new International. Communist parties at this time existed only in a few countries; on the other hand there were in Spain, Portugal, France, Italy, Holland, Sweden, Germany, England and the countries of North and South America syndicalist organizations, some of which exercised a very strong influence. It was, therefore, the deep concern of Lenin and his followers to win these particular organizations for their purpose. So it came about that at the congress for the founding of the Third International in the summer of 1920 almost all the syndicalist organizations of Europe were represented.

But the impression which the syndicalist delegates received in Russia was not calculated to make them regard collaboration with the Communists as either possible or desirable. The dictatorship of the proletariat was already revealing itself in its true light. The prisons were filled with Socialists of every school, among them many Anarchists and Syndicalists. But above all it was plain that the new dominant caste was in no way fitted for the task of a genuine socialist construction of life. The foundation of the Third International with its dictatorial apparatus and its effort to make the whole labor movement in Europe into an instrument for the foreign policy of the Bolshevist state quickly made plain to the Syndicalists that there was no place for them in the Third International. For this reason the congress in Moscow decided to set up alongside the Third International a separate international alliance of revolutionary trade unions, in which the syndicalist organizations of all shades could also find a place. The Syndicalist delegates agreed to this proposal, but when the Communists demanded that this new organization should be subordinate to the Third International, this demand was unanimously rejected by the Syndicalists.

In December 1920 an international Syndicalist conference convened in Berlin to decide upon an attitude toward the approaching congress of the *Red Trade Union International,* which was prepared in Moscow for the following year. The conference agreed upon seven points on whose acceptance the entrance of the Syndicalists in that body was made dependent. The importance of those seven points was the complete independence of the movement from all political parties, and insistence on the viewpoint that the socialist reconstruction of society could only be carried out by the economic organizations of the producing classes themselves. At the congress in Moscow in the following year the syndicalist organizations were in the minority. The *Central Alliance of Russian Trade Unions* dominated the entire situation and put through all the resolutions.

In October 1921 an international conference of Syndicalists was held in Düsseldorf, Germany, and it decided to call an international convention in Berlin during the following year. This convention met from December 25, 1922 until January 2, 1923. The following organizations were represented: Argentina by the *Federación Obrera Regional Argentina,* with 200,000 members; Chile by the *Industrial Workers of the World* with 20,000 members; Denmark by the *Union for Syndicalist Propaganda* with 600 members; Germany by the *Freie Arbeiter Union* with 120,000 members; Holland by the *National Arbeids Sekretariat* with 22,500 members; Italy by the *Unione Sindicale Italiana* with 500,000 members; Mexico by the *Confederación General de Trabajadores;* Norway by the *Norsk Syndikalistik Federasjon* with 20,000 members; Portugal by the *Confederacao Genral do Trabalho* with 150,000 members; Sweden by the *Sveriges Arbetares Centarlorganisation* with 32,000 members. The Spanish C.N.T. at that time was engaged in a terrific struggle against the dictatorship of Primo de Rivera and had sent no delegates, but they reaffirmed their adherence at the secret congress in Saragossa in October 1923. In France, where after the war a split in the C.G.T. had led to the founding of the C.G.T.U., the latter had already joined Moscow. But there was a minority in the organization which had combined to form the *Comité de Defence Syndicaliste Revolutionaire,* representing about 100,000 workers, which took part in the proceedings of the Berlin congress. From Paris the *Fédération du Batiment* with 32,000 members and the *Fédération des Jeunesses de la Seine* were likewise represented. Two delegates represented the Syndicalist Minority of the Russian workers.

The congress resolved unanimously on the founding of an international alliance of all syndicalist organizations under the name *International Workmen's Association.* It adopted a declaration of principles which presented an outspoken profession of Anarcho-Syndicalism. The second item in this declaration runs as follows:

"Revolutionary Syndicalism is the confirmed opponent of every form of economic and social monopoly, and aims at the establishment of free communities and administrative organs of the field and factory workers on the basis of a free system of labor councils, entirely liberated from subordination to any government and parties. Against the politics of the state and political parties it proposes the economic organization of labor; against the government of men it sets the management of things. Consequently, it has for its object, not the conquest of power, but the abolition of every state function in social life. It believes that, along with the monopoly of property, should also disappear the monopoly of domination, and that any form of the state, including the dictatorship of the proletariat, will always be the creator of new monopolies and new privileges; and never an instrument of liberation."

With this the breach with Bolshevism and its adherents in the various countries was completed. The I.W.M.A. from then on travelled its own road, held its own international congresses, issued its bulletins and adjusted the relations among the syndicalist organizations of the different countries.

The most powerful and influential organization in the I.W.M.A. was the Spanish C.N.T., the soul of all the hard labor struggles in Spain and later the backbone of the resistance against Fascism and the social reorganization of the country. Before the triumph of Franco, the C.N.T. embraced a membership of about two millions of industrial workers, peasants and intellectual workers. It controlled thirty-six daily papers, among them *Solidaridad Obrera* in Barcelona, with a circulation of 240,000 the largest of any paper in Spain, and *Castilla Libre*, which was the most widely read paper in Madrid. The C.N.T. has published millions of books and pamphlets and contributed more to the education of the masses than any other movement in Spain.

In Portugal the *Confederacao Geral do Trabalho,* founded in 1911, was the strongest labor organization in the country, and based on the same principles as the C.N.T. in Spain. After the victory of dictatorship, the C.G.T. was forced out of public activity and could only lead an underground existence.

In Italy, under the influence of the ideas of French Syndicalism, the syndicalist wing of the *Confederazione del Lavoro* left that organization on account of its subservience to the Socialist Party and formed the *Unione Sindicale Italiana.* This group was the soul of a long list of severe labor struggles and played a prominent part in the occurrences of the so-called *Red Week* in June 1913 and later in the occupation of the factories in Milan and other cities in Northern Italy. With the reign of Fascism the whole Italian labor movement disappeared along with the U.S.I.

In France the Anarcho-Syndicalists left the C.G.T.U. in 1922, after that organization yielded entirely to the influence of the Bolshevists, and formed the *Confédération Génerale du Travail Syndicaliste Revolutionaire,* which joined the I.W.M.A.

In Germany there existed for a long time before the first world war the so-called *Localists* whose stronghold was the *Freie Vereinigung deutscher Gewerkschaften,* founded in 1897. This organization was originally inspired by Social Democratic ideas, but it combated the centralizing tendencies of the German Trade movement. The revival of French Syndicalism had a great influence upon the F.V.D.G. and led to its adoption of pure syndicalist principles. At its congress in Düsseldorf, 1920, the organization changed its name to *Freie Arbeiter-Union Deutschlands.* This movement rendered a great service through the tireless labors of its active publishing house in Berlin which printed a large number of valuable works. After Hitler's accession to power the movement of the F.A.U.D. vanished from the scene. A great many of its supporters languished in the concentration camps or had to take refuge abroad.

In Sweden there still exists a very active syndicalist movement, the *Sveriges Arbetares Centalorganisation,* the only syndicalist organization in Europe which escaped the reaction of Fascism and German invasion during the war. The Swedish Syndicalists participated in all the great labor struggles in their country and carried on for many years the work of socialist and libertarian education. The movement has at its disposal a large daily paper, *Arbetaren,* in Stockholm, and its internal organization is very efficient.

In Holland the syndicalist movement concentrated in the *Nationale Arbeids Secretariat;* but when this organization came steadily under increasing Communist influence, nearly half of its members split off and formed the *Nederlandisch Syndikalistisch Vakverbond* which joined the I.W.M.A.

In addition to these organizations there were Anarcho-Syndicalist propaganda groups in Norway, Poland and Bulgaria, which were affiliated with the I.W.M.A. The Japanese *Jiyu Rengo Dantal Zenkoku Kaigi* also joined the ranks of the I.W.M.A.

In Argentina the *Federación Obrera Regional Argentina*, founded in 1891, was for many years the center of most of the big labor struggles in that country. Its history is one of the most tempestuous chapters in the annals of the labor movement. The movement ran a daily organ, *La Protesta*, for over twenty-five years and quite a number of weekly papers all over the country. After the coup-d'etat of General Uribura, the F.O.R.A. was suppressed, but it carried on underground activity, as it does now under Peron. In May 1929 the F.O.R.A. summoned a congress of all the South American countries to meet in Buenos Aires. At this congress, besides the F.O.R.A. of Argentina, there were represented: Paraguay by the *Centro Obrero del Paraguay;* Bolivia by the *Federación Local de la Paz, La Antorcha* and *Luz y Libertad;* Mexico by the *Confederación general de Trabajo;* Guatemala by the *Comite pro Accion Sindical;* Uruguay by the *Federación Regional Uruguaya.* Brazil was represented by trade unions from seven of the constituent states. Costa Rica was represented by the organization *Hacia la Libertad.* At this congress the *Continental American Workingmen's Association* was brought into existence, constituting the American division of the I.W.M.A. The seat of this organization was at first at Buenos Aires, but later, because of the dictatorship, it had to be transferred to Uruguay.

These were the forces which Anarcho-Syndicalism had at its disposal in the various countries before the Reign of Fascism and the outbreak of the second world war. The International Bureau of the I.W.M.A., which was transferred during those years of reaction and war to Sweden, is at present occupied with the preparations for an International congress of the reorganizing syndicalist forces.

BIBLIOGRAPHY

ANARCHISM

ANDREWS, S. P.: *The Science of Society*, New York, 1851.

BAKUNIN, M.: *L'Empire knouto-germanique et la révolution sociale*, Geneve, 1871.

BAKUNIN, M.: *Dieu et L'Etat*, Geneve, 1882.

BAKUNIN, M.: *La theologie politique de Mazzini et l'Internationale*, Neuchâtel, 1871.

BAKUNIN, M.: *Gosudarstvenost i Anarchüa*, Zürich, 1873.

BERKMAN, A.: *The Bolshevik Myth*, New York, 1925.

BERKMAN, A.: *Now and After*, New York, 1929.

DE CLEYRE, VOLTAIRINE: *Selected Works*, New York, 1914.

DOMELA-NIEUWENHUIS, F.: *Le Socialism en danger*, Paris, 1893.

ELTZBACHER, P.: *Der Anarchismus*, Berlin, 1902.

FABBRI, L.: *Influencias burguesas sobre el Anarquismo*, Barcelona, 1918.

FABBRI, L.: *Dictadura y Revolucion*, Buenos Aires, 1921.

FABBRI, L.: *La Crisis del Anarquismo*, Buenos Aires, 1921.

GODWIN, W.: *An Enquiry Concerning Political Justice and Its Influence on General Virtue and Happiness*, London, 1793.

GREENE, W. B.: *Mutual Banking*, West Brookfield, Mass., 1851.

GREY, J.: *The Social System, a Treatise on the Principles of Exchange*, Edinburgh, 1831.

KROPOTKIN, P.: *Paroles d'un révolté*, Paris, 1885.

KROPOTKIN, P.: *La conquête du pain*, Paris, 1892.

KROPOTKIN, P.: *Fields, Factories, and Workshops*, London, 1899.

KROPOTKIN, P.: *Mutual Aid—A Factor of Evolution*, London, 1902.

KROPOTKIN, P.: *The French Revolution*, London, 1909.

KROPOTKIN, P.: *La science moderne et l'anarchie*, Paris, 1913.

KROPOTKIN, P.: *Ethics—Origin and Development*, London, 1924.

LANDAUER, G.: *Aufruf zum Sozialismus*, Berlin, 1913.

LANDAUER, G.: *Die Revolution*, Frankfurt, 1907.

MALATESTA, E.: *La politica parlamentare nel movimento socialista*, Mantova, 1890.

MALATESTA, E.: *L'Anarchia*, Geneva, 1891.

MELLA, R.: *La Anarquia, la Federacion y el Colectivismo*, Sevilla, 1891.

MELLA, R.: *Lambroso y los Anarquistas*, Barcelona, 1896.

MERLINO, S.: *Socialismo o Monopolismo*, Naples, 1887.

PISACANE, CARLO: *Saggi storici—politici—militari sull' Italia, Terzo saggio: La Rivoluzione*, Milan, 1860.

PROUDHON, P. J.: *Qu'est-ce la propriété?* Paris, 1841.

PROUDHON, P. J.: *Idée générale de la révolution au XIXe siècle*, Paris, 1851.

PROUDHON, P.J.: *De la justice dans la révolution et dans l'eglise*, Paris, 1858.

PROUDHON, P. J.: *Du principe féderatif et de la nécessité de reconstituer le parti de la révolution*, Paris, 1863.

Proudhon, P. J.: *De la capacité politique des classes ouvrières*, Paris, 1865.

Reclus, Elisée: *Evolution et Révolution*, Paris, 1892.

Reclus, Elisée: *An Anarchist on Anarchy*, London, 1894.

Reclus, Elisée: *L'homme et la terre* (6 vols.), Paris, 1905-1908.

Rocker, R.: *Nationalism and Culture*, New York, 1927.

Spreading, Ch.: *Freedom and Its Fundamentals*, Los Angeles, 1923.

Spooner, L.: *Natural Law or the Science of Justice*, Boston, Mass., 1882.

Spooner, L.: *An Essay on the Trial by Jury*, Boston, Mass., 1853.

Stirner, Max: *Der Einzige und sein Eigentum*, Leipzig, 1845.

Tcherkesoff, W.: *Pages of Socialist History, New York*, 1902.

Thompson, W.: *An Inquiry into the Principles of the Distribution of Wealth, etc.*, London, 1824.

Tolstoi, L.: *My Confession*, London, 1879.

Tolstoi, L.: *What I Believe*, London, 1884.

Tolstoi, L.: *What Shall We Do Then*, London, 1885.

Tolstoi, L.: *The Kingdom of God Is Within You*, London, 1893.

Tucker, B. R.: *Instead of a Book, by a man too busy to write one*, New York, 1893.

Warren, J.: *True Civilization: a subject of vital and serious interest to all people, but most immediately to the men and women of Labor and Sorrow, Boston*, Mass., 1863.

HISTORICAL AND BIOGRAPHIC WORKS

Nettlau, M.: *Michael Bakunin. Eine Biographie*, London, 1896-1900.

Berkman, A.: *Prison Memoirs of an Anarchist*, New York, 1912.

Goldman, Emma: *My Disillusionment in Russia*, New York, 1923.

Goldman, Emma: *Living My Life*, New York, 1931.

Guillaume, J.: *L'Internationale, documents et souvenirs*, Paris, 1905-1910.

Kropotkin, P.: *Memoirs of a Revolutionist*, London, 1899.

Lorenzo, A.: *El Proletariado Militante*, Barcelona, 1902-1923.

Mackay, J. H.: *Max Stirner, sein Leben und sein Werk*, Berlin, 1898.

Nettlau, M.: *Errico Malatesta: Das Leben eines Anarchisten*, Berlin, 1924.

Nettlau, M.: *Bibliographie de l'Anarchie*, Paris, 1897.

Nettlau, M.: *Elisée Reclus, Anarchist und Gelehrter*, Berlin, 1927.

Nettlau, M.: *Der Vorfrühling der Anarchie*, Berlin, 1925.

Nettlau, M.: *Der Anarchismus von Proudhon zu Kropotkin*, Berlin, 1927.

Nettlau, M.: *Anarchisten und Sozialrevolutionäre*, Berlin, 1931.

Rocker, R.: *Johann Most, das Leben eines Rebellen*, Berlin, 1924.

Rocker, R.: *El Pensamiento liberal en los Estados Unidos*, Buenos Aires, 1942.

ANARCHO - SYNDICALISM

Baginski, M.: *Syndikalismus; lebendige, keine tote Gewerkschaften*, Berlin, 1925.

Besnard, P.: *Les syndicats ouvriers et la révolution sociale*, Paris, 1930.

BUENACASA, M.: *El movimiento obrero español,* Barcelona, 1928.
C.N.T. (published by): *Les oeuvre constructive de la Révolution Espagnole,* Barcelona, 1937.
CORNELISSEN, CH.: *Ueber den internationalen Syndikalisimus,* Leipzig, 1910.
FABBRI, L.: *Sindicalismo y Anarquismo,* Valencia, 1908.
GRIFFELES, V.: *L'action syndicaliste,* Paris, 1908.
LAGARDELLE, H.: *La grève générale et le socialisme,* Paris, 1905.
LEVINE, L.: *The Labor Movement in France,* New York, 1912.
MANN, T.: *Prepare for Action,* London, 1910.
MANN, T.: *Symposium on Syndicalism,* London, 1910.
PATAUD AND POUGET: *Syndicalism and the Co-operative Commonwealth,* London, 1913.
PELOUTIER, F.: *L'organisation corporative et l'anarchie,* Paris, 1896.
PELOUTIER, F.: *Histoire des Bourses du Travail,* Paris, 1902.
PIERROT, M.: *Syndicalisme et révolution,* Paris, 1908.
POUGET, E.: *La Confédération du Travail,* Paris, 1908.
POUGET, E.: *Le Parti du Travail,* Paris, 1909.
POUGET, E.: *Sabotage,* Paris, 1911.
ROCKER, R.: *Der Kampf ums tägliche Brot,* Berlin, 1925.
ROCKER, R.: *Anarcho-Syndicalism,* London, 1928.
ROLLER, A.: *The Social General Strike,* London, 1902.
ROLLER, A.: *Die direkte Aktion als Gewerkschaftstaktik,* New York, 1906.
SANTILLAN, D. A.: *Reconstrucción social,* Buenos Aires, 1933.
SANTILLAN, D. A.: *El organismo económico de la revolución,* Barcelona, 1936.
SANTILLAN, D. A.: *La revolución y la guerra en España,* Buenos Aires, 1937.
SCHAPIRO, A.: *The International Workingmen's Association: Aims and Principles,* Berlin, 1933.
SOUCHY, A.: *Spain,* New York, 1937.
SOUSA, M. J.: *O sindicalismo en Portugal,* Lisboa, 1931.
TOBLER, M.: *Der revolutionäre Syndikalismus,* Zürich, 1922.

X.
Agrarianism

THE IDEOLOGY OF THE PEASANT MOVEMENTS

Editorial Note

The following two chapters on the peasant movement were written by Mr. Victor Zenzinov, theoretician of the Russian radical peasant movement, also known as the Social Revolutionary Movement, (SR), and by Dr. George M. Dimitrov, leader of the Bulgarian Peasant Party and Secretary General of the International Peasant Union.

The Social Revolutionary Party was a broad, democratic peasant and intellectual movement directed against Tsarist tyranny, and toward a free and democratic commonwealth of Russia. The Social Revolutionaries commanded the majority of the Russian peasantry during the first stages of the Revolution, before the Bolshevik minority succeeded in gaining control of the old Russian empire.

The Social Revolutionary Party was the historical Russian peasant party; the Bulgarian Peasant Party, the party of the late Stamboliiski, is the historical democratic party of Bulgarian peasantry. Both Mr. Zenzinov and Dr. Dimitrov are prominent in their movements. It should be noted herein that, with the exception of Russian Social Revolutionary ideology, peasant ideologies in eastern Europe were not particularly well-developed, and the peasant movements had more of a concrete, practical program than any real philosophy.

In his chapter, Dr. Dimitrov analyzes the ideologies of eastern European peasant movements, known, in some countries, as "Agrarianism." Dr. Dimitrov employs the term "Agrarianism" for all progressive peasant ideologies of the eastern European region.

There was not, however, any one accepted and recognized ideology of the eastern European peasantry similar, for instance, to Marxism. Nevertheless all democratic peasant movements had political attitudes and programs which were remarkably alike:

radical land reforms, small land ownership, peasant cooperatives, social justice, economic and social democracy achieved through democratic and cooperative peasant organizations, and devotion to true democratic institutions. These principles formed the core of almost all peasant programs and ideologies.

Dr. Dimitrov is one of the foremost ideologists of contemporary eastern European peasant movements. His bio-materialistic interpretation forms an important contribution to Bulgarian peasant ideology. Although not all eastern European peasant movements had an equally well-developed philosophy, and had (and still have) foundations other than bio-materialism, probably all of them were strongly empiricist and pragmatic.

The second portion of Dr. Dimitrov's discussion treats the history of eastern European peasant movements.

Mr. Victor Zenzinov gives an outline of Russian peasant ideology in the final chapter on this topic. Russian peasant ideology originated much earlier than the non-Russian, eastern European system, and had a more extensive philosophy and deeper historical background. Russian peasant ideologists—the "Narodniki" and the Social Revolutionaries—had an idealistic philosophic background, unlike that of the materialistic Marxist-Socialists. Fifty years ago, violent ideological battles were waged in books and periodicals between the Narodniki, or Social Revolutionaries, and the Orthodox Marxists.

In short, Mr. Zenzinov represents the idealistic philosophy; Dr. Dimitrov represents the bio-materialistic which, however, contains idealistic elements.

Since the chapter of Dr. Dimitrov has been written, representatives of eastern European peasant movements in exile have resurrected in Washington, in the summer of 1947 *the "Green International," a democratic and progressive "International Peasant*

Union." As was mentioned before, Dr. Dimitrov has been elected its Secretary General.

The reader is also referred to Chapter I. "Mechanics of European Politics," which contains a psychological and sociological analysis and comparison of peasant and labor movements in Europe; to Chapter II. "Communism"; Chapter V. "Consumer Cooperation and the Freedom of Man"; Chapter VII. "Liberal Tradition in Russia."

F. G.

X.

AGRARIANISM

by

GEORGE M. DIMITROV

IN ITS FUNDAMENTAL principles, Agrarianism tends to be an ideology of political and economic democracy based on the idea of cooperative syndicalism. It is an ideology of social justice which repudiates the communist idea of the dictatorship of the proletariat and upholds that of the private and cooperative ownership of the means of production and of its results for the laboring classes. Thus Agrarianism may be defined as cooperative syndicalism.

In its present tendencies, Agrarianism is undoubtedly one of the most recent and progressive ideologies, in spite of the fact that its origins are to be found in the past—in the struggles of the masses for freedom and social justice—in struggles of the tillers of the soil for land and of the industrial workers for participation in the ownership of the factories and in the shaping of the conditions of labor, of production and of the distribution of material wealth. Naturally, being recent, Agrarianism does not yet possess a systematic doctrine of fundamental principles or a coherent philosophical structure of values. Nevertheless, as may be seen even from this brief account, its ideological and theoretical argumentation tends to rely on the dynamic scientific attainments of the age taken as a whole. Starting from the treatment of the human problem in classical ancient philosophy Agrarianism moves toward the sociological efforts of modern thought and the attainments of cooperativism and economics. However, the most vigorous and reliable dicta of the Agrarian ideology have been derived from practical life and from the uniformities of nature. Thus Agrarianism is a practical rather than a theoretical ideology; its doctrine is being developed gradually on the basis of practical experience. Agrarian ideologians have aimed to observe and penetrate as deeply as possible the conditions of practical existence in order to ascertain the uniformities of phenomena rather than indulge in the composition of abstract philosophical treatises and utopias.

In principle, the Agrarian ideology upholds the idea of the materialistic explanation of natural phenomena to the extent to which the natural and experimental disciplines have established their material character. However, fundamentally, the Agrarian outlook relies primarily on the biological principle for the explanation of the historical, social and economic complexes of life in general and of the individual in particular. Agrarianism maintains that neither history nor economics is capable of explaining the phenomena of nature and their dynamics without the assistance of biology. Thus the Agrarian ideology tends to become a biological materialism which conceives the uniformities of natural phenomena in terms of a biologico-materialistic parallelism.

Biology is a comparatively new discipline but its attainments are fundamental because they deal with the most profound manifestations of life reflected in the phenomena of nature. Biology is the discipline of organic life: it unfolds the dynamic process of this life—of the organic matter which determines the development of human faculties. To what extent the organic principle dominates nature is shown in the fact that for the characterization of the earthly world men employ the term *life* rather than that of *matter*. Thus it would appear that Morley Roberts is quite correct to argue that "instead of history elucidating sociology, sociology based on biology will elucidate history."[1]

The Biological Factor in Social Phenomena

Cultural man, whose positive and negative characteristics have their source in his organic nature and his animal origin and who

[1] Morley Roberts, *Bio-Politics*, London, 1938, p. 20.

rises above nature primarily because of the development of his nervous system and his intellectual capacities, is destined to dominate the earth. Man tends to occupy the position of control which belongs to him and to exercise over other creatures as well as over nature itself (insofar as he has come to know them) a domination which is conditioned only by the negative traits of his own nature.[2]

What is the potency that has guided and assisted man during the long period of his primitive struggle with the brutal forces of nature? Reason?—No, his rational faculty was undeveloped then. Even after the slow and gradual differentiation of the rational function its share in the struggle for existence remained insignificant to the point of impotence. In other words, if it is true that there is no significant rational function without the existence of language, the primitive human could not have availed himself of the rational potentialities of his brain especially during the centuries when adjustment to the natural milieu has been one of his most difficult problems. During all these years of ignorance and animal helplessness man managed to move forward pushed and guided by the living force of the *instinct* inherent in the original organic aggregate of which he is a descendant and which is responsible for his survival. The dynamic of the same biological factor is illustrated by the behavior of infants at a stage when there is no room for manifestation of the rational faculty. When the infant reaches for the bosom of its mother for the first time, it makes a move dictated by the inherent requirements of its organic existence which is dominated by instinct rather than reason.[3]

The instinct has been the subject of reflection from the time of ancient philosophy to that of modern scientific thought.[4] For contemporary philosophy, biology and psychology it appears as a fundamental primordial organic impulse—as the living dynamic

[2] A. Buechner, *Energy and Matter*, Sofia, 1931 (Bulgarian trans.).

[3] Henri Bergson, *L'evolution creatrice*, Paris, 1909.

[4] Thomas Hancock, *An Essay on Instinct and its Physical and Moral Relations*, London, 1823, pp. 130 ff.

stream inherent in the germinating cell itself. The instinct is conceived as the creative organic kinetism which, from the condensed potential of the cell protoplasm and the chromosomes, in collaboration with the surrounding milieu, shapes and generates the progressive development of the animal and human organisms. It is the fundamental moving force in the differentiation of all functions inherent in organic existence and development and necessary for self-preservation and perpetuation of the species. Therefore the instinct may be said to be one of the fundamental elements of the uniformities of nature involved in the genesis of living matter. Dealing with inert matter, reason may effect the movement to a certain extent but interference beyond that leads to the destruction of the living creature.

Without the primitive impulse of life inherent in primordial organic matter—without the instinct—this matter would have remained inert and neither animal nor human life could have come into being.

Without overestimating the importance of the instinct and underestimating that of the rational faculty or of the surrounding milieu as factors in the progressive development of man and of human society, biological materialism holds that the instinct is a fundamental faculty. Regardless of the degree of development of the rational faculty and of degree of perfection of the nervous system which take place under the influence of the surrounding milieu, the dynamic potentialities of the instinct remain. They are the original creative potencies which have manifested themselves in the first living cells and which will be extinguished only with the death of the last ones. The instinct is active consistently[5] and therefore it is the eternally alert and true agent of human life. To extinguish the instinct for self-preservation and perpetuation of the species means nothing short of extinguishing life. Therefore no matter what the ascent of the rational faculty, it can not ever displace completely the functions of the instinct. On the contrary, one may say that even in the spiritual life of man the

[5] A. Nesard, *La vie et la mort des instincts*, Paris, 1923, p. 53.

instinct for self-preservation and perpetuation of the species plays a fundamental part. "Without being in the sphere of the rational faculty," says Bergson, "the instinct is within the limits of the spiritual function."[6] Under the conditions of primitive existence, without the active assistance of an adequate rational faculty, the instinct alone has been successful in overcoming the negative potencies of the surrounding milieu. If it is capable of being extinguished or made inactive, it could not have survived the centuries of the past. Therefore biological materialism holds that even during the era of the omnipotence of the rational faculty, the instinct for self-preservation and perpetuation of the species is one of the factors of human existence. Knowledge can not create synthetically either humans or animals—such a presumption means nothing less than the destruction of humanity. Humans are individuals—they are not inert matter capable of being molded in standarized forms.

The living instinct is the fundamental factor in the function of the human organism. It is the mysterious phenomenon of nature and the source of life in it. In coordinated interaction with the rational faculty and the surrounding milieu, the fundamental biological factor, the instinct, continues to supply the impulse of the movement which is life. And this movement follows the residuary tendencies of the complex interaction of the instinct, the rational faculty and the surrounding milieu. The uniformities to which this movement is subject are not merely those on which the dynamics of inert matter depend. It is consideration of all factors that leads toward the equilibrium and harmony of human existence. The study of human phenomena should therefore be approached not from a purely materialistic viewpoint but from a bio-materialistic one capable of establishing their interrelations and their functionally dynamic character. It is only thus that the knowledge would be useful for the purpose of subserving the requirements and interests of man and equalizing the conditions of social existence. Only thus will it be possible to effect the condi-

[6] Henri Bergson, *op. cit.*, p. 190.

tions for the social cooperation of individuals and their harmonious co-existence. To treat living men as inert matter is to subject them to physical and moral degradation—to deprive them of their human individualities and to push them backwards into social chaos and a struggle of self-extermination. Considerations as these have imposed on the Agrarian ideology to reject the traditionalistic materialist viewpoint and to adopt the bio-materialistic conception.

Bio-Cooperativism

Human generations have succeeded one another in a continuity, transmitting the results of their experience and progressive attainments. Thus primitive man has been transformed into the contemporary rational human. The inactive and clumsy primitive man has thus come to acquire the art and skill of creating modern means of defense and of producing material wealth. The biologically crude characteristics of his organism have disappeared and have been replaced by ones better adapted to the conditions and requirements of modern existence. The biological cooperation of the instinct for self-preservation of the species with the rational faculty and the potentialities of the surrounding milieu tends to direct the human individuals toward a conscious and free social cooperation, toward a preference for social equilibrium and harmonious co-existence. The older forms of social organization yield to the pressing need for new ones. Social mobility gives rise to the complex of political parties, social classes, professional aggregations—the forms of privilege yield to the popular ones. The heterogeneous formations of the old political parties which have been identified with domination aiming to accomodate the exploitation of certain strata by others are yielding in turn to the progressive cooperative aggregations which are being created for the protection of similar political and economic interests. Thus humanity is moving toward the form of a cooperative, equalized republic consecrating freedom, social solidarity and cultural progress.

Life does not always flow gently. It often fluctuates violently and passes through great crises—revolts, wars, catastrophies, strikes, etc. However, for bio-materialism these are not unavoidable; they do not take place as a matter of fatalistic necessity in the transition from one state into another,[7] but are simple deviations due to factors obstructing a normal social cooperativism. In the social process certain groups or strata, when conditions permit, tend to manifest tendencies of unreasonable egoism which upset the harmonious co-existence and social cooperation. But such a state of affairs is capable of being remedied by measures calculated to re-establish the equilibrium. Phenomena as these if construed fatalistically would amount to a repudiation of the usefulness of any social knowledge. Quite the opposite is the case. Advanced knowledge of the conditions of social existence facilitates social cooperation by shaping the rights and obligations of individuals so that unhealthy pressures are eliminated and the social equilibrium maintained. In this manner, without repudiating unconditionally the possibility of violent upsets, bio-materialism does not consider them as involving fatalistically the element of necessity. In fact, it is for the purpose of avoiding them that it adopts the idea of equalization through cooperativism.

Man has not leaped from the primitive state into the modern cultural one by a single stroke but has attained it by means of a long biologico-evolutive process in which social cooperation has played an important part. "The liberation of the laboring class from the oppression of capitalism" does not necessarily imply that it "is attainable only by means of revolution,"[8] but is perfectly possible without it. Moreover not every revolution is progressive in its aims or attainments. One may easily maintain that in principle violence is regressive in its results and reactionary in its

[7] Joseph Stalin, *The Questions of Leninism*, Moscow, 1939 (11th ed., in Russian), p. 537.

[8] *Ibid.*

tendencies. It is an entirely different matter to speak of a "revolution" in the social order attained by means of politico-economic cooperation and legal expedients. Such "revolutions" have taken place in the past and are taking place today. There are scores of democratic and socialistic regimes which have been introduced by the free choice of the masses. There is a great deal of evidence which demonstrates abundantly that social existence is not necessarily a violent "struggle of opposites."[9] There are antagonisms but there is also cooperation. Marxism is extremely onesided in this respect. Cooperation and social equalization are the expedients of Agrarianism, the aims of which are social justice in a labor society of free individuals and not of slaves pushed around in the name of their own imaginary welfare.

Bio-Materialism

Humans and their social aggregations could not and should not be shaped arbitrarily and schematically because the results of such a procedure are nothing short of physical and spiritual degradation which would be destructive to human and social progress. The doctrines which deal with the problems of the substance and the forms of social existence must be based on knowledge derived from the cognition of the factors involved including the biological foundation of humanity. "In the act by means of which it constitutes itself, every species tends toward what is most convenient for it."[10]

An ideology which does not take into account the potencies of the surrounding milieu as well as those of the inner living principle of men is bound to be one-sided, fantastic and socially dangerous. "Ideologies are perfectly legitimate in their place and their objectivity depends on the degree of knowledge they translate . . . the sociological approach must account for both subjective and objective factors."[11] The strength of the Agrarian ideol-

[9] Vladimir Lenin, *Works*, XIII, Moscow, 1938 (in Russian), p. 301.

[10] Henri Bergson, *op cit.*, p. 1342.

[11] C. D. Kojouharoff, *General Theory of Law and State*. A review in the "Tulane Law Review," December, 1945, pp. 298, 301.

ogy is in the fact that it aims to rely on positive knowledge and that it overcomes the one-sidedness of traditional materialism. The fact of the matter is that the importance of biology is recognized at present even by the most extreme bolshevist materialists: "The science of the history of society, regardless of the whole complexity of the phenomena of social existence, is capable of becoming an equally exact science as, for instance, biology is capable of utilizing the laws of development of society for practical applications."[12]

The ideology of Agrarianism has in view a cooperative society based on the principles of social justice and social equilibrium coordinated with the requirements of freedom, capable of securing to the individual and humanity a harmonious existence and progressive development. Relying on its bio-materialistic outlook and employing the expedients of cooperativism, Agrarianism is fighting for the establishment of a new social structure involving a number of fundamental propositions.

In the first place, Agrarianism considers that *man is the supreme value* of the social order, that his requirements are the *aim* while the latter is the *means.* Man is the central figure in economic development, in cultural advancement and in the transformation of social institutions. Thus all modifications in the forms of social organization and all progress in the economic and technical fields have to be considered in the light of the attainments of knowledge with the aim of subserving man rather than making man subservient to them. The pressures which tend to upset harmonious social existence are due primarily to tendencies to ignore this truth. Man is capable of understanding and evaluating properly the forms of political and social organization and their adaptability to the conditions of existence, to his interests and to his spiritual requirements. He resists the efforts to impose on him forms which go counter to his needs and eventually overwhelms them. One of his fundamental requirements is that of freedom insofar as this is compatible with the social aspect of his existence—

[12] Joseph Stalin, *op. cit.*, p. 544.

freedom of belief, freedom of thought and freedom of action. Freedom is the first condition for the proper orientation of man in relation to himself as well as in relation to the phenomena of the surrounding milieu. It is freedom that distinguishes man from animals. Freedom supplies man with wings and permits him to ascend to the heights of spiritual and material attainment. There is no existence without material means but without freedom there is no humanity. "When freedom dies, man lives on his knees. When freedom lives, man walks erect."[13]

For his freedom man has fought and spilled more blood than for his subsistence. Freedom is one of the fundamental requirements of equalized social existence, which in turn is reflected in the struggles for popular rights. A state of equilibrium and social harmony is inconceivable under a regime of slavery even if this is instituted in the name of a perfect equalization. One might say that freedom is a biological requirement and a presupposition of self-preservation and the perpetuation of the species. Therefore Agrarianism upholds the idea that freedom is a natural requirement of man which is qualified only by the social aspect of his existence. Man should first of all be allowed to depend on himself and only to the extent this is incompatible with harmonious and equalized existence should his activities be canalized. To go beyond this and curtail freedom in general as well as suspend the rights of the individual means to take a regressive step capable of generating violence and of excluding the possibility of harmonious social existence. Thus Agrarianism is opposed to every kind of dictatorship; it considers such political structures to be not only utopian but disgraceful—criminal acts degrading human individuality and human dignity. Agrarianism upholds the idea of the popular foundation of authority. It advocates a political structure under which free men are afforded the opportunity to mold a just social order and attain a true cultural progress. So conceived, popular authority is incompatible with forms which concentrate the power in the hands of individu-

[13] H. B. Swope, Foreword to James W. Wise, *Our Bill of Rights*, New York, 1941.

als or oligarchies; therefore Agrarianism favors a republic that coordinates freedom with social justice.

Agrarianism agrees that the economic is one of the fundamental factors in the individual and social existence of man. However, it holds that man and his initiative are equally fundamental. Moreover, differing from historical materialism, the Agrarian bio-materialistic view ascribes the social conflicts to the political and production relationships rather than to the control of the tools of production. It is not the primitive means of production but the relationships between omnipotent slave-owners or feudal lords and slaves tied to the land and deprived of rights that are characteristic of the exploitation structures. The source of social conflicts is not in the progress made in relation to the tools of production but in the structure which accommodates privilege, arbitrariness and the use of force. Not the control of the means of production but the efforts of men to struggle for means of subsistence and for freedom against stubborn irrational egoisms are the source of social and economic crises, revolutions and wars. Such crises are peculiar not only to capitalist structures but also to those which claim a complete levelling in the interest of the proletariat; the Soviet Union has supplied abundant proof in this respect.

Technical advancement derives from the inner creative impulse of man strengthened by the genesis of his rational faculty and the accumulation of experience which together shape the degree of adjustment in relation to the surrounding milieu. The initiative and efforts of man are responsible for the discoveries which make this progressive movement possible. Man is on a constant search for improved means of production, for greater economy, for quantity and superior quality. Communistic materialism maintains that "the new production forces demand . . . more cultured and more proficient workers."[14] The point is, however, that if such workers had not already existed, then there would not have been any "new productive forces." The fact of the matter is

[14] Joseph Stalin, *op. cit.*, p. 557.

that in the discovery, improvement and perfection of the tools of production, there always is an element of human initiative and purpose. Even in the instinctive efforts of most primitive men these elements are always present. Thus the view of Stalinism that the new productive forces and the new relationships of production are generated "not as a result of intentional conscious activity on the part of men, but takes place fatalistically, unintentionally and independently of the will of men" is untenable.[15] Equally untenable is Stalin's assertion that "when men improve one or another tool of production—one or another element of the productive forces, they are not conscious of, do not understand and do not reflect over the social results that should be produced by these improvements—they think merely of their interests, how to facilitate their work and obtain some immediate tangible advantages for themselves."[16]

Views as these appear to be quite out of date. One may say that during the period of primitive consciousness and at the very beginning of mental effort on the part of men, the instinct has moved man unconsciously toward the production of tools for self-preservation and for subsistence. It goes without saying that at this stage the insufficiencies of consciousness and knowledge did not permit him to conceive or foresee the distant consequences of these activities for him and his kind. However, so far as contemporary technical discoveries and attainments are concerned, it would be nothing short of absurd to maintain that all new means of production or of defense and attack are attained unconsciously or independently of the intentions and purposes of men. Such fantastic schematism finds its conclusive refutation in the work on atomic energy and its applications. Stalin himself appears not to be "unconscious" of their far-reaching results and consequences for human civilization as well as for the social existence of man. Under the circumstances is it possible to argue that the scientists who have contributed to the present knowledge

[15] *Ibid.*, p. 559.
[16] *Ibid.*, p. 560.

of atomic energy and its applications were not aware of the consequences of their work or that they were preoccupied with interests of their own and expectations to derive tangible benefits for themselves? The answer to such superficial arguments is obvious. In fact, one may go further and remind Stalin that the United States, in spite of its most efficient means of production, has not experienced either a change of economic relationships or a shake-up of its social structure. Is it not clear then that an economic unit may have new productive forces without a necessary change of economic relationships—or that there may be new economic relationships while the productive forces have remained the same?

In the Soviet Union there are new economic relationships: state-party ownership of the means of production under a Communist dictatorship. However, the forces of production have remained the same as those available to capitalist economies. One observes the opposite in the capitalistic United States: while economic relations have undergone no appreciable change, the production forces are incomparably superior. It is true that man can not foresee all of the consequences of new discovery or of a reform in the conditions of existence, because the complexities of the future reach far beyond those of the present and are therefore incapable of being represented adequately in the ideas of the latter, and because the portals of evolution are open widely for infinite creativeness.[17] Nevertheless, if the social and economic implications of the ever-increasing store of knowledge are followed closely and the new undesirable tendencies of the social process eliminated as soon as detected, there are no difficulties to be anticipated. In this respect the forecasts of the doctrinaires of Stalinism are nothing but efforts to argue under any circumstances the dogmatic assertions of materialism because of the fanatic requirements for orthodoxy. It is in this manner that writers like Prenant could identify themselves with the following naive statement: "At the moment when in capitalist countries there is talk for the ar-

[17] Henri Bergson, *op. cit.*, pp. 112, 114.

resting of technical and scientific progress because it creates misery there, in the Soviet Union this progress is rewarded generously because there it makes useful contributions."[18] This was written in the year 1935, and in the years of the war the Soviet Union had to depend for its salvation on the technical progress and efficiency of production of such orthodox capitalist countries as the United States. Moreover, it was in the United States that in the year 1946 the most important contemporary discovery of atomic energy was made. And all these things were accomplished without any radical changes in the traditional structure or in the existing economic relationships.

In the historical development of the social and economic relationships of men, revolutions neither possess the element of necessity nor are they the desirable rational means for the solution of social problems and economic conflicts. Therefore Agrarianism considers untenable the Marxian assertion that after the forces of production have reached a high point, the existing economic relationships and the ruling classes become a barrier which could be removed only through the conscious effort of the new classes expressing itself in acts of violence; that at that stage only revolution is capable of clearing the way.[19] We hope to have made clear by this time that the forces of production and the economic relationships are capable of development independently of one another, and that the "new classes" quite frequently overcome the Marxian "barrier" without resort to violence—a popular political structure makes this perfectly possible. In this connection it is hardly necessary to remind the dogmatists that during the war in the country of classical capitalism, England, the House of Lords voted voluntarily to place at the disposal of the state all possessions of English citizens; that at the present time a great deal of the capitalistic structure in England is being liquidated by legal means.

[18] M. Prenant, *Biologie et Marxisme*, Paris, 1935, p. 69.
[19] Karl Marx, *Works*, Moscow, 1935 (in Russian), p. 269.

It is man that moves the wheels of both technical and cultural progress. One may say, therefore, that he, rather than the means of production, is the "most revolutionary element" of the social complex. He does not reconcile himself with degradation and a treatment which repudiates his human characteristics and requirements. He has reacted in the past and will react in the future with all his energy against dominations and dictatorships, be they exercised in the name of capitalism or in that "of the proletariat." Once capital and the means of production have been taken from the bourgeoisie and placed under the control of the state—that is, "of the proletariat organized as dominant class,"[20] then this "dictatorship of the proletariat" comes to dominate all other classes in the same (if not more brutal) manner as the bourgeoisie has done in the past. Dominations and dictatorships generate resistance which precludes the possibility of harmonious social existence and tends to overcome all unjustified curtailments of freedom. The ideology of Agrarianism rejects oppression and dictatorship as methods for the solution of political, economic and social controversies, or for the establishment of new political and social structures. Agrarianism maintains that through education of the masses in the processes and principles of social and political democracy it is possible to eliminate the irrational personal and class egoisms; that through cooperation all social antagonisms and economic problems are capable of being resolved into an equilibrium which secures social advancement, cultural development and technical progress. Agrarianism prefers creative, economic and cultural radicalism rather than destructive and bloody revolutions.

Ownership of the Means of Production

Agrarianism maintains that the means of production should be in the hands of those who utilize them and who through them invest their labor in the process of production and become the

[20] Manifesto of the Communist Party, 1938, p. 50 (in Russian).

builders of human culture. It upholds the idea of private and cooperative ownership and opposes every type of speculative accumulation of wealth, be it private-capitalistic or state socialistic, when no immediate labor is involved and the labor of others is exploited. The private right over the fruits of one's labor is deep in human nature—it is a biological characteristic.[21] In his study on Herbert Spencer, A. W. Bateson writes that "the only instinct in our race which is sufficiently universal . . . is the desire to accumulate property. . . ."[22] This remark accords with the views of the Bulgarian leader of Agrarianism, Stambolisky, that "the preoccupation of man with the needs of the future is responsible for the accumulation of wealth which is but the primitive form of private property."[23] If the principle of private property is a fundamental manifestation of the human instinct, then no force is capable of eradicating or suppresing it. "Against the instinct the most powerful intellect or combination of intellects will move in vain."[24] Private property is thus the condition of securing the life of individuals and of perpetuating the species. It is one of the requisites of human integrity and freedom. Possessing the means of production, man is in a position first of all to rely on himself and only then to depend on others. It affords him the experience of a sense of security in relation to the present as well as to the future.

If the individual does not possess property of his own—if he has to depend on others for his subsistence—regardless of whether the structure is capitalistic or communist, bureaucratic—he is not a free individual. He is keenly aware of the fact that the conditions of livelihood are insecure and that he is being placed in the position of a puppet in the hands of others. On the other hand private ownership of the fruits of labor generates personal stimulus and is primarily responsible for the productivity of labor.

21 Morley Roberts, *Bio-politics*, London, 1938, p. 138.

22 Wm. Bateson, *The Biological Fact and the Structure of Society*, Oxford, 1911, pp. 31-32.

23 Alexander Stambolisky, *The Principle of the Bulgarian Agrarian Union*, Sofia, 1944 (in Bulgarian), p. 29.

24 Morley Roberts, *op cit.*, p. 132.

The possibilities to secure the means of subsistence are conditions which determine the degrees of exertion and efficiency on the part of the worker. Thus at the present time there is no doubt that the industrial worker should share in the ownership of the factory, that the farmer should own his land which he tills and that every one should own the home in which he lives. The fact of the matter is that Lenin made use of the urge for private ownership to win the revolution by promising the land to the farmers and the factories to the industrial workers. It is the repudiation of this promise that is the main source of the instability of Stalin's regime, that has been instrumental for the identification of the "dictatorship of the proletariat" with brutal repression. Stalin himself is aware of the fact that the pressures for private ownership in 1936 imposed a modification of the Constitution of the Soviet Union. Thus, in spite of the decrees for socialization and for collectivization of the lands, an attempt was made to meet these pressures by means of the "private land-households" and the "succession in personal property."[25] The pressure of the kolhosnics in favor of the supplementary private property expedient and against the collective ownership of the kolhoses as originally intended demonstrated unmistakably the potency of the tendencies for private labor ownership of the land. As a matter of fact Stalin himself has admitted that much publicly: "It would be a mistake to think that since the kolhoses have been established socialism has already been instituted. And even a graver error it is to think that the members of the kolhoses have been transformed into socialists."[26]

Experience has shown that without the element of personal interest the processes of production and the organizations of economic enterprises are inefficient because the personal efforts for the productivity of the labor and the quality of the product are lacking. Such a state of affairs affects the national economy to an appreciable degree. Extraneous and bureaucratic managements

[25] Constitution of the USSR, 1936, arts. 9-10. On collective farms, Kolhoses, see also chapter XI.

[26] Joseph Stalin, *op. cit.*, pp. 289-290.

are incomparably inferior to the cooperative one. This applies with special force to the agricultural industry in particular. Even under the Drakonian regime of the bolshevist collectivism in the agricultural industry, collective labor demonstrated itself to be impossible to the extent that the Soviet Government was forced to fall back and rely on the labors of small groups and individuals. "The more the labor in the kolhoses is individualized in the form of small groups and individual kolhosnics, the more their industry is materially compensated, the more productive it is in the production of crops as well as in cattle raising."[27] Neither legalized violence nor Communist social utopias have proved or could prove capable of suppressing the impulses of the instinct for security of the means of subsistence expressed in the form of private ownership. In this respect the behavior of Russian Communists when they have had the opportunity to acquire things is a matter of revelation. Both Soviet soldiers in the occupied territories and the leaders in the countries subjected to Communist dictatorships have shown unusual avidity in the acquisition of moveable wealth by legal means as well as by brutal violence.

The Agrarian Cooperative Structure

As a rule the excessive accumulation of wealth is the result of exploitation effected by means of political domination—it matters little whether the set-up is capitalistic or not. In principle Agrarianism is not against the expedient of collectivization. On the contrary, it is aware of its advantages especially in the mechanization of production, in the unification and modernization of the economic effort and the conditions of labor. However, Agrarianism accepts a cooperative collectivism which is compatible with freedom; which retains the institution of private property but equalizes its distribution. Thus the expedient of the cooperatives is fundamental in the social and economic orders en-

[27] A. Andreev, Speech before the 18th Congress of the Bolshevist Party, Moscow, 1940 (in Russian), pp. 29-31.

visioned by Agrarianism—it is the most adaptable expedient for the attainment of social harmony and the comparative equalization of wealth. The cooperatives coordinate the economic initiative of the individual with the social interest. By means of cooperatives the small private economic units coordinate voluntarily their efforts and means of production, retaining their own properties and sharing in the control over the production, distribution and exchange of the produced wealth. In this manner the exploitation of labor and of its fruits are eliminated, while the desirable characteristics of individual economic activity are retained.

Agrarianism upholds the views which condemn the speculative acquisitions of land and the exploitation of agricultural labor: "The land should belong to those who till it."[28] The land should not be subject to speculative transfer but should be privately owned only as a means of investing one's own labor. The value of the land should not be determined by its market price—for the farming owner it has the additional value of stability as to his means of subsistence, of security for the future, of freedom. In other words, if one uses the Marxian terminology, the "absolute rent" belongs to the farmer on the basis of the fundamental requirements of agricultural production.

In the Agrarian structure labor is the standard of value—labor is not only an individual right but also a social duty. It is a physiological necessity for the proper development of the human organism and its normal function. He who is capable to work and does not wish to do so forfeits his title on existence. Agrarianism is thus against social parasitism but at the same time it repudiates any ideas which tend to transform man into a laboring slave. Overwork leads to the degeneration and degradation of humanity; the Soviet Stakhanovism is incompatible with labor hygiene and with the human interests of the laborer. Such schemes of economic activity transform men into slaves and revive out-

[28] Raiko Iv. Daskalov, *The Struggle for Land*, Sofia, 1945 (in Bulgarian), p. 9, iii edition.

grown systems as to the compensation of labor. In order to exist men have to work but they do not exist merely for that purpose; they have also spiritual and cultural needs; they have the right to rest and enjoy the fruits of their labor. Laboring men ought to be masters over their own labor and its fruits.

Agrarianism proposes to realize all these fundamental ideas by means of a comprehensive cooperative structure. Under this regime the farmer is laborer as well as owner of the land and its products, while the industrial worker is made a participant in the ownership of the enterprise for which he works—the labor in the cooperative enterprises is compensated in such a manner that gradually the workers become the owners. Under the cooperative structure neither the land nor industrial enterprises are exposed to speculation; they are merely transferred from one generation of workers to another. This structure eliminates both the money-lender and the brokers of the old order just as much as it steers clear from the oppressors and parasites of the "new" communist order. Through the cooperatives of production, distribution, consumption and credit, directed and controlled by the members themselves, the system eliminates all unnecessary economic waste.

In this manner the cooperative structure of Agrarianism aims to coordinate the maximum of freedom with the necessary degree of equalization in the conditions of economic activity. The Soviet order has destroyed freedom and in practice has abandoned the idea of equalization. "To every Leninist—of course, if he is a true Leninist—it is clear that equalization as to needs and modes of individual life is a reactionary and petty-bourgeois absurdity."[29] Thus the original bolshevist slogan "from every one according to his capacity—to every one according to his needs" was restated into the following proposition: "from every one according to his capacity—to every one according to the quantity and quality of the labor invested and the results from it."

[29] Joseph Stalin, *op. cit.*, p. 470.

Agrarianism conceives the cooperative structure as an organ of political and economic democracy. The traditional political parties as artificial political aggregates of heterogeneous elements for the exploitation of authority are thus condemned to gradual extinction. They are transitory in the manner in which the old order which gave rise to them is transitory. Only the professional organizations are homogeneous and permanent because they represent and uphold similar social interests; they are going to exist as long as the professions endure. Thus it is through unification of the professional organizations and the economic syndicates into a comprehensive social cooperative structure that Agrarianism proposes to solve the social and economic problems of the contemporary complex, to realize the necessary degree of equilibrium and to secure the progressive cultural welfare of a new free and unstratified society. It is obvious these days that the domination of a single class, be it a dictatorship of the proletariat, is incapable of ever realizing such an unstratified society. This is possible only through the willing and active participation of all productive sectors of the masses by means of their free professional and cooperative organizations, that is to say, by means of political and economic democracy. In this manner Agrarianism proposes to realize in fact Charles Gide's ideal of the cooperative republic. By so organized free cooperative republics mankind will be moving gradually toward a world-wide cooperative federation. Agrarianism agrees that the capitalistic structure is "pregnant," but it is with cooperativism, not with communist socialism.

II.

AGRARIANISM IN ACTION

Bulgaria

The embryonic stage of the movement emerging in defense of the Bulgarian peasant-farmer can be traced back to the closing years of the 19th century. At that time a number of modest, "provincial" newspapers, such as "Agrarian Defense," published by the agronomist Yanko Zabounoff in Pleven, and "Agrarian Justice," published by Dimiter Draghieff in Stara-Zagora, almost simultaneously printed editorials designed to disclose the devastation and plunder to which the seed peasant-farmers had long been subjected on the part of ruthless bankers, contractors and greedy middle-men. These valiant but rather segregated and disorganized efforts found enthusiastic support in individuals like Tsanko Bakaloff, country teacher and poet, who subsequently played a major part in the rising Agrarian Union.

The rapid establishment of ideological and political directives was largely due to the development of certain events which followed very closely. Agrarian ideology in Bulgaria was born during the barren years 1897-98; politically, however, the movement received its baptism in the historic battles between peasants and police organs of the reactionary government of Dr. V. Radoslavoff — T. Ivancheff (1899), which had refused the farmers the right to hold public meetings in protest against the recently imposed tithe. Such a heavy and unjust toll had, in the past, been levied only by certain cruel and irresponsible officials of the Sultans—during the 500 years of Turkish domination. Rising in indignation, the farmers planned mass meetings in protest against it. The police, however, had been instructed to use firearms, and hundreds of peaceful farmers were killed and wounded. The clashes were particularly sanguinary in Southern Dobroudja and the districts of Varna and Tirnovo. The material devastation caused by two consecutive lean years, as well as the ineffectiveness or unorganized action to produce a desired result, played a decisive part in convincing the peasant masses of the necessity of establishing an organization in defense of their political rights and liberties and their economic interests. The struggle, consequently, for the creation of an agrarian union in Bulgaria started at the bottom—among the masses, by the people themselves.

Fearful of possible political consequences, the Government and the existing conservative political parties tried to divert the rising mass-movement into purely economic channels. The peasants, however, soon found out that their resolutions and petitions failed to impress distant cabinet members and deputies and were heedlessly tossed into waste-paper baskets. Their problems and requirements remained unsolved and ignored. The establishment of a political and economic Agrarian Union was the next logical step.

This new political element was not composed of heterogeneous ideological elements interested exclusively in the seizures of power. Its primary objective was the unification of the professional agrarian syndicates for the purpose of defending the political and economic rights and interests of agrarian labor. In view of the fact that at this time agriculture was the work of 95% of the population in Bulgaria, the organization was properly named Bulgarian Agrarian Peoples Union.

The Union gradually acquired its own sound economic, social and political doctrine. Ideologically it is based on the conception of political and economic democracy; its economic basis is cooperative. Nature's common biological laws compose its philosophical doctrine. Thus, it acknowledges only the theory and practice of life — *reality*. Consequently, the purely materialistic interpretation of history and historical events is rejected in favor of interpretations based on the biological and materialistic parallelism. Internally, the Union is organized along the lines of an Agrarian Cooperative Syndicate.

The history of the agrarian movement in Bulgaria is inseparably linked with the life and activities of its most illustrious son, greatest exponent and ideologist, Alexander Stambolisky. This former disciple of the agronomist Yanko Zabounoff and fellow-worker of Draghieff, this outstanding leader of the agrarian masses throughout South-Eastern Europe was the first to harness the revolutionary flame of the peasant-farmers into a dynamic struggle for liberty and democracy. Subsequently, he headed the first Popular Agrarian Government and attempted to provide a philosophical explanation for the development of agrarian ideology, which to him was something tangible and real—admirably applicable in life.

Stambolisky emerged early in public life and by 1911 was a member of the Grand National Assembly. The arrogant German prince, better known as King Ferdinand of Bulgaria, was then at the height of his power. And yet, we find Stambolisky in the Grand National Assembly raising a lonely voice in favor of a Republic. His profound love for peace and his incessant struggle against war found concrete expression in endless written and verbal attacks, directed against the proud Monarch during the fatal years 1913-15. His efforts, subsequently, led to mutinies in the armed forces, which were ruthlessly suppressed by firing-squads, and to his own imprisonment for the duration of World War I.

Released from prison for the ostensible purpose of pacifying the troops that had mutinied and left the battle-fields, and aided by his associate Dr. Rayko Daskaloff, Stambolisky placed himself at the head of those troops, led them against the Monarchy and in 1918, within 25 miles of Sofia, declared the First Bulgarian Republic. Short-lived as it was, owing to the intervention of German army units, it nevertheless marked a corner-stone in the political history of the country.

In spite of being constantly embroiled in political struggles, Stambolisky managed to write several books, the most significant of which is *Political Parties or Professional Organizations.* In a simple and unpretentious manner, Stambolisky expounds in it the essence of agrarian ideology. Although at the time (1909) political scientists and philosophers generally were not very familiar with the importance of biology, he laid particular emphasis on the part played by human instinct, and he underlined its colossal significance as basic generator of the social and economic activity of the human being. "The instinct of self-preservation takes precedence in human nature and motivates its entire activity."[30]

[30] A. Stambolisky, *Political Parties or Professional Organizations*, p. 13, Sofia, I edition 1909, III edition 1945.

In the same book Stambolisky explains the advantages of professional organizations as compared to political party organizations and thus prognosticates the future of the Syndicates. "By the establishment of separate professional, political and economic social organizations, the laboring masses will accomplish successfully what the political parties failed to do, i.e. they will stabilize in effect the disputed social and political equality, as their normal existence is impossible without it; and also, by numerous legislative and other actions, they will abolish the economic inequality, which has been so brutally established."[31]

Even in this early epoch Stambolisky appeared as a great sociologist and agrarian ideologist, and his new, constructive and progressive ideas, under one form or another, became later the subject of scientific analysis by eminent professors and scientists such as Adolph Damashke, Leon Duguy, Dragolub Ivanovitch, M. Roberts, H. Bergson, etc.

The dynamics and power of agrarian ideology and of its first exponent, A. Stambolisky, become evident to any unprejudiced person who is desirous of appreciating in full the accomplishments and acts of the government which, to a large extent, applied them in practice.

The Agrarian Union was called upon to take over the government and save the country and the people from the after-effects of three consecutive, catastrophic wars. Unprepared as it was to shoulder the gigantic responsibilities, especially in such critical and fateful times, and conscious of their historic significance, the Union, with Stambolisky at the head, came to the rescue. From the very beginning, the new Government was subjected to relentless attacks from both right and left-wing parties, which not only enjoyed full freedom of expression, but also took advantage of it in a cruel and spiteful manner. Stambolisky, however, instead of resorting to the traditional bloodshed and oppression, retaliated by exposing his legislature to the whole world and placed it in the hands of the people. Each and every new

[31] *Ibid.*, p. 14.

law, before reaching Parliament, was presented to the people, studied, discussed and amended by them at their local agrarian organizations and village meetings. In this manner, what might have been a bloody political revolution turned out to be a purely economic transformation. Liberty took the place of oppression; deeds, the place of vain promises.

Fundamentally opposed to trade and speculation with land and labor, the Agrarian Government of Bulgaria introduced, by means of new laws, land ownership based on labor qualification. Land was taken away from large landowners who were not interested in cultivating it but had it for purposes of trading and speculation, and it was distributed among those who were prepared to work on it alone or with their families. Maximum ownership of land was limited to 30 hectares per farm. In this manner, the land question was solved permanently, positively, and in a just way, because this solution was attained by the people themselves and expressed their desires and wishes. That is why, after the "coup d'etat" of June 9, 1923, by means of which the Agrarian Government was forcefully replaced with a royal and reactionary dictatorship, the former landowners attempted to reclaim the lands taken away from them, but the peasants reacted sharply and kept the land which had been acquired by virtue of law and the right of labor. The statistics of 1934 show 99% of the establishments possess 30 hectares or less, comprising 94% of the arable land, and only 1% of the farms are over 30 hectares, comprising 6% of the arable land. At that, the greatest part of the properties over 30 hectares is owned by Municipalities, Schools, Cooperatives, etc. Bulgaria, consequently, became the state with the most even distribution of land throughout the whole of Eastern Europe.

The Agrarian Government introduced social laws for the protection of labor and provided the industrial city workers with such guarantees of work and conditions of existence for which today, under the Communist dictatorship "of the proletariat," the Bulgarian workers can only dream.

During the Agrarian regime labor became the yard-stick with which the value of economic goods was estimated. The work of the industrial and handicraft laborer was better paid than that of the farm laborer. Workers' syndicates prospered freely. Having created such favorable conditions for the craftsmen, the Agrarian regime helped and encouraged them to form cooperatives and to establish their own political and economic professional unions.

Being fundamentally opposed to war and ardently in favor of peaceful economic construction, the Agrarian Government introduced in Bulgaria (for the first time in the history of the modern state), the institution known as Labor Service. A large part of the existing regular army was transformed into a creative labor army. The cannons and machine-guns were made into plows and scythes, into sickles and shovels and were applied to building schools, hospitals, reading-rooms, roads and bridges. Instead of the old military insignia, the hats of the new labor heroes carried the sign "Labor for Bulgaria." Labor, freely and voluntarily given by every Bulgarian, became not only a right and an obligation, but also an honor and a pride. Great, cultured and ancient states sent special missions to small, youthful but laborious Bulgaria to study the brilliant organization of this unique reformation. An exhaustive and detailed description of this epoch-making reform and the results achieved by it is given by a former Russian minister, the socialist revolutionary Vladimir Iv. Lebedev, in his two books *The New Roadway* and *In the Land of Roses and Blood*.

Opposed to the speculative exploitation of property, the Agrarian regime confiscated buildings which were used for speculation and placed in them the families of workers of government institutions. Simultaneously, however, substantial credits were allowed for the construction of new homes. In one building season alone, entire new blocks sprang up in Sofia and thousands of families found refuge and new homes. The housing problem found a satisfactory solution.

In the same attempt to stamp out speculation, the Government passed a special law dealing with wartime profiteers. Illicitly acquired profits and properties were confiscated and a number of people were sent to prison for unlawful practices.

The Agrarian Union, as symbolized by A. Stambolisky's regime, introduced for the first time in Bulgarian history Progressive Income Taxation. In this manner, the economically weak strata of society was relieved from excessive taxation and the burden fell on the well-to-do classes.

A new Education Law was created, changing from 4 to 7 years the gratuitous primary schooling. Mass education of the population was stimulated by the establishment of free Sunday and Night schools and courses. Within a period of three years illiteracy among the people was reduced to 3% (not including children) and Bulgaria became one of the most literate countries in South-Eastern Europe with a population whose political and social consciousness was enviable.

In an attempt to extirpate completely the speculative exchange of economic goods, a new law was voted favoring the cooperative movement. By placing the production, exchange and distribution of goods under the supervision of the people, a gradual social reconversion was anticipated based upon the political, economic and cooperative syndicate conception.

The rights and liberties accorded to the people were indicated and specified by the modern and extremely liberal Tirnovo Constitution. Everyone in Bulgaria was allowed to work freely and without interference, to speak or to write, to criticize the Government, to pray to his own God, to own his private or cooperative property and to feel certain of his life and subsistence. The feeling of security and stability prevailed.

The King reigned but did not govern the State, as was provided by the Constitution. For some time Stambolisky had been working on his pet project of converting the state to a Republic in a constitutional and democratic manner. Unfortunately, after World War I the Allies had objected to the abolition of the dynasty in Bulgaria.

For the first time in Bulgarian history, the people were their own masters and held their destiny in their own hands.

All this, however, should not create the impression that there were no mistakes or deficiencies in the administration of the state by the Agrarian Government. On the contrary, there were many. Particularly in the application of the newly created laws, divergencies often assumed the form of provocation or sabotage on the part of certain Government employees who were in sympathy with the opposition. The Agrarian Union, as stated before, had been called upon to assume the responsibilities of governing the country while it was still insufficiently prepared for the job, especially at a particularly unfortunate time, after a national and military catastrophe, and it had been compelled to make use of the existing and largely corrupt corps of civil servants. That is one reason why the divergencies mentioned above were mainly directed against the Government itself and the new laws labelled by the opposition as "Bolshevik." The Communist Coryphees in their turn, frightened by the fast evaporation of their influence among the masses, declared the Government of the Peasants as "counter-revolutionary" and launched a mad attack against the Agrarian Union and Stambolisky himself. Partisan passions boiled high. Criticism of the Government was merciless from right and left-wing parties alike, and to say the least, it was often irresponsible.

However, to every unprejudiced and conscientious person it was evident that Bulgaria had started on a new road—a road leading toward cultural, political and economic prosperity, internal peace and order. "The Agrarians fomented among the people the worthy sentiments of idolizing labor, peace and education."[32]

Being an ardent and sincere champion of peace and good-will among all nations, the Agrarian Government abandoned the old

[32] V. I. Lebedev, *In the Land of Roses and Blood*, p. 97, Paris, 1935.

militant and adventurous foreign policy of King Ferdinand and turned decisively toward an understanding, not only with the Southern Slavs and other Balkan countries, but also with all states, great or small. Stambolisky was the first to activate officially the idea of a Balkan Federation. He preached of the United States of Europe long before Aristides Briand. He persistently told the world that a moral disarmament should precede any military disarmament.

Stambolisky, however, was the product of a "small" nation, and his voice did not carry very far. He was not appreciated in time even by the immediate neighbors of Bulgaria, in whose interest it was to understand and support him. This did not discourage the Peasant Leader, for it was in his nature to fight and even die in defense of his ideas and their realization, because he was convinced that they were beneficial not only to his own people but to all humanity.

None-the-less, the new foreign policy of Bulgaria had attained certain results. After a tour by Stambolisky in Europe, which lasted 100 days, the atmosphere around Bulgaria became partially cleared. The question of reparations was solved in a relatively satisfactory manner. Relations with the neighboring states began to improve and Bulgaria was admitted to the League of Nations. The policy of peace and collaboration with the entire cultural world was beginning to pay dividends; a small but healthy and laborious nation was really coming to life after five long centuries of Turkish domination, boldly freeing itself from spiritual and political oppression in an effort to attain peace and liberty.

However, a group of Bulgarian reactionaries, incited by the Dynasty and inspired by the new fascist doctrine of Mussolini, succeeded in over-throwing the Agrarian regime by means of a military "coup d'etat" in June of 1923. Stambolisky was brutally murdered. The resistance which the peasants offered in defense of their democratic government was overcome. Thousands of people died in the impact with the on-coming fascist dictatorship; other tens of thousands were put in prison. But the work and ideology of Alexander Stambolisky remained alive and unconquered.

For more than two decades this same ideology inspired the overwhelming majority of the Bulgarian people in their resistance to the mad attacks of Fascism and Hitlerism and made possible the act of September 9, 1944, when the Bulgarian peasants and workers, intelligentsia and army once more took over the Government.

Faithful to its democratic ideology and principles, the Agrarian Union was ready to participate in the formation of a coalition government comprising all democratic elements and fully representative of the people. Normally, representation in such a government should have been based on the numerical following of each group, in which case the Agrarian Union, being by far the largest single party in the country, should have been given the majority of cabinet posts. However, in the presence of a small but Soviet-sponsored Communist party, this principle was deliberately disregarded and the key positions of the government were seized by the Communists.

Conscious of its own numerical superiority and overwhelming popularity, the Agrarian Union conceded to this arrangement and made a deliberate effort to cooperate with the Communist party. Anxious to reestablish normal conditions of life, the Union introduced an amendment to the Land Law adjusting definitely the question of land ownership and legalizing the cooperative farms, which embraced the smallest landowners.

The Communist party, however, had other plans. Installed in all key positions and backed by the Soviet army of occupation, they embarked on a reign of terror and oppression with the object of eliminating all democratic elements from public life, and the ultimate establishment of a one-party, Communist dictatorship. Cognizant of the support and popularity of the Agrarian Union among the masses, one of their first drives was directed against the unity of the Agrarian Union. The drive failed to produce the desired split, but it disclosed the ulterior motives of the instigators, and the Agrarian Union had to leave the Government and went into opposition.

Numerous attempts on the part of Communist functionaries to create the Soviet-type "collective farm" (kolhozi) in Bulgaria met with stubborn opposition from the peasants. Ignoring the existing law for private and cooperative land ownership, which, incidentally, had been signed by the Communist members of the Cabinet, they often resorted to violence in their attempt to impose the collective farm. By so doing, they disclosed complete ignorance of the elementary characteristics of the Bulgarian peasant-farmer—his inherent and profound attachment to the land he calls his own. Peaceful farmers were killed, but they fought back with such tenacity and ferocity that the Government was compelled to abandon this attempt temporarily. However, it is generally assumed that in the near future the drive for expropriation will be resumed with new vigor, especially with the ex-Secretary of the Comintern, Georgi Dimitroff, at the head of the new Cabinet.

Yugoslavia

The Agrarian movement of Yugoslavia emerged at different periods in the various constituent parts of the country.

In CROATIA the ground-work for the establishment of an Agrarian Organization was started in 1899—the year in which the Bulgarian organization was founded. There, the development of the Agrarian Union was directly connected with the names of the two brothers, Ante and Stephen Radic—worthy successors of the great peasant leader Matija Gubec, who had led the Croatian land-workers in an insurrection in the 16th century. After a newspaper campaign in defense of agrarian rights carried out by the paper *Dom* and the monthly publication *Croatian Thought*, the brothers Radic took up the initiative of founding an agrarian organization in 1905, while the country was still under Austro-Hungarian domination. Of the two, Ante was more of a fighter and ideologist. He died early. Stephen was the apostle-organizer,

Being the first to turn his attention to the farmer and attempt organized action, he won the love and fanatic devotion of the Croatian peasants. To him the peasant was the basic and most stable element in the creation of a healthy, social, economic and cultural unity. Liberty, independence and cultural advancement were impossible in any country without raising and organizing the broad peasant masses. Everything else, in his opinion, was only accessory. Radic hated the cities in the beginning, because there was centralized oppressive power, corruption and speculation. He ended up by becoming the undisputed master of both village and city in Croatia. His peasant fanaticism is evident to this day in the literary works of his successors. Dr. Yuraj Krnevic, secretary of the Croatian Peasant Party, well-known for his western tendencies, wrote in the preface of his recent publication: "Constitution of the Independent Croatian Peasant Republic": "The Statute is based upon justice to every individual, in the manner in which the peasant himself is just."[33]

This Constitution, according to Dr. Krnevic, was written in 1921 mostly by Stephen Radic and incorporated the fundamental ideology of the Agrarian Movement of Croatia. Liberty and Rights to every individual on Croatian territory; abolishment of large land ownership in favor of private family and cooperative ownership. Even the State is not supposed to own more farming land than is allowed the average agrarian labor family. Labor is to become an obligation and a right. The fruits of labor are to belong to the laborers. The administrative organization of the "police" state is to be replaced by an economic and cultural organization. "Instead of a political 'police' government, an economic, cultural and wholesome one is to be introduced."[34] Self-governing, economic village administrations, economic peasant "jupas" and autonomous town administrations are to be established, and thus an Independent Croatian Peasant Republic.

[33] "Constitution of the Independent Croation Peasant Republic," p. 7, Hamilton, Canada, 1946.

[34] *Ibid.*, p. 21.

Characteristic of the Croatian Agrarian movement was the establishment of a special economic organization, called "Gospodarska Sloga," purporting the promotion of assistance among the peasants and capable of fighting their enemies and oppressors by means of peasant strikes and blockades. It resembled closely the professional syndicates, but wielded much greater political power than the ordinary cooperative, economic organizations. These latter had acquired a very impressive status in Croatia and had united in a special Union which was directed almost exclusively by the Croatian peasant political organization.

Radic's motto was: "Faith in God and the Peasant's furrow." This, however, did not prevent him from being anti-clerical and from criticizing bitterly the misuse of the peoples' faith.

Being outspoken enemies of dictatorship, Radic and the Croatian Agrarian movement have for a long time been subjected to its bloody onslought. Reactionaries killed Radic in the hope that they would kill the peasant movement. The death-blow reached not only this great Yugoslavian, but also Southern Slav Unity. The murderers themselves were terrified by the magnitude of their crime, but it was too late. . . .

The successor of Radic, Dr. Vladko Macek, carried on the fight against oppression and in collaboration with other agrarian groups and democratic elements was largely responsible for the elimination of dictatorial regimes in Yugoslavia and the establishment of a democratic government. However, "understanding" and "unity" among the Serbs and Croats came as an imposition from the top ranks and not through the medium of the people's will. Consequently, it proved to be unsound. In this internal controversy the nationalistic element unfortunately out-weighed the social element and the problems remained unsolved.

The Croatian Agrarian Organization participated in short-term coalition cabinets and was unable to introduce and realize a total agrarian program.

Dr. Macek, miraculously saved from Hitler's hangmen and the Communist executioners, as well as all his collaborators, have undoubtedly profited by the mistakes of the past, and the experience gained will in the future direct the Croatian peasants toward brotherly cooperation with the Serbian, Slovenian, Bulgarian and other Balkan peasants in a noble effort purporting the establishment of Balkan and European democratic solidarity.

In SERBIA the Agrarian Organization came into existence after World War I, largely as the by-product of the cooperative movement. The prominent Serbian cooperative leader, Michael Abramovich, was one of the founders. His ideas for a Serbian Union of Agriculturalists were based on the conception of professional syndicalism. Following the pattern set by the Bulgarian Agrarian Organization and under the guidance of prominent political personalities, he embarked upon lively political activity, retaining the cooperative unit as his economic base. He was, therefore, particularly anxious to assume the greatest possible share in the management of the Union of Serbian Agrarian Cooperatives.

At the death of the old statesman Yotza Yovanovic-Pijon, leadership of the Serbian Union of Agrarians went to Dr. Milan Gavrilovic—one of the most intelligent and honest Serbian journalists and statesmen. In old Serbia, however, the Union encountered obstacles and grave difficulties in combating the established authority of statesmen like Pasic and Davidovic, whose political parties had also started among the peasants. At about this time, an enterprising and energetic agrarian promoter, Dr. Milosh Toupanyanin, had succeeded in transforming Bosnia into a peasant stronghold, where, even during the Austro-Hungarian domination, the intelligent defender of the peasants, the poet Peter Kocic, had worked with the same objective. Beyond the river Sava, among the so-called Serbs of Preko, Milan Pribicevic was responsible for the spreading of a doctrine closer to Agrarian Socialism than anything else. Much later, in 1940, Prof. Dragolub Yovanovic established his own Agrarian Socialist group.

In character the Serbian Agrarian Movement was closely related to that of Bulgaria and Stambolisky inspired them both. Comparatively young, the Agrarian Union of Serbia only recently participated in short-lived cabinets and was unable to introduce effectively systematic reconstruction of the State. In common with other Agrarian and democratic organizations it took an active part in the struggle which eliminated dictatorial regimes in Yugoslavia and reinstated a democratic government desirous of reaching an understanding with the Croatians and the Bulgarians.

The Serbian peasants carried on a titanic struggle against the German troops of occupation and with their own flesh and blood inscribed one of the most glorious pages of history. Not any less glorious is the present struggle which these same peasants are waging against the reactionary Communist dictatorship. Relying upon his leftist ideology and an endless source of energy, the ambitious and highly cultured Dragolub Yovanovic made a brave effort to cooperate with Tito's Communist regime and went as far as becoming a member of his "Parliament." However, he was soon thrown out of the so-called "Parliament," out of the University, and was even "expelled" from his own party group, because he had permitted himself to state in jest that the Communist Party should be separated from the State. . . .

Dr. Milan Gavrilovic was sentenced by Tito's Communist courts and sent into exile for "the terrible" crime of being friendly with his colleague in the former cabinet and Serbian patriot Draja Michailovic.

In SLOVENIA the Agrarian movement began as an off-spring of the Cooperative movement—which, incidentally, is the oldest movement in Yugoslavia. It took part in coalition governments but its leaders failed to register any particular political activity. It sustained a great shock with the death of its young, intelligent but rather idealistic leader, Yan J. Novak. But the sober and industrious Slovenian peasants continue to defend with ferocity their own conceptions of liberty, rights and private ownership.

The Yugoslav Agrarian movement in general has had little opportunity to realize its social and economic program, or to even establish its own unity. In spite of that, under pressure by this movement, the distribution of land on the merits of labor took place shortly after the same measure was put into effect in Bulgaria. According to the statistics of 1931, 67.8% of the farms are under 5 hectares. On the other hand, the development of the cooperative movement continues to grow throughout the whole country. Characteristic of Yugoslavia are the sanitary cooperatives. Although limited in numbers, they are doing useful work for the health and welfare of the peasants.

Rumania

Formally released from bondage during 1864, the Roumanian peasants, more-or-less, continued to live in a state of feudal slavery until the beginning of the 20th century. In 1907, the revolution of the poor, landless proletariat, staged against the "boyars"—large landowners—was brutally suppressed and drowned in blood. But the struggle for land and liberty had started and was constantly gaining momentum. The ruling classes were compelled to promise land reforms, which they had no intention of fulfilling, but which served to divert the desires of the Rumanian peasants for active participation in the political life of the country. Generally speaking, the attitude of the ruling classes was reflected in the policies of the two political parties, the Liberals of Bratianu, and the Conservatives of Take Ionescu, which represented the capitalist interests of industrial protectionism and land feudalism. Typical of contemporary Rumanian reality was the attitude of the capitalist ruling class, which, for the lack of colonies, in the words of the Rumanian sociologist M. Zeltin, applied colonial measures "to their own natives—the peasants." Rights and privileges were being administered like medicine—a teaspoonful at a time. Out of a total 183 members of Parliament, the peasants were allowed to elect only 40—by indirect vote, through special representatives.

Until the end of World War I, the Rumanian peasants were barred from education and culture and more than 60% of them were illiterate. Only in 1917, during the most critical period of the war, the King issued a special declaration promising them land and equal electoral rights. Simultaneously, the leaders of the two political parties had "generously" consented to "expropriate" for the benefit of the peasants 2 million hectares of land from the large owners. As usual, these promises were largely theoretical, and not worth the paper they were written on. However, all these machinations were no longer successful in lulling the Rumanian peasants into subordination. Right after the war, under the leadership of Jon Mihalache, Konstantin Stere, Junian, Madgearu and others, the peasants of Rumania proper, considerably influenced by the agrarian movement of Bulgaria and the events in Russia, founded their own political organization on the basis of a very progressive, social and economic program. After the incorporation of Bessarabia, Bukovina and Transylvania in Rumania (1918-19), the organization of the Moldavian peasants, well seasoned by the Russian revolution, joined that of the Rumanians. In 1926, the Transylvanian organization, under Dr. Juliu Maniu, was also incorporated. In character this last was rather nationalistic, owing to the struggle against Hungarian domination, but the vigorous Transylvanian peasants readily accepted the policy of the Rumanian Agrarian Organization. In this manner, the United National Agrarian Organization soon became the most powerful democratic political force of the country and was able to demand the right of participation in the government.

The laws for expropriation and distribution of large land ownerships, originally introduced in 1921 and subsequently amended by various cabinets, actually gave the peasants about 6 million hectares of land. This, by itself, did not improve their economic position. Rather, agricultural production reached a very low level, because the peasants found no assistance in their attempts to procure more up-to-date implements and machinery. Soon the small farmer was heavily in debt and a severe political and economic crisis gripped Rumania in 1927. 50,000 Rumanian farmers held a public demonstration at the historic Congress of Alba Julia and were ready for a "march on Bucharest."

1928 brought Maniu and Mihalache to the head of an Agrarian Government in Rumania. The elections had given them over 75% of the votes. Owing to a constitutional dispute with King Carol, this Agrarian Government lasted only until 1931. But a brave attempt to improve the position of the people and the country was made. It was responsible for the establishment of democratic order in Rumania. Education of the people became widespread and popularized. The establishment of cooperatives was encouraged and modern agricultural tools were introduced. Investment of considerable British, French and American capital was procured, and the general welfare and standard of living were raised. The agricultural reform was widened but not completely accomplished. In 1930, according to official statistics, 74.9% of the farms had under 5 hectares of land, comprising only 35.8% of the total arable land; 24.3% had between 5 and 50 hectares, or 45.4% of the arable land; and 0.8% of the farms had over 50 hectares, or 18.8% of the arable land.

In 1932, Maniu and Mihalache were again in power for a brief period and were again ousted for refusing to accept the unconstitutional acts of the King. This marked the beginning of a long and bitter struggle between Agrarian democratic conceptions and extreme rightist dictatorship. It was terminated by the victorious democratic blow of 1944, which the Agrarian organization instigated and carried out against Hitler's troops of occupation and their subservient Rumanian puppets. During World War II, Maniu and Mihalache had maintained secret contact with the Allies with the object of overthrowing the pro-German regime.

After the Germans had been disposed of, the Rumanian peasants, headed by Maniu and Mihalache, formed the back-bone of the coalition Government in which the Communists participated, in spite of the fact that they represented a very small minority. Relying on the support of the Soviet troops of occupation, in a manner quite identical with the developments in all other Soviet-dominated lands, the Communists lost no time in setting up puppets, such as Peter Groza, in an attempt to suppress and annihilate the Agrarian organization of Maniu and Mihalache and to impose by brute force its own reactionary red dictatorship.

Hungary

Under the revolutionary leadership of Dosza (XVI Century), Kossuth and Petõfi (XIX Century), as well as that of Tildy and Nagy (XX Century), the Hungarian peasants struggled for one and the same thing—Land, Liberty and Rights. It was a bitter and sanguine fight between the landless agricultural workers and small-holders on one side, and the large land-owners, the favorites of the Hapsburg dynasty, some of whom possessed as much as 500,000 acres, on the other. In consequence, the agrarian movement in Hungary started out as one of the most extreme leftist social moevments, assuming the form of Agrarian Socialism. It acquired the shape of an organization after the peasant strikes of 1897, 1905 and 1906. However, its actual beginning can be traced much further back. In 1896, Sanodia Csizma, a young agricultural worker and early promoter of Agrarian Socialism in Hungary, was tried for publishing an article presumably instigating the peasants against the ruling class. "Hunger and misery made me an Agrarian Socialist," he told the court. And this is what Socialism meant to him:

> When I speak of the Fatherland . . . I do not mean a piece of land, because in that case I should have no Fatherland. No matter where I went, if I set foot on any piece of earth saying "this is mine," I should be chased away with the words "get off there, that is not yours." Therefore, when I speak of the Fatherland I mean the existing system and I think I may hate this system—may I not?[35]

In 1897, the agricultural laborers went on strike for greater pay. In 1898, the "Parliament" pronounced agrarian strikes outside the law and voted a reduction of the daily wages. In 1905,

[35] G. Palouczi-Horwat, *In Darkest Hungary*, London, 1944, p. 87.

over 100,000 estate servants stopped work. More than 1000 of them were arrested and 60 were killed. 10,000 foreign workers were called in. In spite of that, a raise in the wages was achieved. In 1906, over 100,000 land workers were again on strike. This time 5000 of them were arrested. Foreign laborers and soldiers were called upon to gather in the crops. At about this time, however, "The Agricultural Labor Association" came into existence and took up the fight against the association of the powerful landowners, known as "The Estate Owners Association" (O.M.G.E.).

The land-workers were mobilized and forced to work without pay. It was even suggested by the large landowners that 100,000 Chinese colonists be imported, but the cost of transportation was found to be too great.

> This is the pre-1914 "liberal" period in the country . . . Bankers, manufacturers, big landowners were permitted to unite and to form organizations, even the industrial workers could build up their Unions, but all attempts by the land-workers to do the same thing were met by prison and the gendarme's bayonet.[36]

The leader of the Agrarian movement, Várkonyi, was put in prison. Andras Achim, a learned and intelligent peasant and member of Parliament (1906), was tried for an article in defense of the peasants. In court he stated:

> The future order for which I am fighting and for which I stand accused of stirring up the people will be one in which only the work done by the individual, the importance of that work and its real value will assign to the citizen his importance in the society.[37]

In the program which he published the same year in his paper, he called for universal and secret suffrage, expropriation of es-

[36] *Ibid.*, p. 90.
[37] *Ibid.*, p. 1.

tates over 10,000 acres and their breaking up into small farms, freedom of speech and the press, progressive income taxation and reformation in the administration. However, in 1911 he was killed. The mass of peasants assembled at his funeral resembled a stormy ocean. During this restless period, 1890-1914, over 1.5 million Hungarians were literally compelled to emigrate, mainly to North and South America.

The attempts for agrarian reforms of Karolyi's Government after World War I, as well as the "socialization" policy of Bela Kun remained scraps of paper. The fatal experiment of the Agrarian leader Stephen Szabo Nagyatadi, aiming to introduce agrarian reforms while he was minister of agriculture in the cabinet of the perfidious Count Bethlen, ended in a catastrophe for himself and a death-blow to his agrarian organization. The peasants were cruelly cheated and until 1930 only 2242 persons possessed more land than 4 million small-owners together.

The inspired peasant-poet Peter Veres preached "freedom of cooperation" and "the way of the free spirit" but the bayonets of the State Police were pointed against him and against the whole agrarian movement. Unperturbed, the Hungarian nobles continued to dispose of the lives and fates of their peasant slaves as they pleased. In 1926, Count Pallavicini levelled the whole village of Doc in order to compel the peasants to leave his estate—consisting of some 60,000 acres. Barbarous acts of this sort continued even as late as 1937.

And yet, in spite of the fact that the struggle was unequal, in the period between 1921 and 1938, over 271,000 hectares of land were distributed among the peasants. However, the statistics of 1935 still showed that 0.7% of the estates possessed 48.3% of the land surface in Hungary, while the remaining 99.3% of the owners had the balance of 51.7%. Even in 1942 Count Sosich stated in Parliament that the theory according to which every Hungarian had the right to possess land was false.

By 1945, the Hungarian peasants, with Tildy and Nagy at the head, had seized power and proceded to allot the lands of the

Counts and the Hapsburgs to landless farmers. The fact that even under Soviet occupation 55% of the votes in the first election went to the peasant organization of Smallholders, points clearly the type of agrarian socialism practiced in Hungary and its determination to withstand any form of dictatorship.

Czechoslovakia

The Agrarian movement in Czechoslovakia was founded while the country was still under foreign domination.

In SLOVAKIA—under the leadership of Dr. Milan Hodza, Stepanek, etc. the struggle of the peasant masses was aimed at (a) the abolition of the Austro-Hungarian domination, and (b) the restoration and distribution of the lands forcefully seized by the foreign favorites and supporters of the Hapsburg dynasty.

In BOHEMIA and MORAVIA the same type of struggle was carried on by the peasants under the leadership of Antonin Svehla, aimed against the despotism of the Kaiser and the "tools," whom he had rewarded with bountiful donations of Czeck lands.

To appreciate properly the accomplishments and merits of the Czechoslovak Agrarian Organization, one should take into consideration the situation of the peasant populations of these countries before they had attained their independence.

In Bohemia 81% of the smallholders owned only one-eighth of the entire land surface. Seven-eights of the population, according to the statistics of 1896, had no land ownership what-soever. At that, 1548 persons possessed two-fifths of the land, and 150 families held one-third of the land.

In Moravia, six-sevenths of the total number of proprietors possessed only one-sixth of the land surface with farms up to 5 hectares. One-third of the entire land belonged to 0.1% of the landowners.

In Silesia, out of 505,980 hectares of land 203,066 hectares belonged to a handfull of proprietors.

In Slovakia; 1000 individuals possessed 2,100,000 hectares out of a total of 5,512,000 hectares.

In Sub-Carpethian Ruthenia, only 750 individuals possessed one-third of the entire land.[38]

To make matters worse "in Czechoslovakia the landowning class was almost entirely German or Hungarian."[39] To name some of the better-known ones, the estates of the Lichtensteins, the Waldesteins, the Dietrichsteins, the Moralas and Huerta, had been created and maintained in the name of foreign oppression. At the same time, 2,300,000 persons, or 23% of the population of these parts, were compelled to emigrate to North and South America, Canada, Asiatic Russia, Vienna, Germany, etc.

All these "favored" foreign and local proprietors were naturally supporters of the Hapsburg dynasty and of German influence in Czechoslovakia, and fought on Germany's side in World War I, while the Czech peasants and their leaders fought and died for the liberty of Czechoslovakia on the side of the Allied armies of liberation.

After the liberation and establishment of the Czechoslovak Republic, the Agrarian Organization participated in almost all of the Governments there. Under the wise leadership of Svehla, Stepanek and Dr. Milan Hodza, the Czech and Slovakian Agrarian Organizations were united and were able to carry out the greater part of their program, in spite of the fact that there was no homogeneous agrarian government. From 1932 until his death Svehla was Prime-Minister of the country with few brief exceptions. During the stormy years preceding World War II, the Slovak leader Dr. Milan Hodza was at the head of the Government in Czechoslovakia.

Under pressure from the Agrarian Organization, the agrarian reforms, which distributed gradually the huge estates of the Austrian and Hungarian aristocracy among peasant-farmers, were first introduced in 1919. By 1931, 98% of the farms in Czechoslovakia had up to 30 hectares of land and only 2% had more than 30 hectares.

[38] "Politica," *The Agrarian Reform in Czechoslovakia*, Prague, 1923.

[39] Hugh Seton-Watson, *Eastern Europe*, Cambridge, II edition, 1946, p. 78.

Financial support of the farms was procured mainly through the Agrarian Cooperatives, which, under the management of F. Klindera, had united in a powerful cooperative union and had become the economic base of modern Czechoslovak agriculture and industry. Along with the development of agriculture, Czechoslovak industry had assumed enviable dimensions and in many respects was in a position to compete favorably with the German industrial output. Modern social legislature accounted for visible improvement of labor conditions and provided the workers with a tolerable existence.

The Czechoslovak peasants, in collaboration with the other democratic organizations of the country, had succeeded in a short time to create an exemplary, free and democratic young Republic which enjoyed undeniable cultural progress.

People who have had the privilege of visiting Czechoslovakia prior to the German invasion are fully conscious of the extent to which the Czech peasants and workers, and for that matter, the entire population, were ready to die in defense of their freedom, their land and all their economic and cultural acquisitions. The Munich Agreement, however, dealt the Czechoslovak people a staggering blow and disillusioned them completely.

In spite of that, the village of Lidice will remain as an everlasting memorial to the struggle for resistance of the Czechoslovak peasants.

At present, with a Government completely under the control of the Communists, the Czechoslovak peasants are forbidden to have their own agrarian organization. In Slovakia they were compelled to enter the new Slovak party and under the leadership of their youthful chief Yanko Ursiny, they managed to poll 65% of the votes in the recent election.

Poland

In the eighteenth century, Poland was partitioned between Russia, Germany and Austria. The revolution of 1848 was a decisive moment in the emancipation of the Polish peasants under Prussian and Austrian rule. In the Russian occupied part of Poland, serfdom was abolished in 1864.[40]

Confirmation of the right of the peasants to own the land they cultivate is to be found already in the revolutionary Manifesto of Tadeush Kosciuszko, issued in May of 1794. These rights were reiterated again in the Manifesto of the Polish National Council (1861) which paved the way of the insurrection of 1863. The Russian Tzar suppressed this insurrection brutally, but found he was obliged to accede the rights and privileges of the peasants as demanded by the Polish national Council. In this manner the feudalism of the middle ages came to an end in Poland.

The Political movement of the Polish peasantry started in the last years of the Nineteenth and the beginning of the Twentieth century. In 1931, the left wing "Wyzwolenie" (Liberation), under the leadership of K. Baginski and Stanislas Thugutt, merged with the moderate "Piast," headed by W. Witos, into one unified peasant party, the PSL (Polskie Stronnictwo Ludowe—Polish Peasant Party). Thus, competition and struggle between the left wing and moderate peasants has been replaced by cooperation in a common struggle for democracy and social justice.

When Poland became an independent Republic toward the end of 1918 and the beginning of 1919, two-thirds of the land was in the hands of small farmers, with an average of 6 hectares per farm.[41] Only one-third of the land still remained in possession of large landowners and social institutions. However, under pressure of the Agrarian movement, in the same year the Constituent Assembly passed a resolution with which large land possessions were to be broken up and distributed among small farmers.

Under the direction of its leader Wincenty Vitos, in 1920 the Polish Peasant Party headed the Polish Government and defended the country with all its might against the onslaught of Russian bolshevism. Participating in various coalition govern-

[40] Feliks Gross, *The Polish Worker*, New York, 1945, p. 21.

[41] Tadeusz Mincer, *The Agrarian Problem in Poland*, London, p. 19.

ments, the Polish agrarians remained in power until the first part of 1926, when Witos was again Prime-Minister. In 1925 his Government passed a new, radical land reform reducing the maximum ownership of land to 300 hectares, making obligatory the allotment of a total of 200,000 hectares to landless farmers annually, conferring the right of cooperatives to own land, providing cheap and easily accessible credit to the peasants from the Agricultural Bank, etc. The creation of an industry was started on the basis of new social legislation. Poland was confronted with numerous difficulties, but the country was definitely headed toward internal and external stability.

In May of 1926, however, Witos and his Government were overthrown by a military "coup d'etat" organized by Marshal Pilsudsky. The Polish Peasant Party began a stubborn fight against dictatorship. In 1930 the dictatorial Government held elections under conditions of bitter terrorism. The leaders of the opposition were arrested and Witos was faced with false charges and convicted. But the Agrarian youth of Poland succeeded in hiding him and getting him over the border into Czechoslovakia, where he spent 8 long years in exile. From there he continued to direct the struggle of the peasants for liberty, land and democracy. In 1935, the authoritarian government of Poland held another "election." The Polish peasants, together with all other democratic parties, decided to abstain from voting. By means of the cooperative organizations, their own publication "Wici," pamphlets, etc., the Agrarian Youth Organization of Poland maintained a most valiant struggle, regardless of the cost in human life and suffering. They warned and attacked the new "Szlachta" of the colonels, which, like the old one, was leading the country toward a new catastrophe. The Government, however, continued its oppression.

In 1937, the Polish peasants went on strike and refused to deliver their produce to the cities. Once again the Government police suppressed the strike by terroristic measures. Scores of people lost their lives, but the Government officially admitted only 42 casualties. The struggle went on and under popular pressure the

Government had to make certain concessions. In the period between 1920-1937, according to official statistics, 2,469,000 hectares of land were distributed among 700,000 peasants, and in 1938 Poland had 4,200,000 individual farmers.[42]

Hitler's invasion of Czechoslovakia in 1939 compelled Witos to return to Poland. The impending catastrophe prevented the Government from taking active measures against him. Shortly afterwards the Polish nation became the victim of Hitler's invasion and tyranny. In spite of the attitude and criminal follies of their government, the Polish peasants demonstrated to the whole world how they could fight in defense of their land and freedom. They were not conquered and subjugated either by Hitler's vandalism or by the Soviet stab in the back. Poland was overrun and partitioned once again, but the Polish love of freedom and proud spirit remained intact and, rising from the ashes of destruction, soon made itself evident in the battle-fields of the Middle East and Europe.

Witos was wounded. The Germans placed him under arrest and subsequently kept him in confinement. His faithful colloborators, Stanislav Mikolajczyk, Prof. Kot, and others, continued the fight until victory was achieved over Hitlerism and Fascism.

At the end of the war they returned to their Fatherland and accepted collaboration with the Communists, Socialists and another democratic group in the attempt to rebuild Poland. In accordance with the decisions and declarations of the "Big Three" at Yalta, Potsdam and Moscow, and in the spirit of the Atlantic Charter, they were compelled to make sacrifices and compromises.

But these remained one-sided, as the Communists had only one desire; to strangle the Polish peasant movement and to establish a dictatorship of their own. Thousands of members of the Peasant Party were imprisoned. Baginski, who had been imprisoned in Poland for his struggle for democracy, and who led the peasant underground during the German occupation, was again thrown into jail, together with many peasant leaders.

[42] *Ibid.*, pp. 74-75.

Finland

The Agrarian Organization of Finland was founded while the country was still under Russian domination, in 1906. It received its baptism in a general strike, bordering on revolution, after the Russian-Japanese war, directed against the tyrannical conduct of Nicholas II, who also held the title Duke of Finland.

The founder of the Finnish Agrarian Organization was the popular peasant writer Santeri Alkio, and his first assistant, Kyosti Kallio, who was an average peasant-farmer from the province of Pohjanmaa. The organization was made up of small farmers in the provinces of Eastern Karelia and Western Pohjanmaa who struggled against a handful of large landowners in possession of the greatest part of the land. At this time 59% of the peasants were share-croppers.

The program and ideology of the Finnish Agrarian movement was based on liberty, national independence and private ownership on the merits of labor; struggle against the domination of the Russian Tsar and the establishment of a democratic Republic; struggle against large landowners and industrialists, who at this time were mostly Swedes and as such became conductors of Swedish chauvinist and cultural expansion. The Finnish Agrarian movement was stimulated by a desire for political, economic and cultural equality based on the cooperative conception. Their program also included the introduction of temperance laws. The most decisive struggle was directed against the existing political parties who were prepared to tolerate the Russian Tzarist regime even at the expense of certain privileges that had already been granted to the people of Finland. The Finnish Agrarians collaborated secretly with the organization engaged in training the youth in preparation of the insurrection contemplated against the domination of Russian imperialism.

The Agrarian Organization of Finland played a major part in the life and fate of the Finnish people and was able to introduce a large part of its program. By 1907 the Finns had acquired the right of having their own free Parliament, elected by universal secret ballotting and Finland was one of the first states to introduce equal rights for women. For a short time in 1927-28 the Agrarian Party had a homogeneous cabinet. By 1929 it had become the most powerful political organization of the country. It participated in almost all of the coalition cabinets. Its prominent representative, L. Kr. Relander, was President of the Republic from 1921 to 1925. Its leader, Kyosti Kallio, had a ministerial post in almost all of the cabinets. In 1937 he became President of the Republic and held this position until his death in 1940. Its prominent members, I. Naukkanen, K. Lohi, Ellila, Dr. P. T. Yutila (present minister in Washington), Dr. I. Kekkonen, E. Tarkkanen, as well as the young and promising V. Suhselainen—now President of the Organization—were for the most part farmers and economists and have proved able leaders and statesmen.

With the agrarian reforms of 1917-18, the large estates were allotted to the peasants, and 90% of the farms became small. From a total of 315,000 farms, only 3300 possess more than 50 hectares of arable land, and 225,000 farms had under 10 hectares. Considering the unfavorable climatic and soil conditions, Finland had acquired a most even distribution of land. Here, too, we have the cooperative principle as a basic economic factor.

In Finland we find a well organized modern industry. The people of Finland are fanatically devoted to their liberty and positively reject any form of dictatorial or totalitarian regimes. All these admirable characteristics have been rapturously described by the Russian author Gregory Petrov, who named Finland "the Land of the White Lilies." These same traits accounted for the astounding heroism with which the proud and laborious Finns defended their country and their political, economic and cultural acquisitions in 1940 against the attack of the Soviet Union.

At present the Finnish Agrarian Organization participates in a coalition government along with Social Democrats, Communists and other political groups. In spite of the fact that Finland took an active part in the war against the Soviet Union, the country was not subjected to military occupation. The leader of the Finnish Communist party, Otto Wille Kuusinen, still remains in Moscow.

Conclusion

Agrarian Movements are to be found in many other countries. In Denmark we have an Agrarian organization of long standing and high repute, with very considerable achievements to its credit. Agrarian Movements exist in Greece, Switzerland, Holland, France, Austria, the Baltic-States. Agrarian Movements will exist wherever there is an agricultural population governed by a democratic regime.

A most powerful democratic Agrarian organization will some day rise in Russia out of the oppressed "kolhoz" workers, who are at present engaged in a heroic struggle for the recognition of their rights, their freedom and their democratic principles. Admittedly, they are severely handicapped by the authoritarian Soviet system, but those who are of the opinion that the peoples of the USSR are psychologically adapted to dictatorial regimes are laboring under a misconception. Such nations do not exist. Even elementary knowledge of history should disclose that the Russian peoples have in the past been responsible for the greatest number of revolts and insurrections and have shed rivers of blood for their freedom, for their land and for their rights.

The peasantry of the world is engaged in a struggle against oppression and injustice and is attempting to establish its own Agrarian and cooperative organizations. The grain producing populations everywhere are united by a common policy and an ideology which is deeply rooted in their biological, psychological and material reality—Free Land, Free Labor, and Free Private Ownership.

Distant and often superficial observers are inclined to see more profound differences between Agrarian organizations of more progressive social policies and ideologies—such as the Bulgarian one, for example—and those of more conservative spirit—such as the Polish and Czechoslovakian organizations. A simple analysis of the conditions and circumstances in which these organizations have appeared and grown will indubitably point out that this is merely a question of a stage in evolution. The Bulgarian people were delivered from the status of feudalism while they were still under Turkish domination and for 66 years have existed as a free and independent nation. The Polish, Czechoslovakian and Croation peoples received their sovereignty only after World War I. Of primary consideration and importance to the Polish, Czechoslovakian and Croatian peasants was the problem evolved by the desire of the Prussian and Hapsburg imperialists to stamp out the Slav elements in their lands. It was, therefore, imperative that states who had yet to solve the problem of national self-preservation and independence should give secondary consideration to their internal, partisan differences. Fortunately, the wholesome instinct of the people is always able to distinguish between greater and lesser dangers. Consequently, the accomplishment of uniformity in Agrarian principles and policies is only a question of time and any existing differences are not due to an organic dissimilarity.

It is made evident by the foregoing survey that Agrarian movements throughout the world have a common historical and evolutionary background. Also, that fundamentally they were inspired, strengthened and sustained by the same ideological principles leading to a common ultimate objective—Land, Liberty, Democracy. Whether in France or in Russia, Holland or Rumania, Finland or Bulgaria, the nuclear cell—the peasant-farmer—is subjected to the same unifying factor—land toil. Regardless of origin, creed or geographic location, custom, manner or language, the hands that hold the plow, toss the seed and reap the harvest have more than callouses and sinews in common—they are engaged in the same beneficient, noble, life-creating work of producing the basic requirements of mankind.

The Agrarian class is a homogeneous professional unity and a basic factor in the historic development of organized human society. In spite of the tremendous industrial development, Agriculture will always remain as one of the solid bases of life, of material and spiritual human culture. Some of the most highly industrialized countries have lately shown distinct tendencies of returning to the land. Prominent French statesmen have made public declarations to the effect that the salvation of France is in agriculture, and British Laborites of today are laying plans for a more rational British agriculture. Perhaps the most striking example is to be found in the younger generations of Palestine. They look upon Agriculture as the salvation of the entire Jewish nation and have in effect established some of the most modern farming enterprises, such as Moshav Ovdim, Kvutza, Moshava, etc., of whose success I am an eye-witness. "What Palestine needs is more farms—not Tel-Avivs" is the accepted slogan of Palestine youths.

Industry and Agriculture will have to develop simultaneously with the object of complementing and assisting one another. In a normal society the Agrarian class should be accepted on an equal footing with all other social and labor classes and no attempt should be made to subordinate it to either the bourgeoisie or the proletariat. It should be remembered that it is by fusion with the virility of the Agrarian class that the poisoned atmosphere of factory and city is refreshed and literally saved from degeneration.

The farmers constitute a struggling, revolutionary class. The efforts of Stalin to refute this particular quality of the peasants are in vain. In his preface to the book *What to Do*, by N. G. Chernishevski, published by the Leningrad section of the Young Guard in 1936, the Soviet writer A. Starchakov says: "The Russian Liberals have never constituted a revolutionary party with the object of fighting against dictatorship. The revolutionary class at this time was the peasantry—the proletariat had only just been established as a separate class. Chernishevski is a consistent Democrat and Socialist, in whose activity and literary works the interests of the revolutionary peasantry find expression."

Agrarian democracy is this very same peasant democracy of Chernishevski. The peasant revolutionary class was in existence before the establishment of the industrial workers' proletariat. The peasants, however, do not consider revolution as fatal, nor as the only means of solving social conflicts. They stoop to armed revolt only when all other legal means have been exhausted. To quote the American Declaration of Independence of 1776, "Whenever any form of government becomes destructive of these ends it is the right of the people to abolish it and to institute a new Government."

There exists no revolution in history which has been successfully carried out without the active participation of the peasants. The Russian Revolution is a very outstanding example. Stalin himself, in speaking of the participation and activity of the peasants in it, clearly concedes that "these preparatory circumstances decided the fate of the October Revolution."[43] And the official Soviet history also concedes that "the outcome of the civil war depended mainly on which side the peasants would add their weight."[44]

Even more erroneous is Stalin's assertion that the peasant class is in a process of deterioration. Such a homogeneous unity as the peasant class cannot deteriorate. On the contrary, powerfully supported by its cooperative and private ownership foundation, it remains the main pillar of liberty and democracy in their struggle against any type of dictatorship. This fact is well appreciated by the Communists, and it explains why they always talk of collaboration with the peasants while it has been notoriously proved that in every instance they have not failed to attack with ferocity their democratic organizations.

In their epic struggles through the centuries the peasants caused the downfall of slavery and feudalism and thus gained liberty and land. They will not tolerate the chains of the modern Communist party feudalism. Struggle against the peasants is a very

[43] Stalin, *op. cit.*, p. 173.

[44] *History of the Bolshevist Party*, short edition, Moscow, p. 223.

dangerous adventure. It might mean hunger, misery and a catastrophe for the protagonists and maybe for the world. The Soviet Union is responsible for starting it and will probably soon be convinced of this truth. Maybe it will try to correct the mistake—if it is not too late, because the victims of the war were millions, but the victims of the "peace" may amount to billions.

After World War I, in 1920, representatives of the Agrarian organization—Stambolisky, Svehla and Witos,—laid the foundations of International Agrarian Solidarity and founded in Prague the Agrarian, also called the Green, International, which was to serve as a fortress of peasant democracy against dictatorships. Today the Agrarian organizations are much more numerous and far more powerful, especially in Eastern and South-Eastern Europe. They are united by their common ideology and in the name of a powerful democratic Agrarian Union. In July 1942, a great part of these Agrarian organizations held a special conference in London and were represented there by prominent Agrarian leaders such as Mikolajczyk, Dr. Milan Gavrilovic, Matsankieff, L. Feierabend, F. Lichner, etc., who established and demonstrated once again their ideological solidarity and laid the basis of a common post-war Agrarian program.

The Agrarian organizations are always eager for collaboration with all other democratic organizations and welcome the support of world democracy for the establishment of democratic, international solidarity and a federation of the peoples. It is to be understood that this federation is to be attained freely, voluntarily and by their own initiative and not imposed by force. To quote Feliks Gross: "It is clear from our recent experience that social justice cannot be imposed from above by decree. Nor can equalization of a democratic pattern throughout this region be so instituted. The peoples themselves must create the democratic pattern, however much sympathey from the outside may aid them to clear away the obstacles to progress."[45]

[45] Feliks Gross, *Crossroads of Two Continents*. New York, p. 53.

In this manner the Agrarian Democratic Union and a Balkan and Eastern European Federation may provide a solid basis for the United States of Europe and, subsequently, a federated peaceful and cultured world. This is one of the grandest objectives of Agrarianism.

BIBLIOGRAPHY

AGRARIAN (*The*) *Problem from the Baltic to the Aegean*, London, 1943.

AGRARIAN (*The*) *Reform in Czechoslovakia*, Prague, 1923 (Reprint from the *Politika*).

ANDREEV, A.: *Speech before the 18th Congress of the Bolshevist Party*, Moscow, 1940 (in Russian).

BATESON, WM.: *The Biological Fact and the Structure of Society*, Oxford, 1911.

BERGSON, HENRI: *L'évolution créatrice*, Paris, 1909.

BERGSON, HENRI: *Le pensée et le mouvant*, Paris, 1941.

BUECHNER, A.: *Energy and Matter*, Sofia, 1931 (Bulgarian tr.).

CHERNISHEVSKY, N. G.: *What to Do?* Leningrad, 1936 (in Russian).

Constitution of the USSR, 1936.

Croatian Peasant Party Council, Canada: Constitution of the Independent Croatian Peasant Republic, Hamilton, 1946.

DASKALOV, RAIKO IV.: *The Struggle for Land*, Sofia, 1922 (in Bulgarian).

DIMITROV, GEORGE M.: *The Fight for Freedom and Independence*, Sofia, 1944 (in Bulgarian).

DIMITROV, GEORGE M.: *The Ideology and Fights of the Agrarian Movement*, Sofia, 1945 (in Bulgarian).

ENGELS, FRIEDRICH: *Anti-During*, Paris, 1926 (French tr.).

ENGELS, FRIEDRICH: *Ludwig Feuerbach*, Paris, 1932 (French tr.).

ENGELS, FRIEDRICH: *Origins of Family and Property*, Sofia, 1927 (Bulgarian tr.).

EVANS, I. L.: *The Agrarian Revolution in Roumania*, Cambridge, 1924.

FABRE, JEAN H.: *Les mervilles de l'instinct*, Paris, 1913.

GARNETT, A. C.: *Instinct and Personality*, London, 1928.

GIDE, CHARLES: *Political Economy*, Sofia, 1918 (Bulgarian tr.).

GROSS, FELIKS: *Crossroads of Two Continents*, New York, 1945.

GROSS, FELIKS: *The Polish Worker*, New York, 1945.

HAECKEL, ERNEST: *Les merveilles de la Vie*, Paris, 1907.

HANCOCK, THOMAS: *An Essay on Instinct and Its Physical and Moral Relations*, London, 1824.

History of the Bolshevist Party, abridged ed., Moscow.

HODZA, MILAN: *Federation in Central Europe*, New York, 1942.

HODZA, MILAN: *Speeches and Articles*, Prague, 1930 (in Czech).

IOVANOVIC, DRAGOLJUB: *Teachers of Energy*, Belgrad, 1940 (in Serbian).

IOVANOVIC, DRAGOLJUB: *The New Antaeus,* Belgrad, 1934 (in Serbian).

KOJOUHAROFF, C. D.: *General Theory of Law and State.* A review in the "Tulane Law Review," Dec., 1945.

LEBEDEV, VLADIMIR IV.: *The New Roadway,* Sofia, 1923 (in Bulgarian).

LEBEDEV, VLADIMIR IV.: *In the Country of Roses and Blood,* Paris, 1935 (in Russian), (first ed. 1923 in Serbian).

LENIN, VLADIMIR: *Works,* XIII, Moscow, 1938 (in Russian).

LODGE, OLIVE: *Peasant Life in Yugoslavia,* London, 1941.

Manifesto of the Communist Party, 1938 (in Russian).

MARX, KARL: *Works,* Moscow, 1935 (in Russian).

McDOUGALL, WILLIAM: *Introduction to Social Psychology,* London, 1908.

MINCER, TADEUSZ: *The Agrarian Problem in Poland,* London, 1944.

MITRANY, DAVID: *The Land and the Peasant in Roumania,* London, 1930.

NESNARD, A.: *La vie et la mort des instincts,* Paris, 1926.

PAINE, M.: *Physiology of the Soul and the Instinct,* New York, 1872.

PALOUCZI, HORVAT G.: In Darkest Hungary, London, 1944.

PETKOV, N. D.: *Alexander Stambolisky,* Sofia, 1930 (in Bulgarian).

PRENANT, M.: *Biologie et Marxisme,* Paris, 1935.

REK, TADEUSZ: *Peasant Movement in Poland,* Lodz, 1946 (in Polsh).

ROBERTS, MORLEY: *Bio-Politics,* London, 1938.

RUSSELL, BERTRAND: *Principles of Social Reconstruction,* London, 1916.

SETON-WATSON, H.: *Eastern Europe,* Cambridge, 1936 (2nd ed.).

SOROKIN, P., ZIMMERMAN, C. C., GALPIN, J. CH.: *A Systematic Source Book in Rural Sociology,* Minneapolis, The University of Minnesota Press, 1930.

STALIN, JOSEPH: *The Questions of Leninism,* Moscow, 1939, 11th ed. (in Russian).

STAMBOLISKY, ALEXANDER: *Political Parties or Professional Organizations,* Sofia, 1934 (3rd ed.; 1st ed. 1909), (in Bulgarian).

STAMBOLISKY, ALEXANDER: *The Principle of the Bulgarian Agrarian Union,* Sofia, 1944 (in Bulgarian).

SWOPE, H. B.: Foreword to JAMES W. WISE, *Our Bill of Rights,* New York, 1941.

THUGUTT, STANISLAS: *Selected Essays and Autobiography,* Glasgow, 1943 (in Polish).

TODOROV, KOSTA: *Balkan Firebrand,* New York, 1943.

TODOROVIC, L. V.: *Sveslovenstvo, St. Radica,* Belgrad, 1938 (in Serbian).

TODOROV, KOSTA: *Alexander Stambolisky,* Belgrad, 1930 (in Serbian).

XI.

The Destinies of the Russian Peasantry

(The Russian Peasant Movement)

XI.

THE DESTINIES OF THE RUSSIAN PEASANTRY
(The Russian Peasant Movement)

By

VLADIMIR ZENZINOV

AMONG THE VARIOUS "*Bylini*" (epic songs) created by the Russian people in ancient times, there is one that cannot fail to leave a most striking and lasting impression on the mind of every student of Russian folklore. This legend reflects the relationship between the peasants' toil and the soil they are tilling, and it is permeated with the fathomless profundity of popular wisdom. During all the centuries of their historical life, the overwhelming majority of the Russian people were peasants engaged in raising products of the soil. This is the prevailing condition of life in Russia also at present. Consequently, the relationship between the toiling peasant and the soil he is tilling represents the most important problem of the Russian people's social and economic life.

The "*bylina*" referred to above concerns the Valiant Svyatogor, one of the senior, i.e., the most powerful, Russian legendary heroes. Once upon a time he went horseback riding for exercise or to challenge somebody to a test of strength. On the way he met a stranger, a peasant, carrying a small bag on his back. Svyatogor set his horse to trotting but the peasant remained ahead of him. Then he rode as fast as he could, but the wanderer remained just beyond his reach. Finally Svyatogor shouted at the top of his voice: "Ho, wanderer! Stop a moment! I cannot catch up with you though I am on horseback!" The stranger stopped, lifted the small bag from his shoulder and set it on the ground. Svyatogor approached the bag and tried to push it aside with his whip. It did not budge but remained as though rooted in the earth. Svyatogor seized it firmly with his hand but the bag did not move. He dismounted, grasped the small bag with both hands and strained until his white face became suffused with blood. In spite of all this effort he succeeded in lifting the small bag only a hair's breadth from the ground while he himself sank knee-deep into the earth.

"Tell me the truth," demanded Svyatogor, "What did you put in this bag?" The wanderer replied:

"The load in this bag is the spell of our Mother Earth."

"And who are you? What is your name?"

"Me? My name is Mikula (Nicholas). I am a peasant and our Mother Earth, our native soil, is fond of me."

That, in a nutshell, is the content of the "*bylina*." It is easy to grasp its meaning. After he seized the peasant's small sack with both hands and strained mightily, the legendary hero was able to lift it only a hair's breadth, a barely perceptible distance. At the same time, the peasant carries this very load on his back with such ease that the valiant hero on horseback is unable to overtake him. Pondering this ancient tale, one must recognize that the profound popular wisdom has thoroughly weighed and appreciated all the details which are immensely important in grasping the very essentials of the people's life. The spell of, and the bondage to, the soil are of overwhelming magnitude. When the valiant hero tried to shake them even imperceptibly, red blood covered his face. Yet the people carry the load of these forces produced by the soil with the greatest of ease as if they were carrying an empty sack. It is hardly possible to give a more striking and graphic picture of the relationship between the earth, the nursing-mother, the primary source of human life, and the peasants who are tilling it. One could imagine no better description of the close ties between the soil and the toil put into it ever since the beginning of

Russia's history than this myth created by the people themselves in times of yore.

Russia, both as country and as state, was created by her peasants, the leading characters on her historical stage. Russia's political unification was not an outcome of planned actions from the top, it rather developed from below, through the toil and efforts of the masses at the bottom layer of her population. It was the movement of these masses towards new frontiers in order to settle in new regions that spearheaded and directed this process of unification. All strata of Russia's population took part in this movement, yet the lion's share of the pioneering work was borne by the peasants. Equipped with axes and primitive wooden ploughs, the peasants persistently and unflaggingly penetrated into the impassible virgin forests and jungles (taiga) of Northern Russia and Siberia. They cleared the forests, tilled the wide areas of deforestated lands and steadily, step by step, worked their way to the North, East and South. In their wake followed warriors with their swords, traders with their money bags and agents of the government. All of them in the main did no more than consolidate the results of the peasants' spade work.

It was the peasants who at first cemented vast spaces of the boundless plain into Muscovite Russia and then became the bedrock of an expanded, united and powerful Russian state.

The famous Russian historian Vassilii Klyutchevski demonstrated that 16th and 17th century developments directed from outside the country had a great bearing and a decisive influence upon the whole organization of the Muscovite state and its social structure. During those two centuries, Muscovite Russia was continuously threatened, harassed and invaded by external foes from the East, South and West (by nomadic peoples, the Tartars, Lithuanians and Poles). The state, therefore, had to be organized on the pattern of a besieged military camp.

The guiding principles of this state structure were the compulsory assignment of definite duties and obligatory services among the various groups of the population and the attachment of each group of the people to the specific service assigned to them. In that way all the strata of the country's population were deprived of their freedom. The traders and craftsmen were bound to their commerce and crafts which became their compulsory obligations toward the Czar; the landowners became tied to the Czar and the state as military and civil servants while the peasants, the overwhelming majority of the country's population, were bound to the landowners, on whose estates they lived, and were compelled to toil for them and to get from their soil the means they needed for the discharge of their service to the Czar.

In that way the peasants' serfdom gradually developed during the 16th and 17th centuries. The peasant became the serf of the landlord because the latter also was inseparably bound to the compulsory service he had to render to the Czar and the state. The peasant's dependence upon the service-bound landlord actually was a peculiar indirect kind of compulsory service the peasant himself had to render to the same state. That is why, by the way, the laws of the 17th century did not grant to the landowner the right to deal with his peasants at his own discretion. Above all, the landowner was deprived of the right to set his peasant free. Though he belonged to his landlord, the Russian peasant actually was the serf of the state.

The Russian peasants suffered heavily under the burden of this twofold serfdom (to the landlord and to the state), and it incited their wrath and thirst for revenge. This is borne out by the mass revolts in the 17th and 18th centuries under the leadership of Razine and Pugatchev respectively.

After the reforms of Peter the Great (in the 18th century) the nobility was relieved of compulsory state service. The peasants' bondage, however, remained in full force and even was tightened during the reign of Empress Catherine.

The first half of the 19th century was marked in Russia by a succession of historic vicissitudes. Napoleon's onslaught led to the epic Patriotic War from which Russia emerged victorious and triumphant. In December 1825, the first attempt at an armed uprising against the autocratic regime was made in the centre of the country's capital, St. Petersburg. Then followed the reign of Nicholas I, a long and uninterrupted period of severe and implacable reaction. Nevertheless, all these manifold turns in Russia's 19th century history notwithstanding, it can be asserted without peradventure that throughout the whole period in question the basic fact that determined Russia's domestic developments and their trends consisted in paving the way for the abolition of the peasants' serfdom. Not only the peasants could not bear it any longer, but it gradually became a heavy burden even on the government itself. It had come to be generally recognized as the main barrier to the country's economic development. This explains the memorable statement made by Czar Alexander II on the eve of the emancipation of the peasants, while their serfdom was still in force: "It is better to set the peasants free by an act of government than to wait until they free themselves by taking matters into their own hands."

Economic and political conditions became more and more entangled until, finally, the knot had to be cut. In 1861 the abolition of the peasants' serfdom was finally accomplished by the government of Alexander II. However, this government was subjected to the unrelenting pressure of the land-owning nobility which was clinging to the privileges it derived from the peasants' serdom and which put forth every effort to preserve most of these privileges. That is why the "Great Reform," the emancipation of the peasants accomplished by Alexander II in 1861, did not do away with the peasant problem in Russia. At that time the problem at hand was whether plots of land should or should not be allotted to the peasants at their emancipation. In other words, should the peasants continue to carry on their husbandry on the same plots of land on which they had toiled up to then or should they be "set free" also from the soil, i. e., be deprived of the lands they had tilled for generations? The solution adopted by the government in 1861 was a compromise. And the result was that the majority of the peasants were allotted plots of land which were too small for the development of a husbandry sufficient to live upon. Considerable stretches of land that the peasants had tilled before were taken from them and given to the landowners. In addition, the peasants had to compensate the landowners for the plots of land allotted to them. The government issued "Redemption Certificates" which were given to the landowners, and the peasants had to make "Redemption payments" which for a period of decades were levied by the government as a special tax. These installment payments proved too heavy a burden for the majority of the peasants.

Most of Russia's peasants were unable to satisfy their insatiable longing for larger plots of land. That is why during the second half of the 19th century also, Russia's political thinking in all its ramifications continued to be focused on peasant and agrarian problems. Just as before, the peasants continued to be the ferment of social developments. Even the labor problem that soon made its first appearance on the social and political scene proved to be closely related to the peasant problem. The majority of the workers in plants and factories at that time were closely connected to the rustic people. These workers were also peasants who left their villages only temporarily. To most of them the work in the shops and plants in the cities was only a fill-in seasonal work during the winter months when agriculture is impossible.

The political attitude of Russia's progressive circles was marked by strong partiality for the peasants and by an eager desire to work for the benefit of the people who were regarded as synonymous with the peasants. In the 1860's and 1870's the peasant and his way of life was the favorite theme of Russian literature. The peasants' cause also provided the clue to the whole political ideology of Russia's various social groups and served as the guiding star of the revolutionary "Populist Movement"' (Narodnitchestvo: "Narod" means "the people") of the 1870's and of all the social movements and political groups of that time, viz. the so called

"Going to the People" (Khozdienie v Narod), 1873-1874; the "Land and Freedom," (Ziemlia i Wolia), in 1877-1879; and the "Party of the Will of the People," (Narodnaja Wolia) in 1879-1881.

Only after the "Party of the Will of the People" was crushed by the government (in 1881-1883) and after the first Marxists and Social-Democrats made their debut in Russia, new trends appeared among Russia's socialist and revolutionary circles. They rejected the traditional pro-peasant attitude and stressed the significance of the labor problem, as co-equal with the peasant problem and, sometimes, as overshadowing it. As the basis of their program the Marxists and Social-Democrats emphasized the interests of the proletariat instead of those of the peasants. During the years that followed, beginning in the late 1890's and the early 1900's until the very eve of the revolution in 1917, the adherents of two ideologies, of Populism and Marxism, fought relentlessly for domination of the political stage.

The attitude toward the peasants was the basic issue which split these two currents of Russian social and political thought. The Populists who, since the turn of the century, were represented by the Socialist-Revolutionary Party (founded in 1901) remained true to the traditions of the progressive school of thought. They maintained that the peasant problem continued to be Russia's fundamental social and political problem and that it could only be solved by placing all the available land at the disposition of those who would till it. Prohibiting the sale and purchase of land as a marketable commodity, its socialization on a nation-wide scale and making it available to all the people who would work it; that was the program of the Socialist-Revolutionaries, cut down to essentials. The Marxists did not share this view. They held that, in the political program, the labor problem not the peasant problem, the interests of the proletariat not of the peasants were to be emphasized. In their opinion, Russia like all the other European countries had embarked upon developing a capitalist economy. Consequently, the social and political program in Russia should be similar to those of the European Social-Democratic parties. In accordance with the Marxian doctrine, as they conceived and interpreted it, they regarded the peasants as a class of small property owners, of petit bourgeois. They, therefore, rejected the idea that the transfer of land for use by the peasants or the toiling masses generally would be a step on the road to social progress. On the contrary, in their opinion the socialization of land would, rather, impede the movement toward Socialism. The Social Democrats were disposed to regard the peasants politically as conservatives ("The idiotism of the peasant's way of life") and in the field of social development as a backward group ("The peasant's anti-collectivist skull"). This was the viewpoint of both factions, the Bolsheviki (i. e. the adherents of the majority of the party convention) and the Mensheviki (i. e. those who sided with the minority of the party convention), into which the until then united Russian Social Democratic Labor Party split in 1902 (at the party's convention in London).

In 1905 it was the peasants who more than the other classes of the population contributed to turning the events of that year into Russia's first revolution. This fact in a measure undermined the Social-Democrats' negative attitude toward the peasantry. Guided by considerations of political expediency, they adopted a more favorable attitude toward the peasant movement. Yet, ideologically their conception of the peasant problem remained unchanged. As before, they refused to agree that making the land available for the use of those who would till it would be a proper solution of the agrarian problem and they declined to adopt such a plank into their political program.

Until 1917 the attitude towards the peasant adopted by the Bolshevik faction of the Social-Democratic Party was definite, and one befitting orthodox Marxists. The Bolshevik program embodied the conceptions of a commonplace variety of Marxism, according to which the peasantry were, first and last, a class of petty bourgeoisie, alien and antagonistic not only to socialist ideals but to all social progress. The proletariat were the sole organ of the socialist ideal, that is to say of the future. Accordingly the party was built up on exclusively proletarian lines. Its program, so far as the peasant was concerned, was restricted to political demands; for any economic improvement of his condition was in their eyes not only without object but even objectionable. Theoretically the peasants, being established on the land and possessing some means for its exploitation, would have to go through a process of differentiation in the course of which the petty holders among them would be absorbed by larger ones. In conformity with this theory of common Marxism, something analogous to the evolution of industry was due to take place in the villages. Strengthening the petty peasant would mean hampering the inevitable social progress. The only thing the socialist party could do for the peasant—said the Bolsheviks—was to help organize the paid agricultural laborers. Such was the Marxist doctrine professed by the Bolsheviks in the purest form.

For long years the Bolsheviks had been waging a tireless theoretical battle against another Russian socialist party, the Socialist-Revolutionaries, whose chief distinction from the Bolsheviks and from the Marxists in general was this: the Socialist-Revolutionaries in their theoretical conception made no distinction between the proletariat and the peasantry; they considered both united in one laboring class, and argued that the socialist program and the socialist movement must be the common cause of these two armies of labor. This theoretical discussion between the Socialist-Revolutionaries and the Bolsheviks went on incessantly.

In 1905 the Bolsheviks were forced to make large concessions in this question. The peasantry, of whom, up to this time, they had thought of as a purely reactionary class, socially as well as politically, showed that they were a powerful revolutionary force. Indeed, the movement of 1905-06 which compelled the early concession of the government of Tzar Nicholas II—"the first revolution," the manifesto of October 17, the Duma—was largely a peasant movement. The Bolsheviks grasped this and made a change in their tactics in regard to the peasants. But only in their tactics, not in their program. To be sure, they officially proclaimed the slogan "nationalization of land," but they did not conceal that to them this slogan was only a tactical move, by which they wanted to lead the peasant to political revolution. As before, they deemed the paid laborers, the proletariat, to be the only class able to carry out a socialist revolution. The peasant in revolt, demanding land, was to them at this historic moment only a traveling companion on the road to revolution.

A great gulf separated the Bolsheviks from the Socialist-Revolutionaries who proclaimed, as their watch-word, "the socialization of the land." To the Socialist-Revolutionaries, "the socialization of the land" was a specific variety of nationalization; the difference consisted in this: while in "nationalization" the state becomes the legal owner of the land, in socialization the people acquire the supreme right to dispose of all the nationalized land, in accordance with a special legislative provision. Besides, the Socialist-Revolutionaries conceived of "the socialization of the land" as a far-reaching social reform creating favorable conditions for socialization and the introduction of the cooperative principle in all the other branches of industry, agriculture and city affairs. In a socialized agriculture, the land is temporarily distributed among the peasants, by themselves, in their own community. "Temporarily" means here, that the land is returned to the local community periodically for free redistribution.

Then came the year 1917. Contrary to the ordinary conception, the real revolution at that time was not created in the cities, but in the villages. The essential content of the Russian Revolution was the tremendous, elemental process which took place among the peasants and resulted in the disruption of the landed estates, the expulsion of the landed proprietors, most of whom belonged to the nobility, from their estates, and the forcible appropriation of all private and state land by the peasants. The thing that many had foreseen as inevitable, namely the satisfaction of the peasants, age-long thirst for the land, took place in an elemental way. The ideas of the Socialist-Revolutionaries on this point were identical with those of the peasants—"the land must be emptied from the exchange of goods," as they put it; and, "the land is the Lord's own, or nobody's; it's a sin to buy it and a sin to sell it," as the peasant said. Consequently, they hoped to have this wholesale seizure legalized in the Constituent Assembly by a fundamental law on the socialization of the land. This was to be worked out in the highest legislative and administrative organ of the country, by deputies from all the people, and the rules thus established would regulate the use of land throughout the country, converting the peasant's primitive conviction of his right into a law obligatory for all citizens.

The Provisional Government of 1917 did not solve the "Agrarian Problem." It was guided by the principle that it was not authorized to carry out a reform of such tremendous importance. It held that this reform should be entrusted to the Constituent Assembly which was to convene in the near future. This Assembly was to be elected by universal suffrage. It would, therefore, be truly representative of the country's whole population and vested with supreme authority. The Provisional Government, nevertheless, formulated some principles on which, in its opinion, the future agrarian reform should be based and which were in full consonance to the traditional ideas of Russia's peasantry. These principles were: 1) All the land should be placed at the disposal of and made available to the entire laboring population; 2) The unproductive owners should cede their estates without any compensation.

As has been mentioned above, a truly elemental agrarian revolution took place in the rural districts of the country and was brought about by the peasants themselves. The way had been paved by the whole course of Russia's history and its imminence became manifest in the raids on and looting of the landowners' estates in 1903 and 1905, which turned into a large scale mass movement on the part of the peasants, and in the numerous riots in the summer of 1917. The revolution finally materialized in 1917 and 1918. The first looting of manor-houses occurred in

November 1917, the second one in March 1918; and in April 1918 all the available arable land was re-distributed and seeded with summer crops. Essentially, this was the very core of the revolution, the clue to all its developments. The problem of the disposition and use of the land and of its re-allotment produced the revolution, the lofty aims and the enthusiasm which it inspired and, above all, its unprecedented range.

It is generally believed that the Russian peasants' revolution of 1917 was a cruel and bloody uprising. This is absolutely false. The revolution was neither cruel nor bloody, and it cannot even be classified as an uprising. On the contrary, it can be asserted with full justification that no other revolution in all world history took a more peaceful course and was accompanied by less bloodshed. Russia's revolution, of which the agrarian revolution was the paramount driving force, was directed not against people but almost exclusively against property. Similar developments (Peasant Risings and Peasant Wars) in France, Germany and England were much more turbulent and resulted in more numerous casualties (just like the peasant and Cossack movements in Russia under Pugatchev's leadership in the 18th century).

In April of every year the inhabitants of the villages in middle-belt Russia witness miraculous natural and meteorological metamorphoses. After several days of sunshine, rainfall, and mild winds, the snow that covered the earth and the ice that bound the rivers for months melt away. The frosty weather that still prevailed during the nights disappears and the frozen earth thaws. In a matter of days, in the course of a week or so, the soil becomes dry, torrents of water rush forward in the streams and rivulets, flowers burgeon in the forests and, in the fields, ploughshares sparkle in the sun while they turn over heavy layers of fat black earth.

In April 1918 a no less miraculous metamorphosis accompanied the natural developments with which the people were familiar. During five consecutive days, probably all over the country, men and women crowded the fields, incessantly shouting at the top of their voices and excitedly gesticulating. Yet, they were not quarrelling with one another, but carrying out a transaction which is completely familiar to Russia's rustic population: i. e., the redistribution of land. This time, however, the situation was different in that the re-allotment had to be carried out on an unprecedented scale, all over the country. The land was distributed among whole villages. Owners of homesteads and wealthy peasants offered no resistance and meekly ceded their surplus lands to peasants with big families. In only one week the new distribution of the land was accomplished and everybody went to the fields to till the new plots. There was a generally shared feeling that a miracle had occurred. The smoothness and speed with which this tremendous land re-distribution was carried out and the degree of leveling of the economic opportunities of those who took part in it were amazing. The peasants' attitude toward the basic problem of the allotment and use of the soil was highlighted by the fact that almost everywhere the landowners whose estates were expropriated by the peasants were also allotted plots of land of the same size as those allotted to the peasants. This was an illustration of the peasants' general belief that every toiler was entitled to a plot of land he himself can till without using hired laborers. There actually were landlords who became peasants as a result of this spectacular land re-distribution.

The land re-allotment was accomplished without arousing any marked opposition because it was generally acknowledged to be just and fair. All the peasants, those who benefited as well as those who lost by this re-allotment, accepted it without qualification as inevitable. The gloomy forebodings that a re-allotment of the land would unavoidably lead to a civil war among the peasants proved to be groundless. It was the Bolshevists who later deliberately fanned the civil war among the peasants by the organization of the "Committees of the Village Poor," and then by the implacable struggle against the "kulaks." And it must be borne in mind that the Bolshevists regarded as kulaks not only actually well-to-do and wealthy peasants but every proficient and thrifty peasant even though he owned no more than one horse or one cow. However, all this happened much later.

The most striking feature of this large scale land distribution was that it was accomplished by the peasants themselves. During the winter of 1917-1918 and even in the spring of 1918 the agents of the new Soviet regime (the Bolshevists seized the state power in November 1917) had not yet succeeded in taking hold of the country's rural regions. The Bolshevist revolution had triumphed only in the towns and cities. During the period in question the peasants were in complete control of their affairs.

That was how this unprecedented re-allotment of immense areas of land was carried out. It was done by the people themselves, without any guidance by agencies of the State Administration and without the assistance of surveyors. The peasants were guided by the "experience in land re-allotment" which was the very essence of Russian rural community (Mir) life.

The All-Russian Constituent Assembly convened on January 18, 1918. It is well known that its session lasted only one night. During this session frenzied Bolshevist soldiers and sailors kept their guns trained on the non-Bolshevist deputies and heaped unheard of abuse upon them. Yet, nevertheless, these deputies succeeded in making history in this single session. At dawn on January 19, at 5 a. m., the Constituent Assembly adopted the "Fundamental Agrarian Law" which was drafted and brought in by the deputies of the Socialist-Revolutionary Party Group. This law provided that all the land should be placed at the disposal of the people, that land should no longer be a marketable commodity and that it should be made available to anyone who would till it without the aid of hired laborers. The Socialist Revolutionary Party Group of deputies had the absolute majority of seats in the Constituent Assembly, viz. 370 of a total of 707. The Bolshevists dissolved the Constituent Assembly by the use of force. Earlier, in November 1917, they had overthrown the Provisional Government and seized the state power. Thus the Agrarian Law adopted by the Constituent Assembly actually was not a law in the usual sense of the term but rather a declaration of the intentions of the Assembly's majority in the field of land reform and of the principles which guided them.

The Provisional Government did not solve the agrarian problem. It lacked the power to prevent the solution of this problem by the people themselves who, acting on their own authority and with the impetus of an elementary force, seized the estates owned by the landlords and the state. The one thing the Provisional Government accomplished in this field was the formulation of some general principles which should serve as the basis of the Consituent Assembly's deliberations on the land reform. During its single night session, the Constituent Assembly only managed to define the basic principles of this reform in more exact terms. After the Soviet government dissolved the Constituent Assembly by the use of force it ignored the Assembly's work. Yet, the Soviet government completely adopted the basic principles which were advanced by the Provisional Government, viz. that all the land should be placed at the disposal of the working population and that the unproductive landowners should be dispossessed without getting any compensation. The Soviet government contributed absolutely nothing of its own to the legislative work concerning the land reform. On February 19, 1918, on the anniversary of the peasants' emancipation in 1861, the Soviet government promulgated the "Basic Law on the Socialization of the Land." This legislative act gave the *de jure* sanction to the *de facto* status which developed among the lower strata of the population during the period when the supreme power over the state shifted from the autocratic Czarist government to the democratic Provisional Government and then to the Soviets.

The basic provisions of this new Soviet law were as follows:

Article One: The private ownership of land is abolished.

Article Two: The land is transferred to the disposal of the working people without any compensation to the former owners.

Article Three: Only people who will till their plots themselves without the aid of hired hands are entitled to land allotment.

Article Forty-five: Transfer of allotted land from one person to another is forbidden.

In order to grasp the actual significance of this law it must be borne in mind that generations of Russian peasants had been longing for a re-allotment of the land and that as a matter of fact it was accomplished a long time before this law was promulgated.

The Bolsheviks themselves never attempted to conceal the true character of the peasant policy they adopted in the first days after their coup d'état. No less a person than Lenin himself several times publicly acknowledged in speaking and writing that the Bolsheviks had taken their decree on the socialization of land from the Socialist-Revolutionaries. "Nine-tenths of the peasants," —he wrote,—"have gone over to our side within a few weeks because we adopted an agrarian program that was not our own but that of the Socialist-Revolutionaries, and put it into execution. Our victory consisted precisely in the carrying out of the socialist-revolutionary program. That is why it was so easy." (Lenin's words on the Congress of Comintern 22. VI. 1921). "Indeed, why shouldn't we borrow from the Socialist-Revolutionaries whatever was really good?"—he used to say with a cunning smile. In doing so he never denied that to the Bolsheviks it was but a means of attracting the peasants or at least neutralizing them politically.

Expressing the same thought Trotsky wrote:[1]

"At the decisive moment, when the struggle for the state power began, the decade long fight against the petit bourgeois Populists provided the Bolshevists with the opportunity to deal a knock-out blow to the Socialist Revolutionists. The Bolshevists appropriated the agrarian program of the Socialist-Revolutionary Party and the peasant masses flocked to the Bolshevist banners. This political expropriation of the Socialist-Revolutionary Party was a necessary prerequisite to the economic expropriation of the landlords and the bourgeoisie."

[1] Leon Trotsky, *Pyat' Let Kominterna* (Five Years of the Comintern), Moscow, 1924, p. 16.

What did the peasants gain from this large scale agrarian revolution? Strange as it may seem at first glance, as far as the enlargement of the plots of land at their disposal was concerned, the peasants did not gain very much in 1917 and 1918 from the transfer of the estates owned by the landlords and the state. It should not be overlooked that before the revolution a great many peasants had no land of their own and that, on the other hand, even greater areas of the land owned by the landlords had come under peasant tenure. As far as the entire rural population was concerned the total land area which became available to the peasants after the revolution was 19.5 p. c. larger than before the revolution. For the most part the size of the newly alloted additional plots of land varied between 0.09 and 0.39 desiatines (2.5—5.5 acres). As a result of developments which nobody could direct or master and quite independently of any "land reform," post-revolutionary Russia became still more a country of small peasant holdings than it had been before the revolution.

Large peasant holdings usually were in the hands of big families. In order to save their land, livestock and household belongings from being taken from them and allotted to peasants who were in need of them, wealthy peasants hastened to divide their holdings into smaller units. In addition, at the allotment of the lands from the landowners' estates, first priority was given to peasants who had no land at all or only inadequate plots of land. The result of all these developments was a considerable reduction of the medium sized peasant holdings which, up to that time, provided the bedrock of the country's agriculture. The number of holdings which produced huge surpluses of grain and other food products for sale on the market decreased considerably. The markets were supplied not only by the landowners' estates which produced exclusively for sale but also by the large commercial type peasant holdings which were operated with the aid of hired hands. Now both the landowners' estates and the large peasant holdings disappeared. In the north and middle belts of European Russia such large holdings constituted only 2 — 3 p. c. of the sum total of the peasant holdings. Yet, together with the landowners' estates they provided almost one half of all the grain which was exported abroad and consumed within the country by the population of the towns and cities.

As a result of the reduction of the average size peasant holding the purely subsistence level of Russia's agriculture was still more accentuated. Larine, one of the prominent Soviet economists, wrote: "Just as before, the peasant sows only enough rye for his own family and, in addition, as much of other crops as he needs for the operation of his holding. At the same time the sowing of those crops which were used mainly as raw materials in industry and in the export trade (flax, hemp, sugar beets, linseed, etc.), or for the needs of the city population is reduced." The peasants were interested in the cultivation of these crops only in so far as they were the source of money they needed for the payment of taxes and the purchase of consumers' goods. They soon realized that the payment of taxes could be discontinued or that taxes could be paid with the devaluated bills they had hoarded in huge amounts and that the consumers' goods they needed could no longer be purchased on the city markets. It was only natural that they lost every incentive to produce more agricultural products than they needed for themselves. "It goes without saying,"—wrote Larine,—"that such a shift in the crops planted in peasant holdings cannot help resulting in a general lowering of the level of Russia's agriculture."[2]

According to Bolshevist authorities,[3] in 1917 no less than 1,400,000 hired laborers were employed in European Russia's agriculture. During the revolution these hired workers became independent small holders who produced only the products they needed for themselves.

As a result of the agrarian revolution the non-efficient and effete small holding gained predominance in Russia's agricul-

[2] Larine, *Otcherki Khozyaistvennoi Zhizni* (Studies of Economic Life).

[3] Strumilin, *Sostav Proletariata v Rosii* (Structure of the Proletariat in Russia), 1919.

ture. More and more the peasants reverted to the conditions of natural economy and reduced their planting.

This steady weakening and decline of the country's agriculture could not but become a matter of grave concern to the Soviet government. These developments menaced the further existence not only of the country but also of the Soviet regime. Gradually, a new idea dawned upon the men at the helm of the Soviet state; namely, the idea of a new land reform on an immense scale. This reform had, on one hand, to compel the peasants to work not only for their own subsistence but also for the needs of the state. On the other hand, the state itself was to take part in agricultural production. The organization of the "Kolkhozy" (collective peasant holdings) and "Sovkhozy" (Soviet estates) was the outgrowth of this new idea.

According to the plan of the Soviet government, the collective holdings, the "Kolkhozy," were to replace all individual and communal peasant holdings. The Soviet estates, the "Sovkhozy," were to be grain producing state enterprises, "grain plants" supplying the state. The collective holdings were to bear evidence of the superiority of communal husbandry over the individual holdings and the Soviet estates should demonstrate the advantages of the large enterprise compared with the small enterprise. Essentially, however, the "Kolkhozy" as well as the "Sovkhozy" had to accomplish the same task, viz. to supply grain to the state. It was this task which peremptorily determined the trend of the Soviet government's agrarian reform as well as the agrarian policy it henceforth pursued.

According to the Soviet government's plans the "Kolkhozy" (the collective holdings of farms, collective farms) had to replace the former independent peasant holdings (the communal as well as the individual ones) whereas the "Sovkhozy" (Soviet estates) had to take the place of the former landlords' estates. These two types of agriculture holdings, first of all, are of different size. A Collective Farm is placed at the disposal of and tilled by a certain peasant community (or by the inhabitants of several settlements or villages). A Soviet Estate can in principle be of any size, yet preference is given to large estates. Soviet Estates are owned, both legally and actually, by the state. In the Collective Holdings the peasants (in the Soviet Union the term "peasant" has been superceded by "kolkhoznik," i. e. "partner of a collective holding") enjoy equal rights in making use of the holding's common land and till it for the sake of the state and of their own. All those who work in Soviet Estates are hired laborers. They are paid wages by the state which is the owner of the estate, as a worker of a factory.

According to the records of the Soviet government, in 1920 the entire land area under cultivation was distributed as follows:[4]

Individual peasant holdings	93.7 p.c.
Soviet estates (Sovkhozy)	4.6 p.c.
Collective peasant holdings (Kolkhozy)	1.7 p.c.

Now, the government itself wanted to take over the management of the country's entire agricultural production for the sake of the state and the newly established regime. It is obvious that under such circumstances the above mentioned distribution of the lands under cultivation ran counter to the government's aims. This distribution could no longer be tolerated and had to be eradicated. The Soviet government did not waver and started a ruthless campaign for the achievement of its new aim, completely ignoring the vital interests of the population. First of all, it was necessary to crush the prosperous peasants because they could offer resistance to the contemplated plans. Then the poor and destitute peasants had to be won over by promising them better living conditions. To this end it was necessary to pave the way for a "civil war in the villages." The government's program frankly proclaimed this aim, and during the 1920's and 1930's this program was being carried out implacably and stubbornly. First of all the "kulaks," i. e. the wealthy peasants,

[4] *O Zemle* (On Land Problems). Collection of articles, pt. 1, pp. 819, Moscow, 1921.

were to be eliminated. Later the so-called "medium holding" peasants were to be added to the list and they too were to be victimized, although they often owned only one horse or one cow. In that way huge numbers of peasants were labeled "kulaks" who were to be eliminated. The Soviet government organized the so-called "Committees of Village Poor" which undertook the special task of carrying on "the struggle against the kulaks as a class." During the period in question, various complex laws were promulgated which were aimed at the kulaks, the wealthy as well as the medium holding peasants. The local organizations of the Communist party also took part in the struggle against these groups of Russia's peasantry. The plots of land, houses, livestock and all the household goods were taken from the well-to-do peasants. Thereafter they and the members of their families were jailed and later sent in special trains into exile. In that way huge masses of peasants were evicted from their homes and driven into Northern Russia, to regions to the east of the Ural Mountains to work in the woods or to build new factories and plants. Others were sent to Northern Siberia or to the distant north-eastern regions of the country, into the horrible concentration camps of the Kolyma province where gold is mined. People perished there by the millions. The plots of land which became available after their former holders were driven away were given to those peasants who remained, and they had to use them collectively. In this way the collective holdings, the "kolkhozy," originated.

The government itself also took a hand in the production of grain. To this end the Soviet estates, the "Sovkhozy,'" were organized. Several of them extended over immense areas (measuring tens of thousands of acres). According to plan, these estates were to become actual "grain plants." Yet, they did not directly affect the peasants' situation.

The government wanted to achieve the collectivization of the peasant holdings in the shortest possible time. That is why it did not shrink from applying any measure it deemed appropriate for this end. The following official figures give a graphic picture of the rapid course of the agricultural collectivization.[5]

Up to July 1, 1928	1.7 p.c.	of the peasant holdings were collectivized.
Up to Oct. 1929	3.9 p.c.	of the peasant holdings were collectivized.
Up to July 1, 1929	4.1 p.c.	of the peasant holdings were collectivized.
Up to Jan. 20, 1930	21.0 p.c.	of the peasant holdings were collectivized.
Up to Mar. 10, 1930	58.0 p.c.	of the peasant holdings were collectivized.

A glance at these figures is enough for the realization of how terrible a catastrophe has stricken Russia's peasantry. In eight months of 1929-1930 more than half of all the peasant holdings of the country were collectivized! Even in the Soviet press of that period can be found many descriptions of the horrible price in livelihood and blood which the peasants had to pay for this experiment. Even the man who according to the assertions of his admirers has nerves of steel, Stalin the Infallible, was for a while shaken by fear and dismay! On March 2, 1930, all the Soviet newspapers published an article by Stalin under the characteristic heading: "Dizziness from Success." In this article Stalin stressed that the local Communist authorities had been carried too far. Now he called for moderation! However, the local Communist organizations were only following the directives of the party's top men.

Irrevocable harm has been done. The collectivization of the peasants' holdings was enforced by high-handed measures. One of the developments which originated in this collectivization was the catastrophic slaughter of livestock and the elimination of peasant animal husbandry. When the Bolshevist authorities began to take away the peasants' plots of land the peasants began slaughtering their own cattle. This was their natural reaction to governmental measures.

According to official figures which were made public by Stalin himself in the official governmental mouthpiece "Izvestiya" of January 28, 1934, the numbers of livestock heads were reduced as follows (in millions of heads):

[5] *Materyaly Pervogo Vsesoyuznogo S'yezda Kolkhoznikov Peredovikov* (Minutes of the 1st All union Convention of Vanguard Collective Holders), Moscow, 1933, pp. 38-39.

	Horses	Horned cattle	Sheep	Hogs
1929........	34.0	69.1	147.2	20.9
1933........	16.6	38.6	50.6	12.2

By 1938 93.6 p. c. of all the peasant holdings had been transformed into collective holdings. By 1940 the individual peasant holdings had almost disappeared. 25,000,000 individual holdings were turned into 236,000 collective holdings.

Since the Bolshevists' rise to power, famines occurred in Russia which had no precedents in all her recorded history as far as the numbers of people affected and the areas stricken were concerned. In 1921 starvation's strangling grip took a heavy toll of the population of the Volga region. In 1932 the Ukraine, the Northern Caucasus and the lower Volga regions were stricken by a severe famine. According to Walter Duranty,[6] from 4 to 5 million peasants died from starvation at that time. The most horrible famine apparently occurred after the end of the recent war. Only now the first reports about this catastrophe are reaching us here.

In order to understand the system of collective holdings and the conditions of life among the collectivized peasants better, it is necessary to ponder some particular details.

What kind of life are those peasants now living who become partners in a collective holding? They have neither land nor agricultural implements of their own. They are working for and paid wages by the state. These wages are calculated by "workdays" on the basis of definite work performance standards. These standards are established by the authorities directing the country's entire agricultural economy, i. e. by the Communist party. The level of the standard work to be performed is very high so that this kind of pay-off actually is nothing but a revival of the infamous sweating system. All the work in the collective holdings is performed as task-work. Every peasant is assigned a de-

[6] Walter Duranty, *USSR*, New York, 1944, chapter 17, "Man-made Famine."

finite daily task. If he does not accomplish the standard daily work, only a fraction (½, ¾, etc.) of a "work-day" is entered into his work-book. The same procedure is applied when a peasant has accomplished the task-work assigned to him but, in the supervisor's opinion, has done it badly (e. g. has mowed at too high a level or weeded out unsatisfactorily). In such a case also, no full "work-day" is entered into the work-book. Moreover, the peasant in question can be fined either by the deduction of a certain number of work-days registered in his work-book or by the assignment of some work without registering it. The kind as well as the measure of punishment rests at the supervisor's discretion exclusively. Apart from punishing by his own discretion, the chairman of the collective holding managing board can hand over a peasant charged with some dereliction of duty to the state prosecutor, and the Communist court can at will send the "defendant" into exile or to a concentration camp for one, two or more years. A strict discipline is maintained in the collective holdings, almost as strict a one as in the army. For instance, partners of a collective holding who have repeatedly been late in coming to work are liable to prosecution by the courts. All the partners of a collective holding are under complete subordination to its Communist administration board. There is no possibility of escape from the collective holding into the towns and cities and to get work there. The government does not grant passports to peasants who are partners of collective holdings and people without passports are not admitted to any work in towns and cities.

Only once yearly, on January 1st of every year, when the harvest is distributed, the final accounts for the work done by each partner of the collective holding are settled. During the whole year each partner's earnings are only entered into his work-book. The managing board of collective holding makes only prepayments which never exceed 25 p. c. of the registered work-days. By January 1st the full amount of the harvested grain is summed up. Thereafter follows a series of deductions. First priority is given to the quantity of grain which has to be delivered to the state. Then follow the numerous taxes (the general tax, the tax for cultural purposes, the contributions to the Social Security Fund, to the Air Defense Organization, the International Proletarian Relief Fund and other "voluntary" contributions), the salaries of the many Communist members of the collective holding managing board and the quantity of grain to be stored for future sowing. The balance remaining after all these deductions represents the real earnings of the collective holding. This quantity of grain is divided by the sum total of the "work-days" registered for the past year. As a general rule, the products which the collective holding partners earn during a year are sufficient for their upkeep for 6 or 7 months only. The balance they must obtain from the vegetable gardens near their cottages (the size of such a garden does not exceed ¼ ha)[7] or else they are doomed to a semi-starvation existence.

The picture would, however, not be complete if we failed to point to the great difference between the prices which the state pays to the peasants for the products they deliver and those which the peasants have to pay for the same products when they purchase them in the state stores. A former Soviet agronomist who was taken prisoner while he was fighting in the ranks of the Red Army in the recent war reported the following prices for 1939:

	State purchase price	When purchasing the same products from the state the peasants paid
Wheat (1 kilogram)	0.08 Rouble	1.92 Roubles
Meat "	0.17 "	19.00 "
Rice "	0.13 "	4.00 "
Butter "	1.80 "	38.00 "
Cheese "	0.80 "	24.00 "

In present-day Russia the peasants who are partners of a collective holding have no rights and almost no property. They are working under sweating system and slave labor conditions.

[7] 1 ha = 2,471 acres.

Truly, they are outlaws and slaves of the Soviet state. Can it, therefore, cause any surprise that their attitude toward the present collective holdings is one of fierce hatred? To them the conditions of life in these holdings, certainly, are worse than those in the times of serfdom, prior to the peasants' emancipation in 1861.

The above mentioned Soviet agronomist had the opportunity to observe the conditions of the peasants' life before the recent war in the Kursk, Orel and Smolensk provinces. He attests to the fact that at the German armies' advance the Communist managers of the collective holdings fled. The peasants felt that they had been freed and immediately divided the land and the agricultural implements of the collective holdings and allocated them to individual holders. This was done with utmost speed and without any arguments. In the course of one day everything was distributed and settled. According to the testimony of the above mentioned agronomist, it was amazing how quickly the system of collective holdings disappeared without leaving any trace. When the Germans arrived they found that all the land and all the implements of agriculture were privately owned. . . . It is highly significant that the Germans restored the system of collective holdings in the parts of Russia under their occupation. By means of this system it was much easier to squeeze the grain from the peasants. From the fiscal point of view the system of collective holdings is much preferable and, in this regard, there was no difference between the Soviet state and the Hitlerite occupants. Reports of the restoration of the collective holdings by the Germans can be found in the Soviet publications as well as in the German press.

The system of collective holdings inaugurated by the Soviet regime instilled a longing among Russia's peasants which they never knew before, viz., an eager longing for private ownership of land. This longing for private ownership supplanted the ideas and aspirations which had taken hold of Russia's peasants as a result of her centuries-old history. This is a new development which will play its part in the future.

The Soviet regime failed to solve the peasant problem. On the contrary, as a result of the Soviet "reforms" this problem has become still more complex. Future generations will still have to deal with it and search for its solution.

BIBLIOGRAPHY

SCHWITTAU, G. G.: *Revolutzija i narodnoye khozjaistvo v Rossii* (1917-1921), Berlin, 1922.

KLIUCHEVSKY, V.: *Kurs russkoi istorii,* 5 tomov. Moskva, 1921-1923.

KIZEWETTER, A.: *Krestianstvo v istorii Rossii.* "Krestianskaya Rossija," II-III, Praga, 1923 Z. Kpoznaniiu proisshedshego. "Russkaya Mysl," 1923, v. III-V.

KPOZNANIIU PROISSHEDSHEGO, Z.: *Russkaya Mysl,* 1933. v. III-V.

PROKOPOVICZ, S. N.: *Russlands Volkswirtschaft unter den Sowjets,* Europa Verlag, Zurich-New York, 1944.

XII.
Catholicism and Politics

RELIGION AND POLITICS

Editorial Note

The relationship between politics and religion forms an important problem in continental European political ideologies. A great many references to it may be found in this volume; however, limitations of space have not permitted us to include more detailed studies of various religions in relation to political movements. Only one had to be chosen as a representative example. Perhaps, in this respect, Catholism is the most interesting, since it has wielded a vast amount of influence upon various political ideologies. Powerful political Catholic parties have been organized, such as the Christian Social Party (Christlich-Soziale) in Austria, and the centrist Catholic Party in Germany.

In his chapter, Professor Mendizábal presents a study of the relations between Catholicism and politics. The reader, however, will find some disagreement between his views and those of other authors (especially Professor Borgese's). Also, in some respects Professor Mendizábal's article will complement, and in others it will oppose, Mr. Napht's article on Falangism.

F.G.

XII.

CATHOLICISM AND POLITICS

by

ALFREDO MENDIZÁBAL

IF WE TRY to determine and analyze the influence of Catholicism on the world of Politics, and more concretely on the Politics of our own century, the major mistake to be avoided is that of confusing such different fields by superimposing upon the first the framework characterizing the second. This could be the fatal result of an approach which follows too close an analogy.

Catholicism is not, and cannot be a political ideology; even less a political movement. Specifically, it is a religion, the Christian religion - almost without contest until the 16th century, since then with the Protestant contest of the Reformation. Former schisms and "heresies" had detached individuals and peoples from the Christian Church. Luther's revolt, being not only a religious but a political revolution, did more than that. Throughout the bitter fight between Reformation and Counter-reformation (the latter cannot be labelled as a mere conservative reaction, since its leaders shared with reformers many of their criticisms of the Church, but looked for disciplinary reform from within), the fundamental principles of the Roman Church remained unchanged. Christianity was divided, and extremely subdivided in reformed areas. Catholicism, however, won strength in unity, while losing in extension. New problems arose in the field of relationship between State and Church. Being of its own essence supernational, and having spiritual aims, quite different from those of the State, the Church had to assert itself in the State, alongside of the State, or against the State, which in turn placed itself with the Church, outside the Church, or against the Church. The most conflicting position indeed was that of one aiming to be over the other, embodying and holding both spiritual and political power.

Every conflict of conscience is, nevertheless, at its root, an individual conflict, which demands solution in human souls. Religious and civic societies both exist through their members only, and every man faithful to the Church in religious matters is, at the same time, a member of the civil society, ruled by the State. Definition of the respective jurisdiction of both spiritual and temporal powers is necessary in order to keep each of them within its natural bounds, but the fact remains that believers give simultaneous allegiance to the Church and to the State, two institutions very different in nature and aims, which can and often do enter into conflict through rivalry or hostility, as well as through intermingling connection. The Church's mission is not to provide a political solution for political problems, but to proclaim spiritual principles capable of inspiring men's thought and action in every moral issue, therefore also in the field of political justice and political morals. But the jurisdiction over society, as such, belongs essentially to the State. Parliaments, not religious bodies, give laws to the State, which is not a divine but a human institution. Christians, nevertheless, did receive the injunction of obeying God rather than men, when men were ruling in opposition to moral or natural law. They are indeed interested in politics, not only as citizens, but as Christians, too. There is a Christian politics, even though a political Christianism would hardly be conceivable, other than as a religious reformation. The Christian as a citizen is and must be interested in the welfare of the community in which he lives. Even if he considers himself as not belonging to the world, he exists in the world, closely linked to his brothers, and he must see all men as brothers, regardless of their color, creed or nationality. He participates in public affairs with the same rights as anyone else, but with more specific duties, if he is conscious of the implications of his faith and of primacy of charity in Christian religion. Now, such an awareness is not widespread enough among Christians to determine the logical pattern of their political attitude. Furthermore, orthodoxy in religious matters does not include a definite line to be followed in civic life. A plurality of divergent solutions appears before each Christian when considering forms of government. God's realm is not of this world. The Church therefore cannot impose any orthodoxy in political matters, in which each Christian is free to choose his way according to the dictates of his conscience; but this conscience, if it really exists, will act according to religious and moral convictions. But we do not see most so-called Christians accepting their responsibilities as such. On the contrary, we often see them acting and reacting according to their interests, determined by class or prejudice, more than by spiritual values. So we are aware of a sharp division among Christians regarding their political and social behavior, depending upon whether or not they are inspired by their faithfulness to the principles; and also of many occasional divisions which are the logical result of their basic liberty to decide themselves among several ways of interpreting those principles *hic et nunc*. This can explain their respective different, and often opposite attitudes with regard to the fundamental political issues of our times, as well as of past times throughout human history.

Catholics and Democracy

Each time the words Catholics and Democracy are coupled together, their association provokes reactions which vary according to the favorable or adverse stand of those who consider such a delicate subject. They deduce either natural harmony or incompatibility between those terms, as suggested by their respective dialectic opinions. The aim of this study is indeed not concerned with the envisaging of religious institutions in their global attitude for or against the political structure known as Democracy.

It merely endeavors to examine the concrete and often divergent positions which Catholics are wont to assume with regard to theoretical as well as practical Democracy.

This is a real problem most frequently approached by combining, not always adequately, psychological complexes and traditional doctrines; and often through strongly impassioned convictions. Perhaps the clue to such a difficult question lies in its dealing with absolutes. Believers in Catholicism, and also believers in Democracy, generally adopt a stand dogmatically implied in their respective faiths, even though this query remains for Christians, along with a great deal of others, outside of dogmatic definition. Nevertheless, some regimes based on civic intolerance intended to correct the orignal liberty of Christians by introducing a strong conformism to the predominant doctrine in force. A typical example of that totalitarian intolerance was furnished by the statement of a Minister of Franco's cabinet, Señor Serrano Suñer, who proclaimed (in his speech at Seville, on April 2, 1938): "We know there is a sector of national policy which belongs to us as fully settled within our own boundaries; it is constituted by matters that God left to the free disputes of men. But as we do not want any more disputes in Spain, these problems have been solved in a definitive manner by the National Movement embodied in the Falange. . . ." Here is a tragi-comic result of divinization of the State in every dictatorial regime of our time: so-called Catholics aim to prove themselves more papist than the Pope, by imposing upon Catholic subjects a strict orthodoxy in matters in which the Church had declared them free. And this with all the compulsory machinery of the State, which will punish political non-conformism as heresy. That which belongs to God is claimed by Caesar.

Since the State which has its specific goals, pretends to spiritual mastery, and endeavors to subdue consciences, Christians find themselves automatically in conflict with it. As a matter of fact, not only Christians. When the State dares to impose itself as a divinized being worthy of worship and forces its subjects to absolute submission of body and soul, all citizens have to resist this tyrannical assumption of abusive powers. Believers of any faith, especially, because the State intends to replace the mere juridical relation existing between ruler and ruled by a religious one not in compliance with their own faith. Non-believers also, because they reject every religious tie, one moreover whose acceptance could not be an act of free will, but rather a consequence of direct pressure from the almighty State compulsory organization.

Totalitarian mythology transfers to the State all duties which the Christian has toward his Church. No one independent Church is tolerated, for the character attributed to the State is basically determined by the mark of *ecclesiasticity*, according to the fascist teaching of Sergio Panunzio, professor of the theory of the State at the University of Rome. In other words, as noted by professor Charles Journet, of the Seminary of Friburg in Switzerland,[1] the State replacing the Church claims to be the supreme spiritual society, embracing all men totally in the same faith, the same political creed; and the party in power plays a rôle which corresponds to that of religious orders in the Church.

World War II, as a universal catastrophe diabolically contrived by the most anti-democratic powers, became a supreme test for western civilization based upon spiritual values proceeding from the Jewish-Christian moral tradition, from the Greek philosophy and Roman law, from the renascent humanism of the Middle and Modern Ages as well as (since 1776) from the proclaimed aspirations for freedom of every person as a bearer of those fundamental human values. Contemporary man acknowledges the strong intimate relationship among such historical ingredients of his consciousness of his own dignity, ingredients which were formerly too often presented as separate and even opposing factors. An uninterrupted line binds those successive stages of the sweeping tidal wave for human liberation, and it is highly significant to observe

[1] Ch. Journet, *Vues Chrétiennes sur la Politique* (Beauchemin, Canada), 1942, p. 17.

the modern convergence of anti-Semitism and anti-Christianism,[2] anti-Humanism and anti-Democracy. *Germanentum* attacked spiritual values on all fronts at the same time. Its aims intended to totally destroy those values. According to a Nazi writer, Jünger: "One of the most cruel and marvelous pleasures of our time is to share in the work of the spade which has to shatter western civilization;"[3] or even clearer, as Hitler shamelessly avowed, including his followers: "We are barbarians and want to be barbarians; it is a title of honor. We have come to rejuvenate the world. The present world is at its last stage of life. Our task consists in plundering it."[4]

One of the most influential thinkers of the contemporary epoch, the Catholic philosopher, Jacques Maritain, points out the relations between Christianity and Democracy: Christianity or Christian faith may not be fettered to any political form, therefore neither to Democracy as a form of government nor to Democracy as a philosophy of human and political life. This is a result of the fundamental distinction introduced by Christ between things belonging to Caesar and things belonging to God. . . One may be a Christian supporting another political philosophy. . . Christianity is not bound to Democracy, and Christian faith does not compel every believer to become a Democrat; but Democracy is bound to

[2] As Jacques Maritain logically concludes: "Nazi anti-Semitism is at the bottom a furious aversion to the revelation of Sinai and the law of the Decalogue. It is above all, as Maurice Samuel, the American Jewish writer has so well pointed out, a supernatural fear and hate (which dare not say their name) of Christianity and the evangelical law, and of that King of the Jews who is the Word Incarnate, the Word Who was in the beginning—the Word and not the Action—and Who took flesh in the womb of a Virgin of Israel, and Who came to bear witness unto Truth, and proclaimed the beatitudes to the poor and the merciful, and will put down the powerful from their thrones, and Whose kingdom is not of this world and Who will judge all of us on love and charity." *Racist Law and the True Meaning of Racism*, in "The Commonweal," New York, June 4, 1943, p. 186.

Volkstum wird uns Gottestum, said a Nazi professor of philosophy, counsellor Schwarz, claiming an heroic notion of divinity. And he added: "Our vital existence gravitates around the axis of honor; All this: sense of eternity, of fatherland, of folk, is superpersonal. There is no connection between it and the personal God of Love of Christians. To him who lives on the eternal values of folk, of honor and freedom, there is no problem in the understanding of God." *Die gläubige Freiheit deutscher Menschen*, in *Blätter für deutsche Philosophie*, Berlin, 1939, p. 386.

[3] Quoted by Alfred Stern, *La Filosofia en el Tercer Reich, instrumento de guerra*, in *Cuadernos Americanos*, Mexico, No. 5.

[4] Hermann Rauschning, *Hitler m'a dit*, Paris, 1939, p. 100.

Christianity, as issued from evangelical inspiration. Here the question is not concerned with Christianity as a religious creed, as a way toward eternal life, but with Christianity as a leavening in social and political life of peoples, as bearer of the temporal hope of men. . . . It is not in the heights of theology—Maritain explains—but in the depth of profane conscience and profane existence where Christianity acts thus, sometimes taking heretical forms or even forms of revolt in which it seems to deny itself.[5]

Too many Catholics are handicapped in the acceptance of Democracy because they remain deeply attached to an old conception of Order, desirous of preserving all their ancient privileged positions even though these perpetuate social injustice and unnatural iniquities. They are prone to consider every advance of the common people in political and social life as an attempt against the "established order" which they are inclined to take for the natural one, since they are themselves comfortably settled in it. They believe that they are traditionalist in acting this way. Instead, they are reactionaries, for tradition implies continuity and therefore evolution, not stopping or regressing. And these stagnant mentalities would like not only to preserve their profitable positions but also to increase their privileges by barring any improvements claimed by the people.

In opposition to the reactionary outlook, other more liberal Catholics have always remembered the Christian principles of equality in human nature coming from the Gospel, explained and spread through the Middle Ages by theologians, moralists and jurists, recalled under Absolutism by many ecclesiastical writers and

[5] J. Maritain, *Christianisme et Démocratie, Editions de la Maison Française*, New York, 1943, pp. 42-44. (A former miniature edition of this work had been widely distributed by RAF planes over occupied France.) The French professor insists on the fact that the sources of the democratic ideal must be sought several centuries before Kant and Rousseau (op. cit., p. 67), and recalls President Roosevelt's and Vice-President Wallace's assertions that Democracy, Freedom and international good faith find their more solid basis in religion and give to religion its best guaranties (cf. FDR's Letter to the American Episcopacy, *Catholic News*, January 17, 1942). "The idea of freedom is derived from the Bible with its extraordinary emphasis on the dignity of the individual," as proclaimed by Mr. Wallace, who even sees in Democracy "the only true political expression of Christianity." (Henry A. Wallace's speech, May 8, 1942).

teachers, and recently by several Popes, principally Leo XIII and Pius XI. But reactionary Catholics did not follow these Christian principles, even though they were emphasized by the heads of the Roman Church. They avoided putting them into force and suspected the aforementioned Popes of being socialists because their respective Encyclicals (*Rerum Novarum* and *Quadragesimo Anno*) were inspired by interest in the working classes and preached as strict duties of justice what the privileged had previously believed to be merely voluntary behavior. The Popes condemned the exploitation of man by man, economic and social inferiority of the workers, and abuses of modern capitalism, in terms somewhat similar to those of moderate socialist criticism, but naturally they did not extol violent upheaval or total abolition of the present social regime as a remedy. They were against the class struggle on both sides, and finally Pius XI issued another Encyclical against Bolshevism. Nevertheless, it is important to make clear that through moral criticism of the Soviet regime, the opposition between it and Catholicism is there highly emphasized because of the "atheist" aspect of communism. Proposing the establishing of a Christian social order as a true solution, Pius XI takes care to prevent a fascist reaction among Catholics, at the same time condemning every kind of totalitarianism, above all German Nazism (Encyclical *Mit brennender Sorge* issued directly in German) as incompatible with the fundamental teachings of the Church and with the basis of the Christian concept of life.

Unlike the Church's concrete social doctrine for justice and harmony between classes, no such constructive official doctrine in the political field has been formulated and assembled as a whole in recent years. As a matter of fact Catholics do possess this through the tradition of the classic thinkers in Christendom, continued, explained and perfected by authoritative Catholic writers and leaders in modern times. Even by taking note of successive condemnations by Pope Pius XI of exaggerated Nationalism, and Fascist, Nazi and Soviet totalitarianisms, they can easily realize what forms of the State are excluded from that black list. But a brief analysis of certain summits of Catholic thought in the historical development of political ideas will give us an impressive result in favor of democratic principles as being in accord with Christian doctrines of human liberty.

Medieval Democratic Principles

The roots of the democratic doctrine of the 'general will' may be found—even in the seventh century—in the text of the Fifth Book of St. Isidore's *Etymologies* which considers law as the fruit of popular decision (*constitutio populi*), made by both the senators (*majores natu*) and the common people (*plebs*). According to Isidore, kings are so called (*reges*) because they must act rightly; such an essential prerequisite that they even lose the name of kings if they fail to comply:[6] "there are those who convert the government into a cruel tyranny, and once they have arrived at the height of their power, they forget their duty, fire their hearts with selfish pride and finally disdain their subjects as if they were nothing in comparison with a king... Such kings should remember the words of the *Ecclesiastes*: Have they made you a ruler? Do not raise yourself above them, but be one of them."[7] The bases and limitations of royal authority are clearly apparent in the Isidorian doctrine and in the decisions and acts of the former Councils of Toledo. The fourth of them, presided by St. Isidore, in 633, set down rules for the election of the king, and protected as far as possible the rights of the nation through the rising popular liberties. An important law of the Sixth Council of Toledo (which became the law XI of the First Heading of the *Liber judicum*) dealt with "breaking of oaths," and among other things declared: "If any king should not want to fulfil the articles set forth in this constitution, may his generation be scorned forever and lose its wealth and distinction in this world, and may he be condemned and punished with his companions in hell." The supreme religious

[6] *Sententiarum*, book III, chapter 48.
[7] *Ibid.*, 32, 1.

sanctions were thus added to mere political ones, by the authority of the Church. The political importance of those Councils in Spain was manifested in their power to submit royal rule to principles of Law, according to the concept: "You will be a king if you act according to justice, and if you do not, you will not be a king."

The Middle Ages considers God as the supreme fount of sovereignty, and the people as its common channel. The struggle between the elective principle sanctioned by legislation and the hereditary principle which the kings tried to impose, was prolonged through the Merovingian and Carolingian dynasties, in France, and far beyond the visigothic epoch in Spain. A Charter of Charlemagne, in the year 806, proves that "the sons of a king did not succeed the father by right, nor by order of primogeniture, but it depended upon the people to elect a successor." When Swintila, master of the whole Iberian peninsula, tried to make the crown hereditary in his family, giving his son joint rule with himself, and also giving power to his wife and brother, the people regarded this attempt as an attack on the national prerogative of election and as a violation of fundamental laws. The king, forced to flee by the people who revolted, was declared, with his family, banished from the throne by the Fourth Council of Toledo, before which the proclaimed successor Sisenand was called, and humbly received the authority of king from the supreme assembly. And the Council established: "When the king dies, no man may take over the reign or make himself king;" and provided for election by "the accord of the bishops, the noble Goths and the people." The first Christian reigns which were formed in the Iberian peninsula after the Arabic invasion in the eighth century, the kingdoms of Asturias and Leon, were modeled on visigothic laws and their kings could not alter in their favor the visigothic tradition. It was only in the eleventh century that heredity through association of the son with the father was established, but the elective system was in force for many years. The great political innovation originated in the twelfth century, the *Cortes* introduced in Leon, Castile and Aragon, as the first parliamentary institution known in

Europe, continued the work of the Councils. It was considerably extended, since the three social classes of the epoch, nobles, clergy and the Third Estate were represented in those assemblies, the latter through the municipalities. Alongside of their fundamental function to discuss, approve or reject the royal petition on taxes, the Cortes exercised a certain legislative power by virtue of their right to formulate petitions introducing laws and revising old ones; and upon receiving the crown, the king had to swear before the Cortes that he would respect the laws and the rights of the country. If the king should die without direct heirs, the Cortes called an assembly which was already called the Parliament, to elect a new monarch.[8]

The Christian Middle Ages carefully developed the political doctrine issued from the famous text of *the City of God* in which St. Augustine deduced human freedom from the natural order prescribed by God accordingly to the Scripture: "Let them rule," said He, "over the fishes of the sea, and the fowl of the air, and over every thing that creepeth upon the earth." He made man reasonable—Augustine explains—and lord only over the unreasonable, not over man, but over the beasts. The great theologians always sought to set up limits to royal power, to close it within, and to denounce as tyrannical any transgression of the legal statute. Since St. Thomas Aquinas (whom Lord Acton called "the first Whig" because of his constitutional theories),[9] the thesis of the mixed regime become generally accepted, including the advantages of the three legitimate forms of government: monarchy, aristocracy and democracy, as defined by Aristotle,[10] constantly seek-

[8] For example, at the Parliament of 1134, in Borja, the Aragonese elected Ramiro as King. When the Cortes were not in session, there was a permanent body called a general deputation which carried on, and which saw to the management of public affairs. When the king was a minor, the Cortes appointed a body of prelates, knights and "good men" to counsel him, "without whom nothing was to be done," as provided by the Cortes of Palencia in 1313, and to receive complaints when anything was done wrong and see to it that the guardians of the king put it right. Cf. *Colección de Cortes,* 37, 4; 38, 14; and R. A. & A. J. Carlyle, *A History of Medieval Political Theory in the West,* vol. V, pp. 125-126.

[9] Cf. J. Clayton, *Democracy in the Middle Ages and Modern Times,* in the volume *For Democracy* published by The People and Freedom Group, London, 1939, p. 41.

[10] *Politics,* book III, chapters IV-V.

ing to avoid those in opposition: tyranny, oligarchy and demagogy. But it was already stated by John of Salisbury in the twelfth century, that "authority in princes has its measure in Law" and "society imperously requires submission of the Princedom to the laws, for Princes must be persuaded that nothing removed from Equity and Justice may be permitted them."[11]

Democratic Tradition and Natural Rights of Men and People

As forerunner of Grotius, the theologians belonging to the Catholic school of Natural Law in the sixteenth century were decidedly defenders of Democracy. Dominican Francisco de Vitoria asserts that "the source and origin of cities and republics comes from nature" but "no man has the right by natural law to force laws on others, since man is naturally free and is dependent only on God."[12] This idea of the natural liberty of men is strongly emphasized by jurists of that period. Let us quote, for instance, Fernando Vázquez Menchaca:[13] "All men are equal by natural law; all are born free. That is, not only is the whole world not subject to the jurisdiction of a man, but no man is or was subject *de jure* to rule by another, unless it is through his own will." Two centuries later the world will believe it is discovering such current topics.[14]

Equality and liberty were recognized as belonging to all men. Vitoria and his followers, practically all Churchmen, insisted upon the fact that infidelity was not a just cause of war. In the same

[11] John of Salisbury, *Polycraticus*, book IV, chapter I.

[12] *Relectio de potestate civili*, No. 7.

[13] *Controversiarum illustrium*, book I, chapter XX, No. 24.

[14] The proverb *per me regnant reges* implies causality—according to Vazquez Menchaca—in the same way that it is said "that, through divine ordinance, rivers flow, fountains spring forth, plants grow, trees germinate, the sun sheds light, the moon and the stars shine, and some men read, some write, some plough, others sow, the leaves of the trees are stirred by the wind, the cat chases the rat, the eagle chases doves, or the dog chases rabbits, and many other manifestations of this nature. Then, in order for the ruler to perform iurisdiction through God's will, it would be necessary that God in the examples outlined above, were maintaining iurisdiction through all those beings." *Controversiarum*, book I, chapter XXIX, No. 4.

way Pope Innocent IV established: No one has the right to force infidels to accept the faith, for each man has the right to follow his own will, and nothing but the grace of God has any importance in this instance. Bartolomé de Las Casas in his famous polemics with the imperialist Ginés de Sepúlveda (1550), declared: "All nations and peoples whether they have faith or not, who have territories and separate kingdoms which they have inhabited from the beginning are free peoples and are under no obligation to recognize any superior outside themselves." Freedom becomes therefore extended to the international community as a logical consequence of the principle of equality among peoples as well as among individuals. The Papacy likewise supported the rights of the "infidels" against too zealous conquerors invoking so-called religious interests in order to enforce non-believers to embrace the faith, or wanting to enslave them. A Bull issued by Paul III in the year 1557, defined and proclaimed that "Indians or any other people, who may be hereafter discovered by Catholics, although they be not Christians, must in no way be deprived of their liberty and possessions, and that on the contrary they may and must be allowed to enjoy freely and lawfully the said liberty and possessions; that they must not be in any manner enslaved; and that, if they be so enslaved, their slavery must be considered as null and void." Analogically, one hundred years later, another Pope, Urban VIII, in his Bull of April 22, 1639, forbade "any person to dare or presume to reduce to slavery the said Indians, to sell them, exchange them, give them, separate them from their wives and children, despoil them of their properties and possessions, take them into other places or deprive them in any manner whatsoever of their liberty, retain them in slavery, as well as to lend aid, favour, or give counsel or succor, under no matter what pretext or excuse, to those who should do the said things, to speak of it and teach it as something permitted, or to collaborate in it in any way whatever." All this "under pain of excommunication."

The Church joined, as we see, the party of freedom against that of oppression, and this was done not only by the head of the

Roman hierarchy, but also by the clergy sent to the new world by the conquerors. It is known that the bishops were entitled the "defenders of the Indian people," and protested energetically before the king each time abuses were committed. Franciscans living in Mexico recalled to Charles V that "God forbids man to do wrong, even if this wrong is to produce the best consequences," and dared to add: "It is even preferable that no native of the New World be converted to our Holy Religion and that the King lose his lordliness rather than to condemn those peoples to slavery in order to obtain their conversion and submission."[15]

Three Jesuits were in the vanguard in supporting democratic ideas at the end of the sixteenth and the beginning of the seventeenth century, Cardinal Bellarmine, Suárez, and Mariana. And they did so opposing every tyrannical attempt of the kings reigning in their epoch. As James I of England asserted that he "owed his crown only to God, and had not received his power from the people," he contradicted the doctrine of Catholic theology upheld by Bellarmine, according to which political power, even though it be by divine right in view of its existence and necessity in society (which would perish without someone to govern), "resides immediately in the collectivity of people, has not been given to anyone in particular, but to the multitude."[16] James turned furiously against Cardinal Bellarmine for having dared to think otherwise. By will of the Pope, Suárez was brought into the controversy and dedicated his book "to the most noble kings and princes of the whole Christian Orb" in order to defend this thesis: "No king or monarch derives, nor has derived (according to common law) political sovereignty from God immediately, or by divine institution, but through human will and establishment," and this is *egregium theologorum axioma* as supported by a great many theologians, jurists and Fathers of the Church enumerated by Suárez, who quoted Augustine's sentence: *Generale pac-*

[15] Cf. G. Mendez Plancarte, *Humanistas del siglo* XVIII, Mexico, 1941.
[16] *Disputationes Roberti Bellarmini*, book III, *De laicis*, chapter VI.

tum est societatis obedire Regibus suis[17] explaining it in the sense that royal rule as well as obedience to it is based upon human will through human contract conferring power.[18]

The *potestas* of princes, said Suárez, is conferred upon them by the community, for "such a power of mastering or ruling the men politically has been given to no man immediately by God"; and "all men are born free by nature; therefore no man has political jurisdiction or power over another one."[19] At last, there is a decisive assertion to be quoted from this theologian: *"Only Democracy can exist without a positive institution,* as a consequence of the *natural order* (*ex sola naturali institutione seu dimanatione*): for political power being naturally, according to reason, proper for any perfect community, it naturally follows that the community owns that power, unless it has been transferred by a new institution to another subject."[20]

To the question, Is the authority of the King greater than that of the whole Republic? Mariana's reply is frankly democratic in nature: "Since royal power, in order to be legitimate, must be born of the people, and only through their consent and will were the first kings put into power in all States, this royal power must be limited from the beginning by laws and sanctions, so that it will not cause harm to the subjects and finally degenerate into tyranny."[21] Mariana does not admit that the citizens have absolutely stripped themselves of their rights when they set up a sovereign and bind themselves to obedience. They have not conferred upon him the right to do whatever he wishes, without excep-

17 St. Augustine's *Confessions*, book III, chapter VIII.

18 Suárez, *Defensio fidei*, book III, chapter II.—The King of England avenged himself on Suárez by having the book burned publicly in London, and he complained to Philip III of Spain, who answered, after having had Suárez' book examined by the most learned scholars of Spanish Universities, that the book was found to contain sane and Catholic doctrine, and that he would defend it and its author "with arms, if it were necessary."—St. Thomas Aquinas (*Summa theologica*, I IIae, q. XC, a. III) conceiving law as an "ordinance of reason for the common good," acknowledged that "the right to ordain anything for the common good belongs either to the whole multitude, or to someone who acts in place of the whole multitude."

19 *De legibus*, book III, chapter II.

20 *Defensio fidei*, loc. cit.

21 *De rege et regis institutione ad Philippum* III, book I, chapter VIII.

tion and without guarantee. And "the king is not superior to the people, just as the son is not superior to the father, nor the brook to the fountain from which it takes its origin." For this reason, Mariana considers it necessary that people defend their rights against tyranny, and that royal authority be limited.

We do not argue with Mariana's doctrine on tyrannicide, because the Church refused to admit it. It is also useless to continue resorting to many other texts from ecclesiastical authoritative writers openly supporting a democratic constitution of civil society, our aim being only to recall how Democracy, human freedom with regard to kings and rulers, and opposition to tyranny are in the genuine tradition of Christian teaching. If particular areas of Catholicism in modern times are obstinate in rejecting such a tradition, it comes from other sources than those; but the phenomenon is indeed worthy of some accurate analysis.

The clash between Catholicism and Democracy, the antagonism between values that seemed to be predisposed to interpenetrate each other, began actually through the progressive secularization of civic life. Since a large part of society refused to be led by the teaching of the Church, and the formulations of natural law became no longer concerned with God as the author of nature, and Reformers as well as philosophers insisted upon "free thought" outside of the Catholic dogma, many Catholics found themselves in opposition to civic society as a whole. Instead of accepting to fight for their attacked principles and reasserting them in their permanent essence compatible with the new conditions of the world, they often preferred to forsake the political field. So the Christian moral basis of human politics was more and more removed, according to Machiavellianism. Catholic thought became weak, unable to continue the strong tradition of the sixteenth and seventeenth centuries, and it happened that a motto so deeply Christian as that of "Liberty, Equality, Fraternity" could be turned against Catholicism because of the apathetic attitude of too many Catholics in defending it as their own. Conservative Catholics are generally behind the times, and they neglect to assert the lasting vitality of Christian values.

Church and Modern State

Since the State had become embodied in representative forms by adoption of the principles of Democracy, it was obvious that its management needed organization of the liberties of men who had to co-operate actively with the regime. On the other hand, citizens realized the importance of safeguarding and protecting their freedom, without which the increasing power of the State machinery could crush them. That freedom was invoked by citizens in a two-fold way, from the Church and from the State. They often saw in the union of both supreme institutions, spiritual and temporal, the threat of the two old "swords." Actually the Church used as its main weapons spiritual ones on account of its disciplinarian power over the whole community of believers. Originally the Church disposed of only spiritual punishments, and even the most terrible sanctions were left to the judgement of God, as being ultra-temporal by nature. So the most serious one that could be imposed on this world was excommunication. But the Church had no power over non-Christians. The sole right of the Church over non-baptized men was that of announcing the Gospel to them, but this peacefully, without forcing them to convert. We see how such a doctrine is recalled by the Council of Trent: "The Church does never exercise any judgement over those who did not enter it by the door of baptism."[22] Despite the efforts of many theologians, in medieval Christendom spiritual and temporal social orders appeared not only united but often confused. What the Church regarded as an ideal to be obtained by persuasive ways, the unity of men in the same faith, Kings frequently used to accomplish by force, compelling non-believers to accept an imposed faith and then persecuting them because of their logi-

[22] Cf. Charles Journet, *Le pouvoir coercitif de l'Église*, in *Nova et Vetera*, Friburg in Switzerland, July-September 1937, pp. 303-346.

cal insincerity in practicing their new religion. The Inquisition was a fruit of that confusion of attributions, understandable enough in its epoch, even though not justifiable, and unimaginable in the primitive Church or in our time. It was exploited in fact more by the State than by the Church, and more as an instrument of policy than as a religious one. But it contributed enormously to discredit Christian Churches (both Catholic and Protestant, which used such a cruel proceeding), and also the State as indirect judge and direct punisher in matters of faith.

There were many reasons to hope that a distinction of competence and jurisdiction between State and Church could put an end to that medieval confusion which could no longer be prolonged since European society had ceased to be united by ties of the same faith. The separation however began with a constant rivalry in the absolutist period, to be converted into rupture and reciprocal hostility in the revolutionary and constitutional epoch. The deeper the influence of the clergy in absolute monarchies, the more anticlerical was the revolution. Constitutionalism, like the consecration of revolutionary conquests, was frowned upon by the Church insofar as the social role of the Church became threatened with nullification by the revolutionaries.

One cannot be astonished that the Papacy was opposed to the French Revolution. At that time such a feeling was shared in every European court—the "Terror" had naturally terrified them. And then, the Church was hostile to the liberties claimed as a whole, as they implied equality for all cults before the State, as well as the free spreading of doctrines against the faith and ethics of Christianity. "The most active and most intolerant current of the Catholic clergy and hierarchy declared itself against every Constitution (at the time of Pius VII) and connected closely with reactionary parties and absolutist courts, especially Vienna."[23] The more and more inflexible attitude of the Holy See, throughout the nineteenth Century—as recalled by Don Sturzo[24]—the

[23] Luigi Sturzo, *L'Église et l'État*, Paris, 1937, pp. 478-479.
[24] *Ibid.*, pp. 483.

monarchism of many bishops penetrated with old absolutist and royalist theories, as well as the anti-liberal campaign of the Jesuits and other congregations, all led to confuse morally acceptable Constitutionalism and political liberties, with naturalist and revolutionary philosophies. It contributed to the creation of an even deeper gap between the Church and the people wanting liberty. Each "liberal" was regarded as anti-religious, while reactionaries leaned upon the Church in order to use it as a tool of power and a means of struggle.

It was a fact, a characteristic fact of the Modern Ages, that a Catholic State, that is, a political community which is composed exclusively of Catholic subjects and which recognizes Catholicism as the only true religion[25] no longer existed.[26] A divided society caused a divided State. Tolerance was often claimed by dissidents in each Nation; it was hardly practiced by rulers. The Protestant principle: *Cuius regio eius religio,* was generally adopted by both Protestant and Catholic States. Freedom of conscience, of worship, of opinion, were anxiously asked for. In the minds of many people these notions became absolute and boundless. Here is where the strife with the State and with the Church took place. The State opposed unrestricted liberties by accepting the principle but limiting as much as it could the concrete liberties acknowledged in the constitutional epoch. The Church whose theologians had supported popular liberties such as rights against rulers, emphasized the doctrine of liberty, and rejected the new secularized bases attributed to the claimed freedoms, as well as their conceited boundlessness. The natural rights of man had always been defended by Catholic doctrine, founded on Natural Law, and deriving from the Eternal Law and the Divine Rule of the World. Since Nature appeared to men as if it were independent of or unconcerned with its Creator, the Church looked upon it as deprived of any basis. Fundamentally, discussion came less from

[25] As defined by J. Pohle, article on *Toleration* in *The Catholic Encyclopedia.*

[26] "The intimate connection of both powers during the Middle Ages was only a passing and temporary phenomenon, arising neither from the essential nature of the State nor from that of the Church." J. Pohle, loc. cit.

the pattern of the concrete liberties than of their philosophical implications. This made it inevitably more bitter.

In 1884, Leo XIII's Encyclical *Humanum genus* condemns that doctrine of secularized "Naturalism," as a form of Liberalism: "The Naturalists hold that all men have the same rights and are in every respect of equal and like condition; that each one is naturally free; that no one has the right to command another; that whenever the popular will changes, rulers may be lawfully deposed; and the source of all rights and civil duties is either in the multitude or in the governing authority, when the latter is constituted according to the latest doctrines." The average reader will find therein an accusation of the principles of both the Bills of Rights and of authoritative Catholic writers who supported "natural rights," especially throughout the sixteenth and seventeenth centuries, in behalf of the Church. He who wants to conciliate texts like that quoted above with a "reasonable liberalism," will argue that when Popes condemn such propositions, for purpose of rejection, they are wont to choose the most absolute form, the most exaggerated thesis; and then, it is sufficient to withdraw any extremist incidental sentence (for instance, the words "in every respect" from the beginning of the text) and the proposition becomes no longer condemned. Unfortunately the average reader does not become convinced in every case by such a keen argument. Let us examine the most significant debate in this matter.

The Quarrel on the "Syllabus"

There is a document issued by the Vatican in the last century, that has always been thrown in the face of the Catholics as obvious evidence of intolerance: it is the *Syllabus* of 1864. Wielded at the same time by conservative Catholics against their more progressive fellows, and by every foe of the Church against this institution itself, it marked the high tide in the struggle between Rome and Liberalism. Endless polemics were opened since its publication and they are not yet closed. Let us briefly see why.

On the death of Gregory XVI, in 1846, Pius IX was elected Pope and such a choice produced general enthusiasm not only among believers, but also among people outside of the discipline of the Church. They thought him a liberal and placed a lot of romantic hope in him. Guizot dared to believe that the new Pope, in opposition to the policy of his predecessor, would accomplish the reconciliation of the Church and "modern society." The strong popularity of Pius IX as well as his first decisions might encourage such a confidence. The famous Theatine Father Ventura, a constant friend of Lamennais, was called to Rome, and his sermons, believed to be inspired by the Pope himself, provoked a tremendous sensation because of their frankly liberal tendencies. But the "idyl between Church and Liberty," as remarked by an ecclesiastical writer[27] ended very soon. The so-called "modern society" was fiercely anti-clerical and even anti-religious, and Pius IX wanted no compromise with it. A catalogue of its "errors" was ordered by the Pope, to be prepared in 1852. Two successive commissions shared in this work until 1864, when the Encyclical *Quanta cura* was published and, at the same time, in charge of the Pope, the Secretary of State Cardinal Antonelli sent to all bishops a *Syllabus* "containing (as its title reads) the most important errors of our times, which have been condemned by our Holy Father Pius IX in Allocutions at Consistories, in Encyclicals, and other Apostolic Letters."

Two principal aspects should be commented upon the *Syllabus*—the way of its promulgation, and its contents. About the latter, no doubt that it is extremely severe for each and every current thesis among non-orthodox thinkers, and even for some that were supported by certain Catholic liberals whose condemnation appeared suddenly and formally. Indeed the Encyclical of 1864 proscribed Gallicanism, according to which the acts of the popes concerning religion were required to be sanctioned by civil

[27] Don Luigi Sturzo, *L'Église et l'État*, Paris, 1937, p. 507. Cf. also V. M. Crawford, *The Rise and Decline of Christian Democracy*, chapter IV of the volume *For Democracy*, by "The People and Freedom Group," London, 1939, p. 60.

power[28], and also absolute Liberalism which claimed for every citizen total liberty to express publicly his opinions, no matter what they might be, by way of speech, the press or any other means, without any possibility of curtailment or limitation by ecclesiastic or civil authorities. But the *Syllabus* seemed to condemn all liberties as proclaimed by philosophers and established in Constitutions and Bill of Rights, especially freedom of conscience and everything that was proudly considered the appanage of "modern society." It seemed the bitterest answer to those who had harbored a hope, of course exaggerated, based on the so-called Pius IX's liberalism.

Its eighty condemned propositions dealt with various theological, moral and political subjects. Some of them caused great astonishment among liberals, both believers and non-believer. For instance, the 15th, declaring erroneous that "every man is free to embrace and profess the religion he is led by the only light of his reason to find as being the true one." And the 80th, declaring it to be false that "the Roman Pope can and must agree with progress, liberalism and modern civilization." Catholics themselves were afraid, for the literal interpretation of such principles created an embarrassing situation in which the Church could lose all connection with the society upon which it was nevertheless called to act. And such a situation became more burdensome since reactionary Catholics took the *Syllabus* as a weapon against less narrow-minded co-religionists.

A French bishop, Msgr. Dupanloup undertook the job, no easy one, of eradicating the misunderstanding. He hurriedly wrote and published, in January 1865, a clever comment on the Vatican documents.[29] Based on the current distinction accepted by theologians between *thesis* and *hypothesis*, Msgr. Dupanloup demonstrated that the Pope envisaged the ideal of an entirely Chris-

[28] Gallicanism, Josephism and "regalism" were always restrictions to the liberty of the Church. It is to be noted that, in 1868, the *Conseil d'Etat* at Geneva refused Msgr. Mermillod his title of bishop under the pretext that it had been granted by the Pope without participation of the State.

[29] *La Convention du 15 septembre et l'Encyclique du 8 décembre 1864.* Cf. Lagrange, *Vie de Monseigneur Dupanloup*, vol. II, Paris, 1894, pp. 291-293.

tian society, but he left believers free to act according to the conditions of the political society actually existent. Replacing each proposition of the *Syllabus* into its context, he presented them in the sense in which one must understand them, always a just and reasonable one.[30] Many papers opposed to the Church cried out that the Bishop of Orleans "transfigured" the Vatican texts. But the Pope himself wrote to Msgr. Dupanloup: "You have rejected errors in the same meaning that We have done so."[31] Dupanloup's statements were immediately accepted by no less than six hundred and thirty bishops of many countries offering him the most enthusiastic congratulations for his work. The very authoritative Jesuit review *La Civiltà Cattolica,* which had just been placed under the direct inspiration of the Vatican, supported the same attitude. Its writers had already asserted that in the field of the "hypothesis," modern liberties might be legitimate, and Catholics were allowed to love and defend them.[32]

Reactions in other countries were similar. Theologians applied themselves to give a little more liberal interpretation than that too literal one embraced by either conservative or anti- Catholic minds. In a very subtle manner, Archbishop J. B. Purcell,

[30] Msgr. Dupanloup explained that the *Syllabus* did not condemn progress as such, but a certain so-called progress, a certain so-called civilization: "These sublime words (progress, liberalism, civilization) that you denaturalize, we have taught them to you in their true meaning. . . . In spite of you, each of these words has had, and still conserves, and will conserve forever a perfectly Christian sense." Lagrange, loc. cit.; Mourret, *Histoire générale de l'Église,* vol. VIII, Paris, 1921, pp. 496-498.

[31] Pius IX's *Letter to Msgr. Dupanloup,* February 4, 1865.

[32] *La Civiltà Cattolica,* October 17, 1863. In the same way, a very learned Spanish priest and philosopher, Jaime Balmes, and the great French tribune Montalembert had tried to show no incompatibility but rather conciliation existing between Catholicism and Democracy. They devoted themselves to distinguishing between *dogmatical intolerance* in matters of faith, and *civil tolerance* proclaimed as necessary to society, as a way to preserve peace among men.

With the very useful doctrine envisaging not thesis but hypothesis as applicable to the actual conditions of life in our times, the position of Catholics, living in this "hypothetic" but real world becomes indeed simplified. As Msgr. Dupanloup said: "When as a matter of fact the unity of doctrine has been broken in any country, a political law may be established on that fact. For this reason the Pope does not necessarily condemn any Constitution in which freedom of cults is granted." What the *Syllabus* means is that such a situation is not "the ideal one" for the Church (whose ideal was all men professing the true religion). "The same for political liberties—Dupanloup continues—: the question is not to know if Catholics must embrace as a thesis, as an absolute truth, but simply if they may accept as laws or, on the contrary, reject modern political liberties as such;" and his solution is that "considering laws and institutions needed by a country or at a certain time, no one word of the *Syllabus* or of the Encyclical condemns them," (Lagrange, loc. cit.).

of Cincinnati, in his polemics with Th. Vickers, Minister of the First Congregational Church of the same city[33] said, concerning the Eightieth condemned thesis: "I believe that the Pope has no need to reconcile himself to progress or true Christian evangelical liberalism, for he was never, and is not now, opposed to either."[34] On the Fiftieth proposition of the *Syllabus showing* it as an error to say that "the Church ought to be separated from the State, and the State from the Church," Archbishop Purcell's comment was categorically: "I do not want a union of Church and State. I deprecate such a union. I prefer the condition of the Church in the United States to its conditions in Italy, France, Spain, Austria, Bavaria."[35] With keen prudence the Dutch Jesuit Father A. Haag recommends an analysis of each of the propositions included in the *Syllabus* "according to the laws of scientific interpretation."[36] Its form is a negative, not an affirmative one. Telling in each case what proposition is rejected, it does not provide its contrary as admitted by the Church. And even each proposition is given generally, in an absolute sense, and is to be referred to its source. Thus the often quoted Eightieth proposition must be explained with the help of the Allocution on March 18, 1861, in which the Pope expressly distinguishes between "true and false civilization" and affirms "that, if a system designed to de-Christianize the world be called a system of progress and civilization, he can never hold out the hand of peace to such a system." According to the words of this Allocution, then, "it is evident that the thesis of the *Syllabus* applies to false progress and false liberalism."

[33] Edited in pamphlet under the title *The Roman Catholic Church and Free Thought*, Cincinnati, 1868.

[34] Loc. cit., p. 33: It could also be said that the Eightieth proposition was only concerned with the Pope and presented as if he *could* and *might* (both terms together) reconcile *and* harmonize (both too) with progress, liberalism, and with modern civilization (with all the three); and that lacking only one of these terms, the thesis would be changed and therefore no more condemned. Casuistry possesses inexhaustible resorts.

[35] Archbishop Purcell, loc. cit., p. 32—If it is an "error" that the Church and State *ought* to be separated (as an ideal for every country and every time) it does not imply that they *ought* to be united, either in abstract or *hic et nunc*.

[36] *The Catholic Encyclopedia,* vol. XIV, p. 369.

J. Elliot Ross[37] invokes Cardinal Newman's *Letter to the Duke of Norfolk* published in 1879, as the best treatment of the relations between Church and State, demonstrating that no incompatibility exists between the teaching of the Catholic Church and a Democracy: In the *Syllabus*, the condemned proposition number 80 is universal and positive; the proposition implicitly affirmed by the condemnation of that will then be particular and negative: "sometime, somewhere (for instance, in Vatican City or the theocratic State of Solomon) Church and State should not be separated." Both chosen examples are deeply significant of the wideness of such an interpretation.

Cardinal Newman had openly settled, aside from the question of the contents of the *Syllabus*, another one upon which discussion had been introduced among theologians and canonists—the question of what were doctrinal authority and binding power of the *Syllabus* over the Catholic world.[38] Cardinal Antonelli, the Secretary of State had sent the document to all the bishops, jointly with the Encyclical which was of course a direct act of pontifical teaching. Nevertheless, the *Syllabus* was not signed by the Pope himself. It had been prepared and issued by order of the Pope. Was it an act *ex-cathedra?* Many theologians denied it. Among them, was Father Newman, who wrote in the open *Letter to the Duke of Norfolk*: "The *Syllabus* has no dogmatic power"; after which Leo XIII appointed him as Cardinal. Pius IX, as well as Leo XIII considered it an act of the Holy See; but not precisely an act *ex-cathedra*. "So long as Rome has not decided the question, everyone is free to follow the opinion he chooses. . . . There is no agreement on the question whether each rejected thesis is—for the Catholics—infallibly false, merely because it is condemned in the *Syllabus*."[39] An Austrian Bishop, Msgr. Fessler, the learned canonist De Angelis, and many other authoritative ecclesiastical writers refused to acknowledge a dogmatic character

[37] *The Religions of Democracy* (Judaism, Catholicism, Protestantism in creed and life), New York, 1941, p. 166.

[38] Cf. Mourret, op. cit., vol. VIII, p. 501.

[39] Cf. article *Syllabus*, in *The Catholic Encyclopedia*.

to that document, issued by Cardinal Antonelli in charge of the Pope.

The Church and the Totalitarian State

In practice the difficult question of the relations between the State and Church is easier than in theory. The church, inflexible in its principles (the "thesis"), is more conciliatory when dealing with established regimes (the realized "hypothesis"). Strict application of the alliance between both institutions being only available in the case of a completely Catholic State, and there being "good reason to doubt if there still exists a purely Catholic State in the world" according to modern theologians,[40] "when several religions have firmly established themselves and taken root in the same territory, nothing else remains for the State either to exercise *tolerance towards them all*, or, as conditions exist today, to make *complete religious liberty* for individuals and religious bodies a principle of government."

We are far enough from the times of rupture which created strong hostility between the temporal and spiritual powers. Democracy has been put into practice in many countries, in almost all civilized ones, through historical vicissitudes. And it is worth noting that the more and better such a regime is loyally applied, the more effectively religious liberty is granted and protected. No Church may be persecuted where Democracy enacts its own liberal principles. On the contrary, the further a State separates itself from the liberal and democratic concept of power, the more precarious becomes the status of believers and Churches. Religion and Churches in our times have been persecuted only by dictatorial States. Either they frankly opposed every religion because they try to supplant religious dogma by their own, covering the full field of consciences (like Sovietism and Nazism), or they intended to exploit, to their benefit, the acknowledged values of

[40] J. Pohle, on "Toleration," in *The Catholic Encyclopedia*.

religion and the Church (like Fascism and Falangism).[41] At any rate, persecution or deformation is all the Church can expect from any anti-democratic dictatorial regime.

Since the Church has no political form of civil society as its own, because of its supera-temporal mission which deals with leading souls towards "God's City"—no matter what the pattern of the "Earthly City" may be—Catholics remain free to prefer one or another among the legitimate regimes. There is no political dogma: the "realm of Christ" is not of "this World." It does not mean that Christians should be absolutely unconcerned with political life and action. Even though, as Christians, they are not *of* the World, they exist indeed *in* the World, and must be conscious of their responsibilities as citizens of their respective States. Neither their religious faith however, nor their allegiance to the Church, may imply any supplementary political attitude as needed. They may be for Monarchy or for Republic, for Aristocracy or for Democracy. No orthodoxy binds them, no declaration of heterodoxy threatens them in their free choice, provided that the ruler does not attack religion, nor oppose Christian moral principles. And even in this case the Church is wont to distinguish between regime and legislation, by recommending subjects to fight lawfully against laws or acts of persecution, but meanwhile respecting legitimately established regimes.[42] Only when a regime

[41] Italian Fascism combined both systems—destructive and corruptive—in its fight, now open and then palliated against the Church. Mussolini could not neglect the importance of the Catholic factor in Italian life. So he looked opportunistically for compromising. Spanish Falangism declared in its official *Program*, paragraph 25: "Our movement incorporates the Catholic sense—of glorious and predominant tradition in Spain—for national reconstruction." And prevented all "intrusion" of the Chuch "offending the dignity of the State," without granting any reciprocal attitude on the side of the State which actually endeavored to obtain annexation, submission and utilization of Catholicism under color of protection.

[42] Resistance to oppression is very carefully regulated by Catholic doctrine, in both passive and active ways, according to the Evangelical principle: "It is better to obey God than men." Nevertheless, sedition is generally forbidden to Catholics, through the teaching of Popes. Pius XI recalled the common doctrine in his *Letter to the Mexican Bishops* on March 28, 1937: "The Church condemns all unjust insurrection and violence against established governments. . . . It is quite natural that when even the most elementary religious and civil liberties are attacked, Catholic citizens do not resign themselves passively to giving them up. However, the vindication of these rights and liberties . . . by legal and appropriate methods . . . only justifies actions that are lawful and not actions that are intrinsically bad. . . . If means ought to be proportionated to the end, we must only use them in the measure

identifies itself with anti-religious struggle, does the Church condemn it as incompatible with the natural rights of consciences. Priority and superiority of the natural rights of man with regard to the State are recognized by Catholic doctrine. No legitimate State may be founded on systematic violation of such essential rights. The State is viewed as a simple means for human social life, never as an end in itself. If it intends to upset that order between means and ends, it contradicts natural law. When the State, by its own divinization, claims to occupy in the souls of its subjects the place that believers reserve to God, conflict with the Church becomes unavoidable. All the strife between the spiritual and temporal powers in contemporary times is settled there. Politics becomes religion, the State changes itself into a Church, civic allegiance turns to faith, discipline is implied in political dogma, non-conformism is punished like heresy. It is the typical phenomenon of the totalitarian State.

A whole system of myths is set up by modern Totalitarianism. Worship is imposed upon men in behalf of the Nation, the Party, the Class, the State or Race. Infallibility is attributed to the supreme Leader, who like the absolute Kings "can do no wrong." He appears as a superman, and even as a god in the eyes of the simple people.[43] Against all these aberrations the rebuke of Pius

in which they serve to obtain the end, or to render it possible in whole or in part, and in such a way that they do not cause the community greater damage than that which one wishes to repair."

A peculiarly puzzling case, resulting in deep trouble in consciences, is that of the position of the Church in Spain during the last fourteen years. When leftist Republicans succeeded in imposing upon legislation certain principles denying Catholics the rights of equal liberty proclaimed as fundamentals for all citizens, the protest of the Church against such unjust measures was as firm as it was lawful. Formally and unanimously the Spanish bishops kept believers away from the paths of sedition. But when sedition was started out by the Army, in 1936, most of the same bishops accepted and even blessed the military uprising from the beginning, so contradicting the instructions given five years before to the Catholics.

[43] Blasphemous tenets are current ways of stating an idolatric submission in totalitarian regimes. So Becker, Director of the Nazi Workers' Front, dared to assert: "Christ was great. but Adolph Hitler is greater," (*Frankfurter Zeitung*, October 10, 1935). Dr. Engelke went even further: "God has manifested himself not in Jesus Christ but in Adolph Hitler." (Reported in the *Manchester Guardian*, July 15, 1938. Cf. *Nazism and Christianity*, by the Rev. John A. O'Brien, Huntington, Indiana, 1941, p. 21.)

Two forms of parody of the Christian Creed were recently launched in Germany and Spain. The former was published in the *Reichswart*, as follows: "I believe in

XI remains in all the strength of its expression: "Anyone who takes race, or people, or State... and divinizes them through an idolatrous worship, overturns and falsifies the order of things... He who dares to lift a mortal man to the same level as Christ, and even over and against Him, deserves to be told he is a prophet of nothingness, to whom the words of the Scripture are applicable: "He who lives in Heaven jeers at him."[44]

Man, sovereign lord of all things and all powers on the earth. I believe in the German, lord of himself, conceived under the nordic sky, who has suffered under Papists and Mammon's disciples, has gone down into hell, under rods and calumnies of all kinds of devils, is resurrected from the darkness of national death after tens of miserable and hopeless years, who ascended to the heaven of Eckhardt, of Bach and Goethe, where he is sitting down beside his brother of Nazareth, at the right side of the Eternal, wherefrom he will come to judge alive buried and dead people. I believe in the Holy Ghost of Humanity, in the Holy Church of the future, in the communion of all serving not themselves but the weal of the country, in the foregiveness of all faults, in resurrection—under more perfect appearance—to an eternal life in future as in the past." The second Creed, more personal in the Spanish "caudillo," was published in the Falangist press by Isidoro Rodrigálvarez. Here is its absurd text: "I believe in Franco, the almighty man, the creator of a great Spain and of Discipine in a well organized Army; crowned with the most glorious laurels, liberator of dying Spain and modeller of the Spain rising in the shade of the most rigorous social justice. Son of the people and born from the people, he lived with the people; he endured wants and difficulties peculiar to workers' families; he was born from the entrails of the Motherland Spain, he suffered under Azaña's tyrannical power, he was tortured by the members of a despotic and partisan government, he was badly regarded and exiled. I believe in Property and in the greatness of Spain, which will preside the walk along the traditional road thanks to which all the Spaniards will have something to eat. I believe in forgiveness for those whose repentance is sincere, in resurrection for ancient guilds organized into corporations, and in lasting tranquillity. Amen." No commentaries are needed on these demonstrations of mental disturbance, too frequently found under any totalitarian climate. Its examination is, of course, useful to the diagnosis of psychiatrists.

[44] Encyclical *Mit brennender Sorge*, March 14, 1937. In 1931, the same Pope had already condemned and called the ideology of the Italian Fascism a "Statolatry" ("which clearly resolves itself into a true, real pagan worship of the State"); and severely blamed the tendency to subject all rights and all education to the service of that conception of the State which "cannot be reconciled by a Catholic either with Catholic doctrine or with the natural rights of the family." (Pius XI's Encyclical *Non abbiamo bisogno.*) Despite these clear words from the Head of the Church, one of the "prophets" of Spanish Fascism, Ernesto Giménez Caballero, for whom Fascism is the true Catholicity, impudently wrote that: "Catholicism should henceforward support itself on this new Catholicity" since the Church "in the last three centuries has gradually lost its Catholicity . . . by dint of compromise with heretics, revolutionaries and philosophers, by dint of Concordats and modern culture" (*La Nueva Catolicidad*, Madrid, 1933, pp. 107-108, 118); he exalted idolatrous worship of the Hero, "the human gate of action opening on the divine, the ideal goal leading to God;" and even added: "the worship of the Hero is similar to that offered to Almighty God. . . . The hour has arrived for setting up this image of the Hero before the youth of the whole World, and for commanding all to kneel before it" (pp. 143-144). We can easily see how also in Catholic countries Fascism is always deeply anti-Christian because of its genuine pagan roots.

The Rise of Catholic Parties

Catholics in several countries have found themselves, in the last Century, faced with the vital problem of their participation as such in political life and rule. If they wanted their principles on political and social ethics not to be neglected, they had to share and direct the responsibilities of government, through an adhesion without mental reservations to the fair play of Democracy. On the other hand, they had to be careful not to compromise either supreme principles of religion or the authority and prestige of the Church, in hard strife of parties. A solution came only from liberty. This liberty had to be conquered against the rest, but at first against themselves. One knows the difficult beginning of the policy of the Catholics in several European States whose Constitution inspired by democratic radicalism was viewed as in opposition to the Church, or whose rulers openly persecuted the Church.

The Centrum Partei started in Germany from the struggle between Catholic universalism and German *Weltanschauung of* Bismarkian *Kulturkampf* supported by the Hohenzollern. Throughout many vicissitudes, this Party as well as the Bavarian Catholic Party played a very influencial role in the Weimar Republic, in co-operation (and often in dissidence) with Social-Democracy, but always witnessing the presence of Catholics in public life, co-working with the rest at watching over the commonwealth of the temporal community. One also knows the extreme difficulties created for Catholics in Italy by the special situation of the Vatican which refused to recognize the Italian State and Savoy dynasty issued by "usurpation" of the Pontifical States. The Papal prohibition to Catholics from participating in politics, signified by sustained *non expedit,* challenged for a long time any political activity of believers. And this *non expedit* that was the answer given in 1874 by the Vatican to the question raised by Italian bishops asking if Catholics might take a part in the election of deputies to the Chamber, after the abolition of the temporal power of the Pope, was only revoked in 1919, thanks to the admirable tenacity and clearsightedness of men like Don Sturzo, the founder of the *Partito Popolare*. The enormous vitality of this organization permitted the *popolari*, in that same year, to obtain 99 Deputies from a total of five hundred which constituted the Chamber. At the same time, the activity of Catholics in the social field succeeded in creating the powerful Confederation of Christian Workers, gathering one million two thousand members, while the Socialist Confederation figured one and half million.[45]

It is a known fact how French Catholics in France struggled to integrate themselves within the Republic, despite persecution and misunderstanding. The Alger toast of Cardinal Lavigerie contributed to the necessary appeasement, asking Catholics to *rally* "sans arrière-pensée" to the regime. And what was for many of them a kind of resignation, became for many others an enthusiasm for the possibilities of infusing a Christian policy and essential principles into public life and institutions, without falling into clericalism. The spread of the French Christian Democracy in its twofold ways (social, by the Christian Workers organization, and political, through Parties, even though non-confessional, inspired by Christianity) has been magnificent in recent years.[46] And we must remark that the condemnation of a Catholic movement like *Le Sillon* was not based on its democratic doctrines but on its theological interpretations, from an analogical point of view to that which led to the former condemnation of Lamennais.

[45] Luigi Sturzo, chapter entitled "Ma vocation politique" in *Les Guerres modernes et la Pensée catholique*, Montreal, Canada, 1942. Cf. his works *Italy and Fascism*, *Politics and Ethics*, where valuable personal views teach us the fidelity of this exemplary priest to both Church and Democracy.

[46] Progressive Catholics have reached, in the social field, a degree of unity still lacking in political matters. As an example, we can mention the *Social Code* issued in 1927 by the "Union Internationale d'Études Sociales" founded in Malines Belgium) under the direction of Cardinal Mercier. This organization was, to a certain extent, the continuation of that of Fribourg (Switzerland) which worked from 1884 to 1891, under the direction of Cardinal Mermillod, for the preparation of principles then embodied in the Encyclical *Rerum Novarum* by Leo XIII. Those participating in the drafting of the *Social Code* included an élite of social-minded Catholics of several countries: Belgium, England, France, Italy, Netherland, Poland, Spain and Switzerland.

As a matter of fact, something was changed with the intervention of Catholics in Democracy. Leo XIII himself had urged French Catholics to the policy of *ralliement.* In his Encyclical *Au milieu des sollicitudes* (1892) he established that "Catholics, like all other citizens, are free to prefer one form of government to another," that was acknowledgment of political liberty for believers. And the Pope added: "the Church in her relations with political powers makes abstraction of the forms which differentiate them and treats with them concerning the great religious interests of nations... When new governments are constituted, their acceptance is not only permissible, but even obligatory, being imposed by the need of social good which has made and which upholds them. This is all the more imperative because an insurrection stirs up hatred among citizens, provokes civil war, and may throw a nation into chaos and anarchy." Then, the Pope attacked frankly the crucial question by saying: "But a difficulty presents itself. This Republic—it is said—is animated by such anti-Christian sentiments that honest men, Catholics particularly, could not conscientiously accept it. This, more than anything else, has given rise to dissensions, and in fact aggravated them." He gave as a solution the distinction between "constituted power" and "legislation"; accepting the former as legitimate, and concentrating the political action in the quality of laws, which "will be good or bad according as the minds of the legislators are... guided by political prudence or by passion." For this result participation in Democracy was obviously the only way. And obstacles had to be removed, little by little. Already in 1885, Leo XIII's Encyclical *Immortale Dei,* accepting diversity of forms of government, considered Democracy as not only permitted but advantageous and sometimes due to citizens.[47] Later Popes successively authorized Catholics to integrate into political parties. Either constituted exclusively by Catholics (and then, as confessional parties as well

[47] "Neque illud per se reprehenditur, participem plus minus esse populum rei publicae; quod ipsum certis in temporibus certisque legibus potest non solum ad utilitatem sed etiam ad officium pertinere civium." Encyclical *Immortale Dei,*, November 1, 1885.

as non-confessional but inspired by Christian principles), or in the form of other open democratic parties counting on the co-operation of many or few believers, it was a fact for many years that Catholics as such participated in the representative system and rule, and even priests and prelates entered or headed governments, as in Austria, Czechoslovakia, etc.

The conciliation of the Italian State and the Vatican, through the Lateran Treaty, signed on February 11, 1929, was an event which the Church had hoped for during many years. It had been prepared before Fascism came to power and was, nevertheless, accomplished only under Mussolini's rule over Italy. This coincidence was bitterly deplored by many Catholics throughout the world since it would afford pretext to the enemies of the Church to accuse it of complicity with the fascist regime. Benedict XV had been about to accept a settlement of the "Roman question," but the conversations in this respect between the Nitti Cabinet and Cardinal Gasparri ceased in 1920 upon the fall of that government. Fascism considered and exploited the signing of the Treaty and concordat as a success of its own. The spirit which inspired it came to the surface a few days later when Augusto Turati, Secretary General of the Fascist Party, publicly reiterated the divinizing doctrine of the State, brutally proclaiming: "Let it be well known that the State, which all of us must adore on our knees, shall never suffer limitations nor diminishings, and shall remain absolute master of all and everywhere." Some months later on May 13, 1929, Mussolini himself reaffirmed the fascist nature, "solely and essentially fascist" of the State and menaced the Catholic organizations with annihilation if they dared combat fascism. Count Carlo Sforza, who remembers these events and who had intervened in the pre-fascist period in several conversations headed toward a reconciliation of the Vatican with the Italian State, also evokes that Pius XI said during the last days of his pontificate: "Late, too late in my life, have I discovered that the dangers for religion lie not only on one side, but also on the opposite side."

Condemnation of Nazism

Totalitarianism came to ruin all the democratic progress. Catholic Parties and all others were banished, as well as Catholic Workers' organizations in any country where the dictatorship of a single party was imposed. After a long period of lack of confidence, Catholicism had been considered compatible with Democracy. But the totalitarian State does not tolerate it.[48] So it is well demonstrated that incompatibility exists in doctrine and fact only with Totalitarianism, which allows no place to any independent social activity. An extensive battle has for some years been waged between destructive anti-democratic forces and supporters of the essential values whose bearer is the human person. Alongside of democrats, the Churches, Catholic, Protestant and Jewish, led the spiritual resistance of men threatened with a definitive loss of the supreme goods of life.

As it is impossible to report here the great number of pontifical and episcopal condemnations of totalitarian doctrines and regimes, let us recall that not only atheistic Communism, but also Italian Fascism and German Nazism were formally opposed on several noteworthy occasions by Catholic authorities. Pius XI, in his allocution to the Cardinals, in December 1926, denounced that which separates Fascism from the Catholic concept of the State: "it makes the State an end unto itself and citizens mere means to that end, absorbing and monopolizing everything." And this came after the famous definition of Fascism delivered by Rocco, Mussolini's Minister of Justice, who asserted, in his address at Perugia, August 20, 1925: "For Fascism, society is an end, individuals the means, and its whole life consists in using individuals as instruments for its social ends... Individual rights are recognized only in so far as they are implied in the rights of the State." Ap-

[48] Neither so-called Catholic Fascism can tolerate any autonomous Catholic organization. Franco Dictatorship forced Catholic Unions to dissolve as well as the Catholic Students Confederation, whose members were compulsorily transferred to the Falangist organizations.

proving the thesis of his Minister, Mussolini had said that Rocco "presented in a masterly way the doctrine of Fascism." Pius XI answered by defending human freedom as well as Catholic principles.

National-Socialism had been condemned by the German episcopacy, since 1930, at a time when many people failed to see the enormous dangers of such a doctrine. The Bishop of Mainz forbade at that time the reception of sacraments to any Catholic professing the principles of the Party, some of which "no one Catholic may embrace without betraying his faith... Hate of other races is anti-Christian," said the Bishop, and refused "to adapt Christian ethics to German moral sense," for "the cultural politics of National-Socialism are in opposition to Christianity." The Archbishop of Breslau, Cardinal Bertram, confirmed the attitude of his colleague of Mainz: "We do not acknowledge any religion of race, nor any national Church. Catholic means universal." All the bishops of Bavaria, as well as Cardinal Schulten with all the bishops of his archdiocese condemned Hitler and his followers, in 1931. A certain appeasement was created by the first attitude of the Führer after taking the rule in his hands, as he announced his intention to negotiate with the Church, considering "both Christian religions (Protestant and Catholic) as the two most important factors for moral conservation." But even after the sinister von Papen was sent to Rome and after the Concordat itself, condemnations of religious and moral errors of Nazism were made by the Church.[49]

The Encyclical *Mit brennender Sorge*, issued by Pius XI on March 14, 1937, is however the most significant condemnation of Nazism by the Catholic Church. And it was not indeed an isolated declaration.[50] Under the most serious conditions, most of the bish-

[49] Cf. A. Mendizábal, *Una mitología política: los principios anticristianos del racismo*, in the review *Cruz y Raya*, Madrid, August, 1933.

[50] After various and repeated condemnations of racist thesis in several documents and speeches, a concrete measure was issued at Rome in August 1938, by the Congregation of Studies and Universities. On that occasion, the supreme organ of control of higher ecclesiastical education commanded that teachers in Catholic institutes and schools, "to the utmost of their powers, should arm themselves with biology, history, philosophy, apologetics, and the juridical and moral disciplines to reject

ops of Germany, Austria, and then of the other countries later submitted to the tyranny of Racism, did not fail to resist its moral evils. Throughout the last war, despite the harsh censorship of the Nazi authorities, some independent voices have arisen from the German Catholic hierarchy itself, condemning Hitler's methods. For instance, the 1941 Lenten Address of the Archbishop of Freiburg-in-Brisgau, Msgr. Conrad Gröber which denounced "the reign of the Anti-Christ in the Great Reich as unlike Christ's reign as water and fire." On July 6, 1941, the Collective Pastoral Letter from the German episcopacy convening at Fulda, was read in every church of the Reich.

Catholicism and Anti-Semitism

The most brutal manifestation of the destructive doctrines and criminal practices of modern totalitarianism—all to the shame of our century—has been the openly declared anti-semitism started by Hitler Germany, and transplanted to many countries as a seed and as the touchstone of the Fascist orthodoxy patterned by Nazism and then accepted by Italian Fascism itself, after being denied any basis by Mussolini in one of his typical speeches.

This is perhaps one of the issues of Fascism which managed the least to attain the treacherous goal of Fascist attitudes among the Catholics. At the very beginning of the anti-semitic campaign, before Hitler's rule, Pope Pius XI approved a decree of the Congregation of the Holy Office, issued on March 25, 1928, recalling that " the Catholic Church has been in the habit of always praying for the Jewish people," that "the Apostolic See has protected this people against unjust oppressions," and clearly stating that "she *condemns* most especially the hatred against that people, once

validly and learnedly the absurd dogmas" of Racism, listed in a kind of "Syllabus." Among those "errors" to fight against: "(2) The vigor and blood purity of the race are to be preserved and cherished by every means possible. . . . (6) The first source and highest rule of the entire juridical order is the instinct of race. . . . (8) Individual men exist only for the State and on account of the State; whatever rights may pertain to them are derived solely from the concessions of the State."

chosen by God, that hatred which nowadays is commonly called Anti-Semitism."[51]

No sooner had Nazism risen to power in Germany than the ecclesiastical hierarchy unequivocally condemned persecution against the Jews. One needs only to recall the decisive attitude of Cardinal Faulhaber[52] which the fearless prelate fenced against the hatred of official Germany.

The doctrinal merit and personal courage of his sermons consisted in his not only upholding Christianism as against Racist Neo-Paganism, but also confronting Judaism and Germanism at the same time, defending the superiority of the religion of Israel over the ancient Nordic Paganism which was attempting to restore itself. Cardinal Manning had said to an Israelite: "I could not understand my religion if I did not revere yours." This was the very attitude of the Archbishop of Munich, who, under Nazi rule, proclaimed the incompatibility of the Hitlerian doctrines with Christianism; the German bishops insisted upon this thesis in their collective Letter of June 7, 1934, declaring the racist doctrine to be a "radical negation of Christianism." In defending the principles of its ethics, the Church was upholding the rights of the human being. The human being keeps his own worth with regard to the State, Cardinal Faulhaber asserted; and the individual cannot be devaluated, nor expropriated, nor deprived of his rights to benefit the State; he cannot become blotted out or turned into a slave of the State, without any rights.[53]

Later, in the face of the increasing persecution of the Jews, Pius XI proclaimed in September 1938, that "Anti-Semitism... is a repugnant movement, a movement in which Christians can have no part." And he concluded, emphasizing the fact that, for

[51] *Acta Apostolicae Sedis*: Decretum De Consociatione Vulgo "Amici Israel" abolenda, vol. 20, p. 104.

[52] Cardinal Faulhaber: *Judentum, Christentum, Germanentum.* Adventspredigten gehalten in St. Michael zu Muenchen. 1933. (Graphische Kunstanstalt. A. Huber, Muenchen, 1934.)

[53] *Judentum, Christentum, Germanentum*, pp. 62-63.

Christians, "Anti-Semitism is not admissible," since "Spiritually we are Semites."[54]

The general attitude of the bishops, the priests and the European Catholics with regard to the persecution of the Jews has been one of open opposition courageously expressed, not only by verbal protests, but by an efficacious and model program of aid to the persecuted; the religious monasteries and the Christian homes served as refuge for the multitude of Jewish families who had to hide from the executioners who were lying in wait for them.[55]

In France, when the imposter's government, headed by Pétain, unreservedly accepted the Anti-Semitism ordered by Nazism, and practiced the horrors of the Hitlerian methods in the non-occupied zone, without heeding the protests of the Vatican, formulated by the Papal nuncio in Vichy, the voices of the bishops such as Msgr. Saliège, in Toulouse, Msgr. Théas, in Montauban, and Msgr. Gerlier in Lyons, expressed the utmost condemnation, and instructed the Catholics with regard to their fraternal duties toward the persecuted people. On August 30, 1942, the Bishop of Montauban said: "I am making known the indignant protests of the Christian conscience, and I proclaim that all men, no matter what their race or religion, are entitled to the respect of individuals and States. The present Anti-Semitic measures are being taken in violation of the most sacred rights of the person and of the family." "They are our brothers," the Archbishop of Toulouse proclaimed, on August 26, of the same year, "a fact which a Christian cannot forget." And the Archbishop of Lyons, primate of France, asked all Catholics not to abandon the children of the Jews to the authorities, while other Episcopal instructions begged the Catholics to give all possible aid to the Jews." Catholic writers, like Jacques Maritain, Francois Mauriac, Wladimir d'Ormesson

[54] Cf. *Catholics and Jews,* A Study in Human Relations, by Rev. Gregory Feige. (The Catholic Association for International Peace, Washington, 1945), pp. 89-90.

[55] See John M. Oesterreicher, *Racisme—Antisémitisme—Antichristianisme* (New York, Editions de la Haison Française, 1943) pp. 199 and following; Ecole Libre des Hautes Etudes, *Le Droit raciste à l'assaut de la Civilisation,* especially the chapter "L'application du Droit raciste en France" by Paul Jacob (New York, Editions de la Maison Française, 1943).

showed themselves to be champions of the liberty of the Jews, in face of the unleashed hatred brandished against them by the racist tyranny.

Among so many mistakes which the Catholic masses have committed in our century in political matters, that of Anti-Semitism has in general not been committed, thanks, in this instance, to the purely Christian attitude of the hierarchy. Anti-Semitism was the most brutal of the natural consequences of Fascist totalitarianism. The horrible sight of the gas chambers and of the sadism of the torturers was instrumental in opening the eyes of a number of Catholics who certainly had not shown themselves to be clairvoyant with regard to the totalitarian tyranny which was the cause.

Catholics and Authoritarianism

Politically and socially, the Catholics of our time are profoundly divided between two currents of thought and action, which we may name respectively the progressive tendency, which is disposed not exactly to accept with resignation, but to propel and drive the lifting of the working classes to the full exertion of their rights and social responsibilities; and to recognize and practice democracy as a regime of liberty and justice, with equality of rights for all and with the maximum respect for the dignity of the human person; and the narrowly conservative tendency, or rather reactionary, opposed to all social advancement and to the full participation of the people in the affairs of State. Since the pontifical condemnations of totalitarianism in its various branches made the conciliation difficult between a profession of Catholic faith and the upholding of totalitarian regimes, the Catholics of reactionary tendencies tried to find a ground for compromise in those regimes which, while not proclaiming themselves openly totalitarian, defined themselves as being authoritarian; and upheld especially the systems called "corporative," whose main fault was the non-existence of really independent corporations. Such a position was, actually, rather difficult to justify. Italian

Fascism, which created the myth of the Corporate State, defined itself as being totalitarian at the same time; and was even the founder of the totalitarian formula of State absolutism: "Everything in the State; nothing outside the State, nor against the State." The non-totalitarian regimes, nonetheless strongly authoritarian, of Austria under Chancellor Dolfuss, and of Portugal under Oliveira Salazar, were founded on the suppression of civil liberties. The Spanish dictatorship of General Primo de Rivera followed similar principles. What the partisans of authoritarian regimes who did not accept the frankly totalitarian regimes in their entire crudeness, did not see or did not like to see, is that from one to the other type of regime there is no more than a step's difference, and that a government which is on the slope of authoritarianism soon, by virtue of historical conditions and the internal dialectics of the system, arrives at the practice of totalitarianism, since the man or group who exerts a power without limits, naturally tends to abuse it and to increase it to the utmost; and as soon as there are no obstacles to political power, like those checks which democracy imposes by means of the vigilant intervention of its citizens, the power becomes total, and the regime is converted into a totalitarian one. Thus, authoritarianism is a temporary disguise for totalitarian tendencies; and the Catholic reactionaries who accept it are willingly or unwillingly servants of Fascism, which, by its very nature, is totalitarian.

Those groups of Catholics who are enthusiastic over the dictatorial totalitarian policies and who have to recognize the fundamental incompatibility between totalitarianism and Christianism, are looking for the escape of their difficult doctrinal position in a formula which, considered objectively, is a lamentable aberration: since the totalitarian anti-Christian regimes are unacceptable for believers, they believe that if the dictator is Christian and ostensibly protects the Church, the objection which the Church raises to totalitarianism will be automatically erased. Those who think in this manner are perhaps defending the material "interests" of the Church, but it cannot be said of them that they are serving the "spiritual" cause of religion. "A Christian dictator" is a *contradictio in terminis*, for, if he is really Christian, he cannot be a dictator, that is, the bearer of an absolute and total power, which disregards and affronts the dignity of the person by suppressing essential rights. In a broadcast beamed to Spain (which was very significant indeed) on July 27, 1944, the Vatican Radio bitterly condemned existing dictatorship by totalitarian governments in various countries. The speaker quoted the Pope as condemning "those who dare to place the fortunes of whole nations in the hands of one man alone, a man who as such is the prey of passions, errors and dreams." Pius XII opposed tyranny which "attributes to the man who holds the necessary physical strength the power to make use of it without any consideration for the rights of human beings." Such a statement was clear enough for Catholics supporting so-called "Christian dictators," but the natural addressees of this message did not consider that it alluded to them, and on the contrary, continued to think that the pontiff was referring to others, and continued willingly to close their eyes to truths as Christian as these: that Liberty is a necessary condition for our human and transcendent destiny, and its recognition in the political order is parallel to that of free will in the ethical order; that Equality means the acceptance of the essential worth of men, of each man, without any possible lessening on account of the color of his skin or the color attributed to his convictions; and that the most genuine Brotherhood is expressed in religious terms by embracing all men as God's sons.

The exploitation of the most respectable religious sentiments to serve the interests of a dictatorship oppressing consciences, is a profanation and an overturning of spiritual values; and it cannot legitimately base itself upon a reaction against the anti-Christianism of other forms of dictatorship. As a Review of English Dominicans fearlessly recorded: "Christ on His Cross has a dignity and a moral power which no Marxian hatred can dispel. But Christ the servant of a totalitarian State, granted grudging liberty of cult which will take the minds of the poor off their misery, yet forbidden to open His mouth against violence, injustice and the denial of His social teaching... must tear the heart of every true Christian."[56]

The conflicting ideologies of our time led too many people toward the stupid dilemma: Fascism or Communism, two issues which are not exactly two solutions, but rather two evasions of the primordial problem. Fascism and Communism are not antipodes, but neighbors, bad neighbors and therefore in conflict... until they reach an understanding; right and left of the same tyranny, of the same dictatorship against man; two arms of the same Moloch demanding inhuman human sacrifices. Such a stupid dilemma created the brutal tension which split the world by leading the peoples toward that universal civil war whose forerunner and sinister rehearsal was the Spanish War.

The Spanish Test

From 1936 onward, not only the Spanish Catholics but those of the whole world, were deeply divided in view of the phenomenon of the Spanish military insurrection which, with the efficient aid of Hitler and Mussolini, resulted in the setting of the Franco regime in Spain, after a war of nearly three years' duration. It would be simplifying matters too much to consider this schism between the lines of the battle fronts, as an opposition between the supporters of Franco, helped by Germany and Italy, and the supporters of the Spanish Republican Government, helped by Soviet Russia. The division between the Catholics of Spain and the world took place, basically, between those who accepted Franco as if he were the savior of his country and the leader of Catholicism, and those who considered him as the destroyer of his country and of all ethical precepts, and especially of the religious ones, which he invokes at every instance. Nevertheless, it is not a matter of a schism between Catholics who support Fascist and Catholics who would support Communism, but between Fascist Catholics and

[56] *Blackfriars*, October 1936, from the Canadian Catholic paper *Social Forum*, August, 1936.

Democratic Catholics. The latter, in confronting Franco, were not defending a form of totalitarianism opposed to his, but on the contrary, for they rejected the absurd dilemna of Fascism-Communism, and were fighting on two fronts, against any form of totalitarianism, that of the left or of the right. If, in the case of Italian Fascism, the Democratic Catholics, inside and outside of Italy, had taken a stand in frank opposition to Mussolini's regime, why could not a similar phenomenon have arisen in the case of Spanish Fascism? The question was more difficult in the latter case, because Franco, unlike Mussolini, offered himself as champion of Catholicism and was supported by the ecclesiastical hierarchy and by a large majority of militant Catholics. But, despite this, many Catholics and numerous ecclesiastics and some prelates in Spain, refused to admit the validity of the military insurrection, the justice of the war, and the horrible crimes which were committed against the dissidents, as well as the ends pursued and put into practice by those who called themselves "crusaders of a Holy War." Most of the Basques, whose Catholicism cannot be doubted, fought openly against Franco's troops and against the Italian divisions which took part in the war. Franco had indeed gone to great lengths in showing considerations and apparent respect to the Church, as a means of making use of it. When, as in the Basque country, the Church did not appear disposed to submit to the dictator's violence, he persecuted it, expelled the Bishop from the Diocese of Vitoria, together with hundreds of priests and religious men, who are now scattered throughout the world; 19 Basque priests were executed by Franco's authorities and 53 others were still in the prison of Carmona at the time that the socialist leader Besteiro died there, in 1940. Not all the Spanish bishops signed the "collective letter" which Franco expected of them to support his propaganda, and Cardinal Vidal y Barraquer, Archbishop of Tarragona, who had refused his signature, died in exile in Switerland.

Nevertheless, the instructions which the Spanish Catholics had received from their Bishops, as early as 1931, were positively clear. The instructions formally and unanimously given by the Bishops during the early years of the Republic aimed to keep the Catholics away from the paths of sedition. Just after the vote of the Constitution, whose anti-Catholic bias had created deep unrest among believers, the Collective Declaration of the Episcopate on December 20, 1931 recalled that: "The Church has never failed to inculcate the respect and obedience due to constituted power, even in those cases where its holders and representatives have abused it . . . To cooperate by participation of abstention, in the ruin of the social order, in the hope that from such a catastrophe a better condition may emerge is a reprehensible attitude which, by its fatal effects would amount to treason against religion and country . . . It is not by a seditious and violent attitude that Christians will remedy those ills which weigh them down." Why should those sound principles expounded in 1931, condemning sedition—to be feared as a catastrophe and to be qualified as treason—not be valid in 1936, just when the opportunity to apply them presented itself? Why should the person who directed the "treason against religion and country" have received the title of savior of religion and country? The supporters of that "seditious and violent attitude" will claim that they tried to remedy the evils of society. Before the war, in the first half of 1936, rightist leaders denounced in Parliament political crimes under the Popular Front Government, amounting to 182 killings. The "remedy" to this, coldly chosen and prepared, and brutally administered by the "saviors of the nation" was infinitely worse than the evil. It is enough to consider the atrocious course of the Civil War and of the regime which succeeded and which is still in power. The triumph of violence could not assure peace, but only the perpetuation of violence, in the service of a dictatorship, defined by its leader, from the beginning, as being a totalitarian one.[57] Only too late the Episcopate and many Catholics began to realize the meaning

[57] On October 1, 1936, Franco, assuming the functions which his co-insurgents had so liberally conferred upon him (enthroned by General Cabanellas by the words: "I confer upon you the absolute powers of the State") formally declared "Spain is organized according to a vast *totalitarian* concept."

of the Falange's totalitarianism as well as the fact that solidarity with such a regime compromised the Church to a great extent in Spain. When Pope Pius XI issued his encyclical against Nazism, the Spanish newspapers were unable to publish it, because the German censorship, which was set up in the Peninsula, prevented its printing. Only in the final months of the Civil War did Cardinal Goma, Archbishop of Toledo, dare to protest publicly against "the divinization of the State." But scarcely had this disagreement arisen when Cardinal Goma found himself forbidden to publish his instructions to the faithful, as the Franco regime did not allow the slightest criticism, even from an ardent collaborator.

In its reaction against martydom in one zone, the hierarchy had accepted submission in the other, and submission to a totalitarian system which, in its own program, declared its intention of making use of the social force which the Church represented in order to annex it and incorporate it into its nationalistic frame. Franco dissolved the Catholic organizations of workers and of students, in favor of the sindicatos of the Falange. The Catholic leader, Gil Robles, despite having himself ordered the dissolution of his party at the beginning of the military insurrection, and being disposed to favor it, soon found that he was expelled from Spain and is still living in exile in Portugal. Many Spanish Catholics (Republicans, Monarchists, Traditionalists), are living in exile or in Franco's prisons, or have been deprived of the right to practise their professions. But we must make a basic distinction between those Catholics who supported the counter-revolution and who were then persecuted for not showing an absolute conformism with the regime, or for incidents of a personal nature, and those other Catholics who, from the outset, opposed totalitarianism and whose attitude is based on deeprooted democratic convictions. Some day, when the Franco regime has fallen into defeat, if a genuine democratic movement of Christian inspiration is able to arise in Spain, this will be on account of those Catholics who have always upheld a decisive attitude of opposition against the dictatorship, in defense of liberty.

The Rebirth of Christian Democratic Parties

After World War II, in which so many worthy as well as unworthy things have been demolished, millions of Catholics have finally understood their task and assumed it in political and moral reconstruction. Prejudices which had formerly separated them from democracy have been perhaps forever banished, since Catholics now realize that Democracy, while being only a way, can lead better than any other way to the accomplishment in political life of moral values which Christians rightfully deem themselves obliged to preserve. Religion is outside and above every policy, but it is not wrong to think that Democracy today is the instrument to govern men without neglecting their most human aims and even guaranteeing by equal liberty the advent of a real brotherhood in which Christians will be able to fill their temporal mission.

Too many people, when faced with the phenomenon of the springing up of strong democratic parties of Christian inspiration, believe that this is something absolutely new. However, what is new are not the parties, but their present strength.

Since 1924, the Popular Democratic Party, existed in France with only about fifteen representatives; one of its leaders, M. Champetier de Ribes was a cabinet member for several terms; there also existed a paper called *L'Aube*, published by a team headed by Francisque Gay and Georges Bidault. The heroic conduct of this group in the Resistance is what gave to these men and to their ideas the national and international resonance which they had not had before. Their firm decision in the fight against the invader and in favor of the principles of Christianity and of Democracy, is what has brought them to power in the postwar period. In the general elections of 1945, the party which obtained the greatest number of votes was the "Popular Republican Movement,"[58] the successor of the Popular Democratic Party, directed by the same leaders, of which the best known nowadays is Georges

[58] 4,887,000 votes (a few more than the Communist Party, and considerably more than the Socialist Party).

Bidault due to his being entrusted with the Office of Foreign Affairs almost without interruption since the liberation of France and his being Prime Minister under especially difficult circumstances.

The democratic seed of *L'Aube*, of the former Popular Democratic Party and of its younger brother, the party of the "Young Republic" had fructified, through an intellectual elite which, between the wars, had published papers which were highly interesting, from the doctrinal point of view, like *Esprit*, *Temps Présent*, *Politique*, *Res Publica*, *La Vie Intellectuelle*, etc. Without being the organs of any party, these publications spread the democratic doctrine among the Catholic French and prepared a democratic movement and a conscience whose ripeness is now clearly appreciated. In 1940, at the time of the French Armistice, only 80 members of the Parliament refused to vote against the Republic. They belonged to the Socialist Party and to the Popular Democratic Party. In the past, the Catholic-political groups were considered as belonging to the right. Nowadays, they find themselves politically in the center and socially to the left. In France, nationalization of certain industries and the banks has been backed by the Popular Republicans, in conjunction with the Communists and Socialists; and even though the philosophy of that party is different from, and even opposed to the Marxist philosophy of the other two, the consideration of the "commonweal" has made the Catholics cooperate loyally with the other groups in the government and in the material and moral reconstruction of the nation.

The Italian Popular Party has been reborn in Italy under the new name of "Christian Democratic Party" with leaders like Prime Minister Alcide de Gasperi, Guido Gonella, Salvatore Aldisio and others, disciples and followers of Don Luigi Sturzo, whose return to Italy in 1946, after twenty-two years of exile, was of triumphal significance and character. Don Sturzo, during this time, has been the guide not only of the Catholic Democrats of his country, but also of those of other European and American countries; and his pure religious orthodoxy, linked with his sound democratic standing, has given him his unique prestige.

The participation of the Christian Democrats in the government of Italy, alongside with Communists and liberals, was not an easy task. One of the first problems, which were to test the democratic loyalty of that party, was the question of the form of government. Many Catholics were inclined towards the conservation of the monarchy, but the Congress of the Christian Democratic Party decided in favor of the republic in 1946, by a majority of 69% of its delegates. In Italy, like in France, Belgium, Holland and other countries, the Catholic Democrats had gained the respect of the other groups, due to their opposition to Fascism when it was in power and because of its resistance to Nazism under the German occupation.

It would be a mistake to assume that the democratic attitude, nowadays so widespread among the Catholics, was common to all of them. In France, during the Vichy regime, there were many, in fact too many, of the Catholics who backed Marshal Pétain, himself a Catholic, admirer and follower of Fascist methods. The difference between Catholic conservatives, or rather reactionaries, and Catholic progressives, defenders of freedom, is now more obvious than ever.

In Portugal, the dictatorial regime, military in its origin, and established after a period of political disturbances, was headed since 1928 by a notorious Catholic economist, Oliveira Salazar, former professor at the University of Coimbra. The events in Spain without doubt impelled Salazar to assume positions parallel to those taken by the Italian and Spanish Fascism. During the Spanish civil war he considered that his own regime was linked to Franco's fate; even though the Imperialism of the Falange could have made him fearful of the risk which its expansion would mean for the Portugese freedom. Salazar is perhaps the least aggressive of all dictators—a dictator "malgré lui"—but in any case a dictator of fascist type, which he would nevertheless characterize as semi-fascist, with a corporative facade. "We are anti-parliamentarian, anti-democratic and anti-liberal," wrote Salazar in the introduction of his book *Doctrine and Action* (London, 1936). The discontent of numerous Portuguese Catholics has manifested itself on repeated occasions, and Cardinal Cerejeira, patriarch of Lisbon, erstwhile a personal friend of Salazar, has withdrawn himself from the regime and has favored the separation of the Church from the State, preferring poverty for her upon renouncing the support of the State for the cult and clergy, in order to avoid the "utilization" of religion as a government weapon.

In Spain, shortly before the establishment of the Dictatorship of Primo de Rivera in 1923, the "Popular Social Party" was founded by a group of Catholic democrats, which the Dictatorship did prevent to develop. Under the Republic two parties of democratic type developed: the "Basque Nationalist Party" and the "Democratic Union of Catalonia." Because of its exclusively regionalistic character, their influence was limited to only the Basque country and Catalonia, respectively. But their firm democratic standing outlived the severe trial of the civil war and Franco's dictatorship. The "Christian Democracy Group," which existed in Madrid before the civil war, aimed only at social studies without connection to the field of political democracy.

It would be now too early to judge upon the political standing of the Germans after the war. The military occupation of their country and the resulting political influence of the big powers lead the Germans, who were for so many years isolated from the currents of thought in the world, to vote when they have the occasion of doing so, without knowning what is going on, or guided by opportunistic views, lacking any sincerity.

In Germany and Austria, as well as in the most of Europe, three main forces appeal to the public opinion: Communism, Socialism and Christian Democracy. But none of these in occupied countries can claim its voters as adepts. The majority for one or another party mainly depends on the occupation power of each zone. However, the elections held until now outline the trends of the future, which nevertheless might entirely change when fascist currents now forced to hide themselves would arise anew. In the meantime, millions of former supporters of Hitler are voting for their opponents.[59]

Franco, Pétain, Salazar, have had the backing of many Catholics (and not only in their own countries), but in opposition to them and in favor of democracy, many other Catholics have given testimony of their political independence, without involving the Church, like the others had done frequently. The Church must necessarily remain out of the parties, but the Catholics as citizens can and even must, through parties, as instruments of government, intervene in politics. From its inception, the Italian Popular Party insisted upon its autonomy and independence from ecclesiastic control, calling itself not a Catholic party but a party of Catholics, a distinction not sufficiently appreciated by many who often did refer to the party as if it were the very arm of the Vatican, even at times when the Vatican was not very sympathetic to that movement.

In order to provide for a common ground the various democratic groups inspired by Christian civilization, a *Secretariat of Democratic Parties of Christian Inspiration* was founded in Paris in 1925, and later, in 1940, an *International Christian Democratic Union* was established in London, through the initiative of the *People and Freedom Group,* one of the most active and useful instruments of Christian Democratic thought and action.

In the middle of the last war, Pope Pius XII issued, through his Christmas Message of 1942, a body of sound principles of Christian ethics aiming to "reconstruction of what is to arise and must arise for the good of society." Among such fundamentals proposed to the post-war world, the head of the Catholic Church stated the necessity of "giving back to the human person the dignity given to it by God from the very beginning," claiming as basic the personal rights. Requesting for the rights of man not only

[59] The final tabulation of 30 million post-war votes in the four zones of Germany gave these results: Christian Democrats, 10,598,241; Social Democrats, 7,778,313; Socialist Unity Party (Communist dominated), 5,093,144; Communist, 1,247,340; Basse-Saxe Party, 1,002,718; Center, 459,425. When in November, 1945, Austrians elected their Federal Parliament and provincial bodies, the Popular Party (former Social-Christian) won 1,574,587 votes and 85 seats; the Social-Democrats, 1,420,862 votes and 77 seats; the Communists only 176,671 votes and 3 seats.

declaration but also implementation "by the authority of the courts," the Pope stated the principle that "the State and the functionaries and organizations dependent on it are obliged to repair and to withdraw measures which are harmful to the liberty, property, honor, progress or health of the individuals," in order to restore the State and its power to the service of human society" with full recognition of the "respect due to the human person" against "the errors which aim at deviating the State and its authority from the path of morality." The above mentioned principles were in opposition to those on which totalitarian dictators of every brand founded their regimes. Reactionary Catholics therefore decided to skip the statement or to understand it as directed only against leftist dictatorships. Catholic democrats welcome the Pope's declaration and its full significance.

The Christmas 1944 message of Pope Pius XII was even more significant in favor of democratic principles. "Taught by bitter experience," the Pope said, the peoples are opposing "the concentration of dictatorial power that cannot be censured or touched." They are calling "for a system of government more in keeping with the dignity and liberty of the citizens," and such a demand "cannot have any other meaning than to place the citizen ever more in the position to hold his own personal opinion, to express it and to make it prevail in a fashion conducive to the common good." Pope Pius XII evokes the democratic government as it appears to many "as a postulate of nature imposed by reason itself." And a great Catholic and democrat, Professor Francis E. McMahon comments: "Both democracy and Christianity are being assailed by the same enemy. . . . Totalitarianism would wipe both off the face of the earth. There would have been no Totalitarianism if both had remained joined together. Now, by the force of a common threat, they have been united in a fashion. But the task of cementing the union has yet to be achieved . . .Christianity and democracy must cease going their separate paths or contemplate the destruction of their common world."[60]

[60] Francis E. McMahon, *A Catholic Looks at the World* (New York, Vanguard Press, 1945), p. 185.

BIBLIOGRAPHY

EPPSTEIN, JOHN: *The Catholic Tradition of the Law of Nations,* London, Burns Oates, 1935.

FAULHABER, CARDINAL: *Judentum, Christentum, Germanentum,* Muenchen, Huber, 1934.

FEIGE, GREGORY: *Catholics and Jews,* A Study in Human Relations, Washington, The Catholic Association for International Peace, 1945.

JOURNET, CHARLES: *Vues Chrétiennes sur la Politique,* Montréal, Beauchemin, 1942.

LEO XIII: *Encyclicals.*

MARITAIN, JACQUES: *The Things That Are Not Caesar's,* New York, Scribner's, 1930.

MARITAIN, JACQUES: *True Humanism,* New York, Scribner's, 1938.

MARITAIN, JACQUES: *Christianity and Democracy,* New York, Scribner's, 1944.

MARITAIN, JACQUES: *The Rights of Man and Natural Law,* New York, Scribner's, 1943.

MCMAHON, FRANCIS E.: *A Catholic Looks at the World,* New York, Vanguard Press, 1945.

MENDIZABAL, ALFREDO: *Una Mitologia Politica,* Los principios anticristianos del racismo, Madrid, Cruz y Raya, 1933.

MENDIZABAL, ALFREDO: *The Martyrdom of Spain,* New York, Scribner's, 1938.

NEILL, THOMAS P.: *Weapons for Peace,* Milwaukee, Bruce, 1945.

OESTERREICHER, JOHN M.: *Racisme—Antisémitisme, Antichristianisme,* New York, Editions de la Maison Française, 1943.

PEOPLE AND FREEDOM GROUP: *For Democracy,* London, Burns Oates, 1939.

PIUS XI: *Encyclicals.*

PURCELL, J. B.: *The Roman Catholic Church and Free Thought,* Cincinnati, 1868.

RYAN, JOHN A. and BOLAND, FRANCIS J.: *Catholic Principles of Politics,* New York, Macmillan, 1940.

ROSS, J. ELLIOT: *The Religions of Democracy* (Judaism, Catholicism, Protestantism in Creed and Life), New York, 1941.

SCOTT, JAMES BROWN: *The Catholic Conception of International Law,* Washington. Georgetown University Press, 1934.

STURZO, LUIGI: *Politics and Morality,* London, Burns Oates, 1938.

STURZO, LUIGI: *Church and State,* New York, Longmans, Green & Co., 1939.

STURZO, LUIGI: *Less Guerres modernes et la Pensée catholique,* Montréal, Editions de l'Arbre, 1942.

STURZO, LUIGI: *The Catholic Church and Christian Democracy,* New York, Social Action, 1944.

The Catholic Encyclopedia.

VERMEIL, EDMOND: *Hitler et le Christianisme,* Paris, Gallimard, 1939.

XIII. Nationalism

XIII.

NATIONALISM

by

THORSTEN V. KALIJARVI

Our Age

Since we live in a time when political ideas and doctrines are the subject of general discussion, it is important to recognize that many of the current doctrines and theories so freely discussed today are so explosive that they could have been held only in secret or cherished only in the face of inimical philosophies or doctrines a generation or two ago. Many of the ideas and ideals, which we hear over our radios today, if uttered forty years ago, would have incurred immediate punishment.

One of the most explosive political phiosophies is nationalism. It is also one of the greatest forces of our civilization. Although it in reality looks far back into the dim regions of history, nationalism has become a mighty current only since the end of the eighteenth century. Today in its many variations it is perhaps the most potent political force in all Europe; and, as we watch the shifts in population and the efforts of one European country to free itself of the racial minorities of another, the appeals of a common race and all the concomitant paraphernalia overshadow everything. Nationalism is both a constructive and destructive force, which fact will become clear as our discussion proceeds.

At the outset, it should be noted that the sentiment of nationalism is not simple. In the process of evolution it has developed more and more complex and intricate forms. Thus the Irredentism of Garibaldi in Italy looks very simple in comparison with current Communism, Fascism, National Socialism, Hispanidad, and other nationalistic ideologies. Furthermore the old and new nationalisms are inextricably intertwined. Look at any of the national songs, folkways and poems, and note how they survive changes in government and even migrations of people from one territory to another.[1]

Nationalism Defined

There are so many views on nationalism, and there are so many terms, which are so closely related to it, that a definition is required here. We must not confuse it with national, nationalitat, nationalismus, nationality, state, or government. In general nationalism means the sentiment or sympathy which binds a group of people together through common institutions and common culture, and thus gives unity to the group.[2] It is a spiritual manifestation of the people of a state whereby their loyalty to country and their patriotism—the love of local institutions—are translated into bases of social and political action. In its dynamic sense, nationalism is composed of all the cultural activities and ambitions of a state; while in its static sense it represents the existing state system in the world.[3]

Nationalism should be distinguished from the word nation. Nation refers to a group of people inhabiting a definite territory and believing that their members constitute a distinct cultural society. The bond, which ties this group together—nationalism—becomes especially marked when the group is threatened by other men or groups of men who do not share its particular beliefs and senti-

[1] See introduction to Alfred Zimmern, *Modern Political Doctrines*, New York, Oxford University Press, 1939, pages I-XXXII.

[2] *Royal Institute of International Affairs, Nationalism*, London, Oxford University Press, 1939, pages XVI-XX.

[3] Harry Elmer Barnes, *History and Social Intelligence*, New York, Knopf, 1926, page 145; also see C. J. H. Hayes, *Essays on Nationalism*, New York, Macmillan, 1926, and Bernard Joseph, *Nationality: Its Nature and Problems*, New Haven, Yale, 1929.

ments.[4] In this sense the nation, its customs and traditions are often combined with demands for racial amalgamation, racial purity, which in turn are based upon racial awareness of common destiny and common blood.

Nationalism should also be distinguished from a state, which is an established organization consisting of a group of people inhabiting a particular territory with a particular form of government, which group is held together by the consciousness that in its entirety it constitutes a state..

Nationalism also differs from patriotism and loyalty, which mean love of the fatherland. Nor is nationalism government, which means the political organization that controls and directs the political community.

Nationalism is not synonymous with society, for society is the term which is applied to all group actions of communities no matter what the organization may be.

Parker T. Moon points out that nationalism is loyalty to the state of which one is a subject accompanied by a desire for security, prosperity and the greatness of the country in which one is born. This sentiment tends to insist upon uniformity of language, religion and institutions. It feeds upon an intense pride in national institutions, manifested in the desire that all people who speak the national language shall be included within the national state. It also strives to encompass within the national state those areas to which claim can be made historically, geographically or economically.[5]

Summarizing these thoughts, nationalism is a form of group feeling related to other kinds of group feeling, be they community, family or religious. It is concerned with political power which places the individual at an advantage when he belongs to the community and places him under disadvantages when expelled from the community. Nationalism is based upon the differing

[4] Thorsten V. Kalijarvi, *Modern World Politics,* New York, T. Y. Crowell, 1945, 2nd ed., page 59.

[5] Parker T. Moon, *Syllabus on International Relations,* New York, Macmillan Co., 1926, page 9.

of groups. It is a sentimental political concept directly related to the struggle for power, which respects the individuality of states, recognizes the variations in law and government, and segregates group from group on the basis of a common core of ideals and beliefs.[6]

Nature of Nationalism[7]

Burns points out that national differences are due to heredity and environment. When nationalism as a group feeling is analyzed as to its component parts, it is found that it is not a primary instinct, nor can it be classified as such. It is the outgrowth of several characteristics of man. The first is man's gregariousness. His pugnacity also must be taken into account. Likewise group preservation and group aggrandizement, through which nationalism is often expressed, are the results of human egoism and desire for self preservation and self aggrandizement. Nationalism incorporates man's submissive characteristics or man's tendency to follow leaders. In short, while nationalism is not instinctive with man, it does grow out of the emotional and instinctive characteristics of modern society, and as such, in many instances it is not a product of reason, but of feeling aroused by the effect of current affairs upon several of man's primary instincts or characteristics.[8]

Forms of Nationalism

There are many forms or concepts of nationalism. France and the Latin countries identify it with a spiritual bond growing out of culture and religion and similar influences. However, countries like Finland, Switzerland and Belgium tend to identify national-

[6] C. Delisle Burns, *Political Ideals*, London, Oxford University Press, 1932, pages 179-181.

[7] *Ibid.*, p. 175.

[8] W. McDougall, *Social Psychology*, Boston, Luce & Co., 1916; also Sydney Herbert, *Nationality and Its Problems*, London, Methuen, 1920; Gustave LeBon, *Psychology of People*, London, Unwin, 1899.

ism as the spirit which characterizes people who live together. The Nazi philosophy identified it with the race and the state citizenship with which one had been endowed. In the United States and Great Britain, nationalization is characterized by definite social aims, loyalty to the state and the constitution under which it operates.[9]

It is not difficult therefore, to observe that as groups of men differ from each other and as each group has its own individual characteristics, nationalism will differ with each group, and eventually it will acquire the idea of political independence, especially among subject minorities. Nationalism is distinguished as it represents different people, institutions, laws, governments and sentiments. Nationalism is also given particular characteristics as it it affected by the contact of group with group and the attendant friendships and conflicts between groups. Thus one group imitates its foe for the purpose of overcoming him.

COMPONENT PARTS AND BASES

Nationalism is also in part a habit, for it grows out of habits. It is a product of the past living in the present. We are what we are because of what has happened to our forebears. Nationalism rests on several foundations.

(1) One of them is a strong group feeling, which develops among those who inhabit the same territory, especially if they are isolated from other people.

(2) Another is the solidarity which arises out of the belief that people belong to the same race.

(3) Closely akin to this feeling is that which grows out of a common language.

(4) A fourth bond or foundation is comprised of the traditions and the great events of the past history of a group in which every member takes part and shares with others.

[9] Joseph Roucek, "Nationalism and Minority," T. V. Kalijarvi, *Modern World Politics,* New York, T. Y. Crowell, 1945, 2nd ed., pages 61-62.

(5) Religion also may be a binding force as may be observed in Eastern Europe.

(6) The temperament and character of the people may be a base.

(7) It has also been seen that great works of art, especially literature—music, stories and songs of the greatness of a people, plays about national heroes and dances—induce national solidarity.[10] Let us examine some of these in greater detail.

Strong Group Feeling

J. S. Mill in his *Representative Government* has an interesting observation to make on the first point. He says,

> A portion of mankind may be said to constitute a nationality if they are united among themselves by common sympathies which do not exist between them and any others—which make them co-operate more willingly than with other people, desire to be under the same government and desire that it should be government by themselves or a portion of themselves inclusively.[11]

Since this definition may also be true of cities, trade unions and other groups, it is necessary to add that the sentiment must be such that the group concerned considers itself a nation with national characteristics.

Race

In considering the second point, namely race as an important factor in the formation of nationalism, it should be emphasized that race cannot by itself create a new nation. Something more is needed. This is amply illustrated in Europe, where not a single pure race can be found, but where nationalism nevertheless abounds.

[10] T. V. Kalijarvi, *Modern World Politics*, New York, T. Y. Crowell, 1942, 1st ed., page 45.

[11] J. S. Mill, *Representative Government*, chapter XVI.

There are many racial mixtures in England and the Balkans, Switzerland and elsewhere in Europe. While one may attribute, for example, tallness and blond features to the Scandinavian people, one also finds many brunettes among them. Racially the French, German, and English peoples are mixtures. In spite of this, European nationalism in a very substantial measure depends upon a widespread popular belief that a nation is, or ought to be, a racial unit. This old concept goes back to primitive tribes where blood relationship was basic to tribal membership. When this racial idea is carried to its logical nationalistic conclusion it develops into the idea of master races and inferior races. Here in our own country we have not been immune to its influences because, for example, we believe that aliens are inferior to native Americans. Sometimes the concept of race goes so far as to state that war eliminates unfit races and only the fit races survive.[12]

So strong has the feeling of race become during the last decade that violent conflicts have occurred over it. We know that all Frenchmen are not temperamental, all villains are not dark foreigners, all Irishmen are not witty, nor are all Americans lovers of the almighty dollar, yet most of us act as if this were true, and out of these racial ideas emanates much modern nationalism.[13]

Language

Point three was that the possession of a common language is also basic to modern nationalism. It is closely related to the idea of racial kinship. How strong a hold the sentiment of a common language has on a nationalistic group may be seen in the claims to border lands put forth by Poland and Czechoslovakia at the end of the First World War.

[12] See Y. A. Novicow, *War and Its Alleged Benefits*, London, Heinemann, 1912, chapter 4.

[13] See H. F. K. Günther, *Rassenkunde Europas*, Munich, 1926, 2nd ed., translated by G. C. Wheeler as *The Racial Element of European History*, New York, Dutton, 1928; also T. Lothrop Stoddard, *The Rising Tide of Color*, New York, Scribner's, 1920; and Ruth Benedict, *Race: Science and Politics*, New York, Modern Age, 1940.

Men may err in the belief that a common language gives title to the area inhabited by people of the same language. It is true that the assumption is often erroneous, but that makes small difference in world politics where belief is basic to the policies and the strategies of states. Moreover the identification of language with race and thus with nationalism is a potent emotional force, whether it is correct or wrong.

As a rule uniformity of language tends to make for group solidarity while diversity of language makes for misunderstanding. Yet some states develop strong nationalism in spite of many languages. That is true of Switzerland with four languages—French, Italian, German and Romansch. Some nationalistic states like Italy have only one language while other equally nationalistic states like Finland have two or more languages. Finland has both Swedish and Finnish.

Sometimes the political program of a state within whose boundaries several languages are spoken may advocate the imposition of language uniformity on all minority groups. Examples of this were the Russification and Germanizing of subject peoples by Russia and Germany before 1914, and the present Russification of the people of Turkestan.

But while uniformity of language is often a component part of nationalism, as has been seen, it is not always essential to a strong nationalism. Most European languages are not "pure" but have been derived from vernaculars or popular spoken tongues which have been spread through the activities of the printing press. In some strongly nationalistic countries such as Norway many dialects are spoken. There are also instances of conquered people upon whom the conquering people have forced the victor tongue, yet the conquered have maintained a strong nationalism in spite of the loss of their native tongue. The Irish in spite of speaking English, have never been tied to the English by any mutual national feeling.[14]

[14] See L. Dominian, *The Nationality Map of Europe*, Boston, World Peace Foundation, 1917; also K. L. Guerrard, *Short History of the International Language Movement*, London, Unwin, 1922.

Customs, Traditions, Institutions, Ideals

Perhaps the strongest single force making for a powerful nationalism is the fourth mentioned at the outset, or community of customs, traditions, institutions and ideals. These enter a country's policies, aims, hopes, and aspirations. Such institutions are national anthems, holidays, games like baseball and cricket, costumes, and national dances. Their promotion and preservation are considered vital because they create fondness and loyalty for the State. We may not be able to determine exactly what a United States citizen means[15] when he speaks of the American way of life, but the term connotes to us American traditions, customs, ideals and institutions. Therefore it is a real force. It is not so important that the precise character of a nation's institutions shall be known, as it is that the people shall believe that there are such institutions.

Family, religion, business, law and free economic opportunity are institutions for which persumably we stand. We are aroused to indignation when alien dogmas propose to abolish them. We are strongly opposed to the institutions in other countries which are inimical to our own. This attitude is reflected in our relations with the states in which the objectional institutions are to be found.

Closely connected with a state's institutions is the memory of its people as they take pride in past wars, in heroic exploits of great leaders, in patriotic sacrifices and in national obstacles surmounted. People love to look back to bygone times and recall great events in their history. Memories are a vital part of the consciousness of a people that they belong to the State. This consciousness makes them capable of great sacrifices and holds the State together in times of crises. Institutions, memories, traditions and ideals, may be translated into policies such as American neutrality, German struggle for a place in the sun, Italian

[15] For more views on this subject see D. L. Crawford, *Can Nations Be Neighbors*, Boston, Stratford, 1932.

longing for "unredeemed" territory, British preponderance of sea power, and French determination to recover Alsace-Lorraine after 1871. These are component parts of nationalism.

Since no two groups have the same traditions and since a widespread difference in beliefs prevails in this world, national ideals are often more important to nationalism than language or race. True it is that we may encounter difficulty in determining what they may be; but in spite of this they place their individual stamps upon groups, which derive happiness because they exist.[16]

Religion

Our fifth base was religion. In some cases the racial, linguistic, traditional and institutional bases of a state's nationalism also include a religious component.[17] The racial boundary between the Poles and the Germans is also the religious boundary. One of the complaints of the Germans prior to the second World War was that Catholic Poland controlled Protestant Danzig. However, it would be possible to emphasize this matter too much as may readily be seen by noting the loyal Catholic element in the otherwise Protestant Switzerland, or by reflecting on the religious heterogeneity of the United States.

Religion may furnish a base for nationalism, but it may also transcend national frontiers as a great international force. We need only recall some of the great religions of the world and where they are to be found in order to realize their international and counter-nationalistic aspects. Many Christian creeds are spread over the world. Hinduism is found everywhere in the Far East, especially in India; so are Buddhism and Brahmanism. Confucianism is encountered in Ceylon, China, Tibet and Japan. Greek Catholicism is scattered over the Balkans. Mohammedanism is in-

[16] Here for example see D. J. Hill, *Americanism, What Is It?* New York, Appleton, 1916; G. Ohlinger, *Their True Faith and Allegiance*, New York, Macmillan, 1916; and Edward M. Hulme, *Renaissance and Reformation*, New York, Century, 1915, pages 52-53.

[17] R. A. Goslin, *Church and State*, New York, Foreign Policy Association Headline, 1937.

fluential in Africa, Asia and the Near East. These religions are not national; they are world forces. Some of the world's greatest nationalistic movements, however, have been closely intertwined with religion, for example Pan Islamism, the Pan-Arabic movement, and Christianity.

One reason why the Europeans obtained political supremacy over the world may be found in the dynamic character acquired by the Christian religion as it struggled for survival in ancient Rome, as it established its supremacy throughout Europe, as it fought for the recovery of the Holy Land during the crusades, and as it spread its missionaries everywhere. Christian missionaries in the new world, Africa, Oceania and the Far East have at once been agents of the church they represented and also powerful advance representatives of the states from which they came. History abounds with examples. There is by way of illustration the colonization of the New Hebrides Islands and the resulting quarrel between the missionaries of France and of England for control of the islands.

Religion then plays an important part both in nationalism and in world politics, as it did in medieval times. British, Russian, French, German and American leaders call upon God to help them in their fight upon each other. The rôle of the Roman Catholic church in the Spanish Civil War of 1936-1939 is still a fresh memory. Mussolini used the church to forward his program, and he could not succeed without its friendship. The struggle of the Roman Catholic Church in Mexico—the Papal Encyclical *Acerba Animi of* Setember 29, 1931; the expulsion of the papal legate Ruiz y Flores by the Mexican Chamber of Deputies as "a pernicious foreigner," these indicate that religion as a force in world politics is far from dead. And, if we look back to the 16th and 17th centuries we shall find the Anglican church of England, the Presbyterian church of Scotland, the Dutch Reform church of the Netherlands, the Lutheran church of Germany were all strong forces in the creation of the nationalisms of those states. At the same time they stimulated increased nationalism in Catholic countries.

How the religious factor has been injected into nationalistic ideals may be seen in the Irish Catholic opposition to English Protestantism. But the close tie between religion and nationalism today may also be seen in Japanese Shintoism, Jewish Zionism, and the Islamic Holy War.

But even in countries where religion seems so closely allied with nationalism there may be lack of religious uniformity. Irish Protestants in many instances have found no trouble in joining Irish Catholics in the fight upon England. Anti-Semitism is generally condemned and the Ku Klux Klan is in bad standing in the public opinion of the United States. Thus while religion does form an influential part of nationalism, a common religion is by no means an indispensable condition of nationalism.[18]

Geography

Geography may play a strong part in nationalistic sentiment. Even though different races at different times have developed different cultures in the same localities, there is little doubt that humans are moulded by geographical and climatic conditions. In this sense geography may be fundamental to nationalism. This is especially true if a group is subject to geographic isolation, in which case their nationalism may become strong by feeding upon itself. It may be true that the world is not divided into geographic units identical in nature, and that geographical boundaries are often purely artificial, yet, as Burns correctly says,

> One family differs in blood from another, and as the group we call a nation is a more or less permanent association of families, we may suppose that one nation differs from another. National surroundings, climate, and the resources of the country soon make considerable differences in any settled state of society, although their influences are somewhat exaggerated by such writers as Bluntschli.[19]

[18] F. Matthews, *Patriotism and Religion,* New York, Macmillan, 1918.
[19] *Supra cit.,* page 176.

Influence of Man on Man

When an individual belongs to a group possessing a particular type of nationalism he usually adopts the belief of his group. The crowd mind, overemphasized by Le Bon in France, or the soul of a people, overemphasized by Bauemler in Germany, places its stamp on the ideals and the nationalism of a group. It does not take long for the individual to absorb the ideas growing out of the tradition and the background which go into the making of nationalistic ideals.[20]

History

Most nationalisms have historical objectives. For instance the historians, particularly of the nineteenth century, Treitschke, von Sybel, Macaulay, Seely, Michelet, Palacky and Bancroft, contributed to the love of fatherland. They sang the praises of their countries and reveled in past glories. Battles, wars, heroes, great statesmen, enter into the making of greater pride in national unity and feeling. Historically, too, the hatred of another country may constitute a bond among the hating people. The Irish are held more closely together because of their feelings against the English; the French are closer to each other because of their antipathy for the Germans and the Baltic people are more united because of fear of the Russians. The soul of many national aspirations is historical.[21]

Economics

While nationalism, as a rule, is emotional, it may have an economic aspect. The desire to expand territory, to acquire economic self-sufficiency, to promote the business interests of its citi-

[20] Gustave LeBon, *The Psychology of People*, London, Unwin, 1899), also W. McDougall, *Social Psychology*, Boston, Luce & Co., 1916, Section 2, chapter 10, "The Operation of the Primary Tendencies of the Human Mind in the Life of Society."

[21] A. Guilland, *Modern Germany and Her Historians*, London, Jerrold & Son, 1915.

zens will often lead a state to bolster its economy through subsidies, protection of investments abroad, use of its consular service as an advance economic agency, and support of private business enterprises abroad. These economic appeals to patriotic citizens are so closely related to nationalism as to be inseparable from it. One of the components of modern nationalism consists of dynamic search for raw materials. This struggle is supported by the group. Cecil Rhodes was the advance agent of British imperialism which was the nationalistic expression of England at the time of Disraeli through the latter nineteenth century.[22]

Political Doctrines and Ideologies

During the last generation conflicting ideologies and warring political doctrines have entered more potently than ever into European nationalisms. They challenge the early revolutionary democratic nationalism which went on the assumption that the wishes of the people were being served by government even though the people themselves might not always have the opportunity to voice their views. Democratic allegiance had gradually come to depend upon choice; but the newer ideologies now determine allegiance by birth, not choice, thus giving voice to a patriotism much older than modern democracy. Today, democratic nationalism has to share its hold on the people of the world with Communistic and Fascistic ideologies, which contradict democracy.

Obviously these conflicting ideologies raise conflicting sentiments and ideals, and since they constitute basic parts of European nationalisms these latter will inevitably conflict in so far as they reflect political ideologies.

Propaganda

While itself an instrument for spreading sentiment and beliefs, propaganda must be considered a component part of nationalism.

[22] See R. G. Hawtre, *The Economic Aspects of Sovereignty*, Boston, Longmans, Green, 1930; also, *Strategic and Critical Raw Material*, Army Services Manual M104, Washington, D. C., Government Printing Office, January 15, 1944).

In many instances it not only articulates beliefs but it spreads them and is in its own right a means of popular education and a device for the teaching of patriotism. A moment's reflection will show that the press, the moving pictures, the radio, and other instruments of public opinion are potent factors in arousing and spreading national sentiments. Patriotic societies, military groups, political leaders, spokesmen on nationalism arouse the emotions which make nationalism.[23]

War

Nationalism finds its most powerful expression during wars, since nationalistic forces are easily stimulated in times of danger. Indeed the world seems to be caught in an endless cycle in which nationalism leads to war and war to nationalism. Look at some of the causes of war, if there is any doubt on the point. There are wars for independence, self-determination, irredentism, imperialism, economic growth, protection of citizens abroad, in defense of national honor, and as a basis of militarism and navalism. While most nations theoretically are opposed to aggressive wars, they are willing to fight a war in self-defense, and self-defense comes pretty close to being nationalism. As a rule states in their own eyes only fight wars of self-defense. Seldom do we see any state admitting that it is an aggressor. Thus current wars are nationalistic struggles.

II.

HISTORICAL ORIGIN

Beginnings

The sentiment of nationalism, which now dominates states, is essentially a modern development. It has no exact counterpart

[23] *Modern World Politics, Supra cit.*, 2nd ed., chapters I and XVI.

in the past except perhaps the loyalty of the Greeks to their city state. However the roots go back even farther than Greece to primitive times when group was separated from group and each acquired its own characteristics, moulded by environment and experience, and reflected in racial, linguistic, and religious group unity.[24]

Ancient Greece

In Ancient Greece this group unity took on distinct political form as loyalty to the city state. Geography was responsible. The mountainous area of the small Greek peninsula made it possible for the many small city states to develop their own individual institutions and sentiments. The Athenians loved Athens; the Spartans were loyal to Sparta; and every city state had its own particular allegiance and loyalty which was rendered by its subjects. It was an international world of small Greek states with its own international law, nationalisms, imperialisms, and diversity of culture, language, and institutions.[25]

Rome

When Rome succeeded Greece as mistress of the Western World the Roman institutions were well advanced. Originally they had had much in common with the Greek and the Italian peninsula was dotted with small city states, each with its own institutions like those of its Greek prototype. But Rome early in its history achieved a single state unified by common experience. With unification, city-state particularism and loyalty disappeared. In their place came a world empire based on the idea of a single universal empire. Thus, as Rome became a world state, the earlier narrow Roman nationalism gave way to ideals of univer-

[24] Burns, *Political Ideals,* chapter 8.

[25] W. A. Dunning, *Political Theories, Ancient and Medieval,* New York, Macmillan, 1902, being vol. 1, chapters I-IV.

sality and the concept of nationalism slumbered for several hundred years.[26]

Middle Ages

The Middle Ages continued to be unpropitious for a revival of nationalism. The Roman concept of a universal empire was joined with the idea of a universal religion; and consequently nationalism had no place in the scheme of things. There were occasions such as that of the appearance of the Franks, when common traditions and diversity of languages encouraged group diversification; but these were not sufficiently strong to revive nationalism. Even Charlemagne received his title of Emperor from the church. The idea of a universal state did not yield room for the national state and its outgrowth—nationalism—until the Renaissance. Not until the One Hundred Years War did national feeling become evident. The great instance of loyalty during the Medieval Ages sung by the bards of that time was the *Song of Roland,* in which it is told that Roland laid down his life at Roncevaux in 778 to cover Charlemagne's withdrawal from Spain. But Roland did not lay down his life for a Frankist state but for Charlemagne himself to whom he owed personal loyalty.[27]

Revival[28]

The end of medieval universalisms came gradually as the result of many forces which tended to break Europe into states rather than nations. The control over the world which had hitherto been vested in the Papacy and the Empire began to dissolve. Heresies and Protestantism, mingled with racial confusion, separated group from group. The people of Wessex and Northumbria became

[26] R. H. Murray, *The History of Political Science from Plato to the Present,* New York, Appleton, 1926), chapter II.

[27] W. A. Dunning, *Political Theories,* vol. 1, chapters V-X.

[28] E. M. Hulme, *Renaissance and Reformation,* New York, Century, 1915, chapter 3.

Englishmen. The Normans became Frenchmen. The Catalonians became Spaniards. Everywhere the rising royal power, which grew strong at the time of the Renaissance, challenged the idea of a universal empire. Vernacular languages replaced the universal Latin. The new despotism challenged the old social order.

It was in France that modern nationalism first made its appearance with the advent of the national state. The historic instance occurred when the French people arose to support their King Phillip the Fair, in his struggle against Pope Boniface the VIII. Here, for the first time in hundreds of years, a people rallied to their king as against the universalism represented in the Papacy. The French people defied Papal excommunication and won. Then came the One Hundred Years War and the leadership of Jeanne d'Arc which produced a stronger French state and the first national France in history. Similar trends occurred in England, where King Edward I, whose reign began in 1272, gave unmistakable proof of a preference of English people for English customs. Scotland, in the struggles of Wallace and Bruce for independence, Bohemia, in the struggles of the Hussite Movement, Spain, in her fight against the Arabs, and in the union of Castile and Aragon wrote finis to the Medieval idea of a universal lordship, to the Holy Roman Empire. Simultaneously they bespoke a welcome to the new national state and to the new national monarch. The Reformation following the Renaissance succeeded in centralizing the administration of law and enhanced royal prestige which grew stronger as it emphasized the peculiarity of national institutions and languages and thus of the new nation states. Herein lay the broad beginnings of modern nationalism.

The old Roman world had marked Europe between the fourth and fourteenth centuries with the idea of unity. When it went to pieces the New Europe was made up of several nation states tied together into a family of nations and regulated by a philosophical international law. As nations responded to the call of nationality and as slumbering national consciousness awoke, many states could achieve national statehood through national revolutions.

Benevolent Despots[29]

As the new nationalism took its expression in popular support of the king usually as against efforts to enforce religious uniformity, the new nationalism was closely tied into religious conflict. After the Peace of Augsburg of 1555 and the acknowledgement of *Cujus regio ejus religio*, it was the ruler who determined the religion of a state. But that did not mean that the ruler might choose the religion of his people capriciously. He could do so only in conformity with their wishes. Henry VIII would never have succeeded in breaking away from the Catholic Church if the English people had not been ready for him to do so. Henry's move bore clear testimony to the new-born English nationalism which rejected any universal hold upon England of either the Church or the Empire. And so it was with Queen Elizabeth of England, Catherine de Medici, and the other rulers of the time. When they spoke as the so-called benevolent despots, they did so because they voiced the wishes of their people. The nationalism of the time expressed itself through the rulers.

The Age of Revolution

This was true until the latter half of the eighteenth century when the despot had outlived his usefulness. By that time the ruler had grown away from his people until he no longer embodied their national aims, ambitions, and longings. The efforts of the people to express themselves took the form of throwing off the yoke of benevolent despotism. National longings were identified with democratic institutions attainable only by revolution, such as the American Revolution and the French Revolutions. Through these

[29] W. A. Dunning, *Political Theories, from Luther to Montesquieu*, vol. 2.

the people gave voice to their wishes, beliefs and sentiments; and the people justified the revolutions as means of achieving national ambitions and satisfying the sentiment of the group. Popular participation in government and the acknowledged responsibility of government to the people became the heart of all democratic nationalism.

Napoleon

These sentiments did not end with the establishment of democratic government. A direct outgrowth of French revolutionary nationalism was the imperialism of Napoleon. Its evolution was clear. When France was menaced from the outside the French people rallied to throw out the invaders, and on the surge of this emotion came the first instance of the nation in arms. The enemies of France were defeated. But the sentiment was so strong that Napoleon easily won leadership of the French armies which he led from one conquest to another. These conquests only aroused counter nationalisms in England, Germany, Italy, Spain and Russia. Democracy, constitutionalism and internationalism were increased in intensity by the newborn democratic nationalism which began its great sweep, that sweep in the midst of which we still find ourselves today.

Nineteenth Century

Even the reaction of Metternich's times only served to intensify the new nationalism in central Europe. The need for national self-expression aroused Belgium to revolt in 1830, the German states to struggle for national unity between 1813 and 1871, Italy to seek liberation and unification between 1869 and 1871. Underneath the surface smoldered Polish, Finnish, Lithuanian, Czech, Roumanian, Bulgarian, and Greek desires for freedom and independence as well as those of many other nationalities .They only awaited the proper moment to burst the bonds which held them.

Twentieth Century

Most of the Balkan states secured their independence early in the twentieth century as a result of burning nationalisms. At the end of the First World War a number of smoldering nationalisms flared up in new states; Poland, Czechoslovakia, Hungary, Finland, Estonia, Latvia, Lithuania, Yugoslavia, and Ireland. Meanwhile Irredentism flourished in Alsace-Lorraine, Moresnet, Malmedy, Eupen, Schleswig, the Saar Basin, Danzig, Upper Silesia, Teschen, Memel, Transylvania, Macedonia, Thrace, Dobrudja, Epirus, the Dodocanese Islands and in other spots in Europe. Thus while the Peace Conference at Paris was an effort to rationalize and settle the nationalistic conflict, it was to no avail.

From the First World to the Second World War and After

By 1917 Communism had taken hold of Russia and had begun its campaign of anti-liberal nationalism. To this Germany replied with National Socialism and Italy with Fascism. Suddenly all along the line democratic nationalism was challenged by anti-liberal and totalitarian nationalism of different varieties and intensities.

During the Second World War nationalistic ideologies were used by all parties. Under the guise of a struggle for peace and the solution of the nationalistic conflict all parties advocated a new world order in which uniformity of national ideologies was the key. The world was thrown into an even more intense conflict of nationalism than it had ever experienced before. The war destroyed the League of Nations and substituted for it a United Nations Organization dominated by nationalistic thinking. The war did not end nationalism nor did it bring universal peace. All it did was to eliminate Germany, Italy and France from the roles of powerful world states. Russia was as nationalistic as ever. So were Britain, and the United States. New irredentas were created by Russia as she absorbed the Baltic states. Millions of people were shifted from one state to another in hopes of eliminating future irredentas, but this only created new ones. As Europe had once risen to destroy Napoleon, she had risen with the aid of the United States to destroy Hitler. But there it ended, for nationalism was more than ever a willing dynamic force whose propagation continued to be one of the most potent sources of international dispute. It unified the states and caused them to nationalize foreigners within their borders. If the foreigners could not be nationalized the practice was established of driving the foreigners over the border. The newest nationalism disrupted existing states and created new ones. It shattered colonial empires and created others in their stead. It was an inducement to the revolt of people held in colonial and political subjugation and underlay the principle of self-determination and the struggles of minorities with irredentist yearnings.

Not a Simple Form

Thus it will be seen in its historical aspects and from a study of its component parts that nationalism is a sentiment which differs from state to state. It is one of the most complex social and political forces of our times.

III.

MINORITIES, IRREDENTISM AND NATIONAL SELF-DETERMINATION

Majority-Minority Relationships

One of the main problems of nationalism is the majority-minority relationships. These take two forms principally: (1) the struggle of national minorities for self-expression and self determination, (2) the efforts of the majority to control the national minorities within the group. Sometimes as in the case of the Magyar in the 1914 Hungarian Empire, a powerful minority may be able to control a large majority in a national state. Professor Roucek has said; "A lack of national unity is always productive of tension." This generally leads, as in the cases of Poland, Yugoslavia and Greece and other countries of Central-Eastern Europe between 1920 and 1935, to efforts of one group of nationalists to impose their exclusive views upon other groups within the state. Thus a controlling or ruling group may impose its will and sentiments upon other groups, with the result that anyone who stands in opposition to the views presented is usually branded as a traitor or outsider.

While the majority can impose its views by a resort to power, the national minorities may live within the state intermingled with other minorities as do the border people in present Russia; or minorities, when they form compact blocks or islands of population, may rule a part of the state, as do the Jews in Palestine; or they may remain unabsorbed by a surrounding people as in the case of the Welsh in England; they may be intermingled with the general population as are the immigrants in the United States; or they may be lost in a larger state because they lack sufficient numbers in which case they may create fifth columnists or belong to groups of refugees. The views of such groups always constitute a potential force if not an actual one in the state.[30]

Irredentism

Irredentism is a broad term for the desires of one country to include within its borders the so-called "unredeemed" minorities of its own nationalism located in another country. A host of illustrations immediately rise to mind, such as the Poles in Russia,

[30] Robert E. Park, "Views on the Power of the Press," *American Journal of Sociology*, vol. 47, no. 1 (July, 1941), pages 1-11; G. Borsky and others, *Enemy Within*, New York, Hutchinson, 1943; and Francis J. Brown and Joseph S. Roucek, *One America; Our Racial and National Minorities*, New York; Prentice-Hall, 1945.

the Lithuanians in Poland, the Hungarians in Transylvania, the Yugoslavs in Austria-Hungary, the Greeks in Turkey, and the Italians in Dalmatia. The arguments used by states to support their claims for the reincorporation of irredentas run the entire gamut of nationalistic arguments, including language, race, history, economics, religion, historical boundaries, geography, strategic frontiers, and popular desires. Obviously it is and will always be impossible to draw European frontiers so as to eliminate all irredentas. Moreover the irredentist claims are woefully inconsistent one with the other. Some European irredentas can be settled only by creating new ones.

Problem of Minorities

National minorities always constitute a problem. A discontented minority always has its own nationalism which conflicts with the nationalism of the majority group, and therefore that minority is always a danger to the security of the major powers. Such minorities are by no means helpless. They may seek help from their co-nationals in other states, as the Sudeten Germans did before the Second World War, when they appealed to Germany for help. They may secure privileges from the majority group as did the Catalans in Spain before Franco, or they may succeed in bringing about a complete separation of their territory from the major group as the Memellanders succeeded in breaking away from Lithuania before the Second World War. The demands of these minorities are ceaseless and ultimately lead to majority-minority conflicts.[31]

Examples of such conflicts are numerous. A few selected at random arose over Poland, Northern Schleswig, Alsace-Lorraine, the Polish Corridor, and over the Russian subject peoples, especially the Poles, Lithuanians, Estonians, Ukrainians, and Armenians. Violent conflicts arose over the Magyarization policies of the Hungarian government before 1914 as they were applied to

[31] *Royal Institute of International Affairs, Nationalism,* pages 283-295.

the Rumanians, Slovaks, and Yugoslavs. Contemporary instances are the efforts of the Jewish minority to take over control of Palestine and the emancipation of the Poles, Czechoslovaks, and Yugoslavs. The list is far too long to exhaust here. In our own country we have the unassimilated Japanese and Negro.

Practices of the Majority and their Relations With the Minority

There are three principal ways in which the majority ordinarily deals with minority problems; (1) coercion whereby the majority will is imposed on the minority; (2) discrimination whereby the minorities are permitted to carry on their function but under disadvantages as compared with the majority, thus having inferior schools, special institutions and labor rights; and (3) toleration and equality, whereby the dominant nationality accords equality to the minority as is characteristic of the United States.

When substantial minorities exist within a state and when they achieve a unity of their own, it is almost impossible for the majority group to assimilate them. When assimilation does take place, it can do so only over a long period of time.

Recent international efforts to solve the problems of the minorities, especially through the League minority agreements, have not been very successful. Today expulsion, massacre and economic attrition are resorted to by some states to eliminate their minority problems. Over half the people of Europe have been subjected to these procedures at one time or another during the last ten years. All in all there has been a reversion to the more primitive and drastic methods of enforcing group will upon recalcitrant minorities.

NATIONALISM IN THEORY AND IN LITERATURE

If we are to understand this century's political ideals we cannot escape a backward look to Fichte's *Addresses to the German Na-*

tion which reflect a clear understanding of national character as a force in history, and to Görres' *Germany and the Revolution,* which sets forth nationalism in its democratic form. Mills' *Representative Government* and Renan's *Qu'est-ce qu'une Nation* contained a popular appeal combined with tradition, and Mazzini's *Duties of Man* made clear that a united Italy could only grow out of the Italian people themselves. Mazzini gave the best expression possible to modern nationalism. And he concludes that a nation is great not with reference to its size and territory but according to the ideals for which it stands. A country is not territory; it is an idea from which the country takes its birth. Thus ideological struggles are not philosophical quarrels but wars to the death. The sentiment of nationalism is the state itself.

The State as a Sovereign[32]

One of the basic theories of the present time, which runs back into the 19th century, is that a state is a sovereign person. This is a German idea which hies back to Hegel, and it is still the basis upon which most of Europe operates. Princes and governments are the instruments of the people and the state grows through the self-consciousness of the people. Schleiermacher advanced the idea a step further than Hegel; so did Bluntschli. To their views must be added those of the Historical School of German political scientists including Dahlmann, Georg Waitz, and F. J. Stahl. To them the state was the people in all their physical and spiritual personality. The views, wishes, and sentiments of the group determined the type of government and the program of a country.

Nations as a Unit of Race and Language[33]

Another school of political scientists believes that the nation constitutes a unit of race and language. The last state of this

[32] W. A. Dunning, *Political Theories, from Rouuseau to Spencer*, pp. 299-311.

[33] H. F. Gunther, *The Racial Elements of European History*, New York, Dutton, 1928.

doctrine or its *ultima ratio* may be seen in the National Socialist program of Germany with its *Rassenseele* and *Blut und Boden.* This doctrine, however, is not new. Its beginnings are to be found in the systematic and powerful writings of Fichte, again in the *Addresses to the German Nation.* One of Fichte's successors, Savigny, asserted that the nation is a manifestation of a social aggregate or of a group of people which takes its character from the role it plays in the scheme of universal existence. Both believed that it was character which made one nation superior to another. Purity of race and language were important determiners of national greatness. However, it was the inner urgings of people which marked the basic differences among them and consequently the differences in their nationalism.

Nation as a Geographic Unit

Still another theory, which goes farther back in history than the previous one, is that the nation constitutes a geographic unit. This is excellently put forth in Edmund Burke's *Appeal from the New to the Old Whigs* when he said his country was not only the physical locality in which he lived, but all the institutions with which he had been born. The same idea was held by Schleiermacher; likewise by Hegel in his *Philosophy of History.* As the science of geography grew Humboldt and Ritter combined ethnology, philology, and anthropology with geography. Sociology was brought to bear upon geography as the basis of national individuality and national characteristics. A more scientific basis for nationalism had been found. And today the last step in this evolution is the appearance of geopolitics.

Nation and Nationality

As nationalisms grew and theories of national greatness abounded, Jeremy Bentham, Cornwall, Lewis, Austin and others attempted to distinguish between nation, people and state. Some of their distinctions are still in use. The Swiss Bluntschli defined a nation as

> masses of men of different occupations and social strata in a hereditary society of common spirit, feeling and race, bound together especially by language and customs in a common civilization which gives them a sense of unity and distinction from all foreigners, quite apart from the bond of the state.

Like Hegel and Fichte he adopted the state of mind as the ultimate factor in nationalism. He also distinguished a people in this sense from the people in the political sense, and thus he gave a clear background for the distinction between, for example, the German state and the German people.

The National State[34]

But in spite of these efforts the distinction between state and nation was not clear. As far back as Thomas Hobbes the Utilitarian theorists had held that nationality and political independence were inseparable. Nationalism was the striving for freedom and self-expression by a people. Much of the same idea might be found in the thinking of the American John C. Calhoun and in his *Disquisition on Government.*

In the second half of the nineteenth century nationalism in Germany, Italy and the United States took the form of struggles for freedom and independence. These struggles determined the nationalistic philosophies of the countries in question. In Italy the objectives were freedom and independence. In Germany the striving was for unification expressed in common race, language, and geography. Elsewhere nationalisms evolved about struggles for freedom from Napoleonic control, about efforts to unify Germany

[34] See Mazzini's *Essays* as translated by Okey.

under Prussia, about the search for independence from Austrian rule and about the war waged incessantly by the Balkan states against the Turks.

Renan observed all this, and found the soul of a people first in its common heritage of memories, of sacrifices and suffering, and secondly, in the desires of individuals to live together and to receive the transmitted heritage.

The nationalism of the twentieth century is only the nationalism of the nineteenth century. With the latter as background, D'Annunzio sang the Italian people into World War I and into the seizure of Fiume. He revelled in the past glory of Rome, preached the Italian occupation of the Irredentist areas in 1910 while Italians formed national associations and while in 1915 Italian nationalists formed a political party which won six seats in Parliament. The Irredentist movement as applied to Trentino and Trieste became a code of Italian nationalism. In 1915 the Italian people demanded these areas in the London Treaty and succeeded in securing a promise that they would be granted to Italy. This nationalistic code was all ready for Mussolini to put into action, a code supported by four million people. It was both intensely nationalistic and openly imperialistic and it reached its height when on November 30, 1938 Farinacci in the Chamber of Deputies demanded the return to Italy from France of Corsica, Tunis, and Nice.

SCHOOLS OF NATIONALISMS[36]

Humanitarian Nationalism

The nationalism of our day in its theoretical aspects can be divided into schools, which run back one hundred fifty years or more. According to the eighteenth century "enlightment," na-

[35] C. J. H. Hayes, *The Historical Evolution of Modern Nationalism*, New York, Richard Smith, 1931. This is the standard treatise of the whole subject.

tural law was substituted for supernatural forces, and science for theology in the belief that the whole universe of matter and mind is guided and controlled by natural law. Into this enlightened humanitarianism were injected new ideas. The role of government, was to do good and to correspond with the spirit of a people, giving voice to their special genius. The principal exponent of this doctrine, Bolingbroke, who in his *On the Spirit of Patriotism* and in *The Idea of a Patriotic King*, did not use the word nationalism, but spoke and discussed "the spirit of particular nationalities." He found in the British a special genius for constitutional government with guarantees for British liberties. His nationalism was both political and aristocratic.

J. J. Rosseau in his *Le Contrat Social* pointed out that people might be distinguished into cultural nationalities, and that only people, who share a community of language, customs, and historic tradition, can be distinguished from other people. In his *Considération sur le Gouvernement de Pologne* he stated that it is the national institution which forms the genius, the character, the tastes and the customs of a people, which make one people and fail to make another, which inspire the ardent love of country founded on habits and customs impossible to trace back to their sources. It was Herder who said of the national soul that,

> As a mineral water derives its components parts, its operative powers, and its flavor from the soil from which it flows, so the ancient character of peoples arose from the family features, the climate, the way of life and education, the early actions and employments that were peculiar to them.

"The most natural state is one people with one national character."

At the end of the eighteenth century it might be pointed out that theories of nationalism had reached the point where they could be divided into (1) aristocratic, (2) democratic and (3) neither. Democratic nationalism became Jacobin. Aristocratic nationalism became traditional; while the nationalism which was neither democratic nor aristocratic became "liberal."

Thus out of the enlightened eighteenth century came the decapitation of the French king, and there arose the French cries of liberty, equality and fraternity, the composition and singing of the *Marseillaise,* and there emerged a new French national ferver, which infected all Europe. The evolution of nationalism from that day to this has been constant and uninterrupted.

Jacobin Nationalism

Jacobin nationalism took its beginnings in the theory of humanitarian democratic nationalism of Rousseau. It took its impetus from the Girondist and other apostles of Republicanism during the French Revolution. And as the French people in 1792, went to war against the invaders of their country they were fighting a new kind of war to make the world safe for democracy and for French nationalism. It was not a war between dynasts, but between the French and other peoples, and between French despots and the French people. The French

> national assembly proclaims that the French nation is faithful to the principle consecrated by its constitution, not to undertake any war with a view to conquest nor ever to employ its forces against the liberty of any people. It only takes the vows for the maintenance of its own liberty and independence that the war which it is forced to prosecute is not a war of nation against nation, but the just defense of a free people against the unjust aggression of a king; that the French nation never confuses its brethren with its real enemy and it will favor all foreigners who adjure the cause of the enemy. It will try to reduce the curse of war.

The Mountainist group were forceful nationalists, who under the guidance of Barere stirred the French people to hate their enemies and distrust leaders. The Dantonists spoke of patriotic "audacity" in the face of foreign and domestic enemies. The Hebertists were fanatically anti-Christian, devoted to the religion of reason, and imbued with ideas of nationalistic terrorism.

Jacobin theory was clear where Rousseau was vague. The theory of the French revolution and its attendant terror set the pattern for the twentieth century nationalisms of Russian Communism, Fascism, and National Socialism. Jacobin nationalism was suspicious and intolerant of internal dissent. It favored rooting out and destroying factions suspected of liking a free world. It became fanatically religious and adopted symbols and ceremonies which played up the national flag, the national anthem, national holidays, national shrines, liberty caps, altars to the state, tablets of national laws, public baptisms and funerals, and solemn parades and eulogies.

Barere said, "In France the soldier is a citizen and the citizen a soldier." Thus Jacobinism was the prototype for the later national conscript armies, public schools, public instruction, controlled journalism, and lip service to freedom. "La Patrie" was God in the Jacobin hearts. When Napoleon used the ideas of a nation in arms, the nation in school, and censored newspapers, he was following Jacobin nationalistic theory. French newspapers never mentioned his defeat at Trafalgar so long as Bonaparte was in power. Barere was his minister of propaganda against the English. Napoleon capped the Jacobin patriotic societies with the famous Legion of Honor.

Traditional Nationalism

Traditional nationalism, whose theory was evolved by Edmund Burke was occasioned in part by the latter's revolt at the excesses of the French Revolution. The Traditionalists believed that nationality and the state had just evolved, and it was idle to discuss how they began—perhaps by contract. The state was no mere partnership to be made or suddenly dissolved at pleasure. It was a partnership not only between those who are living but between those who are living and those who are dead and those who are to be born. The people, the nationality, were not distinct from their government and they had no right to break the social tie which linked them to their forefathers. Burke's nationalism glorified the aristocrats, flaunted the genius of the English lords, feared the despotism of the multitudes, and believed in loyalty to family, locality, and region.

In France, the Vicomte de Bonald held with Burke. In Germany, Friedrich von Schlegel was of the same theory.

If traditional nationalism opposed Jacobinism it was no less warlike. It was the motive force of the growing resistance on the Continent as exemplified in the nationalistic awakenings in Germany, Holland, Portugal, Spain and Russia. If Napoleon Bonaparte and his marshals were the product of Jacobin nationalism, then the Traditional nationalism flowered in Castlereagh, Nelson, Wellington, Archduke Charles and Alexander—and the battle of Waterloo was a battle between Jacobinism and Traditionalism, and of course it ended in a victory for Traditional nationalism.

Liberal Nationalism

After 1815, particularly under the reaction of Prince Metternich and originally spurred by Czar Alexander of Russia, Liberal nationalism came into being. It stood midway between Jacobinism and Traditionalism, and was originated in England by Jeremy Bentham in his *Fragment of Government.* The theory was that states should respect economic liberty, freedom of the individual to engage in any profession or industry, to enter any contract at will with the employer or employee, and to trade with whomsoever he would. The worst thing in international relations was war and every effort ought to be made to eliminate it. It was logical for him to advocate a program of universal peace. This included a world organization, disarmament, and an international court.

His internationalism spread to Germany where Humboldt and Baron Stein became strong proponents. In France, François Guizot upheld it. Perhaps nowhere was Liberal nationalism more forcefully enunciated than by Theodore Welcker in Germany.

But it was Guiseppe Mazzini in Italy who gave the final wording to this type of nationalism. "God and the People," was the motto of his young Italy. In his *Autobiography*, in the *Essays on Duties of Man*, in *Nationality* and in *Faith and the Future*, he declared that French Jacobinism failed because it stressed the rights and not the duties of man. The French Revolution was selfish; its rights having begun in the declaration of man it could only end in man. The man was Napoleon. In contrast with this he emphasized that the nation was a God-appointed instrument charged with the welfare of the human race. Fatherlands were the workshops of humanity. The state must educate and train its members in the light of moral law, and it must arrange and direct its activities in behalf of humanity at large. Nationalism is what God has prescribed to each people in the work of humanity.

A number of liberal nationalists were Garibaldi, Cavour, Gagern, Schmerling, Lasker, Michelet, Victor Hugo, Casimir-Perier, Ledru-Rollin, Austin, Grote, Francis Place, John Mill, Korais, Bluntschli, Kossuth, Palacky, and Daniel O'Connell.

In general, Liberal nationalism stood for an independent constitutional government to end despotism, aristocracy, and ecclesiastical influence, and thus assure every citizen that through its exercise personal liberty would be achieved. Each state will serve its true interest by following national policies of free trade, anti-militarism, anti-imperialism and international cooperation. Some even went so far as to justify intervention in the affairs of foreign countries in order to free people from the despotism of alien oppression. Liberal nationalism survived the World War of 1914-1918, and it was against this Liberal nationalism that Communism, Fascism, and National Socialism were fighting regardless of the sides the belligerents happened to be on. But before our own day Liberal nationalism had already given birth to a new type of nationalism: namely, integral nationalism.

Integral Nationalism

Integral nationalism was a term applied by Charles Maurras to designate the nationalistic doctrine of his small and hysterical political body in France.[36]

It also indicates certain significant elements in Italian Fascism, in Russian Bolshevism, and in German National Socialism as well as doctrines held by many other national groups not addicted to the theory. Maurras defined nationalism as

> the exclusive pursuit of national policies, the absolute maintenance of national integrity and the steady increase of national power, for a nation declines when it loses military might.

Maurras is not so much interested in the oppressed or the subject nationalities, but rather in the nationalities who have already gained their political unity and independence. This type of nationalism was hostile to the internationalism preached by the humanitarians and the liberals. It made the nation not a means to humanity and not a stepping stone to a new world order but an end in itself. It put national interests above those of the individual and above humanity. It refused cooperation with other nations except as such cooperation might serve a nation's own interests. Obviously it became the instrument of jingoists, of militarists and of imperialists. In domestic affairs it was highly illiberal and tyrannical because all citizens must conform to a common standard of manners and morals and share the same unreasoning enthusiasm for it. They must subordinate all personal liberties to its own purpose, and if the common people should murmur it would abridge democracy and gag it in the name of national interests.

That is the course much nationalism has taken during the twen-

[36] See his *Action Française.*

tieth century. Integral nationalism as seen in Russia today began as an economic and social reform with loud protestation against militarism, imperialism and nationalism. As it discovered that the nations of the world were not ready for its "Messianic mission," it ended by converting its own peculiar brand of integrated nationalism into a nationalism of the Union of Soviet Socialist Republics. This was used as the basis for an unreasoning enthusiasm of the masses to see the world plotting their overthrow. Integral nationalism is similarly to be observed in the pre-Second World War dictatorships in Hungary, Poland, Turkey, and Yugoslavia. And of course the arch example of the time was the National Socialist party in Germany and its doctrines supporting Adolph Hitler, the Fuehrer.

Theorists of the Integral nationalism look back to August Comte, the founder of positivism and the founder of sociology. Comte, while not a nationalist, repudiated Rousseau and Jacobin doctrinaires. He based his political organization not on metaphysical concepts like the general will, but on the positive fact of force, material force, as a permanently dominating thing. Government is power, essentially material, arising from rank and wealth. Force is essential to every human society. Similarly H. Adolphe Taine, a misanthrope, defended aristocracy, monarchy and religionalism. He believed with Schlegel that race is fundamental to a nation, but like Schlegel confused races and linguistic groups. Also, Barres, a precocious youth, spoke of the honor of "la Patrie"

> as embodied in the marching ranks of a regiment; all the military fanfares carry us back to the conquered soil; the waving of the flag seems to us a distant signal to the exiled; our fists clench, and we have only to make ourselves provocative agents.

He had nothing but veneration for Taine and Renan.

Thus had the ideas and theories of the last two centuries changed from a praise of man to the enhancement of national egotism. In the place of Bentham's Utilitarianism the world had developed the flaming oratory of D'Annunzio, and the impassioned pleas of Hitler. As Bolingbroke had once spoken of the genius of British aristocracy so Mussolini spoke of the grandeur of Rome.

OUTGROWTH AND CONTRADICTIONS

Imperialism

The natural outgrowth of modern nationalism and one which seems to be a contradiction of nationalism is imperialism. The logical conclusion of nationalism is that there shall be territory for each national group with an independent existence for the group therein. However, as we have seen, the tendency as a state grows is to seek to include within the state the greatest possible number of people. To make a state strong it requires territory, security, people, raw materials, economic resources and other objects of imperialism. The belief soon develops that a great state is of necessity a large state which possesses a large territory and has a large population. Inevitably minority groups will be absorbed in its people. Thus modern imperialism is the logical result of nationalism.

Internationalism

So too it is with current internationalism. The conflict of group with group and the division of the world into national states has given rise to the idea of the family of nations and a law governing the relations of the members of that family one with the other. It is obvious that current nationalism is both the cause and the result of wars. If it is to be curbed, it is logical to think of doing so by a superior force or power above the national state. Thus by a super-national or international force a more peaceful world will be created. Thus internationalism is the logical outgrowth of an effort to control the unbridled nationalistic states in their struggle for power.

Pacifism

In many ways pacifism is likewise the outgrowth of national strivings and yearnings. It is observed that nationalism leads to war. Peace can be achieved only through the elimination of war and thus the struggle for peace inevitably is a struggle either to control and subordinate nationalism or to eliminate it as an active force.

NATIONALISM OF THE TWENTIETH CENTURY[37]

A Surging Movement

The sentiment of nationalism is one of the greatest single political forces of modern times. It permeates every political philosophy be it national, pan-national, imperialistic or international. The sentiment of national consciousness has entered a crusading phase so powerful that every dogma of the state and of peoples in general is linked with it. It has taken as complete a hold on modern thinking and attitudes as did religion and theology on the thinking of the Middle Ages. Its manifestations and ramifications are bewilderingly manifold. The political scene is dominated by nationalistic leaders and the quest for peace during our time is a search for the solution of the perplexing problems of conflicting nationalism often expressed in terms of bellicose ideologies. National consciousness has been moulded into dogmatic philosophies identified with ideological strivings. Nationalism today belongs to the people of the world. It finds full expression in the efforts of politically divided nations such as Germany to achieve union into a single state; in the strivings of national minorities

[37] There is a vast field to explore. Only some of the major phases of twentieth century Nationalism in Europe have been selected for discussion. Excellent bibliographical background may be found in O. Douglass Weeks, "Recent Nationalism" in J. S. Roucek, *Twentieth Century Political Thought*, New York, Philosophical Library, 1946, chapter IV.

and irredentas to win autonomy, self-determination, and independence; and in the struggles of independent states to achieve greater wealth, territory, people, and power. In short, nationalism is a form of mass psychology, of relatively recent origin and for the purposes of this chapter it has taken possession of all the peoples of Europe.

Democracy

Up to the end of the First World War democratic nationalism, particularly of the liberalistic type dominated the world. It had first appeared during the revolutionary period in France and in the United States. After that it spread its influence so extensively that prior to the First World War the conviction was generally voiced that all countries in the world would eventually become democratic. During the Second World War, except in the case of Communist Russia, democratic nationalism won its fight against totalitarian nationalism.

Nationalism and Education

Modern nationalism is developed through the educative processes. Democracies, through free public universal education, have spread the belief in democratic nationalisms. How effective this work has been may be seen in the way in which the United States and Great Britain were able to stand up under totalitarian assaults during the Second World War. But education as a vehicle for the spread of nationalistic ideals is not confined to democracies. From the start, the Russian, German, Italian and other totalitarianisms have operated on the basis that education and propaganda are means of spreading doctrines. Most totalitarian leaders have asked for one generation in which to convert the fundamental outlook of the state to their way of thinking. Thus was Russia converted to Communism, Italy to Fascism, and Germany to National Socialism, during the generation between the two World

Wars. National systems of education, whatever their objectives, have been the means of spreading and inculcating people with nationalistic doctrines.[38]

Propaganda

Fundamental to the spread of nationalism and to its development during the twentieth century have been the newly developed techniques of public opinion and of propaganda control. There are many publics with which the state must deal, all depending upon the subject which is involved. Propaganda in times of war as well as in times of peace is one of the great instruments of modern nationalism.[39]

Nationalism and Geopolitics

One of the more recent subjects to receive the attention of the twentieth century has been political geography. As geopolitics it has tied together geographical and political concepts and used them to further the physical interests and powers of the state. Geopolitics used geography as a means of enhancing national ideals and longings. It embraces nationalistic strivings for autarchy and Lebensraum and thus plays an important role in current nationalism. Kjellen, Haushofer, and many students of the subject have had a marked influence on the nationalisms of the last decade in particular.

THE IDEAL OF NATIONALISM

Its Value

The tremendous power which is modern nationalism is neither pure blessing nor pure curse. It possesses a number of funda-

[38] Edward H. Reisner, *Nationalism and Education since 1789*, New York, the Macmillan Company, 1922, also Joseph S. Roucek, *Sociological Foundations of Education*, New York, Thomas Y. Crowell, 1942.

[39] T. V. Kalijarvi, *Modern World Politics*, 2nd ed., chapter 16.

mental values. It permits a nation within its own borders to develop its own character. It is doubtful that in the long run any national group or state can impose its will upon another group without serious damage. When people retain their own characteristics they are bound to create a more productive and progressive world. Nationalism, therefore is consistent with humanity and with nature. It is only found that when any nation seeks to impose uniformity of belief or doctrine on the world, no matter how good its doctrines may be, that effort is not only egotistical, impractical, and boresome, but it is also in the interests of mankind that it should fail. The failure of Nazi Germany and imperialist Japan was therefore in the interests of the world. Similarly, it was in the interest of the world at large that the efforts of Russia to impose her institutions upon Poland, Lithuania and the border states failed during the nineteenth century. It is in the interest, not only of individual states but of the world as a whole and of human society, that each nation should be permitted to develop its own characteristics. As Burns says: "For the human race is not at its best when every man and every group is a copy of each other."[40]

Its Drawbacks

The difficulty with modern nationalism is that there are no limitations placed on it until it becomes destructive. If means were found for correcting it at the point where it becomes destructive, then indeed the world would be in a position to proceed at a faster pace, ever expanding to the comfort and convenience of man. Nations need not be expanded at the expense of others. The difficulty lies in the present belief that national self-sufficiency is the only solution for national problems. Peace and world order are achievable, but only when man realizes that national groups can be so regulated in their relations with each other that points of difference can be settled by other means than by conflict. If

[40] C. DeLisle Burns, *Political Ideals*, page 194.

modern nationalism can be stripped of its bellicose actions, peace can be achieved. It is fantastic that states which demand freedom for their nationalism should simultaneously demand the right to impose their own nationalisms upon others and to govern other peoples. Some of these inconsistencies must be ironed out. The chief difficulty of the present moment is lack of political imagination.

Indeed, the chief difficulty about modern nationalism is that it has a moral outlook which insists upon nationalistic preponderance and superiority. Fascism is one of the most unfortunate developments of modern nationalism, but chauvinism, imperialism, and the hatreds characteristic of the more intense nationalism are retarding influences also.

Shall It Be Eliminated?

It has been suggested that if nationalism were eliminated wars would be ended. Such reasoning is unrealistic. Long before modern nationalism came into existence wars raged among men. Men have not fought exclusively over nationalistic ideals. The religious conflicts of the late Middle Ages were not nationalistic. Nor were the Crusades. Examples could be multiplied. Nationalism is a part of our world. We cannot eliminate it if we would wish to. What we need is to learn how to control and eradicate its harmful manifestations.

One Nationalistic Idealogy for the World?

Likewise no uniform political doctrines or nationalistic doctrines would be suitable for the world. The big problem is to create an international environment in which many nationalisms can live without eternal bickering and conflict. And that, in general, means the finding of some peaceful curb and developing toleration for other nationalisms than our own. This in its turn can only rest on the guaranteed security of our own.

BIBLIOGRAPHY

BARKER, ERNEST: *National Character and the Factors in Its Formation*, London, Harper and Brothers, 1927.

DEMISHKEVICH, MICHAEL: *The National Mind—English, French, German*, New York, American Book Company, 1938.

BURNS, C. DE LISLE: *Political Ideals*, London, Oxford University Press, 1932.

BRADY, ROBERT A.: *The Spirit and Structure of German Fascism*, New York, The Viking Press, 1937.

HAYES, CARLTON J. H.: *Essays on Nationalism*, New York, Macmillan Company, 1926).

HAYES, CARLTON J. H.: *Historical Evolution of Modern Nationalism*, New York, Richard R. Smith, 1931.

DOMINION, LEON: *Nationality Map of Europe*, Boston, World Peace Foundation, 1919.

KOHN, HANS: *Nationalism in the Soviet Union*, New York, Columbia University Press, 1933.

KOHN, HANS: *The Idea of Nationalism*, New York, Macmillan, 1944.

LENIN, NIKOLAI: *Über die nationale Frage*, 2 volumes, Berlin, Rewohlt Verlag, 1930-1931.

MARX, KARL and ENGELS, FRIEDRICH: *Correspondence: 1846–1895: A Selection with Commentary and Notes*, New York, International Publishers, 1936.

MEINECKE, FRIEDRICH: *Weltbürgertum und Nationalstaat, Studien zur Genesis des deutschen Nationstaates*, 7th, Munich, R. Oldenbourg Verlag, 1928.

ROUCEK, JOSEPH S.: *The Politics of the Balkans*, New York, McGraw Hill, 1939.

ROUCEK, JOSEPH S.: *Twentieth Century Political Thought*, New York, Philosophical Library, 1946.

SALVEMINI, GAETANO, *The Fascist Dictatorship in Italy*, New York, Holt, 1927).

STALIN, JOSEF: *Leninism*, 2 volumes, New York, International Publishers, 1928, 1933.

STALIN, JOSEF: *Marxism and the National Question*, New York, International Publishers, 1942.

Nationalism, Royal Institute of National Affairs, London, Oxford University Press, 1939.

BROWN, FRANCIS J. and ROUCEK, JOSEPH S.: *One America: Our Racial and National Minorities*, New York, Prentice Hall, 1945.

ASCOLI, MAXHAM FEILER: *Fascism for Whom*, New York, W. W. Norton, 1939.

FLORINSKY, MICHAEL: *Fascism and National Socialism*, New York, Macmillan, 1936.

WILLIAMS, FRANCIS: *Democracies Battle*, New York, The Viking Press, 1941.

ZIMMERN, ALFRED: *Modern Political Doctrines*, London, Oxford University Press, 1939.

XIV.
Regionalism and Separatism

XIV.

REGIONALISM AND SEPARATISM

by

JOSEPH S. ROUCEK

ACCORDING TO HEDWIG HINTZE, regionalism is difficult to characterize. In a very general way, it may be defined "as a counter movement to any exaggerated or oppressive form of centralization."[1] But regionalism, according to Hintze, must not be considered "solely from the viewpoint of political control or governmental administration," for regionalist problems arise in a combination of two or more such factors as geographical isolation, independent historical traditions, racial, ethnic or religious peculiarities and local economic or class interests. "Regionalism must be distinguished from nationalism in that it recognizes a higher national unity and superior national interests transcending the attachment to the local region. It must be distinguished also from mere sectionalism in that it is not based exclusively on regional economic or class interests but involves certain ethnic factors, such as cultural, traditional or linguistic peculiarities, which provide a basis for what is often termed a subnationality."

It is obvious that these involved definitions of Hintze are none too helpful and up-to-date. In the first place, we have learned in recent years that regionalism is not necessarily a counter movement to "exaggerated or oppressive form of centralization." From this point of view, it can be seriously debated whether the regionalism and separatism of the Slovaks was really caused by the "exaggerated or oppressive form of centralization" of Prague; the same

[1] Hedwig Hintze, "Regionalism," *Encyclopedia of Social Sciences*, XIII, 208-18.

applies to the problem of the Sudeten Germans. In fact, the agitation and maneuvres of Hitler were more important factors than the policies of Prague. Secondly, regionalism can hardly be distinguished from nationalism, for the most troublesome difficulties of regionalism and separatism have been caused during the last two or three decades not so much by economic or class interests as by the nationalistic agitation.

In fact, the basic factor of regionalism of contemporary Europe has been the problem of nationalistic self-determination; although the economic, religious and other factors have played their part, the arguments provided for regionalistic and separatist claims have been underlined primarily by the nationalistic ideologies.

France—The Classic Land of Regionalism

Hintze's concept of regionalism is, however, of some value, if we recall that the study was written in the thirties, when the intensification of the nationalistic tendencies on Europe's horizon was not yet clearly discernable. In this respect, France served Hintze as the "classic land of political unity and administrative centralization," as well as "the classic land of regionalism," and, as a consequence, "the French regionalist movement may be used as a paradigm for regionalist movements of other lands."[7]

Since 1789, including the years of the French Revolution, the process of unification of the French State steadily gained impetus and, finally, centralization was accomplished by Napoleon Bonaparte.

The new centralistic system met with opposition, and a decentralized, federalist principle found such strong French supporters as Proudhon, Comte, and Le Play. At the beginning of the second half of the nineteenth century, a group of poets organized a regionalist movement to revive the Provençal language; this was the starting point of a regionalist revival in France which eventually found organized expression in the *Fédération Régionaliste*

Française, a movement directed against the centralist system. French regionalism gradually grew sufficiently strong to cause certain changes and reforms in favor of decentralization.

Separatism of various brands was evident, in the same period, in Corsica, Béarn and particularly in Brittany; the language question played an important role especially in French Flanders; in the three departments of Moselle, Haut-Rhin and Bas-Rhin, "sentimental" and "administrative" regionalism was related to the language question. The Alsatian autonomism was based on strong local feeling and directed chiefly against the rigorous manner in which the French language was taught in the schools and used in the administrative offices. Alsace, in fact, represented a type of cultural autonomism and a desire for self-government.

The Problem of Alsace-Lorraine. The incorporation of Alsace and Lorraine in the seventeenth and 18th centuries, respectively, involved France's expansion beyond the naturally-defined limits of France, for, while the Lorraine Plateau is intermediate to the Paris Basin and the Rhineland, Alsace turns away from France and is an essential part of the Rhine Basin. By their inclusion within political France the two provinces were prevented from working out an independent life, as at one time seemed possible, on the basis of the longheld traditions of the Duchy of Lorraine. While the French Kings respected the local rights, and notwithstanding a measure of gradual assimilation to France, the German character of the region was preserved in general. The French Revolution marked a change; the local rights were abolished and the administration fully equalized with the rest of France, the country being divided into three départements. Nevertheless, the Alsatians heartily welcomed the revolution, as it freed them from feudal bondage.

Restored Kingdom, Second Republic and Second Empire continued the policy of unification and assimilation in the region. The Alsatians were loyal French citizens, and many of them rose to high posts in the French state administration. After the German-French war of 1870-71, the reestablished German Empire annexed the three *départments*, uniting them into the province of Alsace-Lorraine (German name: *Elsass-Lothringen*). Municipal and local councils passed resolutions protesting against the annexation (the "protest movement"); they protested even against the introduction of the German language in the schools. Germany retorted by withholding self-government for Alsace-Lorraine and keeping the provinces as "Reichslande" (Imperial Territories), under a dictatorship of a strong military flavor. In the 'nineties, the protest movement ebbed, and the Alsatians joined the various German parties, mainly the Catholic Clericals (*Zentrum*). An Alsatian Constitution was granted in 1911, providing for a Diet with limited autonomy. While a large section of the population seemed ready to acquiesce in cooperation with Germany, there was also a renewed pro-French current under Wetterlé. Incidents like that of Zabren in 1913 (outrages of the military against the Alsatian population) perturbed the bid for reconciliation, and the Diet was in permanent conflict with Berlin. During World War I, pro-French sympathies flared up again, and more than 20,000 inhabitants were deported by the German authorities on political grounds.

When the French armies, in accordance with the terms of the Armistice, marched into Alsace-Lorraine in November, 1918, they were enthusiastically welcomed. By the Treaty of Versailles, the provinces were reunited with France, and a German demand for a plebiscite was turned down.

The French restored the three *départements*, Haut-Rhin, Bas-Rhin and Moselle, and embarked on a policy of assimilation; French was introduced as language of instruction in schools. As during the period of German rule the population had learned to feel as a territorial unit and had become conscious of their ethnical character as German-speakers, an autonomist movement arose and gathered momentum by the government's action in 1925 which was intended to introduce French lay legislation instead of the still valid German legislation favoring the Roman Catholic Church. The plan had to be dropped on account of the strength of Catholicism. An autonomist movement known as *Elsass-Lothringer Heimatbund* (Home League of Alsace-Lorraine) was launched in 1926 on a program of "home rights," including recognition as a national minority, political autonomy within the framework of France, an Alsace-Lorraine Diet with a separate administration, German schools, equal rights of the German language alongside with French, and protection of local economic interests. A group of autonomists, including the leaders Rossé and Ricklin, were tried at Colmar in 1928, and sentenced to prison—but soon pardoned. Reinforced by Catholic elements under Father Haegy and democratic ones under Dahlet, they won a success in the 1929 elections. More important became their indirect influence, as the autonomist program, or parts of it, penetrated all the local parties. By the start of World War II, the autonomist party proper, styling itself *Elsass-Lothringische Partei,* had no representative in the French parliament, but a number of autonomists (describing themselves as *heimattreu,* hometrue) were found within a variety of parties. The strongest Alsatian party, the clerical *Union populaire républicaine,* formed, with 2 smaller groups, the *Action populaire indépendente* in the Chamber, numbering 15 members and comprising pro-French members (such as the leader, Michel Walter) as well as such autonomists as Rossé.

The Nazi propaganda was at the same time quite active, and produced various crypto-Nazi organizations, suppressed by the government in 1939; one autonomist leader, Charles Philippe Roose, was executed for espionage.

Last of the lost provinces to greet the troops of liberation, Alsace stood first in the heart of France in November, 1944. Paris had plans at that time to eliminate, progressively, the special status that prevailed in this German-speaking province before the war, that the time had come to prevent the future recrudescence of autonomism.

The whole problem of Alsace-Lorraine indicates the point which we emphasized at the beginning of this chapter, that the outstanding aspects of the questions arising from the existence of regionalism are those of nationalism.

This characteristic is more and more apparent as we progress, geographically, from western to Central and Eastern Europe. But the growing nationalistic aspects of this problem during the twentieth century have been a burden to the westernmost state, England, where regionalism of cultural kind has been submerged to a remarkable degree to the interests of the United Kingdom—with the exception of Ireland.[2]

Ireland

Ireland was divided into a number of Celtic kingdoms with a high king (whose authority was doubtful) up to 1152, when one of the sub-kings invoked the aid of the Anglo-Normans in a struggle with the high king. This led to the first landing of the English in Ireland, and henceforth English rule was extended until Henry VIII assumed the title of King of Ireland. The Irish were in constant opposition to English rule and the racial cleavage was deepened by the religious rift after the reformation of the English Church when Ireland remained Roman Catholic. Very serious fighting occurred under Cromwell who subsequently ordered the evacuation of the northern counties, now known as Ulster, by the Irish population, and settled Protestant Englishmen and Scots there. An Irish Parliament, subordinate to that of England, subsisted till 1800, when union was proclaimed and the United Kingdom of Great Britain and Ireland was created. By that time Ireland had become largely anglicised, the Gaelic Irish language had almost vanished, but the national consciousness of the Irish survived.

In the 19th century, the Anglo-Irish dissension was aggravated by social and economic oppression of the Irish. Most of the land

[2] No attempt is made here to deal with the background of England's regionalism and separatism—only Ireland. For such related problems as that of Scotland, see any standard text on England, or brief summary in Frederick E. Graham, "Great Britain, Ireland, and the Empire," Chapter VI, in Joseph S. Roucek, Ed., *Contemporary Europe* (New York, D. Van Nostrand Co., 1947).

had become the property of English noblemen in the course of the centuries and the Irish peasant was holding it only as a tenant. The Irish question was eventually tackled by the Liberal Gladstone government, and in 1866 and 1893 the first Irish Home Rule Bills were introduced. Though they were rejected, Gladstone was more successful in settling the Irish land question, and the work initiated by him in securing the peasants' tenure of land was substantially completed in 1903. In 1912, a New Home Rule Bill was introduced by the Liberal Asquith Government, which met with passionate opposition in Ulster. Sir Edward Carson raised the Ulster volunteers, while Irish volunteers for Home Rule were organized in Southern Ireland, and civil war in Ireland was imminent. The Home Rule Bill was twice rejected by the Lords, and in the meanwhile the Great War of 1914 broke out. The Home Rule Bill was then passed but its operation delayed until after the war.

A group of radical nationalists, who became known as the Sinn Fein Party (Gaelic, meaning "We ourselves") cooperated with Germany in preparing an insurrection. They claimed to be a continuation of the Irish Republican Volunteers who seceded in the number of 12,000 from the Southern Irish Volunteers (total number 160,000) in 1914 over the question of participation in World War I, carried out the Easter Week Rising in Dublin in 1916, proclaimed the Irish Republic, and fought the Free State Government in the Irish Civil War of 1922. They clung to the fiction that this Irish Republic continued to exist, and they regarded themselves as its army. They rejected the Eire Government, aimed at the reunion of North Ireland and Eire, and complete secession of Ireland from the British Commonwealth. Condemned by the Government of Eire, they carried on continuous bombings in London and other English towns until World War II.

World War I over, another Home Rule Bill was passed, providing for a Northern Irish Parliament at Belfast and a Southern Irish one at Dublin; the Radical Irish Nationalists, however, started civil war. They started a campaign of shooting the Irish

Constabulary man by man, and organized terror throughout Ireland. Britain retorted by sending in a special police force known as the Black-and-Tans, and a period of guerilla warfare followed. The 73 Sinn Fein members of the British Parliament (out of a total of 105 Irish M.P.S.) withdrew from Westminster and gathered at Dublin as Dáil Eireann or Irish National Assembly. This dark period came to an end in 1921 when the Anglo-Irish Treaty was concluded between London and the Dáil Eireann. The Home Rule Bill was repealed, and the Irish Free State Act of 1922 created a Dominion known as the Irish Free State in Southern Ireland (Eire). Northern Ireland remained a part of the United Kingdom but was given a degree of self-government—and represents a definite problem in regionalism.

Spain

Spain has always been troubled with the regionalistic and separatistic problems. Catalonia is a region in the northeastern corner of Spain, inhabited by the Catalans or Catalonians who speak a language akin to, but substantially differing from, Spanish.

Catalan regionalism has its roots as far back as the twelfth century. For centuries, regionalism, and often separatism, was a dynamic issue in Catalonia. During the twelfth century, when Spain became a nationalistic state, Catalan regionalism experienced a revival; with it appeared a strong tendency towards a renaissance of Catalan culture. As in France, these regionalist tendencies coincided with federalist tendencies.

Piy Margal, Prime Minister of the Spanish Republic (1873-4), who was influenced by Proudhon, was in favor of a cantonal autonomy and a federative principle for Spain.

In the new Spanish Republic, the autonomous and regionalistic demands of the Catalans, Galicians and Basques played a significant role. Under the Republican Government, with whom they sided in the Civil War of 1936-39, the Catalans won autonomy; but Catalonian nationalists and anarchists, the latter being traditionally strong in the region, displayed sectional tendencies in the course of the war; finally the Republican government took control of Catalonia. In January, 1939, General Franco started his offensive on Catalonia, resulting in the conquest of Barcelona and the collapse of the Republic. The Catalonian privileges were suppressed by the victory and centralist Spanish rule was reestablished.

The Basques. A similar course of development took place in the region of the Basques, a people of about 2,000,000 on the northern coast of Spain, with a branch in southwestern France, speaking a language quite different from Spanish and not related to any other European tongue. The Basques (living in the provinces of Alava, Bizcaya, and Guipúzcoa) maintained a separate existence in the Spanish monarchy for a long time. These privileges were known as the Basque *fueros.* The movement reached its apex at the beginning of the 20th century. A student, Sabino Arana-Goiri wrote *Bizcaya por su independencia* (Bilbao, 1892), and in 1895 the nationalist Basque party was founded, declaring itself for "the tradition, the church, the ancient laws and institutions of the land, language and art of the people." After World War I, the Basques obtained autonomy. But defeated by General Franco, their country was occupied in 1937 by the Spanish nationalists; all their privileges and linguistic rights were suppressed.

With a view to reviving Galician as a cultural tongue, the movement centering itself around the old University of Santiago de Compostela.

Italy

In Italy, the problem of regionalism has usually tended to become that of federalism or separatism.

Italian regionalism reverts to the times of Risorgimento. Among its most important writers, Mazzini deserves particular mention; he advocated a regional-federal system for Italy. Despite regionalistic projects, however, a centralistic system was established in the Italian Kingdom. After World War I, the tendency toward regionalism became increasingly popular, but the establishment of Fascist rule has practically destroyed all hopes for a decentralized, regional system.

Sicily may be noted as a good example of Italian separatism and regionalism.

"Independence of Sicily" has always been Italy's gravest national problem.[3]

The movement resembled, at the end of World War I, that for the separate Moslem state of Pakistan in India. Furthermore, Sicily was the first place the United States forces liberated in Europe, and it is a good example of what disturbing forces liberation was setting free in the Old World from which America's people came. There are more Sicilians and Americans of Sicilian descent in the United States than there are Sicilians in Italy.

Like everything else connected with Sicily, separatism is an extraordinarily complicated phenomenon. It cuts across all party lines like republicanism and monarchism and there are separatists even in the communistic movement, which is fundamentally the greatest enemy of the independentists. The motives behind it are mixed with genuine idealism, selfish personal interests, political designs, trouble-making, sincere convictions and innocent hopes. The Maffia, that peculiarly Sicilian institution, which is almost a government to itself, is also deeply involved.

As its name implies, the movement seeks to separate the island from what every Sicilian calls "the Continent," meaning the mainland governed by Rome. The chief leaders of the movement—lawyer and former Deputy Andrea Finocchiaro-Aprile, who is President; Lucio Tasca, whom Colonel Charles Poletti made Mayor of Palermo and who was removed by Rome after eleven months, and his brother Alessandro, who is probably the largest landowner on the island—want first, the creation of an indepen-

[3] Herbert L. Matthews, "Separatist Crisis in Sicily Is Acute," New York *Times* (February 4, 1945).

dent sovereign state, and second, the formation of a federation between Sicily and Italy. However, there are extremist elements, particularly students and intelligentsia, who oppose the federation, while there is also a moderate wing willing to accept a large degree of autonomy under the Rome government. According to the dominant ideology of the movement, Sicilians are a race apart from the Italians of the mainland. They claim a long historic background of separation or aspirations for independence and interpret all their great revolts from 1282 to the uprising against the Bourbons in 1848 in terms of separatism. They charge neglect and exploitation by Rome and northern Italy since the Risorgimento and unification, and provide convincing statistics to support their case right through the Fascist regime which prevented the development of industry and did little or nothing to relieve agricultural distress. Even before the collapse of the monarchist regime in Italy in 1946, they had been, potentially and essentially Republicans, since the Monarchy stood for unity.

Germany

Regionalism and separatism have been connected with the whole history of Germany. In modern times, these problems appeared in various forms such as the Junker or Bavarian problems, not to speak of numerous others. We shall have to limit ourselves to the consideration of the "Free Rhineland," and Schleswig-Holstein movements.

Free Rhineland. The dispatches of 1946 from Germany told of the establishment of a "Free Rhineland" movement presaging more trouble for the inhabitants of the battered German lands in the west. The new group, called the Rhenish People's Party, is the spiritual descendant of a number of organizations which, in their efforts to set up a Rhineland Republic kept that region in a state of turmoil in the years following the end of World War I. In fact, Dr. Fritz Opitz, a journalist, who headed the new party in 1946, admitted his movement was begun by former followers of Dr. Hans A. Dorten, president of the short-lived Rhenish Republic of 1919. One element, however, in this sequel to the 1919-24 events appeared to be lacking: the presence of foreign support for the separatists. While the French were certainly not unsympathetic to the Rhenish People's Party, they took no part in 1946 in sponsoring the organization. But the French quite firmly proclaimed their desire for an independent Rhineland. This, with internationalization of the Ruhr, they felt, would end the long-standing German threat to their security. After World War I, the French played a considerable role in the numerous attempts to sever the Rhineland from the Reich, their efforts culminating in the formation in the winter of 1923-24 of a Rhenish state, dubbed the "Revolver Republic," by the German populace.

The moves of France in the '20's were supported by Marshal Foch, and those two other leaders of a resurgent France—Georges Clemenceau and Raymond Poincaré; the British and Americans opposed such a proposal in drafting the Treaty of Versailles, by which the French were forced to settle for temporary occupation of the Rhineland.

Not to be balked at the peace table, however, France turned to propaganda and more forceful means of accomplishing her goal. Even before the Treaty had been signed on June 28, 1919, a campaign had begun in the Rhineland, whose people were told that they not really Germans, but "Celts, comme nous"—"Celts, like us." And General Charles Mangin, French Army occupation commander and a foremost exponent of his nation's Rhine policy, secretly met with Dr. Dorten, an obscure Wiesbaden lawyer, to discuss the financing and arming of a band of men to establish a Rhineland republic.

The attempt to convince Rhinelanders of their Gallic affinity was doomed to failure, but intrigue with separatists was to be a contributing factor to the continued unsettlement of Germany for years.

Schleswig-Holstein, a province in North Germany, was taken from Denmark by Prussia in 1864. The Danish population in the northern part claimed return to Denmark over half a century, and in 1920 a plebiscite was held under the Peace Treaty of Versailles, resulting in the return to Denmark of North Schleswig. The district was thereafter called South Jutland; it included a German minority of 35,000 enjoying broad rights and having German schools. But German aspirations to the reacquisition of the province continued, and were realized under Hitler. In 1946, the British Military Government announced the province was designated a *Land* (State) on a par with the Land of Hanover and the Land of North Rhine-Westphalia. With this step, the British accomplished the federalistic reorganization of their zone into three *Laender* (States) in addition to Hamburg along the lines of the American zone, which was divided into three *Laender*. At a session of the Schleswig-Holstein advisory council (September 16, 1946), which was told about the decision, the members voted 53 to 2 to decline further discussion of a motion to permit South Schleswig, north of the Eider River, to secede and form a separate province directly under the military government.

Hitler's Pan-Germanism. A chapter in this volume covers the Pan-Germanic ideologies and tendencies of the modern age, and it is not necessary to deal here with the relation of the German minorities to the problems of regionalism and separatism. Sufficient to point out that everywhere, under the influence of Nazi propagandists, the German settlements started claiming special privileges as branches of the Germanic race, and in such cases, as the Sudeten Germans, culminated their movement in separatistic demands from their states. According to the theories of Hitlerism, the German was defined as all Germans of German parentage or near-descent, whether speaking German or not. By this definition Germany, under Hitler, had roughly between 90,000,000 and 100,000,000 "abroad." The Reich also claimed blood kinship with additional so-called German minorities of France, Romania, Hungary, Yugoslavia, Italy, Latvia, Denmark, Lithuania, Estonia, Belgium, the Crimean Soviet Republic, and the Ukrainian Soviet Republic. German-speaking inhabitants of these lands were estimated anywhere from a million and a half in France to about 16,000 in Estonia. Certain European nations were either 100 per cent German-speaking (such as Liechtenstein and Luxembourg) or held large Germanic minorities, like Switzerland, where some three-fourths of the people speak German. Some of these Germans evolved a culture and tradition of their own, different from that of their racial cousins. Such, for example, was the German group settled along the middle Volga River of Soviet Russia, and comprising more than half the population of the autonomous Volga-German Republic. Another, nearer to the Reich, is the independent little principality of Liechtenstein, which is well satisfied with its ruler and the country's economic ties with Switzerland.

Central-Eastern Europe

The regional and separatist movements of the European states between Germany and Russia have all been characterized by the nationalistic aspects of such demands. The national movements of these states and nationalities all have certain main characteristics in common; they can be summarized as follows:[4] (1) These national movements have been ultimately, if indirectly, derived from independent political existences at some day past, more or less remote (although these earlier organizations could not be described as "national states.") (2) The super-structures over these various nationalities built up by colonization or conquest did not succeed in obliterating the loyalties and the sense of distinctness which the earlier independent political structures had created. (3) These nationalistic memories failed to be obliterated because the political superstructures (or empires) were headed by aliens and invaders who, both socially and politically, kept the upper positions strictly to themselves, and who failed or neglected to form a strong and permeating central authority. (4) Many of

[4] Royal Institute of International Affairs, *Nationalism* (New York: Oxford University Press, 1939), Chapter VI, "Other European National Movements," pp. 81-113.

the leaders of the national movements could not show any hereditary connection with those who had lived under the earlier states; a large number of the leaders came of the stock of the alien invaders. (5) These national movements were often related with a revival of the native languages, which had survived as peasant dialects since the days of independence. Eventually these dialects were unified, grammars and dictionaries created, and the vocabulary enlarged to make the language suitable for purpose of literature and government. (6) The literary revivals were the products of small bodies of intellectuals, many of whom belonged to the dominant race, and most of whom had taken advantage of its educational system and culture. (7) The inspiration for these revivals came from abroad, particularly from Germany (Herder[5]), and the political ideas of Western Europe from England (Ireland, Italy), France (Poland, Rumania, the Czechs), or Germany (Latvia, Estonia, Croatia). (8) The literary revivals became politically important because they emphasized the sense of distinction already felt on a social basis; the Western concept of self-determination was accepted because it offered the possibility of liberation from rule that was socially oppressive. (9) These national movements were also related to the growth of the capitalist system and the Industrial Revolution. (10) Nevertheless, the middle classes here remained comparatively small and played a limited part in the growth of the national movements. On the whole, the professional classes (clergy, teachers, lawyers, doctors) were much more important than those engaged in commerce or industry. (11) Due to the weak middle classes, the national movements here had to look for support to a number of different groups—professional men, industrialists, small gentry, peasantry—which were bound together by the desire to be rid of alien rule. (12) Political independence brought these nations face to face with a number of serious questions, both political, social, and economic, on which the differences of opinion went deep. These dif-

[5] R. R. Ergang, *Herder and the Foundations of German Nationalism* (New York, Columbia University Press, 1931).

ferences handicapped the establishment of a democratic form of government, especially as most of these nations had had no background in self-government and lacked the relatively high material and cultural standards of the western states. The difficulty was strengthened by the fact that few of these nations gained independence by their own exertion, but owed it in nearly all cases to foreign aid.

To treat all the main and minor problems of regionalism and separatism in this part of the world would obviously mean the discussion of all the nationalistic aspirations of all the nationalities living here. We shall have to limit ourselves to the currently outstanding problems in this region: Austrian South Tyrol, Czechs and Slovaks, Ruthenes, Yugoslavia, and Macedonia.

Austrian South-Tyrol

Although Tyrol is only one of Austria's provinces, it has left a deeper impression on the imagination of the world than almost any other European region. It has always stood for untouched nature, pine woods, pastures, and a bewitchingly beautiful and majestic mountain landscapes. It is a country of mighty mountain ranges which, as in Switzerland, have produced a hard-working, pious, stubborn, and freedom-loving people—the Tyrolese.

The territory was annexed by Italy from Austria after World War I. The southern half was inhabited by Italians while the northern half, including the towns of Bozen (Bolzano) and Meran, was inhabited by 267,000 German Austrians. This area came to be known in Italy as *AltoAdige.* Italy insisted on its possession for strategic reasons, particularly on account of the Brenner Pass. While the South Tyrolese enjoyed liberal minority rights until 1924, they were subject to forcible Italianization by the Fascist regime; some looked to Germany for help, but Hitler renounced South Tyrol as the price of Italy's friendship. In August 1939 the German South Tyrolese were offered an opportunity to assume German nationality and to emigrate to Germany; 185,000

Germans chose to go to Germany, while 82,000 decided to stay.

Unlike all other disputed territories of Europe, Tyrol has never known different masters, with the exception of a short period under Napoleon. Never in its long history was the south separated from the north; it has been an individual state unit since the 7th century, when it was settled by the forefathers of the present-day Tyrolese. The long traditions of independence produced the fighters who in 1809, guided by their peasant leader Andreas Hofer, inflicted the first crushing defeat on Napoleon at a time when even the most powerful nations of Europe were still willing to submit to him.

Although the capital of Tyrol, Innsbruck, has developed in the north, the ecclesiastical capital was at Brixen (in the south), and the Archbishop of Brixen remained the head of the church in the entire Tyrol even after the partition of 1919. From a cultural viewpoint, the south was even more productive than the north, and the great names of Tyrolese civilization, the great painters and poets like Walter von der Vogelweide came from South Tyrol. (The very name of Tyrol originated at Meran).

During all these centuries the Tyrolese inhabited their land in a solid block which reached as far as Salurn, where we find the oldest and sharpest nationality line in Europe. Today, ethnically the country belongs to Austria. But throughout 1946, Rome and Vienna were arguing over the possession of the region.

Czechs and Slovaks

Czechs and Slovaks, united in a struggle for national liberation, overthrew at the end of World War I the feudal Empire of Austria-Hungary and created modern Czecho-slovakia. But the problem of the regional and eventually separatistic tendencies of Slovakia provided one of the greatest problems of the new state, especially when the issue was seized upon by Hitler for his purposes of driving through Czechoslovakia on the way to the Balkans and the Near East, along the "transversal Eurasian Axis."

For the purpose of our topic, it is sufficient to notice that both the Czechs and the Slovaks have the same origin, that they are the same people. But history separated the Slovaks from the Czechs when the Magyars seized Slovakia in the tenth century.[6] Their history thereafter was, for a thousand years, a record of living as an unwilling province of the Kingdom of Hungary—while the Czechs formed their independent state, and lived between 1620 and 1918 in Austria. In 1918, the Slovaks were far behind the Czechs in cultural and political development and there were few among them who recognized the significance of the 1914-1918 struggle until it was over. On the brink of national extermination in 1914, the Slovaks had scarcely more than 500 Slovak families who were nationally conscious, and it was not until 1918 that the Slovaks began to take an active part in the leadership provided for them by such people as General Stefánik who worked with Masaryk and Benes for liberation of Czechoslovakia.

Slovakia's separatism had a slow start. The religious issue was in part responsible. Slovakia had a serious shortage of men and women who could take the place of the Hungarian officials, teachers and priests after 1918. Czechs came in large numbers; many of them were Protestants and free thinkers and offended the religious feelings of the Slovak peasantry. (This was fomented by the Hungarian priests who remained, and to this day they are partly responsible for misunderstandings between Czechs and Slovaks). At first the Slovak Clerical (Autonomist) Party, under Father Hlinka, and the Czech Clericals cooperated; but after a while this link was severed, and Hlinka started a serious opposition to Prague, partly for personal and partly for political reasons. He was a Roman Catholic priest and exercised great influence over the quick and sensitive Slovaks; in pre-war Hungary, a brave and devoted Slovak patriot, he carried his early fighting spirit into the Czechoslovak Republic and preferred "Slovak" to "Czechoslovak" patriotism. When he died in 1938, his place as leader was

[6] For more information on this problem, as well as all other problems of Central-Eastern Europe, see: Joseph S. Roucek, Ed., *Central-Eastern Europe* (New York, Prentice-Hall, 1946).

taken by Tiso, also a Priest, and later by his right-hand man under Hitler's regime, Tuka.

The party demanded Slovak autonomy in 1938, and with Hitler's help created an autonomous, "free" Slovak state in 1939, which collapsed with the Russian invasion of Slovakia at the end of World War II. While Tuka was hanged as a traitor, the separatism of Slovakia received a definite recognition from Prague, which inaugurated the new regime by allowing Slovakia a definite set of powers for self-government.

Yugoslavia

If there was a state in the post-war Europe cursed with the most burning regional problems, then it was Yugoslavia. To speak of Yugoslavia as a whole would belie facts. The country presents the most baffling mixture of race, language, custom, and belief imaginable. Here are Serbs, Croats, Macedonians, Magyars, Slovenes, Albanians, Moslems, Romanians, Germans, and Jews; here are Mohammedans, Protestants, Roman Catholics, and members of the Greek Orthodox Church. All these aspects had their regionalistic and separatistic tendencies, focused particularly around the problem of the Serb versus the Croat. The crux of Yugoslav politics, from the very formation of the new state in 1918 to this day, has been the alternative of centralization and federalism—the Serbs fostering the notion of "Greater Serbia," and the Croats advocating regionalism. The conflict between the Serbs on the one hand and the Croats and Slovenes on the other hand reached a climax in 1928 when several Croat leaders were shot by a Serb deputy in the National Assembly. It was this incident that led to King Alexander's dictatorship—a system of government which tried to supplant regionalism by a strict centralism.

What was in the background? The reply is simple. Yugoslavia was enmeshed in a tangle of regional nationalisms, nursed by different historical experiences of each region, antagonistic creeds, and contrasting cultures, while being faced at the same time with exasperating economic and international problems demanding a strong central government. The new state was unable to create spiritual unity among its constituent parts because its Slavic population had lived too long under different sovereignties —Austria, Hungary, Serbia, Montenegro, and Turkey; during the era of division, the Yugoslavs had been unable to participate in the same political, economic, cultural, and religious development. The geopolitical conditions of the Balkans intensified centrifugal tendencies; they emphasized differentiation and diffusion rather than integration. When the old dream of national unity had come true, tribal and regional interests were already too deeply rooted to give way to broader allegiances.

The movement was headed by the Croats who resented the domination of Serbia's Belgrade. Zagreb, ancient and obstinately self-assertive Croat center, strongly Catholic, objected to the rulership of Belgrade's centralistic administration. Although Serbs and Croats have the same literary language, both consider themselves separate cultural groups. The Croats and Slovenes use the Roman alphabet, while the Serbs write in Cyrillic. Memories of the early Croat Kingdom and the wide autonomy enjoyed by the Croats in prewar Hungary, taught the Croat his own conception of regional justice. "States rights" in the American sense became his gospel; he was jealously defending the status of his province, suspicious of Serb interference. After the relentless fight against Magyariazation, what could be worse for him than to become "Balkanized?" Too long had autonomy been the cherished weapon of national self-defense to make the Croat yield to Belgrade even in minor matters. Religious differences made the contest deeper. As Catholics, Croats and Slovenes had their objections to the domination of Serbia's Orthodox Church. Then there were cultural differences. Belonging to the "Western" cultural zone, both Croat and Slovene were convinced that theirs is an "older" and "higher" civilization than that of the Serb, who, in their eyes, is little more than a modern "barbarian," a ridiculous and brazen upstart.

The demands for regional autonomy were voiced by Radich, murdered in 1928, and since then by Dr. Matchek, who found himself, in 1946, in exile. On the opposite side of the fence stood Pashitch, Serbia's great statesman, and after his death, other pan-Serbs, symbolized in King Alexander and then King Peter.

The matter continued to disrupt the state up to the very beginning of World War II. The invasion of Yugoslavia by Hitler's hordes gave a chance to the Croats to form their own "independent" Croat state, on the lines of "independent" Slovakia, under the leadership of a Quisling, Ante Pavelich. With the end of World War II, the Croat question was submerged in federal plan of Marshal Tito, which, theoretically, gave Croatia autonomy—although, in practice, the pro-Communist Tito's regime was just as centralistic, if not more, than that of the late King Alexander.

Macedonia

The fateful importance of Macedonia has been due not only to the persistent regionalistic and separatist agitation of the Macedonians, but also to the geographical aspects of the problem, since Macedonia lies in the very heart of the Balkans—and the possession of Macedonia has been the common objective of the nationalist and strategic ambitions of three Balkan powers—Bulgaria, Serbia (Yugoslavia), and Greece. Each has tried to impose her own culture on the Macedonian portions belonging to it, while jurisdiction over the territory has been shifting back and and forth as one or the other claimant won a round in the intricate contest for balance of power in the Balkans.

The location of Macedonia can be indicated by drawing on the Balkan map a semi-circle with a radius of about 150 miles around the port of Salonica as a center. Racially, Macedonia is a medley of peoples; but the majority are Southern Slavs, who belong to the Orthodox Church. This makes the matters worse, for the Macedonian dialect is neither Bulgarian nor Serbian. Hence the Serbs are prone to classify the Macedonians as "Old Serbs" or

"South Serbs," while the Bulgars consider them pure Bulgars, and the Greeks "Slavophones" (Slav-speaking Greeks).

The ideological beginning of the Macedonian struggle for independence goes back to 1893, when Damo Grueff, Sofia University student, and Pera Tosheff, founded, in the fall of 1893, in Ressen (Resna), the first central Committee of the Macedonian Revolutionary Organization according to the example of the Carbonari Societies of Italy. This *Imro* has been active, in varying degrees, ever since in the Balkans, usually murdering its opponents or its critics. While the *Imro* proclaimed "Macedonia for Macedonians," the Vrhoven Committee, founded in 1894 by Stojan Mihailoff, supported the acquisition of Macedonia by Bulgaria. After the second World War, another organization arose, aiming to support the Communist federation of the Balkans, with Macedonia at its head.

The movement was lost in bloodshed, forgetting its original aims to liberate Macedonia, or to secure for it at least some form of autonomy from the three states holding various parts of Macedonia. In 1934 the movement was suppressed by the Bulgarians, a step cheered by the Yugoslavs troubled for years with the Macedonian terror. The problem reappeared again when Marshal Tito made Macedonia one of the parts of the autonomous Yugoslavia. But the fate of the Macedonian portions of Greece remained one of the biggest questions facing international statesmanship in 1948.

Russia

Some observers believe that Russia has found a formula of solving the problem present by the existence of regionalism, separatism in a strongly centralized state.[7]

The problem was the subject of theoretical discussions among the Bolshevist leaders before the party came to power in November,

[7] Bernhard J. Stern, "Soviet Policy on National Minorities," *American Sociological Review*, IX (June, 1944), pp. 229-35.

1917.[8] The disintegration of a multinational empire under the force of rampant nationalism, which was already in full swing in Austria-Hungary, seemed to be in the shaping also in Czarist Russia, with her some 140 ethnic groups. To be sure, only a few among the many ethnic groups that composed the Russian population displayed, around the turn of the twentieth century, nationalistic sentiments of an intensity comparable to the heat of nationalistic feelings in Central-Eastern Europe. Apart from the Great Russians, the Poles, the Finns and a few other nationalities, the national consciousness of the Russian people was not yet definitely crystallized. Needless to say that the leaders of the Bolsheviks were not interested in maintaining the Czarist Empire, but were interested in preserving the existing political framework of Russia, and scented in the disruptive force of nationalism, or rather ethnocentrism of regionalism and separatism, a serious threat to the socialist cause for which the party stood. This caused Lenin and lesser Bolshevist theoreticians to give special considerations to the problems of nationalism. Among the contributions of the minor Bolsheviks, Joseph Stalin's essay on "The National Question and Social Democracy," written and published in 1913, holds an eminent place.[9] Stalin wrote this essay in Vienna which, at that time, was torn by national strife. Stalin's arguments can be gathered from Stalin's conclusion that the Jews do not constitute a nation, since their fate has been dispersion rather than communal life, be it in linguistic, territorial, or economic terms. Stalin stressed that the nation is a historical phenomenon, and that this process lies outside the province of government, and should be left undisturbed by governmental interference. The nationalities policy of the government of a multinational state should be guided by the laissez-faire principle. The task of the socialist is not to stimulate nationalism, not to strengthen national distinctions, but rather to

[8] Erich Hula, "The Nationalities Policy of the Soviet Union," *Social Research,* XI (May, 1944), pp. 168-201.

[9] Republished several times; see Joseph Stalin, *Marxism and the National and Colonial Questions* (New York, n.d., Marxist Library, Works on Marxism-Leninism, Vol. 38, ed. by A. Fineberg), pp. 1-61.

break them down and unite the population "in such a manner as to open the way for division of a different kind, division according to class." In Stalin's view, the form that best serves this purpose is regional autonomy, the autonomy of territorial units with an ethnically diversified population. Common, not separate, institutions promote the spirit through which common purposes are achieved. Thus Stalin defined the equality of nationalities in terms of the equal rights of their several members. The endeavor to make use of common institutions in order to check separatist tendencies of the nationalities is even more conspicuous in Stalin's insistence on a single proletarian party.

When we look at the present conditions in Soviet Russia, let us notice that the Union is not a national state in the sense in which the word has come to be understood in Central-Eastern Europe. It is nationally neutral, and none of the national groups is legally recognized as a dominant nationality. Nevertheless, the Union is still an "inter-national community" as regards the relationship among its component ethnic groups. Article 1 of the Constitution (1936) defines the Union of Soviet Socialist Republics as "a socialist state of workers and peasants," without circumscribing their nationality, and the very name of the Union still includes no reference to its ethnic elements. Its legitimacy rests not on any title of nationality, but on its claim to be the instrument of a class. The Soviet Union regards itself as a class state, not a national state.

Actually it is not so much a class state as a party state. The legally and actually privileged group which rules the country is the All-Union Communist Party. And in view of this political reality, particular importance attaches to the fact that the purposes of the Communist Party itself are related to all nationalities alike. The party wields power over the Union not with a view to furthering the special interests of any of the many nationalities but with a view to achieving social ends and to maintaining the unity of the political system. Accordingly it tries to steer a nationally neutral course and to insure, as the party program promises, "the fullest equality of all nationalities" (Point 9 of the program).

The Soviet regime has gone much farther than the imperial government ever did in trying to approximate the administrative political set-up in the national structure of the population, at least in the southeastern and eastern parts of the country. But the fact also remains that neither the Union republics nor their territorial subdivisions are ethnically homogeneous. Even more striking is the ethnic mixture in the autonomous republics; some of them derive their name not from the majority, but from a minority group.

All in all, then, regionalism and separatism play a minor role in Russia today, although they are not hindered—as long as the nationalities concerned do not in any way hinder the plans of the Soviet economy. Conversely, if the regionalistic or separatistic tendencies in any way threaten the welfare of the Soviet Union, radical steps are taken. Thus the Germans were deported from their settlements on the Volga at the beginning of World War II, and in 1946, Moscow revealed that two of the autonomous Soviet Republics (of the Crimea and the Chechen-Ingust in the Northern Caucasus), had been heavily disciplined for treachery in the face of the enemy. They had been liquidated as autonomous republics, reduced to the status of provinces, and many, apparently a large proportion, of their inhabitants resettled in other parts of the Union. Evidently, in Soviet Russia, nationality and politics are inextricably tied up with one another, and the solution demands the price of Communist centralization.

BIBLIOGRAPHY

Anderson, E. A.: *Nationalism and the Cultural Crisis in Prussia, 1806-1815*, New York, Farrar & Rinehart, 1940.

Carr, E. H.: *Conditions of Peace*, New York, The Macmillan Co., 1942.

Chadwick, Henry M.: *The Nationalities of Europe and the Growth of National Ideologies*, New York, The Macmillan Co., 1947.

Hayes, Carlton J.: *A Generation of Materialism, 1871-1900*, New York, Harper & Brothers, 1941.

Pinson, K. S.: *Bibliographical Introduction to Nationalism*, New York, Columbia University Press, 1934.

Royal Institute of National Affairs: *Nationalism*, New York, Oxford University Press, 1939.

XV.

Zionism

ZIONISM

Editorial Note

Space limitations deny the separate treatment of various national and nationalist movements, country by country. However, Zionism differs strongly from so many other national movements that it deserves a special chapter. A nationalistic struggle for independence is generally waged by an oppressed nation in a determined territorial area against a determined national oppressor which has invaded their country.

Zionism started as a movement of the Jewish people who were scattered throughout the world and not in Palestine fighting an oppressor. Their original Roman oppressors (in Palestine) died centuries ago, and the Jews survived them, as they did so many other oppressors. This, then, was not a struggle such as the Serbs' against the Turks for five hundred years, or that of the Poles against Czarist Russia for one hundred and fifty years. These examples are of nations with definite enemies on a particular territory.

Beside these specific differences, Zionism became a significant movement after World War II and, because of the tragic plight of European Jewry, has assumed sufficient importance to be dealt with separately. Aware of the importance of other Jewish political movements, we were unable to treat them in a detailed manner, due to space limitations. However, mention should be made of such important movements, before World War II, as the Jewish Socialist Party ("Bund") which, at that time, was highly influential in Poland. This Socialist movement shared many common ideas with those discussed by Mr. Algernon Lee in his chapter on Socialism. The "Agudas Israel" is an important religious political movement of orthodox Jewry which should be mentioned, too, as are the "Assimilationists," who tried to merge both culturally and nationally with the nation in which the Jews had lived for centuries; they were particularly influential in the nineteenth century, especially among the intellectual and professional classes. Finally, the Territorialist Movement should be noted. Headed by Dr. I. Steinberg, its aim is to build a Jewish home in any fertile, peaceful strip of land (not necessarily in Palestine). Logical and dynamic though it is, it lacks the emotional values of a social myth which Zionism possesses in such great measure.

F. G.

XV.

ZIONISM

By

JACOB LESTCHINSKY

Institute of Jewish Affairs

Historical Background

IT IS SCARCELY possible to find another socio-political movement in the world that is as deeply rooted in the soul of the people as Zionism. Attachment to Palestine, the dream of redemption and the faith in a Messiah as the redeemer of Israel primarily, have been cherished by Jews since the destruction of their Temple. These emotions have been guarded with such piety and devotion that until the emancipation they constituted almost the sole content of the psyche of the Jewish people. Three times a day during their prayers and three times a day while saying grace at table, the Jews prayed for the redemption of Israel, an event which in their mind connoted the return to the Homeland and the restoration of independence. The highest expression of this unique yearning of a people for redemption was to be found in *Tikun Chatzoth* (a special midnight prayer). Jewish folklore was almost exclusively woven about Palestine, Jerusalem and the Messiah. Studies in the religious schools concentrated the attention of the Jewish child on the milieu of ancient Palestine or about events in Palestine. No history of Jews in the dispersion was taught in these religious schools; only the Bible and the Talmud. These dealt only with the history of the Jews from the Exodus from Egypt to the destruction of the second Temple. The entire Jewish literature beginning with the Talmud up to the period of the emancipation and including the Chassidic works of the eighteenth and nineteenth centuries are filled with references to the merit of living in Palestine and praise of the country. It is true that during the past two thousand years Jews also produced secular philosophic and poetic works, but they were quantitatively few and could not compete in the consciousness of the people with the religious works. Yehuda Halevi viewed Palestine as the land whose climate produces prophets. To die in Palestine was the most devout hope not only of pietists but also of such educated persons as Maimonides and Yehuda Halevi. This national desire for redemption through a return to Palestine was so deeply rooted that even a man like Lord Beaconsfield (Disraeli), who had broken with the Jewish people, reflected it in his novels, (*David Alroi* and *Tancred*).

Thus one can account for the fact that throughout almost nineteen centuries since the destruction of the Temple, Palestine was at no time devoid of Jews. During the first seven or eight centuries of this period large numbers of Jews continued to live in the country and a number of rebellions occurred in an effort to regain Jewish independence. When Palestine was occupied by Khalif Omar (637 A. D.) between three and four hundred thousand Jews lived in Palestine. The country passed from one ruler to another, from Rome to Byzantium, then to the Arabs. For a short time it was ruled by Christians after the first Crusade, then it passed to the Turks. Persecution of Jews in Palestine continued in various degrees but never ceased entirely. Nevertheless, Jews were continually drawn to the country. The Jewish traveler, Benjamin of Tudelo, found only about a thousand Jews in Palestine. Following upon the expulsion of the Jews from England, France and many cities of Southern Germany at the time of the Crusades, migration to Palestine increased. After the expulsion of the Jews from Spain (1492) this migration assumed a mass character. During the sixteenth century Safad became the center of the Cabbalists and more than fifteen thousand Jews lived in that city. At that time some practical attempts were made to colonize the country. Don Joseph Hanassi, who had fled Portugal and had become an intimate of Sultan Selim II, obtained permission to colonize Jews in Tiberias and the neighboring villages. This effort proceeded at a slow pace and later was abandoned altogether because of changes in the political situation. After the Chmelnitsky pogroms (1648) the migration to Palestine again assumed large proportions. These immigrants were active in the Sabbatai Zvi movement. In the eighteenth century the Chassidic movement brought about a resurgence of the migration which involved thousands of families. Under the leadership of the *Gaon* of Wilno, many others, though opposed to Chassidism, followed their example.

The large number of false Messiahs—as they are referred to in Jewish historiography—could not have enjoyed their successes had they not found a highly receptive mood among the masses. It was only natural that such Messiahs should appear in the wake of catastrophes: David Alroi in the twelfth century and Abraham Abulafia in the thirteenth marked a reaction to the Crusades and the expulsion from Western Europe; Reubeni and Shlomo Molcho in the sixteenth century followed upon the expulsion from Spain; Sabbatai Zvi appeared after the Chmelnitsky pogroms. All of these found a deep faith in redemption and a readiness to start out for Palestine alongside the moods of despair which the catastrophes had engendered.

It should be noted that within the Christian world, especially in the Anglo-Saxon countries, there flourished in recent centuries a belief in Jewish redemption and an interest in the restoration of a Jewish state in Palestine. In 1621 a book appeared in London which weighed the necessity of a Jewish state in Palestine on a practical basis (Sir Henry Finch, *The World's Great Restoration*, London, 1621.) During the eighteenth and nineteenth centuries scores of authors and statesmen advocated projects for the establishment of a Jewish state in Palestine. The most interesting of these plans was the establishment in 1844 in London of a society named "British and Foreign Society for Promoting the restoration of the Jewish Nation in Palestine."

In 1799 Napoleon issued an appeal to the Jewish people, "to the Rightful Heirs to Palestine," to hasten and establish a Jewish state there. He wrote: "Hasten! This is a moment which may not recur in a thousand years."

Emancipation, which engendered a measure of disintegration within the Jewish communities in many countries and led to apostasy and mixed marriages, let alone to cultural and linguistic assimilation, also fostered a greater degree of national initiative and a more dignified attitude toward the uniqueness of the Jewish position and against humiliations practiced against Jews. From the ranks of assimilated Jews many projects for a Jewish state were advanced. As assimilated persons they naturally stressed the state aspect of their plans, rather than Palestine. The first of these projects was that of the famous American Consul in North Africa who was recalled from his position because of his Jewishness. At any rate, this is the way he interpreted his recall. He was Mordecai Emmanuel Noah, journalist, playwright and political figure. He evolved the plan to create a Jewish state within the United States (Grand Island). In 1840 there appeared a pamphlet in Berlin entitled "New Judea" written by one S. L. K. The author of this pamphlet was apparently an educated man, trained in politics. He outlined a detailed plan for the establishment of a Jewish state in a sparsely inhabited country. The nineteenth century, he maintained, the century of the reconstruction of peoples and countries, must also provide a home for the Jews. But if "Palestine was the cradle of the Jewish people, the home must therefore stand elsewhere," in a larger and better country. Finally, there were Leon Pinsker, the author of *Auto-Emancipation* (1881), and Theodore Herzl, the creator of modern Zionism. Both of these men had been assimilated Jews and both began as territorialists.

Orthodox and nationally self-conscious Jews spoke of the restoration of the Jewish state in the Holy Land, which was sacred to them not only because of the Temple but also because of the Prophets. The most prominent among them were Moses Montefiore, Rabbi Kalisher, Moses Hess and Eliezer Ben Yehuda.. All of them preached redemption in the traditional sense, yet tried to do something concrete about it. In 1878 a group of Rumanian Jews founded the first modern Jewish settlement, Petach Tikvah—Gate of Hope. This was a promising beginning.

Chibbat Zion

Immediately following the Russian pogroms of the 80's, while the sound of broken window panes in Jewish homes still vibrated, two movements came into being which, while partially agreeing in principle, differed in methods and purposes: *Bilu* ("House of Jacob, let us arise and go") and *Am Olam* ("Eternal People"). The principle common to both these movements was the reconstruction of Jewish life on a sound economic basis, eliminating the use of outside labor and achieving economic independence. But, whereas Bilu primarily thought of the redemption of the Jewish people which should rebuild its life on labor foundations within its homeland, Am Olam dreamed of a pure socialist society in the form of model socialist settlements. The first, therefore, streamed toward Palestine, the latter, toward America where they hoped to found a new socialist society in the free and uninhabited areas far away from cities.

In scores of cities in Russia, and later in other countries, groups bearing the name of Bilu were formed. These soon changed their name to *Hovevei Zion*—"Lovers of Zion." The further development of these groups regrettably justified this change of name, for this movement rapidly assumed a philanthropic nature.

The chief ideologist of Hovevei Zion was Leon Pinsker, author of the book which remained the Gospel of the movement until the appearance of political Zionism, and to some extent even after that. Pinsker's diagnosis of the Jewish problem later became the foundation of all Zionist theories — both left and right wing. Homelessness was declared to be the chief weakness, hence the main problem, of the Jewish people. Deprived of a home, the

Jewish people wandered like a shadow among the nations of the earth which were all organisms wedded to the land and would therefore not tolerate this disturbing exception. Hence Jews must cease to be an exception. They must become the people of a land. A country, a home—this was the fundamental and sole solution to the Jewish question. Later Pinsker joined the Hovevei Zion because he realized that an abstract theory without an appeal to existing folk sentiment and without a bond with historic traditions could find no echo within the people, while the call to colonize Palestine soon united hundreds of young Jewish intellectuals, many students and scholars, and led to immediate practical steps.

In fact a number of Jewish settlements soon were founded in Palestine (Rishon Lezion, Rehovoth, Hedera and others). But colonization in a terribly neglected country by persons both inexperienced and unused to manual labor could not bring about the desired results. The work encountered political difficulties on the part of the Turkish Government and physical hardships from the Arabs who at that time were not opposed on any political grounds but simply engaged in looting.

The movement soon declined to the level of philanthropy and lost the great influence it had exerted on wide circles as the beginning of a significant trend.

But Hovevei Zion could boast of a small, fanatically devoted, group of followers who dedicated their lives to the idea of the redemption of their people and by their stubbornness prepared the ground for the great movement which eventually became a people's movement in the full sense of the term.

This small group of idealists consisted of three segments which performed different functions in laying the foundations for the large mass movement that later emerged. One segment stubbornly and with great material and spiritual sacrifice continued the colonization work in Palestine. They suffered defeats, malaria and other diseases ravaged their ranks, some were killed by Arabs, yet their courage remained undaunted and they did not lose faith in their ultimate success. A second group concentrated about Eliezer Ben Yehudah who undertook to transform Hebrew into a living tongue, basing his effort on the correct assumption that, without a common language and culture, Jews reaching Palestine would prove to be a Babel of tongues and dialects that would only demonstrate to the world the breakdown of the Jewish people. The third group remained in the Diaspora and concentrated about Ahad Ha'am and his so-called Spiritual Zionism. The historic role of this trend did not maintain that Zionism could not or should not strive to solve the Jewish political and economic problems, but rather that it should concentrate on the solution of the Jewish national-cultural problem through the establishment of a spiritual center in Palestine. It set itself the task of preserving the basic principles of Zionism, of preparing cadres of devoted idealists to present the idea to the people and preserve its purity, sanctity and essence. Indeed, in later years disciples of Ahad Ha'am were to be found in all Zionist parties. They had abandoned the main idea of their leader—that of a spiritual center—but otherwise observed the moral commandments of his teachings to serve the people and to devote their lives to them.

Zionism

During the last quarter of the 19th century certain manifestations ripened which forced the more sensitive and thoughtful emancipated Jews to pause and consider. Emancipation was almost a hundred years old and it was time to examine its results.

It became apparent that emancipation did not result in that absolute merging of Jew and non-Jew so desired and dreamed of by some Jewish and non-Jewish elements alike. It became evident that it was very difficult to absorb a group with so well-defined and firm a traditional psyche as the Jews possessed. Neither did the object of the assimilatory process display as great an eagerness to vanish as Jews as had been promised by the early advocates of assimilation through emancipation. Opposed to the extreme assimilationists who practiced conversion and mixed marriages, there came into being an extremely orthodox element which strongly hindered the assimilatory process. An additional factor evoked an echo within a certain sector of outwardly assimilated Jews of Western and Central Europe—the resurgence of Eastern European Jewry which was outspokenly national in character. This echo roused dormant sensibilities and wakened longings hibernating under heavy layers of assimilation.

But far more effective and influential was the fact that the non-Jewish side refused to abandon its age-old attitude of considering the Jew an alien, a neighbor who was perhaps gifted and accorded political and economic rights but nevertheless not a complete equal and therefore not of the same worth. Intensive Jewish participation in the political and cultural life of the assimilating nations was met with less sympathy than their participation in the economic fields of action. The more assimilated among the Jews felt this especially keenly since they were so eager to serve their fatherlands in every sphere of endeavor without any reservations. And their accomplishments were far from negligible indeed. The more sensitive assimilated Jews felt humiliated by the repeated venomous reminders of their duty to be thankful for the emancipation which had been granted to them as a gift. These also sensed the falseness of their statutes of "slavery within freedom," as Ahad Ha'am so brilliantly defined it. From beneath the accumulated tiers of assimilation new manifestations of national pride began to appear. Moses Hess expressed this feeling in *Rome and Jerusalem.* Some decades later Nathan Birnbaum voiced it in his Zionist writings which advocated Herzl's ideas a decade before Herzl appeared on the scene. Max Nordau described the position of the assimilated Jew, who feared to admit his Jewishness even while his neighbors considered his as such, as one of "moral need." This need began to torment the conscience of the new type of Marrano.

Anti-Semitism, which suddenly gained a new aggressive lease on life, exerted an even greater influence on the revision of the attitude toward assimilation. In the very midst of the process of assimilation, even as Jews participated intensively in the capitalist development of their countries, the new violent anti-Semitism emerged which stemmed precisely from the Jews' participation in the capitalist development, and their share in destroying the outlived feudal and semi-feudal forms of life. Jewish liberalism in politics, science and the arts fed it. The new social class—the middle class—took the lead in this anti-Semitism. The intellectuals of the middle class spearheaded it. Treitschke in Germany, Drumont in France and Lueger in Austria became its prophets. They sounded a warning to the Jews that their romance with assimilation had come to an end and a new era of modern anti-Semitism in the tempo of the new times was commencing, based on economic interests and fought primarily with political means.

These developments in the aforementioned countries were in harmony with the moods of Eastern European Jews and created a common ground for common strivings. In the countries of Eastern Europe, too, there operated not only negative factors such as pogroms and lack of rights but also organic processes of the auto-emancipation of Jewish spiritual energy. The field for new national stirrings was therefore of considerable scope. In the countries of Central and Western Europe the negative factor was the more potent. Individuals blessed with the sense of anticipating historical events reacted to it. Eastern European Jewry provided the mass sentiment, "the hewers of wood and carriers of water" who were true to tradition and zealously guarded historic values. Western Europe provided the planners, the political architects and leaders, the diplomats.

Among these chosen ones Dr. Theodore Herzl was the elect. A prominent European journalist, dramatist and essayist, a typical Viennese Jewish intellectual, a doubter and melancholy modernist, he gained vision when he became absorbed in the Jewish question. His being burned with the problem. In the course of a few weeks he wrote a small book which was to mark a new beginning in the destiny of the oldest among nations. The name of the book was *The Jewish State*. It left an indelible impression, especially in Eastern Europe where the soil had been prepared by the Hovevei Zion, and the organic development of the new liberation movement was awaiting the appearance of a leader and guide, of an inspired visionary possessing the talents of an organizer.

Herzl was remote from Judaism and from Jewish life. He therefore had no traditional bonds with Palestine. He did not know of the Hovevei Zion or of the beginnings of colonization in Palestine. Only when he saw his ideas accepted primarily by these traditional bearers of the movement for rejuvenation did he agree to unite these with his great political plans.

The Jewish State was remarkable not because of the aim it advocated. This aim had been popular among Hovevei Zion even earlier. It was distinguished by the practical methods it outlined for the realization of this aim. Herzl's political scope and the statesmanship of his approach were new. The masses gravitated toward him as the potential "Jewish King," a personality fit to occupy the throne of leadership, a redeemer on a modern scale who approached the Jewish question from a political standpoint that was in keeping with the political trends and methods of the time. The charm of Herzl's personality exerted its influence in Central and Western Europe on those elements who had become disappointed in the redeeming quality of emancipation. In Eastern Europe his influence was enhanced especially by his European aureole and the fact that he came from a strange and distant world.

However it would be erroneous to assume that only the charm of his personality roused to drastic and far-reaching action. There was something fateful in his appearance on the scene. The Jewish masses sensed that he had voiced that which they, being politically inarticulate, had not dared to enunciate, but bore deep within their hearts as an unuttered dream. Manner is no less important in politics than in art. Old truths assume an explosive character when uttered by a person who knows the secret of resurrection, who possesses the key to the era. Herzl was such a person.

Herzl formulated the Jewish question in the following manner:

(a) The Jewish question is national in character. It concerns all parts of the people and touches upon every aspect of their life, political as well as economic, material as well as spiritual. Return to Judaism must therefore precede return to Jews.

(b) The Jewish question is international and must be solved on an international basis.

(c) The Jewish question is political. Political rights guaranteeing the basis and scope of the Jewish State must precede the practical work of colonization.

(d) Only an organized Jewish people, equipped with the necessary political and financial apparatus, can carry out the great historic objective of establishing a Jewish State. A world Jewish Congress must be formed to undertake the establishment of the institutions necessary for the realization of this task.

These were the main ideas of the small book which laid the foundations for the Zionist organization and created the political atmosphere leading to the Balfour Declaration, the Mandate and the international recognition of the Jewish Agency as the organ of the Zionist movement.

Nor was Herzl satisfied merely to indicate the ways and means of politically organizing the scattered Jewish people and of establishing a political apparatus for landless Jewry. He also gave a concrete description of how to organize the work which would lead to a Jewish State and to train the Jewish people so that the State should be founded on progressive trends of European social thinking. This concretization of aim as well as of ways and means had a great effect, since it was expressed in simple and sober terms yet with such conviction and faith that great masses were enchanted by it and were ready to follow Herzl wherever he led. Jewish intellectuals, and the orthodox as well, were moved by the solidity of his plan, the depth of his faith and the ripeness of the moment for the establishment of a Jewish State. The immediate result was the first world Zionist Congress, which was without doubt a turning point in the history of the Jewish people.

The Zionist Congress

In 1897 in Basle the first Zionist Congress took place which laid the foundation for the present day movement and became a stabilized international political organization of the Jewish people.

204 delegates as well as several hundred guests were present. The delegates came from many different countries and represented Jewish communities scattered throughout the world. The gathering was a conglomeration, not only of languages and cultures, but also of physical types, clothes, manners and customs; Jews from many lands, from different economic walks of life and cultural levels; Ashkenazi, Sephardic, Arab, assimilated, half assimilated, nationalistic and orthodox. In a word, a true Tower of Babel.

The first Zionist Congress keenly demonstrated two things: It showed how the homeless Jews, torn asunder and scattered the world over, had become estranged from each other. Yet at the same time it also demonstrated how deep rooted were the common national feelings and mutual bonds, how strong was their belief in their common creed and redemption; and how alike was the destiny of Jewish minorities in different countries despite all their economic, political and cultural differences.

Listening to the reports of the representatives, one became increasingly aware of the sameness of the Jewish problem in all countries—the world accepts the Jew as an alien and treats him accordingly; and not in a single land do the Jews feel at home or have they any sense of security. Only in the degree of homelessness did the situation vary; in essence it remained the same for the Jews the world over. The picture was clear—the problem was to find a home for a homeless people. And history has long since chosen this home. The land where this people awakened to national consciousness; where the most inspired page of history was written—the page of the Prophets and monotheism. This is the land that people carried in their hearts through exile and inquisition, through pogroms and persecutions, and only on this historic soil is its continued vital existence as a people possible.

Herzl believed that the Zionist Congress was the Jewish Government en route—and there is much truth in this. During the course of the 50 years of the existence of this Organization, only once did a group break the discipline and withdraw. This was in 1933, when the Revisionists, a right-wing political group headed by Vladimir Jabotinsky, split the ranks and attempted to create a new parallel Zionist organization. Despite the frequent sharp differences of opinion and principle, despite the bitter fights between the various groups—ideological and social—the internal national and moral discipline was nevertheless so strong that the minority was always willing to accept majority opinion. The movement kept growing; it developed subsidiary institutions and enterprises with budgets and large important economic investments. But it never came to a serious internal rift. This manifestation of free national discipline demonstrated the great moral strength of the national ideal.

The program accepted at the First Zionist Congress was decisive. "The aim of Zionism is to create for the Jewish people a home in Palestine secured by public law. In order to attain this object, the Congress adopted the following means:

1. The systematic promotion of the settlement of Palestine with Jewish agriculturists, artisans and craftsmen.
2. The organization and federation of all Jewry by means of local and general institutions in conformity with the local laws.
3. The strengthening of Jewish sentiment and national consciousness.
4. Preparatory steps for the procuring of such government assents as are necessary for achieving the object of Zionism."

Any Jew who accepts this program and buys a Shekel (fifty cents) is entitled to membership in the Zionist Organization.

Stages of Development of the Zionist Movement

The development of the Zionist movement was molded and influenced by three basic factors:

(a) The situation of the Jews in the Diaspora.
(b) The drive of the Jewish masses to emigrate from European countries and the immigration possibilities in new lands.
(c) The absorptive capacity of Palestine and the prospects for the achievement of national political independence.

The influence exerted by these three factors was not always uniform and harmonious. As a result, the development of Zionism did not always forge ahead, but zigzagged, falling, in general, into three major periods:

(a) From the First Zionist Congress (1897) to the Balfour Declaration (1917)—political failures, and meager colonization achievements.
(b) From the Balfour Declaration to the Hitler debacle (1933)—intensive immigration into Palestine, tremendous increase of Palestine's absorptive capacity but an inadequate influx of capital which retarded the economic progress of the country.
(c) From the beginning of Nazism until the present day (1947)—tremendous drive of Jewish masses to Palestine, influx of capital, intensification of industry, and intensive growth of the absorptive capacity of the country.

The Zionist Congresses called forth a great national awakening in the Jewish world. This reinvigorating spirit was felt on all levels of Jewish life—a stream of new blood bringing to all Jewry renewed strength. Ideological contacts and mutual interactions between Jewish communities became more intensified and fruitful. Frequent meetings of Zionist leaders from all over erected new bridges from Jewish center to center—bridges which had been destroyed by emancipation. National consciousness grew, winning large portions of assimilated Jews back to the national fold even in those lands were assimilated Jews were the majority.

But politically, the efforts of Herzl brought no results. By 1903 it became quite evident that there was no hope at all for a Palestinian Charter from the Turkish Sultan. This gave rise to a serious crisis in the movement, sharpened all the more by the death of Herzl (1904), on whom the masses had bestowed their blind allegiance.

This critical period in Zionism coincided with the tremendous growth of revolutionary trends in Russia. The Jews were strongly attracted by the Russian Revolution; hopes for political emancipation and even for broader national rights became so wide-spread that even extreme Zionist circles embraced this blinding illusion. The Socialist-Zionist parties actively participated in the Russian Revolution. The Russian General Zionist Organization, then the strongest and most influential of the parties within the World Zionist Organization, initiated a broad national program of activity in the Diaspora (Helsinki, 1906). Even the few hundred pogroms in the days of the 1905 October Revolution did not deter the Russian Zionists from their energetic program in the Diaspora. The prospects for immigration to Palestine were at that time very weak.

And such was the political mood not only in Russia. In Galicia, too, which boasted the second strongest Zionist movement in the world, the local national program was accepted enthusiastically by the Jewish masses. The Zionists had to reckon with the prevailing mood of the masses and go along with them. The Socialist-Zionists were particularly active in this work. There were extreme elements within the Zionist movement that fought against the Diaspora illusions. Thus, Jabotinsky wrote: "There is no middle road —either exodus or assimilation! Either our own home or national disappearance." (*Raswiet*, No. 13, 1907).

At the same time, the gates of the immigration countries in the world were wide open. To the extent that the Jewish masses sought ways of escaping poverty and persecution in most of the Eastern European countries, they had many refuge opportunities other than Palestine, and under better conditions. From 1897 to 1914, more than one and a half million Jews emigrated from Europe—almost a fifth of the total Jewish population. Of this tremendous number of emigrants from Europe, scarcely 30,000-35,000, or 2 percent, came to Palestine.

But a pioneering immigration to a barren wasteland must not be measured by numbers alone, for qualitatively, just in the years after the unsuccessful Russian Revolution, a great upheaval took place in the composition of the immigration to Palestine. This was the small but famous *Second Aliyah* (ascension) which played so great an historic role in the development of Palestine.

The first generation of immigrants to Palestine—from 1882 to 1907—although making great physical and material sacrifices, nonetheless did not succeed in completing the pioneer period of colonization. This generation did not manage to create such colonization forms as were appropriate to the extremely difficult conditions in the barren and stony land of little rains and a primitive local population; nor did they establish the colonization forms required for the rebirth of a people that for centuries had been far removed from agriculture. The early colonists, whose fields and gardens were watered with Jewish sweat and blood, were eventually forced to hire Arabs for the work requiring agricultural skills and physical strength. A most complex and unfortunate situation resulted—the Arabs constituted the majority in those Jewish colonies which were destined to establish a Jewish National Home. To overcome this crisis and create the conditions necessary for a mass influx, a new element was needed with fresh idealism and modern methods. They appeared in the few years prior to World War I.

The complete failure of the Russian Revolution, the re-awakened reaction and tendency to confine Jews to the ghettos, the 700 pogroms and more in the few days of the October Revolution, the more violent pograms of 1906 in Bialostok and Sedliez—all this shook the Jewish population of Russia to its roots and produced two results: larger masses fled overseas, especially to America; the disappointed Jewish intellegentsia increasingly sought means of organizing and directing the energies of the wandering masses toward a radical solution of the Jewish problem. In the first four years of the twentieth century, 160,206 Jews from Russia and Poland emigrated to the United States; in the next four years (1904-1907), their number more than doubled—410,098.

During these same years various territorial projects and organizations came into being which approached the Jewish problem as if it were solely one of immigration. They believed that favorable colonization conditions in a free land were sufficient to attract the Jewish masses to any given place which would then become a home for the homeless Jewish people. Those Zionist circles, however, whose approach to theJewish problem embraced all its historical complexities and took cognizance of the inherent desire for the vital continuity of a people, aware that such a folk instinct could be put to good advantage in mobilizing the accumulated spiritual well-springs of world Jewry—these circles remained loyal to Palestine. But they had to seek new ways and means to conquer the difficult colonization obstacles in Palestine. It was at this point that the idea of *Chalutziut* (pioneering) emerged; in its deepest sense, it embodied two basic ideas: self-employment and collective work. *Hachsharah* (physical and spiritual training for Palestine in the Diaspora); the work cult as an ideology; Hebrew as the only language of the new settlements; socialist education of the younger generation in the Diaspora and a socialist society as the objective—these were all by-products of the central theme of Chalutziut.

All these idealistic moods and collectivistic ideas were forged in Russia in the left-wing Zionist circles who had been reared in Achad Ha'am's ethic Zionism and in Russian Socialism, which was more nationalistic than the purely proletarian Socialism of Western Europe.

Although the trickle of Chalutzim into Palestine was not too strong, nevertheless the contribution they made to that which was later created there is beyond evaluation. In a few short years these numbered folk-idealists laid the foundation of the colonization forms which later became the model for the entire agricultural program. Life changed and corrected much in the early collective settlements, and today Palestine offers the entire scale of Socialist colonies from extreme communistic, which include cooperative kitchens and a cooperative child education system, to colonies based on a minimum of cooperative principles, such as cooperative buying and selling, and cooperation in agriculture. But the great influence that the first collectives had on the development of the entire economy of the country, including that of the cities, was most important. This cooperative principle, to the extent that it has been realized in Palestine, is not to be found anywhere else in the world. About two-thirds of the agricultural produce of the country, other than citrus fruits, are produced in collective settlements of one socialistic form or another. Approximately half the Jewish population of Palestine is organized in consumer cooperatives. Almost all building and construction is done through cooperatives. Transportation is practically entirely in the hands of cooperatives. These last two economic branches include many thousands of workers. The credit corporations are well represented throughout the country. And even about ten percent of the country's industry is cooperatively run. The effect of the cooperative principle goes far beyond its actual economic participation in the business of the country, for during the war, the cooperatives regulated and controlled prices and prevented the development of wide-spread speculation. The numerically small immigration of the first period played a most decisive role in the development of the entire community; it prepared the blueprint not only of the economic structure of the country, but of the entire social structure of the national organism. It was from this small group that the nucleus of teachers and leaders arose who later became the guides and founders of all financial and political institutions which were constantly growing and increasing in number and scope. It was this group, too, who created that inspired communal atmosphere in which the movement grew.

The first world war and the European revolutions changed the economic and political structure of Europe to its very foundations, and even more radically affected the situation of the Jews in Europe. The most significant positive achievements were: the Balfour Declaration, the Palestine Mandate, and the system of national minorities rights in the countries of Eastern Europe guaranteed by the League of Nations.

The Balfour Declaration begins with the following passage:

> His Majesty's Government view with favour the establishment in Palestine of a national home for the Jewish People and will use their best endeavors to facilitate the achievement of this object.

This was presented by the British Government through Lord Rothschild with instructions to submit it to the Zionist Organization of England (November 2, 1917). Further developments brought about an even more important political document—the Mandate, the second paragraph of which reads:

> The Mandatory shall be responsible for the country under such political administrative and economic conditions as will secure the establishment of the Jewish National Home.

While Paragraph 4 reads:

> An appropriate Jewish agency shall be recognized as a public body for the purpose of advising and cooperating with the administration of Palestine in such economic, social and other matters as may affect the establishment of the Jewish national home. The Zionist Organization, so long as its organization and

constitution are in the opinion of the Mandatory appropriate, shall be recognized as such agency.

The Declaration, which basically recognized the historical right of the Jews to Palestine and actually promised a Jewish State as the final goal, was greeted with enthusiasm by all classes of world Jewry. Even greater was their joy because the atmosphere surrounding the granting of the Declaration demonstrated that it was not being donated as the gift of a benevolent government; on the contrary, it was quite clear that the British Government was anxious to win over to the Allies the sympathies of the large Jewish masses in Russia and the United States. The Mandate was further proof that Jews were being recognized as a national entity, that the throes of deliverance were over and the Jewish people was now entering the stage of factual self-determination.

Immediately following World War I, therefore, Zionist activity followed two directions: on the one hand, feverish preparations for ambitious constructive plans in Palestine, especially for the reception of large waves of immigration; on the other hand, organization of the Jewries of the European countries and creation of that new community set-up that is a prerequisite of a fruitful national autonomy in the Diaspora. Wherever there were democratically elected Jewish community organizations or central land organizations, the Zionists were in the majority. Such was the case in the Ukraine, which for a time was independent; in Lithuania where the Jews were autonomous for a while; in Latvia where there was an autonomous Jewish school system.

At this time, however, there were also other factors which diminished the enthusiasm of the Jewish people. The war ended with the dissolution of the Russian and Austro-Hungarian Empires. This, in turn, led to the disintegration of that historic Jewish center which numbered about 8 million Jews, and which for hundreds of years had been the main-spring of Jewish national energies. Instead of living in two large empires, the Jews were now divided up and scattered in tens of larger or smaller states.

In the Ukraine, where a bitter conflict raged between the Ukrainians and Russians, more than 2,000 bloody pogroms against the Jews took place. This was a painful and costly demonstration of the abnormal position of the Jewish minority within the fighting nations among whom they lived. The Ukranians blamed the Jews for Bolshevism and Russification, and the monarchist armies blamed the Jews for Bolshevism and Ukranian sympathies. And both groups inflicted pogroms on their "enemy," the Jew.

Those peoples who became politically independent, whom the Jews had greatly aided in their struggle for freedom, and who had during the period of combat promised the Jews civil and national equality, actually forgot all their promises on the day after victory, did an about-face and immediately began waging their own fights against the Jews: an economic struggle so as to usurp their economic positions; a political struggle so as to isolate Jews from those progressive non-Jewish elements who had remained loyal to their liberal ideas; a national struggle so as to dilute the Jewish concentrations in the cities and make of them a minority where they had previously been a majority. The conflict took various forms in different countries, the methods being more or less severe; but the end goal was everywhere the same: to poison the life of the Jews to such an extent that they would be forced to flee. Physical insecurity mounted. Economic displacement assumed dangerous proportions. Social isolation increased the stifled atmosphere. The goal had been reached—the Jewish drive to emigrate was ever increasing.

The Bolshevik Revolution, with its nationalizations and confiscations, ruined more than half of the Jewish population of Russia. This was concrete proof that socialism must, in its early stages, adversely affect Jews more strongly than non-Jews; belonging as they do to the urban social classes, Jews must necessarily be the first victims of the change from capitalism to socialism.

In countries neighboring on Russia, a few hundred thousand refugees gathered, fleeing from the pogroms and the Bolshevistic regime. There were more than enough of real and potential immigrants in Europe, and the numbers were constantly mounting. Jews set out to all corners of the world, seeking a place of refuge. But as early as 1920, the United States, the main country of absorption, began imposing immigration restrictions—and in 1924 quotas were imposed which practically closed the doors to the Jews of those countries from which they wanted most to flee.

In the four years from 1921-1924, 180,000 Jews came to the shores of the United States, while in the following four years (1925-1928), just 43,000 entered, even though the need for emigration from Europe had increased tremendously during this short period.

This was just one side of the picture; but real life is many-sided, often complicated and conflicting. During these very years of unrest and disappointment in the Diaspora, there were also a number of incidents of cultural re-awakening.

The new life being evolved in Palestine had a profound effect upon the Diaspora community: Jewish youth went to Palestine in droves, but large masses stayed behind and began to prepare themselves, physically, occupationally and cultural-linguistically, for *aliyah* (immigration to Palestine). The word *aliyah* was magic to the ears of the youth. The countries of Eastern Europe became dotted with tens of hachsharah (agricultural) places, hundreds of chalutz kibbutzim (urban collectives), with Zionist sport organizations, with Hebrew schools—folk schools, high schools, evening classes. The Zionist movement sprouted new wings. Its activity grew from day to day. It not only did not negate the Diaspora, but, on the contrary, threw itself into a prodigious folk-work: reorganizing the *Kehilloth* (Community organizations) on democratic foundations; creating institutions for economic self-help; conducting schools and courses for handicraft workers, etc.

The upsurge of Zionist activity carried forward the activity of all other Jewish social organizations. But not this alone. There were other positive factors which intensified Jewish social potentialities in the ten years following World War I—those very years when the heavy tread of the pending disaster was already to be heard.

The unused and pent-up revolutionary energies of those Russian Jews who had been cut from Russia sought their expression in the newly formed states in which they now lived. Although the political and economic conditions in these new countries were not perfect for the development of revolutionary ideals, they were nevertheless better than those existing under the Tsarist regime. And indeed, a feverish activity began on all levels of social and cultural life—in Poland, in Luthuania, in Latvia, partly in Rumania, and in Hungary.

In these countries, schools in Yiddish and Hebrew were established; literature in both languages made great strides; the Yiddish press became richer in content and increased in its influence on the masses; the unions of various occupational organizations grew stronger; the Jewish communities became more highly organized, more deeply nationally aware, Zionists and non-Zionists alike. The age-old rule of Jewish history was in force here, too—the more the Jews are persecuted, the more nationally conscious they become, the more productive does the work in their own backyard become.

For the first time in the long history of the Jewish Diaspora immigration to Palestine assumed large proportions. Of the 680,000 Jews who left Europe between 1919 and 1933, 135,000 (20%) went to Palestine, a percentage ten times that of the pre-World War I period. Immigration into Palestine grew from year to year. Two factors worked to effect this steady multiplication: the immigration restrictions in the American countries, and the rising absorptive capacity of Palestine.

Economic development in Palestine now proceeded much more intensively than before the Balfour Declaration, but with frequent interrupting crisis. The influx of capital was meager since over 90 percent of the newcomers were from the poorer classes of Eastern Europe, primarily youth and laborers.

During these years, however, the Palestine community became more and more crystallized in its economic and cultural structure. The collectives were gradually becoming self-supporting. Especially in the field of agricultural techniques were tremendous strides made. The Hebrew language became so rooted in the life of the country, that the newcomers were forced to learn what had now become the language of the country. The Zionist institutions, the Bank, the Funds, succeeded in strengthening the operation of their machinery and improving the organization of their national campaigns. The Hebrew University was established and the National Library grew steadily. A rich daily press sprang up which played its role in cementing the heterogeneous Jewish elements from the many countries and language areas of Europe. The Jewish Agency was created (1929), including non-Zionist members, which gave it greater authority in the eyes of the outside world. The National Council (*Vaad Leumi*) was established, the autonomous organ of the Jewish community in Palestine.

The workers' organizations and institutions displayed an extremely progressive, intensive development both in numbers and in quality. The Federation of Jewish Workers in Palestine, *Histadruth*, established in 1920, acquired tens of thousands of members and set up many new workers' institutions, such as *Kupath Cholim* (Sick Fund), a large daily newspaper, a press, schools, and many others. The Histadruth became the most important factor in the progress of all facets of the Community, particularly in aliyah.

The Zionist Organization ceased to be a "Jewish Government en route" and assumed its role as the Jewish Government in the making.

The picture of Jewish life in Europe in the third period (1933-1939) in its negative aspects was very similar to the situation described, only ten and twenty times worse. Hitler came to power. The liquidation of German Jewry began. The Zionist Organization was the only body to realize what the further development and significance of this fact would be, and purposefully began to organize the methodical emigration of Jews from Germany. Due to this activity, which was strongly opposed by the assimilationist groups on the one hand, and on the other, by the anti-Zionist socialist elements, tens of thousands of German Jews were saved, among them many of the youth. Hundreds of millions of German marks were also salvaged which were utilized for construction work in Palestine. Many hachsharah camps were established in the countries of Europe where thousands upon thousands of German Jewish youth were trained for eventual emigration to Palestine.

The poison of Nazi anti-Semitism began spreading throughout the countries of Eastern Europe. Although it did not assume the same murderous forms and degrees as in Germany, it nevertheless evidenced the same tendencies—expulsion of Jews in one form or another. It was an untenable, suffocating situation. Physical pogroms increased. Small excesses and radical attacks on Jews became daily occurences.

Under such circumstances, it is easy to understand how quickly and intensively the trend to emigrate from Europe grew among the Jews. But it was just in these awful, fateful years in the history of European Jewry that the gates of the immigration countries were more tightly barred to them. Jews fled to all corners of the world—Jews could be found wandering in the most remote and foresaken lands, across all the seas and oceans, often without destination, but with the hope that somewhere they would find a place in which to settle. The flight to Palestine began to assume the proportions of a mass movement. And so it continues to this very day. Of the 440,000 Jews who left Europe in the years between 1934 to 1946, 210,000, or 47.7 percent, entered Palestine. In 1939 the British White Paper appeared which severely restricted immigration to Palestine. But "illegal" immigration, which began in 1933, accounted for increasingly larger numbers and, by the end of 1947, included over 50,000—30,000 of whom are now interned in camps on the island of Cyprus.

The heavy influx of private capital during these years, as well as the increase in the number of Jewish industrial engineers and merchandising experts, made Palestine an industrial country.

Differentiation

It was quite natural that the Zionist organization, as a national movement, should become divided into various groupings—first, according to social classification of the people, secondly, according to differences in ideological precepts. From the very beginning it was obvious that, in regard to the political problems of the Jews in the Diaspora, there must necessarily be great differences of opinion between the leaders of the Labor Zionists and of the bourgeois sectors within the movement. An attempt was made to exclude the concrete political, economic and cultural problems of the Diaspora from the framework of Zionism and consider it merely an organization concerned with the exodus of Jews from the Diaspora. The idea was that the Zionist movement must not interfere in any of the local political or class conflicts. But it soon became apparent that because of the slowness of pace and multiplicity of problems raised by the "return to Zion," this would mean suicide to the movement. It would remain suspended in mid-air, and would have no membership when the time for liberation finally arrived. It was exactly through the fight for political freedom in the Diaspora, and due to the national awakening in the Diaspora, that the movement created the social atmosphere necessary for the stupendous work of re-building their homeland.

These cardinal questions were especially vital to the labor Zionist circles, who were enthused by the general European socialist movement and particularly by the Russian revolutionary struggle. A synthesis had to be found between Diaspora work and Palestine colonization; between the struggle of the working class for their immediate economic needs and the goal of Zionism which was so distant both in time and space. This internal conflict in the movement—the tragedy of the struggle for rights and freedoms, and the simultaneous preparation and up-building of a national home in another land, on another continent—this abnormal situation of the Zionist movement did but demonstrate in striking relief the abnormal situation of the Jewish people itself which, despite having no soil of its own, nevertheless remained alive as a people, and was forced to use its creative powers in two directions.

In the further development of Zionism, the problems of class struggle penetrated to the colonization work. While the bourgeois elements based their theories on private initiative, labor Zionism emphasized collective economy. But here, too, a tragic conflict ensued: on the one hand, the concrete immediate needs and interests of the working class and its socialist ideals, on the other hand, the national interests of the Jewish people which demand sacrifices from all classes and do not always coincide with the special interests of the working class. Here, too, it was necessary to find a synthesis, a compromise between class interests and national interests. Concretely, this meant maximum encouragement of the collective economy and, at the same time, non-interference in the development of private economic ventures to the extent that they contributed to the progress of national reconstruction, to the upbuilding of a national territorial home.

We cannot go into the details of all the forms of differentiation developing in the movement here. Briefly, a left-wing group emerged, closer to communism, which underlined the class struggle and believed that the positive national work could be relegated to the bourgeoisie. There also grew up an extreme right wing which stressed the national aspect and demanded that Jewish workers forget the class struggle and devote themselves exclusively to the great national task of building a home for the Jewish people. The largest workers' party, the Right Poale Zion, here displayed a historical intuition—without theorizing, they found the necessary synthesis; practically, they always solved the problem with such a compromise that produced the maximum results in the interests of the people as a whole, and with a minimum of sacrifice of the interests of the working class.

It is thus that this party became the outstanding group in Palestine as well as in the entire movement. In the process of setting up socialist forms within the Palestine economy, they not only did not hinder the advance of private enterprise, but even welcomed and supported it. They advocated competition between the two factions rather than conflict; and it was this that helped produce the fine results.

In the ranks of bourgeois Zionism, too, a differentiation took place. An orthodox element—Mizrachi—has grown up which aims at imposing religious forms on the community. In the first years of Zionism there was a group which preached Achad Ha'amism—the idea that Palestine must become a spiritual center for the Jewish people, that Zionism is incapable of solving the economic and political problems of world Jewry. An extreme right wing also developed which at one time imitated certain fascist ideologies such as opposition to the class struggle, the "Fuehrer" principle, negation of the claim of Diaspora Jews to attain rights as Jews. But even within the bourgeois elements there was always a center which tried to live more or less in peace with the proletariat elements. Here, too, the healthy compromise which supported the positive elements of Labor Zionism was victorious.

BIBLIOGRAPHY

DUBNOW, SIMON: *Weltgeschichte des Juedischen Volkes,* Berlin, Vol. 9-10.
COHEN, ISRAEL: *The Zionist Movement,* New York, 1946.
LOCKER, BERL: *Stiff-Necked People,* London, 1946.
AMERICAN PALESTINE COMMITTEE: *Christian Point of View Presented to the Anglo-American Committee on Inquiry,* New York, 1946.
ZIMAN, J.: *Revival of Palestine,* New York, 1946.
HESS, MOSES: Rome und Jerusalem, Leipzig, 1899.
PINKSER, LEON: *Autoemancipation,* Berlin, 1920.
SOKOLOW, NAHUM: *History of Zionism,* London, 1908.
HAAM, ACHAD: *Ten Essays on Zionism and Judaism,* London, 1922.
BOEM, ADOLF: *Die Zionistische Bewegung,* Vienna, 1935.
HERZL, THEODOR: *Zionistische Schriften,* Berlin, 1923.

HERZL, THEODOR: *The Jewish State,* London, 1936.
NORDAU, MAX: *Zionistische Schriften,* Cologne, 1909.
Palestine, A Study of Jewish, Arab and British Policies. Published by Yale University Press, New Haven, Conn., 1947.
LORD BALFOUR: *Speeches on Zionism,* London, 1928.
JABOTINSKY, VLADIMIR: *The Jewish War Front,* London, 1940.
LOWDERMILK, WALTER: *Palestine, Land of Promise,* New York, 1944.
NATHAN, ROBERT: *Palestine: Problem and Promise,* Washington, D. C., 1946.

XVI.
Anti-Semitism

XVI.

ANTI-SEMITISM

by

Jacob Lestchinsky

Introduction: Before XVIII Century

Before the emancipation period the Jewish question was—for Jews and Gentiles alike—a religious and economic one. For the Jews it was a question of how to be tolerated in the Christian or Mohammedan world despite their different religious creed, and how, being strangers and temporary guests, to secure their subsistence. Mentally, the Jews were not willing yet to regard themselves as citizens of the Diaspora countries; they looked upon the Diaspora as a temporary condition and firmly believed that the Messiah would come and guide them back to the land of promise; and they would become a united and independent nation again.

The same problems existed for the Gentile world, only as it were, with inverse signs, namely; Should aliens belonging to a different creed be tolerated? And will their economic activities be profitable enough for the whole nation to justify the "sacrifice" of tolerating "godless" people in their midst?

All this makes it understandable why the Jews felt little inclination to become an organic part of the economic life, and, even more, a part of the cultural life of the countries where they found only unstable and insecure residence. Besides, Jews were forbidden to own land or to be active in agriculture in all European countries; only trade and finance were open to them; yet both these activities were only slightly developed in the pre-capitalistic era. In the majority of the European countries, Jews were also excluded from the handicrafts (with the exception of only a few which they needed from the ritual point of view, like baking, tailoring, or even butchering). The Jews felt that their property, as well as their very lives, were always at the mercy of a sudden whim of a ruler or violent outburst of a religious fanatic, and since they always had to be ready for a sudden, quick escape, they kept their possessions in "liquid" form, easily transportable.

The emancipation of the Jews (18th - 19th century) brought about a radical change in the relationship between the Gentile world and Jewry. For the first time in history the Jews in Europe were looked upon as citizens of equal rights in the countries of their birth and residence; and, for the first time, also the Jews became conscious of their rights: not only their right to exist, but their right to play some part in the cultural and political life of the Diaspora countries.

In the words of the Declaration of Independence, "All men are born equal," there was given the simplest and, at the same time, the highest formula, politically and morally, of all European revolutions of the 18th and 19th centuries; yet the materialization of this formula, the virtual admission of Jews to all fields of social and economic activity, was a result of a relentless struggle, and the process of the virtual emancipation of Jews was largely different in scope and tempo in different countries.

Since the Jews belonged, both socially and politically, to the underprivileged groups, they had everything to gain and nothing to lose from the establishment of democratic institutions in the Diaspora countries. The Jews belonged neither to the politically dominating groups nor to the feudal class; nor, as a matter of course, did they share any privileges of the clergy. Therefore, the overwhelming majority of Jews was progressive minded as far as political and economic questions were concerned. Throughout Europe they were intensely involved in political and cultural struggles; everywhere they felt the impact of the traditionally anti-Semitic minded domineering groups and classes; several internationally famous fighters for freedom and equality for all men, such as Marx and Lasalle, Heine and Boerne, came from their midst. The Jews also played an important part in the development of modern capitalism, especially in the countries of Central and Eastern Europe: But, since the development of industry and trade jolted some groups of artisans and small shopkeepers from their economic positions, the Jews were blamed for all their mishaps, and new fuel was added to the anti-Semitic feelings.

Gentile society, like all societies, is certainly not uniform, and its attitude toward the Jews runs the whole gamut, from grim hatred, to sincere sympathy, to equal association. In normal times the Jewish question represents just one of many problems around which the political, economic and ideological struggle is concentrated. In times of severe crisis and sharp social encounters, however, the deeply rooted hatred for Jews sweeps over society; and that movement which sees in radical anti-Semitism the only solution of the Jewish problem usually carries the day.

Derivation and Definition of the Concept "Anti-Semitism"

The word, "anti-Semitism," means hatred and hostility against the Jewish people. Although the literal meaning of the word is hostility towards Semites in general, it is now commonly accepted that it means hostility toward Jews exclusively.

The German Journalist, Wilhelm Mahr in his pamphlet, *Der Sieg des Judentums ueber das Germanentum vom nicht konfessionalen Standpunkte* (1873), was the first to coin the word "anti-Semitism," and the first to preach hatred against Jews from the racial point of view.

Concurrence of Several Factors

The history of anti-Semitism shows that several different factors concurred in the creation of hostile feelings against Jews:

repulsion and enmity to aliens, religious fanaticism, and economic competition. Later, in the era of emancipation, when the Jews became incorporated into the Gentile society surrounding them, to a greater or lesser degree, and commenced participating in the political and cultural life of this society, new factors of a political and cultural nature were added to the group of motives which inspired anti-Semitic feelings. And every time in history that the anti-Semitic feelings were condensed to such a degree that acts of mass violence against Jews have occurred, these events resulted from specific conditions; they depended, first, on the nature of the dynamic factor which was, in every case, the driving force leading to mass violence and, second, on the active social group which made use of accumulated hostile feelings against Jews, turning the passive hatred of the masses into acts of violence. Thus, for instance, in the Middle Ages, the driving force of the massacres and persecution of Jews during the Crusades and bubonic plague was religion, and the clergymen were the active leaders of the instigated masses. On the other hand, if we take the anti-Semitism of the emancipation era in the countries of Central and Eastern Europe, we will find that the main factors leading to it were of a political and economic nature, and that its leaders mainly came from the lay "intelligentsia."

In harmony with the positivistic and naturalistic spirit prevailing today, the anti-Semitic movement has replaced the religious element with the racial one—and this is even more useful for the purpose of eliminating Jewish competition. In addition, the new orientation on the principle of race prevents certain circles of assimilated Jews from deserting the creed of their fathers.

Latent and Dynamic Anti-Semitism

We must define the difference between the following two forms of anti-Semitism: latent and passive, and dynamic and active anti-Semitism. Latent anti-Semitism, which is rooted in the feelings of repulsion against aliens and hostility to the "godless," is many hundreds of years old; it is instilled in the souls of Christian children when they are still of tender age and their minds are very susceptible to all sorts of influence. Thus, hostile feelings against Jews became wide-spread in the largest majority of nations where the Jews lived. This latent stratum of hatred, although it may appear passive and innocent, still offers the best basis for dynamic anti-Semitism; the latter represents deliberate action on the part of certain social or political groups, guided in their struggle against Jews by specific political or economic interests.

The latent anti-Semitism did not represent a sufficiently strong obstacle to keep the Jews from enjoying the closest economic and cultural relations with the Gentile world, as well as from occupying high economic and social positions among the Gentiles. But as soon as conditions grow difficult and restlessness prevails; when economic crisis, intense political struggle, disastrous epidemics and hunger jeopardize a nation, dynamic anti-Semitism immediately tries to utilize the disturbed situation, the excited mood and nervous strain of the masses. It swerves the inclination of masses towards murder and looting, which is natural in such times, against the Jews. No matter how innocent Jews may be of the misfortunes of a nation, the instigators of pogroms easily discover a spark to kindle that powder-barrel of hatred which lies uncovered in the soul of the ignorant and eagerly awaits such a spark to explode in jubilant violence.

Dynamic anti-Semitism shows, despite all its variance through various times in various countries, the following two general and permanent traits:

(a) While conditions remain more or less quiet it fights for all kinds of restrictions of Jewish rights; it tries to limit their freedom of residence, their economic activities, even their rights of education. Throughout Europe, until the end of the 18th century, Jews were excluded from all universities but two: Padua in Italy and Leyden in Holland; and even in these two universities Jews were only permitted to study medicine. Even at the beginning of World War I, educational restrictions still existed for Jews in Russia.

(b) In troubled times anywhere, dynamic anti-Semitism always assumes catastrophic forms and dimensions: persecution accompanied by looting and confiscation of property, pogroms, mass expulsion, outright massacre.

Factors and Motives

Political parties and groups dislike admitting that their struggle is mostly inspired by plain egotistic interests; they prefer to hide these interests behind grandiloquent ideologies, and they resort to slogans which appeal to the higher, moral inclinations of men. This becomes particularly clear in the history of anti-Semitism: the lower and more egotistic were real motives of the Jew-baiters, the higher and more inspiring were the slogans they threw to the masses. Thus, when the pious Catholic king of Austria, Leopold, yielded to the request of the Viennese citizenry and ordered the expulsion of 3,000 Jews in 1670, those "arch-enemies of Christendom," the egotistic interests of the "*civitatis Viennensis et mercatorum*" were also expressly and fully satisfied.[1]

The Jews as a Unique Social Phenomenon

The history of the Jews reveals traits which mark them as a unique, historical phenomenon: the Jews are the oldest minority; they are spread all over the world; and there is no country in the world where they would represent anything more than a minority; they belong to the weakest and most helpless social groups, all over; and, at the same time, they are comparatively the richest.

Even while the Jewish state existed, only slightly more than

[1] Hans Tietze, "Die Juden Wiens," Vienna, 1933, pp. 68-69.

twenty per cent of all Jews lived in Palestine and for almost nineteen centuries now the Jews have been living in complete Diaspora. They survived persecutions and attempts at their annihilation; they withstood the process of assimilation, despite their stormy history.

The Jews live as a minority in more than ninety different countries. In the past, the Jews have lived in every civilized country at every epoch. And in the 15 years during which the situation in Europe gradually became more and more difficult and, finally, quite intolerable for them, they penetrated into every colony, every habitable island, every "hole" which was not hermetically sealed against them.

Many nations have lost their political independence, but they either regained it or were slowly absorbed by the conquering nations. During the nineteen centuries of their scattered existence, the Jews were never capable of rebuilding their own state, and at the same time they were never completely assimilated by any nation. They lived as a minority everywhere in the world.

Being a minority without political strength anywhere, Jews were often chosen as scapegoats. Robert Redfield, professor of anthropology at the University of Chicago, said: "He (the Jew) has been an international scapegoat so long that in any situation that requires a scapegoat he is likely to be the unfortunate candidate."[2]

In the past, the Jews have represented a strong religious unity; they were very slow in assimilating other tribes, just as the groups of Jews who lived amidst other peoples withstood any attempts to become assimilated themselves. The Jews were the only monotheists in a world where the religious creed was mingled with magic. They preached a religion based upon reason and righteousness; the Ten Commandments of Moses outlined the very foundations of all human society and were accepted as such by almost all civilized nations. And, in the preachings of the prophets, the highest moral values were revealed to mankind. All this provoked

[2] "Scientific Monthly," September, 1943, pp. 193-201.

other nations, and at an early date accusations were levelled against Jews that "their religion differed from others." Cicero accused Jews of "atheism and exclusiveness."[3] The sharpest accusations were brought against Jews because, while living in the midst of other nations, they refused to change their religion and accept other gods. The first anti-Jewish pogrom was carried out in Alexandria in 38 A. D., and the reason given was the refusal of the Jews to put a statue of Caligula into the synagogue. To the Jews a king could not be God; a king was only a servant of his people, not their Lord.

Modern Anti-Semitism

Germany is the classic country of modern anti-Semitism. Jews played a very important part in the development of capitalism and general economy in Germany; furthermore, they penetrated deeply in all spheres of cultural life, in science, literature, journalism, politics, and social movements. The active bearers of modern German anti-Semitism were the professional "intelligentsia" and the middle class. The church relinquished her role as leader of anti-Semitism, and even the priest, Stoecker, the founder of the Deutsche Christlich-Sociale Partei in 1879, based his anti-Semitic ideology not only upon religious but social economic motives. He addressed his propaganda to the petty bourgeoisie and craftsmen, two social groups which suffered the most from the stormy development of industry and big business.

At the same time, the "foreignness" of the Jews was now explained: not by their "godlessness" but by a false theory of racial inferiority and harmfulness. This theory claimed that the Jews were a non-creative group, not particularly gifted, and incapable of conceiving original ideas. Progressively, the stage was reached when the anti-Semites asserted that the Jews were originators and bearers of all that was evil in mankind or the individual.

[3] "The Idea of Nationalism" by Hans Cohn, New York, 1944, p. 592.

Modern anti-Semitism is well-organized socially and clearly demarcated politically. Several anti-Semitic parties were founded in Germany, Austria, Poland and other countries during the 20th century. The Jewish question became an important issue in the political struggle of Europe, and anti-Semitism was used as a weapon by almost all conservative parties, including those which did not openly admit their anti-Semitic character.

However, Hitler's Third Reich was the first to make the Jewish question an affair of State; it assumed great importance and created an anti-Semitism unparalleled in history. This anti-Semitism reveals the following eight fundamental features:

1. It is thoroughly *ideological* "The conception of a purely national state, born out of the idea of race, is the final criterion of our judgment on all that we are doing on earth."[4]

2. It is *racial.* It is guided by the principle that a person of Jewish "blood" cannot possibly avoid the consequences of being a Jew, no matter to what acts of volition, abjuration or renunciation he resorts.

3. It is *integral.* Contrary to other forms of state anti-Semitism, it does not intend to "cream" the Jews of its country in order to absorb those Jewish elements which it judges are the best. Fritz Haber, the Nobel prize winner, whose research rendered immense service to Germany during World War I, was exiled from Germany and died in misery. The list of a few honorary "Aryans" is not large enough to constitute an exception from the general rule.

4. It is publicly *proclaimed.* It is an official doctrine of the government. It is by no means camouflaged or confined to administrative practice or "spontaneous outbursts" secretly encouraged. It sharply cuts off the tradition of the Czars, Petlioura, or Polish reactionary governments which consisted in denying any responsibility for anti-Semitic violences.

5. It is *juridicial,* inscribed into law. It is not merely a policy carried out by the government in disregard of codes ruling the

[4] Alfred Rosenberg. Quoted by MacGovern, p. 637.

country. Anti-Semitic ordinances become laws in the same manner as all other ordinances, and the courts administer justice by applying them.

6. It *pertains to the state* and is a monopoly of the government or the Nazi party. The masses have no right to indulge in pogroms, a state of affairs which was encouraged, at certain times, by the Czarist regime. In the Third Reich the anti-Jewish outbursts were organized and carried out by the official or semi-official agencies of the government or party.

7. It is *total*. It embraces all realms of the political, civil, military, economic, social, and intellectual life. A Jew is refused admittance everywhere.

8. It is *expansionistic*. It does not limit its authority to the subjects of the Reich. Anti-Jewish laws are equally applied to those aliens of Jewish blood who sojourn or reside in Germany. The allies, friends and vassals of the Third Reich have to accept its anti-Semitic doctrine and put it into effect. As far as this article of faith is concerned, no compromise is admitted. It became an anti-Semitism of *extermination*. The Nuremberg Trial clearly showed that approximately six million Jews fell victims of the Nazi anti-Jewish campaign.

Anti-Semitic Movements in Various European Countries

Europe politically, economically and culturally represents an agglomeration of countries which differ considerably from one another. And no less different are the forms of anti-Semitism we find in these various countries. The whole picture is so variegated that some degree of generalization is unavoidable in its description; the simplest method is to divide Europe into three spheres: Western, Central and Eastern Europe.

(a) Western Europe, comprising all countries west of Germany: These countries are characterized by highly developed capitalism and some by large colonial possessions; there is an influx of raw materials, and foreign markets are available to them; the masses here have a comparatively higher standard of living and a higher level of political and cultural education; liberal-democratic traditions are strongly developed—and all these factors together created a stable political life there and kept the class struggle within constitutional limits.

The Jewish population of these countries is small, almost less than one per cent everywhere—in Norway and Sweden, .1%; in Denmark, .2%; in England and France, .6%; in Belgium, .7%; and, in Holland, 1%. The anti-Semitic traditions of these countries are very weak, since their Jewish immigration coincided with the rapid rise of liberal-democratic ideas in Europe; whereas no Jews lived there in the dark times of the Middle Ages. Furthermore, when the Jews began their immigration to these countries, economic development was already in high gear there, so that in no branch of industry and trade did they reach a dominant position. Only comparatively few of them (such as those whose ancestors lived there for many generations), played an outstanding part in the economic and cultural life of those countries; the great mass of them, only newly immigrated, remained at the bottom of the social scale.

(b) Central-European countries, especially Germany: The retarded consolidation of the German people as a united national state; the retarded capitalistic development; the backward policy of gaining colonial possessions-all this created in the German people the desire of overtaking and outstripping countries which are far ahead of them in economic development.

The flagrant contradiction between Germany's intense economic development, the meager achievements of her policy of acquiring colonies, and the difficulty encountered in securing raw materials and markets for her industry created in the German people a feeling of insecurity and a desire to achieve an international position more adequate for its potential power.

The very low political development of the German masses; the complete absence of any kind of democratic traditions; the compromising revolution which left political power in the hands of the feudal classes, junkers and large land owners, all this made the German policy inflexibly stiff and reactionary.

The extremely high development of German science and literature aroused in the German people exaggerated ambitions and pretensions that they had to enjoy the pre-eminent position in the world.

Germany's Jewish population was much larger than that of the Western European countries: one per cent of the total population. Yet, still more important than this number, was the role the Jews played in all fields of German life. During several centuries in the Middle Ages, the Jews were prohibited from staying in Germany, but since Germany was divided in so many independent kingdoms, duchies, palatinates and cities, the anti-Jewish policy was not uniform and not equally severe in all parts of Germany. Therefore, Germany never became quite free of Jews ("Judenrein"). And when Germany's stormy economic development commenced, the Jews played a dominant part in all the vital branches of its economic life: in banking, railway construction, export and import, etc. At the same time, the ruling, feudal class in Germany carried the old strong anti-Semitic traditions into the 19th century, and they still regarded Jews as slaves and inferior people.

(c) Eastern European countries: They were economically very backward rural countries with weakly developed capitalism. They were politically uneducated and without any democratic traditions. There was a very high percentage of illiteracy and a thinly spread layer of intelligentsia; hard working conditions in the factories without protection of labor existed all over. The rural question stood in the center of the social struggle, and this question attracted the intelligentsia of the higher-classes or impoverished groups of these classes.

The majority of the Eastern-European countries were nationally enslaved by Russia, Austria-Hungary and Turkey, and all three of them, despite other great differences, followed the same policy of rejecting any capitalistic development in their peripheral territories.

At the end of the 19th century, this huge part of Europe became involved in an intense rural and political struggle for liberation. Large masses of the population were pulled into this struggle; they became more active politically, and this made them more active, ambitious and experienced in economics.

Eighty-six percent of all European Jews and over 60 percent of the world Jewry lived in this part of Europe (in 1900). The Jews there were the main bearers of trade, industry and craftsmanship. In some regions, the Jews comprised 80 to 90 percent of all shopkeepers; in many places even more than 90 percent.

The development of anti-Semitism assumed very different aspects in Western, Central and Eastern Europe.

In Western Europe, scarcely any anti-Semitism existed before World War I. At least, no organized anti-Semitic parties with their own press organs, conferences, and so on, were in evidence. In France, the anti-Semites tried to utilize the Suez-Canal scandal and the Dreyfus Affair in order to overthrow the young French Republic. This was the first important attempt to utilize the Jewish question in general political struggle, but the French liberal and radical circles were perfectly aware of the impending danger for their republican regime and decisively defeated the anti-Semites. All remained quiet for several years, and only in the thirties of the twentieth century, when an acute economic crisis and unemployment threatened France with social conflicts, did anti-Semitism rear its head again, and the *Cagoulard* demonstrations in 1936 and 1937 were aimed at the Jews, as well as at the overthrow of the Republic. But this time again the sound instinct of the French people, strongly supported by organized labor, beat back all attacks. Only the Nazi occupation gave the French anti-Semites all the freedom of action and all the opportunities for aggressiveness they desired.

The situation in Germany was quite different. The central government of Germany, as well as the governments of the separate states comprising it, kept a tight rein on the several anti-Semitic parties and dozens of anti-Semitic organizations which were founded in Germany since the last part of the 19th century. No sanguinary pogroms were allowed, although these governments tolerated the wildest and most dishonest propaganda against Jews and all that was Jewish. All attempts made by individual Jews and organizations to arraign the libellers met with no success whatsoever. At the end of the 19th century, the German authorities even carefully planned anti-Jewish riots, providing that these riots consisted only of destroying and looting Jewish property, without indulging in any bloodshed. They themselves practiced an anti-Semitic policy by not admitting Jews as officers to the army and navy, by sharply restricting the number of Jewish teachers at the universities, colleges and high schools, and by strictly forbidding the employment of Jews as state officials.

At the beginning of the twentieth century, the economic situation in Germany was so prosperous that soap-box anti-Semitism visibly abated, but the anti-Semitism of the German intelligentsia greatly increased. The high achievements of German Jews in science and literature-Jacob Wasserman, Feuchtwanger, and Zweig in literature, Cantor, Klein and Curant in mathematics, Hertz and Einstein in physics, Ehrlich and Wassermann in medicine and many many others-kindled the envy of the German intellectuals, and they began to question the "fairness" of "aliens" occupying prominent positions in the cultural life of Germany. The prestige of the Jewish-owned liberal press in Germany, *Frankfurter Zeitung*, *Berliner Tageblatt*, *Vossische Zeitung*, and the influence it gained in the world, the large number of Nobel prizes awarded to Jews—all this irritated not only the German anti-Semites but even such liberals and intellectuals as Sombart or Avenarius, who suggested in 1912 that the Jews should voluntarily abandon the leading roles they were playing in the cultural life of Germany and retreat to the background, or it might produce disastrous consequences for them.

The defeat of Germany in World War I came as a quite unexpected and violent shock to the German people, and, without exaggeration, one might say that Germany as a whole became hysterical. The Germans looked for a scapegoat and for a victim upon whom to vent off their wrath; they found both in the Jewish people. When, a few years later, a severe economic crisis gripped Germany, (with six million unemployed workers, many thousands of jobless lawyers, physicians, journalists, and writers, and her entire economic life thoroughly disorganized), the stage was completely set for Hitler's appearance.

The plight of Jews in the Eastern-European countries was of a different nature. In Russia and Rumania, in the last portion of the 19th century the governments kept the Jewish population in a permanent state of fear of pogroms. In 1871 there occurred the first pogrom in Odessa, and between 1881 and 1882 there were about two hundred pogroms in as many different places. The dreadful pogrom in Kishinew (1903) shocked public opinion throughout the world and evoked energetic protests on the part of the American and British governments. How effective these protests were may be revealed by the fact that in 1905, 700 pogroms took place in Russia. The situation of the Jews in Rumania was very similar. The anti-Jewish program of the Russian government there was clearly formulated in the following words of a leading statesman:

> "One third of the Jews will have to emigrate; another third will die out; and the rest will become Gentiles."

In Russia and Rumania, anti-Semitism was primarily of a governmental and social nature; in the "Congress-Poland" (that part of Poland that belonged to Russia before World War I), anti-Semitism was primarily of an economic nature. The National party, which was founded in 1897 and openly proclaimed anti-Semitism as one of its main goals, demanded in its program that all Jewish-owned industry and trade should be transferred into Polish hands. A national motive also played an important part in stirring anti-Jewish feelings: The Jews, especially those who were expulsed by the Czarist government from Russia and found refuge in Poland, were accused by the Poles of supporting the policy of Russianization of Poland.

This national motive played an even larger part in Ukrainian anti-Semitism. The Russian language was the only one permitted in the Ukraine, and the Jews could receive general education and instruction only in schools conducted in the Russian language. Since the Jews had a richer background and were more vitally interested in obtaining a thorough education than the Ukrainians, they outstripped the latter in all fields of cultural activities; this resulted in unfounded accusations that the Jews were trying to Russianize the Ukraine.

Thus, in all these countries new hostility and accusations against Jews arose to augment the already latent anti-Semitism especially religious anti-Semitism which was very strong in Russia with her 75 per cent illiterates.

The plight of the Jews in all other countries of Eastern Europe, such as Hungary and Galicia, was similar. Jews everywhere were squeezed between domineering and oppressed nations; they evoked the hatred of the domineering nations by their economic competition, and the hatred of the oppressed nations by their alleged support of the assimilatory tendencies on the part of the ruling nations.

World War I brought liberation to some of those oppressed nations, but the plight of the Jews grew even more desperate. Poland, Hungary, and Rumania took up the old tradition of keeping the Jews in a permanent state of fear of pogroms, thus forcing them to emigrate. In Poland, for instance, some pogroms took place as early as 1919 and 1920, and the pogrom atmosphere remained there continuously, with only a few short interruptions, until the outbreak of World War II. The 1930's brought about a marked aggravation in the situation: numerous bloody attacks on Jews, looting and picketing of Jewish-owned shops, beating up of Jewish students, introduction of "ghetto-benches" at the universities and exclusion of Jews from all the liberal professions. All this had the full blessing of the Polish reactionary government which did not tolerate an abundance of bloody anti-Jewish excesses but still permitted pogroms so numerous and severe that Jews were forced to emigrate or at least to abandon their economic position.

Anti-Semitism as a Political Weapon

At the 19th and the beginning of the 20th century, anti-Semitism became an instrument of great national and international importance. The acute national and social struggle of that period, the political differentiation and strong ideological controversies in the social life of that time, the participation of the masses in the political struggle—all this created a favorable atmosphere for the utilization of anti-Jewish feelings as a weapon which political parties applied against each other. Thus, anti-Semitism was used as a means against democratic revolutions in all European countries. In Germany, Austria, Russia, and Poland, the feudal classes waged their struggle against the liberal movements of the 19th century and originated the idea that the Jews are solely responsible for liberalism and democracy, and that they would use these liberal movements exclusively to their own advantage. Later, the remainder of the feudal classes united with the bourgeois classes in their common struggle against the socialist movement, and popularized the notion that Socialism was a purely Jewish invention by which they, the Jews tried to rule the world. The rapidly growing international, economic, political and cultural complications, and the manifold influences of modern methods of agitation and propaganda campaigns even trespassed the borders of government activities, crossed seas and oceans, and opened new and broad vistas for anti-Semitism. The tendency to use the weapon of anti-Jewish hatred in international politics became ever stronger.

The Russian Czarist government actively employed anti-Jewish hatred in its struggle against the revolutionary movement. As is well known, Russia experienced a strong wave of pogroms in the years 1881-1882, immediately after the assassination of Alexander II. Jewish participation in this assassination, as well as in the whole revolutionary movement at that time, was almost infinitesimal. And, as Leo Tolstoy wrote in a letter which was widely circulated abroad and even distributed in Russia in mimeographed form, the pogroms came to pass in the following manner: "So ging's in Balta, in Kiev, in anderen Staedten zu, und gerade dieses Sachverstaendnis, diese Planmaessigkeit, gerade diese kaltbluetige und verstockte Verbrecherart der Organisatoren ist der beste Beweis, dass die Herren der Ordnung selber die Niedertraechtigkeit veranstaltet haben. Entweder verkleidete Polizisten in eigener Person oder mit ihrem Segen versehene Menschen".[5]

One cannot deny that in 1905, during the first Russian Revolution, the Czarist regime began directing the wrath of the masses toward anti-Jewish pogroms which took place in more than 700 cities and towns.

The following interesting fact illustrates the tragic plight of the Jewish minority. The Russian revolutionists of the group *Narodnaya Volya,* the same group which carried out the assassination of Alexander II and which it would be ludicrous to accuse of anti-Semitism, published a proclamation addressed to the peasantry (1880) calling for anti-Jewish pogroms. The motivating idea was that Jewish pogroms would be the quickest and easiest way to shake the Russian peasantry out of its apathy; as soon as the peasantry discarded its customary inertia, it would be possible to direct its wrath against the landlords and the government, and thus carry out revolutionary upheaval. Jewish blood as a lubricant for the wheels of the Russian revolution!—This later became a popular

[5] "It happened like this in Baltic countries, in Kiev, and in other cities. It is just this expertliness, this planned program, just this sort of cold-blooded and bull-necked crookedness of the organisers, that is the best proof that the gentlemen of order have themselves created this bastardliness, either as disguised policemen in person or as persons that have received the former's blessings." Tolstoy published this article in Germany since, because of Tsarist censorship, he was prevented from publishing it in Russia.

slogan; it was quite clear that every unsuccessful riot against the Czarist regime would be quelled with Jewish blood. And this was virtually so—all pogroms in Russia from 1881-1921 attempted to divert large masses from the Czarist regime and, at the same time, served as a magnet to gather the masses in their common struggle for national independence. Petlura, a Ukrainian Socialist revolutionary, used anti-Jewish pogroms to bring the Ukrainian masses into the cadres of the Ukrainian army, fighting for the separation of the Ukraine from Russia. Denikin permitted anti-Jewish pogroms because it was the best method of organizing his fight against the Bolsheviks.

In all Eastern European countries in which agrarian reform had not been carried out during World War I or were carried out only on a very limited scale, the land-owning class very skillfully played upon anti-Jewish feelings.

The appalling poverty of Eastern European peasantry was caused by the scarcity of the three basic pillars of its economic structure: arable land, live stock and machinery. The resulting conditions led to the spilling of Jewish blood. The peasantry, in its ignorance, believed that taking over the small and dirty stands in the suburbs where Jews toiled for 18 hours a day and hardly earned a crust of dry bread would solve the problems of its poverty.

However, anti-Semitism had already expanded beyond the borders of national governments. Hitler brilliantly showed the world how easily betrayal, espionage, quislings, and fifth coloumnists can be propagandized and won over to the cause of Nazism with the help of Jew-hatred. He used anti-Semitism to establish special agencies throughout the entire world; these agencies were to serve Germany in peace, as well as in war. Anti-Semitism was the iron bridge by means of which Hitler was trying to achieve his goal of dividing the population even in such traditionally democratic countries as England, France, Holland, Belgium, and Denmark. With the help of anti-Semitism, Hitler set up centers of Nazi propaganda in South America, North Africa, and virtually the whole world.

During the first period of its development in countries with a small percentage of Jews and with strong democratic tradition, Fascism was not at all anti-Semitic. As is well known, Mussolini scoffed at Hitler's race theory and not only admitted the Jews to the Fascist Party but even appointed them to high Party and Government positions. Oswald Mosley, the father of English Fascism, declared in 1933:

. . . "the British Union of Fascists is not anti-Semitic. Attacks on Jews in any shape or form were strictly forbidden within a month after the movement was launched. Fascism stands for religious and racial tolerance. We have no quarrel with the Jews as Jews, as we have no quarrel with Catholics as Catholics".[6]

In Holland, too, Fascism was not based upon anti-Semitism at the outset, and the Germans were displeased with Mussert, whom they rebuked in their magazine. (*Information on the Jewish question*, September, 1939).

The situation in Belgium was quite different. There, the Flemish felt a national animosity toward the Jews, an animosity which was strongly reminiscent of conditions in Eastern European countries. The Flemish in Belgium are a small and weak minority group, and since the Jews showed more inclination toward French culture than Flemish, they were accused of attempting to assimilate the Flemish part of Belgium.

Hitlerism intended to exploit anti-Semitism to the fullest degree for political ends. And, as in all its undertakings, in this case, too, it displayed extraordinary energy and achieved outstanding results. It employed three methods:

(a) Large subsidies were granted all Fascist organizations throughout the world, provided that anti-Semitism was accepted as obligatory.

(b) Stupendous propaganda among the German colonists was disseminated throughout the world; it was always conducted in

[6] The Jewish Economic Forum, July 28, 1933—Quoted from Prof. James Parkes's book, *An Enemy of the People: Antisemitism*, New York, 1946, p. 55.

the language of the country and directed from the central office in Germany.

(c) Leaders of the local Fascist and generally reactionary organizations were won over to the belief that anti-Semitism was the best and most appealing means of arousing the masses and achieving their goal of attainment of political power.

As early as 1924, the Nazi Party founded a large magazine, *Der Weltkampf*, which outwardly gave the impression of being a scientific publication; it attempted to prove the anti-Semitic theory scientifically. This magazine was distributed throughout the world, and especially within German colonies, even before the Nazi Party established a special nucleus in many German colonies in Europe, America and Africa. But only when they came to power in 1933 did they develop a strong international machinery to spread anti-Semitism, allocating hundreds of millions of dollars for this purpose. They recognized the spread of anti-Semitism as one of their most important tasks and an effective means of preparation for all the other goals which Hitlerism attempted to achieve. These goals were indeed very far-reaching, since they not only aimed at making Germany strong and powerful, but at ruling the world. The Germans they felt, are allegedly the most courageous and gifted nation in the world, and therefore the throne of the world ruler must belong to them. Since these goals were of an international nature, the Germans selected the Jews as the most appropriate scapegoat.

No sooner had the Nazis become the rulers of Germany than they established a special Ministry of Propaganda under the leadership of Goebbels, and a special office under the leadership of Alfred Rosenberg.

At that time approximately 40,000 German unions existed abroad, dispersed over all continents. More than 300 German newspapers and magazines appeared abroad. All these unions and press organs immediately felt the impact of Nazi pressure. Many of them had been connected with the Nazi Party before 1933. Some were connected with the Stuttgart Institute for

Germans Abroad. Hitler personally authorized Streicher to become the head of German Propaganda abroad. In 1934, the International Congress of Antisemitic Organizations was convened in Munich. To this Congress, delegates came from several countries which had fought with Germany for centuries; there were delegates from Hungary, Rumania, Austria, and many other countries. In 1935, the International Anti-Semitic Congress convened in Belgium, a country which had suffered so heavily from the German invasion of 1914-1918. The Germans did not appear openly at these Congresses, but took a highly active part behind the scenes and assumed the leadership. Soon the Germans began to disseminate anti-Semitic literature throughout the world. The two books which were most widely distributed were Hitler's *Mein Kampf*, which had a printing (in 1943) of 9,840,000 copies,[7] and the notorious *Protocols of the Elders of Zion.* Germany supervised the translation of the Protocols in scores of foreign languages.

In 1934, in Erfurt, the *Weltdienst* was launched; its main function was close cooperation with all anti-Semitic parties and groups abroad. This publication first appeared in eight languages (German, French, Russian, Polish, Hungarian, Danish and Spanish), and in 1940 the number was increased to twenty, including Arabic, Bulgarian, Croatian, Dutch, Greek, Italian, Lettish, Norwegian, Rumanian, Serbian and Ukrainian.

Information on anti-Semitism was distributed throughout the world. Furthermore, all available anti-Jewish material was used for the purpose of international politics. A very strong link with all anti-Semitic organizations was established. All correspondents and collaborators of the publication throughout the world received excellent salaries and, in this way, a network of agencies was created which were all dependent on the German center.

This network later became very helpful in espionage activities which the Nazi Government so skillfully organized throughout the world. In Germany alone, three institutes with scores of pro-

[7] Max Weinreich, *Hitler's Professors*, New York, 1946, p. 24.

fessors were established for the sole purpose of studying the Jewish question. Two tasks were undertaken by these institutes:

(1) To prove that the Jews dominated the world financially, economically, culturally and spiritually.

(2) To prove that the Jewish race exercised a bad influence upon all nations wherever they lived.

The Nazi "professors" performed their task with great zeal and perfidy. They published hundreds of books in which they tried to prove the thesis that the Jews provide the greatest misfortunes to the world; and that the recovery of the world from all catastrophies would come only after the extermination of the Jewish people.

That the Nazi Government clearly paved the way for the coming war and felt the necessity of winning converts in all countries was clearly shown in the *Weltdienst* of September 1, 1939. The headline of this issue read: "Everyone should respect the country of other people, but should love his own country." This was written after the occupation of Austria and Czechoslovakia. By then all plans for the invasion of Poland had been completed by the Germans. That issue of the *Weltdienst* appeared shortly after the International Antisemitic Congress of 1939. It brought greetings from France, Italy, Rumania, England, Russian refugees, Hungary, Yugoslavia, Belgium, Poland, Holland, Denmark, Spain, Argentina, United States, North Africa, Canada, and Portugal sixteen nations, in all.

Among these countries were those which Germany attacked and enslaved less than twelve months later. The main issue at this Congress was that since the Jews were allegedly preparing the way for war, all other nations should unite and organize themselves in order to prevent the impending catastrophe. This subject was thoroughly discussed at public conferences.

In September, 1939, after the outbreak of the war, an issue of the *Weltdienst* appeared with the following sensational headline: "To all friends of the *Weltdienst*. To all Patriots of their countries." All these patriots were invited to explain to their people that Germany had not attacked Poland, thus starting the war, but that the Jews were waging this war against the "Aryan race." All the governments of the world: the English, the French, the American, etc. were either in the hands of the Jews or bought by the Jews; therefore, the Jews declared war on Germany and on the entire Aryan world.

Today, we realize that all these patriots and friends of the *Weltdienst* often betrayed their countries and helped Hitler to enslave the very nations to which they belonged. In all the twenty countries which Hitler occupied or conquered, he found friends, collaborators, quislings and fifth coloumnists. Professor James Parkes writes: "Quisling in Norway, Mussart in Holland, Degrelle in Belgium, Cagoulards and similar groups in France—all had been the spearheads of anti-Semitic movements in their countries; all of them were distinguished from other extreme nationalist movements—such as the Flemish movement in Belgium, by the fact that when the crisis came they willingly acted as traitors in the German interest."[8]

In all the American countries, too, the Black Shirt and Yellow organizations of Argentina, Brazil, Uruguay, Paraguay, etc., were at Hitler's disposal. And, in the United States, a network of spies existed which was intensely active and widespread, as had been proved by scores of documents found in the archives of the German Embassy. At the trial of the traitors in Washington, it was established that as early as 1938 Bund members distributed leaflets asserting that the Jews are responsible for all trouble and that the United States would also be forced into war against Germany and Japan.[9]

The same leaflets said that "The press, radio and movies, all controlled by the Jews, filled the whole country with propaganda aiming at a war against Germany. The Americans do not want any war with Germany or Japan. The Americans do not want any war with anybody. And the Germans as well as the Japanese

[8] L. C., p. 59.

[9] New York Times, June 28, 1944.

do not want any war with the Americans. The only people who drive towards war are the Jews."[10]

This was written in 1938, when Germany was the only country feverishly preparing for war and when Goering boasted that Germany possessed the strongest airforce.

[10] *Ibid.*

BIBLIOGRAPHY

Essays on Anti-Semitism, New York, 1946.

PARKES, JAMES: *The Jewish Problem in the Modern World*, New York, 1939.

SARTRE, JEAN-PAUL: *Portrait of the Anti-Semite*, New York, 1946.

VISHNIAK, MARK: *An International Convention Against Anti-Semitism*, New York, 1946.

COUDENHOVE, GRAF HEINRICH: *Antisemitismus*, Vienna, 1932.

Anti-Semitism—A Social Disease, New York, 1946.

VALENTIN, HUGO: *Anti-Semitism*, New York, 1936.

FENICHEL, O.: "Psychoanalysis of Anti-Semitism," *American Imago*, 1940.

Hitler's Ten-Year War on the Jews, Institute of Jewish Affairs, New York, 1943.

WEINREICH, MAX: *Hitler's Professors*, New York, 1946.

LIVINGSTON, SIGMUND: *Must Men Hate?* New York, 1944.

XVII.

The Origins of Fascism

XVII.

THE ORIGINS OF FASCISM

by

GIUSEPPE ANTONIO BORGESE

THE EIGHTEENTH BIRTHDAY of Fascism was celebrated on October 28, 1940. The ritual of celebration adopted in 1941 was the attack on Greece. Thus the celebration was no doubt interesting for both the countries directly concerned, Italy and Greece. It had scarce repercussions, if any, in the world at large. The date October 28, 1922, the birthday of fascism, has not yet reached the universal fame it deserves.

A general tendency is noticeable in the average man and even in intellectual circles considerably above the average to push the Italian factor of the present world situation into a rather restricted corner of the perspective. As a whole, the conventional observer and the automatic thinker would feel happy if they could think that fascism is a German invention exported to Italy and accepted by Italy in a spirit of submission, more or less spontaneous, to the dictate of her powerful neighbor. A substantial amount of this happiness is achieved by a subconscious mental operation which modifies the proportions and almost overlooks the chronological sequence.

There cannot be any inclination in the general mind to recognize the leading and decisive part which the Italians have played and still are playing to some extent. This distortion of the observers' attention is largely due to the fact that the general mind, even during these eighteen or twenty years, has been under the influence of the two following assumptions. The first is that the world role of Italian culture and action had come to an end with the end of the High Renaissance, say with the sack of Rome, 1527, and with the fall of the Florentine Republic, 1530. It follows, then, that nothing really important such as the creation of fascism could have originated in a second-class nation. The second assumption is that the Italian people are well-known and always were well-known for their keen individualism, which positively accounted for much of Italian culture and art while negatively it accounted for the Italian lack of discipline and efficiency. It follows, then, that a totalitarian ideology and movement welding all the forces of a national group into one purpose and endeavor could not possibly originate in such a highly differentiated and at the same time unorganical country.

Yet facts must be taken for what they are, even when they run counter to habits and expectations. The fact is that fascism in its formative period is an Italian phenomenon. A second fact, correlated with the first, is that practically nothing in the Nazi mentality and action can be explained without the Italian antecedent. Hitler, of course, is the most authoritative witness. His fundamental acknowledgment in *Mein Kampf* reads as follows:

> In those days—I admit it openly—I conceived the most profound admiration for that great man south of the Alps who, full of ardent love for his people, would not deal with the internal enemies of Italy, but pushed their annihilation in every way and by all means. What will rank Mussolini among the great of this earth is the same determination not to share Italy with Marxism, but to save the fatherland from it by dooming internationalism to annihilation.
>
> How wretchedly dwarfish our German State yes-men appeared in contrast and how nauseating it is when these nonentities undertake, with boorish conceit, to criticize a man a thousand times as great; and how painful it is to think that all this goes on in a country which, barely half a century ago, might still call a Bismarck its leader.

This acknowledgment by Hitler of fascism and Mussolini as his fundamental inspiration goes at least as far back as 1926, when

Mussolini had not yet to his credit any final accomplishment except the totally autocratic seizure of his native Italy: a man rather of words than of deeds, and the neologist forger of winged and felicitous slogans such as Fascist, Totalitarian, Corporative. But he seemed already very great to Hitler, the obscure rioter in a Munich Bierhalle, the untiring scribbler in a Bavarian fortress.

It was on March 23, 1919, that a small group of malcontents under the guidance of a second-class editor gathered somewhere in Milan and formulated a sweeping program, offering happiness and glory to everybody. It was on that evening that the word fascism definitely entered history—at first a national, nay, a local section of history. It was three and one-half years later, on October 28, 1922, that the central powers in Rome yielded to a threat of armed revolt and called fascism to share in the government. It was three more years later, on January 3, 1925, that absolute dictatorship was officially proclaimed. It was between 1925 and the end of 1926 that a system of restrictive laws and a wholesale authority conferred on the secret police made of the proclaimed dictatorship an unshakable condition of Italian life. Ideologies and forms of fascism were thus mature at least seven years before the accession of Hitler to power.

What were the components of fascism in its formative stage? What inherited inclinations and contemporary circumstances made its rise and victory possible in its native country? We shall divide our short survey into three main items: (1) the centuries-old complexes of the Italian mind; (2) the religious background; (3) the circumstances generated by the World War and its immediate aftermath.

The terms inferiority complex and superiority complex so often used and misused in the common psychological talk of our time cannot be avoided when we try to determine the essential tendencies of the Italian mind, especially in as far as the ruling classes are concerned. Italy arose as a nation as did almost all the other nations of Europe at the close of the Middle Ages. Her birth, however, was different. She was not the creation of kings and warriors. She was the creation of poets and dreamers, and of one above the others—Dante. His political life had been a failure and the particular situation in which Italy found herself between the universal drive of the Roman Church and the universal drive of the Holy Roman Empire of the German nation hampered to the point of disaster her attempts to build a factual national unity of the kind that was meanwhile developing in France, in England, and in other European regions. This frustration is at the foundation of the Italian intellectual tradition. The concept that dominates Dante's political speculation is that Rome is divinely predestined to be the center of the world and to contain both kinds of world-ruling authority, the religious and the political. At the time of Dante, however, and in the all-human vastness of his conception, the nationalistic or parochial components of this assumption were still counter-poised by a feeling of universality. This also happened because at the time of Dante the world unity of the Church and the Empire had still elements of reality or possibility. They both went to pieces in the fourteenth century. The followers and continuators of Dante in the expression of the national mind, did not have any support in historical reality or political possibility. Thus frustration expressed itself in day dreams; bitterness and ambition became decisive components in Italian political speculation.

Of course, literature cannot be considered as a field of politics and history; it is, however, a most striking experience of collective feeling. The expert in Italian literature insists especially on the Canzoni of Petrarch extolling the primacy of Rome and of the Italian people bidding for world supremacy, inciting the Italian princelings to revive the ancient glory or even staking preposterous hopes on such attempts as Cola di Rienzo's to rebuild the Roman Republic and Roman Empire. The next epoch-making document is Machiavelli's *The Prince,* written about 1513 at the eve of the collapse of Renaissance Italy. Whatever political scientists may think, the inspiration of *The Prince* is mainly literary and emotional. Its closest source is in Petrarch's Canzone *Italia*

Mia. The basic motives are distress and anger at the inferiority of Italy as compared with the rising nations of Europe, and the medicine that is proposed to make up for such a decadence consists of the restoration of Roman pride and virtue.

This complex was never deleted or considerably weakened.

Exceptions can be listed, but they remain exceptions. Even the greatest among the Italian poets of the nineteenth century, Leopardi, starts from the same antimony of superiority and inferiority national complexes that had ruled the Italian mind in the preceding centuries. The conclusions of his poetry and of his thought seem to be conditioned by supranational and supratemporal situations of the human heart and mind. They seem to appeal to the permanent qualities of sorrow, hope, and despair. But the origins of his attitude are clearly stated in his early poems. It is again the restlessness and dissatisfaction of the heir to Rome whose life and energy are wasted in mediocre and humiliating circumstances. The Risorgimento—that is, the movement that led Italy to the establishment of her political independence in the United Kingdom proclaimed in 1861—was the work of prophets and heroes, some of whom tried new paths. Yet even the one who was the most revolutionary-minded among them could not wean them from the suggestions of Roman superiority. Even in Mazzini's scheme of a federated mankind, Rome and the Italians were assigned a central place, and the mission which was assigned to his own nation was, after all, of a sacerdotal and hegemonic nature. The name itself, *Risorgimento*—resurrection—points again to the ineradicable Italian idea that the past is good and beautiful and that no hope for the future can be substantiated with anything that is not the reinstatement and the revindication of the past.

There is no necessity to beautify with lenient words the moral and intellectual error of such an attitude. The claim to the matchless nobility of Roman heritage and to the endless mission of world command entrusted to the direct offspring of Rome includes an unmistakable amount of intellectual and moral guilt. Of course, he who is without sin should cast the first stone. This drive toward group superiority has been and is the curse of all group actions. Nationalism and parochial pride are not the particular inventions of the Italian people. What is particular to the Italian people is the definite historical conditions in which its complexes of inferiority and superiority matured and festered. During the centuries from the decline of the Middle Ages to the modern era its complexes of pride were more unsound than those of any other great nation of Europe, due to the political helplessness and impotence of the Italian nation. The forbidding disproportion between desired and objective power was to become operative also during the rise and progress of fascism. It is operative even today in the mutual relations between Italian ideology and German action. The origin of the intellectual error lies in the unwarranted identification of Italy with ancient Rome plus the assumption that the ancient Roman Empire can be resurrected.

The moral error, on the other hand, whatever the matchless achievements of the Italian mind in practically all fields of human endeavor, belongs to the category of selfishness and vanity. In Italy as anywhere else the real root of the complex of national superiority is in the personal lust for personal greatness. It is here, after all, that lies the seed of any kind of nationalism and racialism.

The habitual or automatic thinking insists on the undisciplined or even loose individualism of the Italian character. It has insisted for many generations on the lack of religious conviction, and on the noncommittal or even pagan attitude of the Italians toward Christianity and Catholicism, in spite of the fact that the historical seat of universal Christianity has been in their country. Obviously there is a point in this contention if we consider separate individual experiences and the surface of things as they appear to the momentary observer. There are, however, other points if we look at the historical sum-up of Italian behavior and if we consider in the Catholic Church the elements of its political structure rather than the theological and ethical elements that the Roman Church owes to primitive Christianity. The definition according to which the Roman Church is the ghost of the deceased

Roman Empire is all too sweeping. But there are well-known elements in its structure that work and have worked for centuries as the continuation of the administrative build-up and of the bureaucratic legal structure of the Roman Empire. World unity is essential to it; Roman, and by implicit or explicit inference Italian, primacy also is essential. The quality of Italians as a chosen and superior people in the administration of Christianity was frankly stated by Innocent III and implicitly or explicitly admitted by other popes. A hierocracy of Catholic Christian content and discipline making of all the world a Christian unity was more or less by definition and almost constantly by fact an Italian and Roman hierocracy. The prevalence of Italians on the Papal See and in electoral College of Cardinals has been overwhelming through the centuries. It is overwhelming even now. From the strictly national and nationalistic point of view the Christian Catholic Apostolical Roman Church is a Roman Italian Church with world-wide expansion. In its kernel it is an Italian spiritual bureaucratic empire.

The third element that must be kept in mind besides the two elements of world unity and Italian primacy is authority. Through a long and consistent process of centuries the authority of the Roman Church on the minds, and when possible on the bodies, of its members became sacrosanct and irresistible. The right to dissent was gradually limited until it was completely obliterated. As a reaction to the dangers involved in the Protestant movements of the sixteenth century the theory was formulated according to which the individual believer in the Catholic Church must be like a "corpse," passively subject to whatever the superior authority decides concerning matters of faith and rules of behavior. It seems apparent that the unity of the Roman Church could not be preserved after the Protestant upheaval if not at the price of the strictest intellectual and ethical discipline. After the storms of the early sixteenth century the organization of the Church was stabilized as a foursquare authoritarian and totalitarian system with the main authority acting as an imperil power and with the main orders, prominent among them the Jesuit order, acting altogether as an army and a police, although the army was not necessarily armed with physical weapons and although the police could not always count on secular help.

It is true that the attempts of the city-states in the late Middle Ages gave glorious inspirations to the modern theories of democracy and political freedom. There may still be a point in the romantic theory of Sismondi, according to whom modern freedom was first invented in those brilliant communities of central and northern Italy between the eleventh and the thirteenth century. It is true that some of the leading trends of the Risorgimento in the nineteenth century had kept clear of the Roman complexes of world authority and Romano—Italian primacy, and that spirits like Manzoni and Cavour and Garibaldi did not care for anything but a dignified and free life of the Italian nation in the brotherhood of the other nations.

It also is true that the confused but powerfully creative movements of the Italian Renaissance had contributed decisively to the formation of modern individualism. The Renaissance, however, collapsed and its continuative outcome was the establishment of the political tyranny in the country, whether of inner or of foreign origin, and the final establishment of the universal authoritarianism in the Roman Church. In other terms, the problem should be formulated as follows: are there elements of freedom and individual initiative prevalent in the psychological build-up of the Italian mind from the collapse of the old Roman Empire to the rise of fascism? Or is the contrary true? The most enduring experiences came from the authority of the Roman Empire and from the authority of the Roman Pope, from Caesars and high priests. These two sets of experiences were practically unbroken through about fifteen centuries. The others were comparatively fragmentary and temporary. On the whole, the Italian mind was prepared by the longest experience in centralized authority which Western history records—to submission both in things of the faith and in things of action.

On the whole, the trends toward liberal attitudes have remained on the surface. They have expressed themselves in whims or riots or personal and momentary rebellions rather than in one enduring and consistent effort as in English history from the Magna Charta to yesterday, or even in French history from the eighteenth century, at least, to the collapse in 1940.

As for his specific attitude toward the Roman Church, the average Italian of the ruling classes has mixed feelings. There certainly were reformatory endeavors, from the mystics of the Middle Ages to Dante and further. There were half-atheistic and half-jocular inclinations of middle-bourgeois freethinkers, anticipated, for example, in the open world of the *Decameron.* But even such people—and Boccaccio himself—wanted, as a rule, reconciliation with the Church on the most important occasions of their personal lives and especially in the hour of death. All centrifugal attitudes remained as a rule on the margin. The Italian as a nationally minded man could not forget, indeed, that it was the Church and the Pontifical State, stretching like a forbidding barrier across the Peninsula, that made political independence and unity impossible. He knew or felt that the Church neither succeeded in establishing a large political empire of its own nor could it be brought in line with Italian national aspirations. Hence the anticlerical mood of so many Italians through the centuries. Hence the many attempts of short-lived Roman revolutions to get rid of the papacy. Hence the final achievement of the Italian Risorgimento in occupying Rome and in expelling the papacy from all Italian territory except the Apostolic palaces—which were not even acknowledged to be under the unrestricted sovereignty of the Popes.

But, on the other hand, the power and glory of the Roman See were a constituent part of Italian and Roman glory and power. A complete disintegration and humiliation of the Catholic Church would have been felt as a heavy loss in the share of Roman power and glory that still was assigned to the Italian nation.

The reactions of the Roman Church against the Risorgimento and the deadly danger that according to the Holy See was implied in the laicization of Rome and in the final triumph of the free-thinking spirit originated in Renaissance, Reformation, and Enlightenment and the defensive-offensive strategies when the Church adopted to offset the danger have not been considered enough in their fargoing and world-wide import. The final triumph of liberalism and the seizure of Rome by the Italian liberal state marked at the same time the start of a second Counter Reformation. As the danger of dispossession came closer, the defensive attitude of the Church stiffened; and from hesitancy and helplessness—nay, from a short-lived attempt, 1846-1848, to collaborate with the Italian Risorgimento and to assume leadership in it—it changed into an attitude of aggressive challenge. The reaction to the Protestant reform in the sixteenth century had been a deflnite crystallization of discipline and authority within the Catholic Church. The reaction to the final triumph of enlightenment and liberal thought, implicitly Protestant, in the Italian history of the nineteenth century was a further and stricter proclamation of the authoritarian system of the Church.

The most important document and the one which should be considered as the official inauguration of the second Counter Reformation is the Syllabus of Errors of 1864. Hannibal was *ante portas*. The Italian liberals and anticlericals were at the gates of Rome. The Church powerless as far as its military defense was concerned, exercised whatever power it had in an uncompromising condemnation of the philosophical and political principles in which the triumphant liberal civilization was grounded. It is sufficient to quote Articles 77, 78, 79, and 80 of the Syllabus of Errors. According to Article 77 it is expedient "that the Catholic religion shall be held as the only religion of the State, to the exclusion of all other modes of worship." According to Article 78 it is unwise and subject to anathema "that it has been provided by law in some countries called Catholic, that persons coming to reside therein shall enjoy the public exercise of their own worship." According to Article 79 "civil liberty of every mode of worship, and the full power given to all of overtly and publicly manifesting their opinions and their ideas, of all kinds whatsoever, conduce to corrupt the morals and minds of the people and to the propagation of the pest of indifferentism." According to Article 80 "the Roman Pontiff" cannot and ought not "to reconcile himself to, and agree with, progress, liberalism, and civilization as lately introduced."

A few years later and exactly on the eve of the occupation of Rome by freethinking Italy the Dogma of Papal Infallibility was promulgated. This formulation established on an unshakable basis the authoritarian and totalitarian quality of the Roman Church.

At that time this seemed to liberals to be nothing but wet lightning. It was not so, however. No challenge of this import and power had ever been flung against the civilization of rationalism and liberalism. Modern civilization seemed to be beyond and above any danger. And indefinite automatic progress was the common belief of the Western man. The effects of the challenge were to be seen in the forthcoming epoch of crisis, although nobody at that time, and perhaps not even Pius IX, the Pope of the Syllabus, could foresee how close at hand such an epoch was.

This epoch is characterized by the disturbances of the first World War, 1914-1918, and of its immediate aftermath. Passions were inflamed and interests were subverted. The passive discipline of months and years spent by millions of people in the trenches offset to a considerable extent the former experiences of freedom and initiative. On the other hand, the economic security which was offered for the duration of the war to the combatants and their families developed a tendency toward the preservation of this advantage, which was obscurely considered as a minimum reward for the past dangers and efforts. Adjustment to renovated conditions of competition and initiative was made extremely difficult by the disorganization of peacetime enterprises and by social and economic perturbations of all kinds, among them even the ravages of epidemics at the end of the war and by the pathetic return of the combatants to their homes. The helplessness of the outcome of the war, compared with the promise of victorious democracies in building a new and durable order on foundations of ethical fairness and intellectual consistency was perhaps not yet clear to observing minds, but it was in some way present to the stirred and dissatisfied emotions of the masses.

All this is very well known, yet the problem remains why and how it happened that a world phenomenon like fascism started in Italy, why, in other terms, the morbid conditions created by the war proved more promptly and more effectively operative in that country than anywhere else.

Specifically the situation in Italy, especially during the last period of the war, from, say, the spring of 1917 to the autumn of 1918, had been from the alimentary and social point of view considerably worse than it had been in France or in England. On the other hand, it had been considerably better than in Austria-Hungary, in Germany, or in Russia. It remains to be explained why fascism did not rise in any of the latter countries. Russia reacted to its disastrous conditions with the Bolshevik revolution, which, at least for many years, was directed toward intentions and aims that seemed and largely were diametrically opposite to the intentions and aims of fascism. Austria-Hungary and Germany went through an experiment in republicanism and liberalism of the left.

It seems clear, then, that the particular economic situation of Italy does not account for the rise of fascism, not even if one takes into account the comparative weakness of the middle classes. The middle classes were much weaker in Russia than they were in Italy. The merely political military explanation, founded on the alleged failure of the Italian military effort and on the alleged frustration of Italian diplomacy in the negotiations for peace, looks more impressive at first, but it does not stand the test of factual examination.

Of all battles that were fought on the Italian sector of the World War by far the most famous is Caporetto, October, 1917.

A sudden and brilliant maneuver of envelopment performed by the Austro-Hungarian army with some German help broke the Italian front along the Isonzo and forced the entire Italian army to a precipitous withdrawal, which at certain moments assumed the aspect of a desperate flight. Yet this flight and the advance of the enemy invasion were stopped in a very few days at a comparatively short distance from the earlier alignment. Not even Venice was lost.

Resistance proved effective and unbreakable on the river Piave. Help from the allies, France and England, was all but nominal. The effort and pride of successful resistance were virtually entirely Italian. Successful resistance was followed by the splendid defensive-offensive victory of the Piave in June, 1918. This happened to be the first decisive victory on the side of the Allies. The following contributions of the Italian forces to the common victory may have been more or less well timed. At any rate, from June to early in November it was a series of successful operations and the end of the war was smashingly victorious. The French at Charleroi, and later the English in March, 1918, and the Russians at the Dunajec had undergone defeats no less severe than Caporetto. No victory had been better earned on any section of the Allied front than the victories on the Italian front in 1918. Yet no other country was chosen by destiny as the birthplace of fascism.

The losses of Italy during the war were appalling. The dead alone numbered between six and seven hundred thousand. It certainly was an enormous loss; but if we should consider it as the determining cause of fascism, the problem arises why the French, the Russian, and German losses, which were even greater than the Italian, did not work as a determining factor for fascism in the respective countries.

The diplomatic territorial outcome of the war was unsatisfactory for each and all of the parties concerned. Russia was severely mutilated and virtually deprived of any European role by the treaty of Brest-Litovsk. The nationalistic plan of the French patriots, aimed at the secure Rhine frontier and at the splitting of the German unity, was flouted. England annexed some additional colonial territories but saw the ties within the Empire dangerously loosened. America started immediately after the armistice her complaints about having been exploited and plundered by the Allies without any gain for herself. Yet none of these countries was elected by destiny as the birthplace of fascism.

Of all the combatant nations, Italy was the one who saw her so-called hereditary enemy, Austria-Hungary, go to pieces. She acquired a continental frontier of mountain ridges than which only the ditch around the British Isles could be considered more comfortable. Around her frontier only minor states, Jugoslavia and Switzerland—not at all dangerous—remained alive, and France at the west. No aggressive intention whatsoever could be attributed to France. Italian colonial acquisitions were small or altogether irrelevant, but no real national passion stood behind the colonial demands. They had been slighted by Italy herself in her treaties with the allies concerning the rewards of victory. They were never insisted upon by the Italian delegates at the conference of Paris after the armistice. When possibilities of this kind, like a partial occupation of Asia Minor or even of Georgia, appeared during the negotiations, it was Italy herself that refused the honor and the burden.

Thus a diplomatic interpretation of the rise of fascism, if tested on the edge of factuality, works as badly as the social or the economic interpretation. the motives were much deeper. The most important among them belong to the two trends of thought which have been outlined in the earlier sections of this summary. It is true however, that such motives would not have become operative if they had not been energized by passionate references to the immediate results of the war. This happened, and it was one of the most magnificent manipulations in history. We shall not go into details, which would sound comparatively outdated today. An immense wave of propaganda was started about a few cliffs and villages on the eastern shore of the Adriatic. These were central Dalmatia—with little more than five hundred thousand inhabitants, overwhelmingly Slavic and with about ten thousand Italian-speaking persons among them. The most importan urban conglomerations were two townships with a few charming mememtoes of Venetian architecture; their names were, in Italian spelling, Seberíco and Spálato (Slavic, Sibenik and Split). The immense majority of the Italians did not even know how to pronounce the two Italians names; almost all of them insisted on saying Sebénico and Spaláto, with wrong accents.

This wave of nationalistic and irredentistic propaganda provided the spark for the outburst of the emotional complex which stood behind the whole disorder. Military victory, however, interspersed with defeats and diplomatic victory, however, qualified by disappointment, was transmuted into military and diplomatic disaster and the Italians were provided with the make-up of a defeated nation. Caporetto was emphasized by the Italians themselves and the previous and following victories pushed into the background of the emotional perspective. Such reactions to the artificially provided complex of defeat might have gone the Russian or the German way, toward Bolshevism or toward social-democratic Republicanism. They went the other way, toward the earth-shaking invention of fascism, because the emotional and intellectual background of the ruling classes in Italy was prepared for something of that kind. Their inferiority and superiority complexes—pivoted around the myth of Roman primacy—found a propitious terrain in the disturbances of the war and postwar years. Their historical experiences in authoritarian discipline, through both allegiance to Caesarism and submission to the papacy, weighed heavier in the moment of crisis than their interrupted endeavors in liberty and individualism.

Thus the hour struck. Resistance against fascism in its early stages proved stronger in Italy than it was to prove a few years later in Germany. It was, however, ineffective. The governmental and capitalistic centers were virtually ready to surrender as soon as the movement started. There was no revolution, only a sequence of *coups d'état*. The first and most decisive, October 28, 1922, was a compact between monarchy and fascism. The seizure of Rome by fascism was no military operation, no revolutionary deed. It was a coarse parade or celebration, a black carnival.

I shall quote from an earlier essay of mine, *Six Kings*, written before the outbreak of this war:

> Hitler now overtowers both the inspirers of his vigil, Bismarck and Mussolini. Much more, however, than the Prussian chancellor, the Latin Duce had been and remained paramount in the Fuehrer's formative years. A Southerner and a Catholic by birth, Hitler's mind was steeped in schemes of Latin and Roman rather than of Northern Protestant make. One annotation among others is suggestive in the Alvin Johnson edition of *Mein Kampf*. We learn from it that the "Senate chamber and study in the Brown House, Munich, are proudly displayed as examples of the Fuehrer's (artistic) work. In the first, which is primarily a study in red leather, the Swastika serves as an allusion to the SPQR of ancient Rome (Senatus Populusque Romanus)."

This is indeed the repetitious story of Roman-German political intercourse from the deepest Middle Ages, at least as early as Charlemagne, and earlier, to our daily news. Whatever the Latin imagination brewed on behalf of the resurrection and perpetuity of Roman Empire and Roman unity, the Germans stole home, elaborating the politico-literary plagiarism into a thing of flesh and blood, and whipping a feeble daydream into a galloping nightmare.

No sooner had the outmost provinces of Italy been liberated than a remarkable little editorial was printed in a Catania tabloid, the *Corriere di Sicilia, August* 25, 1943. The wrong of fascism, it stated, was to look backward, to ancient Rome; hence the wreck we contemplate in Rome and the world. "The only possible Roman Empire of today is world cooperation, with all the other Romes partaking equally in the common task." He who worded such plain truths so plainly was presumably an American soldier-writer of Latin descent and background.

His words anyhow had a familiar ring for Italian ears. Elizabeth Barrett had voiced them in her Mazzinian English, from the Florence that is no more, nearly a century ago. "Civilization perfected," she said, "is fully developed Christianity." She said to the Italians of her day:—

> Rise: prefigure the grand solution
> Of earth's municipal, insular schisms...
> Bring us the higher example; release us
> Into the larger coming time...

In slightly different terms: as the curtain, or tombstone, falls on Fascism, we gain a more comprehensive insight into its character and career. It was perversion and dementia. It was the fact, or imagination, of power substituted for the idea of justice. It also was a diagnosis of real diseases that lamed and lame the half-civilization we call democracy, with total brutality offered as the remedy. It also was the wrong answer to a right problem. The problem was: How shall we make order and establish authority in the anarchy of the nations? The answer was: Roman Empire, German Empire. That answer is dust. The problem is bequeathed by the dying to the living; as all epilogues are prologues.[1]

For Bibliography see next chapter.

[1] The above essay on the *Origins of Fascism* had been first written as a lecture for Oberlin College on the invitation of President E. H. Wilkins, four years after the publication of Borgese's *Goliath, the March of Fascism* (1937). It had been included, immediately after the nineteenth birthday of Fascism (October 28, 1941) in a Symposium, *Democracy Is Differcnt* (Carl Frederick Wittke and others, Harper & Brothers, New York).

Another essay, by the same author, *Commemoration of Fascism*, was published in *The Atlantic Monthly*, February, 1945.

The opening paragraph, a reference to the twenty-second—and last—birthday of Fascism, echoed the opening lines of the previous essay: "There was no celebration in Rome last October of the March on Rome—birth date, back in 1922, of Italian and World Fascism."

The closing paragraphs framed in the new events—and new fears, and hopes—the statements and analyses of the *Origins of Fascism* as well as of *Goliath* and of other books and essays by the same author.

XVIII.
Fascism

XVIII.

FASCISM

What Is a Fascist Economy?

by

Guenther Reiman

On the Nature of the Corporate State

The economic system of fascism has been a controversial subject since the early days of Mussolini's totalitarian regime. The controversy has never ended, though the first fascist State, born during the critical years which followed the first world war, is a thing of the past. It was easy to agree on the political nature of Fascism: (1) the one-party State (though the ruling party in a totalitarian State has lost the character of a political party or movement); the ruthless suppression of all other parties and movements, and any actual or potential groups and organizations which were not directly regulated and controlled by the State; (2) the monopolization of all political power by one ruling "party"; (3) the centralized hierarchic structure of the State bureaucracy.

As a political system, Italian Fascism very closely resembled Hitler's National Socialism and the Russian totalitarian State.

To what extent do the similarities in the political system also reflect basic similarities in the social and economic system? This depends on the character of the economy that exists under totalitarian rule. It is easy to point out various phases in the economic development of Fascism. In Italy, for instance, the system started with an economy that did not differ greatly from the private capitalism of the Western world. The corporations were founded only at a later stage, in 1929, during the last year of the prosperity era of world capitalism, during the inter-war period, 1918-1939, and at the beginning of the great pre-war depression. But the Corporate State remained a mere myth for several years. Only when it became clear that the great depression was not a mere cyclical crisis of capitalism, and that permanent mass unemployment and lack of profitable investments for "idle capital" imperiled the economic foundation of the State, the Corporations became active organizations. They were to control and regiment all producers and distributors, all the members of social classes, except the State bureaucracy itself; the working class as well as the industrialists and agrarians.

Thus, the Corporate State was officially created in 1929. But, in October 1932, Mussolini still declared that the Corporate institutions were not going to change the economic system. On October 16, 1932, Mussolini said about the Corporations:

> Those who are seeking miraculous remedies for the depression are mistaken. Either the present depression is a periodic depression with the economic system, in which case it will be overcome, or it represents a transition from one stage of civilization to another.

A year later, he had written off capitalism as the system of Fascism. On October 7, 1933, he announced:

> I want to establish the corporate regime. . . . The corporation will be called upon to regulate all problems of production. A policy of unregulated production is folly and generally catastrophic. . . . I have accomplished these essential political reforms, and my hands are now free to modify the economic system. I intend to experiment as Roosevelt and Stalin are doing.[1]

Must we therefore conclude that the political regime started a social revolution and replaced capitalism with a system of national planning?

[1] Quoted by G. Salvemini, *The Fascist Dictatorship in Italy*, 1927, p. 141.

We pointed out before that the political system of Fascism in Italy, of National Socialism and of totalitarianism in Russia were very similar, indeed, during the early years of Fascism. At that time, the economic system of various totalitarian States differed greatly. We may now point out that the economic system of Fascism—state economic regimentation of all social classes and groups, national planning and government channelling of new investments—often resembled State policies in countries where the government still was subject to Parliament. The American New Deal had many similarities to the State economic intervention in Fascist Italy and Nazi Germany. But "everything is fluid," and we have to consider the possibility that the structure of an economic system may be in conflict with the political methods of rule. Then, either the economy must be changed or the political system must be modified in accordance with the structure of the economy.

Therefore, it is not easy to answer our question: Must fascism have a special economic system, and if we give a positive answer, what are its main characteristics?

Corporate State—as a Myth

The first school of thought with which we are dealing here believes that Fascism is only a system of political reaction, the tool of big capitalists who seek to smash labor unions and to "atomize" the working class. Fascism is represented as a tool of the big capitalists. This was a popular theory among Communists. It was the official thesis of the Communist International during the early stages of Fascism, and also later. Many non-Communist Leftists adopted the same theory.

A former leading figure of the Communist International wrote in the middle twenties:

> In reality, Fascism has added nothing new to the traditional program of the bourgeois politicians (A. Bordiga, p. 177).

At that time, Fascism had, indeed, no program and did not pretend to make any change in the social system. The inauguration of the Corporate State appeared as a mere response to the longing of the måsses for social reforms which once were promised by Fascist propaganda.

Then, at the end of the American prosperity period, the time had arrived when Mussolini officially proclaimed the program of anti-capitalist revolution through State economic planning. The Corporations were of no practical importance except in the sphere of relations between the workers and management, or labor and private capitalists, during the first few years of the Corporate constitution. The syndicates were absorbed by the Corporations. The workers lost the right to strike or to bargain for higher wages.

John Strachey wrote, in 1935 when he was still close to the official theories of the Communist Party:

> The truth is that Fascism is always and everywhere the instrument . . . of the great capitalists using the petit bourgeoisie as its dupes.[2]

In the early stages of the corporations, the State used the Corporations in the sphere of labor, and to a great extent, also against the middle class organizations, while the big industrialists and bankers still retained much independent influence and were permitted to elect the leaders of their own organizations.

Two years after the inauguration of the Corporate State, the latter appeared as a mere myth and the claim for basic social and economic changes a mere fake.

> The term "corporation" has been used, if not invented, to arouse a sense of wonder in the people, to keep them guessing, to provoke inquiry, and to contrive, out of sheer mystification of an unusual word, at once to hide the compulsion on which the Dictatorship finally depends and to suggest that a miraculous

[2] John Strachey, *The Nature of the Capitalist Crisis*, New York, 1935, p. 357.

work of universal benevolence is in the course of performance ... "Corporate" state is a tool of propaganda.[3]

But the privileges of the big industrialists were largely lost at a later stage. It had become impossible for private capitalists to convert money into political influence by financing election campaigns, buying or controlling newspapers, or by buying special favors from the bureaucrats.

The contributions to the Party or to the totalitarian State bureaucracy were greater than whatever was given before to professional politicians or for political purposes. Yet, the big private industrialists and bankers had to be subservient to the Party leaders or State bureaucracy, too. Otherwise, even they risked the loss of their fortunes and worse punishment.

Therefore, Salvemini wrote:

> The Fascist Party is no longer an organization of mercenaries in the service of capitalism, but has been an independent force... If the capitalists stopped playing with the policy of the Party, the Party could easily steer to the Left. Thus, although the employees are privileged (?), they are intimidated at the same time. It is not the first time in history that mercenaries have been the masters' masters.[4]

In 1930-31, it seemed that Mussolini's social promises had been overshadowed by the promises of the New Deal in America and by Russia's Five Year Plan. Therefore, Mussolini suddenly declared in 1933 that the Corporations were not to be mere organs of control or mere ornamental institutions of the State, but tools of a social-economic revolution which would pave the way to a new civilization.

Within the Corporate institutions a turn towards the "Left" was made by the Party bureaucrats. Private capitalists lost their last independent positions. The Party leaders fortified their authoritarian power by tightening the state controls over all individ-

[3] Quoted by Gaetano G. Salvemini, *ibid.*, p. VIII.
[4] *Ibid.*, p. 379.

uals and economic establishments. Mussolini said in a speech to the Senate on January 13, 1934:

> Corporative economy introduces order even into economy. If there is a phenomenon which ought to be well ordered, which ought to be directed to certain definite aims, it is precisely the economic phenomenon, which interests the whole of the citizens. Not only industrial economy ought to be disciplined, but also agricultural economy, commercial economy, banking economy, and even the work of artisans.
>
> How must this discipline be carried into practice? By means of the self-discipline of the interested classes. Only at a later moment, when the classes have not found the way to reach agreement and equilibrium, can the State intervene, since the State represents the other term of the equation...[5]

This meant in practice that the power of the Party hierarchy was increased to such an extent that it could overrule the Army and the old conservative Civil Service bureaucracy.

The terms "Left" and "Right" only refer to the relative strength of the bureaucracies; the Army and Civil Service professionals, on the one hand ("Right") and the "plebian" party bureaucrats on the other hand. The latter has at first deprived the working class of all means of self-protection. Thereafter, the party oligarchy became the self-appointed "guardian" of the "rights" of labor." But the authoritarian party bureaucracy must reconcile its own selfish interests with the requirements of the Army. Compared with the power of the State bureaucracies, the old private capitalists—insofar as they manage to survive— are only of second-rate importance. The political power structure is overruling the formerly leading economic powers. The economic foundation becomes subservient to the superstructure. The latter must satisfy the economic needs of the political powers.

[5] Guiseppe de Michelis, *World Reorganization on Corporative Lines*, London, 1935.

The Corporate State—A Planned Economy?

Another interpretation of the economic system of Fascism (and of any totalitarian regime) has become popular in recent years: Fascism as the fulfilment of socialism, or of a planned economy. Accordingly, the corporations are mere planning agencies with the General Council of Corporations as a national central planning board, similar to the Central Five Year Planning Board in Russia, Goering's Five Year Plan Agency in the Third Reich.

Then, the Corporate State would effect an anti-capitalist social revolution: the fulfillment of national socialism, the managerial society, the replacement of capitalist anarchy with state planning. Private ownership of the means of production ends, and the State becomes sole owner of all productive forces. Surviving private enterprises are of no importance; for they must act in accordance with State regulation to such an extent that they are only part of one gigantic State economy. Industrialists, bankers or other business men become mere agents of the State. Their private existence has only a formal or transitory character.

It is easy to point to certain facts which apparently confirm this theory. Originally, the Corporate State put only labor under stringent state control. During this stage, the Corporations did not change the economic system. The Corporate State appeared as a mere fake. Thereafter, however, the industrialists and bankers and all other private individuals were put under the control (or "national discipline") of Corporate organizations. Finally, a program of regulation of all productive activities, especially of new investments, and of the exploitation of national economic resources and their development "in the interest of the State" and in accordance with a Plan was formally accepted.

But a real national plan of production and distribution of the social products was still missing. Such a plan was finally prepared during the last stage of Fascism as a conversion to a war economy.

The defenders of Fascism themselves were eager to point out the "socialist" character of the Corporate organizations. In the old capitalist world, Socialists fought for State intervention, for State ownership and State economic planning, and often vulgarized the meaning of socialism by identifying it with "planning" or a system of State intervention.

Bernard Shaw, for instance, welcomed Mussolini's Corporations as the beginning of socialism in 1934, as follows:

> Some of the things Mussolini has done, and some that he is threatening to do go further in the direction of Socialism than the English Labor Party could yet venture if they were in power. They will bring him, presently, into serious conflict with capitalism; and it is certainly not my business nor that of any socialist to weaken him in view of such a conflict."

This was not an isolated view.

The chief editor of *The Daily Herald*, organ of the Labor Party, wrote on June 6, 1934, after a visit to Italy:

> The corporation is to be the means whereby the workers' organizations secure not only the right to bargain on hours and wages, but also the right to share in a control and management of industries ultimately to divide control with the technicians, eliminating capitalist management altogether. On the other hand, the... industrialists hope to find in the corporations an instrument by which they can keep the workers more effectively under control, and by which they can free themselves from such of the government and party interference of which they complain bitterly today.[6]

The idea of centralized planning has stirred the imagination of many Socialists and has been popularized by "socialist" State interventionists.

Then the suppresive measures of the Corporate State appear as mere by-products of centralized planning. For the latter requires

[6] Quoted by Salvemini, *ibid.*, p. 370.

the subordination of all personal activities and interests to the "social interests," and the latter are expressed by the "plan."

A similar view is expressed by those who acknowledge the hierarchic structure of fascist society, and the destruction of all values of Western civilization. But this retrogression of civilization appears to them as a mere result of centralized economic planning. Fascism or totalitarianism is to be the beginning of a social revolution which supersedes capitalism.

> It was in the third period—after 1929—that the true significance of fascism became apparent. The deadlock of the market system was evident. Until then fascism had been hardly more than a trait in Italy's authoritarian government, which otherwise differed but little from those of a more traditional type. It now emerges as an alternative solution of the problem of an industrial society.[7]

We may summarize this line of thought as follows:

The political "revolution" of fascism also becomes an economic revolution. The supremacy of the political powers over the economy would be a mere fiction. In reality, the economic character of the fascist society also determines the political system. The fact that Italian fascism started without a program of economic changes would only prove that Italian fascism was not yet fully developed. Even when the Corporate State was formally introduced, fascism had not yet shown its real nature. This only happened when the Corporate organizations became tools of national planning.

Thus fascism is represented as the beginning of a new Civilization which supersedes the old Western world.

The Imperialist Nature of the "Corporate State"

It is easy to quote the practice of Italian fascism in order to prove their theory—the Corporate State as a myth, with the poli-

[7] Karl Polanyi, *The Great Transformation*, New York, 1941, p. 245.

ical leaders in authoritarian supremacy, or the Corporate system as an anti-capitalist national socialism, with the political agents only as organizers and protectors of the "new society."

In Italy, in particular, but also in other fascist countries, the new system passed through various phases—from relatively little State intervention in the economy to complete regimentation and blueprint planning of all individual activities.

But these changes in economic policies were always dictated by the economic needs of the State: to get enough financial resources in order to keep the gigantic inflated State bureaucracy (or bureaucracies) intact, and to finance its huge unproductive expenditures.

Guerin and others have pointed out that the political methods of fascism are designed to increase the rate of profits for the private capitalists, or at least for "big business." But actually, Fascism increases the unproductive parasitic expenditures of the State enormously. It orders new investments in spheres which sustain the power of the State without too much concern for the rate of profit. Shortly, Fascism must requisition a huge portion of the profits, with the result that most capitalist enterprises are threatened by bankruptcy.

The rate of profit continues its decline, and many private capitalists must think in terms of their rate of losses. They may be forced by the State to continue work and production though they cannot realize a profit.

The following passage of the *Cartd del Lavoro* was originally not taken seriously when it was written, but it became of practical importance at a later stage:

> The right of the state to intervene in economic production if the private initiative is lacking or unsatisfactory.......

There is some justification in the claim that the Fascist State has solved the market problem of private capitalism. But another problem arises of even greater acuteness; the problem of deficit spending, and over-consumption or underproduction. Therefore, the fascist State must nationalize private monopolies, or organize a new system of national monopolies, not for the purpose of social planning, but in order to increase the taxation of the private individuals and also of private enterprises. Price policies are planned from the same point of view. Thus all totalitarian powers have established a system of control of agricultural prices. State monopolies require the crops of the agricultural producers at low prices while other State organizations sell them to the consumers at exorbitant prices. The margin of profit is higher than the commercial profits of private capitalism. But these profits no longer are private capitalist profits. They belong to the State, they grow to such an extent that the incentive for the producers to produce, and for the workers to work shrink, and finally may decline to such an extent that personal initiative can no longer be encouraged by the State. Many individuals seek to circumvent the controls of the State in spite of terrific risks. They are unwilling to produce. Therefore, the State must organize special organs of control and coercion.

This was one of the original tasks of the corporate organization in Italy, and one of the reasons for their foundation.

But these organizations contribute to the growth of the bureaucracy and of unproductive expenditures. The system works with a dwindling margin of success. Then new national monopolies must be organized, and the latter fuse with the organizations of control and coercion.

We may therefore define the Corporate State as a system where an authoritarian State bureaucracy must rely on national monopolies as a means of exploitation of the national economy, and on coercive measures in order to force unwilling producers to produce for the State with little or no return.

The predatory character of the fascist State also creates a new drive for imperialist expansion: the totalitarian spheres in the struggle for "fields of investment." The aim is not to create bettor opportunities for capitalist investments. The need for imperialist expansion arises from the urge to gain new or greater national monopolies so that more individuals and more national economies can be exploited by the authoritarian state bureaucracies. The national economy is too narrow a basis for the authoritarian state bureaucratic parasite.

But whenever fascist imperialists seek new foreign expansion, the spheres of foreign powers are threatened.

The centralized monopoly rule of the fascist bureaucracy facilitates the organization of a war economy. It encourages the rise of militarism. It is experienced with the incorporation of all enterprises into a centralized economic system. But militarism and war also increase unproductive expenditures and reduce the private incentives for the producer. A State that can rely on the voluntary support of the majority of the people can create such a war economy without drastic curtailment of personal rights and freedoms. When the voluntary support ceases, the coercive measures must be extended and tightened. Then national plans become necessary. Therefore national planning under fascism is apt to increase economic deficiences and the insatiable hunger of the State for national products and services. Then partial controls or a mere system of national monopolies is no longer sufficient. Then the Corporate State must replace the system of national monopolies with a system of national planning. The Corporate State reaches therefore its ripest stage at the time of its greatest crisis. If it could survive this crisis, it would have to rely on a system of national monopolies rather than of national planning.

The universal nature of Fascism—with revival of nationalist traits and extreme nationalist propaganda also as a universal feature—will be more clearly recognized after the second world war than before. During the first years of fascist rule in Italy or National Socialism in Germany, the character of Fascism was obscured by mysticism and mere political methods of suppression. It seemed that Fascism was only a change of political methods of rule without attempting to change the economic foundation. The Fascist leaders themselves did not conceive any social or economic revolution. They were out to conquer political power, and to hold it forever. The monopoly of political power not only had to be defended against political opponents, but also against the danger of an economic breakdown.

As long as the economic foundation—private capitalism—was able to provide the means for the maintenance of the huge inflated political machine of Fascism, intervention of the State in the sphere of economics did not go further than in many non-Fascist states. But when private capitalism was unable to guarantee the economic existence of the Fascist State, State intervention in the sphere of economics became necessary. The Fascist government was better prepared to intervene and to change the economic foundation than capitalist countries where parliamentarian rule made it difficult. Here it is possible for social classes and group interests to exert independent influence and to act as pressure groups. Their complete suppression under Totalitarianism has been a common feature of Fascism in Italy, National Socialism in Germany and also of "Communism" in Russia.

This "universal" phenomenon has been accompanied by the establishment or introduction of institutions and "plans" which were to change the economic system from top to bottom; replacement of the private capitalist economy by a system of national planning. Thus, the monopoly holders of political power, the regulators of production, fuse with the industrial or agricultural managerial class. The State would thus become some kind of State trust with the dictator as supreme Chairman of a giant corporation.

This conception of "managerial revolution" is in our view only a trend which reaches its highest form in times of war—as the fulfillment of the war economy. But this State trust does not solve the conflict between the need for political monopoly rule and an economic foundation which provides the means for the political power. In a war economy, this conflict reaches its highest intensity, with the political power greatly extended and the economic foundation greatly weakened.

The bureaucratic fascist, national socialist or nationally planned state is like a gigantic parasite who must eat up more than the exploited economic body can deliver, yet, the parasite cannot become the provider himself. Therefore, Fascist corporations are tools of the State that must control, suppress and regiment the private producers, but they do not necessarily change the economic foundation.

The Corporate institutions—as we know them—are of a transitional character. At first they are a myth, then they are used in order to establish strict "discipline" over hostile social classes and also over social groups which are no longer permitted to remain in an independent position, finally they become part of a war economy, or tools of "national planning."

In theory, it is possible that they could change their character again, and become some kind of caste-like organizations, organized as a new form of "guild," which must pay a heavy tribute to the State though they may have functions of their own. Such a transformation is, however, possible only if national fascism could form a world-monopoly state. Then the fascist hierarchy could form an international foundation for itself.

This form of "world fascism" can only be realized by wars not only between fascist and non-fascist powers, but also among the totalitarian States themselves. The entire structure of world economy may disintegrate during such wars to such an extent that the basis for any kind of world organization would disappear.

BIBLIOGRAPHY

Bonomi, I.: *From Socalism to Fascism*, 1924.
Borgese, G. A.: *Goliath: The March of Fascism*, 1937.
Ferrero, G.: *Four Years of Fascism*, 1924.
Matteotti, G.: *The Fascisti Exposed*, 1924.
Mussolini, Benito: *The Political and Social Doctrine of Fascism*, 1935.
Nenni, P.: *Ten Years of Tyranny in Italy*, 1932.
Nitti, F. F.: *Escape*, 1930.
Nitti, F. S.: *Bolshevism, Fascism and Democracy*, 1927.
Salvemini, G.: *The Fascist Dictatorship in Italy*, 1937.
Sforza, C.: *The Real Italians*, 1942.
Sturzo, L.: *Italy and Fascism*, 1926.

XIX. Hispanidad and Falangism

EUROPEAN FASCIST MOVEMENTS

Editorial Note

Fascism has scattered its seeds throughout Europe. Fascist and Nazi ideologies existed in almost every nation, although there were discrepancies and variations between them. However, Italian Fascism with some Nazi tinge was the popular pattern. Spain had its "Falange"; England, Sir Oswald Mosley's "Black Shirts"; France, the "Cagoulards" and the "Croix de Feu"; Norway, the Nazi "National Samling" headed by Quisling; Roumania, the Iron Guard, led by Codreanu; Hungary, Szálasi's Arrow Cross; Croatia, the "Ustachi" commanded by Pavelitch; Poland, the National Radical Organization (ONR) and the "Falanga"; and Slovakia, the autonomous movement commanded by Tiso with the Hlinka Guard. It is beyond the scope of this volume even to enumerate the barbaric sympathizers and followers of Hitler and and Mussolini who have now disappeared from the scene; but they are still capable of disseminating hate and violence. Their ideas are not yet dead, and democratic forces must remain on constant guard against the resurgence of their deadly ideologies, unless total collapse of our morals and our culture occur.

Since separate treatments of each movement were technically impractical and since, as a whole, they are generally similar, only a single representative "minor" Fascist movement was chosen, the "Falange." Due to its connection with Hispanidad it appeared to be a particularly interesting example.

F. G.

XIX.

HISPANIDAD AND FALANGISM

by

STEPHEN NAFT

LIKE ITS ITALIAN and German prototypes, the philosophy of Spanish totalitarianism has two facets: one concerned with domestic reconstruction—Falangism, and the other aiming to justify the expansionist ambitions of nationalist megalomania—*Hispanidad.*

Hispanidad is as closely related to and as much one of the principal tenets of Falangism as the theory of the superiority of the German "Nordic Aryan race" is part and parcel of Nazism and its past activities and aspirations.

Expansionist Pan-Germanism existed as a theory long before Hitler became its most active and, for a while, its most successful promoter. Before the advent of Mussolini, Enrico Corradini preached the necessity of reestablishing for Italy the power of ancient Rome, beginning with proclaiming the Mediterranean as the *Mare Nostrum.* And Hispanidad, the revival of the dream of reestablishing Pan-Hispanic rule over the Western hemisphere and all territories once discovered or possessed by Spain, was also conceived before the active organization of Falangism.

Nazism, Fascism and Falangism improved on the theories and, particularly, on the practice of their super-nationalist forerunners. While the latter wanted or dreamed only of enslaving or subjugating other nations, the Fascists of the various countries and shirt colors varied or amplified that program by beginning with the enslavement of their own compatriots.

The Falangists seriously believed that they would get their share of the world—the Western hemisphere at least—after the victory of the Axis powers, of which they were fully convinced.

A few years before the organization of the first groups sworn to the destruction of the Spanish Republican regime and before the creation of the word "Falangism," a series of articles entitled *Defensa de Hispanidad* appeared in the monthly magazine *Acción Española,* beginning with its first issue in 1931. The author of these articles and the editor of the magazine, legally published under the tolerant Republic, was Ramiro de Maeztú, the son of a Cuban father and an English mother. In his youth he sympathized with and was even literarily active in the anarchist movement, but in later years he became an ardent Catholic and monarchist, and the Spanish monarchy rewarded him with the post of ambassador to Argentina.

His articles in the Acción Espãnola, later collected in a volume, became the evangel of Spanish Falangism and Hispanidad, almost as much as Hitler's *Mein Kampf* became the evangel of Nazism, and Lenin's *What is to be done,* that of the budding Russian brand of totalitarianism.

Maeztú's book contains a map showing the Spanish empire at the time of Philip II, and there was no doubt in Maeztú's mind that the manifest destiny of Spain was to regain the lost empire. There is, however, a slight difference between Maeztú's rationalization of the aspirations of Hispanidad and Hitler's justification of German world rule. Maeztú rejects the racial principles of the Nazis. He bases the right of Spain to rule again over half the world, including all peoples which once were under Spanish rule, on the combination of tradition, history, religion, and "spiritual heritage," regardless of race, color and language. Thus we read in his book (third edition):

> Hispanidad, of course, is not a race . . . the 12th of October (Columbus Day in the United States and "Dia de la Raza" in all Spanish speaking countries) is wrongly called *Dia de la Raza.*

It should be accepted in the sense that we Spaniards do not attach any importance to the blood or the color of the skin, because what we call Raza does not consist of these characteristics which can be transmitted by vague protoplasmic mysteries, but by those which are the light of the spirit, such as language and faith. Hispanidad is composed of men of all races, white, black, Indian and Malay and its mixtures, and it would be absurd to seek characteristics by the methods of ethnography. ...Neither by those of geography. Hispanidad is not restricted to one territory; it has many and very different ones....The climes of Hispanidad are in the whole world. And this lack of geographical and ethnographical characteristics is one of the most decisive features of Hispanidad...its spirit is not the attribute of one single country or any definite race.

Is it history which defines its scope? All peoples of Hispanidad were ruled by the same monarchs from 1580, the year of the annexation of Portugal until 1640 the year of its separation, and before and afterwards by two peninsular monarchies, since the year of the discovery until the separation of the nations of America. All these owe their civilization to Spain and Portugal. ...The community of Spanish peoples cannot be that of voyagers traveling in the same boat, who, after having lived together for a few days, say good-bye to each other never to meet again. ...All of them conserve their sentiment of unity, which does not consist in merely speaking the same language, or in the community of historic origin. Neither can it be expressed adequately by saying that it is solidarity; the Dictionary of the Academy understands "solidarity" as a conditional adhesion to the cause of others, and here is not a conditional adhesion but a permanent community....

A historian once called the Spanish-American republics the "disunited states of the south" in counterdistinction to the United States of the North. But much worse than the lack of an organ of unity is the constant criticism and the denial of historic sources of the community of the Hispanic peoples, namely the Catholic religion and the rule of the Spanish Catholic monarchy (pp. 36, 38, 39).

Maeztú is, however, not satisfied with the return of the former Spanish possessions. He looks beyond that:

> Hispanidad is the Empire based on the hope that the inhabitants of unknown countries can be saved as we have been.

Maeztu's hope lies in the emulation of Mussolini:

> The Rome of Mussolini is again becoming one of the hub centers of the world. Will not the old building stones of Hispanidad do something similar for us? (p. 289).

The book has a fifty page appendix entitled "Apologia de la Hispanidad" by Dr. Isidor Gomá y Tomás, Cardinal Archbishop of Toledo, Primate of Spain. This appendix is held in the same high esteem as a theoretical guide for the adherents of Hispanidad as Maeztu's text itself. The words of the Archbishop were intended to give weight to those of the author. The Archbishop denies that the end of the Spanish empire in America was due to "desire of liberty by some peoples enslaved by the mother country" and attributes it to the fact that the eighteenth century was destructive to the spiritual principles which guided the colonies as well as the metropolis—religion, authority and monarchy:

> Atheism of the Encyclopedists and the ideas of the demagogic French Revolution were smuggled into America in Spanish ships, the old sympathy for Spain turned gradually to France; Madrid was supplanted by Versailles, and the Evangel by the Encyclopedia, the old respect for the authority of the King by an itching to try new democratic forms of government (pp. 332-333).

A few pages further on the Archbishop continues:

> ...having defined Hispanidad, I say that it is a great inducement and a duty for Spaniards and (South) Americans to accomplish the Hispanization of America. A temptation in the good sense because every being strives for its aggrandisement, and

> America and Spain invite each other more than other countries of the world toward wide horizons of expansion.... We have conquered and colonized and lived together in the Spanish spirit, and we shall have to reconquer our own spirit which begins to disappear in America (p. 336).

Falangism, the most recent form of European totalitarianism, was created about ten years after Mussolini's ascent to power, or about the time of Hitler's first subjugation of a nation—that of Germany. Onésimo Redondo, a doctor of law of the University of Salamanca and for some time instructor at the University of Mannheim, Germany, published for the first time in Spanish chapters of Hitler's *Mein Kampf.* In 1931 Redondo started in Valladolid a pro-fascist weekly *Libertad,* in which he hailed Hitler as the new Charlemagne. He announced that the swastika was the eternal forerunner of the Latin cross of Christ. In August of the same year he formed a *Junta Castellana de Actuación Hispánica,* and three months later his group and a group created by Ramiro Ledesma Ramos, who had launched a *Manifiesto Politico de la Conquista del Estado,* founded the *Junta Ofensiva Nacional Sindicalista,* henceforth known as the *JONS.* Ledesma Ramos became its chief.

National Syndicalism

The name *Nacional Sindicalista* was chosen in imitation and was an adaptation of Hitler's calling his anti-democratic, anti-labor and anti-socialist party "National Socialist Labor Party." The reason was obvious. In Germany before Hitler, the Socialists had the greatest influence among the workers, while in Spain most of the workers adhered to the syndicalist ideas and organizations. Thus the choice of the name was one of the impostures of these fascist parties to win, by a party name, the confidence of the large masses of the workers who had traditional and ideological attachments to these denominations.

In May 1933 the magazine *Revista JONS* appeared, and at the end of October of the same year, José Antonio Primo de Rivera, the son of General Miguel Primo de Rivera, Spain's dictator under Alfonse XIII between 1923 and 1930, founded the *Falange Española*. In 1934 the *Falange Española* and the JONS amalgamated into the *Falange Española y de las JONS*, and José Antonio Primo de Rivera was proclaimed Supreme National Chief of the Spanish Falangists.

In an interview given in 1933 to the editor of the Madrid Daily *Ahora*, Antonio de Rivera said:

> The world must again be ruled by three of four racial units. Spain must be one of these three or four. It is situated in a most important geographical keypoint and has a spiritual content which entitles it to aspire to one of these places in the world. And that is what we should fight for....Not to be a country of medium importance because a country is either a large powerful nation which fulfills a universal mission, or it is a degraded people without inner values. To Spain must be returned the ambition to be a country to rule the world.

That the principles of Falangism, in spite of its various changes of name, alterations and addition of words for the purpose of satisfying the various component groups, were simply and frankly fascist from the very beginning appears indisputably from the declaration of its first leader Antonio de Rivera. The only difference is its emphasis on its loyalty to the Catholic Church. In the only issue of *El Fascio*, published in March 1933, Rivera's first fascist publication, he wrote:

> We are Fascists because we find our origin in Mussolinian principles; we are Nazis because in National socialist doctrines vibrate our faith and doctrine. But above all we are Spaniards. The National Sydicalist State, corporative and totalitarian, is of Spanish type.

In an article, later hailed as the "Announcement of a New Age" by the devotees of Hispanidad, Redondo wrote in 1935:

> ...A united Germany is the beginning of a strong alliance between all German countries...and a united Spain will be the bastion of revivified Hispanidad....Thus, as the Germany of Hitler has recovered the Saar and sooner or later will conquer the will of Austria, so National-Sydicalist Spain will restore the United Empire of all nations that speak Spanish....Spain will resume her historic task of redeeming the barbarous peoples and the Spanish-German alliance will be placed at the head of the world.

The official program of Spain's ruling Falangist party is not less outspoken. Points one to six of the fundamental "*Twenty six points of the Program of the Falange Española*" reads:

> 1. We believe in the supreme reality of Spain. To strengthen it, to enlarge it, is the urgent collective task of all Spaniards. Toward the realization of this task the interests of individuals, groups and classes must be subordinated relentlessly.
>
> 2. Spain is a unity of destiny in the Universe. Any conspiracy against this unity is criminal. Any kind of separatist movement is a crime which we shall not forgive....For this reason we demand its immediate and thorough extinction.
>
> 3. Our aim is the Empire. We affirm that the historical destiny of Spain is the Empire. We demand for Spain a predominant place in Europe. We submit neither to international isolation nor to foreign mediation. Concerning the countries of Spanish America we aim at the unification of culture, of economic interests and of power. Spain affirms its status as spiritual axis of the Hispanic world, to claim its right to predominance in universal enterprises.
>
> 4. Our armed forces on land, on the seas and in the air shall be as powerful and as numerous as will be necessary to guarantee to Spain at any time its complete independence and its place in the world hierarchy to which it is entitled.
>
> 5. Spain will again seek its glory and its riches across the seas. Spain must aspire to be a great maritime power for danger

> and for trade. We demand for our country the same predominancy (hierarchy) in the navies as in the air.
>
> 6. Our state will be a totalitarian instrument and will relentlessly abolish the system of political parties with all its inorganic suffrage, representation by opposing groups and parliaments.

Among the twenty six points of the Falangist Program, which by decree of General Franco became the basic law of the State, point twelve shows a slight diversion from the traditional policy of unreservedly supporting the interests of the large feudal landowners, by making, at least theoretically, a concession to popular demands of land distribution. It says:

> 12. We shall enrich agricultural production by the following means: We shall demand that a large part of the population concentrated in the cities be returned to the fields to supply them with sufficient labor, in return for the intellectual and commercial services...and the units of tillage be apportioned, in order to eliminate wasteful oversized landed properties, as well as very small farms, which, due to their poor yield, are uneconomical.

In other words the falangist program provided for the return of many city dwellers to the country to reestablish a rural economy, for the profit of the "intellectual and commercial services" of the metropolis. This may be partly a compliance with Hitler's announced program to transform the conquered or vassal countries into agricultural colonies to supply foodstuffs and raw material to Germany, which alone should have the right to manufacture industrial products. This was the economy which imperial Spain enforced in its colonies in America and one of the principal economic reasons why they revolted and seceded.

On page 161 of the *A B C Político de la Nueva Espana* by Francisco Moret Messerli, published in 1940 under official falangist auspices, we read the following definition of the falangist conception of their "cultural" Empire:

> ...Our historical past and vigorous spirit of the race impels us and places on us the obligation to conceive the word Empire in its genuine and original sense. Empire for us is rank, hierarchy and power. The rank which corresponds to Spain in world politics, the hierarchy established by frontiers abroad and the power which is due to a great nation in the world. Our Empire will be the expansion of our culture, the realization of our irrevocable national destiny....Our Empire is the legitimate call for power, the inexorable resolution for command and predominance. The Empire requires, in addition to its moral and cultural justification, a territorial basis. Without the territorial basis there can be no Empire, because we cannot give this name to a melancholy pilgrimage of harmless cultural missions. Thus is defined our Empire, our will for Empire. We affirm that the historical will of Spain is the Empire, that is, that we shall only attain our pinnacle and our proper place when we are in the central position, when we have the directing role, when we place our country at the head of the world.

José Pemartín, National Chief of University and Secondary Education in the Franco government wrote in his book: *What is new in New Spain. Consideration on the present Spanish situation,*" published in 1938:

> We insist that Spain's final aims are absolutely peaceful...but, to continue, its imperatives are the following:
> ...To extend, to expand our great Hispanic, Latin Christian culture and our political jurisdiction and leadership, particularly over the South American countries of Spanish Iberian soul and language (p. 137).

And, on page 139, we find the following footnote:

> Spain, in fact, has no material, colonial or imperialist aspirations. It is only through the most nobly disinterested cultural imperialism of propaganda of its magnificent culture, the most Christian and the most civilizing, and through its political leadership (maestrazgo) that it will attain its imperialism and its destiny.

On July 17, 1936 the Falangist and militarists insurrection was started against the Republican government. Antonio de Rivera was captured and executed in November of the same year. After the outbreak of the insurrection the Carlists also joined the revolt. The Carlist movement began in 1833 following the conflict over the succession of the throne of Ferdinand VII. Since that time there were several revolts and civil wars initiated by the Carlists against the more or less constitutional monarchy for the purpose of reestablishing absolutism and the inquisition, as they openly proclaimed in their newspapers.

Carlist Traditionalists and Falangists

The Carlists, who call themselves *Tradicionalistas*, organized in 1936 armed forces known as *Requetés* and joined the insurrection against the Republican regime. At first there was a certain friction between them and the Falangists, but soon General Franco, explaining that no divergent parties could be tolerated in a totalitarian state, ordered the unification of all forces opposing the Republic. The Carlist party, whose official name was *Comunión Tradicionalista*, was incorporated into the Falange and the full and official name of the united party became, and remained thereafter, *Falange Española Tradicionalista y de las Juntas Ofensivas Nacional Sindicalistas* or *FET y de las JONS*.

The name of the official organ of the Falange is *FE*, and the paper explained that these two letters, the initials of *Falange Española,* express its principles at the same time by the word *Fé,* meaning faith.

The program of the traditionalist Carlists is the reestablishment of the absolute autocracy of the monarchy and the Church, including inquisition. That this program is being put into practice appears clearly from the constitution of the "New Spain," which stipulates that General Franco is head of state, Generalissimo of the armed forces, Premier of the Cabinet, National Chief of the ruling Falangist party, and "since he is the author of the new historic era, in which Spain acquired the possibility of realizing its destiny, the Chief assumes in its entire plenitude the most absolute authority. The Caudillo is responsible only to God and history."

The establishment of the falangist regime in Spain had been proclaimed as the creation of the "New Spain." How new this Spain was to be, and actually did become, appears in a sentence of remarkable precision in another official publication of the Falange published in 1937, and entitled *Falange y Requeté-Organicamente Solidarios* by W. Gonzales Oliveros, Professor at the University of Salamanca. The purpose of the book was to reconcile the clerico-absolutist Carlists with the Nazi-fascist Falangists, who occasionally had bloody clashes with the former. It contains the following sentence on page 30:

> The Requetes were the Falangist of the past and the Falangists are the Traditionalists of the present.

No statement of the Falangist intention of turning back the clock of history towards absolutism of the past centuries can be stronger than this frank admission.

The same book also contains the following passage:

> ...The imperial aims of Spain are not the imperialism in the bad sense of the word, that is insatiable, immoral or amoral, coveting what belongs to others, such as money, lands or rule. It is not, it cannot be anything but an action of recovery, an imperious (rather than imperial) demand of restitution, an imperative of justice (p. 179).
>
> Everybody knows that that which can be reclaimed is that which is "ours," and is unjustly in the hands of others. We shall from now on place ourselves in a position, should the opportunity arise, to regain what is inalienably *ours* (p. 180).
>
> The true authentic Spanish American League of Nations or the Spanish version of the British Commonwealth under the unified

control of a king or Emperor. . . because in an Imperial union, Spain cannot be just one of the republics or another little republic (p. 182).

In its February issue of 1937 the Falangist official magazine *Fe* said in an article signed by Miguel Gran:

> For the America of our culture, our faith and our blood, we wish more than just living together, more than friendship. We desire unity, unity of mind, unity of economy, *unity of power*. We desire to put an end to "Monroeism" in order to replace it by our affirmation "Lo Hispano para los Hispanos" (What is Spanish to the Spaniards).

The falangist constitution of Spain includes also a "Fuero de Trabajo" or Charter of Labor.

Article XI, alinea 2 says: "Individual and collective acts which in any way may disturb the normalcy of production or any attempt against it shall be considered as crimes of treason against the country."

Article XIII, alinea 4 says: "The leadership of the trade unions well be reserved to militants of the Falange Española and the JONS."

In other words any attempt at striking for better working conditions would be considered and punished as treason to the State —that is by death. And the officials of the so-called trade unions will not be elected by the members of the unions but will be appointed by the falangist party leaders.

That the Falangists and their most authoritative spokesmen, even those of the High Clergy who in Spain supported them, were not averse to advising the use of illegal means and of force, to destroy democracy and its basic means of expression, universal suffrage, appears clearly from the passage of a benediction by Cardinal Isidor Gomá y Tomás, published in a special anthology issue of Maeztu's *Acción Española* of March 1937.

> And since it was evident to us by reasoning and knowledge that democracy and universal suffrage were embryonic forms of communism and anarchy, we clamored that they must be fought by all licit means—even legal means we quoted—in order to make it understood as best we could through the censorship; that if we consented to put into practice the methods of legality—formal, but illegitimate—granted to us (participation in elections, etc.)—it was only to prepare the path for those who would one day march toward honor and glory, leaving behind them legalistic scruples. We had therefore to fight against the erroneous idea propagated at times in certain Catholic circles, regarding the illegality of insurrection and the use of force.

In a proclamation issued in Salamanca on April 18, 1937, announcing the unification of the Falangist and the Carlist Requetes, General Franco declared:

> ...We refer to all secular efforts of the Spanish reconquest which found its expression in United Spain under Charles V and Philip II. That Spain which united to defend and expand over the world the Universal and Catholic idea, a Christian Empire, was the Spain which gave the ideal pattern for the later steps which have been made toward recovering the sublime and perfect goal of our history...

In an interview to the correspondent of *La Prensa* of Buenos Aires, published in November 1939 Franco said ". . . our desire of fusion with all Spanish peoples is at this time the essential part of our program, of our longing for the future" . . .

In a June 1940 edition of the "Informaciones'" of Madrid there was the following paragraph:

> Inevitably this empire will have territorial meaning. We demand the lands discovered and conquered by our conquistadores, which our missionaries have baptized with good Spanish names, names which the pirates cannot even pronounce, and which soon will enjoy the honor of being reincorporated in our empire. Is it necessary to say that we have fought for this empire? Is it

> necessary to recall that we have shed enough Spanish blood for this enterprise?

The monthly magazine SPAIN published in English during the War under the auspices of the Spanish consulate in New York, carried in March 1939 an article by Julian Martin Rubio, President of the University of Valladolid, in which he said:

> Nationalist Spain is bound to Latin America by a triple bond—the past, the present, the future.... It is immortal Hispanicism. It is the Spain of the past once again placed on the road to its mission in Latin America. Nationalist Spain does not take a single step without considering the motherland and Latin America simultaneously, because we want to triumph and conquer in our war in order to share the victory with our brothers across the Atlantic, and if necessary to give it to them so that they may be saved.

All totalitarian states created new emblems. The Nazis have their swastikas, Mussolini's Fascists have their executioners ax surrounded by the bundle of rods (for minor punishments), and the Falangist government of Spain accepted the emblem of the double yoke with arrows across. The yoke as a party emblem is characteristic enough, but the arrows in the emblem are the same used in the sixteenth century by Spain to symbolize the conquest of the Americas.

Consejos de Hispanidad

The Falangist idea of Hispanidad did not remain a pure theory to be enunciated as a dream or an aspiration in fascist and falangist newspapers and magazines. The Franco government proceded to organize its practical activities by creating on November 2, 1940 the *Consejo de Hispanidad,* and placing it under the personal direction of the then Minister of Foreign Affairs, Ramon Serrano Suñer, the most outspoken admirer of Hitler in the Spanish government and the Falangist Party of Spain.

Among the 73 members appointed to the directing body of the Consejo were the Subsecretary of the Ministry of the Navy, the Subsecretary of Press and Propaganda, the Director of Maritime Communications, the Delegate of the Foreign Service of the Falange, the Prior of the Dominicans of the Convent of San Sebastian of Salamanca (it was the Dominican Order which was in charge of the Inquisition), the Prior of the Convent of Rabida, the Spanish ambassadors to Argentina, Chile, Cuba, Mexico and Peru, and a few aristocratic grandees owning immense landed properties, and among the falangist luminaries José Pemartín, Franco's Minister of Education and author of the book quoted in previous pages.

In his decree creating the Council, Generalissimo Franco said it would be a continuation of the *Council of Indies* which governed Spain's one time American empire. The Council received jurisdiction over relations with the Latin American countries and the Philippines, and the external division of the Falange would have to coordinate its activities with that of the Council.

The magazine *Civilización* of Baranquilla, Colombia, published in October 31, 1941 an article entitled *Diatriaba de Hispanidad* by Jorge Padilla, revealing the five points of the program of activity of the *Consejo de Hispanidad*:

1. Vindication of the conquest and the Spanish colonization of the Indies (what is called to day Latin-America).

2. Reconsideration of the historic process of independence of the Spanish colonies.

3. Struggle on all fronts against the philosophical and political principles of the French revolution.

4. Fight against Pan-Americanism and particularly against the policy of economic cooperation among the countries of Central and South America with the United States.

5. **Re-establishment of the Empire and of the unity and destiny of Hispanidad.**

The *Consejo de Hispanidad* was created in 1940, shortly after the return of Serrano Suñer from Berlin, where he held prolonged conferences with General Wilhelm Faupel, who had been Hitler's ambassador to Franco Spain from 1937 to 1939. In the same year 1940, Vigo, the westernmost Spanish seaport on the Atlantic was greatly enlarged and modernized. In connection with the improvement of this Spanish naval base, nearest to Latin America, the most important falangist daily *Arriba* of Madrid wrote in its issue of December 26, 1940, that by this fact

> clearly appears the reality of an authentic, powerful Spain... The enlargement of such ports as Vigo is done for such purpose. Spain is looking once more at America, remembering her tradition and her eternal road, and demonstrating to Hispanic America her unfailing love.

When, in 1940 plans were discussed in the United States to establish air and naval bases in South America, the open and secret falangists organizations campaigned violently against any kind of defense plans in the Latin American countries and against hemisphere solidarity in general. (In this they were supported at the other end of the political rainbow by the Communists before the Nazi invasion of Russia in June 1941). In their newspapers and their meetings the falangists painted in dreadful colors the fate awaiting the Latin American nations if they allowed the establishment of such bases. These projected plans were described as the first step of the United States and Great Britain to deprive the Latin Americans of their independence and freedom, which only Franco and Hitler are willing and able to protect.

There was falangist Hispanidad propaganda before the creation of the Consejo de Hispanidad. But these groups operated without official connection and status with the Spanish government. After the creation of the Consejo de Hispanidad and its branches in this hemisphere, the falangist groups surrendered all their files and documents to the Consejo branches, and falangist

Hispanidad propaganda became an official Spanish government activity.

Enrique Cantos, the chief of the Falange of Cuba, explained in a public speech made in Havana in November 1940, the maximum and minimum postulates of Falangism and Hispanidad:

"It is only natural" he declared "that the Latin American countries should eventually come again under Spanish rule."

Cantos was thereupon expelled from Cuba, and his successor, and the more cautious apologists of Hispanidad, explained that this was only the private opinion of Cantos.

The German Origins of the Consejos de Hispanidad

The *Consejo de Hispanidad,* as was mentioned before, had its origin in Berlin. Its prototype and forerunner was also in Berlin.

In 1924, at the time of the Weimar Republic, the Latin American department of the University of Bonn, known as the *Ibero-Amerikanisches Forschungs-Institut der Universität Bonn;* began to publish a quarterly under the name *Ibero-Amerikanisches Archiv,* devoted mainly to historical studies on Spain, Portugal and Latin America. In 1930 the organization changed its name to *Ibero-Amerikanisches Institut.*

After the accession of Hitler that Institute was detached from the Bonn University, transferred to Berlin and became a separate government organization. Its director, a former Minister under the Republic, Dr. Boelitz, was dismissed, and General Faupel was put at the head of the Institute and of the magazine, for which a Nazi editorial staff was appointed. Faupel was Germany's leading specialist on Argentina, where he was Professor at the Military Academy from 1911 to 1913. During World War I he was in charge of German espionage and sabotage in Spain. After the defeat of Germany, Faupel held the post of chief adviser to the Argentine General Staff and Inspector General of the army from 1921 to 1927. In 1927 he became instructor of the Peruvian army. When Hitler's star rose he returned to Germany.

When, in November 1937, General Faupel was appointed Hitler's ambassador to Franco's Junta in Burgos, another general became the head of the Institute. Thus, significantly, two generals were directing in succession Germany's "cultural relations" with the Spanish speaking countries. At the end of 1939 General Faupel returned from Spain where he helped to direct the Nazi and Fascist forces fighting for Franco's insurrection against the Republican government. In 1939 he resumed his post as director of the *Ibero-Amerikanisches Institut.* One of the principal "cultural" activities of the Institute was the printing of pamphlets on Hispanidad and the necessity of its realization in Latin America. It was disclosed that shortly after the outbreak of the war between Japan and the United States, the Japanese steamer Ishiu Maru arrived in a Brazilian port to unload cases of falangist Hispanidad propaganda printed in Spanish in Germany and consigned to Argentina.

The Nazis called, or still call, any country in which there are Germans a *Gau* (canton). The falangists, copying this system, call every one of their groups in Latin America "provincial falange." But due to the identity of language, religion, family relations, tradition and certain customs, the falangists have much greater facility of exerting influence, particularly among the upper classes and among some intellectuals or intelligentsia groups than the Nazis.

Falangism and fascism repeatedly proclaimed the principle of "hierarchy," hierarchy within the nation and hierarchy of their nation over the other nations. Thus Hispanidad, as understood by the falangists, cannot mean a free association of Spanish speaking nations, but a subordination of the former Spanish colonies to the ruling nation Spain, on the basis of the principle of hierarchy as in the past centuries.

What the Latin American countries could expect after again becoming Spanish dependencies if, tired of Spanish rule, they would once more try to regain their independence, appears in the words of one of the theoretical leaders of falangism and Hispanidad—Onésimo Redondo. In an article published in 1939 he wrote:

Merciless struggle against the proponents and followers of any kind of territorial separatism until their total extermination.

Falangism in Latin America

During the height of the Nazi victories many falangist organizations were formed all over Latin America. Other organizations not outspoken falangist, but of similar ideologies, mainly emphasizing or demanding greater power of the Catholic Church, closely cooperated with falangist or pro-falangist organizations.

For some time they were quite strong in Cuba, until their organization was dissolved by the government. They were also in considerable strength in Puerto Rico, where they functioned under the protection of the democratic laws of the United States.

The Spanish colony in Mexico numbers about 150,000, and in Cuba there are still about 300,000 persons who, after the liberation from Spain in 1898, chose to retain Spanish citizenship. In Puerto Rico there are still about 6000 persons, mostly of the well-to-do upper classes, who preferred to retain their Spanish citizenship. Their sentiment can be judged from the fact that during the Franco insurrection they sent more than $1,000,000 to Franco to help to overthrow the Spanish Republic. In Cuba the Falange was able to influence the masses of the poor by establishing soup kitchens and charity organizations called *Acción Social.* When the Cuban government dissolved these organizations, they were resuscitated under the name of *Fundación Española.*

In other countries, when falangist organizations either lost prestige or found it more appropriate not to operate under their true flag, they adopted more innocuous names, such as *Fundación Española* in Montevideo, *Hogar Español* in São Paulo, *Círculo de Acción Española* in Santiago de Chile, and *Casa de España* in Buenos Aires. They still seem to have considerable influence among the aristocratic Catholic youth, who in Buenos Aires formed an institution called *Cursos de Cultura Católica.* Their enthusiasm for Hispanidad is accompanied by all the other tenets of European fascism, such as strong opposition to all forms of liberalism, democracy, masonry, British and North American "imperialism," and their professed conviction that all the evils of this world are due to the Jews. They also glorify the memory of the ruthless Argentine dictator Juan Manuel Rosas, who one hundred years ago organized the "mazorca," the Argentine equivalent to the Nazi Gestapo, for the purpose of assassinating all those suspected of liberalism or opposition to the dictator Rosas. Their ideas include the restoration of the old Viceroyalty of the Rio de la Plata, by which they mean the annexation to Argentina, of Uruguay, Paraguay, Bolivia and Chile.

In Colombia, the falangists and their Hispanidad ideal have sympathizers among the extreme conservatives led by deputy Laureano Gomez, the publisher of the large conservative daily *El Siglo* of Bogotá. Gomez once said in Congress: "I believe in Hitler and hope for his victory." Though the liberals were in power in Colombia from 1930 to 1946, in that year's presidential vote a conservative president was elected. He, however, does not share the extremist views of Laureano Gomez.

In Mexico the falangist movement and its Hispanidad propaganda increased considerably in 1939 after Franco's assumption of power in Madrid. Falangist groups held meetings in many Mexican cities to celebrate Franco's victory, and the German, Italian and Japanese diplomatic representatives attended the celebration in Mexico's capital.

When Mexico's President Cárdenas ordered the deportation of the three Spanish subjects who directed the activities of the Falange in Mexico, a Mexican citizen of Spanish origin, one Augusto Ibañez Serrano, became the director of the movement. On his visiting cards he called himself "Franco's official representative in Mexico."

Most Mexican falangists were recruited from the Catholic Association of Mexican Youth. (*Asociación Católica de Juventud Nacional*) and the *Acción Nacional*, which claimed 50,000 members among the upper classes and the "old families" of Mexico.

Another falangist inspired group is the *Partido Autonomista Mexicano*. The strong arm of the movement is the *Escuadra Tradicionalista.*

But the mainstay and force of the pro-falangist movement in Mexico resides in the *Sinarquista* Party, which claims more than 500,000 members recruited mostly among the native Indian peasants. The leaders of the party maintain that they are completely independent of the Spanish falangist movement, but except for avoiding the Hispanidad issue, their ideas, aspirations and slogans are identical with those of the falangists.

Each foreign Falangist group is required to keep a card index of all Spaniards in its district, showing their residence, their political affiliation or political opinion, details of their private life, their business and their financial standing. All this information is sent to San Sebastian in Spain, the headquarters of the foreign department of the Falange. The information is passed on to the SIM (*Servicio de Inteligencia Militar*) established in every Latin American country. The latter sent its information in diplomatic pouches back to Spain and from there to Germany.

Anyone joining voluntarily or under compulsion an organization controlled by the falangist or the Madrid government, such as their falangist labor unions, boy scouts, etc., had to take the following oath:

> I swear by God, Spain and Franco and our National Syndicalist Revolution to serve my country above anything else. I also swear to fight unhesitatingly for the spiritual and material reconquest of our lost empire in Asia and America, for the creation of a Spain, United, Great and Free, which has been given to us by the victorious sword of Caudillo.

BIBLIOGRAPHY

A. Books

Anonymous: *Doctrina e Historia de la Revolución Española*, Barcelona, 1939, A. Nuñez, 74 p. (This book contains the "26 Points" of the Falangist Program and the complete text of the "Fuero de Trabajo," the Falangist Chart of Labor.)

Beneyto, Pérez Juan: *El Nuevo Estado Español. El Régimen nacional-sindicalista ante la tradición de los demás sistemas totalitarios*, Madrid-

Cadiz, 1939, Biblioteca Nueva, 267 p. (Bibliography).

BRAVO, MARTINEZ FRANCISCO: *Historia de la Falange Española y de las J.O.N.S.*, Madrid, 1940, Ediciones FE, Editora Nacional, 214 p.

CANALDA, ELIAS OLMOS: Sin Caretas. *Democracia? Totalitarismo? Demofilia?* Valencia, 1940, Tipografia Moderna, 283 p.

ERBLER, DR. JUR. HANS: *Spaniens nationalsyndikalistischer Verfassungs—und Sozialbau. El Fuero de Trabajo und das Program der nationalsyndikalistischen Bewegung.* (Spain's national-syndicalist constitutional and social structure. The Chart of Labor and the national-syndicalist Program.) Weimar, 1936, Schriften des Instituts für Arbeitsrecht a.d. Universität Leipzig, Heft 42, 220 p.

FRANCO, FRANCISCO: *Palabras del Caudillo,* Barcelona, 1939, Ediciones FE. Editado por la Delegación Nacional de la Falange Española Tradicionalista y de las JONS, 319 p. (Speeches of Franco between April 19, 1937 and December 31, 1938.)

GONZÁLEZ OLIVEROS, W.: *Falange y Requeté—organicamente solidarios,* Valladolid, 1937, Imprenta Católica F. G. Vicente, 228 p.

MAEZTU, RAMIRO DE: *Defensa de la Hispanidad,* Valladolid, 1938 (3rd edition), Libreria International, 22 and 368 p. (Contains map entitled: Lands and peoples of Hispanidad under Philip II. Also includes Appendix of Cardinal Gomá y Tomas: Apologia de la Hispanidad.)

MORET MESSERLI, FRANCISCO: *A B C político de la Nueva España,* Barcelona, 1940, Editorial Salvat, 254 p.

PEMARTIN, JOSÉ: *Que es "lo nuevo"—Consideraciones sobre el momento español presente,* Santander, 1938, Cultura Española, 385 p.

PETTINATO, COCETTO: *La Spagna di Franco,* Milano, 1939, Istituto per gli studi di politica internazionale, 208 p.

REDONDO, ONÉSIMO: *El Estado Nacional,* Barcelona, 1939, Ediciones FE, 169 p.

B. PERIODICALS, NEWSPAPERS

"*Acción Española*" (Semi-Monthly), Madrid, 1931 to 1937 (Editor: Ramiro de Maeztú).

"*Ibero-Amerikanisches Archiv*" (Quarterly), Bonn and Berlin, 1934-1939, Volumes 8 to 13 (Director: General Faupel).

"*Spain*" (Monthly), published by Spanish Library of Information (Spanish Government Office), New York, 1939 to 1942.

"*Cara al Sol*" (Weekly), published by Spanish Library of Information, New York, 1939 to 1942.

CASARIEGA, J. E.: *Significado de la Hispanidad*—in: "El Siglo" (conservative daily), Bogota, Colombia, January 6, 1942.

LEDESMA RAMOS, RAMIRO: *La Conquista del Estado.* Articles of October 3 and 10, 1931. Numbers 20 and 21 in his weekly "La Conquista del Estado," reprinted in *Doctrina e Historia de la Revolución Española,* Barcelona, 1939.

PIZZARO MOLINA, RICARDO: *A Propósito de la Hispanidad,* in: "El Pampero" (pro-Nazi daily), Buenos Aires, October 28, 1941.

SAENZ, DR. MARIO: *Hispanoamericanismo,* in: "Revista Juridica de Ciencias Sociales." Buenos Aires, October, 1925, (p. 39 to 45).

SUAREZ, JOSÉ LEÓN: *El Ibero-americanismo,* in: "Revista Jurídica de Ciencias Sociales," Buenos Aires, October, 1925 (p. 31 to 38).

XX.
Pangermanism

PANGERMANISM AND NAZISM

Editorial Note:

The chapter on Pangermanism was written by Professor Friedrich W. Foerster, and that on Nazism by Mr. Friedrich Stampfer. Professor Foerster was the leading German humanistic philosopher, and former professor at the Universities of Munich and Vienna. A prominent German pacifist, he was proposed for the presidency of the Reich, during the early years of the German Republic, by the pacifist left-wing republicans. Professor Foerster was the spiritual father of that courageous group of German pacifists which included Helmut von Gerlach, Osietsky (winner of the Nobel Prize, who later died in a concentration camp), Hainz von Kraschutski (editor of "Das Andere Deutschland), General von Schonaich, and others. These men staunchly opposed German militarism and never yielded to nationalism; often, they paid for their convictions with their liberty and some with their lives. Professor Foerster resigned as Bavarian envoy to Switzerland, so that he might be wholly free to warn Europe against the rising tide of German militarism. A close friend of the late president of Czechoslovakia, Thomas Masaryk, the latter frequently invited him to discuss international problems, as well as problems concerning Germany, with him. Upon the occasion of Professor Foerster's seventy-fifth birthday, the Czechoslovak Foreign Minister, Jan Masaryk, said:

> *. . . "For fifty years Professor Foerster has been warning the world against the Bismarckian way of life, against Pangermanism and vulgar Prussianism. The world, with certain notable exceptions, was either deaf or hard of hearing. . If my father were alive today, he would be among the first to think of Foerster with genuine friendship and great admiration. It is not generally known, perhaps, that the first president of Czechoslovakia and Frederick W. Foerster co-*

operated closely and intimately for a generation. I remember many years ago my father telling me: "If you want to understand Germany you must read Foerster, and I repeat it to you who are listening to us today: You must read Foerster."

Mr. Friedrich Stampfer was one of the most prominent leaders of the Social Democratic Party. Editor-in-chief of the largest Socialist daily in Europe (and the world) "Vorwarts," (Berlin), he was one of the leading personalities in democratic Germany. Mr. Stampfer was also a member of the Reichstag, the German Parliament. He was a strong opponent of the Nazis, and tried to consolidate all the democratic forces in a giant struggle against Nazism.

Professor Foerster and Mr. Stampfer represent entirely different schools of thought concerning the German problem. In debates, as well as in writings, their ideas often clashed.

In his article, Professor Foerster discusses the German origin of Pangermanism, which was the godfather of Nazism, and he, like Lord Vansitaart, asserts that the forces of German democracy are very weak; Nazism and Pangermanism are still highly dangerous, he believes, and cannot be overcome solely by the strength of German democracy. Since Mr. Stampfer deals only with Nazism in his chapter, and, also, since Pangermanism is treated by Professor Foerster, the former limits his analysis to the origin of Nazism, and devotes himself mainly to its foreign, non-German background.

It is true that various forms of exaggerated nationalism can be traced to various European countries; but never in history had nationalism exhibited so monstrous a form as in Hitler's Germany. The specific and terrible difference between German and other nationalism can be found in the cold statistics of twelve to fifteen million persons who were executed in the gas chambers, on the gallows, firing squads, and guillotines. In the concentration camp of Oswiecim alone, four million people were exterminated—men, women, and children, old and young, without mercy.

Very few people realized such uncivilized behavior could be instigated in a nation as civilized as Germany. However, there were a few who predicted it: Heinrich Heine, in his "Letters on Germany," wrote: "Do not fear, however, you German radicals, the German revolution will not be any the milder and gentler because it was preceded by Kant's 'Critique,' the transcendentalism of Fichte, or even by natural philosophy. Through these doctrines revolutionary forces have been developed which only await the day when they can break forth and fill the world with horror and admiration. Armed disciples of Fichte will appear on the scene whose fanaticism of will can be tamed neither by self-interest nor fear.

"Kantians will come to light who will reject any reverence whatsoever, even in the material world, and who will pitilessly plow up the soil of our European life with sword and axe in order to grub out even the last roots of the past." And further," . . . Christianity has, to a certain extent, moderated the brutal German delight in war. But it could not eradicate it, and when once the magic power that tames it, the Cross, is broken, the savagery of those old warriors will burst forth anew. Then Thor will spring up with his gigantic hammer and smash the Gothic cathedrals . . ."

We cannot help but bow our heads in humility that we belong to the human race which has produced Nazism. If such forces of brutality and cruelty are still in existence, then tremendous efforts are needed to develop forces to counteract Nazism and Fascism—and not solely in Germany. Unfortunately, these two evils are far from being dead. We must remain constantly alerted against bigotry and prejudice in any form; for these may provide the stimuli of political magic which, at critical moments, may again steer disoriented and ignorant masses along a terrible path of destruction. Sir James Frazer wrote in "The Golden Bough," "We seem to move on a thin crust which may, at any moment, be rent by the subterranean forces slumbering below. From time to time a hollow murmur underground, or a sudden spit of flame into the air tells of what is going on beneath our feet."

F. G.

XX.

PANGERMANISM

by

FRIEDRICH W. FOERSTER

CLEMENCEAU ONCE ALLEGEDLY stated that there are twenty million Germans too many in the world. This was not intended as a suggestion to free the world of these twenty millions; it was merely a statement of fact that a disquieting disproportion existed between the ethnic elements in Europe. The overwhelming quantity and vitality of the Germans will always act as an impetus toward the enslavement of other nations. Clemenceau hoped that the probable effect of that disproportion might be prevented by the entrance of the United States into the system of European balance; but this was a vain hope which perished in rivers of blood.

In what light did the Middle Ages consider the danger? The great Pope who crowned Charlemagne foresaw that Europe would be enslaved or torn asunder unless a center of federation were created, and Germany firmly linked with both the Western and Eastern worlds. Thus, he entrusted the Germans with the responsibility for preserving the unity of Europe. The German Emperor at that time was not a Pangerman overlord imposing German law upon the remainder of Europe, but a President of a League of Nations and the holder of an international office, who had to coordinate the equal rights of autonomous nations. The very fact that two of the emperors of that League of Nations, called the Holy Roman Empire, were Czech Princes proves this supernational character of the function. It was, therefore, a complete contradiction of historical facts for the intellectual and political representatives of the Pangerman idea to reclaim for the national German State all those European zones which, although formerly contained in the supranational Empire, had never actually belonged to the German nation. But it is apparent that this great European function of the German Emperor has contributed largely to Pangerman dreams, justifications, and plans for world conquest, due mainly to profound and general ignorance concerning the exact supranational nature of the first Reich. Modern German nationalists fell into a kind of German "Provincialism," imagining they were entitled to continue to play a dominant European role, without realizing that this role was conditioned by the fact that it included a tremendous moral elevation which, in itself, repudiated any type of world-Germanization. German history's first important act had been *Europeanization of the Germans* which, for centuries, provided the Germans with a universalistic and cosmopolitan trend; but the modern German attempt at *Germanization of the Europeans* was inevitably doomed to failure, because every ethnic group in Europe revolted against a pattern which aimed at the annihilation of the numerous, deeply-rooted varieties of national types living on the European continent.

The Rise of Pangermanism

After the final destruction of the Holy Roman Empire in 1806, two tendencies of German political evolution were felt: first a disposition towards reconstruction of a European federation. Such great German Catholic writers as Goerres, von Radowitz and Constantin Frantz, the Federalist, all agitated in that direction. Secondly, a nationalist tendency inflamed the Germans to demand a Greater Germany which would incorporate all the Germans in Europe in one vast National State. But it became apparent that the German world was a particular creation of European history, and could not be dealt with solely from the national viewpoint. As a result of the inheritance of the supranational Reich, there was so great a mixture of ethnic elements that no tracing of national boundaries was possible. Only a supranational federation was equal to the tremendous task. No one, however, understood the true nature of Germany nor the fact that national unification of a nation dispersed all over Europe would prepare the way for a European catastrophe. The Pangermans were the only ones who foresaw the actual consequences. Ernst Moritz Arndt, the founder of Pangermanism, in his book, *Germanien und Europa,* written over one hundred years ago, declared: "Germany needs a great military tyrant capable of exterminating entire nations."

Here, in a nutshell, is the entire program of Adolf Hitler. The necessity for destroying "entire nations" is considered justifiable because the nationalist principle, if applied to the Germans, cannot unify the innumerable number of Germans dispersed all over Europe unless the States to which they belong are utterly destroyed. This destruction was the logical consequence of a principle which was totally unfit to solve the extremely complicated German problem. Even Bismarck did not realize the full consequences of the principle he had adopted; but by embracing the nationalist idea, and by exalting "might over right," he created a situation which gradually prepared the nation for its ultimate conflict with the rest of the world.

According to its own logicians, Pangermanism developed in three stages: (1) The unification of the various German "tribes"; (2) The expansion of the German frontiers in order to include in a greater Germany all German minorities in Europe; (3) Those Germans dispersed throughout the entire world were summoned to enter a world-wide German solidarity. Thus, Hitler demanded that every German, regardless of where he lived, should consider himself an active citizen of the Reich, allegiance to which took precedence over any loyalty allegedly due to the State whose citizenship he had acquired.

As noted in Ernst Moritz Arndt's declaration, it is interesting to observe that the Pangerman passion had already possessed the German people long before Hitler. In 1832, Edgar Quinet, the French Protestant whom the *Revue des Deux Mondes* had sent to Germany as its correspondent, commented upon the extent to which this passion had overwhelmed and overruled all the great spiritual traditions and interests of Germany's cosmopolitan era. In one of his reports to the publication, in 1831, he stated: "Unity is the deep-seated ideal, inevitable and constant, which moves the country and pervades every department of the national life. Religion, law, commerce, freedom, despotic rule, everything alive across the Rhine tends in the same direction. This unity is no temporary harmony of conflicting passions which may dissolve the next day. It is the inevitable development of northern civilization." Unfortunately, it was not only northern civilization but, as Ferdinand de Bac said in his memoirs of an "exile," a community of appetites which opened the south to northern aims and proposals. Quinet continues: "In Prussia, the old universalism and political cosmopolitanism have given place to an irascible nationalism. This Prussian despotism is intelligent, active and enterprising. It needs nothing but a man who will clearly see his star. Between the people and the rulers of Prussia there exists a secret conspiracy to postpone political emancipation, to combine in adding to Frederick's inheritance, and to avenge upon France the disgrace, so long endured, of the Treaty of Westphalia." This statement concerning the hidden solidarity of the "democratic" people with the military leaders is highly revealing, because it shows how deeply-rooted in new German history was the connivance of the so-called Weimar Republic in regard to the secret rearmament of reactionary Germany.

Both quotations shed a penetrating light on the well-founded power of the Prusso-Teuton anti-European conspiracy. Pangermanism has been considered as representative of only a small circle of political extremists; this is correct if one views only the small group founded in 1890, the Alldeutsche Verband. But the passages quoted reveal that Pangermanism was the natural and logical expression of the modern nationalist idea when it was translated into German, and contradicted all previous German history which had been devoted to the organization of Europe on federative lines. Between 1850 and 1870 continued resistance was forthcoming from the defenders of Germany's supranational and federalist traditions, but the entire trend of the times opposed them; Germany was doomed to de-Germanization by western nationalism and Prussian militarism. In 1884 Constantin Frantz sent his book on Germany and Federalism to Richard Wagner, the great composer, who replied: "Too late, too late; all is running toward the abyss. I foresee for the midst of the next century the return of mankind to barbarism."

Almost forty years before Hitler's advent to power, an anonymous book appeared in Germany in 1895, entitled, "*Great Germany and Central Europe About* 1950. Its author wrote: "After a certain lapse of time, eighty-six million Germans will dominate one hundred and thirty million Europeans who will be condemned to baser kinds of work. The Germans will have exclusive right to acquire land, to enjoy political rights, and to be entrusted with administrative and military functions."

This is but one typical example of thousands of similar professions of faith. Extracts from many of these may be found in such books as *The German Chauvinism* by Professor O. Nippold, published at the end of the 19th century, and *Know Your Enemy* by T. H. Tetens, published by the Society for the Prevention of World War III, 515 Madison Ave., N. Y. C. The reader will be impressed by the growing intensity of Pangermanism which is revealed in these books.

The Rise of German Nationalism

Toward the close of the 19th century, Germany's political insanity mounted with dizzying rapidity. A typical symptom of the new Germany was Treitschke's course at the University of Berlin. In 1893, Hermann Bahr, the Austrian author, described the inflammatory atmosphere in Treitschke's auditorium; it bears a striking resemblance to the atmosphere at Hitler's meetings four decades later, and proves conclusively that "Hitlerism" existed long before Hitler. Bahr writes:

"As soon as I left the quiet of the philosopher Zeller's lecture-room and entered the steaming atmosphere of the vast auditorium which could scarcely hold the huge crowd of Treitschke's students, another Germany smoulderingly descended on me: Treitschke, already almost completely deaf, was unable to master the cataract of speech which poured harshly though hesitantly from his barking lips. What savagery there was in his eyes which, as it were, gazed inward and boiled over with the visions of his ferocious passions—what paroxysms of a will which seemed almost debased! Old Testament, but beyond that, Teutonic fury! But the fact that we were able to derive from his fuming enthusiasm something almost tainted or corroded, perhaps the agonized sigh of some mysterious longing for a withered period in which the Germans were still a suffering people—this very fact gave him even more power over a youth which divined that it was destined to surge forward over gravestones into the darkness of a mist-covered, uncertain future!"

This is a starkly significant picture of that terrible union between teutonic fury and Prussian militarism which was incarnated in a man such as Treitschke, the former liberal idealist, who hailed Bismarck as the man who best realized the German dream, and who infused the new generation of university students with a contempt for Germany's spiritual past. Treitschke exalted violence as the only creative political power, and his wildly stimulated audience became the fathers of the Hitler Jugend; in fact they *were* Hitler Jugend long before Hitler.

Prussian militarism has always been considered an essential cause of the two world catastrophes. Certainly, the Prussian war policy was a vital factor, but Pangermanism was no less guilty. Both Pangermanism and Prussianism were two giant trees deeply rooted in German history which grew into one gigantic tree under the sign of the swastika. Hitler was the South German who felt that the Pangerman vision could not be realized without Prussian militarism. In Hitler, Maria Theresa espoused Frederick the Great or, as Werner Sombart succinctly said: "German militarism is the complete union between Weimar and Potsdam—it is Beethoven in the trenches."

Even before World War I the German diplomat, Baron von Eckardstein, declared in the preface to his memoirs that never in history had a great nation been so deceived by official lies than the German people. If we contemplate the innumerable number of "official" German lies which were spread during the first war and after it, particularly in the Hitler era, we realize how great a contribution towards the rearmament of the German nation was made by this gigantic effort to distort the truth; not only did it rearm Germany morally and physically, but it tended to disarm the neighbors Germany was threatening. Mussolini called this type of propaganda the "white war" which preceded the red, bloody war. Germany constantly lied about her true intentions, and appealed to her neighbors' ideas of democracy in order to influence them towards her own schemes for so-called equality and liberation; such propaganda paved the route to Germany's big "surprise."

Psychological Conquest Preceded Military Occupation

The necessity for such grand-scale German propaganda resulted from the great difficulty a belligerent group encountered in attempting to justify their ruthless policy to a peaceful people devoted to economy, science, and art. Prussia's neatest trick was to falsify every act of aggression which its leaders committed by terming it a necessary defensive measure. Thus, Prussia succeeded in arousing the emotional Germans to a pitch of wild hatred. As early as 1866, the German historian, Otto Klopp, writing to Princess Eleanor of Schwarzenburgh, gave an impressive account of this propaganda:

"Prussia has set herself systematically to win intellectual Germany to her service. Unfortunately, she has been only too successful, particularly in regard to the historians whose works influence political sympathies and antipathies so strongly. Nine-tenths of German historical writing is steeped in the Prussian spirit. And that spirit is the same here as in the domain of practical politics, a spirit of inveracity and falsification; but also indeed, for that very reason, a spirit of aggression in every shape and form—and, above all, against Austria. Long before Austria was defeated on the battlefield of Koeniggraetz, Prussia's silent emissaries, books and pamphlets pregnant with her spirit of falsehood, had made their way into Austrian palaces and cottages, had confused and deceived men and had fettered their consciences. Falsehood is labeled truth, and truth falsehood. A power that has arisen and grown only by injustice and violence at the expense of Germany and the genuine spirit of her people, is depicted in these writings as the protector of Germany."

This picture of the achievements of German propaganda in Austria, long before the Nazis undermined the Danubian country by open Pangerman agitation, presents a clear version of the insidious manner by which Austria was mentally prepared to accept ideas and plans which were contrary to her whole tradition. But Austria's fate was not unjust; it was due recompense for a blind heedlessness which revealed a deplorable weakness of character and dullness of soul.

By the end of the nineteenth century, Pangerman propaganda in pamphlets, magazines, and books had become so abundant that an entire library could have been formed from this literature alone. It was a literature which poisoned the nation not only by distorting all the issues in the field of foreign policy, but by incessantly repeating German vindications for "a place in the sun." Unfortunately, there was not sufficient sunshine on earth to satisfy their limitless vindications.

Pangermanism Destroyed Czechoslovakia

The destruction of Czechoslovakia was as logical as the annexation of Austria, from the Pangerman point of view. German elements in Bohemia had enjoyed friendly relations with the Czech population before 1866; after that year, resentment grew and soon a very real hatred found explosive expression in the Austrian parliament. Hitler is the direct result of this "pathology of the frontier." By 1899 the German-Bohemian delegate, Türck, was declaring in the Vienna Parliament that "the eternal German inheritance outside Germany's frontiers must be reunited with Germany, as was the case before 1866." A custom-union with Germany will be the first step. Then it is necessary that civil war break out between the German and the Czech citizens of Bohemia, and the Prussian army will march in and teach its lesson."

But, what Türck neglected to mention was that Bohemia never actually belonged to Germany; like the latter, she was merely an independent member of the supranational Holy Roman Empire.

It all came true forty years later. It is interesting to observe that in 1896 Masaryk foresaw the probability of such a counterblow from the Germans, should independency be re-established. "We are not so simple," he declared," that we do not know that we would not be able to defend an independent Bohemia against Germany if the German minority should oppose us." After Germany's defeat in World War I, the first President of the Czechoslovakian State supposed that he hoped the crushing collapse of Pangermanism would prevent its reappearance. He died too soon to have seen the extensive deceptions inflicted upon his country by the Munich peace and the events following it. A great deal of agony might have been spared the peoples of the world if the threatened nations had not accepted these deceptions and lulled themselves with pathetically false illusions about Hitler's ultimate aims and about the so-called German people; the latter had lost any real political substance, and were putty in the hands of their political and military leaders.

Pangermanism in the United States

The background of American Pangermanism is highly interesting. Like all backgrounds, it provides perception for essential and permanent trends, and presents valuable aid in our present practical dealings with the results of a long evolution.

The United States, of course, is not an Anglo-Saxon country. Its population is comprised of all races from all parts of the world, but the political community and cooperation of these various elements is cemented and protected by the great tradition of English law and liberty. Thus, at a period of nationalist madness, America demonstrates the possibility of human community above the bonds of blood and history. This fact is difficult for the Pangerman and imperialist mind to comprehend. In 1847 a German author, Franz Loeher, published a book entitled, *History and Situation of the Germans in America,* wherein he concludes with the following program:

"Indeed, it would form a beautiful historical picture, full of life, probably even the greatest ever offered: Old Germany in Europe and Young Germany in America, powerful exchanges of influence. Old Germany holds the center of Europe and, for a long time, has dominated that continent spiritually and politically. She lacerated herself and became exhausted; now she is driving to new unity. She concentrates her forces and rises to regain her dominant role—will Young Germany, too, hold the center of North America, and will it dominate this continent some day?" It is interesting to note that in a book written in 1847, a peaceful, non-agitating scholar naively expresses the blunt conviction that Germany is entitled to dominate Europe and America, and that this conviction is based on the assumption that by the Middle Ages Germany had already exerted this legitimate domination! This mingling of Pangerman domination with the Holy Roman Empire is the grievous error of the Pangermanists. Loeher inquires about the fate of the Germans in America, and then answers his own question with the declaration that "they will become Americans, efficient republicans and efficient business men; they will mingle with and marry non-Germans and they will adopt some of their characteristics. But their essence and expression will remain German . . . they can establish a German state, in which their language will be the language of the people as well as the official language, just as the English language is now, and there the German nature will live and work, judge and govern, just as the English do now everywhere. The next question is: where will this German state come into existence? The usual answer is: the North-West will become German; that means the states of Ohio, Indiana, Illinois, Missouri, Iowa, Wisconsin, Michigan and upper Canada,—Pennsylvania with its foreland and part of New York and Virginia on one side, Texas and Arkansas on the other side, those will be the German states which connect with the ocean,—the Yankee states in the North and the Slave states in the South will be cut off and border with the German states, whereas the dominating part of North America will be the center, between the Ohio and Missouri rivers."

The book, *Our America,* published some years ago by the Nazi agent, Colin Ross, who was forced to leave America because of his agitation here, is even more incredible and startling. The following is a typical quotation:

"Expressed in the briefest form, our idea is simply this: America is ours. America is ours not only because German blood flows in the veins of at least twenty or thirty million Americans . . . but because in its origins America is a creature of the German spirit. The question is whether these millions of Germans recognize their hour of destiny, whether they are unaware that a decisive moment has struck. Without fear of criticism, we may justifiably say of the New World across the Atlantic created by us: Unser Amerika (Our America")."

The same author published another book, *America's Fateful Hour,* in which he asserted that the time had come for America to make up her mind whether she would continue to impose the inherited English form on all elements of non-English origin, or whether she would draw the consequences from her rapidly changing ethnic composition, and renounce the English pattern. Then the thirty million Germans, aided by other anti-British minorities, would soon conquer the leading position in the country. Actually, this means the complete dissolution of the United States and civil war between the various ethnic groups. As a result, America, the refuge of humanity, would disappear, and racial separatism would hold sway. The real depth of this separatism among Pangermanists and extreme nationalists may be noted throughout Franz Loeher's book, published one hundred years ago. He writes:

"The Germans could create a civil order which would liberate America from the chains and confusion of the near-dying English law which is a mockery of the young Republic, and striking testimony to American inefficiency."

These hopes, expressed in 1847, were buried for decades. But the growing power and expansion of the Pangerman center in Europe revived them, and eventually fresh and unexpected hopes rose with Hitler: there seemed a strong possibility of a victorious German war which would elevate the German element in America to its long-awaited position of dominance.

Concerning this possibility, Rauschnigg's report, "The Voice of Destruction," relates that Hitler told him with great assurance: "We shall soon have an S. A. (storm trooper organization) in America." Hitler remarked to Rauschnigg, in outlining his campaign for the conquest of America, years ago:

"We shall train our youth and we shall have men whom degenerate yankeedom will not be able to challenge. Into the hands of our youth will be given the statesmanlike mission of the great Washington, which this corrupt democracy has trodden under foot."

When Rauschnigg asked, "Do you think that the German-Americans rejuvenated by National Socialism will be called upon to lead a new America?" Hitler replied:

"That is exactly what I mean. . . . America represents the last disgusting manifestation of a corrupt and outworn system." He continued: "National Socialism alone is destined to liberate the American people from their ruling clique and give them back the means of becoming a great nation. . . . I shall undertake this task simultaneously with the restoration of Germany to her leading position in America."

The Achievement of German Propaganda

The intelligent vision and artistic temperament of Germany gave the Prussian enterprise an incomparable weapon. German propaganda, which is a unique product of German intellectual force in the service of the German General Staff, may be likened to the two types of human intelligence in Goethe's Faust: one, in the service of truth and inspired by the passionate longing for truth; the other, in the service of the devil. Similarly, one also finds in the new Germany great achievements of high-minded scientific research, guided by an insatiable love for truth, as the eminent chemist, Liebig defined it; but one finds, as well, German intelligence and erudition devoted to the systematic distortion of historic truth, in order to whitewash the true and ultimate aims of Germany's policy, to deceive the world about Germany's economic situation, her war-potentials, her secret rearmament. The gullible German people, as well as the outside world, had to be fed lies and more lies to conceal the realistic facts.

Hitler's success was due, in a large measure, to the unceasing efforts of Mr. Hugenberg who had purchased the popular newspaper chains and succeeded in poisoning German mentality in a manner which simplified the great demagogue's drawing up practical political conclusions—and, ultimately, whipping the entire nation ino a frenzy.

Therefore, one cannot understand the extraordinary dynamics of modern Pangermanism unless one has previously grasped Prussia's gift to the union; nor, on the reverse, can the dynamics of the modern Prussian system be fully comprehended unless the tremendous impetus provided by the pangerman passion is taken into account. With the advent of Hitler, the sentimental, romantic, emotional German people, who had been anti-Prussian for a long time, now entered into the Prussian system and made of its war-tradition a new religion, a new Islam without Allah—a strange cooperation of intelligence with insanity, of virtue with vice, and of order with anarchy.

The Unknown German Soldier and the German General Staff Find Each Other

A photograph of Hitler, taken two months before the German defeat of 1918, shows him seated on a tree-stump surrounded by his comrades-in-arms. He appears thoughtful, as if he were contemplating the mistakes which caused Germany's collapse when sweet victory seemed imminent. Hitler once called himself Germany's "unknown soldier," and he was determined to prove that, unlike his French counterpart, the unknown Reich soldier was not buried under the Arch of Triumph, but was alive and eager for revenge. Hitler, the representative of the "common man," believed that he personified a nation whose leaders had failed to live up to the heroic devotion and perseverance of its people. During four years of desperate fighting in the North, South, East, and West, he had convinced himself of his own inexhaustible strength and the superiority of the Prussian military machine. The causes of defeat, he believed, lay in the leaders' failure to provide inspiration and vision for their unexcelled human material. The machine had not been fully utilized, the military command had missed its opportunities, the political leadership had lacked coordination. The people were not aware of the prizes at stake, nor the golden chance being offered to Germany.

It is interesting that this man, "one of the nameless mass of the German people," as he liked to call himself, who was obsessed with a burning desire to weld a permanent bond between the German people and their military leaders, met General Haushofer in Munich. Haushofer, the founder of Pangerman geopolitics had, by his own experience, arrived at a similar conclusion: the German people did not realize the full significance and potentialities of the conflict and, therefore, had failed to take their destiny in their own hands. The brain-truster of the German General Staff had returned from Japan, where he had been deeply impressed by the extraordinary unity which, under a mystical authority enthroned above all common dissension, had welded together the entire nation. Haushofer believed that the creation of such a mystical, popular authority in Germany was indispensable; it would bring the whole nation on the side of the military leaders, and it would arouse their enthusiasm for the re-establishment of Prussian power—in the service of the Pangerman program. Haushofer converted Hitler to this program; he even visited him in the fortress of Landsberg every Wednesday, in an effort to explain to him the possibilities and means for conquering the world.

Thus, the master-mind of the defeated General Staff and the Unkown Soldier, representative of the German people, found each other. This fact is particularly important because it throws a searching light upon the great problem of Prussian militarism and the German people. Goering was correct when, after the "day of Potsdam" where this new union was sealed and fêted, he declared: "From this very moment the step of the Potsdam grenadiers has become the step of the German people."

The Racial Element in Pangermanism

The American sociologist, Hyslop, states in his book, *Democracy,* that no metaphysical idea has had such tremendous political consequences as that of the doctrine of the immortality of the individual soul. According to the author, this doctrine is behind the whole evolution of individuality, individual right, and responsibility in the life of modern nations—not as a conscious reference, but as a political consequence of man's spiritual evolution. While in the last centuries of the Roman Empire and during the medieval period an immense mixture of ethnic elements occurred and the longing for universality dominated the world, the Italian Renaissance opened the era of individualism, but at the cost of unity, community, and universality. Mankind entered the phase of separation which invaded even the Universal Church. The legitimate evolution of individuality also encouraged the lower kinds of emancipation, and favored anarchic liberty and self-deification. What Pascal termed "Le Moi haîssable," the disgusting self, was translated into politics. When the modern nation consolidated itself, its tendency toward unity aroused the desire for racial homogenity and led to hatred and persecution of divergent racial elements. Pangermanism, a movement in favor of a racial purge, was a natural and unavoidable consequence of an irresistible aberration. But a permanent, shameful blot will remain on the record of the German Christians because so many of them not only participated in this kind of purge, but, as was the case in Austria, even their leaders accepted an un-Christian persecution. As Hitler himself declared, the demagogic anti-Semitism which brought the Austrian Christian Socialists to power, was largely responsible for his own racial propaganda.

In Indian philosophy, an idea cannot be overcome unless its *Karma,* its deepest germ and content, is brought to full display and evolution. The Germans were the logicians of modern disintegration; and Pangermanism was, and is, the chief bearer of that process which still continues.

Pangerman Propaganda Abuses the Word "Pro-German"

During any discussion on Germany, much confusion is caused by the lack of an actual definition of the terms "Pro-German" and "Anti-German." The so-called Pro-Germans should be asked to express themselves with complete clarity. I would put it to them thus: Towards what kind of Germany are you working? What kind of Germany do you wish to restore? Do you favor the old, constructive Germany, or the new, destructive Germany? That old, great, spiritual Germany, which for a thousand years was the center of European federation, or that recent Prussianized Germany which became the center of European disintegregation, transformed Europe into a military camp, and was doomed to fall into utter depravity? If you honestly want to revive the former, you must oppose the latter with all your strength. You must be ruthlessly radical in depriving the new Germany of all means for organizing a third aggression. Such a merciless shearing of her war-potential is being loudly denounced as anti-German; but, in fact, it is not only the sole effective protection for the world against Germany, but also the most efficacious manner by which Germany may be rid of the cancerous evil which gnawed her mind and body.

The Pangerman Menace Still Exists

Through its secret assistants and open propagandists throughout the world, Pangermanism is once again on the political offensive. Let us not deceive ourselves: it is more menacing than ever today, because its plotters have the advantage of knowing and avoiding their past errors.

The Pangerman and Nazi conspiracy is no longer confined to the German Reich. Today, it has at its disposal well-prepared bases in many parts of the world. The centers of the conspiracy are in Spain and Argentina. These two countries are the breeding-grounds of World War III which is being hatched by German officers, industrialists, and scientists working in close collaboration with pro-German dictators and the world-encircling Falange.

The Pangerman Scheme to Split the Allies

While the victorious powers remain united and maintain a strict and forthright policy toward Germany and her satellites, it is doubtful whether any new German conspiracy could survive. The Pangermans and the extreme German nationalists throughout the world realize this fact and therefore use every opportunity to create dissension among the Big Three. They hope to kindle an atmosphere of enmity which could easily be fanned into war hysteria. If they succeed in their aims, Pangermanism will have won half its battles. The Madrid-Buenos Aires Axis will then be in a position either to conclude an alliance with the Russians against the United States, after the pattern of the 1939 pact, or to form a world front with the Anglo-Saxon powers against Russia. Any such move would be the signal for a German comeback.

According to the German geopoliticians, every war shatters the status quo. Formerly powerful states are destroyed or condemned to play the role of second-rate or third-rate powers, while dynamic states have an opportunity of winning new positions of power. The German militarists and geopoliticians hope that the third world war will result in the destruction of the United States and the "liberation of Europe from America's tutelage" as well as the "menace" from Asia.

Pangermanism in South America

Pangermanism in the United States is now a potential danger; it will explode into overt action when American pangerman forces join with corresponding South American groups. When the possibility of World War III is discussed, most people immediately think of the tension between Russia and the West. But the South American threat is particularly menacing because it is so distant from the great centers of modern world history where every move can be controlled and registered. The control of preparations being made in German laboratories in some remote corner of South America is almost impossible. Germany's master-minds are thoroughly experienced at secret preparations for war. After the German defeat at Stalingrad and the Allied occupation of North Africa, the German High Command realized they had lost the war. They continued fighting because they desperately needed time to complete their gigantic financial transfers to neutral and friendly countries. Production plans for German secret weapons, chemical formulae, laboratory equipment, even the experts themselves—in short, all the material and physical assets of German war industry were transported safely to Spain and Argentina.

When all prospects of German victory had disappeared, the pro-German officers in Argentina established an open dictatorship in the summer of 1943. The Argentine accomplices of the German High Command had to seize power hastily in order to be prepared for the transfer of the disintegrating Berlin-Rome Axis to Madrid and Buenos Aires. Peron's "Colonels' Lodge" in Argentina has been working for years as an agency for the German General Staff. Today, Argentina is the militaristic, turbulent Prussia of the Western Hemisphere who is determined to bring all Latin America under her leadership, either by persuasion or by force. Within a few years, Argentina will be one of the leading industrial nations in the world, and she will have been developed and led by the foremost German technical and military experts. Since we shall have to cope with a powerful, German-dominated, Latin-American bloc in the future, how can the United States or even the UNO possibly control the production of rockets, atomic bombs, and other secret weapons produced in the Andes Mountains, and in the jungles of the Chaco or the Amazon?

German Financial Support of Organizations and Newspapers in Argentina

During the last war, a prominent Nazi leader asserted that should Germany lose the war in Europe she would continue it in America. The Nazis considered the European front as only one facet of their great enterprise of world conquest; the second and future front is in South America where, for several years, they have maintained high industrial positions and are able to continue their work without any restrictions. General Haushofer wrote that South America would be the great stepping-stone towards the decisive world conflict over German supremacy. Germany has associated herself with the great political and military revival of the Latin world (Hispanidad), and is lending it her military skill, intelligence and experience. Obviously, they hope to ultimately become the true leaders of the United States of South America, just as they hope to Germanize North America. It would be disastrous for the rest of the world to allow them to prepare their destructive monster unmolested, and then awaken to its full horror when it is too late.

Auguste Comte, the French positivist philosopher, said that the living are governed by the dead. Actually, Spanish-German collaboration may be considered a revival of Emperor Charles V era; even the Nazis referred to this first phase of Spanish-German Empire politics. But the period of Empire politics has vanished—our present-day problems are far too complicated to be thus solved. Human problems cannot be disposed of by tyranny, separatism, sectarianism, or a vast bloc-policy. Only the genuine spirit of universality and democratic cooperation is equal to this great task.

The Hidden Enemy

The best book on Pangerman agitation was written by a German refugee, H. Pol, and is entitled, *The Hidden Enemy*. Despite the clamor the Pangerman movement has produced, the extension and the greatness of the real danger has not yet been fully realized, either in Germany or abroad. In his book, Pol related that he attended the great demonstrative meeting in which the "Alldeutsche Verband," a highly organized Pangermanistic group, celebrated the fortieth anniversary of its foundation (1930). He was struck by the fact that leading bankers, industrialists, and prominent delegates from all over the world were present, representing the élite of far-flung German power. Mr. Hugenberg, member of the Krupp Board of Directors, greeted Hitler's storm-troopers as "the incarnation of future Germany." The cry went up: "Long live Pangermany!" The author, impressed by this demonstration which he considered an alarming threat to the world, sent a report to the leading liberal newspaper, the "Vossische Zeitung," on it. The report was thrown into the wastebasket, and Pol was told, "We won't publish propaganda for these people. You must not take the shouting of this Pangerman clique too seriously. In a few months, no one will remember them." Such was the typical blindness of liberal Germany.

The Republicans considered the Pangermans impotent shadows, and completely underestimated this "Great Germany" who awaited her hour behind the scenes. Two years later these shadows dispersed the Republicans, and a year later the storm-troopers had their day. But Minister Severing of the Interior had declared: "If ever these people risk a revolt, I do not need my police. I shall disperse them by fire-engines."

The menaced nations were even more blind. Toward the very end of the war the "American Mercury," which obviously reflected the views of certain official circles in Washington, published the following:

"We will refuse to deal with any member of the Hitler gang, but we will deal at any time with any responsible element ready to overthrow the Nazis and to disarm the German army. We will sign a treaty with the Prussian Junkers if and when they are ready."

Fortunately, the Nuremberg trial furnished all the necessary documents to prove that the army and the Junkers had produced Hitler. He was merely the popularizer and executor of their plans; and General Keitel, later hanged, was the symbol of that solidarity.

A German general, when asked his opinion of Hitler, is alleged to have replied: "Hitler is the fulfillment of the prayer of a soldier." In truth, Hitler was the logical expression of the entire historic trend of the Prussian robber-state; he unmasked the bandits disguised as military knights. For this reason, Justice Jackson justifiably told the General: "Hitler's crimes are your crimes."

Nationalist Germany is like the legendary serpent whose poison-swollen mouth produced a new head for every one destroyed; Pangermanism is the mouth, and Hitler was the latest head. Unless we open our eyes in time, they will produce a rich harvest of new heads.

For Bibliography see next chapter

XXI.

Nazism: Its Spiritual Roots

XXI.

NAZISM: ITS SPIRITUAL ROOTS

by

FRIEDRICH STAMPFER

Revolution and Counter-revolution

THIS WRITER STILL clings to the opinion that man is somewhere on the way from the animal to a "Supreme Being." History proves that he is able to increase his knowledge of the forces of nature and his power over them. Although he will never become "almighty" and "omniscient" he can become mightier and wiser. Whether he is able to improve the relations between man and man in the direction of divine kindness (which so far he has not been able to do) is still an open question. However, the course of human history is full of heroic attempts toward that goal, followed often by distressing failures and miserable disillusionments. An optimistic view, in this respect, is common to Christianity, Liberalism, and Socialism. Although disagreeing in many other points, they are united in their conviction of human ability to improve human ethics.

In the terminology of the nineteenth century, we call man's every step in the direction of increased power and knowledge "progress." The swift and turbulent stages in this progress are "revolutions," and movements of the same speed and tumultuousness in the opposite direction are "counter-revolutions." In consequence, the so-called "national socialist revolution" appears to us as the most brutal and disastrous counter-revolution of all times, and as a product, not so much of a particular "national character," as of extremely vehement tensions within the structure of the German nation in the first decades of our century.

It is a well-known fact that every political revolution on the European continent was accompanied, interrupted, or followed by counter-revolutionary movements. Counter-revolutions are the wars of revenge among the civil wars, and this is one of two facts which cause their extreme cruelty. The other one is the intellectual and moral inferiority of the masses, brought into action by them. These masses consist, generally speaking, of bold adventurers and illiterate, backward people, led by lust for booty and by superstition. The great French Revolution deserves its name not for the cruelties committed in its course, but in spite of them. It was a heroic attempt to improve the relations between man and man with *Liberty*, *Equality*, and *Fraternity* as the ultimate goal. Robespierre was a greater revolutionist when he pleaded for the abolition of the death penalty than some years later, when he became the leader of "la Terreur." Out of the Great Revolution came the great adventurer Napoleon, the regime of the sabre and the nationalist "gloire."

The movements of 1848 were crushed everywhere in Europe, even in the most revolutionary-minded country, France. France, at this time, experienced the first attempt of a revolution which was not bourgeois but proletarian, not only democratic, but also socialistic. The frightened upper classes reacted with utmost cruelty and mass slaughter. France put the clock back, and (after an interregnum of two dynasties and one short-lived Republic) the Empire re-appeared. Napoleon le Grand was followed by Napoleon le petit, a figure whose similarities with Hitler have been stressed by many historians. Both of them shrewd demagogues, they founded their power on plebiscites and ruthless suppression of the opposition. Both were favored by periods of economic welfare and military and diplomatic triumphs. Both succeeded in thwarting all attempts to overthrow them from within. Both were crushed by a final military defeat.

It may be dubious whether the Commune, the insurrection of the workers of Paris in 1871, was not rather an act of sheer desperation than a revolutionary uprising. Nevertheless, it was suppressed by outrageous acts of vengeance which, according to Marx, have had no parallel in history since the days of Sulla.

It is quite true that the revolutions in Germany never eventuated in much bloodshed and triumphant victories. However, the spiritual and even the political revolutions of the last two hundred years had no less far reaching consequences in Germany than in any other country of Europe or America. Heine, comparing Kant with Robespierre, found that the former was the greater revolutionist of the two, because it was he who dethroned God himself, and not only a king. The great philosopher of Koenigsberg, remained faithful to the French Revolution, even in the time of the terror, when most of his disciples, like Schiller, turned away with horror. On the other hand, it was the same Friedrich Schiller who popularized Kantian liberalism and humanism. The French Revolution came to the Germans with the sword of the conqueror. The impact of the Napoleonic era was not strong enough to kill the humanitarian and cosmopolitan spirit of the eighteenth century, but strong enough to split it up. J. G. Fichte, although preaching equal rights for all human beings, became the most ardent apostle of the "war of liberation." George F. W. Hegel's philosophy gave the strongest support not only to those who believed in the irresistibility of human progress but also to those who admired the reactionary Prussian State as the embodiment of Reason. In the course of history it became apparent that liberalism and nationalism were brothers—brothers like Abel and Cain.

The bourgeoisie in the time of its ascent, and later on the proletariat, followed the "left" trends in the spiritual development of Germany, whilst the ruling classes adhered strongly to the "right." Both had their own interpreters and interpretations of the difficult language of the German philosophers. However, Marx and Engels were right in asserting that their "scientific socialism" was heir not only to the French and English utopians, but also to the German classical philosophy.

At the turn of the century, Germany was held to be the focus of social revolution. The theory of Marx and Engels, not yet adopted as the state religion of a despotic imperialism, gained adherents throughout the world. The Social Democratic Labor Movement of Germany gave the pattern for all similar movements, striving for democratic socialism by legal or revolutionary means. The German party itself preferred peaceful progress to violent revolution, without excluding the possibility of the latter. In the last years before World War I, even representatives of the moderate wing advocated a general strike with its possibly bloody consequences, in order to win universal suffrage to the Prussian Diet and to smash the power of the Junkers.

Defeat was followed by revolution. Imperial and royal crowns fell into the dust like dead leaves. The Social Democrats succeeded in the creation of a German Republic which had, as they said proudly, "the most democratic constitution of the world." For the first time in German history, men from the working classes were called to the highest official duties, reserved until then to a small aristocratic minority. Trade unionism made heavy gains by obtaining a new charter for Labor. Organized workers remained as members of the varying governments until the accession to office of the von Papen government in 1932.

The fourteen years of the first German Republic were characterized by the efforts of the progressive elements to foster peaceful progress inside Germany as well as outside it. It was of symbolic significance when the Social Democratic "Vorwaerts" celebrated the entry of Germany into the League of Nations with the same words with which the pan-German "Taegliche Rundschau" had greeted the entry into the first World War: "This hour we longed for. Now it has come, this sacred hour." It was no less significant when the Social Democrats struggled for the abolition of the death penalty. When the Social Democrat Hermann Mueller was Chancellor of the Reich in 1929, just four years before the beginning of the Nazi reign of terror, not a single execution took place. It is obvious that in Germany, at that time, there was no "Jewish question" at all. Assimilation, in progress for many decades, seemed to be almost total. In government as well as in business, in the press, and in art, Jews won prominence, partly because of their ability, partly because they were the most progressive elements among the intelligentsia. There was no doubt about their faithfulness to the republic, whereas many University graduates of another creed or origin still clung to the old ideals of monarchy and reaction. The revolution of 1918 completed the transformation of Germany to a democracy of the Western type. It was no less a revolution because it did not destroy all the remnants of the old constitution and the old society. No revolution in history was a definite total success.

There are many reasons why this revolution did not go deeper to the roots of imperial Germany. One of them was, without any doubt, the outspoken aversion of the Social Democrats to bloodshed. You may call it, if you wish, "weakness." Another reason was their respect for the rules of democracy. There was no majority in the parliament for the confiscation of the big industrial plants or for the expropriation of the big estates. Moreover, there were, in fact, good reasons for the postponement of such measures. Private property was respected by the law of Nations, and the law of Nations was still in effect, to some extent at least, at that time. Nationalized property, on the other hand, could be transferred easily into the possession of the victorious allies, as reparations. It was also obvious that the expropriation of the big estates and their partition into small farms could not be accomplished without diminishing the crops and increasing the danger of starvation. But in spite of these good reasons, the shortcomings of the revolution of 1918 were fatal in their effect. The big industrialists and landowners, most of them hostile to the republic, retained a tremendous economic power. There were, on the other hand, the dismissed young officers who knew no other business than war, and the middle class people, ruined by the inflation, all of them dissatisfied with the state of the nation and "novarum rerum cupidi." These were the elements out of which emerged the army of the counter-revolution.

The alliance of the deposed ruling classes with the "lumpenproletariat" or mob, for the purpose of regaining power, is by no means a new experience in human history. Neither is the dictator, called "tyrannos" by the Greeks. Aristotle in his "politics" remarked that in the early days of Ancient Greece the famous generals often became "tyrannoi," but later they were replaced by popular rhetoricians. Although the danger of historic comparisons is obvious, who can refrain, upon reading the sentences of this old Greek philosopher, from thinking of Hindenburg and Hitler? It is easy to understand why the German counter-revolution assumed the form of an overexcited nationalist movement. Nationalism is, as will be shown later on, an international phenomenon of the nineteenth and twentieth centuries. Lust for revenge is always one of the consequences of defeat. Arbitrary annexations always have been answered by ardent irredentas. Military occupation instigated the desire for liberation from foreign domination. It was the German Republic which had to bear, after the downfall of the monarchy, the heavy burdens of a lost war, and which could easily be made responsible for the misery of that time. Moreover, the victors of World War I were the great democracies of the West, and their standard bearer Woodrow Wilson had promised a just peace, founded on the principles of democracy and national self determination. Thus the enemies of the German Republic found themselves in an enviable position. They could accuse the Western democracies of having betrayed their principles, and they could accuse the German democracy of being the dupe of shrewd enemies who spoke of liberty and meant exploitation and suppression. What could the unfortunate rulers of the German Republic do? Theoretically, they could defend the peace of Versailles as democratic, just and as a consequence of the German war guilt. However, they could not do so without being confronted with many outstanding personalities of the allied countries who emphatically denied the unilateral war guilt of the German people and decried the peace of Versailles as undemocratic, unjust, and as a source of future wars. And they could not do it—which is even more important—without being disproved by open facts which weighed heavily on the German people.

Opportunity not only makes the thief, but also the demagogue. What an opportunity for the demagogue, in those times!

It is quite true that the immediate cause of the Nazi success in 1932 was not the Treaty of Versailles, but the economic crisis. However, it would be misleading to suppose that the masses which went over to Hitler in 1932 had been, until then, pacifists and internationally minded. There had been on the contrary, a strong nationalist opposition since the signing of the treaty. The nationalist opposition had already succeeded in 1925 in electing Hindenburg president of the Republic by 14,700,000 votes, one million more than Hitler gained in 1932 at the height of his legal victories. The only effect of the impact of the economic crisis was to aggravate the situation, to make the masses of the nationalist opposition more radical and to give the extremists the opportunity of taking over the leadership. In the meanwhile, there was no other way open to the rulers of the Republic than to fight against what they felt was unjust in the treaty, and to insist on alleviation. If these efforts had succeeded and had been followed by economic recovery, the Republic could have been saved. It was one of the most unfortunate events of History, that the partial reform of the treaty coincided with the most formidable economic crisis of all times. Now again the former ruling classes faced bankruptcy and the danger of revolution. Again the middle class people trembled for their bare existence. Now the industrial workers seemed to them a privileged class, favored by the laws of social security. The workers themselves stood before closed factories and emptied war chests. Defenders of democracy by tradition and education, the working class was weakened economically and divided politically by the communist demagogy. There was despair, confusion, disorder, tumult. But above everything sounded the trumpets announcing the coming of the savior. Time was ripe for counter-revolution and dictatorship.

The Theory; French Influences

Revolutionary movements of the past, liberal as well as socialist, were initiated by revolutions of political philosophy. The liberal revolution of the end of the eighteenth century is unthinkable without the spiritual preparation by Rousseau, Voltaire, and Montesquieu. The socialist Labor movement could not start and win power without the brainwork of a great thinker like Karl Marx. Searching for the intellectual preliminaries of the German counter-revolution, you will find neither a theoretical system complete in itself, nor an imposing personality. In spirit, the so-called "national socialist revolution" lived from hand to mouth.

Nothing is more significant for this theoretical opportunism than a casual remark of Hitler in his standard work *Mein Kampf*. There he told us how he, as a young man, attended a lecture of Gottfried Feder, a once popular dilettante in economics who later sank into complete oblivion. The core of Feder's theory was that it was not the industrial capital, owned mostly by Gentiles, but only the financial capital, owned by Jews, which was the real foe of the German people, and that the power of this Jewish capital could be destroyed by abolition of capital interests. Hitler, as he told us himself, was fascinated by this scientific elucidation. "I grasped it at once," he remarked triumphantly. What the demagogue "grasped at once" was not the truth—for he was, by no means, in search of it—but it was the excellent opportunity for mass propaganda. Thundering against the "raffende Kapital," the "robbing capital," of the haute finance, he could spare the "schaffende Kapital," the "working capital," of his industrial sponsors. He could please the middle class people, the big landowners and the peasants who longed for liberation from the burdens of their debts. And he could confuse the workers by pretending to be a socialist, too. In discovering the propaganda value of Feder's scientifically worthless theory, he revealed his gift of intuition as a shrewd demagogue, unscrupulous in the choice of his means. Obsessed by the idea of power, Hitler and his henchmen had nothing but contempt for the power of ideas. Small wonder that the theory of the "national socialist revolution" never grew up to scientific heights but stuck fast in a kind of opportunistic eclecticism. Hitler's contempt for any kind of political theory was characterized also by a story told by Konrad Heiden in his excellent book *Der Fuehrer*. When Alfred Rosenberg had finished his book *The Myth of the Twentieth Century*, he gave the fat manuscript to Hitler, for it contained some rather daring passages which Rosenberg, thinking of the party's reputation, did not want to publish without Hitler's approval. Hitler took the pages home and put them on his night table where Rosenberg, when he called, saw them lying untouched. This went on for a year. Then the author grew impatient and asked to have the manuscript back. Hitler gave it to him and said: "I feel sure that it's all right."

It is a paradoxical fact that nothing is more international than nationalism. The two great figures adorning the foundation of the theory of true teutonism are a Frenchman and an Englishman: Count Arthur de Gobineau (1816-1882) and Houston Stewart Chamberlain (1855-1927). The fundamental importance of these writers was acknowledged by no lesser an authority than Professor Ernst Hasse, a well-known protagonist of pangermanism. In his book "Deutsche Politik" (1905) he accused liberalism of disrespect of the idea of racism which, however, was rediscovered by Gobineau and Chamberlain "who felt themselves Teutons and assigned to the Germans the highest rank among the Teutons."

Gobineau found his German prophet in Ludwig Schemann. He translated Gobineau's standard work "Essai sur l'Inégalité des Races Humaines" into German, and wrote a voluminous biography of his hero. It goes without saying that Schemann, with German thoroughness, started by examining the ancestry of Gobineau who was, of course, not only a gifted writer but also a member of the old French nobility. Schemann was sincere enough to confess that everything that Gobineau himself had written about his ancestors was based on mere phantasy: "For after all he deemed himself to be a son of Odin." Gobineau, proud of his alleged Nordic ancestry, proclaimed in his work the superiority of the white race over the colored races, the supremacy of the Aryans among white men, and the Nordic race among the Aryans. "All his life," writes Schemann, "was a matchless protest against humanitarianism which has no comprehension of or appreciation for nationality, against a spirit of enlightenment which has no respect for the most sacred forces of history, against a democratic mania of levelling which is unwilling to recognize in the spiritual as well as in the social world, the difference between heights and depths, between individuals and masses."

In France, Gobineau's theory was developed to pure race anti-Semitism by Maurice Barrès. It was Barrès who greeted the condemnation of the Jewish Captain Alfred Dreyfus "with immeasurable joy." "That he is capable of treason," he wrote, "I conclude from his race." For the courageous action of Emile Zola in favor of the innocent he had only one explanation: that Zola was not a Frenchman. "Zola thinks quite naturally as an uprooted Venetian," he proclaimed.

Maurice Barrès, called by his disciple Charles Maurras "the first organizer of the nationalist doctrine," was an antiparliamentarian and avowed militarist. "We are clearly and resolutely in revolt against, and in despise of, the parliamentary system," he said. "We are here, I hope, in agreement on admitting the morality and legitimacy of the iron method." Like the Nazis he tried to win the workers for his ideas of a Caesarist plebiscitary republic—and tried in vain.

Charles Maurras separated private ethics from the ethics of the state. Words, spoken in Germany many years later, "Recht ist, was dem deutschen Volke nuetzt," "right is what is useful for the German people," had their predecessors in his writings: "Politics is not morality. The science and art of conducting the

State is not the science and art of guiding men. Where men in general may perhaps be satisfied, the particular State may be ruined . . . The order of politics and the order of conscience are distinct." (Mes Idées Politiques) I. P. Mayer in his book "Political Thoughts in France" remarks correctly: "The idea of the nation, once torn from its individual root, easily becomes a cloak to cover any abuse." According to his political ideas, Charles Maurras found nothing wrong in Colonel Henry's forging of "new proofs" to condemn Dreyfus. "Among his improvised judges," he wrote, "some sincere nitwits thought, as good bailiffs, that the legality and morals of private life regulate all things—not knowing that there exist particular and unwritten laws, a sphere of morality, higher, more rigorous, and more extensive for human consciences which are charged with certain general obligations." The only fault of Henry, in Maurras' opinion, was letting himself be found out. "The irregularity, I will not say the crime, has one excuse: in success. It must succeed. It ought to succeed." Maurras criticised Marxism as incompatible with nationalism. "But," he added, "socialism freed from the cosmopolitan and democratic element can fit nationalism like a well-made glove on a beautiful hand."

The ideological affinity of the French Rightist with the German National Socialist, their common contempt of morals in politics, their common hatred of the principles of the Great French Revolution make the weakness of French resistance to the aggression of 1940 more understandable. Charles A. Micaud, in his book "The French Right and Nazi Germany, 1933-1939," has this explanation for the phenomenon: "For the extreme Right, democracy was the enemy as much as communism; the coming war appeared to them as a struggle between the democratic ideal of the republic that they had always condemned, and their own conception of authoritarian government, which was defended by the enemies of France."

Arthur de Gobineau's influence on the Nazi mentality was deep and decisive. The same cannot be said of Barrès or Maurras,

Their examples may be used only to show that this mentality is not a product of a particular German "national character," but a phenomenon which can be observed at the same time in different countries. However, there is another French writer whose immediate influence on the Fascist and Nazi ideology is evident. His name is Georges Sorel (1847-1922). From him the Nazis inherited the ideas of the "myth" and of the "élite." They overbade him in contempt of ethics, hate of liberalism, and adoration of violence.

For Sorel, the French Socialist thinker, the "myth," of course, had another meaning than the Nazis. His "myth of the Twentieth Century" was the general strike. Now the general strike is known to us not as a "myth," but as a reality. It was tried in Europe several times either with success, as in Germany in 1920 when it smashed the Kapp-Putsch against the democratic Republic or, as in many other cases, with failure. Many years before, it was widely discussed at Trade Union and Party conventions as a weapon in class struggle, and passionately advocated or coldly opposed. In Germany, for instance, in the time before the First World War, a rather realistic appreciation prevailed, which was expressed in the slogan: "Generalstreik ist Generalunsinn," "general strike is general nonsense." For, so argued the "realists," if we are numerous and well trained enough to organize a general strike, we shall no longer need it. Then we shall have other means as, for instance, victory in general elections through which to impose our will on the ruling classes. On the other hand, if we should start a general strike without thorough preparation, we would not only be beaten but annihilated by the victorious ruling classes.

In order to cut off such too "rationalistic" discussions, Sorel created the "myth" of the general strike. For him the general strike was not so much a reality as a fascinating idea, a luring phantasy which could inspire the workers with an unbending will to fight. Sorel despised the masses and mass democracy. Only a thoroughly elected and educated minority could gain, in his opinion, enough insight and willpower to gather the masses around them and to win victory. This creed of a conscious minority, an élite, leading the unconscious masses, became common to the Fascists and Nazis as well as to the Bolsheviks. Mussolini, whose great future as a national leader he had prophesied as early as 1912, confessed to be a disciple of Sorel. Mussolini was the first one who replaced the myth of the general strike with the myth of the nation. In his famous speech of October 1922, before his march on Rome, he said: "We have created a myth. It must not be a reality; it is an impulse, a creed, a courage. Our myth is the Nation, the Great Nation which we intend to make a reality."

Less harmonious were the relations between Sorel and Lenin. Sorel celebrated Lenin as a true leader, as a "Great Czar," in the same manner as he had celebrated Mussolini as a "condottiere." Lenin, however, disdainfully, called Sorel a muddle head.

There was irreconcilable antagonism between Georges Sorel and Jean Jaurès. The latter was a studied philosopher and historian, true to the humanitarian ideas of the eighteenth century. He founded his socialism on ethics and humanitarian principles. Sorel, on the other hand, despised the era of enlightenment, the American War of Independence, and the Great Revolution. In his book *Les Illusions du Progrès,* "The Illusions of Progress," he quotes Condorcet on the Declaration of Independence. "There can we see," said Condorcet, "the first time in human history, a Great Nation, freed from her chains, giving herself peacefully the constitution and the laws which are, in her opinion, the best for her well-being." This is, in Sorel's opinion, nothing but "a lot of nonsense." Saying so, he cannot refrain from remarking: "For Jaurès, of course, this is admirable. His admiration of the verbiage of Cordorcet is quite natural." Finally he comes to this conclusion: "All our efforts must have the only aim of seeing to it that the ideas of the bourgeoisie do not poison the rising class, (i.e. the proletariat). For that reason we never can do enough to break connections between the people and the literature of the eighteenth century."

From there it is only one step to the burning of the works of Condorcet, Voltaire, Rousseau, and—who can tell?—perhaps also of Karl Marx.

We cannot consider the influence of French political thinking on German nazism without mentioning Gustave LeBon (1841-1931) and his work "Psychology of the Masses." This book, widely read in its German translation and frequently quoted in the German press, could hardly escape the attention of the Nazi leaders. Although it was by no means written for this purpose, it can be used as a primer for demagogues. Democracy is founded on the opinion that it is possible to argue in public meetings with logical reason, and that the results of elections and plebiscites are, or at least can be, the product of individual reasoning. Gustave LeBon vehemently opposes those democratic creeds. In his opinion, the masses can never be moved by logical and scientific arguments but always only by symbols and catchwords. Now we can observe from all systems of dictatorship, particularly of the Nazi regime, a deep contempt of the masses, combined with the strong conviction that it is impossible to govern without being backed by a broad "Mass-basis." Consequently, the Nazis were eager to learn from the church, the army and the theatre how to win the masses without making an appeal to their ability of thinking. However, it would be unjust to conceal the fact that the Nazis were not the only ones to go the way which turned out to be fateful for democracy. In the years of the Republic, Germany was overflowing with political uniforms, brass bands, party flags, and badges of all kinds. There was a race to win the masses not by arguments, but by a skillful combination of music, noise, crowds, heat, color, and inciting speeches. The Nazis became the winner of this race because they were the most consistent and the most unscrupulous. Their meetings had no similarity with the solid sobriety, not to say dullness, of political rallies of former times. They were thoroughly prepared performances, splendid shows with speeches which were dramatic scenes rather than statesmanlike utterances. Hitler's real greatness lies in his consistent turning away from reason and in his genius of leading the masses by irrational means. He was neither a statesman nor even a politician of average intelligence but the greatest political stage manager and popular actor of all times. There is no evidence that he or his skilled co-manager, Joseph Goebbels, had read Le Bon's "Psychology of the Masses" themselves. However, many passages of "Mein Kampf" appear to be nothing but coarsened paraphrases of Le Bon's ingenious remarks.

English Influences

Among the authors of British stock who influenced the political thoughts of nazism, Houston Stewart Chamberlain is the most important. This Englishman is the real counterpart of the Frenchman Arthur de Gobineau. Both of them were extreme nationalists, not for their own nation, but for the Germans or Teutons. As foreigners they were invaluable witnesses of the superiority of the German or Teuton race. How could that superiority be doubted when even French and English writers confirmed it? National selfcomplacency, combined with the traditional respect of the Germans for Western civilization, created the new religion of German nationalism.

However, before dealing with the ideas of Houston S. Chamberlain, it is necessary to mention another British writer whose influence on the Nazi theory is undeniable: Thomas Carlyle. When at the time of the beginning of the German Social Democratic Movement, sixty or more years ago, the apostles of the new creed argued with German professors about the philosophy of history, it was impossible not to focus on Carlyle in those discussions. The point in question was the importance of great personalities in history, vehemently denied by the Social Democrats and ardently affirmed by the professors. The Social Democrats were strong opponents of the so-called "Personenkult," worship of personalities. According to their philosophy of history those great personalities were more the creatures of the great social developments than the creators, more the occasional toils of history than its studied artisans. This was not only a consequence of the Marxist philosophy, but even more a ready-made theory in order to combat the worship of Bismarck, the "iron chancellor," which was, in that time, the political religion of the German bourgeoisie. However, the priests of this religion, the professors, never failed to quote the sentence of Treitschke "Maenner machen die Geschichte"—"it is men who make history"—and to refer to Thomas Carlyle, the admirer of Frederick the Great, and author of the famous book "Heroes and Hero Worship." It was Carlyle indeed who foresaw the authoritarian state when he wrote: "Find in any country the ablest man that exists there; raise him to the supreme place and loyally reverence him; you have a perfect government for that country. No ballot box, parliamentary eloquence, voting, constitution building or other machinery can improve it a whit. It is the perfect state, the ideal country." William M. McGovern in his book "From Luther to Hitler" is right when he remarks: "When we read Carlyle and then look to the later developments in European politics, no one can fail to be struck by the fact that Carlyle's works appear to be little more than a prelude to nazism and Hitler. Carlyle preached to the English, but his sermons were taken seriously not by the English but by the Germans."

Generally speaking, the German nationalists had been more inspired by British history than by English literature. "The cousin beyond the Sea" was always their most admired and the most envied model as a conqueror of the world. The Boer War, the belated flower of British imperialism, was condemned by the German Liberals as a misuse of strength against a small nation. Not so by the Pangermanists. Their only thought was: "Why not we?" Cecil Rhodes and Dr. Jameson stood high in their esteem. The virility of the poems of Rudyard Kipling had been echoed not only by the German nationalists but almost by all of German youth. There was the prototype of the "Herrenmensch," the Master Man, and again the question arose: "Why not we, the superior race? Why not we, the Germans?"

Now we can better understand the enthusiasm which greeted H. S. Chamberlain, the son of a British admiral, who became a German by his own will and the son-in-law of Richard Wagner, the great composer. If it was true that the struggle of races, the rise and fall of empires is the real meaning of history and if it was also true that the Germans were the superior race—as had been contended by the Frenchman Gobineau and confirmed by the Englishman Chamberlain—the Third Reich, the world wide German empire, could not be far away. No wonder that Chamberlain's standard work "Die Grundlagen des 19. Jahrhunderts," "The Foundations of the 19th Century," became the Bible of the Pangermanists who were, of course, a small sect at that time (about 1900) but are now recognized as the spiritual ancestors of the Nazis.

The great success of the "Grundlagen" was caused not by its scientific value but by the political opportunity it offered. Chamberlain is by no means original in his hostility against the French Revolution: "It is one of the most astonishing errors of human judgment," he wrote," to regard this catastrophe as the morning of a new day, a turning point in history. The Revolution was inevitable simply because the Reformation had not been able to succeed in France. France was still too rich in pure Teutonic blood silently to fall into decay like Spain . . ." There is nothing original in his condemnation of the Declaration of Rights of Man. "It was not the rights but the duties of men that the French had forgotten or despised, and so brought about the national catastrophe . . . This solemn proclamation is based, therefore, from the very outset, on an untruth . . . Let us hope that the day may come when every sensible person will know the proper place for such things as the Declaration, namely, the waste paper basket."

Chamberlain's history is treated accordingly to the dogma that everything that is good comes from the Teuton and everything that is bad comes from the Jew. The Teuton, in Chamberlain's opinion, is "the soul of our culture." It was the German element in Italy which brought about the Renaissance. On the other hand, the Jews are the representatives of cold rationalism, calculated egotism and crass materialism. Foreseeing the objection that Christianism emerged out of Judaism, he contends that Christ was not of Jewish origin. H. S. Chamberlain, the Englishman who became a German writer, was a heavy gain for the Pangermanists. He was hardly as great a loss for English literature and science.

Machiavelli and the Wise Men of Zion

In comparison to the French or the British, the Italian contribution to the Nazi ideology was a small one. Although Mussolini was a forerunner of Hitler, the Italian people, poor in military glory and heroic deeds of world conquest for almost 2000 years, could not be accepted as a pattern for the master race. Even the greatest geni of Italian civilization could not escape that generalizing disdain. Otherwise it would be unthinkable that a man like Niccolo Machiavelli should not be recognized as a great teacher in the art of governing in Nazi style. However, even this brilliant spirit could not find favour in the eyes of so severe a critic as Alfred Rosenberg. It is strange to see that his implacable condemnation of the great Italian thinker is founded more on moral than on scientific reasons. "Such system," he wrote, "based on human vileness and the systematic confession of it did not rise in a Nordic mind." Rosenberg has for the baseness of Machiavelli's mind only one explanation: He was of Etrurian origin, which means that he was almost as bad as a Jew.

It is hardly necessary to defend Machiavelli against the imputation of having Etrurian blood in his veins. This degrading suspicion was founded on the only fact that the region where he was born was populated by Etrurians 2000 years before his birth. Moreover, it was obvious that Rosenberg's knowledge of Machiavelli's work was very slight. Otherwise he would have recognized that this great master of political psychology deserved to be a member of the Teutonic race, as were, according to H. S. Chamberlain, the other great figures of the Renaissance. In reality, Machiavelli was an Italian patriot and republican who was willing to renounce all moral principles in order to attain a moral goal: the liberation of Italy from foreign yoke. His understanding of the fact that self-conscious nations prefer to be governed even by tyrants of their own stock than by foreign rulers is a proof of his intimate knowledge of human history and the human mind. Suppression from without paves the way for despotism within. This experience, not alien to Machiavelli, has been proved by many events of the centuries which followed.

It was, however, in a more complicated way that Rosenberg and his followers absorbed and surpassed the systematic immorality of Machiavelli's book, *The Prince.* This is a curious story that was told in full length in Alexander Stein's book *Adolf Hitler. Schueler der Weisen von Zion* (Adolf Hitler, disciple of the Wise Men of Zion).

In 1846 a French opponent of Napoleon III named Maurice Joly wrote an illegal pamphlet which appeared in Brussels and bore the title: "*Dialogue aux enfers entre Machiavel et Montesquieu, ou la politique de Machiavel au XIX siecle. Par un Contemporain.*" (Dialogue in hell between Machiavelli and Montesquieu, or the politics of Machiavelli in the 19th century. By a contemporary). Aiming at Napoleon III, this underground fighter drew the portrait of a modern tyrant who by the most refined system of cruelty, combined with ruse and hypocrisy, gains the domination of the world. Four years later a German writer Hermann Goedsche, with the nom de plume "Sir John Ratcliffe, the Younger," wrote a crude novel, entitled *Biarritz.* It was a mysterious story about twelve Rabbis meeting in secret session in the famous old Jewish cemetery in Prague. From both these writings an agent of the "Ochrana," the Czarist secret police, named Ratchkovsky, made a concoction which, under the title *The Protocols of the Wise Men of Zion,* won fame as the most fateful falsification of all times. Joly in his witty phamphlet attributed to Napoleon-Machiavelli outrageous remarks against morality and humanity.

Ratchkowsky, in his falsification, put the same remarks into the mouths of Jewish conspirators of his own or Goedsche's invention. Thus the counterrevolutionary propaganda of the "Ochrana" tried to turn aside the wrath of the Russian people from the Czarist government to the Jews.

Alfred Rosenberg, then a young student in Moscow, made the acquaintance of *Protocols* in a strange manner. As he told himself, a mysterious man came to him, silently laid the book on his table and disappeared without a word. Young Rosenberg, impressed by the mysterious appearance, was convinced quickly. At the end of 1918 he came to Germany as a refugee from the Bolshevik Revolution with the *Protocols* in his bag. From then on the circulation of the pamphlet spread like wildfire, not only in Germany but also in England and France. The "Protocols" were published in America, in Italy, in Hungary, in Turkey and Arabia. The effects radiated in two different directions. Old superstitions and hatreds rose anew. On the other hand, some adventurous youngsters in Germany decided to match "the Jewish conspiracy" with its own means and to use the arcanum of world domination, so cleverly explained in the "Protocols," for their own purpose. In any case, this stuff was easier to digest than the works of the Italian philosopher, and they swallowed it eagerly. Machiavellism, so ardently rejected by Rosenberg in his original appearance, had a splendid reception when he came back disguised in a stolen Jewish caftan.

From Hegel to Rosenberg

During the war some attempts were made to teach history of philosophy according to racial lines. If Rosenberg and his school concluded from the race of Spinoza that he was wrong, there were some others who discovered that the German philosophers were Nazis because they were Germans. To prove this for propaganda purposes was easy enough, since the language of the German philosopher is hard to understand. It must be a bad German philosopher in whose writings a clever commentator could not find everything. Earnestly, there is hardly a link between German philosophy and Nazi mentality, Nietzsche to some extent excluded.

The State, worshipped by Hegel, had not the slightest similarity with the Third Reich of Hitler, for it was a State of Right, not a State of Power or to use Hegel's own words "an organized ethical whole." Like Kant he taught: "Each subject, or man as man, has on his own account an infinite value." Fichte who was accused to have premeditated the Third Reich in his *Der geschlossene Handelsstaat.* "The Closed Commercial State," preached the equality of all human beings and urged the Germans to build "a true kingdom of righteousness of which the like has never before descended upon the earth."

There is a gap in the course of German philosophy in the middle of the 19th century. Its glory was overshadowed by the rapid progress of natural sciences. Youth became to speak disdainfully about all metaphysical systems. Du Bois Reymond, a famous physiologist and a German in spite of his name, cut off every discussion on supranatural values with the single word: "Ignorabimus." "We never shall know." Why should mankind speculate on such mysterious things when science, step by step, unveiled all the secrets of nature? The philosophical systems were laid aside and the theories of Charles Darwin were passionately discussed.

What was the meaning of Darwinism? In the first line it seemed to be a splendid affirmation of the theory of progress. Development, as understood by Darwin, was a process which was not yet closed. In consequence, men were able to attain heights never dreamed of before. On the other end, however, this theory was also an affirmation of the merciless wisdom of Heraclitus: "War is the father of everything." Progress was achieved by the survival not of the best in a moral sense, but of the fittest in a physical sense. If this was true not only for the plants and animals but also for human beings a new aspect of social life was given and not a pleasant one. Thomas H. Huxley tried to solve this problem by contending that nature, "red in tooth and claw" cannot give an example for humanity. "Morality involves not so much following the methods of nature as opposing them." Nietzsche drew his consequence to the opposite side. For him everything which promotes the survival of the weak at the expense of the strong was wrong, for the weak is not worthy of such a sacrifice. He preached the master-morality in opposition to the Christian "slave-morality."

It may be doubtful whether the immediate demoralizing effect of that devaluation of all moral values was as great as was prophesied by many of Nietzsche's adversaries. His own life was unimpeachable if we can trust his biographers. It is not a new experience that many teachers of high moral principles do not live up to their own teaching. Why should the opposite not also be true?

The answer to the question whether Nietzsche was a forerunner of Nazism cannot be simply Yes or No. What he did in order to destroy the belief in absolute moral values undoubtedly was preparatory work. On the other hand, his passionate contempt of race theories, antisemitism, militarism and any kind of mob instinct make it sure that, if he had lived to see the Third Reich, he would rather have been an inmate of Dachau than a man on the top.

The same cannot be said of some inferior spirits like Otto Ammon (1842-1916) and Alexander Tille (1866-1912). The first one made a rather amateurish attempt to apply Darwin's theory to the human society. In his book, *Die Gesellschaftsordung und ihre natuerlichen Grundlagen.* "Social order and its natural foundations" he argued that the "higher-ups," by being what they were, had proved their superior abilities and therefore were entitled to govern. They are the "social aristocrats" and it is their task to bridle the unconscious masses. Alexander Tille, in his *Der Geisteskampf gegen die gewerbliche Ertragswirtschaft,"* (The spiritual struggle against the economy of profit), is still more outspoken. He is a sworn enemy of the principle of equal rights, called and spurned by him as "equalism," and of any application of moral rules on the economic life. "There is," he complained, "hardly still a single German whose ideas on economic, social and political matters are not corroded by moral acids." An industrial worker, in his meaning, is a man who was not able to ascend higher grades of social life, and he has to behave and to be treated accordingly. Tille, who had studied in England, was the first to translate the works of Nietzsche into English. On the other hand he painted in his writings the English imperialism in bright colors, as a brilliant example for the Germans. In his private life he was the secretary of Freiherr Carl Ferdinand von Stumm, a big industrialist in the Saar and one of the most ardent apostles of social reaction in the German Reichstag. Tille edited the political speeches of Baron von Stumm which were undoubtedly, in their most effective parts, his own works.

The theory of Alexander Tille can be described as the ideological link between Nazism and the mentality of the big industrialists in the Ruhr and the Saar area. Those of them who paid Hitler, expected of him with certainty that he would help them to restore the "Fuehrerprinzip" in their factories, breaking the resistance of the unions and the works councils.

Speaking of the impact of Darwinism on social thinking, it is impossible to overlook its influence on the world of socialism. It was the most intimate friend and collaborator of Marx, Friedrich Engels, who likened the work of Marx with the work of Darwin, saying that Marx' achievement in sociology had been just the same as Darwin's in natural sciences. There is truth in these words, for Darwinism and Marxism are likewise founded on the principles of evolution through the struggle of existence which appears, in Marx's theory, as a struggle of the classes.

Much was said and written about the role of morality in the theory of Karl Marx. There were ardent discussions between his disciples and commentators on this matter. The orthodox faction insisted that morality is nothing else than a function of human society, changing with his structure, varying in connection with different classes. For them moral codes were hardly more than conventional fashions. On the other hand, there was another faction which tried to reconcile Marx with Kant. "Act so, that you, as well in your own person as in the person of every other, look on man as end and never simply as a means." In this fundamental sentence of Kantian ethics they recognized also the ethical base of socialism. Against the supposed amoralism of Karl Marx they referred to his own life, which was the life of a Saint in the service of the humble and the distressed, and to his flamboyant accusation of all kinds of oppression and exploitation.

Karl Kautsky (1854-1938), entangled in a hard struggle with the Neo-Kantians, wrote in his book *Ethik und materialistische Geschichtsauffassung* (Ethics and the materialistic conception of history). "It was the materialistic conception of history which has first completely deposed the moral ideal as the directing factor of social evolution." Nevertheless, he was forced to confess: "The 'moral ideal' has its function. Even the Social Democracy as an organization of the proletariat cannot do without the moral ideal, the moral indignation against exploitation and class rule." "But," he added cautiously, "this ideal has nothing to find in scientific socialism."

The ambiguity is obvious, and it could not last forever. Later, there was a schism between Social Democracy, which stands for the moral ideal, and Bolshevism, which developed the seeds of amoralism, contained in Marx's theory, to full blossoms. Kautsky took sidewise Social Democracy and was cursed by Lenin and Trotsky as a traitor to the proletariat and a vile bourgeois politician. In their opinion, there is no moral link among all human beings countering the differences of classes; every class has its own morality, and class struggle cannot be mitigated or limited by moral scruples.

Thus the problem of the relation between ethics and politics became the decisive problem of our time. Two camps were formed: on the one side the believers of absolute values, the Christians, Liberals and Social Democrats, and on the other the adherents of the manifold theories of "relativity of morality," Fascists, Nazis and Bolsheviks. There also is the point of contact between orthodox Marxism and fanatic Antimarxism, between Rosenberg and Trotsky. "Les extrêmes se touchent."

It must be said again and again that there was always in matters of ethics a difference between theory and practice. You cannot conclude from the moral philosophy of a man whether he is good or bad. Moral nihilism has its roots too often in disappointing experiences. On the other hand, absolute lack of morals is a phenomenon, seldom to be observed. Obedience to a leader and good comradeship among equals are to be considered as virtues even among the most depraved members of human society. Individuals lacking every kind of morals are mostly too narrow-minded to be a danger to humanity as a whole. This danger emerges rather from a theory of group morality from which there is only one step to the practice of gang-morality. Every philosophy denying the duties of morals in dealing with human beings of different kinds contains in itself the roots of evil and may lead to such monstrosities as we could observe in our time. There is, in this respect, an affinity between the Sermon of the Mount, the "Critique of practical reason" by Kant, and the programs of the democratic socialist parties which recognize, although in a different manner, the moral duties of all members of human society toward each other.

There was no lack of educated people in Germany who foresaw the dangers of lawlessness and anarchy emerging out of the "relativation of the moral values." *(Relativierung der moralischen Werte.")* Unfortunately, their will to prevent the coming evils was not as strong as their ability to foresee them. The fighting will of many of them was paralyzed by a new theory which maintained that the decline and fall of our civilization had to be expected as an unevitable event. Oswald Spengler in his *Der Untergang des Abendlandes* (The Downfall of Western Civilization), fought the same fight against "the superstition of human progress" which Georges Sorel had fought before him. Spengler, however, did not satisfy himself with glittering generalities like Sorel, but he thoroughly worked out a scientific theory, based on a multitude of historical facts. By comparing the different epochs of human civilization in their rise and fall, he found the symptoms of rapid decline in the epoch in which we are living. The prophets of human progress, culminating in Karl Marx, preached the creed of "*der Geschichte ehernes Muss,*" "the iron Must of History." They gave us the creed of victory and the strength to fight for it. Now this optimistic determinism was replaced by a pessimistic one. Spengler did not fight for nazism, but by disarming many of its opponents he became one of its pace-makers against his own will.

However, the most conspicuous answer to the challenge of Oswald Spengler did not come from the old believers in human progress whose creed had been shaken by many disheartening facts. In a defeated and hungry nation there is no climate for a sound optimism but only for the alternative of black despair and blinding illusion. Arthur Moeller van den Bruck (1876-1925) was a nationalist and a conservative, a polyhistor and student of the history of civilization like Spengler; but unable to face the facts, he escaped from reality into mysticism. When he was in Paris, shortly after the war, he met the Russian writer, Merezkovski, and discovered Dostoievski. He was deeply impressed by Dostoievski's belief in Russia's messianic mission. Dostoievski dreamed of the Third Rome, the Russian Rome which would bring about the millenium of Jesus Christ. In conscious or unconscious connexion with this mystical panslavism, Moeller invented the myth of the "Third Reich." His book *Das Dritte Reich* was published in 1922 when Spengler's fame was at its zenith. It was just the time when the French made preparations to invade the Ruhr valley. The young German Republic suffered its hardest defeat and its deepest humiliation. Gone was the short-lived glory of the "Second Reich" of the Hohenzollern, and its successor, the poor Republic, could hardly be more than a temporary expediency, a "Zwischenreich," i.e. the shadow of a Reich, filling the gap between the Second and the Third Reich, the great German Reich of the future.

Hans Schwarz, a close friend of Moeller who wrote the introduction to the 3rd edition of *Das Dritte Reich,* after the author's death, said: "He found men when they were searching for a new creed." This is exactly what he did.

Like all the other apostles of nationalism or racism, Moeller was an ardent opponent of liberalism. "The conservatives and the revolutionaries," he wrote, "have both the same enemies, the liberals. . . . Liberalism has undermined civilization, has destroyed religions, has ruined nations. Primitive peoples know no liberalism."

Moeller van den Bruck did not join the national socialist movement which was at the end of his life just beginning. The Juni-Klub, founded by him and his friends in 1919 was a rather aristocratic society which had its continuation in the "Herrenklub," the "Gentlemen's Club" whose president, Heinrich von Gleichen, was an intimate friend of Moeller. Later on some members of the Herrenklub, like von Papen, helped the Nazis to power whilst others were murdered in the blood purge of 1934 or died on the gallows of Himmler in 1944.

Long before this happened, Moeller committed suicide in 1925. The Nazis inherited one of their most powerful slogans from him, the mystical fascinating slogan of the "Third Reich." It came just in time to be incorporated into the compilation of Alfred Rosenberg.

Speaking of Alfred Rosenberg, the high Priest of the Nazi creed, after his ignominous end this writer cannot conceal his personal feelings. They are, sincerely spoken; feelings of pity rather than of hateful satisfaction. As a member of the German Reichstag and its Foreign Relations Committee, I was for some years a colleague of this unfortunate and had the opportunity of observing him closely. In contrast to the open depravity of a Goering or the refined cynicism of Goebbels, Alfred Rosenberg seemed to be rather a dull fellow. This impression was so strong that I doubted whether the works of Alfred Rosenberg were really his own. However, a thorough study of them brought me to the conclusion that his authorship cannot be doubted. Although a certain ability to collect sentences of other writers to his own purpose and to express his opinion in an understandable language is undeniable, the lack of originality as well as of logical thinking is quite surprising. There is nothing else but a stubborn fanaticism exploding in fallacies and banalities. The personal story of Alfred Rosenberg is the story of a man of less than mediocre abilities who rose through the might of circumstances to a position undreamed of before and, corrupted by the possession of power, fell even deeper into the abyss of calamities.

Therefore the presentation of Rosenberg's ideas cannot be anything but a monotonous repetition of the ideas of others presented on the preceding pages. Houston Stewart Chamberlain wrote *The Foundations of the 19th Century*. The standard work of his disciple, Rosenberg has the title *The Myth of the 20th Century*. The difference is significant. The *Foundations* are somewhat real, material, according to the confidence on science, so characteristic for the 19th century. Rosenberg abolishes the *Foundations* of Chamberlain and replaces them by a word borrowed from Georges Sorel: "Myth." Of course, Rosenberg's "myth" is no more the myth of Sorel, the general strike, nor the myth of Mussolini, the greatness of the rejuvenated Populus Romanus; it is the myth of the superiority of the Teutonic race, the myth of Arthur de Gobineau.

There you can find the same superstitious glorification of the Teutonic or German race as in the writings of Gobineau, Chamberlain and many others. For Rosenberg the source of all evils is the United States because it was there where "the idiotic principle of equal rights was realized the first time in history." "Brother Washington," the Free Mason, is in his eyes the forerunner of the French Revolution which he considers as the destruction of the German part of the French people: "The black mob of Jacobins carried to the guillotine every one who was slim and blond." Arguing against the famous dictum of Schiller "Alle Menschen werden Brueder," "all men may become brothers," set to music in the Ninth Symphony by Beethoven—but without mentioning it—he remarks: "A people of brothers is an utopia and not even a nice one. Limitless brotherhood means the ignoring of all differences of values."

There is no difficulty in proving the superiority of the Nordic race: "The two million dead of the (first) World War prove that in the hearts of the most simple peasants and the most modest workers the ancient myth creating power of the Nordic race is still alive." There one could object that other nations also had casualties, that the Nordic people of Denmark, Norway and Sweden did not fight at all, while thousands upon thousands of German Jews died in action. One could object that, on the other hand, Rosenberg himself was then a Russian student who never tried to die for Germany—but objections of this kind would evoke nothing else but anger and contempt of the self-conscious author.

Rosenberg is weary with arguing, disgusted with reason and facts. "The new myth and the force," he exclaims, "creating new types which now are striving for expression, are not to be refuted at all. They will pave their way. They will create facts."

They created facts. Nobody can deny it. Rosenberg's favorite quotation of "Faust" is a rather casual remark of the hero: "Allein ich will!" "For all that, I want it." Not far from there he could find some other lines fitting better himself. It is Mephisto speaking:

Verachte nur Vernunft und Wissenschaft,
Des Menschen allerhoechste Kraft.
Lass nur in Blend—und Zauberwerken
Dich von dem Luegengeist bestaerken,
Dann hab ich dich schon unbedingt.

(Despise reason and science, the strongest forces of mankind, let yourself be entangled in works of illusion and by the sorcery the sorcery of lies,—and I am sure to get you.)

Nevertheless, you can discern in the educational system of nazism a certain method of indoctrination. It is always an obvious fact which is made the nucleus of a confused heap of lies and sheer nonsense.

For instance, it is an obvious fact that there is a difference between Ludwig van Beethoven and a native drumming on the banks of the Congo river. But this observation does not lead, logically, to the conclusion that Mendelsohn Bartholdy must be a bad composer because he was "Non-Aryan" or that Marian Andersen must be a bad singer because she is a Negro. For Rosenberg and his followers, however, the simple fact of existing differences of race is sufficient not only to attribute to a single nation an innate superiority over all others but also to condemn millions of another race, judged inferior, to an agonizing death.

Or take the case of the "myth." It is a historical fact that myth, i. e. creed, not founded on reality, can become the incentive to useful works and heroic deeds. However, "myth" must lose its spell at the very moment when it is recognized as such and called by its real name. It can be likened, in this respect, to the somnambulist who safely walks in his sleep near the edge of a roof, but falls down if he is called by his name. Moreover, myth, recognized as such and sold to the masses as pure truth, ceases to be myth and becomes swindle and betrayal. Thus the artificially manufactured myth, be it of the efficiency of the general strike, be it of race superiority, is in any case doomed to collapse.

Or think on misusing the word "élite." There is a general agreement that masses cannot rule themselves nor move to a reasonable goal without the lead of a minority. The only question is how to create this leading minority. Such a minority can emerge out of the masses, it may be elected by the masses and controlled by them; it can be bound to the masses by the ties of voluntariness and confidence. On the other hand, it can be an élite of self-styled leaders, or a nominated élite, imposed upon the masses by an allmighty dictator. It is obvious that to Sorel, Mussolini and

Hitler only the last two kinds of élite exist, for the first one is an expression of the detested democracy.

Democracy was the offspring of the revolutions of 1776, 1789, 1848 and 1918. To destroy it was the logical aim of the counter-revolution of 1933. "Destruction of the dishonest democracy" was also the slogan of the dull Rosenberg, but the clever Goebbels added shrewdly: "by the means of democracy." Rightly the Nazis could also say: "We want to destroy the fruits of Revolution by revolutionary means." And they did it. This brings us to the insight that revolution and counter-revolution, although ideological opponents, are practically two components of history intermingled and interwoven with each other in such a manner that sometimes it is difficult to discern where the first ends and the second begins. Moreover, the revolutionary or counterrevolutionary character of a movement cannot be recognized but in relation of its occurence to place and time.

Even the most self-conscious despotism cannot avoid explaining its "raison d'ètre" to the world. Unable to found its power on the will of God it has no other way than to found it on the alleged will of the people. As for Napoleon I and Napoleon III, plebiscite became for Hitler the bridge leading from the land of democracy to the shores of dictatorship. Never did he abrogate the Constitution of Weimar with its fundamental declaration: "The power of State comes from the people." Now he was the "power of State" and it was the people from whom his power had come.

"Dishonest democracy has been destroyed," Rosenberg could exclaim jubilantly, "with the means of democracy" Goebbels could add.

Now let us look at the frequently mentioned "25 Points," proclaimed by the Party in its beginning; as early as 1920, it was called the unalterable program for which the leaders of the movement solemnly pledged their lives. There we can easily see that in that early period of its development Nazism by no means renounced the formulas of democracy. On the contrary, after having denied the rights of citizenship to the Jews, in preceding points, point 6 declares: "The right to choose the government and determine the laws of the State shall be the privilege only of the citizens." Point 25 demand "the unconditional control by the central parliament of the whole State and its organizations."

Until then the "Fuehrerprinzip," the principle of unconditional leadership of a single man, had not yet been proclaimed. Law-making was not entrusted to the Fuehrer but to the people as a whole. The supreme power was embodied not in a single person but in the parliament, elected by the citizens "with equal right and duties," as was provided by Point 9.

This was, of course, still a variety of democracy. Later on, when this variety had been degenerated into naked dictatorship, Goebbels, in his insuperable insolence, called it "a kind of refined democracy." Although the magicians of the Nazi theory had condemned democracy again and again, the shrewd demagogue hesitated to renounce a word whose propaganda value had been proved by experience.

It is just the same with the word "socialism." Like "democracy" its value varied from place to place and from time to time. About 1848 it was so abundantly misused that Marx and Engels preferred to call themselves "Communists." In the time of Bismarck the Socialists were outlaws; to call a person a "Socialist" was equivalent to denouncing him to the police. With the electoral victories of the German Social Democrats—culminating in 1919 when the Social Democrats were in the zenith of popular favor—the propaganda value of the word "Socialist" rose into the clouds. It was an act of mere competition when the Nazi Party adopted the name "Nationalsozialistische Deutsche Arbeiterpartei." It was neither a "Socialist" nor an "Arbeiterpartei" or "workers' party," for it was always the bulk of the working people who resisted the Nazi indoctrination so eagerly accepted by the middle classes and a good part of the higher-ups.

In saying that, it shall not be denied that a certain feeling of the iniquities of the existent social order began also to intrude into the middle classes. Gregor Strasser, once the most powerful leader of the Party next to Adolf Hitler, but murdered in the purge of 1934, called it in a famous Reichstag speech "die antikapitalistische Sehnsucht," "the anti-capitalistic longing." This feeling got its expression in some of the 25 Points, concerning economic problems. Point 11 asks for the abolition of "unearned incomes," Point 16 for the creation of "a sound middle class," Point 13 for the "nationalization of the trusts." Point 18 demands the death penalty for "profiteers." None of these demands were realized when the Nazis had the power to do it except perhaps the last one. For during the war many poor devils who had slaughtered cattle clandestinely in order to sell the meat, were really beheaded. This was done in accordance with the old saying: "Petty thieves are hanged, the great ones go free." The promise, given in Point 17, "to expropriate without compensation the owners of any land that may be needed for national purpose," was not only not fulfilled but also formally dropped. Expropriation never became a means of economic purposes but remained always a weapon against alleged enemies of the Nation, i. e. the enemies of the Party and particularly the Jews.

It is quite true that there cannot be a legal protection of political trade marks and that to no party can be denied the right to adorn itself with pleasant adjectives. However, it can be said rightly that the idea of socialism, in its historical development, is so closely connected with the ideas of humanism and internationalism that it cannot be separated from them without losing its face and meaning.

The parts of the 25 Points which were not only realized, but also enlarged by practice and aggravated into frenzy, are those which serve the preparation for war and express extreme hostility to foreigners—that is, above all, the Jews.

It has been said already that Germany was, before the new era of Nazism, one of the countries where the assimilation of the Jews was the nearest to the saturation point. It may be added that the Jews outside of Germany were in former times one of the most valuable assets of German foreign policy. Most of them understood German and held German culture in high esteem. They were active everywhere in the life of the German minorities abroad, supporting German schools, theatres and newspapers. Nevertheless, you cannot explain the Nazi distrust of the Jews merely in term of mediaeval superstition. The Nazis knew that the Jews with their highly developed spirit of scepticism were not the right stuff for the preparation of the masses for the total war.

The Total War

It was hardly a mere accident that one of the first adherents of the Nazi movement emerged as the herald and philosopher of total war. General Erich Ludendorff, having lost the first World War, clutched eagerly at the legend of the "stab in the back," in order to save his self-esteem and his glory as a great war leader. The "stabber in the back" may say that the cessation of the war before ultimate defeat proved to be an act of wise statesmanship which saved the Reich, that time, from utter destruction. Ludendorff, however, although he had asked for an armistice himself, clung to the theory that the war was lost not by insufficiency of military means but by lack of morale caused by subversive elements, particularly Jews. From there he came to the conclusion that victory cannot be won but by ruthless suppression of all moderating elements.

Carl von Clausewitz, the worldwide famous philosopher of war, seems to have foreseen his unfortunate successor when he wrote in his bible of scientific military leadership *Ueber den Krieg* ("On War"):

"The war of a community—of whole Nations and particularly of civilized Nations—always starts from political conditions and is called forth by a political motive. It is therefore a political act. Now if it was a perfect unrestrained and absolute expression of force, as we had to deduce it from its mere conception, then the moment it is called forth by policy it would step into the place of policy, and as something quite independent of it would set it aside, and only follow its own laws, just as a mine at the moment of explosion cannot be guided into any other direction than that which has been given to it by preparing arrangements. . . . Policy therefore is interwoven with the whole act of war and must exercise a continuous influence upon it, as far as the nature of the forces, liberated by it, will permit."

Clausewitz' war is not a "total" one. It is a war directed and limited by political considerations; it can be stopped by political decisions. Not so Ludendorff's "total war." For him war was a game of pitch and toss with no other alternative than complete victory or loss of everything; a mine, as Clausewitz stated rightly, which explodes into the direction, given to it by preparatory arrangements. It was according to the teachings of Ludendorff that World War II was waged and lost.

"Close spiritual unity of the people," the general wrote, "is the foundation of the total war. . . . International powers like Jews and Rome are destructive elements." He found the ideal of national unity in Japan and the Shinto creed. "The Christian peoples," he complained, "are no more so fortunate to have a creed fitting to their race." Rightly he found out that true Christians are as unfit for total war as the Jews. However, his attempt to create a new Teutonic warrior creed failed miserably. If he were still alive he would certainly write another book maintaining that the Germans had to lose World War II because they were not yet pagan enough.

Ludendorff's theory of "total war" is the logical consequence and culmination of the Nazi philosophy. War is no more, as Clausewitz said, "a mere continuation of policy by other means." It is an end in itself with the only aim to destroy in order not to be destroyed. It cannot be stopped just as a mine cannot be stopped after the explosion.

As the consequence and culmination of a nonsensical philosophy, the philosophy of Nazism, "total war" is total nonsense in itself. War cannot be total because there is neither total victory nor total defeat. "Ausrotten," that means exterminate, wipe out, was the favorite expression of Hitler. However, this greatest exterminator of all times succeeded not even—in spite of systematic mass murder—to exterminate the small, helpless Jewish people.

The consequence of the folly of total war was a vast extent of human misery and the collapse of the Law of Nations, which wiser and more human statesmanship could have avoided. The rules of war, dating back to men like Hugo Grotius and embodied in many conventions, faded away.

Hugo Grotius (1583-1645) told us that his reason for writing his treatise "De jure belli et pacis" was that he "saw prevailing throughout the Christian world a license in making war of which even barbarous nations would have been ashamed, recourse being made to arms for slight reasons or no reason; and when arms were once taken up, all reverence for human and divine law was thrown away, just if men were thenceforth authorized to commit all crimes without restraint."

It was the time when the struggle of denominations, fomented by a fanatical confessionalism, culminated in the 30 years war. Grotius was a believer in a "natural law" which regulates or ought to regulate the relations between man and man in the time of war as well as of peace. It is the same "natural law" which we face in the writings of Locke and the French encyclopedists. Kant confessed to have learned from J. J. Rousseau respect for the common man. It was an offspring of the same spirit which led the hand of Thomas Jefferson when he wrote: "All men are created equal and endowed by their Creator with certain unalienable rights, among which are life, liberty and the pursuit of happiness."

The gruesome devastations of the 30 years war were followed by an uprising of mankind against cruelty and oppression. The spirit of humanity and tolerance grew stronger than at any time before. The more the churches were imbued with this new spirit the closer they came back to the very sources of Christianity. No

Catholic or Protestant of our time can imagine that their differences in worshipping God could be reason enough to kill each other.

Such considerations lead to the conclusion that certain reasons of war and barbarism lose their virulence in the course of time, in order to be replaced by others. In our time, confessionalism has been replaced by racism. The superstitious belief that there were races so superior to all others that they are destined to rule the world, and other races so wicked that they must be destroyed to the last man, woman and child, had the same devastating effect on the morals of our time as the fanatical confessionalism on the morals of the 17th century. We cannot destroy German racism without destroying racism of every kind. We cannot abolish war without abolishing oppression everywhere in the world. Otherwise it would always be impossible to draw a correct line between wars of aggression and wars of liberation.

The world was shaken by the spectacle the German people offered during the time of Hitler. A nation, held in high esteem as one of the most civilized of the world, seemed to be changed into hordes of savages drunk with lust of murder and sadistic cruelty. The German people, as a whole, have sinned much and suffered much and, as usual, the suffering of those who sinned the least or did not sin at all was the greatest. "Quidquid delirant reges, plectuntur Achivi." "However the kings"—or the demagogues—"are raging, it is the common people who get the beating." The same can be said almost of every European people entangled in the never ending struggles of that unhappy continent. There seems to be no other choice than to kill in order not to be killed, or to oppress in order not to be oppressed.

A revival of the national socialist ideology in its old form is very improbable. But the evil spirit of nationalism will continue ravaging Europe as long as a just formula for the living together of so many nations in a relatively small space is not yet found, and the principal reason of any kind of fanaticism, economic misery and starvation, is not yet abolished. Both these problems are interdependent and can have only one solution: the union of all peoples in a common effort to alleviate the evil consequences of war and to foster common welfare. This however, cannot be achieved but in a spirit of "liberty, equality and fraternity," so hated and despised by the Nazis and by all the other counter-revolutionaries of other countries. This cannot be achieved without recognizing some absolute moral values binding together all men of every race, nation, creed or class.

It was hardly mere accident that the clandestine resistance movement within the Third Reich was called by its adherents "*die Gesellschaft der anstaendigen Leute,*" "the society of honest people." It was indeed the abhorrence of the moral insanity of Nazism which brought Catholics, Protestants and atheists, Conservatives and Radicals, capitalists and socialists into a common front. They all were united in their belief in absolute moral values and the dignity of man. They did not forget their differences of ideas and interests but they were determined, although fighting against each other, to obey certain rules of honesty, common to all of them.

"Love your enemies," is the most revolutionary sentence spoken at any time. It is a challenge for our human nature. It points to the remotest goal. Men who could follow that rule would hardly be still human beings; they would reach the limits of divinity. We recognize this obvious truth. We may know, however, that we are not born to lie and to betray, to hate and to kill, but to behave as honest people. Man is somewhere on the way from animal to a Supreme Being, sometimes progressing, sometimes regressing. But it is not written in the stars that he has to go back to the jungle.

BIBLIOGRAPHY

AMMON, OTTO: *Die Gesellschaftsordnung und ihre natuerlichen Grundlagen,* Jena, 1900.

CARLYLE, THOMAS: *Heroes and Hero Worship.*

CHAMBERLAIN, H. ST.: *Foundations of the 19th Century* (translated by John Lees), New York, J. Lane Co., 1912.

CLAUSEWITZ, CARL V.: *On War* (translated by Co. J. J. Graham), New York, E. P. Dutton, 1918.

GOBINEAU, ARTHUR DE: *The Inequality of Human Races* (translated by Adrian Collins, New York, G. P. Putnam & Sons, 1915.

GOEBBELS, JOSEPH: *Wesen und Gestalt des Nationalsozialismus,* Berlin, 1935.

GROTIUS, HUGO: *De Jure Belli et Pacis.*

HASSE, ERNST: *Deutsche Politik,* Muenchen, 1905.

HASSE, ERNST: *Die Zukunft des deutschen Volkes,* Muenchen, 1907.

HEIDEN, KONRAD: *Der Fuehrer, Hitler's Rise to Power* (translated by Ralph Manheim), Boston, Houghton Mifflin Co., 1944.

HEIDEN, KONRAD: *A History of National Socialism,* London, Methuen & Co., 1934.

HITLER, ADOLF: *Mein Kampf, Muenchen,* Franz Eher, 1933.

KAUTSKY, KARL: *Ethics and Materialist Conception of History* (translated by John B. Askew, Chicago, C. H. Kerr & Co., 1906.

LE BON, GUSTAVE: *La psychologie des foules,* Paris, 1895.

LUDENDORFF, ERICH: *Der totale Krieg,* Berlin, 1935.

MARX, KARL: *Der 18. Brumaire des Louis Bonaparte.*

MARX, KARL: *Die Klassenkaempfe in Frankreich.*

MAYER, I. P.: *Political Thought in France from Sieyès to Sorel,* London, Faber & Faber, 1942.

MCGOVERN, WILLIAM: *From Luther to Hitler. The History of Fascist-Nazi Political Philosophy,* Boston, New York, Houghton Mifflin Co., 1941.

MICAUD, CHARLES A.: *The French Right and Nazi Germany,* 1933-1939, Durham, N. C., Duke University Press, 1943.

MOELLER V.D. BRUCK, ARTHUR: *Germany's Third Empire* (translated by E. O. Lorimer), Introduction by Mary A. Hamilton, London, Allen & Unrin, 1934.

National Socialism. Basic Principles, etc. Prepared in the Special Unit of the Division of European Affairs by R. E. Murphy, F. B. Stevens, H. Travers and J. M. Roland, Washington, D. C., United States Government Printing Office.

ROSENBERG, ALFRED: *Der Mythus des 20,* Jahrhunderts, Muenchen, 1930.

ROSENBERG, ALFRED: *Wesen, Grundsaetze und Ziele der NSDAP,* Muenchen, 1933.

SCHEMANN, LUDWIG: *Gobineau. Eine Biographie,* Strassburg, 1916.

SIDGWICK, HENRY: *Outlines of History of Ethics,* London, Macmillan & Co., 1931.

SOREL, GEORGES: *Les illusions du progrès,* Paris, 1908.

SPENGLER, OSWALD: *Der Untergang des Abendlandes,* Muenchen, 1922.

THIBAUDET, A.: *Les idés politiques de la France,* Paris, 1932.

TILLE, ALEXANDER: *Der Geisteskampf gegen die gewerbliche Ertragswirtschaft,* Berlin, 1910.

XXII.
Panslavism

Editorial Note

Russian progressive and liberal ideologies are discussed by Mr. Elias Tartak in his chapter, "The Liberal Tradition in Russia," and by Mr. Vladimir Zenzinov in his chapter, "The Destinies of Russian Peasantry."

The reader is referred to these two articles, as well as to to Mr. Max Nomad's on "Communism."

F. G.

XXII

PANSLAVISM

By

WACLAW LEDNICKI

1. The Slavophils

IN CONNECTION WITH the Panslavistic trends which appear within the frames of modern Soviet foreign policy it seems justifiable to begin this study with the definition of Panslavism found in the works of Engels and Marx. This is the indeed striking formulation of the Panslavic doctrine, if this word may be applied, which Engels gives: "In the works of several Slavic dilettantes in the field of history there arose an absurd anti-historical current the aim of which was to subordinate the civilized West to the barbarian East, the city to the village, trade, industry and education to the primitive agriculture of Slavic serfs. But behind this comical theory there stood the terrible reality of the *Russian Empire,*— of that Empire which by every movement manifested a pretension to consider the whole of Europe the property of the Slavic tribe and, in particular, of its only energetic part—Russia. That Empire which, with two such capitals as Petersburg and Moscow, is unable to find its center of gravity until the *City of the Tsar* (Constantinople is called in Russian *Tsargrad*), in which every Russian peasant sees the true focus of his religion and nation, becomes the residence of the Russian emperor. . . . The intrigues by which Russian diplomacy supported the recently invented Panslavism are well-known in central Europe—a doctrine which could not better have corresponded to its aims."[1]

Engels and Marx, to whom I shall have occasion to refer later, fought against this doctrine, led by a clear knowledge of problems connected with international policy. And indeed the time of the Crimean War—the period when Marx wrote his brilliant articles devoted to the Eastern Question—was a time when the Panslavic conceptions became particularly timely. In the definition quoted above one finds the most important characteristics of the Panslavic doctrine. However, this definition does not exhaust the whole of it, and simply in order to be faithful to what we call an objective approach I should like, before showing the actuality of Engels' and Marx's opinions in the light of the Panslavistic trends of our days, to present the genealogy of this movement and some of its most important aspects.

Without going as far as Thucydides who, when speaking about the Slavs, whom he designated generally under the name of Scythians, said that "if these peoples ever unite under one chief and one idea, no power neither of Europe nor of Asia will be able to resist them," one may say that, in general, the historians of Panslavism consider the Croatian Jury Križanić (1617-1683) the creator of this doctrine. Whether or not this genealogy is correct is a question in itself, but what remains doubtless is the fact that the Križanić episode has its special picturesqueness and flavor. Indeed that zealous Catholic, carried away by his Slavic sympathies, by the idea of the re-establishment of religious unity, and by admiration for the power of the Muscovite tsar, made his way from Italy via Poland to Moscow. There he tried in vain to organize the Muscovite tsardom against two foreign influences—Greek and German—and to incite Moscow to a struggle for the liberation of the Slavs from under a foreign yoke—a struggle which would unite the Slavic nations under the Muscovite scepter. The enthusiastic propaganda of the learned Croatian did not

[1] Quoted by Vasily Gippius: cf. F. E. Tyutchev, *Polnoe Sobranie Stikhotvorenii*, Leningrad, 1939, pp. 10-11.

succeed in convincing the suspicious Muscovites — they felt a Latin and a Catholic in him, and in accordance with an already well-established tradition they deported him to Siberia. However, that poor Panslavic enthusiast somehow escaped from Siberia and reached the more comfortable Wilno, traveled farther in order to volunteer in the army of Jan Sobieski and to die for the defense of Austria in the Battle of Vienna under the Polish banners which he had vehemently insulted during his Muscovite sojourn.[2]

Indeed, in the Križanić *Politica,* a work written in Siberia, it is possible to find several elements which some 200 years later were crystallized in the Slavophil and Panslavistic systems. As I suggested above, it would be possible to find some even earlier manifestations of Panslavic trends. But first of all we should indeed try to define at least in a general form the essence of this doctrine. I think that by and large Panslavism is a conception which embraces two main, divergent currents: one was connected with the movements of and hopes for regeneration and liberation among the oppressed Slavs; and as such this movement was directed against the two main oppressors of these nations — the Turks and the Germans. Since the Germanization of Bohemia and the disappearance of Poland from the map of Europe there has remained only one independent and powerful Slavic nation—Russia. Therefore one could see quite strong tendencies among Bulgarians, Serbs, some Croatians and Czechs, and a few Poles toward Russia as a possible liberator of the Slavs. On the other hand, among the same nations there developed at certain periods, especially in the nineteenth century, conceptions of a Federation of Slavs around Austria and without Russia.

The other expression of the Panslavic movement is the Russian one. The oppressed Slavic nations were looking for liberation, and their Panslavistic conceptions represented their hopes for freedom. Russia had, of course, a different approach to the

[2] Cf. P. N. Milyukov, *Ocherki po Istorii Russkoi Kultury,* Paris, 1930, vol. 3, pp. 135-155.

same problem—she was to become eventually *the* liberator, *the* protector, *the* unifier. For this reason these two expressions of the Panslavistic idea differ not only in their aims but also in their historical origins.

From the modern point of view—from the point of view of the political implications which the Panslavistic doctrine contains—the Russian aspect is, of course, much more important. Let us, therefore, devote our attention first of all to Russian Panslavism.

The direct ancestor of the Russian Panslavistic conceptions belonging to the second part of the nineteenth century is to be found in the famous school of the Muscovite Slavophils and Messianists. The formation of this school resulted from different sources, and here again one finds interweaving ramifications of Slavic and Western European thought.

If one were to enumerate the different germs of ideas, programs, currents of thought, sometimes divergent and contradictory, which brought about the actual birth of the Slavophil idea in different Slavic countries, one would be obliged first of all to stress the fact that it took place in the nineteenth century and that it was in harmony with the political atmosphere of the rest of Europe. We find its ultimate sources in a variety of places. There was, for instance, the tenet of universal brotherhood which the Masonic Societies in particular had spread at the close of the eighteenth and the beginning of the nineteenth centuries. To the same period belong the works of the German-Russian scholar August L. von Schloezer, the philosophies of Herder, Rousseau, and the Romantics. From the Christian standpoint a kind of Messianism came to the fore with the sentimental attachment of the Romantics to the Bible and with Bossuet's reliance upon the Hebrew prophets. Mention must also be made of the German philosophers Schelling, Fichte, and Hegel. Along with the conception of the unity of the Slav world which arose out of the studies of the European ethnographers and philologists, went the demand for the freedom of the oppressed nations—a demand proclaimed and strengthened by the French Revolution. The movement toward a Slavophil philosophy was fostered by the propaganda of Czechs like Dobrovský, Kollár, and others who championed the claims of freedom for people of good will—propaganda based on affection for the national past and on Catholic conservatism which saw in the Slav world, and particularly in Orthodox Russia, a bulwark against Western Jacobinism. Finally there were many political factors to be taken into account: on one hand, the role of Russia in the Napoleonic Wars and the growing political power of Russia, which was held to be the only power able to win freedom for the Slavic nations; and on the other, the anti-Russian tendencies voiced in the Polish risings, the leaders of which considered the enemy a nest of political reactionaries and a stronghold of violence. All these elements, various and even contradictory though they were, contributed to the establishment of the Slavophil doctrine and at the same time indicated the goal which it might ultimately attain.[3] As far as the purely Russian Slavophil and hence Panslavistic doctrine is concerned, some other factors must also be taken into consideration.

I must start *ab ovo*. For several very important historical reasons the Byzantine political influence in Moscow, in the Muscovite ideology, became particularly potent. I have in mind the fall of Byzantium and some other events bound up with this great catastrophe. In connection with the more and more imminent Turkish menace, in order to save Byzantium, in order to organize a coalition against the Turks, men in the Roman Church began to consider with even more urgency the already existing concept of a possible union of the two churches; and at the Council of Florence in 1439 the union of the churches was accomplished. The whole Greek world accepted this union. The representative of the Muscovite Church at the Council, the Metropolitan Isidor, also adhered to the union; but unfortunately his adherence did not conform to sentiments at home. And when he reached Moscow, after celebrating masses in Cracow, he was confronted by com-

[3] This follows my articles, "Poland and the Slavophil Idea" published in the *Slavonic and East European Review*, London, 1923 29.

plete disaster. He was imprisoned, and Moscow declined the union.

Ever since that time Moscow considered herself as the new and unique center of pure orthodoxy, of pure Christianity. When in 1453 Byzantium was invaded, Moscow's prestige became even greater in her own mind. The Muscovite monks, working out a sort of Muscovite historiosophy and formulating the Muscovite political program, gave a very significant interpretation of that catastrophe: Byzantium had been punished by God for the sin of the Union of Florence. And then came the establishment of the theory of the "Third Rome": "Two Romes have fallen, but the third still remains." This third Rome was Moscow.

Thus was established a Muscovite eastern Messianism. This Messianism became more and more universalistic in its scope. The Muscovite tsars began to consider themselves the representatives not only of their own Orthodox world but of the whole Orthodox community in the world and, even more, of pure, unsoiled Christianity in general. Very soon after the fall of Byzantium and the spread of the Turkish invasion in the Balkans, many Serbian and Bulgarian émigrés, intellectuals of those times, arrived in Moscow with all sorts of Bulgarian and Serbian Messianic and imperialistic conceptions and theories, modeled on Byzantium and on Greek and Hebrew texts. Messianistic honey was collected from these Bulgarian-Serbian-Hebraic-Byzantine hives by various monks and old men like Philotheus. There were fantastic genealogies, orthographical mistakes — consciously or unconsciously committed—daring eschatological solutions of such problems as why the world did not come to an end on March 25, 1492, which escape it was supposed to owe to Moscow for not having acceded to the Florentine union. Greek prophetic legends, exploited by Bulgars as well as by Serbs, legends promising victory for the *rusy* (reddish) race, *xanthos genos,* became *russky* (Russian) race; and so, as Professor Milyukov stressed, "an orthographical mistake became a source of the Russian imperialistic dreams about Constantinople and the Straits." In a word, orthographical errors and boundless imagination, fed on Byzantine and autocratic Imperial doctrines, decided for a long time the style of Russian political thought. Hence, practically, the Moscow Tsar and later the St. Petersburg Emperor became the head of the church of a Byzantine Caesaro-Papist type and assumed the position of a Byzantine theocrat. The conception of absolute power coming from God, absolute in the universalistic sense, meaning that the monarch was the ruler of all material goods as well as of human souls, became established in Russia particularly in the fifteenth and sixteenth centuries, after the period of the Mongolian yoke had excellently prepared the ground for such a conception of monarchical power. As the ultimate result of these events Moscow represented the type of an Oriental despotism with a tendency toward state control characteristic of these organizations (especially at the time of the *oprichnina* of Ivan the Terrible and later) and the equally characteristic tendency towards imperialism based on Byzantine religious and historical premises.

These bonds with Byzantium became particularly strong after, and in connection with, the marriage of Ivan III to Sophia Paleologus, the Byzantine princess in exile whom Ivan III received from Italy. This marriage is also an interesting story. Both Rome and Venice were still meditating a war against the Turks in order to liberate Byzantium. For the realization of this new, grandiose enterprise the help of the already developed might of Moscow appeared very desirable. Moscow had succeeded at that time through all sorts of belligerent activities and political manoeuvres in establishing its predominance among Russian princes and was on the eve of liberating Muscovy from the Tartar yoke. Led by western political conceptions, Rome and Venice thought that the good will of Ivan III could be bought by the offer of the title of *king*, and on the other hand by a marriage with a Byzantine princess who after the death of the legitimate heir to the Byzantine Empire would become vested with the right to the Byzantine throne.

Ivan III was not very much interested in the European title of *king*, which did not mean very much to him. Moscow was so far away from the habits, manners, and international hierarchy of Europe that European distinctions and collaboration with Europe could not awake real interest in the exotic Muscovite state. On the other hand, Sophia Paleologus was considered by the Pope as a zealous Catholic; Ivan III needed a pure Orthodox fiancée. This last thing, however, was settled, and in 1472 Sophia Paleologus, the princess of Byzantium, the presumably zealous Catholic girl, became the Tsarina of Moscow and the most zealous of Orthodox ladies. The offers of the title of *king* interested Ivan, however, from one special point of view, from the very one which caused great discomfort in Cracow. Ivan III was supposed to become king or even emperor of the whole Russian nation *(in tota Ruthenica natione)*. As I have said, Ivan III was not interested in the title, as he was not even very anxious to buy from the direct heir of the Byzantine throne the rights to the throne, and Andrew Paleologus had to sell them elsewhere. But the formula *in tota Ruthenica natione* awakened some interest, curiosity, and appetite in Moscow.

Ivan III had two reasons for being interested in this suggestion. The first one was connected with the fact that some of the lands which belonged to the Polish King and Grand Duke of Lithuania (in one person, as the King of Poland was at the same time the Grand Duke of Lithuania from the time of the union between Poland and Lithuania) represented ancient *votchinas*, appanages, of the Rurikoviches, that is, of the ancestors of Ivan III. Moscow viewed this circumstance as making possible the expansion of the Muscovite Tsardom, and it opened the door to Russian, Muscovite territorial pretensions and demands.

On the other hand the Ruthenians who populated these lands were descendants of people who had been Christianized from the eastern source; therefore, they were Orthodox. The Union of Florence included them, but not to Moscow's thinking. Therefore Moscow saw in them the object of a religious mission, and that was the beginning of the Muscovite tendency to establish a protection extending to a great part of the citizens of the Polish-Lithuanian-Ruthenian commonwealth, which meant an interference in the domestic affairs of the Polish state. This state of affairs led in Poland to the Union of Brześć (Brest) in the year 1596, the purpose of which was to assure the Ruthenian church of Poland an independence of Moscow, which had become especially menacing since 1589 when a patriarchate dependent on the tsar was established in Moscow. However the Act of Brest did not settle this problem, because of disagreements among the Ruthenians and mistakes of the Polish policy. (The marriage of Alexander of Poland and Lithuania with Helen, daughter of Ivan III—she was Orthodox—reinforced the Orthodox feelings among the Ruthenians).

Poland was powerful enough in the era of Ivan III to stop the inappropriate Roman schemes connected with the problem of unifying all the lands that could be called Ruthenian. And the court of Cracow received satisfactory excuses from Rome in the matter. But Moscow did not give up, and in spite of the fact that the daughter of Ivan III, Helen, was married to the Polish King and Lithuanian Grand Duke Alexander, of the Jagiellonian dynasty, Ivan III seized every occasion to insist on his views and his territorial ambitions. And we see that ever since then Moscow has constantly spoken of cities and towns situated inside of the Polish commonwealth, constantly augmenting the number of cities mentioned, adding to these formulations the sacramental phrase "and many other cities and towns." . . . It is justly said by Milyukov that "on even the most cold-blooded reader of these dry ambassadorial reports, these heavy rhythmic strides of the Muscovite 'Stone Guest' may produce the impression of some crushing nightmare."[4]

But what were these lands—Kiev, Smolensk, Polock, Witebsk, "and many others," constantly demanded from the time of Ivan

[4] *Ocherki po Istorii Russkoi Kultury*, Paris, 1930, v. 3, p. 48. Cf. for the story of the Union of Florence, of Ivan III and Rome, the brilliant work of P. Pierling, *La Russie et le Saint-Siège* (1896-1912).

III until Russia could be led to the final partitions of Poland? It would be appropriate to stress here that the project of these partitions started even in the time of Ivan III. To the Emperor Maximilian, he made suggestions which later on, after the similar plans of Peter I, were finally realized by Catherine II, Frederick of Prussia, and Maria Theresa of Austria—and were later repeated by Stalin and Hitler. What are these lands?

At the time when the Tartars invaded Rus, when they were stopped in the west by the Poles at the Battle of Lignica, 1241, when later on the Muscovite principality was established and before the Polish-Lithuanian union, there arose, spread, and developed between Poland and Moscow, the Baltic Sea and the Black Sea, an enormous empire organized by the dynamic, energetic and mighty Grand Dukes of Lithuania. Their ambitions and political horizons were equal to their military prowess. Very often they reached the gates of Moscow, menacing the city itself, and at any rate they had succeeded earlier in seizing from the Tartars all the Kievan Rus, with Kiev and all lands which now are known as White Ruthenia; so that Smolensk, Polock, Witebsk, Minsk, Mohilev, and the whole modern Ukraine found themselves within the borders of the Lithuanian-Ruthenian state.

In 1386 this whole enormous state was, after the Congress of Krewo in 1385, united to the Polish kingdom, and the Grand Duke Wladyslaw Jagiello, following Polish suggestions, married the Polish queen Jadwiga of Anjou. These lands obtained, after the Pact of Horodlo, 1413, and later after the Union of Lublin, 1569 (a sort of confirmation and development of the Pact of Horodlo), a complete equality of rights and privileges with those which were established in the Polish Republic. After the Union of Lublin, Poland and the Grand Duchy of Lithuania (including White Ruthenia and Ruthenia) had a common parliament. And each successive King of Poland had to be elected by the Grand Duchy of Lithuania as Grand Duke of Lithuania.

While Ivan III and later Basil, and finally Ivan IV (the Terrible) were trying to justify their territorial attempts on Poland, centuries passed during which these lands were living in completely different political and social conditions. The regime of freedom, religious tolerance, and local autonomy became so strongly and solidly established in the Polish-Ruthenian-Lithuanian commonwealth that even Pskov and Novgorod, those peculiar republics accustomed to their freedom, menaced by the Muscovite despotism, made efforts to join the commonwealth. They paid very dearly for these desires; Ivan III and later Ivan IV uprooted these political dreams by the most terrific terroristic acts.[5]

Returning now to the Muscovite Slavophils, one thing must be stressed—that the first period of their activity was connected with more or less Russian historical problems. According to Herzen the moment of the precise formulation of the Muscovite Slavophil doctrine was the year 1836, when the famous *Philosophical Letter* of Chaadaev appeared. Of course it would be possible to find ties between the Muscovite Slavophils and the Shishkovists of the beginning of the nineteenth century, but Chaadaev's Western doctrine, Catholic in its conception, became a kind of catalyzer which crystallized the Slavophil program.

However, it would be difficult to give a precise analysis of the Russian Slavophil doctrine without taking into consideration the so-called *ofitsial'naya narodnost'* (official nationality). This term was originated, I believe, by the famous historian of Russian literature Pypin and applied by him to the official Russian ideology elaborated at the beginning of the reign of Nicholas I by certain high dignitaries, among whom the most prominent was S. S. Uvarov, minister of education. His system was based on three principles: autocracy, orthodoxy, and nationality. Although it is possible that the first two elements of this system may raise no doubts, the third appears less clear. But for Uvarov and his followers it was not so. The concrete significance of the word "nationality" for Uvarov was "reduced," as justly stated by Pro-

[5] Cf. W. Lednicki, *Life and Culture of Poland*, New York, 1944, p. 41.

fessor P. N. Sakulin[6] "to the conservation of serfdom and of forms of life tied with it. Besides, Uvarov realized very well this spiritual relationship between serfdom and absolutism, and he definitely expressed the view that autocracy and serfdom, having the same historical source, must have the same historical fate." When the Chaadaev scandal exploded, Count Benckendorff, head of the Russian police and the closest collaborator of Nicholas I, expressed the following opinion: "*Le passé de la Russie a été admirable; son présent est plus que magnifigue; quant à son avenir il est au delà de tout ce que l'imagination la plus hardie se peut figurer.*"[7]

The establishment of this ideology was not confined merely to official interviews, proclamations, and manifestos. The government had in its hands powerful means with which to imprison the thought of the country within its official ideology. The most efficient weapon was censorship and interdiction of foreign travel. The aim was not only to impose respect for the "three whales" of that ideology but also to eliminate any disaggregating Western influence. I need not mention the fact that in the eyes of the representatives of the *ofitsial'naya narodnost'* the West was considered a source of all kinds of mischievous and dangerous ideas. Strong echos of slogans launched by the official ideology often resounded in the writings of people who from a certain point of view might be considered independent. The most striking example is to be found in the works of a man who, by the way, was one of the closest friends of the Russian Slavophils—I have in mind Nicholas Gogol.

One remembers certainly Chichikov's troika "flying like a whirlwind" on the last pages of the first volume of *Dead Souls*, and one recalls perhaps that the writer compares that troika to a Russia "flying onwards like a spirited troika that nothing can overtake." "The road is smoking under thee," writes Gogol. "The bridges rumble, everything falls back and is left behind. . . .

[6] *Istoriya Rossii v xix Veke*, Izd. A. I. Granata, vol. II, p. 445.
[7] *Ibid.*, p. 445.

What mysterious force is hidden in this troika, never seen before? . . . Russia, whither fliest thou? Answer! She gives no answer. The ringing of the bells melts into music. The air, torn to shreds, whirs and rushes like the wind, everything there is on earth is flying by, and the other states and nations, with looks askance, make way for her and draw aside." Is it possible to read this astonishing "lyrical digression" without being indeed profoundly amazed, especially when one remembers whom Gogol's troika is carrying—Chichikov, Selifan, and Petrushka? This is the Russia for which "other states and nations" must "make way" and "draw aside!" From this point of view Gogol's passage is very characteristic and representative not only as far as the official ideology is concerned, but also the Slavophil. One cannot without amazement see cultivated Muscovite Slavophils like the brothers Aksakov, Khomyakov, Samarin, and many others absorbed in their idealization of the primitive Muscovite institutions and in their disdain for Western civilization.

The Russian philosopher, Vladimir Solov'ev, when criticizing this unjustified Russian messianism and pretension to obtain a privileged situation in the world, asked what benefits Russia might be able to secure to the world. Gogol, of course, had no doubts about this. His *Selected Passages from Correspondence with Friends* gives a very eloquent answer: only the Russian Church "like a chaste virgin has been preserved since the times of the Apostles" in her original immaculate purity, and this Church, "changing nothing in the state," might give power to Russia and become a leader of other nations because of the inefficiency of the Western Church. The tsar is the image of God on the earth; the organization of the Russian State awaits the same state of grace: "The more one scrutinizes the organization of the administration of the provinces, the more one is amazed by the wisdom of the founders: one feels that God himself was invisibly building with the hands of the monarchs."

It is true that some of Gogol's assertions were too strong even for Slavophils, and his book awoke consternation not only among people like Belinsky but even among some of the Slavophils. However, some of their own texts, which I shall quote later, and texts of writers close to them are not less eloquent. This, for instance, is the case with Nadezhdin.

We may find very similar items in a treatise written immediately after the scandal provoked by Chaadaev's famous *Philosophical Letter*. True enough, Nadezhdin wrote his treatise in order to rehabilitate himself after the unfortunate Chaadaev adventure; nevertheless the text remains striking. Here the author stresses particularly the power of Russian unity under the tsar's leadership, Russian health compared to Western disease, and the patience of the Russian people, which brought to their historical development a special character. "Who was the only one who thought and worked exclusively for us? The tsar! When did we write even one line in our history without the order of the tsar? . . . Our history must not be divided into periods of the life of the nation as Europeans divide their history, but into reigns which represent an unbroken stairway of beneficent activity of the tsars and religious humility of the nation. . . . Our spiritual life is not our achievement but the achievement of our wise and protective monarchs. . . . We have populated a space on which there would be room enough for ten and more Europes. Not in vain have we long been separated from the small corner called Europe. Our destiny is not to be the echo of the decrepit dying civilization whose death convulsions we witness, but to develop among ourselves a new, young, powerful, truly Russian civilization which will renew the old Europe." "The tsar is a father and Russians his children." "We are children, and childhood comprises our happiness. Our history has until now been a great poem in which there is only one hero, only one acting character. . . . Remember with religious humility and with noble pride that your existence is concentrated in your holy master. Without him you are only a line of zeros—with that monarchical 'one' these zeros make a billion."[8]

[8] Lemke, *Nikolaevskie Zhandarmy*, quoted by Jan Kucharzewski, *Old Bialego Caratu do Czerwonego*, vol. I, Warsaw, 1923, pp. 301-302.

What is particularly striking is the arrogance of this constant comparison of Muscovite Russia with not only Europeanized Russia, but the whole of Europe. The later Panslavists such as Tyutchev and Dostoevsky will continue to drive in a Gogolian troika. Gogol himself knew Europe and was, I think, very fond of it—especially of Italy. In his *Dead Souls* he showed even a kind of Ukrainian hatred for Muscovite life; yet in his lyrical digressions he sang his peans to the greatness of Russia. There is an element of duplicity and insincerity in this attitude. The same, as I have said, will appear in the case of Tyutchev, for instance, a highly cultivated and profoundly Westernized man. Similar will be the case of Dostoevsky. Both knew the Russian reality, and in spite of that both constantly sought to announce, proclaim, and greet the "coming" of Russia into Europe.

Equally characteristic is another fact—that all these Russian nationalists fought with foreign weapons in their hands. This is a trait which appears continually in Russian nationalistic and imperialistic doctrines. Such was the case of the famous doctrine of "Moscow the Third Rome" and also of the Slavophils and their successors the Panslavists. It is well known that all of them were students and pupils of German philosophy—of Schelling, Fichte, and Hegel. They readily accepted and applied to Russia the German teaching that in different periods of history the universal life reaches its culmination now in one nation, now in another. In their opinion the historical moment for Russia's mission was about to arrive. The teachings of Schiller's *German Greatness,* which may be considered a kind of preamble of Fichte's speech to the German nation, could not but impress the Muscovite dreamers. Schiller explained that the greatness of the German nation is based only on its cultural and moral character. The German spirit is the only one for which "holy things exist." This spirit alone communicates with the spirit of the universe, which has elected the German spirit to work at the imperishable task of culture. "The English look only for riches," says Schiller, "the

French are imbued only with their vain glory, the Germans were called to realize an integral humanity."[9]

The dizzying speech of Fichte in which he launched the metaphysics of Germanism and the identity of Germanism and universalist messianism became, of course, a source of particularly appealing inspiration for the Slavophils. But here again some reservations should be made. Fichte's speech, absurd as it was, was a reaction against Jena—the defeated nation was looking for an ideological compensation. The Slavophils did not need any compensation, but they very quickly used the whole German armament of arguments in their fight against Western Europe and for holy Russia. German philosophical imperialism was directed primarily against the Roman nations. The Muscovite Slavophils expanded that aggression and mobilized themselves against the whole of Europe. Very soon their slogans began to appear. Kireevsky in 1829 compared Europe to a dammed up river which transformed a fertile land into mud. Prince V. F. Odoevsky came to the conclusion characteristic for a Slavophil—that the West needed a Peter the Great who should "innoculate it with the powerful juices of the Slavic East."

The main arguments of the Slavophil program were as follows: the world is divided into two contrasting civilizations: the Eastern—Greek-Slavic, and the Western—Latin-Roman. The Western civilization is a product of the Catholic Church, of the traditions of ancient Rome, and of conquest—the Western states were based on the law of conquest. In the opinion of the Muscovite Slavophils these three factors represent the three original sins of Western civilization. The Roman Catholic Church fell away from the Eastern Ecumenic Church, and since that time it lost its true faith. Rationalism which found its expression in Western Protestantism and atheism developed, the Church lost its universal freedom because of the papal supremacy, and conquest brought the struggle of the classes, political parties, and revolutions.

[9] J. E. Spenlé, *La pensée allemande de Luther à Nietzsche*, Paris, 1934, p. 85.

Quite different was the development of the Eastern civilization. Orthodoxy preserved the purity of Christian faith and teaching, which is established and confirmed by ecumenic councils. The Orthodox theology is the true Christian theology because it is based not on reason but on the revelation of the superior truth. The Russian state originated not by violence and conquest but by a voluntary invitation of the rulers by the people. Russia did not know feudalism, the Russian land never belonged to a feudal aristocracy but to the community, and the Russian people never knew inequality. The tsar was bound to the people by a union of love, and the *Veche* (Popular Assembly) expressed the will of the people. Providentialism and national exclusiveness were at the base of this doctrine.

It would be impossible within the frames of this article to enter into all details of this system, but what was particularly characteristic in the teachings of Khomyakov and the Aksakovs was their conception of freedom which needed no guarantees. They considered treaties, contracts, agreements—in other words any legally established guarantee—evil. In their opinion the Russian people were repelled by juridical norms, and the Russian laws represented an inner truth. They did not care for any external usefulness or formalism. "All classes and groups of the population are penetrated by one spirit, by one faith, by the same opinions, by similar ideas, and by the same need or desire for common happiness." (Constantine Aksakov). Another trait was the complete reduction of the role of the individual which appears in their conception of the Russian land community. The agricultural character of the Russian civilization brought the Russian people to an humble subordination, which, by the way, the Slavophils praised enormously. That choral, primitive, and purely Christian character of the old Russian civilization was what they wanted to preserve. Connected with this was the argument of Russian simplicity. The same Constantine Aksakov stresses the fact that neither did Russian history have any theatrical episode nor did the Russian people like beautiful poses. "Nothing distinguishing in that history," says Aksakov, no "beautiful effects," "bright array," no role for the individual; and because of that, no pride and no memory for individual deeds. Every calamity is considered a punishment of God—every triumph an act of the grace of God. Thus "they do not erect monuments to their heroes, as there are none; but they build churches. . . ." "The history of the Russian people is the unique history in the whole world of a Christian nation which is Christian not only by religion but by its life—at least by the tendencies of its life."[10]

This was the idyllic picture of the Russian past as depicted by the Muscovite Slavophils. They considered that Peter the Great had ruined that beautiful past and brought Russia onto false roads of historical development. They were false first because they betrayed Russian national tradition, and secondly because they brought Russia to the West, which was in a state of decadence. I need not enter into too many details connected with the famous legend about the "rotten West"—a few examples will suffice. One of the leading Slavophils, Shevyrev, compared the West to a man spreading by his breath a terrible contagious disease. For Constantine Aksakov "West" meant violence, hatred, and enslavement; Russia—union, freedom, and peace. In his opinion even Russian paganism had been superior. This was why Russia, deserving it, had obtained a better Christianity; the Russian pagans had a *chayanie* (hope, expectation) of Christianity. The Russians accepted Christianization easily, without any struggle, like a child.

Now and then the Slavophils failed to confine themselves to Russia. They were looking for regeneration, for the restoration of that shining, luminous past, but they were generous enough to spread the benefits of this regeneration outside of Russia too. These benefits should be shared first of all by the blood relatives of Russia, the Slavic nations—and after them by the whole West-

[10] S. A. Vengerov, *Ocherki po Istorii Russkoi Literatury*, St. Petersburg, 1907: chapter on "Peredovoi Boets Slavyanofilstva Konstantin Aksakov," especially pp. 465-469, 470, etc.

ern world. The Slavs, organized around the holy Orthodox faith and under the leadership of Russian autocracy, based on the strong foundations of the Russian land community, would become a powerful political organization strong enough to bring the Western world to the Russian pale.

Here we are already in the center of the Russian Panslavistic doctrine. And this is, by the way, the picture of the whole Hegelian road of the Slavophil philosophy of history: thesis, antithesis, and synthesis. Chicherin in his profoundly interesting memoirs, mocking the Slavophils and especially Constantine Aksakov, says: "He (Aksakov) conceived Russian history according to all the rules of Hegel's logic; the old Russia represented the statement, the new—the negation, and the future announced by the Slavophils was to be the restoration in a superior form of the original statement. This formula could be successfully applied perhaps only to the beard: the beard existed in old Russia, in the new it was shaved, in the future it would be restored."[11]

As long as the Slavophils were busy with their national costumes, traditions, orthodox theology, and glorification of the Russian past, they might be considered more or less independent, distinguished, and inoffensive satellites or offshoots of the official national ideology—but satellites and offshoots who confined themselves to the worship of what they considered Russian national traditions. But when they extended their love to other people and their hatred embraced not only Peter the Great but the West, they became involved in political problems. And at this point some of them degenerated into Panslavism; besides, some new adherents, acting in the purely political field, joined the Slavophil group. Here again we must take into consideration certain other sources of influence and tradition—this time purely political.

Some of the political conceptions adopted by the Slavophils appeared earlier—even at the time of Peter the Great and Elizabeth. From time to time conceptions of the liberation of the "Slavic brothers" emerged, but they developed especially strongly,

[11] *Vospominaniya B. N. Chicherina*, Moscow, 1926, p. 236.

of course, at the time of Catherine II when Russia began the "liberation" of White Ruthenians and Ruthenians from the Poles through the partitions of Poland and finally "liberated" the Poles from themselves. At the time of Alexander I the same conceptions reappeared. V. N. Karazin, a well known liberal of the times of Alexander I, wrote in a memorandum: "Is it possible that the sovereign ruler of free Slavs, the unique protector of the Orthodox Church, can look indifferently upon the sorrow of nations close to them by blood and by religion?" "It is true," says Pypin through whom I quote Karazin, "that Karazin suggested cautious action in order not to offend Austria. But his dreams went very far: he dreamed of the establishment of a 'Slavic Empire' with one of the brothers of Alexander at its head: this empire was, with time, to be extended to the Adriatic Sea in Albania and Macedonia, and on the other side to embrace the southern 'Serbo-Croatian' lands of Austria. . . . This Empire, which would very soon develop and organize, would be bound to the Russian Empire by ties of religion, blood, and thankfulness, and would become Russia's 'storehouse' and natural base for all her activities and relations with Europe and Africa."

The same were the conceptions of other political writers of that time—Bronevsky and General Chichagov. (cf. Pypin, *op. cit.*, pp. 77-79). These conceptions were also discussed in Masonic lodges and even in several lodges of Slavic Unity which had been established in Kiev and in Petersburg. The Russo-Turkish War of 1828 again galvanized these feelings of Slavic solidarity, but this was the time when there began in Russia the great discussions between the Slavophils and the Westerners—in other words, the time when the Slavophil doctrine started its period of crystallization.

I should like to stress the fact that we must have in mind several important historical dates around which the Panslavistic discussion became especially animated. These historical events and dates are: first of all, the Polish Insurrection of 1830-31, the Cracow Insurrection of 1846, the Slavic Congress in Prague in

1848, the Crimean War of 1854-56, the Polish Insurrection of 1863, the Slavic Congress in Moscow in 1867, the time of the Russo-Turkish War of 1877-78, the period preceding the World War of 1914-18 with the so-called Neoslavism and finally the recent movements organized by Russia in Moscow and in this country among the American Slavic population and the Congress organized recently, also by Russia, in Belgrade.

2. The Polish Problem

The first "set" of the Muscovite Slavophils was composed of well-to-do people, people belonging to the Russian landed nobility; they had estates with serfs, they had fine and rich apartments in Moscow. In the beginning they devoted their time either to discussions on historical, theological, and literary problems in Moscow salons or to writings in which they expressed their views. And they also manifested these views in a special national type of domestic life; they wore peculiar hats and *kaftans*, which very often provoked sensations in the streets of Moscow; they ate Russian meals and drank Russian vodka. All these details concerning their private lives and their naïve manifestations of Russianism are very pleasantly related in the memoirs of Herzen and Chicherin. At this stage of their development they were rather innocent and pacific, but they later became strongly intolerant and aggressive. Chicherin gives some episodes characteristic of this intolerance and aggressiveness. This appears particularly in connection with the great Slavic and European problem which the Muscovite Slavophils, by the very fate of their doctrine, were the first to be called upon to solve. This problem was the Polish one. Slavic reciprocity, Slavic sympathy, harmony, regeneration, wars for the liberation of the oppressed Slavic nations—all these slogans, ideas, and initiatives could mean but very little in the face of the still bloody Polish nation under the Russian regime. How could other Slavs who were outside of Russia trust all the great promises given to them by the Russian Slavophils and later Panslavists if these same Slavophils and Panslavists had no solution for the fate of a Slavic nation which was within Russia? As in our days, Poland was a test case, and without a just solution of the Polish problem there was no possibility of offering any more or less satisfactory solution for the Slavic problem in its entirety. And just here the whole system broke; and sympathy, justice, and harmony were replaced by pure violence. The usurping character of the whole doctrine and its demagogical essence became obvious in the light of precisely this problem. As a matter of fact, the Slavophils had a precursor in this field—and a great one. This man was Pushkin. And unfortunately he may be considered ideologically responsible for the direction taken by Russian political thought toward Russian-Polish relations. The intransigent and even ferocious attitude which Pushkin took at the time of the Polish Insurrection of 1830-31 predetermined the attitude of many generations of Russians toward Poland.[12] His anti-Polish and anti-European odes published immediately after the defeat of the Polish Insurrection could not but create an abyss between Russia and Europe. This historical event was especially tragic because of the fact that its creator was the most outstanding and captivating symbol of Russian Europeanism—a Russian who indeed might be considered the Peter the Great of Russia in the field of her spiritual culture. Pushkin refused to see that Russia's annexations in Poland brought her geographically closer to Europe only at the cost of moral separation. In his odes he expressed not only a violent anti-Europeanism and an aggressive imperialism but also traced the lines for broad Panslavistic, Panrussian conceptions. These vociferous odes, belligerent as they were, became a kind of poetical citadel, an arch of triumph under which passed one generation after another of Russian Russificators and persecutors of Poland as well as all Russian Slavophils and Panslavists. These odes became a canon, a national catechism, a kind of lasso thrown by the powerful hand of the great Russian

[12] I cannot enter into details of Pushkin's role in this case. I have devoted a special book to it.—Cf. *Pouchkine et la Pologne*, Paris, 1928.

poet over the heads of Russian politicians, writers, and poets. From this point of view it would be difficult to evaluate the enormity of the moral disaster achieved by Pushkin. And, as I mentioned before, the fact that it was just the great European Russian who assumed the responsibility for this makes it particularly painful. One has the right to say that had Pushkin taken a different attitude, the fate of Russian-Polish relations and therefore partly of Russian-European relations could have been different. It is possible, however, that my point of view is too idealistic and that I evaluate too highly the importance of poetical texts in the life of nations; nevertheless I am not at all certain that I am wrong. When examining the works of the Russian Slavophils and Panslavists—the Aksakovs, Khomyakov, Samarin, Pogodin, Leont'ev, Katkov, Danilevsky, Dostoevsky, and even Vladimir Solov'ev (whose opinions were in many respects opposite to those of the Slavophils and especially the Panslavists), whose views are so actual for our own day, one sees how completely Pushkin's poems were in accord with the basic tendencies of Russian nationalistic historical and political thought, and particularly with its anti-Polish aspects. As a matter of fact, the sources of the historic, philosophic, and religious inspirations of the Slavophils were quite different; Pushkin had nothing to tell the Slavophils in this sphere. Yet it is sometimes difficult to resist the impression that they had him in mind and that his "anti-Polish trilogy" was a sort of poetical noose cast over Russian political thought, the coils of which bound even the most courageous and the most spirited.[13] It appeared that the Muscovite Slavophil system was unable to find any solution for the Russian-Polish problem which would harmonize with the general conception of Slavic unity. The Slavophil systems, both Russian and Polish (to which I shall come later), failed to produce anything positive and creative: the Russo-Polish antagonism in these systems could be dissipated only at the expense of either Russia or Poland; there was no other alternative. This applies especially to the Russian side—to Aksakov, who in

[13] Cf. my article "Poland and the Slavophil Idea," as mentioned above.

the presence of foreigners preferred not to speak of this "family quarrel," and to Pogodin, who, forgetting the ethnographic frontiers of Great Russia, attempted to enclose Poland within ethnographic and "democratic" lines. In Pogodin's opinion the latter boundaries were soon destined to disappear, since the only obstacle to an alliance with Russia lay in the Polish gentry, of "mixed Celtic and Latin origin," which should be destroyed by the Russian government with all possible speed. Aksakov used similar arguments in regard to the old Polish frontiers, while both Strakhov and Katkov attacked these frontiers even more vehemently.[14] Samarin saw in "Latin and Catholic Poland" "not only a historical contradiction of Russia but of all the Slav world." According to him Poland, "having become a poisoned sword and an instrument of destruction in alien hands, has received the same poison into her own flesh and blood." Her only salvation lay in union with Russia, which should become "the historical representative of the Orthodox and Slavic element." This would, in Samarin's view, be the triumph of the one cultural view over the other, although he admitted the possibility of Poland's separation from Russia. Aksakov admitted this separation in the same way, prophesying that in such case Poland would be eaten by Germany. But even here we see the break of the Slavophil conception: the Slavophils indeed did not know what to do with Poland. However, the most characteristic speculations were connected with the analysis of possibilities as to how a real union between Russia and Poland might be realized. The Slavophils were sure that the only obstacle between Poland and Russia was the Polish Latinism and Catholicism—in other words the Polish Western civilization. They thought that this civilization did not penetrate to the masses and that only the Polish inelligentsia—the gentry—represented that civilization. Consistently enough, they advocated the liquidation of this class—a liquidation which would bring into the Russian pale the amorphous masses of the Polish peasantry. This was

[14] The case of Strakhov, however, was less simple in this circumstance. Cf. my article "Russian Polish Cultural Relations," *New Europe*, New York, 1944.

the liberation and regeneration which the Muscovite Slavophils were trying to secure to the enslaved Polish nation. The whole armament of their arguments and weapons may be found in the writings of Aksakov, Pogodin, Samarin, Leskov, Danilevsky, and Dostoevsky. In the light of the present Slav movements organized by Soviet Russia and in the light of the present extermination of the Polish intelligentsia under Russia's "liberating protection" one may see that the most audacious dreams of the Slavophils and Panslavists of the nineteenth century are now being realized. The Russian autocracy was not able to use all means of extermination against the Polish spiritual culture because some of the elements of it were attached to a social regime which the Russian autocracy was bound to protect and preserve in Russia itself. From this point of view Stalin's hands are more free, and his policy of Russification might become more efficient in its destructiveness. However, even at the time of Alexander II and Alexander III, in accordance with the plans of the Muscovite Slavophils and Panslavists the Russian government began certain reforms aiming at the gradual liquidation of the Polish landed gentry through the emancipation of the peasants and through measures favoring the latter at the expense of the former. These reforms would have been entirely justifiable if they had not followed the principle *divide et impera.* Russia was usurping the role of a liberator of the peasants, because the Polish revolutionary national government of 1863 proclaimed the emancipation of the peasants and promised them land without any compensation for the landlords. At this time the Slavophil school became indeed a political one.

And here something very important should be stressed: the Russian democratic and radical groupings were sympathetic to the Poles just because of the democratic character of this insurrection. Such was the attitude of the society *Zemlya i Volya* and of Herzen in his *Kolokol.* They were even trying to prevent the Russian soldiers and officers from fighting against Poles. Herzen at that time published eloquent articles in which he attacked the "patriotic syphilis" which was raging in Russia. The whole of reactionary and nationalistic Russia launched its offensive precisely at this point—the slogan was that the Polish Insurrection was not a national one and that presumably the Polish masses had nothing in common with it. This point of view became the leitmotif of all Katkov's writings, but very soon Aksakov's *Den'* (the organ of the Slavophils) joined Katkov's *Moskovskiya Vedomosti*. The Slavophil phraseology followed that of the government, and Aksakov as well as Samarin explained the Russian-Polish War of 1863 as a war of Slavs against Latinism, as a war of Russia against the Polish landlords. We may see that history indeed repeats itself. The same slogans were used during this war when it was necessary to abolish the legitimate Polish government in London. Herzen understood this situation very well. On January 1, 1864 he wrote in his *Kolokol* as follows: "Having grasped here and there some vague ideas about the social mission of Russia and about her lack of any solid aristocratic principle, our sweet dreamers preach that Russia represents some sort of democratic empire, some sort of kingdom of *equality* and masses, that *she* fights with Poland in the name of the freedom of the peasants against the landlords, etc. Do not be mistaken. . . ."[15]

Sumner in his excellent book *Russia and the Balkans* (Oxford, 1937) brings very correct comments to this development: "The Polish revolt of 1863 unleashed century-old hatred and fears. In the years which followed, the old 'Congress Poland' was mercilessly dragooned within the framework of the administration common to Russia proper while the 'Western Lands' Lithuania, White Russia, and the Western Ukraine were subjected to every measure of Russianism. Meanwhile a campaign was initiated of the same nature in the Baltic provinces and Bessarabia; and, to show without mistaking that Russian meant Great Russian alone, the Little Russian or Ukrainian cultural revival of that time was successfully attacked by Moscow, above all by the prohibition in 1876 of the use of the Ukrainian 'dialect' for any academic or

[15] *Istoriya Rossii v xix Veke*, vol. 3, Z. Lensky, "Polskoe Vozstanie," p. 322.

literary purposes. Symptomatically two of the men most actively associated with this denationalizing, Russianizing policy, were among the most prominent Slavophil or Panslav Muscovites of the day: Prince Cherkassky and Yuri Samarin, a close friend of Aksakov."[16]

Cherkassky, Samarin, and N. A. Milyutin worked at the agrarian reform in Poland, and Cherkassky "distinguished" himself in the campaign for reuniting the Uniates with the Orthodox Church. "Samarin and Cherkassky are significant in the Panslav movement in that, unlike Aksakov or the earlier Slavophils, and unlike the professorial type, represented by Lamansky, Miller, or Grot, they were active in administration and were well-known public figures. . . . Both men are also, above all, significant as representing the transformation of the idea of Panslavism into that of Panrussianism." (*op. cit., p.* 67) Characteristically enough, Samarin was, besides all the traits mentioned by Sumner, a "considerable theologian," the collaborator of Khomyakov in this field.

It is not mere chance that I mention this trait of Samarin's personality. The Slavophil doctrine was from its very beginning deeply rooted in religious thought. The father of the Muscovite school, Ivan Kireevsky, was first of all absorbed by problems of religious and moral categories. Parallel to the pre-Romantics, the Romantics, and the German idealistic philosophers, he was primarily interested in the spiritual structure of the human personality and in the problem of perfecting it. He was fighting for the unity and entirety of the human personality and believed that the superior truth cannot be conceived by rationalism but by the entire spiritual personality in which the factors of feeling and belief were more efficient than reason. M. Gershenzon, in his book, *Istoricheskie Zapiski* (Berlin, 1932), sensationally enough stresses that Kireevsky committed a mistake which became the starting point for the whole Slavophil Doctrine. Milyukov pretends that the century-old Russian trends toward Constantinople and world domination also originated from a mistake—from an orthographic

[16] B. H. Sumner, *op. cit.,* p. 66.

mistake. I shall not try to discover whether or not Gershenzon was right. The point is that Kireevsky's example did not represent any exception. But what was the mistake? The mistake consisted in the fact that conceptions of the law of universal improvements based on a metaphysical truth led Kireevsky and all his followers to the belief that the Russian past, the Russian nation, and Russian Orthodoxy represented the incarnation of that law of universal improvement and of that metaphysical truth. These beliefs led them to their violent hatred for Peter the Great (the brother of Ivan Kireevsky, Peter Kireevsky, hated Peter the Great to such a degree that he was deeply ashamed of the fact that he himself bore the same name) and for Western Europe, and led them to the most simplified and crude philosophical interpretation of the historical development of Europe, which they based, by the way, again on European conceptions—on Guizot's triad: Roman heritage, Catholicism, and conquest. A one-sided rationalism characterized, in their opinion, modern Europe — to which they opposed Russia.

Exactly the same might be said about Samarin, who was, as I mentioned before, plunged in religious and theological speculations and whose philosophy was based on religious personalism and Providentialism. But what is striking is precisely this—that all these men, personally honest and dignified, busy with problems of individual self-perfection, demanding Christianization of international relations, immediately lost and forgot all these speculations as soon as they touched problems connected with concrete political facts. And the respect which they had for the nation, as such, was practically confined to the Russian nation alone, as without Orthodoxy the nation did not mean anything to them. On the other hand, no less characteristic of these self-perfectionists is the dissolution of the individual in their conceptions of the village community and of the choral principle—in the thesis of the Orthodox *sobornost'*. There is hidden their Achillean heel. We shall see later to what ultimate aberrations these doctrines led, for instance in the case of Leont'ev, who praised the "ignorance of the

Russian people" as a guarantee against the dangers of European rationalism.

3. Goldmann, Pogodin, Štur

The above mentioned remarks of Sumner about the role of men like Samarin and Cherkassky illustrate the fact that although in the beginning the Slavophils were not always in *odore sanctitatis* in the official quarters in Petersburg, that situation changed; the government appeared ready to use some of their conceptions. However, similar arguments and weapons for the fight against Poland—sometimes even sharpened ones—were offered to the government from other sides also. We may find a fascinating example of this in the Goldmann episode.

Charles Edward Goldmann, a German and a paid agent of the Russian government, wrote two books: *Die Europäische Pentarchie,* published in 1839 and *Europa's Cabinette und Allianzen,* published in 1862, and several memoirs which he presented to the Russian government. In his writings he tried to prove that the original religion of the Poles was the eastern Greek religion, that this religion had been uprooted by the Latin priests, that the oldest Polish Christian cathedral in Gniezno had been transformed from a Greek into a Catholic one. He attacked and derided the Polish emigration: "Polish emigration?—Does not England hang it *en masse* in Canada, while it dies from starvation in the hospitable England and the French throw it as a prey to the Bedouins, to the roulette, or to the *rouge et noir?* Russia knows very well that England and France in their nobleness and magnanimity would put the emigration next to the lackeys in their state carriage."

Goldmann also gives very valuable advice to the Russian government on how to eradicate the Polish spirit. First of all, Poland must be cut from the West, and Polish scholarship must be submerged in the Russian, the Latin traditions must be uprooted, and above all the Napoleonic Codex which rules Poland must be liquidated; the other Latin institution which must be destroyed is the

Catholic church. Goldmann elaborated a very systematic plan for a consistent and gradual weakening of the Catholic church and its prestige in Poland. I have no space to enter into the striking details of that program which Kucharzewski revealed in his book; enough to say that it was indeed a diabolic program of systematic spoliation of faith through, first of all, confusion of the minds of the faithful. His aim was not only the Catholic Church but also the Uniate Church. Poles, White Ruthenians, and Ukrainians were to become, as Russian subjects, members of the dominant church of the Russian state. In his cautiously elaborated strategy not a single weapon has been forgotten: the building of Orthodox churches, the substitution of Orthodox crosses in the countryside for the Cahotlic ones, the institution of the Greek calendar, the organization of a press of Orthodox propaganda for the people, the appointment of only Orthodox directors and inspectors in the schools, etc. The Catholic priesthood must be weakened by the favoring of sectarianism and material spoliation. "It is difficult," he says, "to secularize one monastery; but the annihilation of 194 monasteries and the refusal of any noviciates in order to create from the unused wealth larger funds for the clergy will find many advocates among the clergy themselves. In general, the state should not hinder but help the clergy to surely and freely ruin and prostitute itself."[17]

This was, in broad lines, the program for eradication of all Polish ties with the West. One is justified in asking if this system which was adopted by the Russian government in Poland was not very close to the main ideas of the Slavophils and Panslavists as far as the problem of Russian-Polish relations is concerned. As was mentioned before, at the time when Cherkassky and Samarin were active in Poland Slavophilism degenerated into Panrussianism. Parallel to this there developed, especially during the time of the Slavic Congress in Moscow in 1867, Panslavic conceptions of the Slavs united under Russian leadership. The most complete and consistently developed program for the sub-

[17] Kucharzewski, *op cit.*, vol. II, pp. 281-297.

jugation of Slavs to Russia was formulated in 1867 by the Slovak, Ludevit Štur, in his book *Slavdom and the World of the Future.* His book, which was republished in 1909 by such modern Russian scholars in Slavic as Lamansky, Grot and Florinsky, who, primarily because of their Slavophil and Panslavist tendencies, considered Štur a "genius of his nation," represents indeed a quite exceptional tribute to the cultural, moral, and political forces of the Russian empire. Štur had, however, predecessors not only in the above mentioned Slavophils but chiefly in the person of the famous Russian historian, politician, and journalist M. Pogodin, who himself represents a bridge between Slavophilism, Panrussianism, and Panslavism. I shall not enter into an analysis of all the voluminous works of Pogodin; sufficient will be his memorandum written in 1838, in which we find items already known to us from Nadezhdin and Gogol and which will reappear in almost similar phrasing in Stur's apology of Russia.

Pogodin writes: "Russia! What a wonderful phenomenon on the world arena. . . . Russia is a population of sixty million people whom it was possible to count in addition to those of whom there is yet no account, a population which increases by a million every year and will soon reach a hundred million. . . . And let us add thirty millions of our brothers and first cousins, the Slavs scattered throughout all Europe from Constantinople to Venice and from Morea to the Baltic and the North Sea, the Slavs in whom flows the same blood as our own, who speak the same language and therefore, by the laws of nature are sympathetic with us, who in spite of geographic and political separation, form one moral unity with us, by origin and by language! Let us *subtract* this amount from neighboring Austria and Turkey, and later from the whole of Europe, and let us add it to ourselves. What will remain with them, and how much shall we represent? One's thought and breath are stopped! A ninth part of the entire inhabited earth, and almost a ninth part of mankind! Half of the equator, a quarter of a meridian! Russia is a state which includes all soils, all climates and is rich in all indispensable products. . . ." Further he enumerates gold and silver, which Europe no longer has, mountains, bread with which they will feed Europe, and forests with which they will rebuild Europe should it be destroyed; they will clothe Europe. He stresses the fact that because of the cheapness of labor and the moderate needs of the workers there is no other place where trade might develop so successfully as in Russia. But all these physical powers of Russia are nothing in comparison with her moral powers. These are common sense, daring, intelligence, patience, military virtues. All these powers form "one enormous machine, organized in the most simple and successful manner, ruled by the hand of one man, by the hand of the Russian tsar, who at any moment, by one gesture may put it in movement and give to it any direction and produce any speed." "I ask, is there anyone who would be able to compete with us and whom we would not be able to bring to obedience? Is not the political fate of Europe and therefore the *fate of the world* in our hands if only *we desire to decide it?*"[18]

The first part of Štur's books is a ferocious attack against Western Europe. He throws himself against Catholicism with Lutheran violence, against Protestantism with perhaps less ardor; he vehemently criticizes European political life, European aristocracy, European bourgeoisie, the spoliations of morals, luxury, demoralization, and economic structure and comes quickly to the Slavic village community, which in his eyes appears to be the magic secret of historical success, prosperity, and happiness. Another factor guaranteeing success and prosperity is a strong government, the lack of which seems to him to be the essential vice of Slavic states other than Russia. Russia represents a glorious exception: "Having taken away from the nobility all political rights, the Russian government by its autocracy rendered an immeasurable service in its time not only to Russia but to all Slavdom"[19] I

[18] A. N. Pypin, *Panslavism v Proshlom i Nastoyashchem,* 1878, "Knigoizdatelstvo Kolos," 1913, pp. 87-88.

[19] *Slavyanstvo i Mir Budushchago, L. Stur,* St. Petersburg, 1909, p. 192.

can not quote all his declamations spread over many pages about the *tsar batyushka* and the love of the Russian people for him.

After these statements he turns his attacks against Austria and destroys the conceptions of Austroslavism. He also demonstrates that Slavs, because of their geographical situation, their religious differentiation, cultural differences, and so on are unable to organize any federation. They are weak, they are simply fragments of one nation, and because of that "the concept of federative states has no sense."[20]

The conclusion is obvious: "There remains a third road, the only one which is sure and has a future—the union of all Slavs with Russia."[21] Then come all kinds of apologetic epithets, comparisons, in which Russia appears as a lighthouse in the dark night, assertions that the Slavs must not start their new life with the declining West but with rising Russia. "Russia . . . is the mother and the leader of all our national family." He is aware, however, of some difficulties as far as the attitude of other Slavs toward Russia is concerned. But he solves them easily according to his assertion that the only Slavs who hate Russia are Poles. By their whole civilization they are opposed to Russia. Poles did not want, as did the Russians, to subordinate themselves to one monarchical will. They did not know how to organize their life, and they had been defeated by Russia, to the great and lasting benefit of all of the Slavs. Had Poland resisted, Russia would have been far away from Europe and would not be able to help the Slavs; and of course the Poles never had any qualifications for leadership among the Slavs.

With the Czechs the situation is less complicated: "In their present prosaic conditions they only weakly attract other Slavs. Although literature is diligently developed, in higher learning, in philosophy and history, nothing outstanding appears, with the exception of Palacký's *History of Bohemia*. And in arts and poetry the Czechs do not possess, with the exception of Mácha, a single

[20] *Ibid.*, p. 129.
[21] *Ibid.*, p. 141.

creative talent . . . material prosperity is the idol toward which the whole nation tends."[22] The Czechs cannot remain in their seclusion or create anything great—therefore they must join a greater entity. The so-called Illyrians and Catholic Croatians—"flabby," "seduced by Austria," "coaxed by Czechs," will be "inspired by the Slavic idea as soon as they rightly understand it." Of course Serbia and Bulgaria will agree. The end of the book is a kind of glorious finale. He brings an enumeration of all the great battles in Russian history. He stresses the fact that the main power of Russia is in the union of the people with the tsar, that the learned people are work-loving and conscious of the greatness of Russia; that the army is deeply devoted to the tsar and to the fatherland; the clergy, "pious and zealous"; the people, "kind, strong and obedient."

Then comes the "Russian Geography"—"Russia represents nine Turkish empires, twenty-eight Scandinavias, twenty-nine Austrias, thirty Germanies, and thirty-six Frances. The power of Russia is spread from the north-eastern corner of Asia, from Kamchatka, to the distant north of America, from the distant European North almost to the Carpathians, Danube, Black Sea, and farther to Ararat itself." Then follow figures concernings export and import, enumerations of Great Russian names, and so on. He concludes that everything works to the advantage of Russia—"Friend and enemy, war and peace, revolts and quietness;—Russia cast off the whole of Europe. She had the decisive voice at the Vienna Congress. . . . With one arm she embraces Asia, the second extends to America; inaccessible to Europe, she is a neighbor of the rotten Austria and the dead Turkish corps." Russia is the agglomeration of great and small things, of things divided and united; she is full of contradictions—Christianity, paganism, Islam, Byzantine churches, mosques, Catholic cathedrals. "She combines Europe with Asia, East with West, the dawn with the sunset, in other words, in the Russian kingdom the sun never sets."[23]

[22] *Ibid.*, pp. 146-150.
[23] *Ibid.*, pp. 150-152.

The final conclusion is that the "immense Russian power pushes ahead, it cannot be quieted, it constantly must look to new arenas for its activity. The Slavic conscience strongly awakens in Russia . . . and it can not longer allow its relative tribes to remain in serfdom and shame. . . . To make of the whole of Slavdom a base is the only natural goal of Russian policy."[24]

4. Danilevsky (1822-1885)

The most radical Russian formulation of the Panslavistic program in its two directions—Constantinople and the Western Slavs —unified by a violent anti-Europeanism, was given by N. Ya. Danilevsky whose book *Russia and Europe* appeared in its first edition in 1871 and in its second in 1888 with a preface by another Panslavist, N. Štrakhov. I cannot quote here the five hundred pages of this book in which the most fantastic idealization of the Russian past is married to the most vehement disdain and hatred for Western Europe and finally organized into a cynical political theory whose aim is to elaborate a system which would secure to Russia a permanent political supremacy in the world. Danilesvky's starting point is the denial of the conception of humanity and civilization as a whole, to which he opposes a conception of struggle between different cultural historical types based mainly on language groupings.

This conception of cultural historical types deserves special attention. Danilevsky combined the theme of Hegel, according to which various nations appear in succession on the historical stage as consecutive and ever more complete incarnations of the universal spirit, with the idea of the German historian Rückert about the existence of separate cultural historical types. "For Danilevsky such a cultural historical type is realized by every tribe or every family of peoples characterized by a separate language or group of languages sufficiently near to each other . . . if that tribe or family of peoples is in general, by its spiritual disposition, capa-

[24] *Ibid.*, p. 158.

ble of historical development and has already risen from infancy. However, not all nations are equally capable of historical development. There are some whose destiny is to serve as ethnographical material to other stronger and more stabilized nations. Those others are God's whips whose mission is to smash from the face of the earth the outlived cultures and nations. Danilevsky gives a series of historical cultural types: Egyptian, Chinese, Assyrian-Babylonian-Phoenician, Indian, Iranian, Hebrew, Greek, Roman, New Semitic, German-Roman or European, and finally Slavic with Russia at its head. Each of these types works out its own culture, and the principles of the civilization of one type are not transferred to another. Various types differ by the degree of versatility of their culture. Danilevsky sees four spheres of cultural-historical activity: the religious, the strictly cultural, the political, and the social-economic. No one of the listed cultural-historical types developed all of these four spheres of activity at once, with the exception of the Slavs and Russians, whose mission will be to accomplish a complete 'four-principled' culture."[25]

The road to that Russian predominance is a purely nationalistic one; and, neglecting any declamation on Russian religiosity and other well known features of the Russian character as presented in the writings of the Slavophils and abandoning all ideas about brotherhood and universal love, he brutally opens the door into the great future of Russia. Russia is destined for that future, but the road to it leads first of all to Constantinople and secondly to the emancipation of the Slavic nations. I shall not bring to the fore all his violent criticism applied to "rotten Europe." The Russian anti-Westernism here reached its climax. The book is supported by quasi-scientific arguments taken from anthropology, zoology, geology, geography, and the social sciences. It might be considered one of the most important scientific manifestos or rationalistic Panslavic theories. However, the most important implications of the book are, of course, the political ones. "Being

[25] Danilevsky, *op cit.*, and article by V. Myakotin on Danilevsky in *the Entsiklopedicheskii Slovar'*, T-A Granat, vol. 17, pp. 552-557.

foreign to the European world because of its internal structure, and in addition being too strong and powerful to occupy the place of one of the members of the European family, to be one of the great European powers, Russia cannot occupy a place worthy of herself and of Slavdom in history other than by becoming the chief figure of an independent political system of states and by being a counter balance to Europe in its entirety. These are the advantages: the utility and the significance of the Panslavic alliance in its relationship to Russia."[26] And this is another programatic assertion: "Sooner or later, whether we want it or not, the fight with Europe (or at least with the greater part of it) is inevitable, and it will be a fight because of the eastern question, that is, for the freedom and independence of the Slavs, for the possession of Tsargrad—for everything which in the opinion of Europe represents an object of illegitimate Russian ambition and which in the opinion of every Russian worthy of that name represents the inevitable demand of Russia's historical mission."[27]

Of course, on his road, Danilevsky fatally met Poland. His fight in this case was very simple. He liquidated Poland with the help of all kinds of historical accusations and political insinuations. In the same way he destroyed every spiritual cultural tie between Russia and Europe. His formula was not at all complicated, and one cannot really deny that this formula is the key to Stalin's present policy. When referring to the theory of political balance he says: "It is not at all difficult to be convinced that between Europe and Russia in this as well as in other respects there exists a direct and complete contradiction. It is precisely the balance of political forces in Europe that is harmful and even fatal for Russia; and the disturbance of this balance, from what ever side it may come, is advantageous and beneficent."[28]

After several historical examples, Danilevsky gives the following formula: "At every disturbance of balance Europe is naturally

[26] *Op. cit.*, p. 437.
[27] *Op. cit.*, p. 474.
[28] *Op. cit.*, p. 486.

divided into two parties—one, the disturbant with those who *volens nolens* are on his side, and the victims of the disturbants who seek to restore the balance. Both parties naturally try to bring to their side the only one strong neighbor who is, by the nature of things (whatever, by the way, might be the forms, words, and appellations applied), outside of their family, outside their system. Therefore both parties flatter Russia. One seeks help from her for the conservation of the obtained predominance; the other one for liberation from the power, influence, and danger coming from the side of the disturbant. Russia may choose of her own will. On the contrary, during the existence of balance the political activity of Europe is directed outside, and its hostility against Russia is given free march: here, instead of two parties one after the other flattering Russia, Europe flows into one entity openly or secretly hostile to Russia. We must therefore abandon the thought of any solidarity with European interests, of any ties with one or the other political combination of European powers, and first of all acquire a complete freedom of action, complete possibility to unite with every European state, on only one condition—that such an alliance should be advantageous for us without any consideration as to what kind of political principle is represented at a given time by this or that state."[29]

It would not be arbitrary to assert that if for the contemporaries of Danilevsky his book was a "catechism" or codex of "Slavophilism" (words of N. N. Strakhov), for us it might be considered the bible of Stalin's present foreign policy. In the light of Russia's present play with England, America, and France, not to mention Germany and China, the guiding ideas of Danilevsky become particularly significant.

From the historical and moral point of view this book cannot resist any critique. Danilevsky followed the Slavophils in their fanatic admiration for the Russia of the Muscovite period. Even from the point of view of Russian imperialism that Slavophil pre-

[29] *Op. cit.*, pp. 488-89.

dilection for the Ivans of Moscow and hatred for Peter the Great were not justifiable. As far as the territorial expansion of Russia is concerned, the Russia of the Petersburgian period did not acquire or "liberate" fewer nations and lands than the tsars of Moscow.[30]

Besides, for every unprejudiced historian one thing is quite clear—that the universal achievements of Russia in the field of spiritual culture were genuinely connected with her collaboration with Western Europe. The Russian national genius was silent or inarticulate for centuries, and only when the magic wand of the West touched the Russian soul did the voice of Avvakum become the melody of Pushkin's poetry. How can we imagine all the great accomplishments of Turgenev, Dostoevsky, Tolstoy, Tschaikowsky, and Rimsky-Korsakov—in other words the Russian culture of the nineteenth century—without Europe and her inspiration? This point of view has been strongly stressed on many occasions by Russians themselves, first of all by Vladimir Solov'ev.

From the moral point of view the ideology of Danilevsky is essentially immoral. Where messianistic arguments are adduced in support love changes quickly and easily into hatred. Danilevsky pays some official tribute to the slogans of "brotherhood" and "Slavic reciprocity" brought to the fore by the first Russian and non-Russian Slavophils. But the essence of his doctrine is pure national selfishness. "Life and theory," says Solov'ev, "somehow very easily and unnoticeably replace the just and human formula of the national idea by the formula of violence and national murder. Not by any means do all the advocates of this idea directly preach subdual and destruction of foreign nations; but there exist roundabout means, softer in appearance although just as murderous in spirit. 'Our nation, by its historical march and by the natural succession of national culture, replaces all other nations who have passed away and are passing away.' This 'replacement' also is not without a cruel, bloody struggle and various national murders, but the final result is attained as if by itself. Such a

[30] This point, by the way, was stressed by Pypin and by Sumner.

softened formula of national selfishness was taken from the Germans by our Slavophils, who applied to Russia that which their teachers applied to Germanism; this view was systematically worked out among us by the author of *Russia and Europe.* Between him and the former Slavophils there is, however, a difference which he himself points out although he does not always observe it. The latter affirm that the Russian nation has a universal historical calling, as the bearer of the final international enlightenment; Danilevsky, rejecting every international task, considers Russia and Slavdom only a special cultural-historic type,—however, the most perfect and complete (four-principled in his terminology), containing within itself the advantages of former types. Difference of opinion, therefore, appears only in abstract terms which do not change the essence of the matter. It must be noted, however, that the orthodox Slavophils (Khomyakov, Kireevsky, the Aksakovs, Samarin), not rejecting universal history and admitting, although only in abstract principle, the solidarity of all mankind, were nearer than Danilevsky to the Christian idea and could affirm it without falling into obvious external contradiction."[31]

I think that there is nothing to be added to this essentially correct critique of Danilevsky's system. One must indeed recognize that from a certain point of view Danilevsky finds himself very far from the first generation of the Muscovite Slavophils who were trying to marry their Russian nationalism and Slavophilism with universal humanitarianism. They had a mystic idea of the nation and a respect for it as for a person, a religious entity. (True enough only for the Russian nation.) Danilevsky lost all these things. There is no spiritualism, no idealism in his approach—just as in the case of another man, Constantine Leont'ev, who was very close to Danilevsky's conceptions and who might be considered the ultramontane of the whole school. Without any great enthusiasm or admiration for the Slavs, but simply guided by a fanatical fear of revolution, liberalism, and Europeanism, stress-

[31] Solov'ev, *Works,* vol. v, pp. 85-86.

ing the fact that Byzantinism was the most definite historical type ("for the state it means autocracy, for religion—Orthodoxy, for the moral world—contempt for earthly things, repugnance for the dreams about the earthly happiness of people, humility") and that the "Byzantine spirit with its principles and influences, like the complicated tissues of the nervous system, penetrated he whole Russian social organism," he proclaimed that: "Russia should be frozen so that she may not decay," as every living process ends in death and decomposition—the state in which Western Europe now finds itself. Although there are no universalistic elements in the Russian past, the Russian civilization must be preserved as it is.

For Leont'ev all means are good as "politics are not ethics." He calls for courage, for people who will not fear the words "reaction" and "reactionary," who will understand "that nothing can be achieved without violence" and that in order to stop the "defrosting" of Russia "retrogressive reforms" are indispensable, first of all "the fight against public education because if Russia has succeeded in her resistance against the spirit of the times, she owes it to the ignorance of the Russian people."[32]

5. Tyutchev (1803-1873)

Perhaps from the purely chronological point of view Tyutchev should have been discussed before Danilevsky. Indeed some of Danilevsky's most essential views were first brought to public opinion in 1869 in the review *Zarya,* in which he said that: "Europe not accidentally but in her very essence is hostile to us. Therefor only when she is in conflict with herself might she be safe for us."[33] In a letter to Aksakov on the second of October, 1867, Tyutchev said: "Civil war in the West is our best political ally."

[32] K. Leont'ev, *Vostok, Rossiya i Slavyanstvo,* vol. I, vol. II, Moscow, 1885-1886; vol. I, p. 81; vol. II pp. 86, 109-120, 78-152, 180, 24-27; quoted by P. N. Milyukov (Milioukov), *Le mouvement intellectuel russe,* Paris, 1918, pp. 400-410.

[33] K. Pigarev, F. I. "Tyutchev i problemy vneshnei politiki Rosii" in *Literaturnoe Nasledstvo,* vol. 19-21, Moscow, 1935, p. 206.

(cf. *ibid.*) However, as early as June 26, 1864, Tyutchev wrote to his sister: "I of course am not one of those who in their gloomy patriotism would like to doom Russia to permanent solitude, isolate and seclude her forever. I admit agreements, but on the condition that they be only *accidental* and that, accepting them, they never forget the truth-dogma, that between Russia and the West there can be no alliance, neither for the sake of interest, nor for the sake of principles, that in the West there exists not a single interest, not a single tendency which would not conspire against Russia, especially against her future, and which would not try to harm us. And this is why the only *natural* policy of Russia toward the Western powers must be not an alliance with one or the other of these powers, but *disunion,* division of them, because, only when they are divided among themselves do they cease to be hostile to us—because of impotence and, of course, never because of conviction. This severe truth will perhaps shock the tender souls, but in the end this is the law of our existence as a tribe and as an empire, and the only way of ignoring this is to cease to be Russian."[34]

The case of Tyutchev is perhaps the most fascinating. Belonging to a distinguished Russian family, a man with intimate ties with the court, a diplomat, one of the most brilliant Russian poets, the poet of the *Last Love,* the poet of the metaphysic fear of "the cosmos" and the universal "chaos," the poet of nature, the poet who created new rhythms and melodies in Russian poetry, the Russian poet who translated Goethe, Byron, Schiller, Heine, Lamartine, and who himself wrote poems in French, a man who was plunged in religious indifference and scepticism, a pantheist, an "ashamed atheist" who was "entirely foreign in his domestic life not only to orthodox customs of the church, but alien to the traditions of the Russian church,"[35] (words of Aksakov), a man who had an arrogant disdain for the "gloomy grey Russian life," in which he saw only "offices and barracks, *chin* and *knut,*" a man

[34] *Ibid.,* pp. 205-206.

[35] A. Lezhnev, *Dva Poeta,* Gos. Izd., 1934, p. 22.

who spent most of his time abroad courting Germans, French, Italians, establishing very friendly relations with Heine, Schelling, and other distinguished poets, writers, and intellectuals in Europe, married to two foreign women who did not know Russian, a cosmopolitan in his private life, "entertaining German barons, poets, and diplomats," always speaking French[36]—Tyutchev became not only in his political treaties, articles, and diplomatic reports but also in his poetry the most violent advocate of Slavophil and Panslavistic ideas and of Russian anti-Europeanism.

There were, of course, slight distinctions between him and the Muscovite Slavophils. The kind of patriarchial democratism which characterized them, their adulation of the Russian peasant, their theory about the Russian village community—for all these things Tyutchev cared very little. His primary interests were connected with foreign affairs. He was the "minister of foreign affairs" of the Slavophils. Therefore the Slavic problem was always important to him. He wrote and published many political poems addressed to the Slavs and to the Czechs and poems connected with the Polish problem,—but again in a very peculiar way. When Murav'ev the "hangman" plunged the Polish Insurrection of 1863 into massacres and blood, Tyutchev addressed to him a homage of greatest thankfulness and admiration. And when the grandson of Suvorov, the famous hero of the Prague massacre in Warsaw in 1794, appeared decent enough to refuse participation in a collective address to Murav'ev, Tyutchev launched a mischievous and sarcastic epigram in which he made fun of Suvorov's misplaced humanitarianism. Besides, he, in 1866 wrote a poem glorifying Murav'ev's memory. True enough that in 1831 his attitude had been a little different. He wrote at that time a poem by which Poles have very often been lulled and which was usually quoted as a Russian pro-Polish text. First of all there is, I think, a kind of moral insanity in bringing the name of Tyutchev as a symbol of Russian-Polish fraternity; the name of the poet who in the most cynical way sang the glory of Murav'ev! Besides, even

36 Lezhnev, *ibid.*, p. 20.

the poem of 1831 gives a rather peculiar consolation to the Poles—this is what Tyutchev says to them: "Believe the word of the Russian nation: we shall sacredly preserve your ashes, and our common freedom as a Phoenix will find its birth in them."

In the recent works devoted to Tyutchev such as those of Pigarev, Gippius, Stremoukhov, Lezhnev, one important detail has been revealed. Both the Slavophils and Tyutchev representing the landed Russian nobility, were deeply impressed by the revolutionary movements in Europe. Tyutchev in his anti-revolutionism, became a kind of Russian Joseph de Maistre and he very soon came to the conception that in Europe there existed two powers: Revolution and Russia. He developed this conception in his articles and poems and for many years he was busy with the organization of Russian propaganda in Europe for the spreading of his political ideas.

One of his most significant poems in this respect was the poem *The Sea and the Rock,* in which he gives a picture of how the gigantic foot of the rock will appease the stormy waves of the sea. The idea which was symbolically presented in this poem was developed in a political language in his article *Russia and Revolution* written in 1848.[37] His conception of the greatness of Russia developed as a function of the mission which he attributed to Russia; and here his imagination becomes boundless. In his famous poem *Russian Geography* he mentions Moscow, Petersburg, and Constantinople as the *capitals* of the Russian empire, in which he sees "seven interior seas and seven great rivers from the Nile to the Neva, from the Elbe to China, from the Volga to the Euphrates, from the Ganges to the Danube—this is the Russian empire."

This was written by a poet who, although he revealed in his lyrical poetry his tenderness for the "original charm" of the "poor villages," "humble nakedness," "boring nature," of the "land of everlasting patience," did not himself care at all for the Russian landscape. This is what he wrote in a letter to his wife:

[37] Pigarev, *op. cit., Literaturnoe Nasledstvo,* pp. 195-196.

"An immense plain—the Scythian plain which you didn't like on my relief map, where it spreads out like an enormous spot, is not more pleasant in reality."[38]

Not less striking than his *Russian Geography* are his historical views and the formulation of the Russian mission which we find in his two French articles *Russia and Revolution* and *Rome and the Roman Question,* and in a large work which he was preparing — *Russia and the West.* In all these writings he draws an apocalyptic picture of the destruction of the Europe of Charlemagne, of the Europe of the Treaties of 1815, of the destruction of the Papacy, Catholicism, and Protestantism. He demands a definitive formation of a great Orthodox empire, "the legitimate empire of the East, which will be realized by the absorption of Austria by Russia and the 'return' (*sic!*) of Constantinople to Russia and by the union of the two churches." The conclusion of these events will be symbolized by the Russian tsar as the Orthodox emperor in Constantinople, as the master and protector of Italy and Rome, and by an Orthodox pope in Rome as a subject of the emperor.[39] In his article *Papacy and the Roman Question* he constantly attacks all kinds of "usurpatory" tendencies of Western thought and seems completely unaware of the fact that his own conception represents the most fantastic historical usurpation—although not at all unreal in the light of our days. This is the way in which he ends his article: "Permit me to recall in conclusion, an incident connected with the visit which the Emperor of Russia made to Rome in 1846. One may still remember perhaps the general emotion with which the Emperor was received upon his appearance in the Church of St. Peter,—this was the appearance of the Orthodox Emperor who returned to Rome after several centuries of absence—and the electric flash which went through the crowd when it saw him going to pray at the tombs of the apostles. This emotion was legitimate. The prostrated Emperor was not alone; all Russia was prostrated with him.

38 Lezhnev, *op. cit.*, p. 24.
39 Pigarev, *op. cit.*, p. 196.

Let us hope that he did not pray in vain before the holy relics!"[40] The *Revue des Deux Mondes* published this article and prefaced it with a small and rather melancholic note: "Charlemagne is no longer in Paris or in Aix-la-Chapelle, he is in Moscow or in St. Petersburg. And one must above all keep in mind the fact that the new Charlemagne coming to Rome clearly pretends to bring, as the former one, a great material power, but he has no intention of coming there to find a spiritual, a moral consecration of his power. Far from that; it is he who, so to say, comes to consecrate the papacy. . . ." "One might make many other reflections upon this subject, and give some peculiar details on the march of ideas in one part of Russian society, and show how the school which formerly had Monsieur de Maistre as its chief and which made its gospel from the doctrines of *Du Pape* arrived gradually, by a kind of national logic, to find that the real pope was the tsar."[41]

But what is especially striking here is that Tyutchev appeared able to marry in his thought and in his heart this conception of a Russian Charlemagne in Constantinople and Rome with his own formula of Russia, a land of "officers, barracks, *chin* and *knut*." Justly asks Lezhnev: "In the name of what is the 'humble Russia' to obtain 'the thunder of earth and sword of heaven?' . . ." "Tsarist Russia spreads like an enormous spot over the map of the world—this is Tyutchev's 'Russian geography'. . . . What is Russia promising to those innumerable nations which she intends to subdue? Nothing but the quietness of the cemetery or of a northern desert."[42] Indeed this whole transformation of "barracks" into St. Sophia and St. Peter is a terrible fairy tale and on this occasion Lezhnev says that the theocratic tiara suits Nicholas I as "a saddle a cow."[43] As we know there are some other candidates for the same saddle. In his poems launched against the Vatican Tyutchev attacks the Pope because of his "fatal word": "the freedom of conscience is delirium." And this was written by

[40] *Revue des Deux Mondes*, January 1, 1850, p. 133.
[41] *Op. cit.*, p. 118.
[42] A. Lezhnev, *Dva Poeta* . . . Gos. Izd., 1934, pp. 13-14.
[43] *Ibid.*, p. 15.

a Russian of the time of Nicholas! Certainly the most deceiving trait in the whole Tyutchev episode is his hypocrisy—that play of his with love and hatred. Repulsive indeed is this Tartuffe who so much resembles Saltykov's Yudushka Golovlev, constantly spreading around him his ointment of sacred hatred. The starting point of all his conceptions, as I showed before, was his fear of European revolution. This also explains in part his attitude toward the Polish insurrections and toward the Hungarian Insurrection of 1848. Russia had to be strong in order to be able to save the world from the catastrophe. We see here the presence of his former altruistic conceptions—Europe is in a state of ideological disaster, the world is in danger—the "Russian rock" of legitimism will save it! However, this was not quite so. Russia's tragic days during the Crimean campaign brought our political Tartuffe to some different views. He consoled himself by the following significant consideration: "In this ultimate fight we should perish if the West were one, but it is two: the red one and the one which must be absorbed by it. We have been opposing it for forty years, and now here we are on the border of the precipice. And now the red one in its turn will save us."[44] This is the best revelation of Tyutchev's universal historiosophic conceptions.

Merezhkovsky once justly observed that "one" of the traits of Russian Slavophilism was its "softbodiness," bonelessness and inability, lack of desire to carry its thought to the end. And Tyutchev "puts bones into the body and dots the *i's;* his logic is merciless." . . . "Tyutchev is clever, and his politics are not stupid; but as far as his conscience is concerned it enters least of all with his politics."[45] Not only hypocrisy but really a complete lack of human loyalty characterized him. During the whole of the life of Nicholas I this "bishop of Russian imperialism" did nothing but spread incense around Nicholas. But as soon as the latter died, after the Crimean War, Tyutchev shouted: "Thou wert not

[44] Pigarev, *op. cit.*, p. 177.
[45] Lezhnev, *op. cit.*, p. 13.

a tsar but an actor" and expressed his indignation about "the monstrous stupidity of this ill-fated man."

This was one missionary of holy Russia, a prophet who appeared before the world with "a crucifix and a dagger" in his hands. Let us now meet one who for the triumph of his Russian truth was ready to change his crucifix into a dagger.

6. Dostoevsky (1821-1881)

Without entering into a detailed description of Dostoevsky's well-known messianic conceptions about the "God-bearing nation" and all his speculations about Russia and Europe, which he develops in his novels and short stories as well as in his *Diary of a Writer*, I shall confine myself to his general philosophy of history. The first thing I should like to stress is that the book of Dostoevsky is a book almost as much about Europe as about Russia—if not even more about Europe. His "Russian boys" are constantly busy with the Russian God—but even more with the Catholic God—with the Inquisition, with socialism, European rationalism, atheism, revolutionism, and so on. And this is so in spite of the fact that in his novels we remain in Russia, constantly in Russian monasteries, taverns, St. Petersburg apartments or streets, or in some provincial Russian towns. Another thing which should be remembered is that Dostoevsky from his very childhood and youth was a pupil first of all of European literature. If one should try to discover in the texts of Dostoevsky any proof of genuine and real sympathy for that European civilization which formed his art and thought, one would undoubtedly be unsuccessful. He very often declaims his enthusiastic love for Europe, but that love is addressed only to the "holy stones" of the "European cemetery." On the other hand the types of Europeans who appear in his novels—French, Italians, Poles—as well as the pictures of Europe taken either from the gambling casinos, London streets, French railways, or Parisian department stores, are deeply repulsive—with some few exceptions: Mr. Astlee in *The Gambler* and

Dostoevsky's feeling for Germany, especially for Bismarck. This obvious antipathy, if not hatred, appeared in Dostoevsky after his Siberian exile. One would be willing to explain this by the negative impression which Europe made upon Dostoevsky when he visited it. However, I think that the motives of his feelings were of a different nature. Dostoevsky was sent to Siberia because of his European infatuations. We know how deeply he suffered during his exile and indeed how unpleasantly he denied his former opinions and appeared ready to embrace less dangerous and less politically compromising roads of thought, although in his situation it was difficult to be heroic to the end. Dostoevsky suffered because of Europe, and I think that this personal motive has to be taken into consideration. It would be useless here to quote all Dostoevsky's astonishing and fantastic conceptions of what he thought to be the real historical relationship beween Russia and Europe. We know that Dostoevsky was always ready to say that "to be a real Russian means to be a real European," and that some of his heroes felt when abroad that they were the unique Europeans among Europeans, that French were French, English English, Germans German, but only Russians besides being Russians were also Europeans, and have I to recall his really incredible and almost absurd speculations about the "Russian seekers"—Onegin and Aleko—in his Pushkin speech? Only an aberration of mind could bring one to assert that Onegin killed his friend and Aleko his wife perhaps because of their longing for universalistic ideals. Dostoevsky's deep belief was that only the Russian thought was able to embrace universalistic goals. By these trends of his beliefs he certainly closely approached the Slavophils and later the Russian *narodniki* as well as the Panslavists; and in his political articles he very often waved the banners of Slavic brotherhood, of a Panslav union under Russian leadership. And one easily remembers his piercing and hysterical shouts: "Constantinople must be ours!" But not all these slogans which, after all, in Dostoevsky's time had become trivial clichés, should interest us here. More significant, as I mentioned before, is Dostoevsky's general philosophy of history, and this has been brilliantly studied and presented by L. Grossman in his study *Dostoevsky and Europe*. Dostoevsky likes to hide the horrible truth about man and mankind with the help of a Russian ikon which miraculously allows him to escape from responsibility. His heroes very often act in the same way, and Dostoevsky usually insinuates that their monstrous moral degradations are due to Western European influences. He constantly uses the method of substitution, attaching European labels to the most ferocious manifestations of his own thought. He very freely uses the author's privilege of disclaiming responsibility for the opinions of his heroes. Shestov, however, seized Dostoevsky in his elusive jumps of thought and brought him to trial. As far as the purely political historiosophic conceptions of Dostoevsky are concerned, Grossman did the same. These are the general conclusions which the "complex philosophy of Dostoevsky" implies: "The mission of the Slavs is to decide and finish the thousand-year old internal conflict of the Roman-German world to the advantage of the Germans and to the mutual domination of the Slavs and the Germans in Europe."[46] Ancient Rome was the source of European civilization; gradually losing its pagan character the Roman idea of universal monarchy was transformed into the European ideal of universal union in Christ. With centuries this great historical conception split— in the East appeared the Slavic idea of union based on the gospel, in the West—the Roman Catholic idea of a universal monarchy with the Pope at its head. The Papacy yielded to the third temptation of the devil and "sold Christ for earthly domination." The next phase of the development of the Catholic idea, and this means the next deformation of Christian ideals, is to be found in France which created Socialism. In this period the definite triumph of materialism over spiritualism was achieved.

To this extreme historical formulation of Western conceptions was opposed the German idea which, from the time of Arminius

[46] L. Grossman, *Tvorchestvo Dostoevskogo*, Moscow, 1928, p. 198. All of Dostoevsky's political system is to be found in the *Diary of a Writer* and in novels like *The Possessed* and in his letters. I follow Grossman for lack of space.

to Bismarck, represented only a negative idea of protest against Rome. This negative "idealism" was the main source of national German inspiration. But at the moment of the final German victory Germany, lacking its object, will be also lacking inspiration, and this will bring her to spiritual death. The final course of this worldly struggle will take on an apocalyptical character. The Pope, having lost his allies in the persons of emperors and kings, will throw himself into the arms of the proletariat, trying to become a socialistic vicar of St. Peter. Against this will rise Germany for the ultimate battle. But the last word will be said by the united East. In alliance with Germany, Russia will destroy the "two-headed monster" of Catholicism and Socialism, and then will be established the domination of the Germans, now inspired by Russia, in the West, and the domination of Russia in the East.[47] As I mentioned before (and Grossman brings many proofs of this), Dostoevsky had a great admiration for Bismarck, the "iron chancellor." He hoped that the creator of the formula of "union in blood and iron" would split Europe with his powerful sword, and that "after rivers of blood and hundreds of millions of heads" the world would accept the new word of the Slavic gospel. And this was to be what Dostoevsky called "The free Panslavic union of Europe."[48] The Franco-Prussian war became a source of inspiration for his conception. "Just like the most aggressive German professors he calls for a march against France" and "wants to enlighten Europe by the light of the gospel, by Bismarck's formula, and by the direct help of the German armies." France will be broken by "blood and iron," "Tsargrad" will be in the hands of Russia, England and France will be defeated by the Russian-German armies, and so the triumph of Russian Christianity will be achieved.[49] In other words he follows the reasonings of his Raskolnikov: "*vive la guerre eternelle*—till the new Jerusalem."

[47] Grossman, *op. cit.*, pp. 199-203.
[48] Grossman, *op. cit.*, pp. 207-208.
[49] Grossman, *op. cit.*

It is true enough that in the very last period of his life as if having lost his hopes for Russia to achieve that universal mission he suddenly called: "To Asia! To Asia!" "To that great mother of all religions, to the original 'neighborhood of God,' to the sacred nearness of the thousand-year-old contemplators of heavenly revelations—to India and Palestine. . . ."[50]

7. Bakunin (1814-1876)

There is a literary theory that Dostoevsky's "possessed" Stavrogin is a fictionized portrait of Bakunin. The author of this hypothesis, L. Grossman, accumulated extremely interesting proofs for his discovery. I shall not enter into an analysis of this theory, but it is quite true that the moral labyrinths of Bakunin's life and political revolutionary career lend themselves very well to this comparison. Bakunin's biographers made great efforts to explain and justify by political Machiavellianism Bakunin's rampant attitude towards Nicholas I and Alexander II, and his behavior in Siberia, which was morally paradoxical to say the least. Therefore, there is no doubt that the ideological prestige of Bakunin's political activities as well as of his writings is strongly contaminated by his very doubtful personality. His *Confession* and his letter to Alexander II surpassed the repentence of the Decembrists, the agony of Chaadaev, and the yielding of Dostoevsky. His infatuation for Murav'ev-Amursky and the role he played in the Irkutsk society are not less astonishing. However, he has his place and an important one in the development of Slavophil and Panslavistic ideas. Bakunin represents a kind of revolutionary Panslavism, but in this field of his political conceptions one may find the same inconsistency that characterized his moral attitude.

National and Slav feelings as well as feelings of sympathy for Poland had been awakened in him by Lelewel, famous Polish historian and geographer, radical democrat and member of the Revolutionary Government of 1830-31, during their meeting in Brus-

[50] Grossman, p. 213.

sels. Lelewel "told him about the primitive democratic Polish municipality, about the agrarian Slavic collectivity, about brotherly institutions and customs distorted later by the class structure and the enslavement of people which came from the West. At that time he conceived a new goal for himself which was "a Russian revolution and a republican federation of all Slavic lands, and the establishment of one indivisible Slavic republic, federative only as regards administration, and politically centralized."[51] At that time, under the influence of western European populism and socialism on one side and, on the other, of his intimate contacts with the Polish emigration in Paris, Bakunin started to crystallize his own Russian populist and revolutionary ideas. The first manifestation of these crystallized ideas took place in Paris in 1847 when he delivered his famous Polish speech at the commemoration of the Polish Insurrection of 1830-31. In this speech he attacked Nicholas I, he asserted that the Russian and Polish nations must be reconciled, that both were paying for the discord introduced by Russian autocracy, and that the Russian revolution would bring freedom to both nations. He said that this task could be realized only through the Russian-Polish alliance: without the liberation of Poland, Russian freedom could not be born. And finally he called for the liberation of all Slavic nations in order to bring about the final collapse of despotism in Europe.

A little more complicated was the atmosphere of the Slavic Congress in Prague, in which he took part and delivered several speeches. At that Congress, as we know, Palacký advocated the idea of a Slavic federation with Austria in which the Czechs would play the dominant role. This idea was not popular among other Slavs, and the atmosphere of the Congress was not at all encouraging.

Bakunin first of all stressed the fact that Russia, by enslaving Poland and especially by giving a part of her to the Germans—the main enemies of the Slavic race—tore herself away from Slav-

[51] J. Kucharzewski, *op. cit.*, vol. II, pp. 161-162; cf. also V. Polonsky, *M. A. Bakunin*, vol. I, Gos. Izd., 1925, pp. 155 156.

dom. She could return to Slavdom only by the liberation of Poland. In this point Bakunin was certainly much more consistent than the Muscovite Slavophils ever were. On the other hand, he tried to warn the Congress against narrow nationalism, against hopes attached to the Austrian dynasty as well as against hopes attached to the Russia of Nicholas I: "Entering the Russia of Nicholas I you would enter a coffin without any national life or any freedom." In several articles such as *The Foundations of a New Slavic Policy, The Foundations of a Slavic Federation, The Interior Organization of Slavic Nations,* and finally in his *Manifesto to the Slavs,* he formulated his view on that future federation. He dreamt about the abolition of tsardom through Russian revolution, which was to be preceded by a Slavic revolution. He thought that the Slavs under the leadership of a free Russia would fight against Austria, Turkey, Germany, Hungary, and even against the whole world if that were demanded by the interests of the Slavic Union. This Slavic Union was to contain not only Slavic peoples but also the Magyars and Greeks. It would be an Eastern world with Constantinople as its capital and it would be opposed to the Western world. The political regime of the Union would be republican but without a parliament, a dictatorship would be established especially because of Russia, which would be unable to reach a higher level of civilization without it.[52]

These articles and his manifesto passed without any great effect. His striking idea of dictatorship representing a kind of anarchical despotism was an idea which obsessed him and which reappeared in different forms on many occasions during his life. He even admitted that a Russian tsar, Nicholas I or Alexander II, or a general, such as Murav'ev-Armursky or Nicholas Ignat'ev, might be a beneficent dictator over the Slavs. The next most important manifestation of Bakunin's Panslavism took place after his Siberian exile, when in 1862 he published his revolutionary *Manifesto to Russian, Polish, and all Slavic friends.* As a matter of fact,

[52] Polonsky, *op. cit.,* pp. 221-227.

he returned in this manifesto to his former ideas—of an agrarian revolution, of the abolishment of bureaucracy and the privileged classes and a federation of Slavic peoples. Characteristically enough, and this is what Kucharzewski stresses in his studies on Bakunin, Bakunin's relationship to Poland was a very peculiar phenomenon. He was attracted by Poles (in Siberia he married a young girl of Polish origin), he always spoke very warmly in his writings and manifestos to Poles, but on the other hand these contacts with Poles each time, just as during his rencontre with Lelewel, aroused in him Russian national feelings. I may add that in his youth he greatly admired Pushkin's anti-Polish odes. When discussing the social structure of the future Slavic federation, he strongly stressed the fact that that structure "will in no way be different from ours." It is clear enough that his manifesto expressing such views on the future of the "Slavs liberated by a revolutionary Russia" could not awake great enthusiasm among them. Hence Bronislaw Zaleski, a distinguished Polish émigré, wrote a long answer to Bakunin's manifesto in which he said that: "Bakunin wants not only the abolishment of despotism but he also wants the destruction of everything which existed before, in other words he wants a deluge—and into the ark, which would save from this deluge a creative idea for mankind, he puts only the Russian village community with its common landownership as it had been formed in serfdom. Hence any individual property must be abolished forever. . . . How many ruins it will be necessary to make in order to prepare that vast pasturage—is what the new reformer does not take into consideration."[53]

Besides this, Bakunin pushed the Russian frontiers of his federation so far into the West that indeed only a very small part of Poland would remain as a Polish entity in the Union. The Polish periodical *Review of Polish Affairs* ended its analysis of Baku-

[53] Kucharzewski, *op cit.,* vol. II, p. 443.

nin's manifesto by saying that "Russian revolutionism is, in its consequences for Poland, similar to Russian despotism."[54]

I shall not enter the further complication of his relations with the Poles, the details of his self-imposed activities in the Polish Insurrection of 1863, nor the mutual deceptions between himself and Poland.

After the Polish Insurrection the Panslavic conceptions played a less important role in the second part of his life with the exception of his program for the Slavic section of the International in Zürich in 1872.[55]

8. Herzen (1812-1870)

Herzen also has some ties with Dostoevsky and these ties are to he found in his critique of the West and in his enthusiasm for the Russian village community which, as we know, was one of the chief objects of admiration of the Muscovite Slavophils though they first heard of it from the German Haxthausen who in 1845 published his work on his travels in Russia. Herzen's cult of the Russian peasant, his populism, made of him a precursor of *narodnichestvo.*

That evolution was not quite simple—Herzen, before his trip to Europe and stay there, was one of the most enthusiastic Russian Westerners, and he very often opposed the Muscovite Slavophils. His stay in Europe changed his opinions, and there he became one of the most violent fighters against *l'esprit bourgeois* of the Western civilization. The conception of the dying Western civilization became a kind of obsession with him and against these constantly drawn pictures of the chaos, agony, and disease of Europe suddenly arose in the mind of this former Westerner his Russian and even Slavophil messianism. To Chaadaev's formula that the past of Russia is empty, the present unbearable, and that she has no future, Herzen replied that the "past of the Russian

54 Kucharzewski, *op. cit.*, vol. II, p. 412.

55 Cf. Kucharzewski, *op. cit.*, and E. H. Carr, *M. Bakunin*, London, 1937.

people is dark; its present is terrible, but it has rights to the future." And he filled that future first of all with the hope that Russia would avoid the poison of Western Philistinism. "Philistinism—this is the last word of civilization, based on the absolute autocracy of property." Russia, by the fact that she knew only communal property, had indeed every possibility of avoiding the poisonous influences of the West.

Certainly Herzen's disgust for European Philistinism was in some degree justified, but the *esprit bourgeois* does not exhaust the content of the Western civilization. It is amazing to see how quickly that former Russian Westerner lost his psychological inclination toward Europe—toward the lights of European thought—toward the intellectual energy of Europe, its philosophy, arts, science, traditions of freedom.

In addition, Herzen had a deep belief in the essentially revolutionary mind of the Russians. "The thinking Russian is the most independent man in the world. What can stop him? Respect for the past? But what is the starting point of the history of modern Russia, if not the negation of nationality and tradition? On the other hand, the past of the Western nations has only a didactic value for us. We in no way consider ourselves the executors of their will. We share your doubts, but your faith does not warm us. We share your hatreds, but we do not understand your attachment to the heritage of your ancestors; we are too oppressed, too unhappy to be satisfied with half-freedom. You are bound by scruples, you are stopped by reservations of mind, we have no scruples, no reservations, we are lacking only in power."[56]

We have here a kind of combination of Chaadaev's pessimism and the Muscovite Slavophils' optimism. The essential idea of Herzen, a very Slavophil and very Russian idea, was that "the western fruit will ripen in the Slavic world." Kucharzewski, whom I quote, very justly states: "The West produces thoughts, Russia utilizes them; to the West is alloted the task of creating, to

[56] Kucharzewski, *op. cit.*, vol. I, pp. 395-396.

Russia—the role of leadership among future mankind, with the help of the ripe fruits of the work of other nations."[57]

When dealing with Herzen as well as with Tyutchev and Dostoevsky—but I think with Herzen even more than with the latter, one is really amazed to see how well and deeply he knew Europe. The more astonishing is, then, that lack of attachment and love for European tradition. They understand everything, but they love nothing.

All these thoughts were developed in Herzen's work *From the Other Shore* (1849), in his letter to Michelet, and a little later, in 1854, in his letter to Riberol, editor of the review *L'Homme*, and in his letter to Linton, editor of the *English Republic.* In this last publication he develops his Panslavic system in connection with the Crimean War. He states that Poland was the one Slavic country who preserved her independence. "Only Poland remained independent and strong, but this because she was less Slavic than the other nations, she was Catholic, and Catholicism is a flagrant contradiction of the Slavic genius. Hence Poland preserved independence by weakening her racial ties and by coming nearer to the Western states."

One must not, forget however, that in 1863 and in 1864, as I mentioned before, Herzen in his *Kolokol* published the most penetrating articles filled with great sympathy and admiration for Poland and the Poles.[58] He greets the Crimean War as "the beginning of a Slavic era, the Slavs will raise the banner of Socialism, and Constantinople will be the capital of the united Slavs. . . . Constantinople is one real capital of the united Slavs, it is the Rome of the Eastern Church, the center of all Slavo-Greeks—Byzantium, surrounded by a Slavic-Hellenic population . . . In any case this war is the *introduzione maestosa e marziale* of the Slavic world into universal history and at the same time *una marcia funebre* of the old world."[59]

[57] *Op. cit.,* p. 397.
[58] Lednicki, W.: "Russian-Polish Cultural Relations," *New Europe,* 1944.
[59] Kucharzewski, *op. cit.,* pp. 399-400.

Yes, Herzen was certainly one of the most brilliant and penetrating singers of the Russian requiem for Europe, but even in this he was a pupil of the Europeans—of the Saint-Simonists, Fourier, Cabet, and Proudhon, who violently criticized contemporary European civilization. They did for Herzen what later in the seventies Renan did for Strakhov. Strakhov filled his book *The Struggle with the West in Our Literature* with Renan's criticism. But Renan did even more—he suggested some ideas to the Russians which they didn't forget. Strakhov quotes one of them: "There still exists in the world a reserve of barbarian forces, which are almost all in the hands of Russia. As long as the civilized nations conserve their solid organization, the role of these barbarians will be almost null; but without doubt, if (from which God preserve us!) an epidemic of selfishness and anarchy brings our western states to destruction, the barbarians will accomplish their duty, which consists in raising the many forces in spoiled civilizations, in producing the vivifying current of instinct which was lost when reflection destroyed subordination, to show that readiness to sacrifice one's life for faithfulness to one's sovereign (a deed which a democrat considers low and absurd) is a source of power and leads to the possession of the world."[60]

The case of Herzen is particularly eloquent: it shows how demoralizing were the Slavophil and Panslavistic conceptions if a man of Herzen's caliber, Europeanism, and superior generosity could find himself in such a moral and spiritual impass.

The ultimate expression of this eastern Messianism suggested by the Russian Westerners is to be found in the *Scythians*, a poetical message which Alexander Blok addressed to the West: "Now rejoicing, now sorrowing, now flowing with black blood, she (Russia) looks at you with hatred and with love. . . . We love everything—the heat of cold numbers and the gift of divine visions, everything appeals to us—the perspicacious Gallic thought and the gloomy German genius. . . . We remember everything—the hell of Parisian streets and the refreshing coolness of Venice,

[60] Strakhov, *Bor'ba s zapadom v nashey literature*, St. Petersburg, 1882, vol. I, p. 324.

the distant aroma of the lemon groves, and the smoky buildings in Cologne. . . . We love the body, the taste and the color of it, and its oppressive deadly odor. . . . Is it our fault if your skeleton cracks in our heavy, soft paws?"

9. Reactions Among the Slavs Toward Panslavic Conceptions

In the beginning of the nineteenth century the Southern Slavs attracted no great attention from the world. However, after the Russian-Turkish wars of the time of Catherine II they began to move more distinctly on the political stage of Europe, as Pypin justly says.[61] The fight of Serbia for her independence, the fight of the Montenegrians against the Turks and their resistance against the French (I am still following Pypin), Illyria established by Napoleon—all this revealed the existence of energetic Slavic elements in the Near East. To this should be added facts as Vuk Karadžić's collection of popular songs in which the deeds of Serbian national heroes were glorified. The fights of the Croatians against the Hungarians, the Russian intervention in the Hungarian Revolution of 1848, the part which Russia took in the liberation of Serbia, all created an atmosphere in which the Panslavistic conceptions could, of course, count on a sympathetic reaction. However, as far as the final results are concerned, Russian Panslavism was not at all successful even among the Southern Slavs. The Croatians, who in the forties when fighting against the Hungarians were dreaming of Slavic unity, very soon abandoned these dreams and looked more and more toward the West for help against Turkey. The Serbs in spite of their religious ties with Russia were returning closer and closer to the traditions of Obradović and of Vuk Karadžić and his reform which brought the Serbian cultural development away from Russian influences, and to conceptions of a national state, and of the building of a national culture. Russia's tactless approaches to Serbia, the Rus-

[61] *Op. cit.*, p. 11.

sian tendency to consider Serbs as merely a new sort of Russians and the Serbian intelligentsia a class which did not represent the real feelings of the people, and facts such as the Russian correspondents calling Serbs "Russians of Belgrade *gubernia*" clarified the situation so that the famous letter of Khomyakov to the Serbs from Moscow published in 1861 created a very unfavorable impression in Serbia; and this found its expression in the answer of the Serbian scholar Daničić.[62]

In Bulgaria the situation has for centuries been even more complicated and dramatic because of the fact that when fighting for their national independence and national culture, the Bulgars had to fight against not only Turks but also Greeks. In spite of the activity of Venelin and the role which Russia played in the restoration of Bulgarian independence and the ties between Bulgarian intellectuals and Russian scholarship, the Panslavistic conceptions could not destroy the existence of strongly nationalistic tendencies.[63]

Among the Czechs and Slovaks, where in spite of their deep and pathetic Germanization there appeared the first great scholars in the field of Slavic philology and history—Dobrovský, Šafařik, Palacký, Havliček, and Jungmann (who, by the way, very often wrote in Latin and in German), the Panslavistic tendencies received a rather cold reception. As I mentioned above, it was only at the time of Jungmann, Rautenkranz, and Puchmajer that the pro-Russian feelings of the Czechs were strong—with Kollár givin the most eloquent expression of these feelings. Palacký, as we know, was an advocate of a Slavic federation but under Austrian leadership. He was too close to the Western traditions to feel any enthusiasm for a conception which would bring all Western Slavs under Russian domination. Such was, by the way, the attitude of the Congress in Prague in 1848. This point of view

[62] Pypin, *op. cit.*, p. 160.

[63] Here must also be stressed the religious pressure in Bulgaria coming from Constantinople and the fact that elements of national consciousness were preserved only among the people and the émigrés. Important, too, was the role of the monk, Paissy, his activity on Mt. Athos, and his collection of Bulgarian legends, songs, historical documents, and his *History of Bulgaria*, of 1762.

was formulated in *The Scientific Dictionary*, a Czech Encyclopedia.[64] The article referring to Panslavism is very reserved. The speculations of the Muscovite Slavophils on the item of Hussism as a purely Slavic movement which presumably had its ties with Slavic Orthodoxy did not appear very convincing to the Czechs.

In general, the Prague Congress of 1848 reduced the Panslavic tendencies to a formula of political organization of Austria which would satisfy the national political demands of the Slavs. In this way was developed a special Austrian Panslavism directed against Russia and later called Austroslavism. The same trends might be discovered in the so-called "Slavic Union" in the Vienna Parliament of 1908. However, under the leadership of the Czech Kramař there developed at the same time the so-called neo-Slavism, which stressed the political solidarity of all Slavic nations on the condition of complete cultural equality, but which certainly contained pro-Russian tendencies. The movement was created in 1908 at the Slav Congress in Prague, followed by a Congress in Petersburg in 1909 and one in Sofia in 1910. There took place only vague and very general formulations of Slavic mutual respect, sympathy, and efforts to calm the inter-Slavic antagonisms —Russian-Polish, Serbo-Croatian, Serbo-Bulgarian, and so on. In spite of the participation in this movement of several important political leaders among the Slavs, it did not reach any concrete results. Most Poles and Russians very soon abandoned it. The War of 1914 brought again to the fore ideas of Slavic union, proclaimed this time by representatives of Russian public opinion and by the Russian government. I should also mention the outstanding activity aiming at spiritual and intellectual collaboration among the Slavs of the brilliant Polish scholar, thinker, and writer Marian Zdziechowski, who established his Slavic Club in Cracow with its review *The Slavic World* before the War of 1914 and who entertained close relations with the Russian sympathizers of these trends, about whom I shall speak below.

[64] Quoted by Pypin, *op. cit.*, pp. 152-153.

Almost at the same time there reappeared in Russia a spiritual, idealistic, mystic approach to the Slavophil conceptions. It was a kind of continuation of neo-Slavic trends. One may find in the writings of distinguished and honest politicians, poets and writers such as V. I. Ivanov, S. N. Bulgakov, and Prince E. N. Trubetskoy items connected with this idealism and mysticism. These trends reappeared during the War of 1914. They were preceded by the old Muscovite "Society of Slavic Reciprocity" which was a quite honorable institution and by the subsequent "Society of Slavic Culture" in which the progressive elements among Russian and Polish politicians and scholars met, such as Professor Korsh, Prince E. N. Trubetskoy, Alexander Lednicki, and some others. The aim of this society was to pacify inter-Slavic relations primarily by the help of cultural activities.[65]

Some of the Czechs belonging to the period preceding neo-Slavism, however, remained faithful to their pro-Russian feelings in face of the opposition of Palacký and Havliček. So Kollár, who even in his *Slávy Dcera* excluded Emilia Plater, the Polish heroine of 1830-31, from paradise "because this sister fought against brothers, a Slav girl against Slavs," and yet, as Kucharzewski observes, granted a place in that paradise to Suvorov and Nicholas I, behaved quite disgustingly at the Slavic Congress in Moscow in 1867, where in the absence of the Poles he did his best to please their Russian persecutors.[66]

Thus the Bohemian Panslavism found practically no expression in the nineteenth century other than a purely scientific one—in the fields of Slavic archaeology, Slavic ethnography, Slavic philology, and Slavic history. I can devote no space to Slavic philology here, but I should like to stress the enormous achievements in this field of, besides the Czechs, Polish, Russian, and Serbian scholars, to whom should be added German, French, Italian, Eng-

[65] Details connected with neo-Slavism, with events preceding the First World War, the policy of Izvolsky, the activities of Count Bobrinskoy on one hand—and on the other, activities of people such as Dmowski among the Poles the attitude of the Ukrainians, and the situation in the Balkans preceding the War of 1914 may be found in Dr. Alfred Fischel's *Der Panslavismus bis zum Weltkrieg*, Berlin, 1919.

[66] Kucharzewski, *op. cit.*, vol. II, Warsaw, 1925, p. 303.

lish, and recently American scholars.[67] From this point of view the Czechs might be considered those who prepared weapons for Panslavism. And even in our days the Czech scholars remain faithful to their conceptions of Slavic cultural unity. It should be stressed, however, that the most prominent advocate among the Western Slavs (with the exception of some Poles) was, as mentioned before, the Slovak Štur, who represents an integral Panslavism practically degenerating into Panrussianism.

10. Polish Reactions

The fate of the Slavophil and Panslavistic conceptions among the Poles has not been simple. Without going too far into the past or refering to Boleslaw the Great in whose policy one may find some elements connected with our subject, I shall abandon the effort to find some manifestations of interest for the Slavs in early polish historians, such as Jan Dlugosz (fifteenth century), and leave aside some Polish plans for political union with Russia in the beginning of the seventeenth century.

A forecast of the full growth of Polish Slavophilism was contained in the interesting "Manifesto" of the Sandomierz confederation or "An Address to the Russian Nation," which was published about 1733, at the time when Poland's political power during the Northern War had begun to decline and Russia's to increase. In this manifesto the Poles, expressing in warm words their sympathy for the Russian nation's "yearning for liberty and freedom, and waiting for a favorable moment to abolish serfdom" "frankly encouraged" Russians "to rouse their knightly spirit." The manifesto stressed that the Polish country "wishes for nothing more than your progress and the freedom of the Russian nation."

67 This information may be found in the studies on Slavic Philology of Jagić, Alexander Brückner, Frantsev, Mazon, Máchal, Lehr-Splawiński, W. Lednicki, A. P. Coleman, in different reviews such as *Archiv fur slawische Philologie*, *Revue des Etudes Slaves*, *Le Monde Slave*, *Swiat Slowiański*, *Przeglad Slowiański*, *Slavia*, *Slawische Rundschau*, *The Slavonic and East European Review*, and *The American Slavic and East European Review*.

However, the really first classical manifestation of Slavophilism in Poland, a manifestation which, by the way, preceded the Muscovite Slavophil school, is to be found in Stanislaw Staszic's *Thoughts on the Political Equilibrium of Europe*, written in 1815. It is a work in which Staszic dealt with the problem of the future of Europe, Russia and Poland. He was aware of the catastrophe threatening contemporary civilization, he saw a possibility for the regeneration of mankind through the Slavs. His views of the three main European races, the Romanic, Teutonic and Slavic, led him to the conclusion that only the last of them was destined to bring about such a regeneration; the Romanic nations had, he held, become exhausted by the controversies which originated in the separation of the state from the church. The Germans, on the other hand, had lost their moral unity owing to their sectarianism, which was based on their "excessive inclination for metaphysics." He further emphasized "their indomitable spirit of conquest and their lust for cruelty, which would always have made lasting peace impossible in the world." The Slavic races were developing intensely; owing to their primitive culture they had suffered less from calamities, their inner union was always durable and they were supported by their "religious unity, which for the most part was blended with the secular power." Among the Slavic nations he gave the first place to Russians whose geographical position rendered them more secure and impregnable than the Poles, and whose Orthodox Church enjoyed a higher type of religion, harmoniously blending, as it did, the secular and ecclesiastical forces. At the same time he attributed great importance to the War of 1812 which Russia "made into a Slavic war," thus showing to the world her inexhaustible power. Poland, in her turn, was destined to reveal that idea of unity which would have been realized by Russia had she overcome the political temptation which had beset the German emperors, for such ambitions would only result "in wars between brethren and in bloodshed." Staszic might be indeed considered the precursor of the Muscovite Slavophils; a still nearer approach to them may be found in the article published by

J. Jaroszewicz in 1826: *On the Influence of the Christian Religion upon the Civilization of the Slavs.* Comparing the influence of Byzantium and Rome, Jaroszewicz found Eastern Christianity attractive, whereas he regarded Rome as a power that had destroyed all native power of the Slavs by forcing upon them the Latin language and foreign clergy. "Thus, although the chains of the new religion bound us (the Poles) to the rest of the European nations, yet after its introduction Poland was educated on foreign models, and the result was that the Poles have become foreign to themselves." Some decades later, "Latin Poland," "the unfaithful daughter of the Slavic race," was to suffer the same reproach from Moscow. On the other hand Jaroszewicz openly acknowledged the beneficent influence on Slavic life of the Greek church. Under that influence the Eastern Slavs preserved the habits and rites that had originated in the pagan period. The conclusion was immediate and plain: it was Russia alone that had kept the ancient tribal traditions.

After the events of 1830 and 1846 Polish political thought reverted to principles which approached the systems of Staszic and Jaroszewicz, but of course very often for quite different motives. Limitation of space does not allow me to go into detail nor to quote the opinions of numerous writers who tried to elaborate Slavophil or Panslavic systems. I shall confine myself to only certain ones. Among them, Count Adam Gurowski deserves attention. For the sake of gain he became an apostate from his nation, and disclaiming his early activity (he took part in the Insurrection of 1831 and was one of the founders of the Polish Democratic Society in Paris), he accepted the amnesty, annoyed Paskevich, the Viceroy of Nicholas I in Poland at that time, by applying for remunerative posts, and wangled money from his acquaintances. Finally, during his stay abroad, in 1841-1848, he published a number of dissertations. Inspired by hatred of the Germans, he defended Panslavism and Panrussianism and tried to prove that the former was a historical necessity and that the Russian conquests aimed only at establishing the total independence of the Slavs from foreign influence. The imperialistic Russian tendencies were only an expression of the principle of defense and of reaction against invasion. He thought that "the archangel of independence seemed to have left old Poland forever; there was, however, some future for the ancient Polish nation if it could be dissolved with no matter how great pain and suffering into Russo-Slavism." He looked with particular sympathy on the Orthodox Church, he thought it much superior to Protestantism, which was split into fragments, and to Catholicism. He considered that the Orthodox tenets depended on a sincere faith in Christ and on tradition. Gurowski considered even that the Polish language when compared to the Russian revealed its decadence and senility. He suggested substituting in Poland the Russian language for the Polish—this to be preceded by the introduction of the Slavic language in order to make the change less drastic.

The views of the second Polish Panslavist of the same period, Waclaw Jablonowski, were very similar. A disappointed monarchist, a pessimist in his views on Poland's future, a man who suffered from a nervous disease, he came to the same conclusion—that the only genuinely Slavic current was that of the East, the Russian and Asiatic, which incorporated the deepest tribal characteristics of the Slavs, who had come from Asia, and belonged to the Asiatic system by their character, their political tendencies and their commercial connections. The views show some likeness to the so-called Eurasian doctrine which appeared among the Russian emigrants between the last two World Wars. Jablonowski was very aggressive. In a French book propagating the idea of a Slavic-Russian empire under the leadership of the Tsar with a capital in Kiev, he suggests the organization of Slavic movements in the Balkans and an invasion of the West: "This movement might very easily coincide with some decisive step in the eastern question. A small army corps may cross the Danube and support movements arising on the other side. Europe, Germany and France, will utter a great cry; the latter will perhaps be obliged to break her alliance. That will be the culmination of the crisis. Then the Tsar will come to Poland, take the title of the Tsar of the Slavs and proclaim the union of these nations. The enthusiasm of the Polish army and of the Polish nation will have no limits. . . . You may believe me that on the day when Tsar Nicholas launches his Cossacks from Cracow at a gallop with the *knut* in one hand and a bag of rubles in the other, the Cossacks will stop only on the other border of the Austrian empire: nothing will resist him on the road. . . . This revolution will fall on Europe like a thunderbolt. . . ." (Cf. J. Kucharzewski, *op. cit.* vv. II and III).

The most original and outstanding Polish Panslavist was Joseph Maria Hoene-Wroński, one of the creators of Polish messianistic philosophy. His philosophy originated in Hegel's dialectic methods and was based on the principles of the threefold development—thesis, antithesis and synthesis—as applied to history by Schelling; and it was in its essence rather teleological. Influenced by the creative philosophy of Fichte and Schelling, Hoene-Wroński replaced the idea of infinite progress by the conception of a purposeful development of humanity which aimed at bringing about God's kingdom on earth and the achievement of immortality. He distinguished three periods. There was first the tendency to realize relative aims. Material welfare, for example was the goal of the Oriental states. Then comes the necessity of securing the welfare attained. This led to the conception of justice, which formed the moral aim of the classical period of Greece and Rome, and to the development of the Christian ideals of the Middle Ages; finally there was knowledge—the spiritual goal of the period which heralded the Reformation. The second period was marked by absolute aims, but this tendency was still immature and split into two ineffective currents of thoughts: one, which regarded feeling and good as the absolute aim, was based on revelation; while the other aimed at reason and truth and rested on experience. The first current became in practical life "illiberal," the second, "liberal," and the conflict between them furnished the basis for the "social antinomy." The third period would represent the union of absolute good and absolute truth. Such is the law of development, and it must be understood if the goal is to be reached. Messianism is but an exponent of this law, that is, a condition of the further development, a factor which can help to create reality. In this way philosophy leaves the field of knowledge and enters the field of action. It is the mission of the Slav world, with Russia at its head, to embark on this philosophy and to realize it. Russia aided by the Slav world is to blend the two contemporary associations of men, state and church, into an "absolute union" which, in its turn, will solve the "social antinomy."[68]

The ideas of Hoene-Wroński were also drawn from his views on the contemporary state of Europe; he thought that Europe was in a critical condition and threatened to collapse. The western nations had produced two destructive ideas which were bound to bring catastrophe,—the French idea of the autocracy of the people, the German philosophic dogma of the infallibility of reason. The Slavs had twice appeared as the defenders of mankind. They had stopped the advance of both Islam and of Jacobinism, proving that they were chosen by God to perform the unification of the different tendencies of mankind: "The absolute destiny of France consists in the realization of the state. The absolute destiny of Germany consists in the realization of the church: the absolute destiny of Russia consists in the realization of their absolute union."[69]

By the way, these ideas about the kingdom of God on earth are an exact anticipation of the analogous views of Vladimir Solov'ev, and an eloquent forecast of the latter's theocratic philosophy of history with its tendency toward Caesaropapism. It would be possible to cite here several other names of writers involved in the same ideas. I think, however, that the three men whom I have mentioned are the most representative. These Panslavist systems, even though not all of them were of the same merit and importance, flowed from a common spring, an excessive concern for national

[68] J. Kleiner, *Zygmunt Krasiński*, Lwów, 1909, Vol. II, pp. 85-87.

[69] *Messianisme ou Réforme absolue*, Vol. I, pp. 22 23.

and European crises. But they had something more in them than that, particularly the system of Hoene-Wroński. At the bottom there was an exaggerated desire for self-sacrifice, a profound love for the misty and chimerical ideas of a universal happiness to which the Slavs were destined to lead mankind, and in particular, the western communities. In the cause of those ideals Poland was to be the victim of a fantastic self-immolation. There we see a significant difference between Polish and Russian Panslavists. The Russian thinkers looked with contempt upon the "rotten West" (while the Poles obviously constructed their systems on behalf of the West). Staszic, and especially Hoene-Wroński had in mind universal aims, but detached from Polish imperialism or Panpolonism. A further difference is traceable to the fact that the Polish Slavophils sacrificed national egoism for higher purposes in their desire to be consistent with their philosophic systems. And thus, whether it was acceptable to the Polish nation or not, they found some consistent solution to the Russo-Polish problem. Finally another difference should be stressed—that the Russian Slavophils and Panslavists were all, in their private lives, honest men and quite independent of the Russian government. The same cannot be said of some of the Poles whom I have mentioned above. It must be added, nevertheless, that the Poles, almost without exception, were different from the healthy, fat, and comfortable Russian Slavophils; they were confused, nervous, excessively sensitive emigrants, sad and despairing exiles who had been compelled to taste of every kind of humiliation and to suffer every kind of trial. There is no need to add that the Polish Panslavists were in disaccord with the majority of the nation, which could not accept the sacrifice of the national self. The best reaction to these Polish political thoughts may be found in the writings of Lelewel, Mickiewicz, Krasiński and Slowacki, in which there will appear different formulations of conceptions of Slavic solidarity and unity; but in all of them the belief in the creative, dynamic powers of the Polish nation will be preserved.

For Lelewel, the Russian-Polish conflict represents the conflict between the ancient Slavic liberty as preserved by the Poles, and the Mongol despotism that has enslaved Russia. He pointed out, however, that Poland, influenced by the magnates and the Jesuits, had run counter to her own republican principles, that this had caused her collapse, and that in her recent fight with tsardom the sympathies of Russian public opinion were with Poland. This, by the way, had been violently denied by Pushkin (Lelewel mentioned his name) who confessed that *"l'accolade de Lelewel me paraît plus dure qu'un exil en Sibérie."*

Mickiewicz went through different phases as far as his attitude towards Russia was concerned. During his exile in Russia he favored some conceptions of "fraternity" of nations and believed in the possibility and, of course, the necessity of the pacification of Russian-Polish relations. However, he was always strongly opposed to Russian autocracy. The Insurrection of 1830-1831, the complications of his personal life, the religious crisis through which he passed during his stay in Rome gave rise to his gloomy opinion of Russia's history in his *Forefather's Eve, Part III*, particularly in the *Digression*. Subsequently he limited his aversion to Russia's political system and tried to overcome his hatred of Russia.

In his lectures at the Collège de France from 1840-1844, he expounded his views on Russia which he now enlarged with historical and political arguments of a precise and penetrating nature. These lectures dealt especially with Poland and the role which she was destined to play in the future of Slavic world. His conception of his native country grew more and more exalted. He regarded her as a martyred nation destined for the sake of humanity to rescue it by her suffering, a nation fated to lead the human race from the "Kingdom of the Old Testament" into that of the Gospel. This view led Mickiewicz to consider Poland as a representative of all that was most creative and fertile in the Slav world, and Russia as the natural "antithesis" of Poland—and hence, the antagonist of the Slav world and of all mankind. He saw the origins of the Russo-Polish antagonism even in the pre-Christian period, expressed in the shape of the two Gods, the "black" and the "white"; their dualism was reflected in the splitting up of the Slavic language into Russian and Polish "dialects." This dualism was strengthened by the alien influences which formed the Slavic states. With regard to the different structural characteristics of the states of the Lechs (Poles) and the Norsemen from their early existence, Mickiewicz sketched the history of the struggle between these two nations for the possession of the northern lands. Catholicism and Orthodoxy only deepened the already existing cleavage. The territory separating Poland from Moscow had been in dispute between them ever since Ivan III. Religion was an instrument, an obstacle, a pretext, but it never was the real basis of the dispute. However, the schism which separated the Greek and the Roman churches had intensified the earlier diversions in the spiritual culture of Russia and of Poland, a cleavage caused by the structures of the two states. The complete dependence of the Orthodox clergy on the secular power nullified any influence which they might have exerted on the spiritual growth of the Russian community. "The Catholic clergy, full of inexhaustible zeal, won in Poland the political liberties which subsequently spread to the other social classes. Whereas the old Bulgarian language segregated Russia from the influences of European civilization, the introduction of Latin among the Western Slavs established a vital contact between Poland and Bohemia and Western civilization, and stimulated the development of the languages and national literatures of these countries."[70]

On the other hand he also stressed the Mongol influence upon Russian mentality. Mickiewicz conclusively proved that it caused that Russian despotism which was fundamentally opposed to the Polish idea of patriotism and Polish traditions of civil liberty. This patriotism and love of liberty, and finally, the conviction that the individual conscience must be the highest form in the national life, were based upon the Christian principle of belief in

[70] I am following here, in general, "Poland and the Slavophil Idea." Cf. Z. Klarner, *Slowianofilstwo w Literaturze Polskiej lat*, 1800-1848, Warsaw, 1926, pp. 175-177.

the close communion of man with God. Hence, whereas Polish political thought is entirely spiritualized, the Mongol principle of autocracy has triumphed in Russia; it has created the immense material power which, if this principle were to prevail, would threaten the world with universal serfdom. In other words Mickiewicz was a pessimist as far as Slavophilism is concerned; the Russo-Polish antagonism broke the unity of the Slavic world. He foresaw, nevertheless, a possible solution. Only by a change from without in her religious mentality could Russia be transformed. Mickiewicz believed in the coming of a new epoch of universal religious rebirth, which was to effect the reconciliation of the divided Slavs. This hope seemed to him quite reasonable. The "heroism of serfdom," Russia's heroic obedience, the intensity of her religious life, allowed him to prophesy that the looked-for religious regeneration would include Russia.

Violently aggressive to Russia were some other Polish Slavophile theorists, eliminating Russia from their systems either because Russia embraced in the early days of her history the political principles of the Scandinavians and worshipped the power of the monarch and the descendants of Odin, and as such was the Anti-Christ of the Slav world; or because of her ethnic consistence: the theory of Duchiński considered Great Russians non-Slavs by reason of the supremacy of their Finnish and Mongolian elements.

A vehemently anti-Russian attitude was taken by Count Zygmunt Krasiński, an aristocrat and conservative, a westerner, a profoundly ardent Catholic and at the same time a messianist, and one of the greatest Polish poets and thinkers. His main idea was that the Polish nation was destined to introduce the gospel into the public law of Europe showing . . . that the incarnate word of God is law for empires as well as for individuals. This idea was later developed by Solov'ev in Russia. Krasiński thought that Polish martyrdom prepared Poland for the practical and concrete foundation of this principle in political life. In his dramas and in his political memoranda he fought against materialism, showing the tragic picture of the European proletariat, "the modern slaves," torn from the cross by a materialism which promised them an earthly paradise, actually unattainable—lacking the light of knowledge and faith, and concentrating all their hopes upon the force of numbers, upon the division of estates, on the abolition of property, upon the destruction of the family, and relying upon violence alone. Only religion could secure individual equality and the brotherhood of nations. He also became in a way a philosopher of the Russian-Polish antagonism. Moscow, which in its childhood dreamed of heroic deeds, "of the western glory of Knights," of "conquering the conquerors," was in later years, "when adolescent," subjugated by the Mongols and could not shake off their yoke. He depicts further the progressive triumph of autocracy, which gradually embraced the whole nation and became settled in space and in time. According to Krasiński there were two main sources of Russian mentality and culture. The first was Byzantium, which seemed to the poet a symbol of the moral decay of the Roman empire in all its aspects, its "validity," its "sense of art," its "acute sensitiveness"; the human soul in Byzantium became so mean that even Christianity became unable to breathe new life into it. The second parent of Russian culture, the Mongol world of Genghis Khan and Tamerlane, "found a sovereign power only in destruction"; it had no idea of God, but it knew terrifying rulers "who changed by slaughter the most fertile and most populated countries into deserts." "In Russian history the passive mother was Byzantine conservatism; the father who made her fruitful was the Tartar invasion; their product, which grew to gigantic proportions, was the Russian government." This government instinctively employed "whatever is evil in good things" whenever liberty declined to the level of violence. It loved not liberty but casual license. It admired and championed any oppression, revolutionary or monarchial, so long as it was oppression. It organized its troops in a Prussian manner, and like the French revolutionaries terrorized its citizens. "Wherever it traced Satan's footsteps in Europe, it stopped to examine them and took its measure from them." "Having made a supreme priest of itself," in the person of Peter the Great, "it displayed itself abroad," that is, it attempted "to destroy the only work of God in Europe." It began to abolish nationalism, which by its body separated Russia from Europe, by its soul kept her from deceiving all the Slavs, by its spirit nullified the probability of a victory over the human race.

Contemplating with horror a future in which Russia might win the victory, Krasiński cast his speech into the form of a prophecy. Thus in the memorandum to Napoleon III during the Crimean War he said: ". . . In case of a pacific solution Russia will find formidable auxiliaries in the fire of anarchy which she will then continue to animate everywhere, and in the very nature of things created by nearsightedness, by wealth, by agitations of misery and by that complete moral prostration about which I just spoke. Therefore all possibility for the future will henceforth be granted to this power. Gifted with an incomparable sagacity, as far as destruction is concerned it will not let escape a single occasion to turn to its profit all the hatreds and envies of our time. It will know admirably well how to exploit on one side the hopes of the legitimists and on the other the fury of demagogy. . . . Then will come the day of the explosion—then there will come another day when Europe, covered with blood and ruins, will collapse under the weight of a thousand crimes and a thousand disasters; then the mistaken conservatives imagining that the Russian government represents order, will indicate it as a liberator and at the same moment the Socialists, recognizing in it their true master, will greet it by the name of the supreme initiator. It will fool everyone and everyone will fall at its feet." In another passage speaking about Russia Krasiński says: "Humiliated and unmasked, but not weakened, she will henceforth try to make use of other weapons and before renewing her unsuccessful attack against Constantinople she will prepare more obscure and more efficient roads. She will stretch out her hand to all secret societies, to all conspiracies, to all shadowy plots from one end of Europe to the other. She will pay them with her gold and support them by her critiques—in a word, she will put her whole power at the service of the social revolution with the aim of precipitating from the throne the dynasties which recently disdained her alliance."[71]

There are indeed some striking passages in this prophetic memorandum. "The whole role which is played by the demagogical party in the breast of every European nation was accepted by Russia long ago and in measure much more gigantic toward all these nations taken together. She also announces an unknown era; she also proclaims another God, another church, the coming of a new society, religion as the slave of the temporal power, the soul subordinate to the body, the destruction of every aristocracy, the obliteration of the individual from the book of life, the realization of absolute equality, it is true at the cost of the most execrable of tyrannies, but unobtainable in a different manner here below; finally, the idea of property erased from the organization of labor—and as a crown for this system, the enjoyments of the brute accorded as a unique consolation to mankind . . . Russia . . . it is the arisen revolution, organized, disciplined, armed with a million bayonets knocking at the doors of the world! If one is not on guard, if she is not stopped in time, sooner or later she will reach her aims. . . ."[72]

Krasiński was aware of the fact that the affinities he stressed between revolution and the Russia of Nicholas I, could appear paradoxical to the people to whom he addressed his memoranda. Therefore in his memorandum to Napoleon III he says that the fact the Russian government had too solemnly proclaimed its principles does not prevent it from following such a course of action. He stressed that "the only principle of that government is to have no principles at all, and that ever since a secret and profound affinity has existed between the Russian Genius and the revolutionary Genius."[73]

[71] *Pisma Zygmunta Krasińskiego*, Vol. VII, Kraków, 1912, pp. 316-317.
[72] *Ibid.*, pp. 317-318.
[73] *Op. cit.*, p. 317.

In his opinion Russia had only one dream—that of a universal monarchy and nothing would ever oblige the government which rules Russia to abandon "the monstrous idea of introducing itself in Europe through interior destruction, wrought by parties which would tear apart the civilized states, and of planting its victorious eagles on the fragments of ruins or on heaps of mud accumulated by the baseness of some, by the unskilfulness of others, and the discord of all. Its very ideal is the triumphal march of Fortinbras at the end of the fifth act of *Hamlet,* arriving almost unknown, where there were none but the dead, and succeeding to them by an unheard concurrence of strange fatalities." (Cf. the article *Deux Puissances.*)[74]

In another article he stresses the same idea that Russia waits for the decomposition of Western civilization; Russia waits for the moment when Europe, "exhausted by cruel wars, social conflicts, injustice, bribery, and spoiliation will call her and surrender to her." "Then with its Asiatic foot she will stamp upon Europe and will give to the Europeans, tubercular, miserable, exhausted, lying in smoking ruins and amidst puddles of blood, the *Knut* to kiss. Then Moscow, convinced that nothing more will resist her, that all the prophesies of Peter the Great are realized, will start to rage but so loathesomely and so inhumanely again that she will awake the last despair in Europe."[75]

It is unfortunately impossible to follow Krasiński further because of lack of space. These examples are striking enough, but actually one may read almost the same things in the articles of Karl Marx published in New York at the time of the Crimean War. Krasiński was an aristocrat, a conservative and a Catholic —and I need not explain who Marx was. Krasiński was led by a fear of revolution organized by Russia. Marx counted on revolution to destroy all despotisms in Europe and first of all, Russian despotism. Who was right, in the long run, that is the question. Before coming to Marx, I should like to add that Krasiński

[74] *Op. cit.*, pp. 175-176.

[75] *Poland in the Face of Storm.* Op cit., pp. 277-78.

might be considered a Slavophil whose views might be compared to the views of the Muscovite Slavophils—with, however, the significant reservation that he attributed to Poland the role which the Slavophils gave to Russia. He eliminated Russia entirely from his system and saw Poland's historical mission in the liberation and preservation of different Slavic nations from Russia's imperialism. To the moral decline of Russia Krasiński opposed Poland which, he maintained, had foreshadowed the future ideal, the unification of republic with kingdom, of democracy with aristocracy, of pagan classicism with the Christian spirit. This unification was manifested in a series of heroes, Zamoyski, Zólkiewski and Sobieski. Poland, in fact, had blended the Roman type with the Christian. These ideas Krasiński expressed in a letter to Montalembert and they represent from a certain point of view the Polish classical formulations of Polish culture. When compared to the conceptions of the Muscovite Slavophils and Panslavists, especially to the conceptions of writers like Aksakov, Nadezhdin, Danilevsky, Tyutchev, and Dostoevsky, they represent a flagrant contradiction.

Of course this was, to say the least, a very abstract idea. In other words, whereas Mickiewicz eliminated Russia from his Slavic system only temporarily, because he believed in her religious and moral rebirth, Krasiński did so irrevocably. The Polish Slavophil systems eliminating Russia as a Slavic state from the other Slavic nations may now be said to have begun. The same standpoint was adopted by Slowacki in his *Letter to Prince Adam Czartoryski* and in the second "rhapsody" of *King Spirit*. Upon the same premises Trentowski, the Polish philosopher, founded his philosophy of history, and the opinions of Tyszyński and Heltman were similar. So, too, the above-mentioned Duchiński argued that Russia was not a Slavic country because of her relationship with the Asiatic nations. Turning for his article to the map of Karamzin, he considered the line of the Dnieper to be the eastern frontier of the Slav world, the center of which was historically Poland. The Polish Walter Scott, I. J.

Kraszewski, and the brilliant essayist Julian Klaczko followed similar lines, in so far as they endeavored to belittle Russia and to represent her as surrounded by other Slav states whose destiny was to check the imperialistic expansion of tsardom. It was this anti-Russian current of Polish political thought which animated the group known as the Democratic Society; and its tradition has survived in certain analogous political tendencies up to the modern times.

But on the other hand one must not forget that the Polish Panslavic conceptions as well as the Russian ones were deeply connected with the weakness of the policy of Western Europe, especially France and England, toward Russia. This weakness discouraged the Poles and encouraged the Russians. Especially critical were, of course, the years of the Polish Insurrections and between them, the years of the Crimean War.

11. Marx (1818-1883)

The policies of the Russian government and of the Western powers affected not only Poles and Russians, but European public opinion as well. I need not recall the fanatic enthusiasm of Paris at the time of the Russians' presence in France after the Napoleonic Wars, the French aristocratic ladies riding horseback with the Cossacks to show their admiration for Russia (the *Cosakée* French girl, to use the expression of Alfred de Vigny), the yielding attitude of the same public opinion in 1831, which provoked indignation among the best Europeans in France, Germany, Italy, Spain and England (cf. my books; *Pouchkine et la Pologne,* and *Life and Culture of Poland*), and later when Tyutchev published his article in the *Revue des Deux Mondes.* A little before that time C. Robert, the successor to Mickiewicz's chair at the Collège de France, started the publication in the same *Revue des Deux Mondes* of a series of articles devoted to Panslavism. He went through a peculiar evolution in these articles. The first part of his study contains elements of acceptance of the Russian interpretation of Panslavism. He stresses the fact of existing mutual understanding between the most distant Slavs, the unity of geography; he constantly mentions the "Greek-Slavic world"; he calls the Russians "the Greeks who emigrated to the North"; he compares the Russian *izvozchiks* to the Hellenes, etc. On the other hand, in the second part of his article he suddenly declares that "there is an abyss between the Spartan Slav of Montenegro and the *mouzhik* of Muscovia."[76] He calls Poland the France of the Graeco-Slavic world, protests against the Russian policy in Poland, Russian "cruelties" in Poland, expresses the opinion that it was only the "apathy and unexplainable indifference of western Europe" which let Russia have such an absolute ascendancy in the affairs of the Slavs, and he comes to the point that Poland should be the representative for Europe of the Slavic world and that Poland has a "sacred right to become the head of the coalition of all oppressed people." Hence his ultimate formula of Panslavism is a union of oppressed Slavs against the tsarist Panslavism. There are here and there in his vacillating study some very just remarks about, for instance, the paradoxical play of geography and culture in the case of Poland: the anti-Slavic enthusiastic Polish Latinism flowering in a completely uncovered and defenceless plain surrounded by the Germans and the Russians. This vision leads him sometimes to pessimism and he is ready to believe that the only condition for Poland's rebirth is Poland's reconciliation with oriental ideas. On the other hand, he perspicaciously loathes the significance of some social and economic reforms and manoeuvers applied by Russia to the conquered provinces, aiming at Russification.

Some few years later appeared, as I mentioned before, Tyutchev's article: *Rome and the Roman Question.* The Polish Library in Paris launched an anonymous answer under the title, *La Russie considérée au point de vue européen.* Unfortunately I do not know who the author was, but he did not confine his polemic to Tyutchev alone—he also had something to say about one of the

[76] *Revue des deux Mondes,* 1846, p. 478.

French collaborators of the *Revue*, M. Desprez, who was in charge of Slavic problems in the *Revue*. M. Desprez represented exactly the same attitude that has reappeared in our times in the form of so-called political realism. He not only accepted the accomplished facts but even justified them. "The Hungarians were broken against impossibility." Russia and Austria represented justice. With Poland—"infernal freedom" was the source of disaster. "To raise Poland again would be the most hazardous enterprise." The enslavement of Poland does not represent any menace for Europe. France could not help either the Hungarians or the Poles, because she would thus compromise her relations with the immense and generous race of the Slavs. In answer to other similar assertions the anonymous author of the pamphlet says: "They insult Poland who has loved France so much, and they adore Russia who asserts that France does not know what she wants. If you lack courage to be just toward Poland, be at least indifferent. Prostrate yourself, if you like, before tsarism, but at least do not spit in the face of the victim; this does not give you any advantage and does not bring you any honor. . . . They fear Socialism and Communism in the West, but Russia is a power which has to a great degree applied Communism; and by the most strange aberration, there are in Europe parties which place themselves under Muscovite protection. . . . In the West it is possible only to dream of or discuss socialism. Russia has it: this is the law of the state. The tsar is the only universal and real proprietor. . . . We do not know whether or not Communism will be established in the West, we doubt it; but if it one day establishes itself, Russia has laid broad and solid foundations for that deadly or beneficent transformation."[77]

One cannot but be surprised to read such texts, realizing that they were written in 1850.

The "disastrous weakness" of the Western powers was also attacked from another side. One may find in the voluminous book of Karl Marx—*The Eastern Question* (London, 1897), containing

[77] *Op. cit.*, Paris, 1851, pp. 21, 41.

his articles written in London and published in the *New York Tribune* in the years of the Crimean War—the most fascinating texts, especially when read in the light of the present day. Let us take this for instance: "Russia has all along been glorified for the forebearance and generosity of her 'august master,' who has not only condescended to cover the naked and shameful subserviency of Western Cabinets, but has displayed the magnanimity of devouring Turkey piece by piece, instead of swallowing her at one mouthful. Russian diplomacy has thus rested on the timidity of Western statement, and her diplomatic art has gradually sunk into so complete a *mannerism,* that you may trace the history of the present transactions almost literally in the annals of the past."[78]

He continues, saying: "Russia now claims occupation of the Danubian Principalities, without giving to the Porte the right of considering this step as a *casus belli.* Russia claimed, in 1827, to occupy Moldavia and Wallachia *in the name of the three powers.* . . . Russia announced in her manifesto, October 10th, 1829: 'Russia has remained constantly a stranger to every desire of conquest—to every view of *aggrandizement.*' "

In another letter he quotes a letter of Count Pozzo di Borgo written on November 28th, 1828, to Count Nesselrode: " 'It is our policy to see that nothing new happens during the next four months, and I hope we shall accomplish it, because *men in general prefer waiting;* but the fifth must be fruitful in events.' " And then Marx says: "Having kept them (the courts of Europe) in this manner for weeks, nay for months, in suspense, Nicholas suddenly makes a declaration that neither England nor France nor Austria nor Prussia has any concern with his quarrel with Turkey, and that with Turkey he alone can negotiate . . . but while he declares that the powers are not to meddle in Russia's concerns, we are informed, on the other hand, that the representatives of France, England, Austria, and Russia killed their time by meeting in conference at Vienna, and in hatching projects for the ar-

[78] *Op. cit.,* p. 48.

rangement of the Eastern question, neither the Turkish nor Russian ambassador participating in these conferences."[79] In this most interesting book one may find striking details showing how the Russian government was organizing its subversive propaganda in the Balkans. The Russian historian, M. N. Pokrovsky, also brings many details connected with the preparation for the Crimean War by Nicholas I, and illustrating that subversive activity of Russian diplomacy in Serbia and Athens. He justly says: "The head of European legitimism quickly stepped into the new role of a revolutionary agitator on the Balkan peninsula."[80]

Not less convincing and even fascinating are the details connected with the same Crimean War brought by the contemporary Russian historian Tarle.[81]

Marx saw the whole situation from a very lucid point of view. He was trying to convince his American readers just as writers in *The New Leader* are now trying to do. Marx asserted that those of his readers who followed his correspondence from London "will have learned before that the idea of Russian diplomatic supremacy owes its efficiency to the imbecility and the timidity of the Western nations, and that the belief in Russia's superior military power is hardly less a delusion." We know how fully Marx's views were confirmed by the events of the Crimean War. How just indeed was Marx when with the genuine emotion of a great political mind he said: "Both (England and France) together have been frightened out of the only policy which would at once have guaranteed the preservation of peace, while maintaining their own respectability. To the arrogance of the autocrat they have replied with the symptoms of cowardice. They have encouraged the very assumptions they have depreciated, just as poltroons always encourage bullies to be overbearing. If at the outset they had used a manly style of language, adequate to the positions

[79] *Op. cit.*, pp. 76-77.

[80] *Istoriya Rossii v XIX Veke*, Vol. III, p. 33.

[81] E. Tarle, "Nakanune Krymskoi Voiny," *Krasnaya Nov'*, nos. 11-12, 1940, pp. 260-270.

they hold, and the pretensions they set up before the world, if they had proved that cluster and swagger could not impose on them, the autocrat would not only have refrained from attempting it, but would have entertained for them a very different feeling from that contempt which must now animate his bosom. . . . There is only one way to deal with a power like Russia, and that is the fearless way."[82]

Marx's optimism had sources very similar to those which inspired the Polish radical and democratic Slavophils and Panslavists and, of course, men like Herzen and Bakunin—this was the hope for revolution. "Russian policy, with its traditional craft, cheats, and subterfuges, may impose upon the European courts, which are themselves but traditional things, but it will prove utterly powerless with the revolutionized peoples." "Western Europe is feeble and timid because her governments feel that they are outgrown and no longer believed in by their people. The nations are beyond their rulers and trust in them no more. It is not that they are really imbecile, but that there is new wine working in the old bottles. With a worthier and more equal social state, with the abolition of caste and privileges, with free political constitutions, unfettered industry, and emancipated thought, the people of the West will rise again to power and unity of purpose, while the Russian colossus itself will be shattered by the progress of the masses and the explosive force of ideas. There is no good reason to fear the conquest of Europe by the Cossacks. . . ."[83]

From the Marxian texts quoted above there appears distinctly first of all the salient Westernism of Marx, and, of course, his anti-Panslavism. He stressed the Western "unity of purpose," and he expresses the conviction that one need not fear the "conquest of Europe by the Cossacks." This becomes extremely significant in the light of modern historical developments. What kind of Marx has been applied by Russia? It is clear that the Panslavic trends favored now in Soviet Russia are in conflict with Russia's

[82] *Op. cit.*, pp. 187-188.
[83] *Op. cit.*, p. 80 and 189.

political gospel. One may wonder what would be the attitude of Marx in the face of present events, and one has some right to wonder if Marx would not now write about the "Soviet Autocrat" and the "weakness of pusillanimity" of the Western powers in exactly the same terms.

The above mentioned Russian historian Tarle quotes, in his study *On the Eve of the Crimean War*, a very interesting letter which Nicholas I wrote to his wife on June 7th, 1844, from Windsor at the time when he paid his visit to England: "Very comical things are taking place here in connection with the Poles. At the present moment there is being collected a subscription for a ball given by swindlers: at the head of the subscription list is the name of the Duchess of Somerset who even offered her house for the ball, and the name of the Duchess of Sutherland. All these events had taken place before my arrival; since I have been here the wind has changed; all these ladies have become afraid that they may defame themselves in the face of the majority of the public which receives me so nicely. And what did they think: the Duchess of Somerset writes to Brunnov (the Russian ambassador) that she is desolate that she permitted herself to be so misled that her name appears on the list and that she has asked to have it crossed off. Many have acted in the same way. I ordered that she be asked not to do anything like that and that even if the subscription does not cover the expenses of this enterprise, I shall be ready to complete the sum. Judge for yourself what was the effect and what was their confusion."

At the same time Herzen wrote in his diary: "Ostrowski (a famous Polish émigré, and translator of Mickiewicz) has been arrested during the sojourn of the Emperor. Such is the *habeas corpus*."[84]

As a matter of fact, although the views of the Polish author of the above mentioned answer to Tyutchev preceded Marx, they are no less significant than the texts of Marx. The unknown Polish author says: "You thought that you had satisfied Russia, having

[84] Tarle, *op. cit.*, p. 238.

given her Poland, and the divine justice has already put you at her feet. Poland resisted and succumbs as a martyr. And what is Europe doing? She is pleased to proclaim her own bankruptcy. . . . The greatness of Russia is not her own achievement; it is the result of the anarchy and inconceivable lack of foresight of the other great powers. . . . In 1815 did they not proclaim that it was the Muscovite Slavs who liberated Europe from French domination? Did they not accord to Russia magnificent aggrandizements? The ambition of Russia does not astonish us at all." And, fascinatingly enough, the unknown Polish author of 1851, overwhelmed by his distress, asks: "Was it not the *Revue des Deux Mondes* itself which made the confession that the Russian power could be broken only by the American people of the United States? And even it doubts it. France, Europe, exist no more."[85]

Comparaison n'est pas raison, one may say; however, the temptation to quote these texts was too strong.

12. Validity of the Doctrine

It would be difficult to enter into all the historical and political details connected with the Panslavistic doctrine and its radiation. I mentioned above the political reactions against Panslavic conceptions among different Slavic nations. The distinguished Russian scholar Pypin, whom I have quoted several times, accumulated many arguments which even from his own Russian point of view are against the Panslavistic doctrine. Even more critical were Solov'ev and Chicherin. Pypin also stressed the fact that the Russian government has not always been willing to adopt this doctrine as a policy of its program. He mentioned that during different phases of her foreign policy Russia had acted against those conceptions and against the interests of the Slavic nations which were under her special protection, such as Serbia and Bulgaria. Russia, for instance, on several occasions guaranteed the integrity of Turkey,

[85] *La Russie considérée au point de vue Européen,* Librarie Polonaise, Paris, 1851, p. 7.

which was against the interests of Southern Slavs whom she considered under her protection. Correct are also the following remarks of Sumner: "Although Russia was undisputably the only effective political and military Slav power, her claims to cultural predominance seemed sin and arrogance in the eyes of many Western Slavs. . . . Despite the reforms of the early sixties, Russian tsardom ran counter to the traditions and aspirations of every other Slav people. Emancipation at the hands of the Russian tsar might mean but an exchange of dominations. Gorchakov, always an opponent of Panslav schemes, was justified in writing: '*Je ne vous dissimule pas qu'il m'est difficile de croire à une sympathie sincère des races slaves pour la Russie autocratique.*' However much some of the Czech leaders might blind themselves to the nature of Russian tsardom, the trees of liberty were likely to have very queer blossoms if transported from the ranks of the Neva or the Moskva. Certainly they were not recognizable along the Vistula."[86]

I have just quoted a distinguished modern English historian. Let us see what is said on the same subject by an earlier historian—C. Robert. "It is principally the South Slavic nationalities that the Russian cabinet works to subjugate. For half a century it has surrounded the schismatic Slavs of Turkey and Austria with quite a special protection. Promises, magnificent gifts, nothing is spared in order to seduce them. Sacred ornaments sent by Russia fill their churches; their most beautiful liturgical books are presents of the Holy Synod of Petersgurg. The principal personalities of Illyria and Bohemia are, so to say, harassed by homages by the Russian agents. The scholars of Prague receive all kinds of gratifications from the tsar, rings with diamonds, even decorations arrive from the Neva as recompense for services rendered for the cause of Slavic literatures. The Muscovite agents know how to hide under this purely literary propaganda one of the most active political propaganda. In the name of the independence of the whole race they call the subjugated Southern Slavs for a coalition with the tsar against their oppressors. Thus they pretend to find a Pan-

[86] B. H. Sumner, *Russia and the Balkans*, Oxford, 1937, p. 269.

slavism of a special order, which would consist of grouping the different Slavic nations under the sceptre of the Romanovs as protected powers. This thought appears from the beginning to the end in the long Panslavist epos of the Slovak poet Kollár under the title *Slávy Dcera.* The poet visualizes the peoples as united to form a sort of Colossus modeled on the Babylonian Colossus of the Bible. Russia forms its head, Poland its heart, Bohemia and Illyria are its hands and feet. It would be imprudent to contest what the ideas have of the seductive and the dangerous, one must indeed recognize the exxistence of a Russian Panslavism, only one may deny its Slavic character and that it ever could possess the eympathy of any independent Slav."

C. Robert stresses another important point when speaking about the activities of the "great protector" among the Danubian and Adriatic Slavs. He would protect them on the condition that they would never follow the example of Serbia and show any pretension for a distinct national existence. "Let one look through the history of these Russian protectorates since the protectorate has been exercised over the last kings of Poland and Georgia to those which the tsar exercises at the present time over the Serbian and Moldavian-Wallachian principalities and over the crumbling Persian empire. One will see that these various protectorates have always had and still have as a unique aim to prevent the protected nations from rising from their humiliation and being reborn to independence."[87] More than that, the same C. Robert observed that during the upheavals in Cracow and Galicia Russia constantly played the role of an ally of Germany.[88]

On the other hand from time to time, as we may see not only in the brilliant articles of Marx but also in the extremely interesting recent publications of the Soviet scholar Tarle connected with the Crimean War, the tsardom was ready to utilize the Panslavic conceptions when they appeared advantageous for it. It is quite true, for instance, that for Nicholas I it was not easy to combine his

[87] *Revue des Deux Mondes,* 1846, pp. 472-473.
[88] *Ibid.,* p. 479.

imperialistic views on Constantinople with a policy which would necessarily favor revolutionary movements among the Slavs and compromise the gospel of his legitimism. Nevertheless, Marx, Pokrovsky and Tarle gave, as we saw, striking examples of this Machiavellism of Russian policy. Let us, however, analyze the doctrine itself and try to see what were the concrete historical and cultural realities which it had to face. We saw that one of the chief problems, that of Russo-Polish relations, has not been and could not have been solved within the frame of Slavophil or Panslavistic schemes. But what was the general picture?

The main argument of unity among the Slavs was of course that of language. The Slavic languages belong to the same family and it is not difficult to prove that certain similar phenomena which appear in different Slavic languages represent not a result of inter-Slavic influences but an independent parallelism of development. For the tenets of the Slavophil doctrine the fact of a common linguistic origin meant very much theoretically. Language is an expression of the relationship between man and the universe, and therefore this expression reveals a—let us say—philosophical outlook. In other words language possesses an ideological value. On the other hand history differentiated the Slavic peoples. During long centuries they went sometimes not only through different but very often even opposite and contrasting cultural influences; and because of that the languages in their turn also differentiated to such a degree that Slavs are no longer able to understand one another. The amusing point here was the fact that the Slavophils of the various Slavic nations used German in order to communicate with each other. This was indeed a paradoxical situation for those who were trying to unite themselves first of all against Germanism. Of course Russia was and still is suggesting that the Russian language be accepted as the common language for the Slavs. But this generous offer has not so far been adopted. The linguistic divergencies become even more salient when we leave the field of language proper and try to apply the methods of unification to the field of belles lettres, especially poetry, even if it be the popular poetry. A synthesis appears absolutely impossible. It would be enough to compare the Czech versification and all the changes it went through with the Russian and Polish to see how great are the differences. Let us take the Russian *byliny* with their assonances, which have no correspondents in other Slavic productions. On the other hand the *Shchedrivky* and the *Koladki* are ritual poems often inspired by historical subjects of a purely Ukrainian character. A quite distinct group is represented by the Serbo-Croatian and Bulgaro-Macedonian popular poetry—heroic rhapsodies which sing of the legendary Serbian hero Kralević Marko, the mother of the Jugović and her sons and many others. This poetry which served the fantasies and mystifications of Mérimée, which enchanted Goethe, Pushkin, Mickiewicz and Nodier, represents a quite special formation and a unique genre in the Slavic world. How different is the medieval Polish poetry, only semi-popular in its most distant origins, with its origin in the Church. Its lyrical starting point is to be found in the *Kyrie Eleison* and *Alleluiah*, refrains of liturgical songs.

Let us abandon for a moment this purely philological statement and turn to a more essential factor which determined the historical development of the Slavic nations: I have in mind religion. Religion divided the whole Slavic world into two parts. Bulgarians, Serbians, Great Russians, Ukrainians, and White Ruthenians embraced Eastern Orthodoxy from a Byzantine source. Czechs, Croatians, Slovenes, Slovaks, and Poles embraced the Catholic religion from its Roman Source. And in addition the Czechs went through Hussism; a part of the Ukrainians and White Ruthenians adopted the Union. The Muscovite Slavophils and Panslavists were fighting against Catholicism. By that very fact they were in opposition to the whole Western Slavic world. Religion determined the cultural differentiation, and if we add to that some other historical factors we shall see that at the time when Russia was under the influence of Byzantium, of the Bulgarian and Serbian messianistic literature which formed her theory of "Moscow the Third Rome," based on all kinds of imported legends and apocryphas, Poland was shining in the sun of the Renaissance. She had her Rabelais—Nicholas Rey, her Ronsard—Kochanowski, and a wonderfully rich and brilliant political literature connected with Latin republican writers, some of which was soon translated into foreign languages, even English.

The Southwestern Slavs, the Croatians, Slovenes, and Dalmatians also took part in the achievements of the Renaissance. They lived that period in contact with Italy while on the other hand Dalmatia was under the influence of several Byzantines. Let me recall the brilliant Italianism of Dubrovnik (Ragusa) of the sixteenth and seventeenth centuries and the flowering of the Dalmatian literature which followed the songs of the provencals troubadours, and of the *Dolce stil nuovo.* The Dalmatian muses found their inspiration in Petrarch, Boccaccio, Guarini, Tasso, Metastasio; this literature knew all genres from *canzone* to the pastoral drama and *la commedia dell' arte.* The Czechs went through this epoch carrying their religious reform—a heavy burden but rich in immense moral consequences. It is probably this reform that gave the definitive form to the moral and intellectual character of this Slavophil and Slavologist nation, least Slavic in its spiritual physiognomy.

The marvellous flowering of the Russian and Polish literatures in the nineteenth century represents again a kind of exception among the Slavic nations. And in spite of a close parallel development, these two literatures very often, following the same roads of literary evolution, in many ways contrast with each other.[89]

So even if one should try to eliminate the purely political barriers separating the Slavic nations, such as the political antagonisms existing between Bulgars and Serbs, Serbs and Croatians, Russians and Poles, Czechs and Slovaks, Ukrainians and Great Russians, Ukrainians and Poles, etc., the problem of spiritual

[89] I have discussed these problems in a more detailed form in my article, "Existe-t-il un patrimoine commun d'études slaves?" Cf. *Le Monde Slave*, Paris, 1926.

unity among the Slavs would still appear very difficult. The cultural differentiation in the march of historical development became so deep that the parental affinities in the Slavic family have been completely lost. And today the cultural type of a Russian differs greatly from the cultural Polish type, and this would be true for all other Slavic examples.

How significant, although in part paradoxical in the light of the events of this war, are the following remarks of Vladimir Solov'ev: "Poland is in Eastern Europe the representative of the spiritual principle which became the basis of Western history. In its spiritual essence the Polish nation, and with it all Catholic Slavs, belong to the Western world. The spirit is stronger than blood; in spite of a blood antipathy toward Germans and blood nearness to Russia, the representatives of Polonism would accept Germanization rather than a union with Russia. A Western European, even a Protestant, is nearer by spirit to a Catholic Pole than an Orthodox Russian. Being the foremost fighters for Western principles, Poles see in Russia the East, hostile to their spiritual essence, an alien and dark force. . . ."[90] "The East," says Solov'ev, "worked out an order of ideas in which man was subordinated to supernatural power. The West created the ideal of the independence of man. In the East the state enslaved the peoples, while Greece elaborated the ideal of the freedom of the peoples. The supernatural element and the predominance of the state have given rise to the idea of resignation. Greece and Rome with their republics developed the principle of spiritual energy and popular activity." (Cf. *ibid.*)

Cultural differentiation represents progress, and the idea of racial unification might be considered as essentially reactionary. And indeed the Panslavistic doctrine is an anti-historical, anti-cultural, and anti-European idea, not only because of its anti-European political implications but because Panslavism refers first of all to theories of racial superiority, supporting them by dubious

[90] V. S. Solov'ev, *Velikii Spor i Khristianskaya Politika.* Cf. *Sobr. Soch. v,* IV, p. 15.

anthropologic speculations. And from this point of view the ideas of Danilevsky, for example, paved the way not only for Stalin's anti-European imperialism but for Hitler's racial conceptions. Besides, Danilevsky's theory of historical-cultural types destroyed the idea of the stability of European culture. From this point of view it was a highly disaggregating, anti-cultural, and belligerent conception of history. The conflict between the Eastern and the Western world was constantly emphasized, and instead of a search for a pacific harmonization of these two worlds, Danilevsky called for a war. This is why he was against the conception of the balance of powers, this is why he was against a Europe in a state of equilibrium and peace. He saw that only a divided Europe, a Europe in a state of conflagration was desirable from the Russian point of view.

Coming back to those conflicting racial and cultural conceptions, we may find many excellent examples which show that a cultural tradition means more than a racial one. If we take the names of some German generals in the last war such as Blaskowitz, Brauchitsh, and Jeschonnek, we may see that their Slavic or even Polish names did not prevent them from making war against Poland. On the other hand, Fabrycy, Januszajtis, Dreszer, Mond, Prugar, Langer, Abraham, and Anders were generals in the Polish army.[91] It would be really impossible to mention all the Poles who played a decisive role in the development of Polish culture and who had names like Copernicus, Chopin, Reymont, Grottger, Andriolli, and so on. What would Polish Slavic philology be without Lelewel, Linde, Kolberg, Baudouin de Courtenay, Kallenbach, Finkel, and Brückner? It would be as difficult to exclude Andrzej Morsztyn, Weyssenhoff, Reymont, and Berent from Polish literature as to exclude Askenazy, Handelsman, Kleiner, Winawer, Wittlin, Tuwim, Slonimski, and so many other Poles of Jewish origin. Is not the Russian picture similar with Pushkin and his Abyssinian ancestry, with Lermontov and

[91] Articles by Jan Wolny "Choroba Slowiańska" in the review *Tygodnik Polski*, New York, nos. 47 and 48, 1946.

his Scotch origin, with Dostoevsky and his Polish origin, and Gogol with his Ukranian descent, not to mention Kantemir, Fonvizin, Delvig, Boratynski, Korolenko, Blok, and so many others? And is it not really stupefying that the ultimate aggressiveness of an Asiatic Scythian Panslavism found its expression in the terrible poem *The Scythians,* written by one of the most European of Russian poets, the above mentioned Alexander Blok?

Let us return again to the Russian Polish problem, which is edifying enough. The Russian Slavophils and Panslavists, who, because they were indebted for their inspiration to European humanitarianism and idealism, seemed to have been destined in theory at least to sanction Poland's right to independence and thereby to redeem the political crime committed by Russia, never proved capable of being true to the dictates of political conscience. They remained blind even to the dictates of necessity, because any attempt to achieve the unity of the Slavic world as long as the Polish question was unsettled was chimerical, just as indifference to Polish national injuries was dishonesty of thought and conscience. No wonder, then, that the Russo-Polish *mariage forcé* was not dissolved by the Slavophils and Panslavists; divorce by collusion was achieved between those Poles and Russians who lacked connections with the Slavophil traditions and represented the spirit of positive Western thought. It is indeed striking to note the absence among the Russian Westerners of any irreconcilable hostility toward Poland. From the brothers Turgenev, who are contemporaries of Pushkin down to Granovsky, Stankevich, Chicherin, and the later liberals, the Westerners, although they realized the difficulties of solving the antagonism, did not succumb either to Slavophil fancies or to an elemental Slavophil hatred for Poland. The Polish problem, as I mentioned above, was from the very beginning the most important obstacle to the advancement of Slavophil ideas, for either the system collapsed or the "unity" of "indivisible Russia" was endangered; consequently the Russian Slavophils and Panslavists were frozen into immobility by the dangers of both alternatives and were unable to pursue their proper course. An exit from this dilemma did, however, exist and was discovered by the Westerners. Characteristically enough, the author of the manifesto by which the Provisional Government of Prince Lvov proclaimed Poland's independence, Professor Milyukov, was one of the most brilliant critics of the Slavophil and Panslavistic doctrines. His collaborator in this field was a Pole, Alexander Lednicki, who also never had any tendencies toward the Slavophil fancies but from the beginning to the end of his life remained faithful to his European orientation.

But perhaps the most edifying Russian example of the overcoming of nationalism and chauvinism by Christianism and humanitarianism is to be found in the "Polish story" of Tolstoy —in the touching tribute paid to the Polish martyrdom which truly inspired this great Russian writer.[92]

13. "Facies hippocratica"

After this rapid course through the thoughts of so many Russian, Polish, Czech, Slovak and other writers and politicians, one unavoidable conclusion is that practically all of them, in spite of their political conflicts, ideological contradictions, and national antagonisms, agreed on one point—the recognition of the moral weakness and lack of moral dignity of Europe. Of course their approaches, motives, points of view, and goals were different. The Russians stated the moral decrepitude of Europe in a more or less speculative way. The Muscovite Slavophils could, after all, take an attitude of indifference and disinterestedness towards Europe. Russia could separate herself from the West and build a life independent from Europe. The Russian Panslavists could try to take advantage of the weakness of Europe for the realization of their Russian imperialistic views. The other Slavs, and especially the Poles, were in a different situation—for them the di-

[92] W. Lednicki, *Quelque aspects du nationalisme et du christianisme chez Tolstoï*, Cracow-Paris, 1935.

lemma, Europe—Russia, was not a question of speculation—it was a question of life or death. What did Europe give to the Poles? Every day of their life was a day of betrayal by Europe of those ideals which Poles considered Polish ideals because of the very fact they were European. This is the main item of the Polish political texts of that period; and perhaps the most eloquent and at the same time tragic expression of these feelings is to be found in the famous message of the Polish National Government of August 15, 1831 addressed to its Western agents: "Truth, seen whole, has appeared before our eyes. We no longer count on the support of the great powers, who could and who would not, who still can and who will not, save us. We can no longer place any faith in the promises which they have made to us and which they belie by their conduct. . . . England and France, then, would not have employed us for the occasion except as an instrument fit to serve the course of their interests. England would not have lulled us with a few illusions except in order to have one more method of establishing the independence of Belgium. And France would not have made promises to us except to win a majority in the Chambers. Will faith, then be wholly banished from cabinets, and the words of a French and English minister be nothing but worthless farthings? . . . If France and England abandon us today and fail to justify the hopes that they have aroused, our ruin will have been brought about, not by the fury of Russia, or the hostility of Prussia, or the indifference of Austria, but by the self-styled sympathy shown us by France and England. . . . If the cabinets lack the courage to help us, let them at least possess enough dignity to acknowledge their barbaric indifference toward our cause. And if they have ignored the duty imposed on them by prudence, morality, and humanity, the Poles will know how to follow him who prescribes to them the sanctity of their rights and the love of their country. . . ."[93]

For Poland was facing not only the loss of her independence but a complete change of her historical mission. For centuries

[93] W. Lednicki, *Life and Culture of Poland*, pp. 212-213.

she was considered the *antemurale christianitatis,* the rampart of Western civilization. An absorption by Russia within the frames of a Panslavistic conception would mean that Poland would become an anti-Western rampart. This is what Count Valerian Krasiński stressed already in 1848, foreseeing the present Polish catastrophe; Krasiński wrote: "If however the Poles will see that they have no chance of receiving from other nations and particularly from the Germans, the necessary assistance for the recovery of their country's independence, and that those nations in granting them some advantages, have no other object in view, than to make use of them as a bugbear to frighten Russia, in order to prevent the consolidation of the internal strength of that country by an intimate union of its Slavonic elements, being themselves ready to sacrifice the Poles as soon as their interests may demand it. If such a conviction becomes prevalent amongst the Poles, and there can be no doubt that it is rapidly spreading, what will then remain to them except cordially to unite with the Russians and to become, from a barrier between Russia and the rest of Europe, the vanguard of the Slavonic race against western Europe and Germany in particular."[94]

There was perhaps some consolation in the fact that the Poles, Russians, and the Slavs in general were not alone in their pessimistic critique of Europe. The Polish catastrophe, which absorbed the Poles and became a test case for all conceptions of Slavic union, was not the single factor that shook all European life in 1830-31 and in 1863. The French Revolution inaugurated a long period of upheavals and perturbations—revolutions, wars were following one after the other and the thunder of social turmoils was constantly menacing Europe during the whole 19th century. Have I to mention here the piercing voices expressing despair and "Weltschmerz," the voices of Chateaubriand, Byron, Alfred de Musset, Alfred de Vigny, and so many others as far as the "period of transition," to use Krasiński's formula, is concerned? Have I to recall the pessimism of H. Taine, the indig-

[94] Valerian Krasinski, *Panslavism and Germanism,* London, 1848, pp. 218-219.

nant admonitions of Ruskin, the anxiety of Renan, not to mention the period of the *fin de siècle* and the modern European pessimism of Spengler's jeremiads?

This does not change the fact, however, that in the light of the events of the 19th century and especially in the light of the present tragedy of Poland, the Polish "message to Europe" becomes particularly poignant. History has repeated itself almost textually with, however, one exception—that the present betrayal of Poland by the Western democracies has followed an even more cynical and indecent road. And has not the same fate overtaken Yugoslavia?

Of course in all Slavophil and Panslavistic texts one may find political hyperbole, exasperation, dreams, vain hopes, idealistic universalistic conceptions of fraternity of nations, beliefs in international justice, aspirations for national independence, imperialistic pretensions, the ideological play with various historical traditions. But as I stressed above, all that Slavic polyphony starts and ends with a dirge for Europe. Indeed we see all of them—those brilliant prophetic writers like Tyutchev, Dostoevsky, Mickiewicz, Krasiński, and so many others, involved in a great ideological battle, in which clashed their most essential thoughts about humanity and civilization, as if petrified by the same vision of Europe which we find in Herzen's terrible suggestions about "*facies hippocratica,* by which the doctors recognize that death has raised its scythe."

14. Post Scriptum

I mentioned on several occasions the fact that we are witnessing a kind of revival of the Panslavistic conceptions under the Soviet sponsorship. Indeed there was created in Moscow in 1941 a new Panslavic committee under the chairmanship of a general, A. Gundorov, and with representatives of different Slavic nations as its members. This committee started to organize first of all Panslavic meetings in Moscow. Then later Panslavic meetings, manifestations, and commemorations in America; in June 1942 such meetings and congresses took place in New York, in Pittsburgh, in Detroit, in Kansas, in Cleveland, in San Francisco, in Oakland, and also in Canada, Argentina, etc., organized by local Slavic committees. These organizations in America and in other countries represent ramifications of the Moscow center; and at each meeting they manifested this relationship by sending addresses and telegrams not only to the Panslavic committee in Moscow but to Stalin, Kalinin, Molotov, and so on. Around the Muscovite center were organized during the war all kinds of Slavic national committees and unions of patriots at the head of which one could find the members of the Panslavic committee in Moscow. These committees and unions were nuclei from which originated the "democratic governments" imposed by Russia to the Slavic and non-Slavic countries (similar committees were organized for Hungary, Roumania, Bulgaria) which found themselves in the sphere of Russia's influence.

For the task of propaganda of these Panslavic ideas of union and fraternity of the Slavs under the protection of Soviet Russia and under her cultural leadership there has been established a monthly review under the title *The Slavs,* published in Moscow in Russian.

It is paradoxical enough that if one takes different Soviet encyclopedias one may find a radical refutation of Panslavic conceptions; the Panslavism of the 19th century has been always qualified there as a bourgeois imperialistic doctrine. It would be very difficult, however, to find any salient difference between the Panslavistic imperialistic conceptions of Tsarist Russia, as far as their essence is concerned, and the Panslavistic policy of the Soviets, even though their motives and ultimate goals are not identical. In order to save appearances the official Soviet press still stresses that difference; so N. Leonidov in his articles *The New Phase in Slav History* published in *New Times* in Moscow in September, 1946, said: "The Russian people never identified themselves with the imperialistic chauvinistic Panslavism of the monarchists." "The slanderous talk about new Panslavism is part of an anti-Soviet campaign."[95]

Of course there are differences. The Russian tsarist government used to change from time to time its attitude toward the doctrines of the Muscovite Slavophils and those of the Panslavists. All depended on the international situation. Besides, in spite of its Machiavellian policy the tsarist government was still bound by precepts of international and public law as well as by international public opinion, and because of that its Russianizing methods and proceedings were still in a certain degree moderated. Therefore in some cases there appeared a divergence of views between the representatives of the government and the most chauvinistic, aggressive representatives of Russian Panslavism as, for instances, the famous apologist of the Russification of Poland—Katkov. Anyhow the Slavophils and Panslavists at that time represented a free, independent initiative. From time to time they even found themselves under a governmental observation that was not very benevolent to them, especially when their Panslavic enthusiasm was bringing harm to the Russian government in its relation with neighboring countries.

It is obvious that the present situation from this point of view is completely different. Everyone knows that there is no room and no possibility for any individual free political initiative under the rule of the *Politburo*. The whole present Panslavic movement has been organized by the Soviet government, and people who are taking part in it are agents of that government. In the beginning the aim was to organize Slavic elements for the fight against Fascism and Hitlerism, against Germany; the unspeakable German atrocities greatly encouraged these activities. Such is the aspect of the first years of the publication *The Slavs*. We find there articles dealing mostly with war events, with German crimes, or with the military history of Russia, articles glorifying great Russian generals like Kutuzov, Suvorov, great Russian tsars or princes like Alexander Nevsky, Peter the Great, some articles

95 Quoted from "Degeneration of Panslavism" by George C. Guins. The article has not yet appeared, but the author has kindly permitted me to use it.

glorifying the outstanding Soviet generals and, of course, men like Molotov, Lenin, "the great son of Slavdom"; and Stalin, "son of the nations of Russia"—it would be rather difficult to make of him a Slav. There are also articles about different manifestations of old and modern Slavic culture, biographies of great Slavs, predominantly Russian. Copernicus, one of them, had a rather amusing fate under the pen of Soviet clerks writing under the *Politburo's* dictates. The *Small Soviet Encyclopedia* (1926) calls Copernicus the "greatest Polish scholar"; and later, its *Great* brother leaves the reader with the impression that he was a German Scholar. Finally, the review *The Slavs* emphasizes his Polish patriotism and the prestige of the University of Cracow!

The activities concerning the further organization of Panslavic meetings abroad have not been abandoned. On the contrary, recently at the end of 1946 there again took place such meetings in America and in Belgrade with the predominant role played by official and unofficial agents and delegates of Soviet Russia, ending with telegrams and addresses expressing loyalty to Soviet Russia, sent to Stalin, Kalinin, and Molotov. All these facts must lead one to the conclusion that we are witnessing here the organization of a new International, of a Slavic International, parallel to the Comintern, and that the numerous ramifications of this organization outside of Russia represent nuclei of a Slavic fifth column in the countries which are outside of the immediate zone of Soviet influence. Within this zone Russia is much less interested in the development of the Panslavic movement through any special organizations, as she has there at her complete disposal the governments of the countries which are under Russian political domination. I do not have to stress what I mentioned before—that Stalin has in his hands means of Russification about which Goldmann and Katkov could only dream.

Not without interest is the fact that the Inter-Slav Bureau of Foreign Contacts had during the war six sections—for the United States, Canada, Central and South America, Australia and New Zealand, the Near and Middle East, and Great Britain. A seventh section dealt with the "occupied countries" and came partly under the jurisdiction of the Bureau and partly under that of the Committee for Active Struggle Against Fascism. In 1942 the All-Slav Committee's budget amounted to 320,000,000 roubles, in 1943 to 400 million, and in 1944, when the financial division had ceased to come under the control of the Secretariate, the Committee's budget had risen to 550 million roubles. The All-Slav Congress which took place recently in Belgrade has afforded some indications of the place which the All-Slav Committee holds in Russia's post-war political propaganda apparatus. The main speech of the Soviet delegate, General Gundorov, was an invitation to the Slav peoples to ignore "the sinister forces of world reaction" and submit to Communist guidance. Two resolutions passed by the Belgrade Congress deserve attention. The first, which makes Belgrade the center of the All-Slav Committee and Maslavitch its chairman, is an indication of the importance attached in Soviet policy to Slav sentiment in the Balkans, where to some extent it is a substitute for nationalist sentiment. The second resolution provides for the participation in the work of the All-Slav Committee of representatives of "the largest progressive Slav organization from non-Slav countries, with the right to an advisory vote."

In order not to be misunderstood I feel it necessary to stress that in spite of some striking parallelisms in the use of Panslavic conceptions by Soviet foreign policy and by the Russian tsarist governement, the differences remain enormous—but not at all in the sense of Mr. Leonidov's views. As I mentioned before, the Russian tsarist government of the nineteenth and twentieth centuries was bound by international and public law; and because of this the fate of the Russian subject of those times cannot be compared to the fate of the modern Russian citizen. Russia was not hidden behind an iron curtain from the world, and foreign travellers could visit Russia and freely observe her life. Poles, Ukrainians, Lithuanians, and Russians were sent to Siberia, but tsarist Russia did not know concentration camps; and the conditions of the exiles in Siberia during the time of the tsars could not be compared to the atrocious conditions reigning in Soviet concentration camps. Besides, the number of people sent to Siberia by the tsars during a whole century never reached even the smallest portion of the number deported by Stalin in one year. The tsars sent individuals there; Stalin transfers whole nations. Finally, one has to remember that free speech was not completely non-existent in tsarist Russia; the Panslavistic doctrines could be and were discussed—and even criticised. Nothing like that, of course, is possible under the Soviet regime. It happened that during the tsarist period Russia realized her greatest achievements in every field of her life. From Pushkin to Tolstoy, from Glinka to Rimsky-Korsakov, from Levitsky to Repin, from Lomonosov to Mechnikov one has pleiads of Russian men who created the great Russian culture and its prestige. Therefore, at that time Russia might indeed represent a spiritual attraction. People realized that Panslavism did not mean exactly Tolstoy and Rimsky-Korsakov but rather a Russian gendarme. This is why Engels wrote that behind the Panslavic conceptions "stands the terrible reality of the Russian Empire." But still the power of suggestion and attraction, to say the least, of the great Russian writers was a concrete fact, and even Russian Emperors like Alexander I, Nicholas I, and Alexander II were not deprived of traits which might captivate Europeans.

How different is the present situation! Where are the great spiritual achievements of Soviet culture? Even if one admits that there is a Soviet literature, that there is a Soviet science, that there is a Soviet music, what would these achievements mean without the background of the great Russian nineteenth century, and what do they mean in comparison with it? What are the promises and gifts which modern Russia would be able to offer to the Slavs, to mankind? What kind of reality "stands" behind Soviet Panslavism?

When one reads the horrifying, really monstrous reports on the abysmal sufferings and tortures which entire nations are enduring cloistered in that terrifying *castrum doloris* which is the present Russia, when one reads the unspeakable stories of the thousands of concentration camps that have been established in Russia one must indeed be terrified by Soviet Panslavic conceptions; *Timeo Donaos et dona ferentes.* St. Augustine once said that he did not like those who speak about mankind because such people do not like man. Neither Slavophil nor the Panslavist systems have any inspiration for the future.

Such inspiration I have found in a courageous Russian review, *Independent Thought,* appearing in Paris under the editorship of S. P. Melgunov. Not a Slavophil but simply an honest Russian, telling the horrible story of the cruel and fantastic co-operation of the UNRRA with the Soviets in their common fight against hundreds of thousands of displaced persons in Europe who did not want to return to the frightening sphere of Soviet domination, writes as follows:

"The fate of the Poles cannot be indifferent to us. We have no right to forget numerous cases when Polish exiles showed a touching solidarity toward their Russian companions in misfortune. So it was, for instance, last year in Bad-Kempten (South Bavaria), when one ill-omened, terrible morning a detachment of American policemen forced their way into the camp of Russian expatriates in order to make extraditions by force. Looking for the last defense, the Russians gathered in the camp church. When the victims were torn out of the church and put on trucks to be taken to the station, the Polish émigrés ran out of their neighboring camp and lay down on the highways blocking the road of the death transport. Taking advantage of the confusion which arose, numerous Russians succeeded in jumping from the trucks and escaped from the American policemen and the disguised Chekists who accompanied them. Then on the day following this memorable application of justice, over all foreign camps in Bad-Kempten, and among them the Polish camp, funeral flags were raised in memory of eighty-six Russians who did not escape repatriation by force and fell into the hands of the NKVD."[96]

[96] *La Pensée Libre—Svobodnaya Mysl'*, No. 6, 1946, p. 37.

The facts and, let us believe, the accidental excesses, reported in *Independent Thought* show the moral impasse in which the ruling political powers of the world found themselves at the end of the war. However, these facts also show something else: that these unfortunate, displaced people, although divided by the political conflicts that separate their countries, were able to forget their dissensions in the name of human solidarity and common European ideals of freedom and justice.

Who knows, indeed, if the sole source of hope for the future does not lie in the misery of these very people, who fought on all the battlefields of the war for their ideals, vainly looking, at the end of their fight, for some recognition of their human rights.

BIBLIOGRAPHY

CARR, E. H.: *Dostoevsky,* London, 1941.

DOSTOIEVSKY, F.: *La Russie face à l'Occident,* edited by André Chédel Lausanne, Editions La Concorde, 1945.

FELDMAN, W.: *Dzieje Polskiej Myśli Politycznej,* 3 vols., Warsaw, 1920.

FISCHEL, ALFRED: *Der Panslawismus bis zum Weltkrieg,* Stuttgart and Berlin, 1919.

GERSHENZON, M.: *Istoricheskie Zapiski,* Berlin, 1923.

KLARNER, Z.: *Slowianofilstwo w Literaturze Polskej lat* 1800-1848, Warsaw, 1926.

KRASINSKI, COUNT VALERIAN: *Panslavism and Germanism,* London, 1848.

KUCHARZEWSKI, J.: *The Origins of Modern Russia,* New York, 1948.

LEDNICKI, W.: *Pouchkine et la Pologne,* Paris, 1928.

LEGER, LOUIS: *Le Panslavisme et l'intérêt français,* Paris, 1917.

MASARYK, T. G.: *The Spirit of Russia,* 2 vols., London and New York, 1919.

MICKIEWICZ, A.: *Les Slaves,* Paris, 1914.

MILYUKOV, P. (Milioukov): *Le mouvement intellectuel russe,* Paris, 1918.

PYPIN, A. N.: *Panslavizm v ego Proshlom i Nastoyashchem* (1878), 1913.

ZDZIECHOWSKI, M.: *Mesjaniści i Slowianofile,* Cracow, 1888.

ZDZIECHOWSKI, M.: *Die Grundprobleme Russlands,* Vienna, 1907.

ZDZIECHOWSKI, M.: *Europa, Rosja, Azja,* Warsaw, 1923.

ZDZIECHOWSKI, M.: *Le dualisme dans la pensée religieuse russe,* Paris, 1924.

ZERNOV, N.: *Three Russian Prophets,* London, 1944.

Also, the works of Vladimir Solov'ev, B. Chicherin, A. L. Pogodin. V. A. Frantzev, etc.

XXIII.

European Pacifism and Internationalism

XXIII.

EUROPEAN PACIFISM AND INTERNATIONALISM

by

NICHOLAS DOMAN

I. Introduction

PACIFISM AS A philosophical and ethical doctrine has its origins outside of Europe. Its most spectacular manifestations in modern times are likewise outside of Europe. Yet, pacifism as a political doctrine has left indelible traces on the history of European politics—it has influenced the development of national as well as international life.

Pacifism as a political doctrine, developed slowly from an ethical conception destined to form the basis of a philosophy of life. The Christian roots of pacifism are non-European, however they represent the first significant effort in our civilization to ostracize force as a social element. The opposition of universalist Christianity to force and violence was not limited to the field of religion. But in spite of the powerful influence of Christianity in the Middle Ages, pacifism both as a practical force and a doctrine, was well-nigh nonexistant in Europe.

Hindu and Buddhist thought and political philosophy were without influence in the western world since the atmosphere of European life was not receptive to Asiatic doctrines. Geographic obstacles have also worked against them.

Gandhi's doctrine of non-violence has proved to be a powerful influence in the life on India. It may have provided limited impetus to European thinking and certain political movements, but it still remains to be proven whether this has been an element of importance in European pacifism.

In evaluating the spectrum of European pacifism, we must operate with approaches which would be wholly inappropriate and defective if the discussion centered around pacifism in America or Asia. Notwithstanding the presence of Christian adjectives in several of the pacifist movements, European pacifism is not a doctrine inherited from early Christianity, and certainly is not an outgrowth of the official position of the various official Christian churches of Europe. Wherever truly Christian influences appear in pacifist doctrines and movements, appropriate attention will be devoted to them. Likewise, we shall not attempt to construct and elaborate a dubious relationship between Gandhiism and European pacifism. It will appear that European pacifism is essentially the product of leftwing political ideology: liberalism, socialism, and internationalism.

Modern European pacifism is not a doctrine or movement based primarily on conscientious objection to war and unqualified endorsement of the doctrine of non-violence. Pacifism in the broader sense includes efforts aimed at the establishment of a peace machinery for the constructive organization of peace. The seasonal pacifists belong to this group. They are pacifists in time of peace, honestly laboring for the safe-guarding of peace and for an international machinery of guaranteeing it, but they join the Armageddon upon the outbreak of wars. They are the practical thinkers and politicians who have only distaste for war but are not morally handicapped from supporting wars already broken out. Their pacifism has moral grounds, but is based not so much on individual morals and conscience as upon their desire to work for the benefit of the community.

Pacifists in the stricter sense reject war as a matter of conscience. They proclaim their opposition to wars in times of peace, and maintain their position in times of war. The pacifists of the conscientious objector type, together with the pacifists of the anarchist type remain logically unassailable when they draw practical conclusions even in times of armed conflagrations from their unqualified opposition to wars.

Pacifists in the strict sense seldom venture into positions of public responsibility. They attempt to accomplish their aims through the media of private organizations or individual action. On the other hand, pacifists in the broad sense, realizing the futility of individual action, seek to further their objectives through organizations of an official character. They are often able to utilize the sounding board of high public position for their purposes.

II. Theories of Pacifism

Depending upon motives involved, several variations of pacifism can be distinguished. Christian Lange, the Norwegian international lawyer ("Histoire de la doctrine pacifique et de son influence sur le development du droit international, Recueil des Cours" 1926, vol. XIII) claims that there is just one pacifism, but with four bases of justification: utilitarian, ethical, practical juridical, and one having the earmarks of natural science, as explained by the German pacifist physician, G. F. Nicolai. The anti-pacifist G. Del Vecchio ("Die Tatsache das Krieges und der Friedengedanke" Leipzig, 1913) differentiates between four peace theories: the ascetic theory of pure Christianity, the imperialistic theory of the Pax Romana type, the empirico-political theory based on co-operation among states, and the juridical theory based on the establishment of a world federation or state on the pattern of the social contract of Rousseau. Max Scheler, the eminent German sociologist differentiates between eight classes of pacifism. Scheler expounded his theory in 1927 after having the opportunity to analyze the behavior of pacifists during the First World War and the defeatist period following. He interpreted the Hague Peace Conference of 1907 as a prelude to the war of 1914-18, and the Washington Conference of 1921 as the prelude to the next world war.

The experiences of the past twenty years, together with the historical appearance of pacifism, suggest the following differentiation among pacifist theories and movements:

1. *Heroic-individualistic pacifism.* This pacifism denies the justification of war in all circumstances; it preaches non-resistance in the case of military aggression, and refusal to render military service. Tolstoy is the outstanding European representative of this school which has few historical roots in Europe, and little affinity to European political doctrines. The intolerance of the European regimes in the past compelled members of pacifist groups to migrate to other continents. Numerous Mennonites—followers of the school of Menno Simons (1941-1561)—fled to America. Rare indeed was the tolerance manifested by William of Orange who, in 1577, ordered the authorities of Middleburg to exempt the Mennonites from military service. The outstanding representatives of this branch of pacifism are found in Asia and America.

In Europe some of the smaller, less representative Christian sects can be grouped in this category, as well as some of the anarchists and modern organizations, such as the War Resisters International. Many representatives of this school have become pacifists on purely secular ethical grounds—often after the repudiation of Christianity.

The anarchists and those who do not believe in social control and the collective power of organized society reject any non-individualist method of solution. Often they are in strategic alliance with religious and conscientious pacifists. These individualists have become sceptical of the capacity of organized society to perform the desired transformation from a system breeding war to a society built on pillars compatible with lasting peace. The individualist pacifist by his refusal to render military service engages in self-disarmament. So far as he is concerned he solved the paramount ethical problem with this gesture, and he disassociates himself from the strife-ridden world. From an individual point of view this may be a self-satisfying attitude, however, society, and particularly those hopeful of organizing a peaceful international society lose the coöperation of those who place individually interpreted ethical comfort above the collective interests of humanity. Advocates of non-violence or non-resistance, with the exception of the followers of Mahatma Gandhi, had no opportunity to test their doctrine in the national orbit. Being unable to influence domestic affairs, they try to use humanity for their political experiments. This attitude has helped to create a Chinese wall between themselves and other sincere exponents of world peace.

None would contend that the organization of world society is a less complicated problem than the organization of a national society. Nevertheless, many European and other pacifists oppose a central governmental machinery without which a modern society of national states cannot exist in relative peace at the present time, while they are much less opposed to national order.

2. *Christian Pacifism or Church Pacifism.* Max Scheler calls Christian Pacifism "half-pacifism." Historically as well as symptomatically there is a clear distinction between the Catholic and the Protestant schools. The pacifism of the Roman Catholic Church is based on the traditional theory of the spiritual supremacy of the Pope. Henri Massis, a popular French political writer, achieved great success with his antithesis of Rome-Geneva. He contrasted the atheistic humanitarian internationalism of the League of Nations with the Christian cosmopolitanism and universalism of the Catholic Church. Although the Catholic Church refrained from opposing the League of Nations, it was felt by some Catholics that the super-national conciliatory role of the Pope was superceded and deliberately ignored by the League.

The structure of international politics has changed momentously since 1503, when Pope Alexander VI arbitrated the territorial dispute in America between Portugal and Spain. Today world politics is less Catholic and less European than it was in the sixteenth century. The world powers of our times are the Protestant Anglo-Saxon countries and communistic Russia which are not likely to select the head of the Catholic Church as the world arbiter. Furthermore, the Islamic nations and the Asiatic powers can be counted upon to reject schemes aimed at the restoration of the temporal power of the church of Rome. It should not be forgotten that the desire of the Catholic Church to establish a just peace and maintain it does not exclude resort to arms for the purpose of defense. The doctrine of St. Thomas Aquinus clearly adopts the concept of "just war."

Non-Catholic Christian pacifism has neither the background nor the organization to render pacifism a practical force. With the exception of comparatively small sects wielding little or no political influence, European Protestantism has neglected to build itself up as an ideological bastion against war. The gulf between the various Protestant churches is too wide, and their alignment with national institutions too overwhelming to permit the emergence of a European Protestant pacifist movement.

To Tolstoy, the ablest representative of Christian anarchist pacifism, the term "Christian State" resembled the words "hot ice." Most Christian pacifists have been unwilling to accept Tolstoy's extreme anarchism. Aldous Huxley and his followers, however, want to sit "on the fringe of the political arena, lest its ends be corrupted by the violences inherent in the politics of the world."

3. *Utilitarian-Liberal Pacifism* has exercised greater practical political influence than have the two other categories mentioned above. Its mainspring is mainly economic. War is rejected not for high sounding ethical or ideological reasons but because it interferes with the material interest of the great majority of the people. Followers of this trend usually believe in the teachings of the positivist school and accept the utilitarian conception of values. This school fully endorses the dictum of Jeremiah Bentham about the "greatest happiness of the greatest number." It draws heavily on other British sources such as laissez-faire manchesterism and the utilitarianism of Herbert Spencer. Because commerce in Great Britain was more advanced than in most of

the continental countries and played a more important role in the economic welfare, it also became a more potent political force. The utilitarian liberal doctrine was not primarily a motivating force in the feudal structure of pre-1939 Poland and countries of similar background.

This school gained prominence in the middle classes, particularly in the mercantile bourgeoise of Europe. It rejected war as a retarding factor of communal and individual life and refused to recognize the economic usefulness even of victorious wars. Economic interest is the foundation of this doctrine which exercises little influence of the historical classes nursed on tradition and non-economic ideological values. It also failed to move the destitute proletariat which could not see the economic blessings of peace based on privilege.

The utilitarian-liberal pacifism was particularly unpopular in Germany. German authors like Hegel, Treitschke, Othmar Spann, and Werner Sombart took great pleasure in contrasting the egotistical individualistic aspects of commerce with the values of nationalism and militarism. Sombart's famous antithesis of "Händler and Held" (trader and hero) revealed a popular German trend of thought.

In the 1920's and early 1930's economic pacifism led to the various Central and Eastern European federal schemes.[1] It was believed that the community of economic interests could overcome political diversity and conflicts, and intelligently interpreted self-interest would eliminate political and territorial friction. The abolition of trade and custom barriers was advocated as a measure of economic internationalism. Unfortunately the breakdown of world economy and the emergence of Hitlerism in Germany cast a fatal shadow over these schemes, which soon lost their economic and political importance.

[1] For a review of the Central European projects and their literature, see Feliks Gross, *Crossroads of Two Continents*, New York, 1945, and Korek-Stark, *Mitteleuropa Bibliographie*, Berlin-Vienna, 1935.

4. *Marxian Pacifism.* Orthodox Marxists are long-range pacifists; they envisage class war against the capitalist state, the temporary dictatorship of the proletariat, and finally eternal peace in a socialist world. Non-communist Marxists, members of the European socialist or social democratic parties, adherents to the Second International, abandoned this conception. Instead they became supporters of international organizations aimed at the maintenance of peace in a world of status-quo. Before the First World War, the great French Socialist, Jean Jaurès, still spoke for the socialist parties of Europe when he charged that capitalism breeds wars, like the clouds breed storms. In Basel in 1912, the Socialists of the world solemnly declared that they considered the coming European war a "criminal and reactionary undertaking of all the governments." But the German Socialist Party and many other socialist parties voted for the war budget in the First World War. "Marxian pacifism" practically disappeared when loyalties and positions had to be decided at the time of the Second World War. The pacifism of the various Communist parties lost its intellectual honesty and became an appendix of the ever-varying Soviet foreign policy. Werner Sombart tried to show that the Soviet Union was developing into a corporative military organization. This accusation had attributes of unfairness when it is considered that the Soviet Union had to embrace military measures in order to survive in a hostile world.

Since the abandonment of the utopistic socialist doctrines and the emergence of the Soviet Union as a world power, the intransigeant *sui generis* pacifism of the Marxists has lost its practical value. According to Marx, Engels, Bebel, and the early Marxists, every war or manifestation of violence against Czarist Russia was justifiable. However, following the establishment of the Soviet Union, every resort to war and violence was rejected unless it worked in the favor of the Soviet Union. Lenin, in his "Socialism and War," excommunicated pacifism and reiterated that wars will persist as long as the systems of capitalism and imperialism continue. He referred to capitalist states when he said: "Whoever wishes a durable and democratic peace must favor civil war against the governments and the bourgeoisie."[2]

The emergence of the Soviet Union as a world power, as well as the need for a war of resistance against the Germany of Hitler, deprived European Socialists of their pacifist tenets and ultimately eliminated them from the roll of pacifists.[3]

5. *Pacifism of International Law and Organization.* After a modest but persistent start in the second half of the nineteenth century, the twentieth century gave birth to a series of international organizations aimed at the maintenance of peace, and culminating first in the League of Nations and later in the United Nations. More and more people have taken the position that the "individual war" of the pacifist individual, the love of peace of the Christian, or the economic self-interest of the bourgeois, are not able to guarantee peace. It was argued that without international law and some world organization, war could not be prevented.

The international organizations of the twentieth century are global—not merely European organizations — though they are based on European doctrines and tradition, and up to the Second World War had their headquarters on the European continent. But the European influence and initiative are on the wane. The Hague conferences were called together by the half European Czar of Russia. The emergence of the League of Nations was due more to the support of Woodrow Wilson than of any other individual.

The supporters of juridical pacifism are sincerely motivated by peace, but by no means do they subscribe to the theory of non-violence and non-resistance. In spite of the great disillusionment caused by the First World War, war-resisting pacifism made insignificant progress. While little confidence was advanced to the League of Nations and its auxiliary institutions, Europeans found no better device for the safeguarding of peace.

[2] There were many reasons why the Soviet leaders decided to break with pacifism. As far back as 1920, Bukharin began to glorify the new Soviet Militarism as "Proletarian Militarism."

[3] For a historical analysis indicating that pacifism and militarism are not the monopoly of any social or economic class, see Nicholas Doman, "The Coming Age of World Control," New York, 1942, pp. 51-54.

Juridical pacifism is not opposed to wars fought in self-defense. Nor is natural law as advanced by Hugo Grotius opposed to "just wars." This type of pacifism appealed to the *beati possedentes* who have been anxious to observe the fruits of past wars in the status quo of peace. It is not mere coincidence that individuals and groups favorably situated in world politics and economics labored so diligently to provide legal foundations for a world which offered them many advantages. Shortly before the First World War the unincorporated socialist-pacifist-anarchist coalition was aided in the struggle to preserve peace by inveterate conservative circles in Great Britain, Austria, and elsewhere. The latter were dubious of war gains and fearful of social and economic repercussions. In the 1930's the conservative circles of Western and Central Europe were among the most persistent proponents of an appeasement policy of peace at any price. This type of pacifism is often an ideology of interest *(Interessenideologie)*. Unconditional pacifists had no use for the League of Nations and for its concept of legalized war in the form of sanctions as expressed in Article 16 of the Covenant of the League of Nations.

6. *Intellectual pacifism.* The glorification of war certainly does not represent the views of the majority of European intellectuals. Moltke, in his assertion that "Eternal peace is a dream and not even a beautiful dream," may have spoken for the formally educated Germans who were thoroughly schooled in the violently nationalist spirit, but not for the great majority of 20th century intellectuals for whom war and progress of civilization are antinomes. Dilapidated reactionaries with a Fascist complex have been popular at certain times and in certain circles, but their worshipping of warrior heroism strikes a discordant tone in the general mental climate of the European intelligentsia. Leon Daudet, Charles Maurras, Jacques Bainville, Othmar Spann, the doctrinaries of Italian Fascism have provoked a resilient echo. At the same time, it would be erroneous to overlook the persistent advance recorded by the exponents of cosmopolitanism, various sorts of internationalism, and federalism. Through their organi-

zations, they have recruited a steadier and more permanent following than have the hit-and-run theorists of the doctrine of violence. Pan-European groups, League of Nations associations, Central European and other federal organizations, developed a great degree of cultural and political "Europeism." Adherents to these groups are not ethical or religious pacifists, but rational and positivist proponents of peace.

III. The Morphology of Peace

Peace has too often been called the absence of war. Even strong advocates of an international order have succumbed to this negative conception of peace. Peace certainly deserves a morphological approach. It would not be out of place to use clinical methods to analyze the problems of peace, to search for its foundations, the causes of organic disturbances, local malaises, and its slow or abrupt dissolution.

The science of peace is the science of international or world government. It has received more attention on the European continent than it has in Great Britain and America. In the 1930's there was a movement at the University of Lyon to establish a chair for the science of peace and to formulate the basic elements for this new science. Although it is never overlooked that Germans pioneered with the science of war, it is rarely recognized that the first significant suggestions for a science of peace also originated in Germany.

Kant's approach to the problem of lasting peace is the source of many of the recent peace doctrines. The status of the world has changed since 1795, when Kant published his work "Toward Eternal Peace," but his philosophical and logical premises retained their significance.

Eugen Schlief's "The Peace in Europe," published in 1892, has given momentum to the modern science of peace. Fried, Nippold, Novicov, Nicolai, and others have kindled the flames of this new science of peace, and tried to formulate a structural outlook for pacifists.

The Viennese journalist, Alfred H. Fried, who received the Nobel Peace Prize in 1911, claimed that his science of pacifism was really a science of internationalism. Max Scheler, following the antique dichotomy, sets militarism against pacfism. To Scheler the love of peace is the motivating force of the pacifists, the love of war, that of the militarists. A more appropriate antithesis is suggested by Leo Gross, an Austrian scholar, in his "Pacifismus und Imperialismus." According to this view, pacifism—the ideal of peace—is opposed by imperialism, the expansive force of nationalism. A brilliant German political scientist, Adolf Grabowsky,[4] claims to find a synthesis of pacifism and militarism in imperialism. To Grabowsky, imperialism is the strongest political force of our time. Pacifism and militarism are merely means to accomplish the end.

Heinrich Rogge, a German political scientist mildly contaminated with National Socialism, puts forward concrete proposals for the organization of a new science of peace. His *Nationale Friedens-Politik* is the most thorough analysis of the theoretical aspects of peace. It is unfortunate that this literary monument has been revised to suit the taste of the Hitler-Papen regime.

Few Europeans would say today that peace is being obstructed by the love of war of the militarists. Pacifism and the organization of peace have failed so far because the spirit of nationalism and the desire for economic domination as organized in our system of national states have been stronger political forces than the desire for peace. The conflict is essentially between these types of particularism and cosmopolitanism. Imperialism is group individualism. This imperialism is not always expansive nationalism—it often parades in the form of economic and social domination, geographical and economic expansion. When conflicting

[4] *Politik*, Berlin, 1932, p. 211. It should be noted that this treatise, published before the advent of Hitler's regime, contains many basic features of the Nazi ideology.

imperialist forces on the great power level clash with each other, peace terminates.

Modern European political thinking at last produced a fairly feasible diagnosis for the peace-war controversy. But so far the results of theoretical contemplation have not influenced the controlling forces of national and international politics.

Not only political theorists, but also practical statesmen have come to realize that without a European or world-wide political authority, great power conflicts cannot be kept from degenerating into wars. According to Kjellen there are no saturated great powers. Grabowsky is subservient to Marxist theories when he claims that the cause of "real" wars is always a "deplacement' 'of power which is not in harmony with the possessions and influence of the state.[5]

Under French leadership, between the two world wars, a great many Europeans paid homage to the classic formula "quieta non muovere," insisted upon and worked toward a static pacifism (organization of international peace under existing power alignments). The majority of German and Austrian thinkers advocated a "dynamic pacifism" in place of the "status quo pacifism" identified with the League of Nations. This divergence in the approach to the problem of peace has sometimes been characterized as the conflict between pacifism through established law and pacifism through power politics. These artificial classifications do not hold water, and it is not possible to maintain the distinction between international law on one hand and so-called "metajuridical spheres" on the other hand.

According to the orthodox Marxist slogan, peace depends on domestic socialization.[6] Many European pacifists have become socialists because they believe in pacifism. Similarly, many socialists espoused pacifism as a doctrine related to socialism. This becomes clear when we think of such names as Ramsay MacDon-

[5] Grabowsky, *op. cit.*, p. 207.

[6] See Rudolf Goldscheid: "Friedensbewegung und Menschensökonomie," 1912, for a rational interpretation of the relationship between peace and socialism. Goldscheid develops the theory that domestic socialization is domestic pacification and this reacts on external pacification.

ald, George Lansbury, and Lord Ponsonby in England; Jean Jaurès, Leon Jouhaux, and Henri Barbusse in France; Karl Liebknecht and Rosa Luxemburg in Germany. Kurt Hiller, a leading figure in the German pacifist movement, portrays the thinking of many Euhopean socialists in the following statement: "We believe that the idea of pacifism cannot be realized within a world organized in capitalism. . . . We are socialists because of pacifism. We regard the realization of world socialism as the condition of the realization of world pacifism. . . . The peace movement will not be the mother, but only the midwife of a social revolution and the social revolution the mother of eternal peace."[7]

IV. Organized Pacifism

The First World War did not toll the death-knell for all pacifist movements operating prior to the war. In the belligerent countries the organization work of pacifism was necessarily stifled, but in some of the neutral countries pacifists were permitted to continue their activities, particularly in Switzerland and Holland. This organizational freedom had been used not only by the scholarly half-pacifist international associations but also by the absolute pacifists who rejected war under all circumstances. An example of this freedom can be seen in the Amsterdam Conference of 1914 where the anarchist-pacifists accepted a resolution offered by G. Rijnders and agreed to oppose every war because of social and personal convictions. In coöperation with the Swiss war resisters, the partisans of the "New Road" movement, and some neomarxist communists, they displayed active propaganda against all wars. Much of this pacifist propaganda is connected with the names of Jules Humbert Droz, Henrietta Roland Holst, and R. de Jong.

In the period of 1918-1921 most of the politically memorable peace manifestations had little or nothing in common with philosophical pacifism or pacifist movements aimed at the organiza-

[7] Kurt Hiller in *Die Friedenswarte*, 1923, p. 14 and 1926, p. 246.

tion of international peace. Incidents like these were motivated by peculiar political conditions:

1918: the sailors of the German Ocean Fleet refused to man the ships when, notwithstanding the armistice, the Admirals wanted to continue to fight in desperation.

1919: the crews of five cruisers of the French Black Sea Fleet revolted against attacking Soviet Russia.

1920: the creation of action committees among British laborers for the purpose of refusing to load munition ships in the war against the Soviet and threatening general strike in case of an official war.

1920: the general strike in Germany which contributed to the fiasco of the Kapp Putsch.

It is historically incorrect and misleading that pacifism should claim credit for, or proximate casual relationship with, these incidents. In most instances, they were connected with domestic political issues or the policy toward the new regime of Russia installed by Lenin.

The atmosphere of postwar Europe in the 1920's provided pacifist movements with an unusually favorable psychological foundation. Pacifist movements of the war resisting type cropped up in large numbers and began to operate beside the already functioning organizations. Among the more representative groups are:

I. War Resisters International, which has enjoyed the benefit of the support of such outstanding men in British politics as Lord Ponsonby, George Lansbury, Laurence Housman, and McGovern, the M. P. of the Independent Labor Party. In Germany, Dr. Helene Stoecker was among its leaders. In Czechoslovakia, Premysl Pitten headed its roster.

Organizations affiliated with the War Resisters International: No More War Movement—later the Peace Pledge Union—organized in 1936 by George Lansbury and his friends in Great Britain; Ligue Pour le Reconnaissance Légale de l'Objection de Conscience, founded in 1924; Ligue Internationale des Refractaires à Toute Guerre, in Paris; Bund der Kriegsdienstgegner, in Berlin; Bund der Kriegsdienstgegner, in Vienna; Movement for Christian Communism, in Prague; Swiss Central Office for Peace Work, in Zurich. Similar affiliated organizations have been active in the Scandinavian countries, Holland, Belgium, and for a limited time, in some of the eastern European countries.[8]

II. International Fellowship of Reconciliation, with headquarters in London, and branches and affiliated organizations all over the world, was an essentially Christian pacifist movement founded in 1914.

III. International Antimilitaristic Bureau Against War and Reaction, with headquarters in The Hague.

Affiliated with this organization was the International Antimilitaristic Commission, also headquartered in The Hague.

IV. International Antimilitaristic Society, with headquarters in The Hague.

V. Women's International League for Peace and Freedom, with headquarters in Geneva.

VI. Tolstoy Federation, with headquarters in Vienna.

VII. International Committee of Democratic Action for Peace, with headquarters in Paris.

At the first meeting of the War Resisters International in 1921, the following declaration was adopted which has since been confirmed at each successive conference: "War is a crime against humanity. We therefore are determined not to support any kind of war and to strive for the removal of all causes of war." The Statement of Principles adopted at the 1925 conference of the International, according to the interpretation of Aldous Huxley's "Encyclopedia of Pacifism,"[9] leaves no doubt that the resort to armed violence, or any form of warfare, is damaging most of all to the "good cause." The War Resisters refused to make special

[8] The War Resisters International was founded in Holland in 1921 and has its headquarters now in Enfield, Middlesex, England. Lord Ponsonby, the Labor peer was its chairman from 1941 until his death in 1946.

[9] An Encyclopedia of Pacifism, edited by Aldous Huxley, Harper & Brothers, New York and London, 1937.

provisions in favor of wars for the defense of democracy or war on behalf of the oppressed proletariat.[10]

In addition to the above strictly pacifist organizations, numerous organizations had been in existence between the two world wars which, while aiming at the maintenance of peace and disavowing war as a political technique, have refrained from identifying themselves with extreme pacifists. Most of these organizations are world-wide in scope and membership, but the emphasis of their interest and the center of their activities are essentially European.

Peace conferences of some type or another had been held since 1843 in London, Paris, Brussels, Frankfort. Most of them were occasions for sentimental manifestation rather than organized reunions of trained political experts and scholars. The peace conference of Paris in 1849, presided over by Victor Hugo, was rather an exception. It had decided political features.

The heyday of the International Peace Conferences was between 1889 and 1914, and again from the early 1920's until 1939. Since 1891 they were called together by the International Office of Peace (Bureau International de la Paix) which was founded in 1891 by the International Peace Conference of Rome. Its funds are provided partly by contributions from Switzerland, Sweden, Denmark, Norway, and Portugal. An International Peace Conference was convoked nearly every year whenever political conditions permitted. Not even the officers of this organization could contend that their meetings and activities have influenced the course of European or world politics. In fact the various army and navy leagues and militaristic societies exercised greater influence on world politics than the more dignified peace societies. This is a significant factor, when it is remembered that we are discussing one of the oldest and most distinguished of the peace organizations. The Nobel Peace Prize was awarded in 1910 to

10 The tyranny and aggressive warfare of Hitler and Mussolini greatly influenced many of the pre-1933 pacifists. The signers of the Oxford Peace Pledge in 1933 vowed to refuse fighting in any future war, even in case of attack. The issues of the Second World War made many of them discard the pledge.

the Bureau International de la Paix, and since 1901, many of their functionaries have been its recipients:

Frederick Passy, France, 1901.
Elie Ducommun, Switzerland, 1902.
William Randal Cremer, Great Britain, 1903.
Berta von Suttner, Austria, 1905.
E. T. Moneta, Italy, 1907.
Frederick Bajer, Denmark, 1908.
Alfred H. Fried, Austria, 1911.
Henri La Fontaine, Belgium, 1913.
Ludwig Quidde, Germany, 1927.

For many years the latter two had been the pillars of the International Peace Conferences.

The Interparliamentary Union is another of the distinguished organizations which is sparsely sprinkled with last-ditch pacifists. It is concerned more with the problems in connection with the organization of peace, and not with providing a forum for individual emotions. It has never served as a platform for extreme pacifists of an anarchistic character; its members are parliamentary representatives of the respective member states, and hence it can be assumed that its conference discussions are not divorced from political realities.

The first Interparliamentary Conference was held in Paris in 1889, under the sponsorship of William Randal Cremer and Frederic Passy. After the First World War the first official act of its Council at the Geneva meeting was a resolution hailing the establishment of the League of Nations with the most profound satisfaction, and expressing the hope "that from now on the Interparliamentary Union will devote all its efforts toward the strengthening and democratic development of the League of Nations."

Before the First World War the Union was a vigorous advocate of international arbitration; it played an important role in the creation of the Permanent Court of Arbitration at the first Hague

Conference and the convocation of the second Hague Peace Conference. After the war its efforts were devoted to the further organization of international society and the maintenance of peace. As a forum for the parliamentarians of nearly all civilized countries, the conferences of the unions were instrumental in creating in the minds of the delegates, a practical appreciation of many problems of an international nature.

The European Center of the Carnegie Endowment was another dignified and scholarly body whose advisory council was studded with names also identified with the activities of the two organizations previously described. This fact might be indicative of the limited number of statesmen and scholars devoted to active work for the cause of peace.

La Conciliation Internationale was established in 1905 by d'Estournelles de Constant, the French Deputy. Its avowed program is "the development of national prosperity in favor of good international relations and the organization of these relations on a permanent and durable basis." Its activities run the gamut of functions familiar in international organizations. Among its French members were Leon Bourgeois, Henri Bergson, E. Lavisse, Charles Richet. While the character of the organization was basically French, many non-French European and other members were identified with it, including Henry Lammasch (Austria), Fr. Nansen (Norway), C. Lombroso (Italy), and F. W. Foerster (Germany).

Among the other international organizations working for peace through better international relations are the World Alliance for Friendship through the Churches (Alliance Universelle pour l'amitié internationale par les Églises), the International Council of Women, (Counseil International des Femmes), and the International Union of the League of Nations Associations. Members of the League of Nations Associations in Europe and elsewhere studied and diffused the principles of the charter of the League of Nations. For many a devout worker of these associations, maintenance of peace was equivalent to the success of the League. Few of them were pacifists of the conscientious objector type. Since the establishment of the United Nations, many of these associations continue their activities as Associations for the United Nations.

The activities of most of the associations centered around university life. In some countries, like France and Great Britain, they also branched out among the citizenry, establishing ties with women's organizations, churches, free mason lodges, etc. It can be said, however, that members of the associations represented heterogenous views on world politics and their only point of unity was the desire to study and understand international relations and peace in connection with the League of Nations and its network of international organizations. The officers of the League cooperated with the associations and regarded them as effective publicity agents for intelligent public opinion. This is evidenced by the fact that resolutions or recommendations of the International Union of the League of Nations Associations were published and given wide diffusion in the official League publication, the *Journal Official.*

The previously mentioned International Committee of Democratic Action for Peace was founded in 1921 at Paris, largely on the initiative of the French Christian-Democratic Deputy Marc Sangnier.[11] This organization is often referred to as the Democratic International. Its members believe that intelligent democratic pacifist education can best guarantee the maintenance of peace. In spite of its French godparents (including Ferdinand Buisson, a president of the Chamber of Deputies), several influential Germans and Austrians joined this group. The strong Catholic flavor of the organization was already apparent when its first conference at Paris extended greetings to Pope Benedict XV.

Primarily interested in international law and the organization of world peace through the instrumentalities of law are:

[11] Sangnier was also the leader of the Catholic Peace group called "Jeune Republique."

L'Institut de droit International—a scholarly group founded in Belgium in 1873, specializing in technical problems of international law such as codification of international law and arbitration.

The International Law Association which, having a more popular character, conducted a successful propaganda campaign for the extension of the principle of arbitration.

V. Practical Pacifism in Time of War

Peace organizations were permitted to operate in countries which had been otherwise unfriendly toward pacifism. This seeming liberalism however, was not carried so far as to exempt conscientious objectors from military service. Few European countries have provisions on their statutes regulating the service of the objectors. Traditionally neutral countries are inclined to be more liberal. Countries which are perennially imbroiled in conflicts are disinclined to distinguish conscientious objection from treason.

The Danish law of 13 December 1917 permitted refusal of military service on grounds of conscience. Instead of military service, the objectors were subject to a so-called civilian service obligation. While the duration of the military service at the time of the passing of this law was six months, the period of civilian service was set at 20 months, with the obvious intention of discouraging refusal to perform military service.

In Sweden the right to refuse military service was granted by law on 21 May 1920. The objector is subject to alternative service. Up to 1925 only religious objections were recognized, but after 1926 the same privileges were extended to non-religious conscientious objectors. Swedish defense law gives the objectors a choice between rendering military service without arms and rendering purely civilian service. The period of service in the first case is extended by one fourth of the duration of the regular military service, and in the second case, by one half.

In Norway, the question of objection to military service is governed by regulations similar to those of Sweden. The number of objectors in both countries ran into several hundred each year before the outbreak of the Second World War.

Since August 1923, Holland has also offered the privilege of alternative service to conscientious objectors. Anarchists, Mennonites, and Quakers have been refusing to serve in the army. Some of the so-called absolutist pacifists have refused even the alternative service, preferring prison terms instead.

In the 1920's Soviet Russia aligned herself with other countries which had manifested a liberal attitude toward objectors. But in the Soviet Union the privilege of objection was reserved only to those who by birth or education belonged to sects which have opposed military service as a matter of basic doctrine. Peasant members of such religious sects could, in many instances, evade military service, whereas intellectuals were not granted the same consideration on the theory that the educated man is not subject to religious prejudices and that only counter-revolutionaries would attempt to evade service in the Red Army.

In other European countries Baptists, Adventists, and Jehovah's Witnesses who have objected to military obligations have, as a rule, been sentenced to prison terms to perform humiliating labor. Catholic countries on the whole have shown less inclination to recognize the principle of conscientious objection than have Protestant countries where, in many cases, free-thinker influences have been responsible for legislation exempting the objectors.

During the Second World War, very few nations actually respected provisions exempting conscientious objectors from military service.[12] When most of continental Europe was under the

[12] In Great Britain an impressive number of persons tried to gain exemption from military service with the plea of conscientious objection. The number of conscientious objectors was around 16,000 in the First World War, while during the Second World War, 59,836 sought exemption up to January 1, 1945. Of the latter, 2,865 were granted unconditional exemption; 22.568—conditional exemption with assignment to certain prescribed occupations, 16,753—noncombatant military duties, and the pleas of 17,650 were re'ected and they were given regular military assignments. (See "The Reporter, " National Service Board for Religious Objectors, III, April 1, 1945.) Thre is no conclusive evidence, however, of the increase in the number of conscientious ob'ectors in Europe, as a whole, since the First World War.

control of Nazi Germany, refusal to render the required military service was settled in a summary way in line with the National Socialist and Fascist approach to pacifism. Members of pacifist groups were sent to concentration caps and subjected to special tortures. The Nürnberg Trial produced authentic evidence in the form of original documents emanating from high German government sources, ordering systematized torture and death for members of sects advocating pacifism. In Buchenwald and many other concentration camps, conscientious objector-pacifists were made recognizable by the violet triangles they wore on their clothes.

It is difficult to generalize the attitude of the European nations toward individual pacifism in the form of conscientious objection. There is little to indicate that the liberal approach of the 1920's will be revived. If any change should occur, it will point rather toward the weakening of the position of the individual pacifists.[13]

VI. Pacifism and a United Europe

It is interesting to note that one of the motivating forces behind Coudenhove-Kalergi's Pan-Europe movement was the fear of Soviet power. The founder of this movement makes it clear that he regards Russia—white or red—as a threat to European freedom. He contends that the geopolitical position of Russia makes her inimical to the interests of the rest of Europe. His book "Pan-Europe" first published in 1923, sounds the prophetic warning: "History gives Europe the following alternatives, to overcome all national hostilities and consolidate in a federal union, or sooner or later to succumb to a Russian conquest. There is no third possibility. Russia is Europe's Macedonia."[14]

13 By the summer of 1946 the War Resister, a publication of the War Resisters International, reported the reorganization of several of its continental affiliates. It also reports that the Friedengesellschaft (German Peace Society) has been revived, with ex-general Freiherr Von Schonaich, the absolutist pacifist, reelected president.

14 English translation: Richard N. Coudenhove-Kalergi, "Pan-Europe," New York, 1926, p. 55.

There is another reason why Coudenhove-Kalergi urges the establishment of a European federal union. He warns that if such a union is not realized "then a Russo-German alliance becomes a mere question of time."[15] Many supporters of the Pan-Europe idea look upon it is a counterbalance to the socialist expansion. Many moderate leftists approved it because it dovetailed with their liberal internationalism.[16] The ambition of the Pan-Europe movement is a peaceful world power extending from Poland to Portugal, excluding the British Dominions and the United Kingdom. For Coudenhove-Kalergi, pacifism is not only a postulate of ethics but also of reason, from the point of view of both "Europeism" and national egoism.

While the program of Pan-Europe is not pacifism, it may fall in our classification of utilitarian-liberal pacifism as opposed to ethical individualistic pacifism. The aim of the movement is to secure peace among the nations of Europe and to arrive at economic prosperity through the unification of Europe. Its motivating forces are economic unity and peace internally, and the emergence of a united Europe as a world power in the game of global politics.

Pacifism should not be confused with the various schemes to establish a United States of Europe. While it is admitted that the strongest and the most predominant single force behind these schemes is the desire to guarantee the maintenance of peace, it would be an error to conclude that a United States of Europe is urged only for the sake of world peace. The drive for a United Europe indicates first of all that political thinkers being aware of the anachronistic nature of the national state system are searching for a realistic substitute. The various projects for a united Europe cleverly indicate that the Haushoferian concept of great area amalgamations has seized the imagination of so many practical thinkers. The advocacy of a United States of Europe by

[15] Richard N. Coudenhove-Kalergi, *op. cit.*, p. 45.

[16] Briand, Painlevé, de Jouvenel, Loucheur, Nitti, Chancellor Marx, Paul Loebe, Sforza, Sforza, Thomas G. Masaryk, Benes, Vandervelde, Karl Renner. Conspicuous were the endorsements of Joseph Cailloux and Msgr. Seipel of Austria, no leftists by any stretch of the imagination.

Herriot and Briand is a case in point. Herriot in his book "The United States of Europe" draws encouragement for his project from the experience of Louis Loucheur who examined the problem of European economic unity under the patronage of the Vienna Chamber of Commerce, and Joseph Cailloux who advocated the establishment of a vast European market within a Pan-Europe organization.

Aristide Briand is another brilliant exponent of utilitarian pacifism, of pacifism through international law and internationalism in general. He, more than anyone, is responsible for the historic memorandum of the French government on the "Organization of a Regime of European Federal Union." On the 9th of September, 1929, the French government invited the European members of the League of Nations to discuss the Briand project for a European union. The memorandum of Briand published in May 1930 represents a radical program compared with the then prevailing national structure of Europe. At the same time it was a modest proposal suggesting "union" and not "unity."

The rhetorical appeals carried little weight. On the 8th of September, 1930, Briand's European Conference met in Geneva simultaneously with the XI Assembly of the League of Nations. Europe's desire for peace was overshadowed by too many other considerations. Words of peace were not enough. Peace fell on the altar of the national state system of Europe.[17]

Disillusionment with the idea of economic union as a gateway to a united Europe and peace, comes among others, from Sir Arthur Salter, who maintains that a United States of Europe must become a political reality before it can become an economic reality.[18] Salter has lost confidence in the utilitarian-economic peace technique parading under the banner of "Zollverein."

17 Briand liked to emphasize the psychological impact of the word "Peace." He told a group of newspapermen: "Ce mot de paix, il ne faut pas que les hommes d'Etat se lassant de la repeter, et vous, Messieurs le journalists, it convient aussi que vous ne cessiez jamais de parler de l'idée de paix, quand même ce serait pour la combattre. Parlez, parlez de la paix, et cela suffira."

18 The United States of Europe, London, 1933.

The governments of Europe, like the governments of the non-European countries are anxious to enter into agreements and conclude treaties and conventions which represent nothing but meaningless rituals designed to please the conscience of the framers of international policy. There is much truth in the cruel phrase of Salvador de Madariaga: "The powers are intent on seeing that the path to international hell is paved with good conventions."

The popular campaign for international arbitration agreements, international organizations, international conferences, the quest for collective security, and high-sounding programs for disarmament failed to touch the essential problems of peace. Behind the curtain of this so-called pacifist phraseology remained the insistence of every national state on the supreme criterion of sovereignty, the *jus belli.* The urge for peace did not abate the intention of any government to insist on the obligation of the citizen to offer himself in "Todesbereitschaft und Tötungsbereitschaft" — readiness to kill or be killed.[19]

VII. Pacifism and Disarmament

Prior to the First World War the quest for peace was, to a large extent, the quest for international arbitration. Such concepts as collective security and disarmament figured much less in the discussions of those who wanted to find the formula for peace. But after the War, peace was sought through disarmament, or at least through the discussion of the subject of disarmament.[20] At first glance the importance attached to disarmament seems subordinate. Individual pacifists, like Berta von Suttner, in her book "Down with Arms" did not fail to see a proximate casual relationship between armaments and war. The diplomatic agencies of the European states and the more digni-

[19] See the clever dissertation of Carl Schmitt on this question in his "Begriff des Politischen," Berlin, 1927.

[20] The subject of this study necessarily relegates to a mere cursory reference such abortive episodes as the Locarno Pact of 1925 and the Briand-Kellogg Pact outlawing war. Such treatment of these pacts may be justified by the footnote like role they exercised on the preservation of peace.

fied societies concerned with international peace gave the question of armaments only cursory attention. This attitude is reflected in the Covenant of the League of Nations. Only two articles of the Covenant, (8 and 9) touch on the problem. Article 8 contained the modest statement that "the maintenance of peace requires the reduction of national armaments to the lowest point consistent with national safety and the enforcement by common action of international obligations."

From 1919 until the failure of the Disarmament Conference in the early 1930's[21] pacifists of every hue and cry demanded disarmament. A legal and moral obligation to disarm was contained in the official Allied and Associated Powers' communique to Germany on the 16th of June, 1919, handed by Georges Clemenceau to Count von Brockdorff-Rantzau: "The Allied and Associated Powers wish to make it clear that their requirements in regard to German armaments were not made solely with the object of rendering it impossible for Germany to resume her policy of military aggression. They are also the first steps toward that general reduction and limitation of armaments which they seek to bring about as one of the most fruitful preventives of war and which it will be one of the first duties of the League of Nations to promote."

After the compulsory disarmament of the Central Powers, France pursued a persistent policy of tieing in disarmament with collective security. The Cabinets of Poincaré and Tardieu particularly pursued this policy, and it was also the principal postulate of the foreign policies of the other French Cabinets between the two world wars. When Leon Blum, as the head of the French Socialist Party became the French Prime Minister in 1936, he hastened to reiterate this tenet of French diplomacy. This may have surprised those who looked upon Blum as the successor of Jean Jaurès, and the leader of a party with considerable pacifist tinge. "Undoubtedly, collective security is the con-

21 The final session of the Conference was on May 29, 1934, but the Conference had been moribund since October, 1933.

dition of disarmament, since no State would agree to disarm unless mutual assistance offered it a degree of certainty; but the converse is equally true. Disarmament is the condition of full collective security, for States must be substantially disarmed if arbitral awards are to be imposed and pacific sanctions are to exert their constraining power."[22]

Other nations only remotely concerned with the German menace did not insist on connecting collective security with disarmament. The effort expanded to guarantee peace through disarmament is impressive indeed, considering the voluminous studies, the establishment of commissions with high sounding names and the holding of innumerable conferences. Genuine pacifists, like Professor Hans Wehberg, and the Norwegian professor Christian Lange, reached to the crux of the problem when they proposed a budgetary limitation for armaments.[23] This suggestion greatly disconcerted the various national governments but of course, remained without practical effect. The much advertised desire for disarmament could not be reduced to practical measures. The supreme political power still resting in the national states, voluntary disarmament had to fail. There is no indication that national disarmament will ever be accomplished until political power is shifted to a supranational authority.

The most significant proposal of the Disarmament Conference came from the Soviet delegate, Maxim Litvinov, who wanted progressive and proportional disarmament with an ultimate view to complete disarmament. Litvinov previously reproached the refusal of the other powers to deal with the question of trained reserves and military materials.[24] Such proposals were received with a grain of salt. Even less innocuous recommendations could not pass the first hurdle. Paul-Boncour vainly insisted on the establishment of an international permanent disarmament commis-

[22] In League of Nations Records of the Sixteenth Assembly, Part II, Plenary Meetings, p. 29.

[23] The Interparliamentary Union discussed this question before the First World War.

[24] Documents of the Preparatory Commission, Series X, p. 19.

sion to inspect and control national armaments.[25] Count Bernstorff demanded a general levelling down of all national armaments to that imposed on Germany by the Treaty of Versailles. Such proposals were futile, particularly in view of persistent rumors about clandestine German rearmament.

Arthur Henderson, the President of the Disarmament Conference, in his attitude to pacifism, stood close to George Lansbury. His statesmanship was no match to the insurmountable diffiiculties which arose.

Intellectual pacifists and absolutist pacifists had been disdainful of the labors of the official representatives of the national governments. They held their own conference against war in 1932 at Amsterdam, through the initiatives of Henri Barbusse and Romain Rolland.

VIII. Pacifism in Great Britain, France and Germany

Pacifism as a political movement, a subject of literature, and as a manifestation of individual conscience, had some appeal in every European country. No attempt is made here to deal with Russian pacifism. The peculiar political position of the Soviet Union, the control of the State over literature, political activities, and manifestations of individual conscience, leave no room for unlicensed pacifism. Pacifist thinking was most fertile in Great Britain, France, Germany, Holland, and pre-Dollfuss Austria. Elsewhere its voice was less articulate than in these countries.

The British Labor Party counted many pacifists and former pacifists among its leaders. At one time pacifism was more in line with the tradition of the party than socialism. Keir Hardie, at the Internationalist Socialist Congress of Copenhagen in 1910 spoke for the most extremist pacifists when he said: "The nation that has the courage to be the first to throw away its arms will win for itself one of the greatest names in history." It took Ramsey MacDonald some time to outlive his reputation as an opponent

25 The United States and Italy were the most conspicuous opponents of this proposal.

of the British war effort in 1914-18. Herbert Morrison, who played such an impressive role in the Second World War was a conscientious objector in the First War. Phillip Snowden, later Viscount Snowden, a close associate and Cabinet colleague of MacDonald in his Labor and National Cabinets was an active pacifist. He often joined pacifists of other nations in demanding the abolishment of all types of military service. Lord Ponsonby, a member of the Liberal Party during the first world war, left his party because of pacifism, and later joined the Labor Party. In 1930 he became his new Party's leader in the House of Lords. Soon afterwards he joined the War Resisters International and in 1943 deserted the Labor Party altogether, primarily because of his pacifist convictions.

The great old man of British pacifism, George Lansbury, a former leader of the Labor Party in the House of Commons, was a pillar in several peace movements, such as the War Resisters International Peace Pledge Union, Peace Pledge Movement, etc. In his later years he lost contact with practical politics as advocated by the Labor Party, and resigned his positions. Lansbury was a Christian pacifist, with a slight Tolstoyian touch. He represented that branch of pacifism which believed that Hitler and Mussolini could be persuaded to become champions of international peace.

Not only British politics, but also British cultural life was deeply permeated with pacifist tones. The luminaries of twentieth century British literature at one time or another embraced pacifism. H. G. Wells, G. B. Shaw, Bertrand Russel, Norman Angell, Aldous Huxley, Laurence Housman, Vera Brittain, and others provided the intellectual touch for British pacifism. Pacifism has never had a more illutsrious galaxy of literary lights in any country, at any time. But we can ask: Where was their influence in British and world politics?

French socialists represented the vanguard of pacifism in their country. With the help of the leftist intellectuals they tried to stem the waves fomented by the revanche mentality of pre-1914 France.

Like most leftists all over the world, after the First World War they supported the League of Nations and the international machinery built around it. There was a certain mental affinity between them and the disillusioned, defeatist spirit that characterized a segment of French cultural life in the 1920's and the early 1930's until the advent of Hitler. In France and elsewhere socialists consistently combatted war propaganda and nationalist outbursts. They fought for disarmament by voting against appropriations for the army and the navy. In the late 1930's a sizable part of the French Socialist Party (S.F.I.O.) desired to remain faithful to the pacifist traditions of the party and favored appeasement and peace at any price with Hitler's Germany and Mussolini's Italy. The so-called neo-socialists under the leadership of Deat were less pacifists than fascists. Their policy culminated in full-fledged collaboration in the Vichy era in both the occupied and the unoccupied zones.

The moderate leftists in French politics were motivated in their pacifism largely by their Europeism. Men like Briand, Herriot, Painlevé, Leon Bourgeois, were Europeans in the best Victor Hugo tradition. At the same time they were the most effective leaders in the peace movements of Europe between the two world wars.

The powerful French trade unions under Leon Jouhaux followed the attitude of the leftist parties, so far as the question of peace was concerned. Jouhaux held the orthodox view that only workers could be depended upon to oppose war. At a public assembly in Geneva in 1934 he claimed that under the present circumstances a general strike was the best method of preventing war. The Second World War gave a resounding answer to this conception. In the United Nations the most dependable and persistent combattants against the former Axis powers were the organized workers.

Unlike Britain, twentieth century France had a powerful anti-internationalist, promilitarist literary clique with devout audience in the middle and upper classes. At the same time the antiwar or pacifist voices in French cultural life were more emotional and vehement. Older Communists of the pre-1917 vintage were prominent among the pacifists. Younger communists like Aragon and Malraux have become active warriors to promote their principles. It is tempting to contemplate what position Henri Barbusse might have taken toward the Second World War had he not died in 1935. The literary pacifists of France were definitely not Christian minded. Men like Anatole France, Barbusse, Romain Rolland were convinced atheists and cosmopolitans. Others like George Duhamel and Victor Marguerite had been internationalists and therefore joined the authors of other nations in demanding the abolition of military training as a means of combatting war. The antiwar novels of Paul Reboux (*Les Drapeaux,* 1921, 1925) and such works as *Le Sort le Plus Beau* of Claire Geniaux, merely portray the disillusioned "esprit" of France in the 1920's without revealing much concern with peace organization or practical internationalism.

The political climate and the underlying nationalist spirit of public opinion has not permitted pacifism, whether allied to socialism or not, to play as prominent a role in public affairs in Germany as it did in Great Britain or France. Pacifism as a program for international policy remained on the fringes of the German political arena. Unlike Bebel and his followers, Karl Liebknecht, Rosa Luxemburg, and their associates among leftwing socialists, were courageous pacifists until the fall of the Hohenzollern Empire. But their pacifism was the half-pacifism or relative pacifism of those Marxists who embraced violence both in national and international politics as soon as the old order began to stagger. Later in the Weimar era German political life failed to produce outstanding statesmen closely identified with pacifism as a technique and categorical program for foreign policy. It would be historically inaccurate to call Walter von Rathenau or Stresemann pacifists, merely because they sponsored international agreements destined to reintroduce Germany into the international community.

More important, however, were the writings of German scholars on international law and politics, the activities of the various German peace organizations, and the pacifist onslaught of an impressive array of German and Austrian authors. With his book, *The Peace in Europe*,[26] Eugene Schlief, a German lawyer inaugurated a new school of thought among German internationalists and pacifists. He demanded an objective-juridical approach to the problem of peace and pacifism within the realm of "Realpolitik." His realistic pacifism is reflected in the writings and activities of Professor Walter Schucking, one of the greatest German international lawyers, and Alfred Fried, the Nobel Prize winning Viennese journalist. In the organization "Neues Vaterland," Schucking was able, during the First World War, to conduct propaganda for his pacifistic views and for an international society organized on principles of law. After the First World War, with his younger colleague Hans Wehberg, he belonged to the small group of German scholars who worked so diligently toward peace within the League of Nations. At the International Peace Congresses together with Senator La Fontaine, Fried, Quidde, and Professor C. van Vollenhoven he argued for the minority point of view, sanctioning defensive wars and the use of an international force in case of disobedience of international arbitration verdicts.[27]

Another outstanding German scholar, Professor F. W. Foerster, a former professor at the University of Munich, in his books, articles and teachings, represented a school of pacifism that was not identified with refusal of military service. For several years during and after the First World War, he successfully defied the militaristic and nationalistic authorities in Germany but ultimately was forced into exile. Foerster gained a large number of followers with his theory that a world organized for peace needs new moral foundations as well as new legal foundations. But perhaps the most effective combination of practical statesman and pacifist is the Austrian Heinrich Lammasch. He was another of

[26] *Der Friede in Europa*, 1892.

[27] See Hans Wehberg's "Die Aechtung des Krieges," Berlin, 1930; and the Bulletin Officiel du XX Congres Universel de la Paix, The Hague, 1913, p. 110.

the so-called juridical pacifists, advocating the establishment of a permanent international court of justice and the extension of the principle of arbitration.

Reference to German peace movements is not possible without tribute to Alfred H. Fried and Professor Ludwig Quidde. Fried, a newspaperman without academic background, became one of the pioneers in modern thinking concerning the role of peace in modern society. He founded the German Peace Society in 1892 and for 22 years edited its monthly "Die Friedenswarte." He was definitely one of the outstanding champions of European peace before the outbreak of the First World War.

In spite of a hostile atmosphere, Quidde was able to build up the German Peace Society (Deutsche Friedensgesgesellschaft) to impressive strength, and reconcile basic differences that existed among German Pacifists, particularly between the practical school of Gerlach and the war resisters of Helene Stoecker and Kurt Hiller. He was the organizational talent not only of German, but also international peace societies.

Hellmut von Gerlach became a peace movement leader in 1908 only after leaving the Reichstag. He never failed to emphasize the practical aspects of peace propaganda and the uselessness of individual action. His school is noted for the concepts which are anathema for the absolutist-individualist pacifist. Like Schucking, he approves defensive wars and wants to secure peace through the rule of law. He justified general strikes in order to avoid wars, but regarded them impractical after the outbreak of war.

Berta von Suttner, author of the popular book "Down With Arms," and Helene Stoecker, were the outstanding feminine champions of German pacifism. The latter represented the small branch of Christian pacifists in the German peace movement, advocating refusal of military service. Kurt Hiller, another of the war resistors, although an extreme leftist, reached the same conclusion on this issue as the deeply Christian Helene Stoecker.

During the Weimar era literature with pacifist leanings enjoyed great popularity. The writings of some authors, like Ernst Toller and Ludwig Renn were filled with communist pacifism. Others propagated a type of cosmopolitan pacifism exemplified by the classics of Stefan Zweig, Fritz von Unruh, and Erich Maria Remarque.

Students and propagandists of pacifism on the whole have been less conspicuous in the other European countries. But everywhere there have been men and women who openly or secretly carried on their campaign for peace. In this connection it is impossible to forget the devotion to the cause of peace of such men as Miguel de Unamuno and Salvador de Madariaga of Spain, Henri La Fontaine of Belgium, C. Van Vollenhoven, and B. de Ligt of the Netherlands, and Christian Lange of Norway.

* * *

It is a curious historic fact that the movements of unconditional war resister pacifists have gained no momentum since the termination of hostilities of the Second World War. The inevitable experience of Hitlerism in Europe weakened the foundations of pacifist movements. The resistance and partisan movements were based on the justification of violence against the oppressors and quislings. In turn the collaborationists and quislings preached the doctrine of peaceful coöperation with the German occupational authorities. Pacifist movements traditionally drew their adherents mostly from liberal and socialist elements, for whom cooperation with German fascism was the apex of anathema. It may not be amiss to say that European pacifism has been badly shaken by the confusion of modern world politics.

It is instructive to compare the period following the Second World War with the years that followed the Crimean War. The Crimean War was a distinct disappointment to the internationalists and pacifists of that era. A period of inactivity characterized the peace movements after 1856, and it was not until 1867 that the peace conferences again manifested noticeable activity. After the First World War extremist antiwar feeling and pacifism were disassociated from the League of Nations and international agencies bearing an official character.

The experience of the League of Nations, however disappointing, helped to channel pacifist activities toward organized internationalism. Furthermore, the emergence of additional technological devices accentuated the control of organized government over the citizenry.

In the face of increased power in the hands of governments, peace efforts are not promising where they are out of line with the established international machinery. Such an observation is bound to be painful to those whose pacifism is predicated upon the power of the moral conviction of the individual, yet it can explain the failure of resurgence of popular pacifist activities in the wake of the Second World War.

Internationalism and world organization have gained apparent emphasis at the expense of pacifism, or in other words, peace has become inseparable from world organization. Political thinking and literary spirit are little stimulated by the idea of peace as existing in isolation from the problems of government. It is unlikely that post-1945 Europe will develop personalities like Tolstoy, Barbusse, or Lansbury.

The United Nations has become the dominant instrument for peace and internationalism. "Private" pacifism, in opposition to, or in ignorance of, official internationalism has taken a back seat. So long as the United Nations remains the primary instrument of peace, it will draw the support and represent the aspirations of most of those who believe in world peace.

BIBLIOGRAPHY

Del Vecchio, Giorgio: *Il fenomeno della guerra e l'idea della pace,* Torino, 1911.

Fried, Alfred H.: *Handbuch der Friedensbewegung,* Berlin-Leipzig, 1911-13; A brief outline of the nature and aims of Pacifism, New York, 1915; *Probleme der Friedenstechnik,* Leipzig, 1918.

Goldscheid, Rudolf: *Friedensbewegung und Menschensökonomie,"* 1912.

GROSS, LEO: *Pazifismus und Imperialismus*, Leipzig-Wien, 1931.

HERRIOT, EDOUARD: *The United States of Europe*, translated by Reginald J. Dingle, New York, 1930.

HUXLEY, ALDOUS: *An Encyclopedia of Pacifism*, New York and London, 1937.

COUDENHOVE-KALERGI, RICHARD N.: *Pan-Europe*, New York, 1926.

KOBLER, FRANZ: *Gewalt und Gewaltlosigkeit*, Zurich, 1928.

LANGE, CHRISTIAN: *Histoire de la doctrine pacifique et de son influence sur le developpement du droit international*, Recueil des Cours de l'Academie de Droit International, Vol. XIII, 1926.

LEONARD, RAYMOND: *Vers une organisation politique et juridique de l'Europe*, Paris, 1935.

LIGT, BARTHELEMY DE: *The Conquest of Violence*, London, 1937.

LITVINOV, MAXIM: *L'U.R.S.S. et la Paix*, Paris, 1939.

MADARIAGA, SALVADOR DE: *Disarmament*, New York, 1929.

NICOLAI, G. F.: *The Biology of War*, New York, 1918; *Aufruf an die Europäer*, Wien, 1923.

NOVICOV, I. A.: *War and Its Alleged Benefits*, translated from French, London, 1912.

RAPPARD, WILLIAM E.: *The Common Menace of Economic and Military Armaments*, London, 1936; *The Quest for Peace*, New York, 1931.

ROGGE, HEINRICH: *Nationale Friedenspolitik*, Berlin, 1934.

SCHELER, MAX: *Die Idee des Friedens und der Pazifismus*, *Berlin*, 1931.

SCHLIEF, EUGEN: *Der Friede in Europa*, Leipzig, 1892.

SCHUECKING, WALTER: *Der Bund der Völker*, Leipzig, 1918; *Die Revision der Völkerbundssazzung in Hinblick auf den Kelloggpakt*, Berlin, 1931.

SIBLEY, MULFORD, Q.: *The Political Theories of Modern Pacifism*, The Pacifist Research Bureau, Philadelphia, 1944.

VAN VOLLENHOVEN, C.: *The Law of Peace*, London, 1936.

WEHBERG, HANS: *Die Aechtung des Krieges*, Berlin, 1930; *Die Fuehrer der Deutschen Friedensbewegung*, Leipzig, 1923.

XXIV.

European Federalism

EUROPEAN FEDERALISM

Editorial Note

A United States of Europe is an old and great social myth. Older even than the idea of a United States of America, it still belongs to that group of social visions which has a good chance of becoming a reality.

The original idea may be traced to the beginning of the fourteenth century, when Pierre Dubois urged a Union of Christian States in his "De Recuperatione Terrae Sanctae" (about 1305-07); this idea was a forerunner of a European Union. Since then, almost every century has brought forth plans for various types of European Unions, such as the "Grand Design" (revised edition, 1638), by Maximilien de Bethune, duc de Sully, and friend of Henri IV, who proposed a plan for a European cooperative system; in 1693, William Penn wrote "Essay Toward the Present and Future Peace of Europe," in which the founder of Pennsylvania proposed an "Imperial Dyet, Parliament or State of Europe." In 1712, Charles Irénée Castel de Saint Pierre advocated a European Confederation, a plan which Jean Jacques Rousseau later supported in his "Project for Perpetual Peace." This chain of great philosophers and talented statesmen who, centuries back, realized the vital significance of a European Union was never broken. Brilliant minds and gifted intellects were constantly attracted to the idea. The celebrated German philosopher, Immanuel Kant, wrote "Zum Ewigen Frieden" expounding his views on a European Confederation based on a republican form of government.

On the eve of the Congress of Vienna (1814), another great Frenchman, Claude Henri Saint Simon, together with Augustin Thierry, the historian, suggested a European Union governed by a Parliament which would be patterned after the English Parliament.

It is not within the scope of this book to present the entire history of European Federalism.[1] *The long history of this ideology proves that it possesses a good deal of tradition among European intellectuals, and is not merely another postwar idea. When R. N. Coudenhove Kalergi started his Paneuropean movement (after 1918), it had a voluminous historical background for its support.*

In his stimulating chapter on European Federalism, Professor Reginald Lang unfolds various visions and plans for a European federal system, with some emphasis on the constitutional aspect of various projects.

During World War II the idea gained further support: democratic European underground literature featured the idea of a European Federation, and the great vision was revived. Such prominent statesmen as the Polish Prime Minister, Wladyslaw Sikorski, and the Czechoslovak President, Benes, realized that a Regional, Eastern European Federation would furnish a foundation, at least, for a European settlement.

Sikorski's and Benes's plea for a federated Eastern Europe was probably the only concrete and specific plan advocated by heads of governments during the Second World War—the former a responsible Prime Minister, the latter a President of the Republic.

General Sikorski had two ambitious desires: one, to establish a lasting settlement insuring permanent peace between the Soviet Union and Poland—to change the HISTORY *of Russo-Polish relations, not solely the temporary* POLITICS; *two, to establish a democratic Eastern European Federation between the Baltic and the Aegean, a plan which Thomas Masaryk, President-philosopher of Czechoslovakia, had favored during World War I.*

[1] A student of the history of European Federalism may be referred to a stimulating volume by S. J. Hemleben, *Plans for World Peace Through Six Centuries*, Univ. of Chicago Press, 1943.

Sikorski approached both problems with courage and sincerity; rather than cautiously discussing his ideas in a diplomatic manner, he propagated them openly with audacity and vision, challenging history for the price of peace. Although history has chosen an entirely different road than that outlined by Sikorski, future historians will undoubtedly recognize him as one of the great and most honest statesmen produced in that tragic era of European history.

Sikorski's plan was to organize a regional federation of eastern European states as a bridge between the West and the East. This federation would form a friendly link between the western democracies and the Soviet Union, without serving as a spearhead against either. Because of the problem of Germany, he was reluctant to propagate a straight European Federation: millions of eastern Europeans were slaughtered by the German Army and the German-Nazis; twice within twenty-five years Germany has infringed upon Belgian neutrality; twice in seventy years German armed forces have marched into Paris. Therefore, reasoned Sikorski, wouldn't a European Federation with Germany in its center mean a German-dominated Europe? Would it be feasible to advocate a direct federation with Germany for those who survived the onslaught of teutonic fury?

Sikorski feared that after Germany's defeat, nationalism would be revived, and a new generation might resume the barbaric march against the eastern European nations. For this reason, as well as those mentioned above, Sikorski supported an Eastern European Federation, above all, and left the problems of a total European Union to the western European countries. The eastern European region in the East, and the western region, with France and England on the western borders of Germany, could thus cooperate in a European Union; Germany would be dealt with in a peace settlement, as a territory under long-term Allied control.

Unfortunately, the "Great Design," a European Union, has been abandoned, and Europe has returned to its prewar system; she is partitioned into separate territories.

Former Prime Minister Churchill renewed his pleas for a European Federation (1947) and launched a European movement. However, the Soviet Union has been in constant opposition to any European federalist schemes, and it has accused Churchill's movement of being anti-Soviet, although it has furnished insufficient evidence for this accusation.

In February, 1947, an international conference was held in London to support a campaign for the United Socialist States of Europe. This conference was called by the British Independent Labor Party to gather support for the United Socialist States of Europe (USSE); delegates from France, Germany, Holland, Spain, and Greece attended the conference. "Europe today," the official record of the conference states, "has come to the crossroads of history. Twice in our lifetime she has been devastated by war. A third World War, waged with the 'total' destructiveness of the atomic age, will finally obliterate her civilization. . . . If freedom is not to perish, the unity of Europe must be based upon libertarian socialism, which is incompatible with any totalitarian regime. . . ."

This movement can hardly be accused of being too conservative, as was Mr. Churchill's. The Congress of the Independent Labor Party was not the only one.

Again in June 1947 a more representative Congress for a United States of Europe of the European Socialist Parties had been called to Paris. Stressing the significance of civil liberties as an inseparable factor for a federal solution in Europe, the Congress spoke in favor of a decentralized European Federation in which political democracy would have its social and economic counterparts. It was also stressed that in order to build a federation, the federal movement should be based on a "sociological force, numerically important and politically conscious"—meaning European labor and free peasantry.

Again in August 1947 at Montreux a Congress of European Federalist met. This was a Congress, which was not limited to one political creed, though not as influential with the European masses as the former. The "Congress of European Federalists" discussed also a broader problem—World Government. The Europeans spoke in favor of a European Federation within a World Federal Union.

A few weeks later the protagonist of the European federal idea, Prof. R. N. Coudenhove-Kalergi, called his international conference in Gstad in Switzerland. His ideas though, follow more the line of Mr. Churchill. This furnishes concrete evidence that a strong desire for a European Union exists and that it may be an invaluable factor in strengthening our chances for a lasting peace.

F. G.

XXIV.

EUROPEAN FEDERALISM

by

REGINALD D. LANG

There have been periods of time in which communities, apparently in peace with each other, have been more perfectly separated than, in latter times, many nations in Europe have been in the course of long and bloody wars. The cause must be sought in the similitude throughout Europe of religion, laws, and manners. At bottom, these are all the same. The writers on public law have often called this AGGREGATE *of nations a commonwealth. They had reason. It is virtually one great state having the same basis of general law, with some diversity of provincial customs and local establishments.*

—Edmund Burke, *Letters on a Regicide Peace* (1796).

The Background of European Federalism

THE IDEAL OF particularism and the ideal of universalism together created the design of European history.

Roman imperialism had articulated the tribal units of Europe into a system of order, but as the Roman system weakened the tribes, now expanded into "nations," established their several dominions throughout Romanized Europe. Charlemagne again gathered them into an empire, but after his death, lacking a universal ideal to cement them together, they broke apart. The ideal of universalism, however, could not be destroyed, and in another century Otto founded a subtle, and not too stable, amalgam that was universalist in symbol, but most particularist in practice. The Holy Roman Empire of the German nations was the heir, but scarcely the successor, of the Roman Empire. Though the disjunctive elements in Otto's creation could only be arrested at intervals by a regenerate imperialism, the Holy Roman Empire, always in symbol, and sometimes in fact, revealed the vitality of the ideal of universalism. Despite the exuberant localism of the middle ages, the ideal of universalism never lost the luster of grandeur, and was never without representation, however inadequate, in medieval Europe.

Modern Europe has gloried in its divisions. Yet the essential unity of Europe that underlay them, while it was denied, could not be ignored. The very imperialism of the modern nations has been an effort of the particular to become the universal. Charles V and Philip II had European ambitions, but the Europe they tried to conquer would have been the lengthened shadow of Spain. Louis XIV would have made Europe politically, as it had become culturally, French. Napoleon, even though a child of the Enlightenment, a European idea, attached his conquests to France, and would have centralized Europe, as he did France, at Paris. The awful abyss to which a national imperialism can sink is the chronicle of Europe's latest years. A part cannot swell into the whole without destroying both. And it is well to recall the terrible forecast of Grillparzer that the way of humanity led through nationalism to bestiality.

During four centuries, Europe has been a system of States which must exist together, if not in harmony, then, it was recognized, at least in balance. And therein lies a recognition of the unity of Europe which does not imply the destruction of its plurality. For the coalitions that always conquered the imperialism of the parts did so in the name of Europe, even though they assembled around the banners of the nations. It was instinctively understood that the nations could nurture and enjoy their diversities only in a Europe that had not been conquered by any one of them. The successive imperialisms of the parts not only menaced the several States; they also threatened Europe. The coalitions could be formed only because there was a common agreement among the nations to preserve a Europe that permitted particularism. This was the negative pole to the positive pole of dynastic and nationalistic imperialisms; both were necessary to the current of European life.

In contemporary Europe, however, the inter-play of the ideals of universalism and particularism are self-destroying. The balance of power no longer protects the corpus of Europe from the swollen imperialism of its parts, and twice the several parts have had to defend their integrity by relying upon non-European powers. An artificial stability can be imposed externally with the apparatus of imperialism, but a natural stability among the States must correspond to their vital needs, and hence it must be an order among them in which they concur. This is the only alternative to wars and preparations for wars against imperialism anticipated or imperialism triumphant. The rivalries of the European nations generated both by attempts at universalism, and efforts to defeat them have made a desert that cannot be called peace. No European nation can become Europe, and Europe will be destroyed in a chaos of nations not related through a principle of order. Europeans, conscious of Europe's unity, now grope for such a principle.

Europe was described by Montesquieu as a nation made up of several. Of Europe west of Russia this remark is especially true. Europe is a society; there are European manners, European customs, European public opinion, European law. The Christian religion gives to European culture a common ethical basis and philosophy of values. Europeans share a common history in the rise and decline of the west Roman empire, in the migrations that followed and in the medieval experience of contests between the Imperium and the Sacerdotium, and the feudalization of both empire and church. Renaissance, Reformation, Counter-Reformation, Enlightenment, Absolutism, Revolution, Romanticism, Realism, Liberalism, Impressionism, Socialism, are all European ideas and mark the course of European thought. Even Nationalism, sometimes supposed to be the antithesis of European unity, is a European phenomenon. It arose out of European conditions.

It is not an alternative to Europe, but a phase of European civilization.

The threat to European unity and civilization does not lie in cultural nationalism but in political nationalism. The alliance of sovereignty and nationalism distorts, and may destroy the latter. Nationalism is of the realm of the spirit; it is a way of thinking, feeling, and acting. Tolerance is of the essence of true nationalism, because respect for *my* national sentiments presupposes respect for *yours*. But political nationalism is intolerant, and thus is self-contradictory; it makes exclusive what should be complementary. Every nation-State in Europe is a denial either present or past of the right of nationalism; every national State grew around a dynasty which absorbed particular groups whose distinctiveness possessed the elements of nationalism. In place of the hundreds of cultural groups once scattered over Europe, there are today only a few national States. Political nationalism is the centralization and absorption of diverse groups around fixed political centers. The nazi attack upon Europe was but the extremist form, and we hope the last, of what has been occurring in Europe since the 15th century. Political nationalism has been, in reality, an imperial weapon exerted upon the European continent by dynasties and organized nations. European history during four centuries has presented a panorama of particularism being puffed to the pattern of universalism; and therein lies its irony. And the troubles of Europe have arisen because there has been no universal power that could check the imperial ambitions of the segments, and yet not absorb the cultural particularism of the parts. The situation is, and has been, essentially cancerous.

The struggle for existence and power among the nations now leads to their destruction in wars of annihilation. Nor is this an accident of science, for ancient history is a catalogue of wars of annihilation. The reason lies in the circumstances. It is a characteristic feature of all religious and civil wars, because they are contests between irreconcileable ways of living that cannot occupy the same space at the same time. European wars are civil wars because they are fought between members of one society, and they partake of the character of religious wars because hostile nationalisms are implacably intolerant. Between 1648 and 1914 wars in Europe, with the exception of the Napoleonic interval, were limited because there was, even among contending dynasts, a feeling of European consensus. This conviction led to the formulation of the principles of the classical International Law, which, by confining wars to a relationship between States, and not men, and by providing for peaceful commercial intercourse between nationals of different States embodied the principle of the European community, namely, that in time of peace, States should do each other the most possible good, and in time of war the least possible harm. But political nationalism has brought unlimited warfare, because between rival sovereign nationalities, as between believer and infidel, and as between established authority and rebels, there is no principle of accomodation.

Therefore, if Europe is to escape an unnatural fate, and not "like the monster of the deep gnaw itself to death," a principle of order, governing the political organization of Europe, that respects alike the ideal of particularism and the ideal of universality must be found.

Whenever the wise and farsighted among Europeans have attempted to reconcile particularism with universalism they have inevitably adopted the federal principle. It is a means for establishing order without sacrificing freedom among States that refuse to be amalgamated but realize that they must be united. Federalism, however, is more than political mechanics; it is also a symbol of union. Where there is federalism, political bodies have decided to accomplish some purpose in common, and, in order that they may do so, have placed their relations with each other, to some degree, under a rule of law. Since the federal structure must rest upon consent as well as a collective purpose, it cannot be imperially imposed. Federalism is simultaneously a political technique and a social synthesis; it is a method and an ideal; a mechanism and a symbol.

Federalism is a principle of order that is both immanent and transcendent. Its transcendent or universal character penetrates, but does not absorb, the constitutent and particular components, while particularism is guaranteed and protected by a universal principle of order. And the interaction of each creates an organic unity that avoids a chaos of dynamic parts unordered by relation to a general principle, or the imposed uniformity of imperial brobdingnagianism. The implicitness of the unifying principle within the parts, a characteristic of a federation, subsumes the parts within the whole. In a proper federation there is no essentian antagonism between the particular and the universal because each depends upon the other; the universal permeates the constitutent parts, and they, in turn, preserve their identities through their common relations to the organs of universality. A federal polity is not the aggregate of its component members; it is not the sum of its local and general governments; it is a synthesis which is greater than and different from the congregation of its parts. Such a political synthesis in Europe would be authentically European. For Europe has accepted universalism only when it insured particularism, and today it is dying from a particularism that cannot be structured into a universalism.

Federalism, the preservation of unity amidst diversity, and the protection of diversity in a union, is the overruling need today for both the nations of Europe and for Europe. An organized polity of Europe is the necessary habitation for the idea of Europe. Although the idea of Europe may not be earth-bound, nevertheless it must have a sanctuary, and only through the preservation of that sanctuary can the idea continue to live. Otherwise Europe may become as Hellas—a memory as of a dream. Those who believe that Europe still can create ideas whose loss would be irreparable to modern civilization must also believe that Europe should be reconstructed, for the idea of Europe cannot endure in a ruined and crumbling habitation. Until federalism becomes the basis of a European Commonwealth, all settlements, where they can be made, of national conflicts are fugitive, and all efforts to overcome the European chaos can be nothing more than ephemeral expediencies.

The reconstruction of Europe as a political program relates to the land west of the Russian frontier. The colonial territories of the European nations would necessarily acquire a special status within a European federation.

The division of Europe today into Russian and non-Russian parts is not the result solely of current and contrasting ideologies. This division is not merely modern; it is Roman. The eastern Roman Empire, centered upon Byzantium, created a civilization distinct from, but not alien to, the west Roman. And Russia was incorporated into the classic tradition from Byzantium.

Between Russia and the west there lies a cultural, as well as political "zwischenland." There eastern and western European cultures mingle, and paralleling this commingling of cultures there has been an uneasy shifting of political policies between Germany and Russia. Nothing shows more vividly the cleavage between eastern and western Europe than the cultural and political confusions in the border-lands between them. It is not only a frontier, but in a sense, is a double frontier, for it points in two directions. Those border-lands are the marches of the east and the marches of the west. It might be said that the gravest problem of *European* statesmanship is the transformation of that frontier region into a link buckling Russia and the west together. It must be neither east nor west, nor a confusion of east and west, but a hinge between them.

In addition, the power of Soviet Russia in relation to the power of any European State would raise the Theban question in a European federation inclusive of Russia in a most aggravated form. A large single State among many small States inevitably creates a hegemonic situation. And hegemony and federalism are utterly irreconcileable. A fear of the unsettling influence of disproportionate power ratios has persuaded the "European Action" organization in Holland to propose that "the federal structure of Europe" should consist of regional federations of small nations, and the reconstruction of Germany "on a federative basis."[1] Europe has suffered nigh unto death from imperialisms and hegemonies, and federalism is proposed as a curative for these afflictions. To incorporate Europe's distress into a federation would be to re-enact the melancholy tale of the Boeotian League, and make the future history of Europe the analogue of the history of Thebes and her client confederates.

The relation of Great Britain to Europe is not readily compressed within a formula. Culturally Great Britain is west European, but she is also insular. The British use of the word "continental" demonstrates that the channel is more than a geographic demarcation. Great Britain is also the center of a Commonwealth, and an Empire, composed of portions of two of the great non-European cultures, Indian and Arabian. Great Britain is related to Europe culturally as well as politically, but only politically to her Empire. For centuries Great Britain feared a Europe imperialized by a dynasty or a nation, but the wars now caused by a divided Europe place her in grave peril. Probably the loss of Calais in 1558 contributed to the security of England during the furious century that followed, but in 1935 a British Prime Minister placed her frontier at the Rhine, and the English retreat from Dunkirk brought an uncomfortable threat of another 1066.

British security lies in a Europe which is neither imperial nor disunited, but united and at peace. The British Empire and Commonwealth do not belong to the corpus of Europe. Should Great Britain, therefore, be a part of a European Commonwealth? This question divides British public opinion. Winston Churchill and Sir Walter Layton reply in the negative, saying that Britain should be linked to, but not comprised within a European polity. Others reply in the affirmative. Could Great Britain be separated from her Empire and interlocked with Europe for the protection of her European interests, and simultaneously separated from Europe and interlocked with her Empire for the maintenance of

[1] Propositions of the "European Action"—a mimeographed copy in possession of the writer.

imperial interests? The British constitution is flexible, and the British are masters of complex procedural techniques. Another question cannot be avoided at this point: Would Soviet Russia willingly be excluded from a European polity that included Great Britain? However the British position in a European commonwealth would of necessity be a special one, and precisely how that uniqueness can be constitutionalized in a European federation is not an imminent problem. The situation needs only to be recognized at this time.

Federalism "in the stream of the world" creates multiform varieties of political forms. So we should not unguardedly identify the general principle with a particular federation, nor overlook gradations between rudimentary and finished forms. The strength of the principle, and its peculiar usefulness for statecraft today in Europe lies in its possibilities for variation. So the federalist should sweep a wide horizon in his search for evidence of federalism.

In ancient Greece, the prototype of modern Europe, the leagues that bore witness to the ideal of Hellas, ought not to be ignored, for there was federalism in them. The Roman reaches for federalism, which unfortunately exceeded their grasp, are instructive because of their incompleteness. The persistence of the Thirty-five tribes, and their division into rural and urban, together with the refinements of Roman control over the Latins as distinguished from their control over other provincials, show that the Republic missed a federal form by a minute margin. And the Augustan arrangements for Gaul and the province of Asia possessed the promise that a portion of the empire, at least, might be federalistic. If, from such a beginning, a European Commonwealth west of the Rhine had developed, how different might the history of Europe have been! Nor should such elementary federal structures as the Lombard League, the Hansa Cities, or the Suabian League be scorned, for they were seeking to achieve common purposes federalistically. The much maligned Holy Roman Empire, even when weakened by the impact of the Renaissance and the Reformation, although not a model of federal government, did reveal the ideal, and occasionally made real, the rule of law among its members. Swiss and Dutch confederations stood firm in the crises, and deflected what appeared to be the irresistible course of European history.

The federal principle is not a mere fashion of an hour; it is a persistent element in the political tradition of Europe. It has been adapted to capricious circumstances; it contrives a multiplicity of forms.

The conspicuous success of federalism in the United States has raised the American form of government to the dignity of a model. Yet the beginnings, more than the fulfillment of American federalism, are most significant for Europe today. When a Crown no longer stood above Parliament and the Colonies, disputes between them were bound to arise, for no longer able to order their relations by submission to a higher authority, the colonies had either to accept the imperial supremacy of Parliament over them, or both colonies and Parliament had to devise and accept a federal division of powers between them. In those early years, however, not only the problem of adjusting powers between political authorities, but also the prior, and more grave and complex problem of finding a central principle to which the federated governments could be made coordinate, and then translating it into institutions of government had to be solved.

American Federalism and Europe

The British imperial system in North America had, by the 1760's, become federalized in practice, but in London there was no federal theory. English authorities, when they theorized, claimed unlimited and imperial power for Parliament. And they could cite the Act of 1649 establishing "A Commonwealth" composed of "the people of England, and of all the Dominions and Territories thereunto belonging," as governed "by the Supreme Authority of this Nation." But to this assertion of imperial power

John Adams retorted that the colonists in America had "got out of the English realm," and were held to England only through a personal union centered upon the person of the King.

But Parliament, for seventy-five years before the Stamp Act had acted "federally," for its legislation affecting the colonies had been confined to commercial regulations, and it had left to them complete power over internal police and taxation. Hence the sudden and unexpected exertions at Westminster to raise a revenue in America, however justified as a policy, provoked the colonists to meet an imperial practice with a federal theory.

In America the federal, as distinguished from the imperial, character of the empire was better understood than in England. John Dickinson, for example, writing in the "Letters from a Farmer," distinguished in the British imperial system of his time between those governmental powers that were exercised by the central, and those that were permitted to the local authorities. This division, he asserted, was not made to detach, but to unite the colonies and England, for "we are but parts of a whole." On the other hand, Governor Hutchinson, expressing the imperial point of view prevailing in parliamentary circles, told the Massachusetts legislature that since Parliament possessed supreme power, all other authorities necessarily were subordinate, and so could exercise only permissive power. To this theory of imperialism, the Massachusetts Council rejoined with a theory of federalism. It declared that subordinate powers could be as supreme in their sphere as the general power in its, because "the two powers are not incompatible, but subsist together."

Edmund Burke, almost alone among British Parliamentarians, comprehended the subtleties of what had become a federal empire, and discerned the contrast between imperial theory and federal practice. Because Burke could think "imperially," he recognized the federalist attributes of the empire, while those who thought only of Britain and the "plantations attached thereto," could not understand the federal character of the empire as a going concern. In a very real sense Burke's admonition that "great empires and little minds go ill together" bore a sharp pertinence to the situation in Parliament. The empire in the capacious mind of Burke was "the aggregate of many states under one head," and in that empire England was only the "head," not the "head and members too." The legalistic monism of the parliamentarians, comparable to the sovereignty argument today, evoked his scorn, and he retorted to their reasoning that "the very idea of subordination of parts" excludes the "notion of single and undivided unity." Burke advised that the "legal competency" of the colonial assemblies to make grants freely to the imperial government should be ascertained. He appealed to English precedents of a day when England was less unitary than in the 18th century. But those precedents, and this is fundamental, rested upon the Crown then legally encompassed with limitations upon its power, whereas during the controversy with the American colonies an omnicompetent and legislating Parliament was claiming supreme power in the State.

The failure of Parliament and the colonists to make constitutional provision for the federalism which had become customary in practice led to the Revolution.

After independence the critical problem of discovering and accepting a principle of order was transferred from Westminster to America. For among the American States there was now neither a Crown nor the urgencies of a war to unite them. Because this problem was evaded, the Articles of Confederation pointed to a negative objective, the maintenance of peace among the States. Consequently the central authority was not endowed with crucial powers of government, but with authority to act as a collective agent in foreign affairs and to preserve peace between the States. While it had some power of legislation, Congress, under the Articles, was not given power to regulate commerce or levy taxes. These were feared as "imperial" powers, for had not the controversies of the pre-Revolution age turned upon them? An economic and social crisis at home disclosed the results of weakness in internal affairs, while menacing actions on the frontiers on the part of Great Britain and Spain, by revealing the necessity for a closer union, created a demand for a consolidated government.

So at Philadelphia the bold step was taken. The framers of the Constitution reconstructed the American polity upon the pattern, with one exception, of the old imperial system as they had understood it. They established a government adequate for all purposes, and made it definitely, unquestionably federal. But, having once divided all governmental powers between two governments, they needed to find a principle which would keep them coordinated. That was the final bulwark against both imperialism and disunion. There was no Crown through which several governing units could be kept in an ordered array. But to create a strong executive, analogous to the royal authority, uninhibited by centuries of a struggle to subject it to legal controls, would be dangerous for a federal government. Yet the whole structure could be paralyzed through an impotent executive. How was a federal government, when constructed, to be held together? What principle would insure order and give unity to a bisected political organization? Within this dilemma the delegates tossed through the summer weeks. More debates took place on the problem of the executive than upon any other, for here they were touching the very core of their federal system.

The solution of the dilemma was accomplished by a daring and creative act of statecraft; the Constitution itself, and not the federal organs of government, was made the cement of the federal union. It embodied the common purpose of the American States and people, and because it was the symbol as well as the instrument of government, around it grew the ideals of American society. Thus the Constitution is more than the supreme law of the land; it also sets a legal pattern for political, economic, and social controversies. Not only are the relations between the States and the Nation, and between the departments of the federal government defined in the Constitution, but the general and normative clauses, such as "interstate commerce," the "due process" and "necessary and proper" clauses are also legalized. In this manner Constitutional provisions involving political and social standards, although generally non-juridical, were made subject to legal interpretation. Consequently, American social transformations have been incorporated within the constitutional system through the process of judicial interpretation. This is the most distinctive feature of American federalism.

The Continental doctrine, on the contrary, since the time of Vattel, who advocated written constitutions as fundamental law, places the interpretation of political clauses in the political department of government. The law-making, rather than the law-interpreting judiciary, is the final authority. Behind this distinction there are centuries of legal and constitutional history, and the contrast between European and English history, notably in the 17th and 18th centuries, can be seen, as in a lightning flash, in that antithesis.

Judicial interpretation is an art as well as a science. It demands imagination and a quickened vision of the purpose of law in a dynamic society. The Roman jurisprudents recognized themselves as intermediaries between the letter of the law and the circumstances of life. They were the custodians of a living law, not merely mechanical practitioners of texts. Judges who are a prey to print fail to understand that law must be elastic if it is not to be broken, and that Constitutional law, especially, since it touches the impulses of social action, must reflect and not constrict the ascendant social influences of the time. In Justice Holmes' striking phrases, a word is "not a crystal, transparent and unchanged, it is the skin of a living thought and may vary in color and content according to the circumstances and the time in which it is used."[2] The amplitude of "interpretation" may seem delusive to narrow and rigid academicians, but what can be more wildly impractical than a legal scholasticism that would see tomorrow in the habiliments of yesterday?

American society was molded within the juridical principles of a supreme law. Hence the principle of federalism that lies at

[2] Towne v. Eisner, 245 U. S. 425.

the heart of our constitutional system has undergone a "legal" interpretation as the means by which it has been adapted to a changeful society. Each political, economic, or social issue, as it arose, perforce became a juridical question. The only dispute which was not settled judicially was finally decided in an armed conflict. In the decade of the fifties the tendons of government were loosened and the slavery issue was breaking up the federal union into an international congeries of sovereign States and embattled sections, because the principle and symbol of union had lost its potency. The exception proves the rule, that controversies which were not settled within the supreme law of a federal union had to be settled by force without benefit of law or federal principles.

So the political law of the Constitution, changing in content from age to age, gave resilience to the charter of government. The great generalities of the Constitution, by making it supple, keep it permanent. The Constitution as the supreme law is the structural framework of the American government; as a symbol of union and a principle of order it infuses American society with a quality of lawfulness.

American federalism has meaning for European federalism precisely where it is least American and most federal. We should distinguish at this point between principles and their effects. American federalism represents a judicially centered federal system. The juridical quality of American federalism accentuates the essentially lawful character of the federal principle. And this has relevance to the situation in Europe today, for the principle of order which alone can preserve European civilization must be one of law. Europeans must elect either to submit to the law of force, or live by the force of law. The legalization of political relations, economic activities, and social problems which has accompanied and governed American history under the Constitution reveals to Europe the promise of federalism as the means for containing European relationships within institutions of government and legal interpretation. This is the distilled essence of American federalism that is beyond the accidents of circumstances.

The American federal system is not a definite pattern of political statics; it is, on the contrary, a series of dissolving views. It has passed through "great varieties of untried being," and is the very reverse of some rigid petrifaction. Moreover, the real character of the federalism of 1787 could not be precisely described even by its creators. Madison, who surely should have known, wrote that the United States was neither a federal nor a national government but a "nondescript to be tested and explained by itself alone."[3] Marbury v. Madison and the Virginia and Kentucky Resolutions do not seem to refer to the same government, and Constitutional texts were used by supporters of both the doctrine of nullification and the doctrine of federal supremacy. The acute French observer, de Tocqueville, in the 1830's described the American system as an "incomplete national government."

Federalism is not a destination but a method of travelling. So we would be unwise to consider what America has become under a federal structure either as a point of origin for a European federal organization, or as an example of the inevitable result of federalism in Europe, or elsewhere. American federalism originated in the colonial practices of an empire; before 1787 it developed as a process of decentralization. After 1787 corporate opposition by the States singly and collectively to the central government was persistent, and at length militant. Moreover events, comparable to the influences that shaped national unification in Europe pushed the American system, especially after 1865, toward a national form. The Constitutional texts could have been used with equal facility to have brought about a more federal and less national polity.

The traditions of European federalism, in general, reveal a different technique than the American. European federations have ordinarily been of a limited purpose type, and so the problem was not how to make one central and many local governments co-

[3] *Works*, Hunt, ed. IV, 420-21.

ordinate, but how to make several central governments associative in an autonomous body. Hence the confederation technique, that is, a continuous correlation of law to carry out federal decisions between the members acting together within the federal institutions, and acting separately within their several constitutional institutions. This differs from the American technique of dividing jurisdictions for all purposes. But confederations, no less than federal unions, must be built around a universal principle of union and order. Otherwise the results of the association are only disguised adjustments of power relationships; the organs of the union become mere procedural devices for the permutations and combinations of power politics. A procedure, however intricate, is not government; it provides for collective agreement to a policy in common, but not for a corporate formulation and enforcement of a common policy. Here the line falls between a League and a Confederation, between procedure and government. In a confederation there is a central authority representative of the whole, in which the component members participate, and through this participation exercise a power greater than any one of them, or the sum of their powers. Participation *in* power, not participation *through* power is the distinction between Confederation and League. In a federal union there is a complete division of all powers between the central and local governments, each acting immediately and with single authority upon individuals.

The difference usually alleged as distinguishing federations from confederations, namely, the individual incidence of the law of the central authority in the former, and its corporate incidence in the latter, is secondary to the primary tehnique. The distinguishing quality is whether there are coordinate governments, central and local, each supreme in its sphere; or whether the central government is one in which the component members participate corporately. The salient difference lies in the process of law-making; not in the method of law-enforcing. Moreover, even in federal unions there may be corporate law enforcement, and even civil war. In a federal union there is direct law-making, and consequently, in general, direct law-enforcement; in a confederation there are levels of law-making, and, therefore, an indirect method of law-enforcement. Moreover the two techniques are not mutually exclusive, and frequently exist together in the same federation. The Achaean League, a federal union type, was confederate in military and taxation matters; those who searched for sovereignty in the German Empire of 1871, an amalgam of confederate and federal union techniques, found it in the Bundesrat, the organ of the States; the president of the United States is elected confederately.

Since a European federation must begin with division and move toward unity, whereas in America federalism was a movement from imperial unity to federal union, indirect law-making and limited purpose federations are more suitable. Nor should this discourage us. If the people, now separated by political boundaries, feel some purposes, but not all, in common, they can act together for special purposes either through direct or indirect law-making, and to that degree become a federal unit. The federal principle, whether applied in the confederate or federal union manner, whether restricted to limited purposes or extended to all purposes is the sole instrument for translating a general desire among several political entities into common and consensual action. In all federations there must be a propulsive and impelling purpose symbolized by the central institutions of government. Those institutions are worth only the sincerity of the constituent governments. The heart of the matter is not legal technique but conviction. There is an amazing parallel between the text of Article 2 of the Articles of Confederation, supposedly the citadel of State sovereignty that obstructed union, and the Tenth Amendment, supposedly the bulwark of States' Rights, which has been almost refined away. Surely in Europe today there is such a yearning for unity that, despite deep attachments to localities, an institution embodying that desire, in which the localities can participate, would be hailed as the instrument of the solidarity of European politics and economics, and the symbol of the unity of

European culture. Where there is solidarity of interests, there ought to be responsibleness and trust; where there is an implicit unity among several political bodies there should be federation.

It is significant that wars of annihilation in Europe evoke, like some contrapuntal theme, the idea of a European Commonwealth. The plans and programs of Sully, Cruce, St. Pierre, Kant, Rousseau, Hugo, Proudhon, Mazzini, Paneuropa, Briand, while not always disinterested, and seldom complete, testify, by their recurrence, to the strength of an idea whose time has been in the future, but which has now come.

Often, it can be observed that ideas recur in similar but altered circumstances, like a theme in a symphony oft repeated with other themes, but always distinct, yet each time more insistent until at length, absorbing all the secondary themes, it sweeps the whole orchestra into its ambit. So with the idea of a federal Europe; it rises again and again, and each time it is more urgent. Will it swell into some triumphant chorale? Or will it vanish irrevocably into the silence of lost aspirations?

Austro-Hungary: Dualism versus Federalism

Deferred hopes, missed opportunities, but unwearied purpose is the substance of our tale. And this is true not only of Europe, but also of its parts. In the microcosm of Austria-Hungary we find the macrocosmic problem of Europe. In the multi-national, multi-state empire of the Habsburgs there was a mosaic of Europe in miniature. In the divisions in that empire and the efforts made to unite the nationalities into a spontaneous union, we can observe the crucial problem of Europe today, and the means for overcoming it. If the Habsburgs had possessed the wisdom and the ability to have symbolized a supranational principle, the empire could have been federalized and so gained unity through the ungrudging support of autonomous and free nationalities. But the Habsburgs, instead, relied upon an administrative centralism, and maintained the power of their House by dividing the nationalities of their empire. Habsburg imperialism was a husk; the Austrian empire, in its latter days, was a skeleton in armor.

The failure to federalize the Austrian empire brought one devastating war to Europe, and the subsequent failure to solve it among the succession States contributed toward bringing on another. As in the attempts to unite the nationalities of the Austrian empire federally we can descry the cure for Europe's present distempers, so in the results of the subsequent failure to federalize its liberated members we can anticipate the ruins that will accompany the protraction of Europe's malady.

The egregious blindness of Austrian policy becomes the more unthinkable when it is understood that the Slavic nationalities, almost until the outbreak of World War I, were not seeking the destruction of the empire, but were seeking desperately, but alas vainly, for a dignified place within it. This was the real meaning of Palacky's famous, and oft-quoted statement, that if the Austrian empire had not existed, it ought, in the interest of Europe, to have been created. The Slav program was not national independence, but a confederation of equal nations. But while the diverse parts of the Austrian empire were clamoring for a concordant unity, the monarchy, that ought to have represented that unity, fatuously believed that its centralized power could only rest upon the disunited parts. The Czech nationalist, Kramar, asked in 1926; "Was not a prudent and honest Austrian policy possible, such a one as our men since Palacký and Havlicék have advocated, because they also wished sincerely the continuation of Austria, a policy which would also have made the Serbs friends of Austria by becoming so just toward them that they would not aspire for a state beyond the frontiers and would estimate as superfluous the arousing of a catastrophe which might have ultimately also a sinister outcome for the Serbs and Slavs . . . ?"[4]

But in the years of crisis there was not total and utter blindness in Austria. A representative Austrian Parliament, meeting at Kremsier during the revolutionary period of 1848, displayed

[4] Oscar Jaszi, *The Dissolution of the Habsburg Monarchy*, University of Chicago Press, 1929, p. 389.

the wisdom that was denied to the Habsburgs. It proposed a federalist plan. This plan preserved the historical kingdoms, but divided the larger territories into districts (kreise) arranged upon an ethnological basis. To guarantee self-government against excessive centralism, local governors were made responsible to local representative bodies. By recognizing the principle of national equality, the representatives at Kremsier planned to transform an imperial monarchy and a centralized bureaucracy into a monarchical confederation united through a supra-national idea. But Francis Joseph refused to accept the labors of the Kremsier parliament; he did not understand that imperial centralization increased centrifugalism among the nationalities, while the decentralization implicit in a federation would have impelled a centripetalism among them.

At the time of the expulsion of Austria from Germany, the Magyars wrung the privileges of dualism from a necessitous monarchy. The slight federalism to be detected in the Ausgleich is spurious, for that agreement divided imperial privileges between two nationalities in the empire. The real character of the agreement is revealed by the privileged position it accorded to the landed nobility in Hungary. The Ausgleich was a pact, something in the nature of a treaty, between the Habsburgs and the Hungarian magnates to govern and exploit in partnership the landless of Hungary and all the other nationalities in the empire. Thus privilege and exploitation and not national freedom and popular government attended the Habsburg monarchy as it moved toward its inevitable doom. Like the House of Atreus it could not escape, either by action or inaction, a design of catastrophe.

The methods of the Habsburgs were essentially those of power politics, not government. And in Europe today, as in the Austria of yesterday, such practices can only postpone, but cannot avert, political disintegration. The establishment of the German Empire in 1871 prompted Francis Joseph to consider placating the Czechs. A German economist, Albert Schäffle, with the support of the Austrian premier, Count Hohenwart, prepared a plan that would have federalized Austrian-Czech relations. One of the articles in the proposed agreement stated that; "All the affairs pertaining to the Kingdom of Bohemia which will not be declared as common among all the kingdoms and countries of the empire belong in principle to the legislation of the Bohemian Diet and will be administered by the Bohemian authorities."[5] Another article made the German and Czech nationalities equal in Bohemia.

This time the Hungarian magnates performed the office of nemesis to the Austrian Habsburgs. Fearful of losing the privileges gained in the Ausgleich, and distrustful of the influence upon Hungary of democratic influences emanating from Bohemia, the Magyars opposed the reform so vehemently that Francis Joseph refused to accept it. Henceforth the struggle of the nationalities within the empire resembled the power politics of the continent; each fought the Habsburgs and each other; the Habsburgs fought all; a war of all against all.

Karl Renner, the present Austrian Chancellor, prepared about 1905 a plan of union which, although it never reached official discussions, has historical interest. Based upon the principle of personality, reminiscent of the middle ages when every man carried his own law, rather than the modern principle of territoriality, the Renner plan guaranteed national autonomy without breaking up administrative unity. Renner did not wish to establish nations *within* the empire, but, rather, to protect national rights transnationally, so to speak, throughout the empire. All the members of each nationality were to be permitted, under the plan, to organize local, intermediate, and central national associations, to be called "National Universities" exercising jurisdiction in cultural and educational matters. Thus each nationality would be united within the empire, and a division of the empire along lines of national cleavage could be avoided. Complementary to, but not parallel with, the national organization of the empire, the plan provided for an administrative structure corresponding to economic divisions within the empire. In some

[5] Quoted in Jaszi, *op. cit.*, p. 113.

local areas the administrative units would coincide with homogeneous national areas, but this was a secondary consideration.

This plan, which identified the supranational principle with supranational economics, with cultural concessions to the nationalities, would in effect have supported the dominant political and economic influence of Austria, and particularly Vienna. Renner's scheme was not genuinely federal; he called his central government a *Staatenstaat,* not a *Bundestaat,* or a *Staatenbund.* But by the early twentieth century the nationalities in the Austro-Hungarian empire were demanding more than cultural autonomy; they were more than "universities"; they were Länder struggling to become *Staates,* in a *Bund* if possible, but *einzelnes* if necessary.

Renner's plan, like Alexander's a century before, could not avoid the taint of hegemony, and as the one seemed to set up a privileged political position for the Great Powers, so the other appeared to confirm the Austrian economic supremacy within the Austrian empire. The universal principle in a federation must not be confounded with a dominant interest, for that would only insure imperialism. The principle that could have preserved the nationalities as political units within the Austro-Hungarian empire must have been one which protected them, and, at the same time, have been the sole means by which they could be free and associated together. It had to be a constitutional principle of order of a federal character. A federal order in Europe will not come solely through European economic conformations, but only by federalizing certain relations between the European States, and among European nationalities. There must be a federal constitutional structure if there is to be federalism.

The struggles for federalism in Austria-Hungary are not only of interest in their bearing upon the problems of Europe today, but they also impinged upon European affairs at a critical point in a critical hour. A confederate Austrian empire could have been a magnetic point of attraction for Slavs and Rumanians beyond the frontiers. And so she would have been an instrument of reconciliation between the Slavs and the Germans in the middle lands lying between aggressive Pan-Germanism and aggressive Pan-Slavism. Thus a frontier could have been transformed into a hinge, and a confederate Austria, composed of Germans and Slavs would have "put friendship between the peoples, and stilled the envy, the secret hatred, hid in their hearts."

As the abyss "yawned sheer," one among the purblind Hungarian magnates, Count Michael Károlyi, had the prescience to apprehend disaster, and the sagacity to know how to arrest it. He advocated the abandonment of Dualism, the inauguration of land reform, the democratization of the empire, including Hungary, and a foreign policy of rapprochement toward France and the Slavs. In 1913 he discussed these matters in Paris with Poincare and Clemenceau.[6] While approving the ideas, Clemenceau pronounced that it was too late. Circumstances which the reason of man had not controlled had at length passed beyond human controls, and events, arising in Austria-Hungary, swelled like a tidal wave overwhelming Europe as "with pomp of waters unwithstood."

As "Succession States" the emancipated parts of the Austro-Hungarian empire attempted to do what the history of Europe during four centuries unmistakeably demonstrated could not be done. As sovereign independent States they were not viable. Conditions of the time "mediatized" those States, to use a term from the constitution of the Holy Roman Empire. Mediatization might be voluntary in a regional federation, or it would be compulsory in a Great Power imperialism. Their choice was limited, either to accomplishing what Austria had failed to accomplish, the federation of central and eastern Europe, or to surrender ultimately, however desperately they might struggle to avert such a fate, to a revived Germany or a reconstructed Russia.

Little Entente

The Little Entente of Czechoslovakia, Jugoslavia and Roumania was formed for three objectives; to prevent any alteration in the

6 Michael Karolyi, *Fighting the World*, New York, 1925, pp. 78-80.

Hungarian frontiers of Trianon, to prevent Anschluss, to prevent a Habsburg restoration. These were all negative; they could be summarized as a policy to keep Austria and Hungary weak. The Succession States moved into the future with their eyes fixed upon the past. Moreover, weakness is a relative relationship, and so the immediate problem facing them was how to make themselves strong when they rejected union. They relied upon French alliances, and national armaments. The European policy, as well as the central European policy, of the Little Entente was also negative, that is, the exemption of central Europe and the Balkans from Great Power rivalries and control.

The Little Entente, because it was an inadequate and unsatisfactory substitute for federation, disintegrated in a time of crisis, as its predecessor, the Autro-Hungarian Empire had dissolved in the storms of war. This region of Europe cannot be divided; if men will not unite it in peace, war will unite them in its common sufferings.

Because it lacked a positive focus, even though common organs were eventually set up, the Little Entente lacked a common will, and was crumbling before it was crushed. Czechoslovakia, Jugoslavia, and Rumania had common relations toward Hungary, but different relations toward Germany, Italy, and Russia. Hence the revival of those powers exerted a deteriorating effect upon the Little Entente which formal schemes of cooperation could not reverse. While Benes announced in 1921 that the Little Entente would found a new order, serving as the "vertebral column" of the Danubian area, the principles, or lack of them, upon which it rested falsified such hopes.

Nevertheless the trend toward closer union which set in as the European situation worsened is of interest to us as another neglected opportunity for federalism in this replica of Europe, and as another ruin marking another turning on Europe's detouring way to federation. In June 1930 at the conference of the Little Entente held at Strbske Pleso, there was added to the collective pact of May 1929 a provision that the Foreign Minister of any one of the States could be authorized to act as the representative of all when exceptional circumstances made it advisable. The trend toward union continued as the European situation approached the crisis phase, and in 1933 in a Pact of Organization the Little Entente States agreed to "the complete unification of their general policy," and, to create "a directing organ of this policy," they formed a "higher international unit." They agreed to set up a Permanent Council of Foreign Ministers, each Minister to be chairman in rotation; a Secretariat, and an Economic Council. The nucleus of the agreement was contained in Article 6 which provided that every political treaty of any one State of the Little Entente, and every unilateral act changing it's relations with another State not a party to the agreement, as well as any economic arrangement involving political consequences, required, henceforth, the unanimous consent of the Permanent Council. Here in Article 6 is the irreducible rudiment of a federal organization; the gristle, if not the bone of a federal structure: namely, that the foreign relations of each member must receive the assent of all.

Surveying the wreck of the storm from exile in the United States, the architect of the Little Entente advocated federalism in central and eastern Europe. "In Central Europe," Benes wrote,[7] "those territories which have associated together most naturally, must be fused into firm blocks. . . . I should expect that with the passage of time, a natural bridge will be established between the northern and southern confederations in Central Europe—that is, between the Polish-Czechoslovak group and the Balkan group. . . ."

Since the war numerous proposals for federation in the Danubian and Balkan areas have been made by statesmen and scholars, and by groups such as the Central and East European Planning Board set up by the Government, Labor and Employers' Delegations to the International Labor Conference, and by the representatives of the Peasant Communities.[8]

7 "The Organization of Post-War Europe," *Foreign Affairs*, Vol. XX, January, 1942, pp. 226-242.

8 Feliks Gross, *Crossroads of Two Continents*, Columbia University, 1945, pp. 18-27.

There has also been official recognition of the need for federations in central and eastern Europe. In the Polish-Czechoslovak Declaration signed in London on January 25, 1942, the two governments express their desire "that the Polish-Czechoslovak Confederation should embrace other states of the European area with which" their "vital interests are linked." The purpose of the Confederation was to assure a "common policy" in foreign affairs, defense, economic and financial matters, social questions, transport, posts and telegraphs. In this document the two States accepted a "common general staff" to "coordinate" the foreign trade and customs tariffs of the members of the confederation, an "agreed monetary policy," coordination of financial and social policies, a "common plan" for the "development and administration" of all transport, "cooperation" in educational and cultural matters, a "full faith and credit" clause, and a guarantee of basic human and political rights by the constitution of each member State.[9]

The Danubian Club of London in 1943 published a plan of federation for east central Europe and the Balkans. This Club, originally the South East Europe Committee of the Fabian Society, expanded its membership and eventually included nationals of the ten States in that region.

The report adopts the federal principle without quibbles. The scheme of government includes a two house legislature, one popularly elected, the other representing member governments; a Council responsible to both Houses; and a Union Judiciary.

The Danubian Club report has unquestionably contributed some fruitful ideas to the cause of federalism in the fields of foreign affairs, international peace, and economics. But the problem of minorities has been a vexing one in central Europe, and any federal system, before it can be successful there, must face and overcome that source of antagonism. A learned scholar and

[9] Text in L. S. Stavrianos, *Balkan Federation*, Smith College Studies in History, Vol. XXVII, Nos. 1-4, October 1941-July 1942. Appendix J, p. 307.

earnest federalist has addressed himself to this problem, and suggests, in addition to a democratic, an "integral" federalism.[10]

Such a federalism would not only federate the economic and foreign relations of States, but also would carry the federal principle to the internal problem of minorities. Integral federalism implies cultural decentralization as it also implies a similarity of economic and social structures. Through providing for an internal cultural federalism, with generous autonomy to cultural groups, it breaks the identity between "citizenship" and "nationality" that has been so productive of dissension. And by "federalizing" the concept of "nationality" within the wider framework of "citizenship" it divides the unitary idea of citizenship into a general political and a particular cultural loyalty, no longer mutually exclusive, but able to exist side by side. This is a logical requirement in Central Europe, for there each State is multinational. And as the relation between the dominant nationality and the minority is one of war sublimated into exploitation, federation is obviously impossible. The corporateness of national feelings among nationals distributed among multi-national States make the external federation of those States depend upon an internal federalism of nationalities.

Balkan Federalism

The pathology of empires that did not impregnate their parts with a sense of participation in the collectivity is the antithesis to a wholesome federalism that incorporates the general and the particular into a comprehensive unity. Perhaps this accounts for the consistent advocacy of federalism as a therapy for ailing empires. Thus, those who wished to preserve a system of political order in Central Europe strove to federalize the Austro-Hungarian empire as a safeguard. And, conversely, the Balkan nations, because they wished to dismember the Ottoman empire, did not propose any federalist devices to prolong it. But, like the Succession

[10] Gross, *op. cit.*, pp. 35-67.

States, after their liberation, although they felt the need for unity, they made only tepid attempts to place their relations with each other upon a federal basis. In those attempts, however, they were expressing their own need and that of Europe; and in their failures they revealed the malaise of Europe as well as their own vexation of spirit.

And nowhere is federalism more needed. The term "Balkan" has come to signify perpetual disorder and fratricidal strife. Imperialism and nationalism, alike, conspired there to accentuate geographic, racial and religious divisions. The Ottoman empire imposed an haphazard and unintegrated system of order upon its diverse parts; it held them together but did not unite them. The gradual disintegration of that empire served only to inflame rivalries among its liberated segments. Moreover, divisions within the Balkans have not only been indigenous to the area, they have also been created by the dynamism of the Great Powers. Power Politics have made the Balkan States either appendages to the Great Powers, or the critical points of intersection between them. And whether dragged in the wake of the Powers, or serving as the foci of their rivalries, the Balkan States cannot be self-determined either in union or apart. Nevertheless the efforts of some Balkan statesmen, and many non-officials, to create a Balkan union upon federal principles in the decade before the war disclosed that this erstwhile "Ottoman territory" was becoming European. And their failure, likewise, discloses that they too suffered from the fretful fever that afflicted Europe during the truce when the nations of Europe were too weak to make war upon one another, but were too strong to make a European peace. So, in this region of the Balkans, as in all Europe, the federal cycle in this terrible age is one of aspiring hopes, ineffectiveness, catastrophe, and renewed hope with a heightened tension of urgency.

In addition to the customary obstacles to federalism, national vanity, vested interests, political immaturity, and intellectual aridity, the Balkan States also encountered the rivalries of the Great Powers which deflected them from their primary Balkan interests, and bitter minorities problems which prevented them from finding and accepting a common Balkan ideal upon which they could all unite.

Following the disappearance of the Austrian, German, and Russian empires in World War I, the time seemed auspicious for Balkan union. The Great Power incubus had at length been lifted. For the first time in Balkan history there was popular support for the idea of federation. Agrarians, socialists, and communists, all traditionally opposed to nationalist wars, adopted the ideal of federation as a part of their programs. But the spirit of division, which seems like a sinister and brooding presence to hover over the Balkans, made these groups in all other things mutually antagonistic. Minorities problems poisoned Balkan nationalism, and irredenta embittered nationalities. Moreover, shortly after the war Great Power rivalries were resumed in the Balkans. France became the defender of the status quo, and Italy spear-headed the revolt against it.

Nevertheless the economic crisis, which fell with such an impact upon the producers of raw materials, persuaded diplomats in east central Europe that national self-sufficiency needed to be supplemented, as a program, with international action. The crisis led Hodza to organize an agricultural bureau composed of the cereal producing countries in eastern Europe. It prompted Papanastassios of Greece, a man with statesmanlike conceptions, to request several international organizations, without success, to sponsor a Balkan Conference. At length the Universal Peace Conference meeting in Athens received his proposal, and its International Bureau at Geneva in May 1930 invited the six Balkan foreign ministers to attend a conference at Athens. The circular invitation declared that "the Balkans will cease to be the neuralgic point of Europe only when . . . they look only to themselves for remedies to the maladies from which they have suffered in the past."

At the Athens Conference the Commission on Organization secured the adoption of a plan for permanent organization. The function of the Conference was defined as the promotion of Balkan cooperation in economic, social, intellectual and political relations as a preliminary to a real Balkan union. Rapprochement, the prelude to and condition of union, would describe in a slogan the objectives of the Conference.

The Conference planned to meet annually in each of the Balkan countries in turn, with the leader of the delegation of the host country acting as president. A General Assembly, Council, Secretariat, and National Groups made up the organs of the Conference. Each country was entitled to thirty voting members in the Assembly, and the diplomatic representatives of the Balkan governments could attend as observers with the right to speak. The Council, composed of the chiefs and two members of each delegation, acted as the executive body. It met between sessions, fixed the agenda for the Assembly, approved the budget, and could take other action considered necessary. The Council of the Balkan Conference conformed to the ancient Greek conception of a second chamber as an executive body, and not to the European idea of second chambers in a federalism as a House of State representatives. The Secretariat was assigned the customary duties. The National Groups, including all members of the Conference, past and present, were obliged to win the support of peace groups and the general public, to aid in the selection of delegates, and to work in their several countries for the application of the Conference resolutions. In this manner a continuity of personnel was assured, and an institutional nucleus from which the influence of the Conference could spread to political circles and among the general public was provided for. The National Groups were an interesting and instructive attempt to cope with the inescapable vulnerability of private associations; a periodic concentration of energies coupled with a continual dissipation of activities.

The First Conference held its closing plenary meeting, significantly, at Delphi, where in the dawn of the brilliant Hellenic day, Greek tribes had learned to unite, and had agreed to refrain from destroying one another, pledging themselves to destroy only the breaker of the bond. At that closing meeting, the minds of the delegates must perforce have gone slipping back to the ancient Amphictyony. Through its principle of union the Greeks had saved themselves from the dark fate of the Thracians, who once inhabited the Balkans, and who, although a large nation, "next to the Indians," according to Herodotus, decimated themselves with internal struggles, and vanished before they could make history because they could not get formed. Were the Balkans to repeat the bloody Thracian episode, or would they move together in a new Amphictyony, a security to themselves and an example to Europe?

The peculiar politico-private half-light in which the Balkan Conference acted was explained by its creator. "Though based on the national groups, composed of politicians, representatives of peace organizations, universities, and professional organizations," wrote Papanastassios, "and though its decisions do not obligate the governments, this organization has nevertheless an official character, not only because the governments of the six countries support the activities of the national groups, but also because the delegations of each country to the Conference are chosen after consultation with the government, and these governments are represented at each Conference by their diplomatic officials . . . in the country in which the Conference meets."[11]

In the Balkan Conference there was no federalism. It was not an order of governments; it was not federal in structure. Numerous draft agreements for cooperation in specific activities were prepared by the four Conferences. They remained unratified; grain and goods, communications and culture internationalism is seriously impeded in the absence of a political framework. However it might have reached governmental proportions, and out of it did come a proposal of genuine federation. So here, as in all European federalism in our epoch, there is a dreary *might have been* caused by political failures; but even in the ruins, there are to be found cornerstones, hewed by those who see beyond the

[11] Quoted in Stavrianos, *op. cit.*, p. 231.

fluctuations of events, upon which a glorious temple of peace can be erected.

To a questionnaire sent to the Balkan States by the Council of the Conference in 1931, the Greek National Group alone replied. The Greeks were reviving the federal tradition of their ancient civilization with energy and purposefulness.

Here was a federal program, a standard to which the "wise and the good could repair." But there was little wisdom in the Balkans, while evil purposes were generating in Europe. Yet, although now faced with an apparent impasse, when our past deeds tower in front of us, we should not be blindly fatalistic, expecting some doom, when we know how to escape it. An acute observer in ancient Greece, who described to a society at strife, with tragic intensity, the horrors of war, and who when contemplating "man's days" found them as a "grey shadow," yet, understanding the elasticity of man's ways, he still had the faith to believe that "the end men looked for cometh not, and a way is there where no man thought."

In the absence of a genuine federalism, political relations followed the conventional modes in the Balkans during the truce era; regular meetings of foreign ministers; a draft treaty of Conciliation, Arbitration, and Judicial Settlement, including the usual stipulations, non-aggression, pacific settlement of disputes, and mutual assistance. But the unprofitableness of these devices was demonstrated when Bulgaria and Albania refused to become parties to a Balkan Pact until the problem of the non-fulfillment of the minorities treaties had been solved. The Greek National Group then proposed that a permanent Minorities Office be established in each State, and, in addition, a Minorities Commission should be set up, composed of representatives of each of the six Balkan States to meet once a year to examine complaints, and refer appeals to the League of Nations in the event of disagreement. This was a constructive proposal for coping with the intractable minorities problem. But it remained unimplemented.

The Balkan States turned from the Conference to a Balkan Entente; from federalism to power politics. The Bulgarian absention from the Conference, because of the minorities problem, revived the diplomatic criss-cross of Balkan foreign relations. A growing rapprochement between Bulgaria and Yugoslavia, outside the Conference, created fear in Rumania, who, to counterbalance it, made a treaty with Soviet Russia. Greece and Turkey, equally alarmed by the Bulgaro-Yugoslav rapprochement, made a pact of mutual guarantee. And out of these several pacts the Entente was formed on February 9, 1934.

It provided that "Greece, Yugoslavia, Rumania, and Turkey guarantee mutually the security of all their Balkan frontiers." Nothing more clearly discloses the hypocrisy of such pacts than the reservations attached during the ratifications—reservations that limited the obligations of the signatories to Balkan aggressions clearly pointed to Bulgaria as the object of the treaty. The Bulgarians characterized the Entente as a "striking contradiction" to the "aspirations of the Conference" by its "tendency . . . to affirm forever the right of the stronger in opposing readjustments by pacific means . . ." and "in attaching no importance to the interests of the two other Balkan countries" which have not adhered to it.[12]

But beyond Bulgaria, as beyond Hungary, there arose the ominous and growing aggressiveness of the revisionist powers, Italy and Germany. Hence the Balkan Entente and the Little Entente, as they approximated their policies to the European dichotomy of a rigid status quo evoking an equally intransigent revisionism, were pulled from their local vortices into the gathering storm that was about to engulf all Europe. Once again the annals of Europe declare the truth, from which Europeans have so persistently turned, that Europe is one in the plenteousness of peace, in the tensions of the truce, in the desolation of war.

Axis domination of the Balkans revived desires and plans for federation in both official and unofficial circles. In the Polish-

[12] Quoted in Kerner and Howard, *The Balkan Conference and the Balkan Entente, 1930-1935*, University of California Press, 1936, p. 136.

Czechoslovak agreement of November 11, 1940 the two "Governments consider it imperative to declare solemnly" their determination after the war "to enter, as independent and sovereign States, into closer political and economic association, which would become the basis of a new order in Central Europe."[13] This was supplemented on January 24, 1942 by a plan for a Confederation in which the guarantee of personal and political rights was a conspicuous feature. The Greek-Yugoslav agreement of January 15, 1942 is the most detailed of official statements. It provides for a Balkan Union with a Political Organ, an Economic and Financial Organ, a Permanent Military Organ, and a Permanent Bureau. The Political Organ would coordinate the foreign policies of the member-States, and undertake a "rapprochement of public opinion." In the Economic and Financial Organ economic activities would be coordinated, and the Military Organ would prepare a common plan for the defense of the "European frontiers" of the member-States.[14]

These official plans, however, possess little federalism. The emphasis is upon "coordination," "common" policies, not upon the "autonomy" of the collective organs, or their "governmental" character. They tremble on the verge between a league and a federation. Resembling what the ancient Greeks called isopoliteia in which the city-states, remaining independent and separate entities, conducted their common affairs in a congress composed of city-state delegates. These plans hold the promise for, rather than the substance of federalism. Common affairs are still managed in membro, so to speak, at a common conclave, not through the corporate organ of a commonwealth. Authentic federations, like the Aetolian and Achaean Leagues, on the contrary, were called sympoliteia, in which a new community was created without prejudice to the autonomy of the members in non-federal matters. In these Leagues the federal authority exerted complete power over foreign affairs and defense. Insofar as its authority

[13] See note 9 above.

[14] Text in Stavrianos, *op. cit.*, Appendix L, p. 311.

extended, it regulated "the" affairs of the commonwealth into which the "common" affairs of the members had been transmuted.

Thus, we can again observe the law of European life: the nations are indissolubly interlocked with the development of Europe as a whole. In a divided Europe no region can be united; particularism, in the absence of a universal principle, may be palliated but cannot be controlled. Europe's law of being, the interaction of universalism and particularism, is violated either by a uniform imperialism that crushes particularism, or a particularism antagonistic to any universalism. Only a European program, European institutions, European law, a European federal government can halt the disintegration of European civilization.

"Pan-Europe"

From Vienna in 1923 the European idea was proclaimed with learning and cogency. Richard Coudenhove-Kalergi, an Austrian and a European, in that year published his book, "Pan-Europe." With clarion eloquence he called the people in Europe to come forth and be Europeans. "This book intends to bring to life," he wrote, "a great political idea which has been dormant in the nations of Europe. Many dream of a united Europe but few are resolved to create it. As an object of nostalgia it remains barren; as an object of will it becomes effective. The only force that can achieve Pan-Europe is the will of Europeans." Within a short time the most distinguished intellectual and moral leaders in Europe were enrolled. Diplomats, statesmen, and businessmen all supported the movement. In October 1926 the first Congress was held in Vienna, and an organization, acting through national groups, was founded.

The Pan-Europe movement recognized that Europe was neither an imperial entity above the nations, nor the sum of the nations' agreements upon common affairs. It was a universal idea penetrating the nations without which they could not exist, and in which they must participate or perish. Hence Pan-Europe is not merely a scheme for uniting Europe, it is the idea of Europe.

The transfer of the central headquarters of Pan-Europe to the United States when Europe was no longer habitable, while bleak proof of the truth of its principles, may also be symbolic of the future. For may it not be the happy opportunity for the United States to support, in Europe, the idea which has been the law of its life, and which is of our European heritage?

The Pan-European Conference, in conjunction with the Research Seminar for European Federation of New York University, issued a Draft Constitution of the United States of Europe in April, 1944. It is called "Articles of Association and Union," and describes the Union as "an association of sovereign states which have decided to establish and maintain common institutions in the interest of their security, prosperity, and liberty" (Art. 2).

This looks to a federal order, for the institutions, not the affairs of the members, are "common." Democratic standards of constitutionalism, (Sec. 2) individual rights, (Sec. 4) and social rights (Sec. 5) which are to be maintained by the several States are particularized. Presumably only the rights granted to individuals are to be enforceable in the Union Supreme Court (Art. 37), for a similar clause is not included for Sections 2 and 5. All disputes between member States must be settled, if of a "juridical nature" by the Supreme Court of the Union, if of a "non-juridical nature" by the Council. (Art. 18) This distinction can provoke controversy; and who is to decide? The organization of defense and the materials of warfare are completely federalized. (Sec. 6) While the Union "shall have power to conduct foreign relations," member States, with the approval of the Union, may exchange diplomatic and consular representatives among themselves and with foreign States. (Art. 54) In economic affairs the Union "shall aim at the unification of the European economy" and within five years following its organization, the Union "Congress is authorized to establish a European customs union with inter-European free trade." (Art. 60) The Union will "assume the unification of the European transport system within a period to be determined by the Congress." (Art. 63) Model legislation in price and wage policies (Art. 62) will be enacted by the Union. Moreover the Union has general power to enact model legislation on any subject "outside of its immediate competence" (Art. 16), and it is to be inferred that it has the same power on any subject within its competence. The Union controls permanent migration. (Art. 17) In the colonial territories of the member States, the nationals of every member of the Union enjoy equal rights and privileges, (Art. 57) and the "governing member state is bound to act in its colonial territory as a trustee for the people of such territory" (Art. 58).

An Assembly elected by popular vote and organized on a plan of weighted representation, and a House of States consisting of delegates from each member State, also according to a weighted plan, "shall have power to deal with all matters falling within the competence of the Union." (Art. 76) In ordinary matters the two Houses are "co-ordinate in authority and their agreement shall be necessary to a decision," (Art. 73) but in constitutional matters they sit together as an Assembly. (Art. 77) The executive organ of the Union is a Council of seven members elected for terms of four years by the two Houses. (Sec. 12) A Supreme Court of fifteen judges elected by the two Houses is the "chief judicial organ" of the Union. (Sec. 13) The Union shall be financed by contributions of members in proportion to their ascertained national income, by proceeds from the "domain of the Union," and "all of the net proceeds of import duties levied by the member states upon their mutual trade, and fifty per cent of the net proceeds of import duties levied upon goods coming from outside the Union." (Sec. 10)

The Draft Constitution is unquestionably federal, yet not over-federal for the conditions now existing in Europe. It is not the law of a utopian Europe with all problems solved, but a constitutional structure in which Europe can solve its problems peacably by European means and for European purposes. Federalism is not a procrustean instrument of force acting compulsively upon nations, it is, on the contrary, an instrument for their liberation from internecine strife, and a guarantee against their absorption into an overruling imperialism. And the Draft Constitution wisely sets up a structure through which Europe can become federal; it does not undertake to federalize Europe forcibly. Europe is a unit from the point of view of war and peace, and so defense and foreign relations are Europeanized. Hence the armed services and materials are placed completely under the authority of the Union institutions in a system of pooled security. International relations are either vested in the Union, or, when conducted by a member State, are subjected to Union control.

The emphasis upon constitutional, individual, and social rights is a recognition of the organic relation between the constitutional ethos and the spirit animating foreign affairs. When, during the 19th century, under the impetus of Liberalism, the trend was toward minimizing governmental action, this intimate connection was overlooked. When political negativity was the desiderata in both internal and external affairs, the singleness of positive policies at home and abroad could not be appreciated. However, in a United States of Europe, constitutional and social rights, as well as individual, should be guaranteed by the Union judiciary, and enforced, when necessary, by Union organs.

The use of a personal, rather than a corporate basis for the election of members to the Council and the Supreme Court, insures an executive and a judiciary which would not become bulwarks of State particularism likely to thwart the general objectives of the legislature. Nevertheless a protection is afforded to the States in the provision that not more than one member of the Council shall "come from the same member state," (Art. 79) and in providing that the "present members of the highest courts of the member states" as well as "a maximum of 100 jurisconsults of recognized standing " (Art. 86) shall compose the lists of nominees.

Here is a project which might well serve as a basic draft for discussion in a European constitutional convention. It might be to the United States of Europe what the Virginia and New Jersey plans were to the United States of America.

Under the impetus and inspiration of Pan-Europe, Briand presented his plan for the organization "d'un régime d'union fédérale, européanne."

Briand Plan

The Briand plan, and in this it bore the mark of the times, represented French policy as well as a European aspiration. And in general the replies of the governments pointed to this vulnerability. And this undoubtedly also explains why the plan approached but never reached a European character. The French were seeking to establish a system in Europe which would give them a feeling of security, for the legal security of pacts piled upon pacts did not allay a nervousness about the future. As "Pertinax," speaking to a British audience in November 1929 said; "Instinctively most Frenchmen do not trust much to all these guarantees, and to me they are not unlike a jigsaw puzzle. When you think you have finished your puzzle, you suddenly find that your last space is empty, and something is missing somewhere. . . ." He explained this uneasiness by asserting that the present system of security was "all more or less based on the most favorable hypotheses," and that it did not "take into account that the worst may happen."[15] The French, laboring like Sisyphus, were seeking additional aid to roll the stone over the hill.

As French policy the Briand plan was a Locarno expanded to Europe, with the light of the Geneva Protocol illuminating the margins like some aurora borealis. One group of alliances in 1929, by focussing on the status quo provoked another focussing on revision. And the French hoped to incorporate all in one grand alliance of mutual guarante. This was a praiseworthy object, but it was not federalism, despite the use of the term. Federalism

[15] Quoted in Survey of International Affairs, 1930, Toynbee, A. J., Oxford University Press, 1931, p. 14.

is not a conjuring word, and its use as an incantation may deceive the unwary but will not persuade the sagacious.

From the European angle of vision the Briand plan was an effort to restore Europe, not to its earlier primacy, but to equality with the peripheral powers After World War I the rise of non-European States to an overshadowing position toward Europe heralded a diplomatic revolution. World War II has accentuated this trend to the point where Europe has been reduced to a colonial status. There ought to be a ratio between European centripetalism and external pressures. Ancient Greece, when encircled and dwarfed by Macedon, Egypt, Syria, and Rome, had to a degree, ceased from her internal strivings and realized for a space the ideal of Hellenic unity which had been created in the period of t he Persian wars, but had thereafter been without an abiding place in Greek political institutions. And, in the early history of Europe, the Italian cities of Venice, Florence, and Genoa were overshadowed by the rising monarchies in France, Spain, and England. Unable to unite, they were for a time pawns in a fierce struggle among the monarchies, but they finally sank to the status of Spanish provincial cities. The Greeks, through their Leagues, postponed their colonial fate for 150 years; but the Italian cities, heedless of the penalties of disunion, delayed their freedom for three centuries. Why from the centers of civilization in Greece and Italy did the cities "rage so furiously together," and why did the peoples who had propelled such thrusts of civilization out into the circumambient world "imagine a vain thing?"

The Briand memorandum signified an effort to enable the nations of Europe "on the plane of absolute sovereignty and of entire political independence" through a "bond of solidarity" to realize the geographical unity of Europe, and to bring about, within the framework of the League, one of the regional understandings which were formally recognized by it.[16] A European union, the memorandum pointed out, differed from customs unions by greater comprehensiveness, for the latter tended "to abolish

[16] Text in Documents on International Affairs, 1930, ed. J. W. Wheeler-Bennett, Oxford University Press, 1931, pp. 61-73.

internal customs barriers in order to erect on the boundary of the whole community a stiffer barrier . . . in practice" against the States situated outside.

The signatory governments, it was proposed, would affirm the "Principle of the Moral Union of Europe" and "place formally on Record the Existence of the Solidarity established between the States of Europe" by promising "to get into touch regularly, at meetings held regularly or on special occasions, to examine in common all questions likely to be of interest primarily to the commonwealth of European peoples." This, it was somewhat hopefully observed, would henceforth put the principle of European union "beyond discussion and removed far above the routine of everyday procedure."

As an organ for accomplishing this task a "European Conference" consisting of "the representatives of all the European governments" that were members of the League of Nations would be constituted. Its powers and procedure were to be settled "at the next reunion of the European States." In addition to the Conference, the plan provided, vaguely, for "an executive body in the form of a permanent political committee" composed "only of a certain number of members of the European Conference, which would act both as the committee of research and as the executive body of the European Union." Its organizations and powers were to be determined "at the next meeting of the European States." The "General Conception" of the European Committee was described as (1) "The general subordination of the economic problem to the political problem"; (2) "The principle that European political co-operation should be directed toward . . . a federation based on the idea of union and not of unity"; (3) "The principle that the economic organization of Europe should be directed toward . . . a rapprochement of the European economic systems effected under the political control of the Governments acting in concert." The memorandum proposed as "Questions of Practical Application" to be studied: the definition of the field of European co-operation; and the definition of the methods of co-operation among European States in European matters, and of European States with non-European States in extra-European matters.

Despite its nomenclature there is no federalism in the Briand plan. The guarantee of absolute sovereignty is inconsistent with a federation which deprives its members of complete discretion in federal affairs. Union implies, as the Netherlands government forthrightly stated in its reply to the memorandum, a limitation of sovereignty. Moreover, not federalism but a Europeanization of the Locarno system was the scheme outlined in the memorandum. A sly parenthetical statement, inserted almost as a caveat after the declaration that the principle of European political co-operation should be the advancement toward a federation, suggests "as a corollary" the extension of the Locarno system. The Locarno system, however, was an unqualified league; it had nothing of government or federalism in it. It functioned at the foreign office level; it depended upon the discretion of sovereign States, not upon a legal order; and the system was enforced by diplomatic not executive techniques. Locarno and federalism are antithetical and nothing more clearly indicates the confusion of the memorandum that the oblique attempt to coalesce them. While it proclaimed the principle of constant solidarity among European nations, the memorandum did not announce any principle of universality that penetrated the parts to unite them. The principle of solidarity is descriptive; it is neither a principle of order nor a supreme law. It is a reason *for* federation, but it is not the rationale *of* federation. Moreover the principle of European union should certainly not be "removed from the routine of everyday procedure," like some astronomical phenomenon related tenuously, if at all, to worldly affairs; it should, on the contrary, be a conditioning and governing influence in "the routine of everyday procedure." The Briand memorandum bowed to the principle of European union, then turned away to be busy with the ways of disunion; it is pointed to the sun, but is rooted in the shadows cast by four centuries of perpetual strife.

The replies of the European governments, similarly, paid obeisance to the moral union of Europe, then promptly criticized the memorandum from the point of view of their special interests. The Netherlands government alone encountered and met the issue of sovereignty. The revisionist powers asked that the plan give equality of status, accompanied with disarmament, and provide for a bold reform of conditions "recognized as untenable" (German reply). In general the replies counselled against provoking inter-continental rivalries and the danger of setting up a rival organization to the League. Many advocated the inclusion of European States not then members of the League; that is, Soviet Russia and Turkey. The British government alluded to the indefiniteness of the organization, while the Italian reply was sharply critical of the proposal for the European Committee.

In the preamble to the plan the "geographical unity of Europe" was opposed to its "territorial divisions," and this was acknowledged as the antecedent, although not the general cause for the proposal. But Europe is not a geographic unit. Geographically it is a peninsula of Eurasia with an undeterminable frontier. The Urals do not divide European from Asiatic Russia. The Elbe-Danube line can be the central axis of Europe, or its eastern geographic and political frontier. The Alps, while they insulate Switzerland, geographically, do not separate Italy from the north. Michelet once declared that Africa began at the Pyrenees; it could be argued that Europe extends to the Sahara. The Bosphorus can either unite Europe to, or divide it from, Asia. The Mediterranean and Black Sea unite the circumjacent shores of continents. Seaways to the East Indies are part of the geography of Holland. Sir Eyre Crowe once pointed out that Great Britain is the neighbor of every country with a seabord. The "geographical unity" of Europe depends more upon political and cultural influences than upon seas, mountains, lakes and rivers. The Rhine, gathering and absorbing the waters of two countries, might be as unifying as divisive; in the trenchant phrase of Romain Rolland, France and Germany "were wedded" in it.

At the heart of the memorandum lay the principle of the subordination of economic to political problems, and all replies referred to this, many to disagree, some to qualify, and others to accept. The economic unity of Europe is a delusive phantom. Approximately one half of its imports and exports, including Great Britain and Russia, are with the non-European world. Because of her deficiency in many basic products, Europe imports nearly all her cotton, about 70% of her wool, 80% of crude copper, and the greater part of her supplies of nickel, chromium, vanadium, and other metals. In a recent economic analysis of Europe the conclusion reached was "that in nearly every phase the industrial as well as the agricultural production of the European countries was to some extent dependent on the import of raw materials, semi-manufactured products, and even some manufactures."[17] The economic health of Europe, therefore, depends upon the prosperous functioning of the world economy.

But, while Europe is not an economic unity, its economy can be so integrated that it will increase the welfare of the European people and contribute to the improvement of the world economy. An articulated, not a unified economy is the need of Europe. The establishment of food processing and of a dairy industry in the Danubian cereal growing countries will lessen the burden of over-population on the land and the dependence upon one crop. Such a program would also bridge the present cleavage between the "two Europes"; the manufacturing and efficiently agricultural west, and the peasant, high cost producing east. A water power project on the Rhine-Danube would unite east and west Europe in a convergent and expanding economy. Inasmuch as mass production of commodities is not suitable to Europe, the organized development of specialized and luxury products would increase her exports and thereby raise the level of her imports. The European economy can live only within the frame of a world economy; the two will rise and fall together; they are mutually dependent. But

[17] Antonin Basch, *A Price for Peace*, Columbia University Press, 1945, p. 10.

a Europe integrated with itself will the more readily participate in and contribute to the world economy.

Hence the issue raised in the Briand memorandum is reduced to the question: Can the European economy be integrated in the absence of political security? Since the disintegration of the European economy, aggravated by political economics, paralleled a growing sense of insecurity, it would seem that although in logic the political and economic elements in a situation are inseparable, in the sequence of time the political is prior. Mercantilism, in the 16th as well as in the 20th century, as a philosophy of political economics, was directed to power as its objective, and is inseparable from power politics. It is significant that the English liberal free-traders of the last century were also pacifists. Economic integration implies diversification and inter-dependence, while power economics aim toward self-sufficiency and economic, as well as political, independence. And the more illusory the possibility, the more intense the efforts. The demonstrable fact that no State can become economically independent, while it should lead to an ordered and planned interdependence, leads, instead, because of the fear aroused through pitiless power politics, to frenzied efforts to capture an ignis fatuus.

Customs unions have been possible only where there was political security. The United States constitution grew out of an effort to remedy economic strife, and only within the political structure it established could this country have become such a free trade area. And even within that system complete free trade is not always possible.

In an insensate nationalist world, economics, no less than all other human relations, cannot escape the nationalist tincture. And since political nationalism is now indigenous in the State-system, it is only in the reform of that system that the tensions can be relaxed, for all social organization is centered upon and constricted within the structure of the State. This is a State age, in democracies as well as in autocracies, and it is *through* the State that the reform *of* the State, and the better ordering of relations *between* States must come. It is the supreme irony of our times, and also a most provocative challenge, that the instruments of our future social salvation are also the means of our present damnation.

Briand was not a European Aratus, and there may have been a dash of Machiavellianism in his project, but in declaring the ideal of European union, and in turning the mind of Europe toward that ideal, however inadequate and disappointing his instrumentation, he was, nevertheless, looking to the light. A century earlier Victor Hugo, a great European as well as a celebrated Frenchman, had eloquently proclaimed the ideal of a United States of Europe. He had also divided mankind into the "luminous and the shady," and surely he would have numbered Briand among the children of light in 1929. As the Briand plan, dismissed with courtesy or impeccable logic, was entombed in archives, a deepening darkness fell upon Europe.

On the morrow of a period "devoted to universal wrack," Europeans, more conscious than ever of Europe, have resumed making plans for it, so that like the city described by the psalmist it will be "at unity with itself." The plans of Pan-Europe, originating after the first World War, and continued into the present, are wide geographically and are wholly federal, (see above). Recently more partial plans, have also been proposed.

The Western European Federation

General Smuts, in a notorious speech in December 1943, demanded a western bloc for the most unfederal of reasons: to balance the United States and Soviet Russia. This, of course, is pivot diplomacy and has nothing of federalism in it. Since the conclusion of the war the idea of a west European federation has been revived, principally because of the division of Europe into east and west, but, more important, between the occupied and the unoccupied. Some fear that an unoccupied and unorganized western Europe will become a zwischenland. This would make western Europe the eastern Europe of the interim between the second and third World Wars. Others, however, fear that a union of western Europe would inevitably become an Anglo-American march against Russia. A frontier is more likely to possess two cutting edges than one.

Among the nations of western Europe there exist many of the ingredients of a federation. They do not feel insecure vis-a-vis one another, but they do feel insecure as the center of rivalries among the Big Three. They have similar social structures. Their trade with one another is approximately 50% of their total. They can readily construct a federation on a common law for common defense, a common foreign policy, and to encourage common economic interests.

The attitudes of Great Britain and France are crucial for its formation. The British Prime Minister has declared that "Europe must federate or perish" but he did not define "Europe." The British government has not disassociated itself from the speech delivered by Winston Churchill to the Dutch parliament in May 1946 in which he hoped that "under the guardianship of a world organization" there should "arise a United States of Europe, both of the east, and of the west, which will unify the Continent in a manner never known since the Roman empire." The Economist, in June 1945, published a series of articles arguing for a western federation. Important sections of British opinion presumably are not hostile to the idea.

Moreover, close, perhaps even federal, connections may yet be introduced into Anglo-French relations. The Churchill proposal of federal union in the crisis of June 1940 was not an abrupt and unanticipated act; it was preceded by extensive conversations carried on in a pre-crisis but urgent mood. Paul Reynaud, in a magazine article, and Albert Guérard, in another,[18] have given us fragments of history which may aid to explain much that is past, and be suggestive for what might come. But this fact indisputably

[18] Paul Reynaud, 165 *Atlantic Monthly,* 445, 1940. Albert Guérard, *Antioch Review,* Spring 1946, p. 136.

emerges: Anglo-French conversations at the highest levels upon the subject of a federal compact between the two countries took place after the outbreak of the war.

The danger of a western combination lies in the possibility that it would be converted into an alliance against Soviet Russia. Yet, on the other hand, if Europe is to federate, a beginning must be made. Preferably that beginning should be continental in scope, but a partial beginning is better than no beginning. And whether or not a western federation develops into an alliance, pointing outward, or into a federal government pointing inward, will depend upon circumstances and not upon texts of pacts.

Russian hostility toward a western federation could create the very thing she fears. But it is a Russian interest, no less than an Anglo-American one, that Europe should be united. For in a divided Europe, Anglo-American and Russian rivalries will breed antagonisms, while a united and autonomous Europe will be closed against Great Power influences. Open, not closed frontiers, infect relations between the adjacent powers. The Low Countries, until as independent States they were closed to rival influences, agitated the European balance for a century. The German States, until they were at length united and consolidated, raised and depressed the European balance as the shifting pivot of the European equilibrium for two centures. In most recent times the European powers gyrated on the vertigo axes of Balkan politics. As long as a divided Europe lies between the Big Three, they will move distrustfully and apart over the "quaking ground."

European Federalists of Today

The European federalists of today, by identifying the political ideal of universalism—Europe—with the philosophical idea of universalism—the humanity of man—insure not only a democratic structure for their federation, but also, by giving it a profound purpose, avoid dedicating it to political ephemeralities. The conjunction of the two universal ideas for which European civilization has long been the symbol should quicken the regenerative elements now concealed or crushed in the ruins made by the negativity of an erroneous idea. This new universalism will transform Europe, and Europeans awakening to a new life should feel the same sense of release that came upon those exiles who, when their captivity was turned, "were like them that dream."

Nor do these latest Europeans overlook, in their zeal for the universal, the need for the particular. And while they recognize the universal of Europe, and the universal in the individual as a human being, they also recognize that these universals are connected through the nations. But the nations, not as sovereign, unassociative, rigid and euclidean corporate bodies, but as cultural units, as wide as civilization yet anchored to a distinct and meaningful localism. The exaltation of the national State that originated either as a reaction against the French imperialism of the Revolution and Napoleon, or as a search for unity where the Revolution had destroyed the traditional and European institutions of cohesion-monarchism, feudalism, and the church—is no longer necessary. For there is no imperialism *in* Europe to be defied, but there is a non-European imperialism that a divided Europe should fear, and the political glorification of uniqueness, it has been learned of late, leads to the destruction rather than to the growth and deepening of diverse national cultures.

The unity of each part as well as of the whole can result only from the acceptance of the true mission of European Civilization —the protection of the spiritual integrity of man, both as a fugitive individual, and as an historic experience with the longest of memories. The incitement of European civilization is the interaction between Europe and its nationalities. And the only political instrument by which Europe can accomplish its civilizing destiny is a federation, because that alone is the political embodiment of the dynamic interaction of the universal with the particular. A federation of Europe is, therefore, most faithfully representative of the community of Europe, and the truest symbol of the idea of Europe.

BIBLIOGRAPHY

BASCH, ANTONIN: *A Price for Peace,* Columbia University Press, 1945.

BRECHT, ARNOLD: *European Federation, Harvard Law Review,* Vol. LV, No. 4; February, 1942, pp. 561-594.

BINGHAM, EDWARD: *The United States of Europe,* Duell, Sloane & Pearce, N. Y., 1940.

COUDENHOVE-KALERGI, RICHARD N.: *Pan-Europe,* Knopf, N. Y., 1926.

COUDENHOVE-KALERGI, RICHARD N.: *Crusade for Pan-Europe,* G. P. Putnam, N. Y., 1943.

DAVIES, LORD DAVID: *Federated Europe,* Gollancz, 1940, London.

GESHKOFF, THEODORE I.: *Balkan Union: A Road to Peace in Southeastern Europe,* Columbia University Press, New York, 1940.

GROSS, FELIKS: *Crossroads of Two Continents,* Columbia University Press, 1945, New York.

GUÉRARD, ALBERT: *Europe Free and United,* Stanford University Press, 1945.

HERRIOT, EDUARD: *The United States of Europe,* Viking Press, 1930, New York.

HODZA, MILAN: *Federation in Central Europe, Reflections and Reminiscenses,* Jarrolds, 1942, London, New York.

JASZI, OSCAR: *The Dissolution of the Austro-Hungarian Monarchy,* University of Chicago Press, 1929, Chicago.

KERNER, ROBERT J. and HARRY N. HOWARD: *The Balkan Conference and the Balkan Entente* 1930-1935, University of California Press, Berkeley, 1936.

LORWIN, LEWIS L.: *Postwar Plans of the United Nations,* Twentieth Century Fund, 1943, New York.

MACARTNEY, C. A.: *Problems of the Danube Basin,* Macmillan, 1942, New York.

MACHRAY, ROBERT: *The Little Entente,* R. R. Smith, 1929, New York.

MACHRAY, ROBERT: *The Struggle for the Danube and the Little Entente,* 1929-1938, Allen and Unwin, 1938, London.

MUIR, RAMSAY: *Nationality and Internationalism,* London, 1917.

NEWMAN, BERNARD: *The New Europe,* Macmillan, 1943, New York.

PADELFORD, NORMAN J.: *Peace in the Balkans: The Movement Towards International Organization in the Balkans,* Oxford University Press, 1935, New York.

PADEV, M.: *Escape from the Balkans,* New York, 1943.

ROUCEK, JOSEPH S.: *The Politics of the Balkans,* McGraw-Hill, 1939, New York.

SETON-WATSON, R. W.: *The South Slav Question and the Habsburg Monarchy,* London, 1911.

STAVRIANOS, L. S.: *Balkan Federation,* Smith College Studies in History, Vol. XXVII, 1942, Northampton, Mass.

THOMPSON, S. H.: *Czechoslovakia in European History,* Princeton University Press, 1943, Princeton.

Epilogue

To participate in battles is praiseworthy
But who is not bold in our brave age?
Everyone fights impudently,
Everyone lies insolently . . .

My hero, may he be first of all—a human being

Alexander Pushkin

The Balance Sheet

..Let us now draw up the balance sheet. We have reviewed a score of various democratic, liberal, and radical ideologies. How much did they contribute to human progress? How much to the improvement of our social, economic and international systems, and to the advancement of our morals?

The postwar upswing of radicalism after 1918 brought radical, socialist, agrarian and democratic parties into power. This was true especially in the defeated countries, and in those countries of Eastern Europe which were liberated from many decades of foreign domination. The "European Revolution" of 1918 was above all a revolution of the defeated. (Victors do not revolt in history; they hail their war leaders and look to a continuance of the status quo). The social change produced positive achievements in many fields. Basic human and political liberties were secured simultaneously with an advance in social and cultural fields. At last, after a long, devastating war, democratic and parliamentary rule was to prevail for a short time all over continental Europe.

Social conditions of the working man were improved. The eight hour day was generally accepted; social security laws and legislation governing women and child labor were passed. Powerful trade unions were in a position to defend the working man's rights. Workers filled the concert halls and theatres, while adult education developed to an unprecedented level. The peasant parties of Eastern Europe, with the support of other democratic movements, succeeded in enforcing land reforms. True, in some countries, these reforms were slow in coming and inadequate, as, for instance, in Poland; and in Hungary the land reforms were entirely upset by the reactionary gentry. Despite these shortcom-

ings, however, the land reforms coming after 1918 constituted a second agrarian revolution in Eastern Europe. (The first was the abolition of serfdom, 1848-1861-1864). These reforms, such as they were, considerably weakened what remained of the feudal system in Eastern Europe. It may be mentioned that the Russian Revolution had an important influence on the general advance and of land reforms; but it is often forgotten that the Tsarist tyranny was overthrown by a democratic revolution, which in turn was overthrown by the Bolshevik Revolution.

These are the achievements, but it would be a mistake to overlook the failures and disappointments. Once the plans for a better society were put into operation, new problems, unanticipated by the social engineers, were created.

Nationalization or socialization of industry also created dangers of totalitarianism—a development which was anticipated by only a few liberals. Moreover, the new socialized forms of industrial management did not necessarily lead to a higher standard of living. Socialization was not a panacea for all social evils as many Marxians believed. A change in the economic organization, without adequate effects on the welfare of the wage earner, provided only a limited interest for the common man. The state economy of the Soviet Union has created a new, privileged elite, a new, unexpected class stratification. A new class division has replaced the old one, and the great problem of economic democracy has emerged as a much more complicated phenomenon than in the writings of philosophers.

Another failure of the socialist governments of Europe was their inability to cope with unemployment. Economists were as helpless as medieval physicians in their fight against the Black Plague. Nor were the democrats of Europe able to make parliamentary government attractive to the masses in all countries. A new problem arose: how to defend a democratic system against violence without the use of violence; and how to defend democracy against enemies who use civil rights and democratic privileges in order to destroy democratic institutions?

In international affairs there were many evidences of good will during the inter-war period. Still, a second world war was not prevented; there was no basic change from the traditional and unworkable international organization of European nations. Nationalism and chauvinism became rampant. Men like Noske had their influence in Germany while Socialists under MacDonald were unable to solve the problem of India and had to wait until Attlee came to power to save the honor of the Labor Party in this particular issue. Moreover, Continental European democrats were unable to lower the tariff walls to form a European Union. On the contrary, Europe became more nationalistic than ever. A foolish tendency toward self-sufficiency developed rapidly in a peninsula which was in great need of economic unity. Left wing socialists during the interwar period did not support the European federal movement; nor did they whole heartedly support the League of Nations. The greatest support for a Federated Europe was to come with the outbreak of the Second World War... ....

Also during this period of the 1920's and 30's the democratic and radical movements of Europe underwent many ideological changes. The long controversy about "Ministerialism" within the Socialist camp finally came to an end. For a long time Socialists had debated whether they should join other parties in coalition governments, thus sharing responsibility for the state, or whether they should avoid any ministerial commitments unless they won a majority and could govern without compromises, according to Socialist theory. European Social-Democrats, however, felt that they had to take responsibility and govern, for no progress could be accomplished by sheer opposition. Austrian Socialists presented a radical program and were able to show constructive achievements in their municipal government of Vienna. In Germany there were groups of Democrats, Pacifists, democratic Socialists and independent Republicans strongly opposed to collaboration with nationalistic groups; they asked especially for tight control of the army and warned the world repeatedly that the surest way to revitalize German nationalism was to strengthen the German Army.

The great defeat came with Hitler's rise to power. Despite the triumphs of Nazism, thousands subsequently showed an inspiring courage and devotion to democratic ideals. They preferred torture and death in concentration camps to a surrender of their ideas. The heroism of the European democratic resistance movement was more than a proof that Fascism and Nazism had not destroyed the deep longing of peoples for a decent way of life.

In the final struggle against totalitarianism, politics again switched to the field of morals. Whereas Fascism and Nazism represented terror, persecution, violence and intolerance, Democratic forces represented human decency. Despite the catastrophic influence of Hitler's madmen, the flame of European culture was preserved by the ranks of the resistance movement.

After the Second World War the democratic European movements emerged revitalized. It was now felt that the old, purely materialistic Marxian theories lacked "something." More specifically, they lacked a humanitarian basis. The Democratic, Agrarian and Socialist movements began to bend toward a new Humanism. France, with the great tradition of Jean Jaurès was the place where the humanitarian trends, especially in Socialism, found a strong expression in the brilliant writings of Leon Blum. In Eastern Europe, Zygmunt Zulawski, the Jaurès of Poland, rejects pure materialism in his "Wealth, Freedom and Morals," written under Nazi occupation, and searches for a moral basis of Democracy and Society. A general rapprochement between the Socialist movements and the Christian Democratic movements, especially in France, is only a symptom of the general trend.

The ideological struggle in Europe today could be presented in a nutshell as the problem of a choice between the primacy of the individual and primacy of the state. It is, in other words, the struggle between the principles of freedom and totalitarianism. On the other hand, on another level, it is a struggle between nationalism and some kind of federalism. It is generally felt that a European Federation is a creative solution for many European troubles.

The contributors to this EPILOGUE do not discuss, as in the previous chapters, any particular European ideology. This following section embodies a normative effort to outline general premises for a democratic, liberal and humanitarian social system. Though ideas presented in the EPILOGUE cannot be regarded as representative of any specific European movement, they do still correspond to a general democratic and liberal trend.

In the chapter on "Parallelism" the problem of a balanced advance in the political and in the economic sphere is analyzed, as well as the progress in political freedom and economic security. In his chapter, "Economic Planning Without Statism," Professor Lewis Corey discusses the problem of reconciling economic planning with the democratic institutions and our civil rights. The humanist basis for a labor movement is outlined in Professor Sidney Hook's chapter. The reader is also referred to R. Gotesky's chapter on "Liberalism."

F. G.

XXV
Parallelism And Progress

XXV

PARALLELISM AND PROGRESS

by
Feliks Gross

European radicals and democrats of the 18th and 19th century knew what they wanted. The objectives were clear. They wanted a world without human misery, without suffering and wars, a new society, harmonious, peaceful and happy. They termed all this "progress." To a worker, to a peasant, to a common man the meaning of progress was clear, too. The life of millions of workers of the 19th century was not happy at all. There were long working hours, low salaries, periodic unemployment, poor housing and hard work under unhealthy, adverse conditions. In most of the European countries, moreover, there was a lack of adequate political rights, and national and political oppression in addition. For those who suffered, it was not difficult to formulate what they needed; to satisfy their needs meant progress for them. Some of the radical idealists may have thought about progress in utopian terms, but for a laborer this meant simply: better living, better housing, a higher standard of living, shorter labor hours, opportunity for education for his children, medical care in case of sickness, political rights, and national freedom for those who were oppressed because of their nationality. People knew what they lacked. The great debates of philosophers and social scientists, who spoke about the illusions of progress, or argued what the word meant, were without any significance for the workers and peasants.

There was a great deal of progress in many fields before the First World War. We saw, in Western Europe, better standards of living than fifty years before. Simultaneously, after 1870, there were more political rights in nearly all European countries, with the least advance in Russia, where except for abolition of serfdom, the path of progress was slowed down. Especially in the Scandinavian and English speaking countries, the road of social and political advance was amazingly parallel: a rising standard of living and economic security was accompanied by a parallel progress in democratic, political institutions. Civil rights did not suffer because of economic and social changes. In the Scandinavian countries, in Australia and New Zealand wages were rising, the eight hour labor day was introduced, social security as an elaborate and wide system of protection of a worker against sickness, disability and unemployment made long strides, and, simultaneously, the working man and the farmer won more and more influence in the government without curtailing the civil rights and basic liberties of his fellow citizens. In all these cases the economic and social welfare of the working masses was considerably advanced, while simultaneously a parallel progress was made in the political sphere.

Parallel advancement in the sphere of economic, social, and political institutions on the one hand, and in the sphere of democratic liberties on the other, is not characteristic of all countries for all times. The initial parallel development in political and social and partially in economic spheres was already upset between 1917 and the 1920's by a growing trend toward totalitarian systems. Communists advocated an unbalanced, anti-parallel system in which advance in economic forms would be achieved at the expense of human liberties accompanied by a definite setback in the sphere of political institutions. Fascists promised glory for the omnipotent national state and fulfillment of the dreams of national megalomaniacs. This glory was to be combined with some type of economic security for their own nationals at the price of war and conquest over foreign nationals. Freedom and civil liberties was the price a man had to pay for the promised Utopia.

Some of the totalitarian states could boast of successes accomplished in certain activities such as road building, industrialization and the attainment of literacy. A good many examples could be found in history when certain reforms and a limited advance in certain segements of human relations were achieved in a despotic, reactionary state ruled by ruthless men whom the Greeks would not hesitate to call "tyrants." The orthodox Marxian school, on the other hand, contends that advancement in an economic sense will automatically bring progress in all other spheres because, as the Marxians argue, the changes in production and in economic forms is the prime mover of social development. Unfortunately, the deterministic Marxian approach has not always found confirmation in historical facts. Technology or economic forms have often advanced with little or no progress being made in other spheres for many years.

When National Liberties and National Glory Coincided With Social Degradation

Times of glory and political independence of a country sometimes have meant a growing oppression for its toiling classes. Times of progress in economic organization have sometimes coincided with a limitation or even abolition of basic civil rights and basic human liberties. Times of great technical advancement harbor dangers of an inner collapse when accompanied by a simultaneous decadence in the sphere of morals as well as in political and social institutions. These lags have become the main illness of progress. The Turks, who subjugated south-eastern Europe in the 15th and 16th centuries, simultaneously partially abolished serfdom there. When Rumania was regaining her national independence and the Turks were losing their foothold in the provinces, Rumanian national progress was accompanied by a re-enslavement of the peasants by their own national gentry. In this instance, the development of a national state meant that the conditions of the common man became incomparably worse than when Turkish foreign rule prevailed. "Surveying with one glance the whole of these changes, political and social . . . they show that in the forties of the nineteenth century, when the Rumanian provinces recovered their national autonomy, their population lost much or most of their social and economic freedom."[1] Thus when Rumania began to regain its national independence, first by receiving national autonomy, peasants fled from their own fatherland to Russia, Turkey and Austro-Hungary, leaving behind them their houses and property. Liberation of Rumania meant for them enslavement. First individual peasants, then whole villages fled across the rivers to Bessarabia, at that time in Russian hands; and by 1834 peasants were fleeing across all frontiers out of their own country into Transylvania, then Austro-Hungary, or to the Turkish territory. Galesco wrote in 1856 that over 100,000 families since 1832 had crossed Rumanian borders illegally, fleeing into Bulgaria, Serbia, and Transylvania. "There is rejoicing among the peasants," he wrote, "when the Danube freezes, for they can escape across its solid surface from their sufferings at home."[2] Liberation from foreign rule did not mean at all social liberation of the peasant masses. To the contrary, liberation in national spheres brought more suffering and less personal liberties to the Rumanian peasants.

Poland is another case in point. Poland in the 15th century was one of the leading European powers under the Jagiellos. It was a country of famous and excellent universities, known at that time for its humanism and religious tolerance in times of religious persecutions in Europe. But it was during this period, in 1496, that the Statute of Piotrkow was promulgated. This was the turning point in the history of Polish bondage and the hard slave system was established.[3] The peasants were not permitted to own

[1] Mitrany, David, *The Land and Peasant in Rumania,* Oxford University Press, London, 1930, p. 38.

[2] Mitrany, David, *Ibid.*

[3] Swietochowski, Aleksander, *Historja Chlopow Polskich,* History of the Polish Peasants (in Polish) Warsaw, 1947 edition, p. 117 and following.

or possess land *for all times;* peasants could have only a tenure. If a peasant had more than one son, only one was permitted to leave his master's village. If a peasant had only one son, he had to stay. Many Polish peasants fled to the Ukraine, to join the Cossacks and escape serfdom and exploitation.

Ivan the Terrible united Russia and introduced Moscow as a great power to world history. His reign, cruel as it was, marks the period of the ascendancy of Moscow. In the time of Ivan the Terrible, the free peasants slowly became enslaved. The rights of freedom of movement were step by step limited, and finally peasants were registered and fixed to the land; they belonged to the owner of the land.[4]

Thus, times of national glory and of a political ascendancy of a state sometimes resemble our Thanksgiving Day festivities. It is a great day for human beings. But for the turkeys which are eaten, it is a disastrous day, a *dies irae.* Glorious days of the early Rumanian national autonomy were disastrous for the peasantry. The same is true of the days of the rise of the Muscovite state. What one class regarded as advance—what might have been regarded as progress even by the enlightened public opinion of the day—was degradation for the peasantry.

When Abolition of Serfdom and Emancipation of Peasantry Was Accomplished by Reactionaries and Tyrants

Was the liberation of peasantry always connected with liberal and democratic governments, with liberal and democratic political reforms? History gives us some strange cases, when the liberation of peasantry has been accomplished by conservative or even reactionary rulers, and when the liberation of the peasantry from serfdom was accompanied with limitations of human liberty

[4] Vernadsky, George, *History of Russia,* New York, 1944, p. 69, also Pokrovsky, *History of Russia,* New York, 1931, chapters III and VII; Kluchevsky, V. O., *A History of Russia,* New York, Vols. II and III.

in other fields, especially in politics and in the decline of democratic institutions.

Liberation of the serfs in Austro-Hungary was accomplished by Alexander Bach, the post-revolutionary (1848) Austrian prime-minister, whom Oscar Jaszi calls "The incarnation of the new reactionary system" and whose regime was described by his former comrade, Adolph Fischhof, as "a standing army of soldiers, a sitting army of officials, a kneeling army of priests, and a creeping army of denunciators."[5] After the collapse of the revolution in 1848, Bach organized a classic police state. His system was a copy of Metternich's. Bach, with his absolutist system, abolished serfdom in the Austro-Hungarian monarchy. This great reform did not transform the absolutist monarchy into a democracy, a police state into a liberal and constitutional system.

A similar historical case was Russia. Abolition of serfdom was an act of an absolutist monarchy. True, Alexander II, an enlightened despot, was of a gentler, more humane character than his father, Emperor Nicholas I. With all his personal qualities, Alexander II was not a liberal, and he ruled without a parliament, even though twenty years later, Melikov, his Minister of Interior, made some plans for a State Council. The fact remains, however, that the liberation of peasantry was not followed by a democratic reform. Alexander II said to the nobility: "Better that the reform should come from above than wait until serfdom is abolished from below."[6] The Manifesto regarding the abolition of serfdom, signed in 1861, was not followed up by a manifesto which introduced a parliament, civil rights and democratic institutions. Russia remained an absolute monarchy until the revolution. In Congress Poland, in that part of Poland which was under Russian domination, a democratic national uprising was cruelly and brutally suppressed, hundreds were executed and thousands were sent in chains to the mines and forests of Siberia. Still, in this same Poland, the same Czar who refused to grant this subjugated na-

[5] Jaszi, Oscar, *The Dissolution of the Habsburg Monarchy*, Chicago University Press, p. 102.

[6] Vernadsky, *op. cit.*, p. 158.

tion any liberties and democratic rights had abolished serfdom. It is not within the scope of this essay to explain the reason for this. The fact remains, however, that a progressive step in social relations, the abolition of what was a European kind of slavery, was not integrated with a democratic, progressive reform in other fields.

Incidentally, neither were the peasants themselves always fighting for their own rights. Napoleon, who brought with his flags of conquest the liberation of serfs from age old bondage, was defeated in 1812 by an army of Russian serfs defending Czarist Russia. They did not fight for their social liberation, but for enslavement. Defeat of Napoleon in Russia delayed the liberation of Russian serfs for fifty years. Still Russian peasantry preferred a national tyrant than a foreign liberator.

Is there much difference between Stalin's policy in the Soviet Union and the reforms of Bach, Stolypin, Alexander II, and Frederick the Great? Industrialization of the Soviet Union and higher literacy has been accomplished in a system which is politically oppressive. Democratic civil liberties have been abolished in Soviet Russia. A minority party rules over a majority. A dictator governs in a ruthless way. Compulsory labor is rampant.

The True Meaning of Progress

True progress is a parallel one. This means that a general advancement can be achieved only if it is accomplished simultaneously in economic as well as in political and moral spheres, when all *essential functions and all basic institutions of a society are affected* by our progressive change. This was well understood by the leaders of the great, democratic peasant movement of Russia who called their movement *Ziemla i Wolja* (Land of Freedom). They understood that neither economic advancement without political freedom nor political freedom without economic advancement will accomplish the ideals of democracy. A peasant

[7] See Max Nomad's Chapter II on "Communism."

who gets his freedom without receiving land cannot enjoy freedom in hunger, and if he gets land without freedom, he will suffer slavery or political oppression, though he will have a loaf of bread for his family. A peasant needs both—land and freedom, bread and democracy.

There is a school of economists and political scientists who are trying to argue that we now have to choose between security and freedom, that we cannot have both. Some will go as far as to argue that misery is the price of freedom. But we cannot gamble bread for freedom or freedom for our bread. We simply must have both, we must solve both problems. Moreover, historical experience, the experience of serfdom, teaches us that we cannot have, in the long run, security in economic sense without freedom. If we lose freedom, we shall finally find that our weekly pay has been reduced to a slave's allowance and finally, once we fall into a prolonged period of misery, we may find that hunger and squalor have made us completely dependent upon those who have the power to sign the check.[8]

Those leaders of totalitarian movements who claim that personal freedom is of secondary importance, that it is "a bourgeois prejudice" or does not exist at all, are always clever enough to secure for themselves the right to abuse the freedom of others. They reserve for themselves more than freedom: lawlessness.

Men today are seeking a general system of security: an economic, political and international security. Economic security simply means security against unemployment, protection against misery, a decent standard of living, decent housing and an eight hour labor day. Political security means security against political abuse, protection against the omnipotent power of the state and the abuse of political power by dictators. Political security consists of our Bill of Rights; political security is our sphere of privacy which nobody is permitted to invade. Furthermore, international security is expressed in our desire for lasting peace.

[8] The problem of reconciling freedom with economic planning is discussed by Lewis Corey in his chapter "Economic Planning Without Statism" (XXVI).

War is threatening everyone today, civilians as well as soldiers. The paralyzing fear of bombings and genocide is a curse of our time. These three basic securities form a condition of human welfare. Their parallel development represents true social progress.

Dichotomy and Balance in our Culture

The tragedy of modern culture is that while we progress in the mechanical sense, we are faced with a disintegration of our moral standards. The Europe of the early 1940's under the Totalitarian aegis retrogressed morally and has not yet recovered from the moral blow of the Fascist and Nazi occupation. We are sometimes misled by the fact that we have more students, more universities, and less illiteracy than ever before in history. The lack of illiteracy does not necessarily mean a more ethical society, nor does the growth of the schools and universities mean necessarily moral and social progress. It seems paradoxical that education and general literacy are, under certain circumstances, dangerous and that developments in formal education may be sometimes contrary to the common interest. What was the advantage for mankind that there was practically no illiteracy in Nazi Germany? Is it not better to have an illiterate people, rather than highly skilled Calibans who know how to use machine guns, tanks, planes, and how to kill thousands? Education has helped Nazis, Fascists, and Japanese militarists to develop a war potential and to mobilize the entire society for a modern war that threatened the whole existence of our culture. Indeed, the last three decades were marked by a rapid development of university education in Europe and an increase in the number of students. More and more laboratories, more and more elaborately equipped, were built. Mussolini could show visitors beautiful schools and universities and campuses filled with Fascist students who admired Marinetti's poetry. It was for them that he wrote: "War is beauty because it realizes the mechanical man. . . ." And when Mussolini screamed from the Palazzo Venezia, holding in one hand a book and in the other a gun, he revealed the purpose of his education to be murder—and proved this in the Ethiopian War.

The invention of the atom bomb brings us closer to the problems of morals than ever before. Today, moral progress is as necessary as total employment. Without moral reconstruction, this world, sooner or later, is doomed. The only lasting safeguard against the dangers of atomic energy is the rise of ethical standards in our society, the moral reconstruction of mankind after this war. A moral humanity will use our great technical discoveries for true progress. Technical discoveries and inventions by themselves, without moral safeguards, can easily be transformed into tools for destruction. Hence, the imperative need for ethical advancement, ethical education and moral balance of science.[9] Man felt instinctively that the discovery of atomic energy brought him close to the great dilemma—to fill the gap between our technical advancement and our moral progress.[10] When the great news about the discovery was broken on August 6, 1945, it was hard to find signs of joy, in spite of the fact that it was clear that this meant the end of the war. There was a general feeling of the great insecurity which is now with us. The man in the street felt immediately the coming dangers as an antelope in the prairies feels the approaching danger. In *The New York Daily News* appeared the shortest editorial probably ever written: "The Atom Bomb is here to stay. But are we?" This was typical of what the people in factories, offices and streets were feeling. In a single issue of *The New York Times*, the printed columns of the "Letters to the Editor" page expressed more fear than on an average day of the cruellest war in history. . . . "Let us dump the whole thing into the Atlantic or the Pacific" . . . we read in the column . . .

[9] This problem has been discussed in "Problems of International Education" by Feliks Gross, *The Journal of Educational Sociology*, September, 1946.

[10] A penetrating analysis of problems of social adjustment and cultural lag has been written by William F. Ogburn in "The Hypothesis of Cultural Lag" in his *Social Change*.

"man is too frail to be entrusted with such power." . . . The cartoonist, Low, editorialized the whole matter in his own way. A large old man holds a little ball (atomic energy) in his hand. He stands on the globe and shows the ball to a baby (humanity). The caption reads: "Life or Death. Baby play with nice ball." The president of the United States said: "It is an awful responsibility which has come to us. . . . I realize the tragic significance of the atomic bomb. . . . The atomic bomb is too dangerous to be loose in a lawless world." And a member of the British Government: "We've opened a door. It is yet to be seen what's on the other side of that door—maybe a treasure house, maybe only the realization of a maniac's dream of destruction."

Here is the problem before us: the great problem of our century—adjustment of our international and social relations and adjustment of our moral standards to the pace of modern technical advancement. We have to check the harmful use of the new discoveries by moral and social advancement, and by new techniques in peace-making. And we will make it. Human culture has developed through the creative influence of human needs. The satisfaction of needs gave impetus to human actions and implemented them with new techniques, with new cultural approaches. Our cultural development is a functional one. A need has now been created for moral advancement. Such an advancement can deter men from the harmful use of atomic energy and of other totally destructive weapons. Advancement of our morals and in the techniques of peace making has a definite function in our new society—to prevent total destruction.

For two thousand years or more, man has been studying the science of slaughter or the defense against slaughter. This science is called *strategy*. Thus far, we do not have a name for a science which would teach us how to make and maintain peace. Inasmuch as "peace" in Greek is called "irene," the science of peace, if it is developed, could be called *irenology*. Beginnings toward such a science were made with the creation of the League of Nations and furthered with the United Nations; and weak as these organizations have been, nevertheless, the creation of such bodies for the organization of peace form a great departure from our "sovereignty centered" thinking. The problems of a World Federation and World Government already are being studied. True achievement in this sphere is still a social myth today, but tomorrow, it may emerge as a reality, or at least as a coming ideology—again an advancement of our study of peace.

We have, then, before us two great goals, closely connected: to achieve parallel advancement in the various spheres of social, political and economic relationships; to create a parallel, a balanced, culture by raising our moral standards and readjusting our social and international institutions to keep pace with our technical advancements. This concept of progress is an organic one. It requires a simultaneous, balanced development in all essential fields and phases, a symmetry of ideas which was so familiar to Greek philosophers in their quest for perfection—*Kalos K'agathos*—both beautiful and good.

XXVI
Economic Planning Without Statism

XXVI

ECONOMIC PLANNING WITHOUT STATISM

Planning in the Framework of Liberty

by

LEWIS COREY

THE CRISIS OF the individual arises out of the crisis of liberal democracy, a form of society built on the recognition of man's right to liberty, personal identity, and moral responsibility. This crisis, in turn, is part of the crisis of a changing social order whose drives may lead to greater liberty, or to an absolute state whose power-needs destroy liberty.

True, liberal democracy has not fully promoted libertarian values, and that is one cause of the crisis. But this is also true: it provides the freedoms and mechanisms that can be used to rid itself of injustices and correct maladjustments.

To live and grow, however, liberal democracy must overcome four dangers. It can overcome them, it is my conviction, only if social change is directed into new libertarian channels.

One danger comes from the diehards of capitalist "economic individualism." Undoubtedly, capitalism, for a moment in historical time, promoted the procedures and values of liberal democracy. The promotion was incomplete, however. And most of the economic individualism of an earlier laissez-faire capitalism is now replaced by a monopoly capitalism that limits or destroys economic freedom as well as human liberty. The diehards' fight to save any and all capitalist economic institutions stands athwart progressive social change. Yet without such change totalitarian reaction and the destruction of all liberties are likely.

A second danger comes from fascism. Fascism is spawned by a liberal democracy not wholly clean of feudal survivals, racial discrimination, and hatreds, and by monopoly reaction against liberty—in brief, by a liberal democracy that has not mastered social change for progressive values. Fascism represents a *frustration* of progressive social change. It is total negation of individual liberty, dignity, and self-development. Fascism is barbarism in scientific technological modern dress.

Communism, a third threat, also destroys liberty and degrades the individual, but through a *perversion* of progressive social change. It arose out of an earlier socialism that throbbed with passion for greater social justice and liberty. But Communism sets up a state that is a totalitarian master, with institutional arrangements that, like those of fascism, suppress the liberal-democratic rights of individuals, including individual workers. It is a society in which the people move and have their being exclusively in the state.

A final, more subtle danger, is the drift of an increasing number of "liberals" toward totalitarian ideas. These liberals, in their rejection of free enterprise, also reject, or at least belittle, the libertarian values identified with free enterprise. They blind themselves to the fact that these values are an enduring contribution to civilization that goes beyond particular forms of economic enterprise. The totalitarian liberals (some are undercover Communists, many more are fellow travelers) think and act as if the final answer to all problems of social change is a constant enlargement of state power. They increase the danger of submergence of the individual in an all-inclusive statism.

Is survival of liberty and the individual—their further development through greater economic, social-political, and cultural freedom—a lost cause? It is not, *providing* we muster every resource of intelligence and social action to master the crisis of social change for libertarian values, to work out new institutional arrangements within which all institutions, including the state, will recognize and expand the rights of man in greater social-economic and cultural fulfillment.

The double-talk from "Right" and "Left" has frightfully distorted the meaning of liberal democracy, especially its relation to capitalism. It is noteworthy that both die-hard capitalist apologists and the Communists agree on limiting what capitalism means to "economic individualism and private profit." To be sure, capitalism brought liberal democracy into being, but the relation is historical, conditional, and relative. We need to reject the either-or absolutes of "Right" and "Left." Liberals must break down today's problem into these specific questions: What particular institutions within capitalism promote liberal democracy? What old institutions must go? What new institutions must replace them to sustain liberal democracy against attacks and further promote its values?

There are five chief factors which shaped the progress *and limitations* of the concepts and practice of liberal-democratic individualism.

(1) Revolution against feudalism began with the revival of trade and the emergence of a merchant class. One ideological manifestation was a demand for recognition of "the rights of property." Since feudal lords in their persons combined absolute economic and political power, this was a revolutionary demand. Once won, the rights of property became the rights of such individuals as owned property, and these limited arbitrary power. A new unlimited state power arose, however, in the absolute monarchy (supported by the big bourgeois merchants) that began state monopoly, restrictions, and controls on economic activity. Free enterprise and the laissez-faire state did not emerge fully (and then only in the countries of Northwestern Europe and North America) until after the democratic revolutions abolished the absolute monarchy and set limits on the state power. Free enterprise did not mean profit-making only; it was a concept of economic self-reliance to liberate men from state tyranny. It meant

free men in the midst of economic and political freedom (including free labor), broadening into cultural freedom.

(2) The merchant class early became identified with religious heresy. The new economic interests and ideas clashed with a feudalism whose binding ideological element was Roman ecclesiasticism. The economic and political revolution moved into religion. Protestant stress on individual conscience and individual worth was used by "Left" heretics, from the Hussites to the Puritans and Diggers, to drive in a social-democratic direction. If men are precious and equal in the sight of God, why, they asked, should not men be precious and equal in the sight of man? To be sure, in its extreme forms, one aspect of Protestantism—the emphasis on individual conscience and direct responsibility to God —became anti-social, providing the justification of an unbridled economic individualism that denied the brotherhood of men. But "Left" heretics repudiated this atomized individualism. They insisted that in early Christian teachings the individual is not an isolated exploiting or to-be-exploited thing, but a social individual whose self-realization comes through service to his brethren and through living that fulfills the independence, dignity, and worth of every human being.

(3) Emerging science also strengthened the revolt against authority and provided new technological weapons for economic progress. The scientific revolution of the 16th-17th centuries was a product of capitalism's liberation of the individual from medieval restraints and taboos. In turn, science shattered the old world of faith and dogma; it broke down absolutes, strengthened the rational approach through emphasis on knowledge for doing, manipulation, and control. In their struggle with the church, scientists developed a supreme individualism which learned to ignore all arguments of authority as to the "dangerous" social effects of their discoveries.[1] In the intellectual revolution that followed,

[1] This historical fact combined with later capitalist disdain for "pure science" to develop an indifference among scientists to the social consequences of their work. But, I may add, the primary trouble is not with natural scientists who are not "social-minded," but with social scientists, who fail to keep social thinking and institutional readjustment in balance with scientific, technological advance.

science opened up new worlds of experience and knowledge. The breakdown of old beliefs stimulated individual self-expression and autonomy, which spread, unevenly, through the intellectuals and artists, to all spheres of human activity.

(4) In its early stages, capitalist society virtually excluded the workers from its values: the change from serfdom to "free labor" was left-handed progress. Under an oligarchical liberal government, workers had no political rights. Under the factory system, the worker had no economic rights except to quit work (an empty right, in many respects, but one from which labor developed the strike weapon). In time free workers answered with labor unionism, an invention of the workers themselves, not of middle-class intellectuals. Liberalism had justified individual property ownership as sustaining independence and liberty. The workers' alienation from property thus excluded them from independence and liberty. Workers now used liberal "freedom of association" to associate themselves in unions. This was not only an assertion of economic needs, it represented a demand for the right to self-government and human dignity. Along with the economic struggle, unions became active in the democratic struggle to give the people equal political rights. They brought constitutional democracy to industry through collective bargaining. Labor unions must be credited with a basic contribution to expanding liberal democracy.

(5) The emergence of the liberal democratic state sums up and intertwines all the other factors. Liberty in the modern world began with the limitation or destruction of medieval statism (lay and clerical), which had centered all economic and political power in the lord and subordinated all individuals to one individual. The alliance of the merchant class with monarchical absolutism was in turn overthrown by a revolt of the lower-middle class of small enterprisers and professional people in alliance with peasants and workers against economic and political monopoly. The limited-power state that arose after the democratic revolutions, while it enlarged the areas of freedom, was a "liberal

oligarchical" state that denied to propertyless persons the right to vote. But later, with the rise of labor, the liberal democratic state came into being.

Individualism was thus the product of a series of interacting institutional, intellectual, and moral changes. It was nourished by economic, political, and cultural *diversity and autonomy*, by a *pluralism* in social institutions and spheres of activity which enabled the individual to have a large degree of freedom of choice and action within capitalism. It is this diversity and autonomy, this pluralism, that must be retained in newer forms if we want social change to promote libertarian values.

It it important, at this point, to note the differences between liberalism and democracy, the two elements which were synthesized in the liberal-democratic state.

The philosophy of liberalism emphasizes the individual's liberty and rights under a government that governs least. But liberal practice, because of unequal distribution of economic and political power, gave particular social groups, classes, and individuals the liberty to promote their interests against that of the mass of the people. Earlier liberals, as a matter of fact, were anti-democratic: the liberal Voltaire opposed a republic in favor of constitutional monarchy on the oligarchical British model. Separation of economic from political power broke the political absolutism of feudalism and brought liberty. But it also brought a private economic absolutism through unrestricted liberty of capitalist property. The theory that "that state is best which governs least" became, in practice, the right of an economic oligarchy to govern most.

Against liberalism, the philosophy and practice of democracy emphasized the majority, the people, equality.

Democracy wanted equal political rights through universal suffrage. It wanted, in addition, a measure of economic equality as the basis of political equality and freedom. Liberalism considered ownership of property as necessary for liberty. So lower middle-class democrats (Jacobins, Jefferson, Jackson) started to use the state to end, or at least to limit, the unequal distribution of property. The propertyless people could limit the economic oligarchy's power only through organization (e.g., labor unions) and, above all, by use of a superior power, *the state power*. Democracy pressed for a state that governs more.

State power also grew with the consolidation of nationalism. Liberal philosophers of the Enlightenment were cosmopolitan in their world-view; the democrats were nationalist. Nationalism was part of the popular democratic revolutions, and its first complete expression appeared in the Jacobin phase of the French Revolution. Later movements for national independence identified nationalism with democracy. Then revolutionary democratic nationalism was transformed into capitalist economic nationalism. Together with imperialism it strengthened state power and intolerance (including people's racial intolerance for other people). Wars further increased this trend. The final misuse of nationalism was its distortion into totalitarian nationalist imperialism.

Democratic emphasis on the majority, the nation, and the state develops a totalitarian potential. The danger of statism arises as majorities, the nation, and state become impatient of the liberal doctrine of inalienable rights, and as the state's powers are enlarged because of its intervention in economic activity.

A totalitarian potential is apparent early in the philosophy of democracy. The democratic state, Rousseau argued in his democratic creed, is "composed of all citizens" and expresses their "general will." Hence this state "can have no interests contrary to the interests of any citizen" and so "*it need give no guarantees to its citizens.*" The "general will" as expressed in the state thus becomes an absolute imperative for everyone, alike for majority and minority, "whoever goes against the general will can be constrained by the whole body. There is no room or need for inalienable rights in Rousseau's state, since that state *necessarily* expresses what is good for the people.

In contrast to this, the *liberal-democratic* state — first formulated by the Levellers (left-wing of the Puritan revolution) and by Locke, and developed primarily in Northwestern Europe, the British Commonwealth, and the United States—attempts the synthesis of liberalism and democracy.

Liberal-democratic government is popular, constitutional, representative government with limited powers, in which liberalism and democracy check and balance one another. The doctrinaire radical argument that the checks-and-balances of the American constitution were intended to thwart the people's will is only partly true. Some of the Constitutional fathers distrusted the people, but all of them distrusted state authority and wanted check-and-balances to prevent tyrannical centralization of political power. And today, for all those who want freedom, not totalitarian dictatorship, a decisive problem of social change remains the problem of how to use checks-and-balances under new conditions to limit state power.

It is the central task of the liberal-democratic state to balance and reconcile the rights and needs of the individual with those of the group, of society. The majority governs, but it must accept definite individual and minority rights as inalienable. A majority may want anti-Semitism and Jim Crowism, for example, but majority will cannot make them right or legal, since they infringe inalienable rights. The majority governs, but the minority can criticize and oppose, organize to change majority decisions, government policy, or government itself. So liberalism and democracy, the individual and the people, minority and majority check and balance one another. The idea of inalienable rights is crucial. They arise not out of "natural law," but out of the experience that there can be no individual liberty and dignity without a recognition of rights that no majority or state can violate.

If liberal democracy never worked fully, it is not because of inherent defects, but because of the nature and limitations of *property relations* in its midst.

The liberals saw in ownership of property the foundation of liberty. Since the majority of the people was propertyless, early democrats urged widespread ownership of small independent property as the *economic foundation of democracy and freedom.* It was a functional conception of property: "What I work I own and what I own I work." The America of 1820's was measurably a liberal economic democracy: about 80 per cent of Americans (excluding the slave South) owned small independent property and so depended on no one for the right to work and live. All this was swept away by the surging tide of industrialism, of large-scale industry and monopoly. Today, upwards of 80 per cent of the American people own no productive property—and depend on a wage-or-salary job for the right to work and live. The liberty-giving quality of property is negated by monopoly; and monopoly property becomes, over large areas of our economy, an anti-liberal parasitism of oligarchical absentee ownership.

Much of recent American political history is the story of efforts by small businessmen, the farmers, and propertyless people to use political power to limit or destroy monopoly by government regulation and control. But monopoly has kept on growing. As it grows it calls forth more government regulation and control, with more regimentation. In turn, unbridled economic individualism of monopoly, operating as an oligarchical power complex, using "free enterprise" ideology to mask its destruction or frustration of truly free enterprise as economic and human freedom, marshals every reactionary weapon of monopoly capitalism to resist "government encroachment"—and we have, as a result, the deadlock which has become the universal crisis of our time.

This deadlock brings economic breakdown. In turns, the breakdown compels government to "plan," spend, and tax in order to make the economic system work (while die-hards of "liberal" economics yell about "restoration of the free market's automatic working and controls"). As government increasingly intervenes in economic activity the state that governed least becomes a state that governs more and more. But more government, using an endless succession of controls that do not work within monopoly capitalism, fails to end the economic crisis and drifts toward statism.

It is at this point that the crisis of capitalism becomes acute. If progressive social change is frustrated and helpless, the path is open for totalitarians of the "Right" or "Left" to break the deadlock—by seizing power to implement reactionary social change. Property rights disappear, and so do the rights of man. Under Communism *all* property is nationalized; under fascism it may survive, temporarily, to become merely the right to levy tribute on production and income.

Thus property, as it becomes monopoly, reacts against its earlier liberating function. And this reactionary trend is also fed, in varying degrees, by the other forces that originally promoted liberal democracy and individualism.

Religion, once liberating, becomes increasingly institutional and a conservative force. Lutheranism conditions believers to a blind acceptance of state authority: man is sinful, hence *any* state, since it is made up of sinful men, is necessarily bad, but its authority must be accepted or society breaks apart. You may pray that the sinful men-of-state may behave better, but you cannot oppose them; only if the state interferes with man's personal relation with God can it be opposed on *that issue* (e.g., Pastor Niemoeller, who fought the Nazi state only on the religious issue). In America, Protestant sects have multiplied and become ingrown, while American "fundamentalism" has become increasingly amenable to exploitation by crackpot fascist groups. As the crisis grows acute, the Catholic hierarchy undermines progressive social action with its overemphasis on the exclusive importance of the individual's direct relation with God, and with its atavistic yearning for political power. Recent returns to religion as a force outside life strengthens the escapist effort to solve the problems of society in other than social terms. (On the other hand, Catholics, and other truly religious people, so long as they keep fresh their faith in the preciousness of the individual, may prove valuable allies in infusing social change with libertarian moral values.) The answer to religious escapism is not philosophical but social: a desirable social change that ends the immoral torture of helpless human beings and realizes the moral unity of mankind.

Similarly, some of the social consequences of science, and some scientists themselves, strengthen the trend away from liberal individualism. The wonders and terrors of science are beyond the understanding of ordinary people, who are made to feel insignificant and helpless. Moreover, too many "social-minded" scientists are totalitarian, looking upon human society as a laboratory and upon human beings as guinea pigs. The scientist-barbarians of fascism are a terrifying omen. On the "Left" too there are omens. A British scientist, C. H. Waddington, one of a small group, in the name of "Marxism" which he misunderstands and distorts, calls for a new *"centralized and totalitarian"* economic system that "perhaps" (only perhaps!) may "combine totalitarianism with freedom of thought." In France a group of Communist scientists (among them Joliot-Curie) is merging science with totalitarianism under the name of "scientism" to "reinterpret" all values. Forgetting that not science, but man in history (which includes science) is the source of all values, they convert science into an absolute that merges with and sustains the absolute Communist state. This danger is strengthened by the belief in "scientific-technological determinism," which argues that science can solve all problems and that "values come from technology; building machines to build more machines comprises all that is worthwhile in human activity." These ideas fit easily into anti-liberal, anti-human totalitarianism.

Out of the limitations of individualism came forces and ideas that react against liberty. Much of the criticism of liberal or "bourgeois" individualism was reactionary, from the feudal-aristocratic criticism of Carlyle to the totalitarian criticism of today. Yet liberal individualism was beset with grave evils. Unrestricted "economic individualism" gave rise to profit-individualists who trampled upon individual human rights. The limitations and frustrations of liberal individualism produced many rootless, disintegrated personalities whose individualism degenerated into atomism. Atomistic individualism became a revolt against the individual human being himself. The work of several generations of artists and writers debased the individual until he is no longer a recognizable human being. This was not only an escape from the social relations of human living but an escape from *the task of reshaping those relations* for a freer, more noble individualism. These perversions of individualism gave rise to the "superman" of Nietzsche, the "new Caesarism" of Rodbertus, and the "revolutionary elites" of Sorel, who exult in violence: they all made their contribution to the totalitarian challenge of today.

At the same time a "democratic individualism" was growing up, which gave the masses of the people increasing self-expression through increasing economic means, political liberty, and leisure. This was largely the work of labor unions. But within democratic individualism is latent the danger of a "mass mind" that may become majority intolerance of individual and minority rights. Moreover, while unions realize and invigorate the rights of workers in relation to their employers, in too many cases workers have few rights in relation to their bureaucratic union leaders. I am not speaking of the tiny minority of racketeering unions; they are *sui generis*. A problem of freedom arises in all unions as they grow bigger and more powerful, with proliferating functions and bureaucratic centralization of power. It is this centralization that small communist groups exploit to get control of free unions and transform them into useful party-state unions that are a support of totalitarian tyranny.

All these specific dangers and limitations are serious; added together, they bulk very large. They give arguments and opportunity to sinister forces, individuals, and ideas — "Right" and "Left" — as old institutions and values crumble, and so long as progressive social change is frustrated. Desperation in the wake of pathological social conditions gives an opportunity for expression to "irrational and destructive potentials buried deep in the human psyche." But these irrational and destructive potentials burst forth only if liberal democracy fails to realize that present failures arise from its failure to transform gradual social changes into a new liberal synthesis through specific social changes.

The error of too many "radicals" is to lump together everything "bourgeois" as bad and reject it. On the contrary, there are libertarian moral values in liberal democratic or "bourgeois" society that must be cherished and strengthened, values that mankind has slowly, agonizingly developed since the Renaissance. The attack on these values themselves as "bourgeois" encourages reaction. From this angle we now see that fascism was more than a reactionary frustration of progressive *social* change; it is a deep-going revolt against all the liberal-democratic *values* whose realization today is incomplete, but whose promise is great. Fascism is the first revolution in history that appeals to all that is ignoble and vile in man and erects this into a state system. The pathology of its power-individualism is fascism's most horrible and revealing aspect.

Individualism is on the defensive, while the material means and the ideas for a finer, more broadly available individual life, beyond anything that men have imagined till now, continue to grow. But if we are to use our productive potential for the benefit of all men, we must first institute changes in economic policy and relationship within liberal democracy. Its property relations no longer sustain or promote (they never fully did) the values of individual liberty; moreover, our economic system is subject to severe and constant breakdown.

Even John Stuart Mill, the great 19th-century liberal, saw that private property relations could not be made an absolute. "I saw private property as the last word of legislation in my earlier years," Mill wrote in his *Autobiography*. But later his "ideal of improvement would classify us decidedly under the general designation of socialists." Mill goes on: "While we repudiated with the greatest energy that tyranny of society which most socialistic systems are supposed to involve. We looked forward to a time when . . . the division of the produce of labor will be made in concert on an acknowledged principle of justice. . . . The social problem of the future we considered to be, *how to unite the greatest individual liberty of action with a common ownership in the raw material of the globe,* and an equal participation of all in the benefits of combined labor."

Mill's acceptance of socialism was a thorn in the side of liberal laissez-faire individualists; they ignored him. But Marxists ignored him, too, for his socialism was libertarian and individualistic. (Marxists also ignored Mill's prophetic warning that "*a yoke of uniformity in opinion and practice*" might be imposed on society as "some particular doctrine in time rallies the majority around it, and organizes social institutions comparable to itself.")

Marx has been proved correct in his major criticism of capitalism: that the dynamics of capitalist production drive toward an economic breakdown that makes new economic institutions inescapable. He advocated state ownership of *all* means of production and distribution in order to realize a society where "free development of the individual is the condition for the free development of all individuals." Lenin agreed; but the Marx-Lenin revolution assumed institutional forms *against* liberty and individual identity. Russian Communism has proved that unlimited state ownership under a dictatorship results in the totalitarian submergence of the individual.

Part of the reason for the failure of the greatest social movement of the past seventy-five years is apparent in the insufficient stress on liberal-democratic and moral values. Of this shortcoming Ignazio Silone wrote in 1942: "Many Marxists have shown a sort of contempt for the inner life. Their ideal, as stressed in the novels of Malraux and Hemingway, is the man of steel, the man of action who never hesitates and has no scruples. This conception derives from Nietzsche, and it has lately been expressed much more compellingly by certain fascist writers. . . . Many Communist bureaucrats, who have lost their faith in the always changing party line, as a result of their spiritual self-mutilation can never return to normal humanity. . . . After being a doctrine Marxism has become a sort of drug, a sedative, a sop to one's conscience. Perhaps some day we shall reach the formula: 'Marxism is the opium of the people.' Socialism, however, will outlive Marxism. Today the problem before us is, What sort of Socialism? . . . I stand for (1) an integral federalism and (2) for an ethical conception of socialism . . . which does not demand a new morality or a new justification for socialism. . . . Human liberty and human dignity are conceptions that will never perish."

Silone is right. While the earlier Marxist movement did, in large measure, emphasize liberal-democratic and ethical values, it fell (in its Communist variant) into the trap of using means that perverted or destroyed the very ends it sought.

The Marxist was caught in the pitfall of utopian belief. Man was by nature good; the wrong institutions of private property and class rule alone made him evil. Eliminate capitalist property and rule, the last evil institutions, and man *will* be good. The consequences of the belief were disastrous. Socialism tended to slight moral values and concentrate on institutional change.

At least as important, however, as the conflict between moral ends and means is the conflict between *institutional* ends and means. Marxism proposed institutional means which, in the language of dialectics, turn into their opposite. Marxism insisted on the proletariat as the exclusive carrier of socialism and on absolute collectivism as the foundation of socialism. Exclusive emphasis on the proletariat necessarily alienated productive nonproletarian groups or classes from socialism. This meant that orthodox Marxist parties never could secure an overwhelming electoral majority to introduce socialism by peaceful democratic means. Hence the practical necessity of the Communist resort to minority violence and dictatorship. The dictatorship becomes a new unlimited power-state whose absolute economic collectivism supports absolute state power and engulfs the individual as economic, cultural, and moral being in an all-inclusive collective despotism.

While Marxists minimized Mill's libertarian humanism, the liberals overlooks his plea for a new economic foundation for liberty. Fascism caught them, as it caught the Marxists, unaware. And as liberals today face the pressure for economic reconstruction they may succumb—some already have—to "liberal" totalitarian means and ideas that emphasize the state.

Earlier liberals had a magnificent faith in the capacity of free men to use liberty and intelligence to solve social problems. Today's totalitarian "liberals," apostates from freedom, mired in power-and-elite realism, totally without faith in the "common man" they orally exalt, and in befuddled fear of mankind's irrationality (they, of course, are always rational), have but one answer to every problem: let the state do it! In discussion with totalitarian liberals I find a frightening contemptuous ignorance or disregard of liberalism's achievements and potential. They sneer at American democracy for its imperfections, while they praise Russian Communism for the imaginary perfections it *may* bring.

We have learned that dictatorship of the proletariat, while it claims to be "temporary," becomes institutional and permanent as it destroys liberal democracy. The state bureaucracy builds and lives by force, becomes a new ruling class through absolute *political* control of all economic power, and inevitably must depend on force to keep the absolute state going. Indeed, absolute collectivism (even without dictatorship, though with quicker finality under dictatorship), recombining as it does *all* economic and political power in the state, must impair, if not destroy, freedom. For by its regimental all-collective uniformity it destroys the diversity and pluralism necessary to nourish liberty of individual and group action.

A large measure of nationalization (or socialization) of industry and of economic planning is inescapable. Recent history shows all nations, regardless of ideology, moving in that direction. But evidence grows that complete nationalization, over-all planning, and the totalitarian state inevitably feed one into the other, at the cost of all individual values.

Hence the basic principles of economic reconstruction must include:

1. The limitation of nationalization, or socialization, to large-scale industry. Socialization of monopoly enterprises, which dominate 70 per cent of American industrial activity, is enough to end the economic crisis and to build a new economic order with a policy of production for human welfare and freedom.

2. In addition to this limitation, socialized industry should be made to assume *functional organizational forms* that promote diversity, self-government, and decentralization within a state that, whatever new economic functions it may acquire, would still remain a limited-power state.

In a highly complex, organized world, organizational forms are important, since—depending on their character—they can support either totalitarianism or freedom. Public enterprises must be prevented from assuming forms that promote absolute centralization of economic power in the state. They can and should be autonomous in organization, operation, and direction, independent of government except for over-all policy. The model is the public corporation of the TVA type, but with greater autonomy and with functional directorates representing management, workers, and consumers. These public corporations or authorities are neither direct state enterprises nor under civil service; they are operated as economic, not political, institutions. They provide the greatest amount of decentralization, with authority distributed on successive functional levels, encouraging employee and community participation and regional self-government, as well as greater efficiency. The public corporations in a particular industry are thus not formed into one "government trust," easily controlled by the state's top bureaucracy; they are independent and compete with one another within the relations of planning. A national government agency with final control can be set up to crack down on public corporations *if and when* they violate the mandates under which they operate.

Such organizational forms of public enterprise prevent an absolute centralization of economic power. At the same time they provide diversity and pluralism with their checks-and-balances. Economic freedom is strengthened by retention of free private enterprise in small independent business and in agriculture, and by encouragement of cooperatives.

There is no economic need to socialize small independent business, in which ownership is combined with management; its existence is no bar to planning for economic balance and welfare. This is also true of farmers, all of whom should become free independent farmers under use-ownership, with cooperatives for large-scale farming and for the purchase and sale of commodities and other purposes. Cooperatives, because of their voluntaristic nature and self-government, can be major supports of economic freedom since they are forms of "social enterprise" independent of the state. Free private enterprise and cooperatives alike serve economic freedom by serving as a check-and-balance to public enterprise and the state. They can serve freedom especially in the opinion industries—film, the press, book publishing, radio—where a diversity of enterprise promotes group, minority and individual liberty of ideas, while absolute state control means their limitation or suppression.

National economic planning need not be absolute or totalitarian. It can be limited to strategic factors of policy, price-and-profit, over-all investment (not all investment), with supplementary resort to fiscal measures for desirable social-economic objectives. There can be decentralization in planning, too, down to the grass-roots level. Planning can draw John Deyey's important distinction between a *total planned* society and a *continuously planning* society.

The institutional basis of the totalitarian state, whatever its ideology, is a combination of union management, industrial management, and government management or administration in *one* centralized bureaucratic power that makes the state unopposed and unopposable. Hence free labor unions, as much as pluralistic economy, are an indispensable element in economic reconstruction for freedom. They act as a major check-and-balance on economic and governmental bureaucracy. Moreover, workers will still need free unions to protect and promote their interests, especially their drive for personal independence and dignity.

Conflicts of group and individual interests will continue to exist; they are part of the diversity of freedom. Only those interest-conflicts that impair or destroy liberal democracy should be abolished. As Horace Fries has suggestively argued, a liberal economic and social democracy will encourage the use of creative intelligence through scientific method of fashion mediation techniques for peaceful, cooperative settlement of conflicts on all levels. Proposals for eternal harmony and final perfection through totalitarian power end up in encouraging brutish imperfection, depending as they do on the intervention of the absolute state dominated by an oligarchy of unlimited power-individualists.

The decisive aspect of the liberal economic democracy or liberal democratic socialism (call it what you will) that I propose is this: It consciously, deliberately *proposes new economic arrangements of a kind calculated to retain and strengthen liberal democracy*. The state must be used to set up the new economic institutions; and these proposed arrangements give government more economic functions than were envisaged in earlier liberal theory. But *the state remains a limited-power state* with all the self-corrective procedures of liberal democracy to promote liberty and security.[2]

Liberty, in the final analysis, is a complex of freedoms that depend on the nature of the state. The politics of liberty are as important as its economics: they are interdependent. One truth must never be forgotten. Absolute state power is the enemy of free moral man. Yet many liberals dismiss this danger as lightly as the Communists do.

[2] For a more complete discussion of these ideas see Lewis Corey, *The Unfinished Task: Economic Reconstruction for Democracy* (1942), especially chapters 17 and 18.

One "liberal" political scientist develops a theory of bureaucracy that is a justification of despotic bureaucratic elites. The representative character of bureaucracy, he writes, is necessary for democracy; this "representative" character "must be sought in a common world view [and] in the officials' commitments to the purposes that the state is undertaking to serve. . . . Bureaucracies, to be democratic, must be representative of the groups they serve . . . must mirror the dominant forces in society."[3] This is only a conditional limited truth. For in this sense every bureaucracy, except in revolutionary times, is representative. A fascist or Communist bureaucracy is "representative," since it has a "common world view," promotes "the purposes the state is undertaking to serve," and "mirrors the dominant forces in society." Yet these bureaucracies are despotic, for they serve an undemocratic state that forcibly creates the "dominant forces," decides and imposes the "world view" and "purposes."

Another political scientist,[4] an active "liberal" apologist of Soviet imperialism, has openly avowed totalitarianism: " 'Caesarism' is the state form of the future. Caesarism means 'socialism'—that is, *military totalitarianism* resting on a dynamic faith and will to action . . . an economy *ruled by a self-conscious, respected and purposeful elite*." (My italics.)

Whatever its class origin or ideology, the unlimited-power state destroys freedom because state and society became identical. Hobbes argued: "The power established to maintain order is sovereign, omnipotent to impose its will . . . doctrines of division of sovereignty, subjection of the sovereign to the laws or restriction by the opinion or conscience of individuals are false." Rousseau's "democratic state" simply puts "the people" in place of "the sovereign," and it, too, gives no guarantees to citizens. Locke, on the contrary, drew a liberating distinction between the state and society. His emphasis was on *liberty in society* alongside of popular sovereignty. Government is *one* institution among many

[3] J. Donald Kingsley, *Representative Bureaucracy* (1944), pp. 274, 282-3, 305.

[4] Frederick L. Schumann in the discussion, "Who Owns the Future," the ***Nation,*** January 11, 1941, pp. 36-38; January 25, 1941, p. 111.

social institutions set up to secure ends that the people want. Liberal democracy imposes restraints upon government to limit its power, otherwise the state becomes identical with society and so destroys the diversity of institutional, individual, and group action without which there is no liberty.

Liberal democracy today needs new economic institutions that go beyond the economics of the early liberals. But the state must remain a limited-power state in *a free pluralistic society*. In the words of Hans Kohn: "The characteristics of the state are enforcement and uniformity; the characteristics of society are voluntary cooperation and variety."

Statism submerges the individual and is the mortal enemy of man. Beneath all institutions there is man, the individual. What counts in man is independence, self-reliance, and initiative: his human sympathy, moral responsibility, and decency—his integrity. . . . These values can flourish only as the freedoms flourish.

XXVII
Humanism And The Labor Movement*

* Reprinted from *New Europe*.

XXVII

HUMANISM AND THE LABOR MOVEMENT

By

SIDNEY HOOK

INSOFAR AS IT is possible to speak of a philosophy of the labor movement, it is the philosophy of humanism. Despite the political and ideological differences that at different time have separated sections of the working class from each other, genuine workers' movements have always been united by certain large beliefs. These beliefs are not the less important for being vague and implicit, for finding expression in action even before they reach the level of articulate formulation. They are; that human values are primary to all others; that social institutions must be judged ultimately not by the intentions or rationalizations of those in the seats of power, but by their effects on the workaday lives of individuals; that all social principles and doctrines must be justified by their fruits in enriching the quality of *personal* experience here and now; and that human beings have the resources in themselves and in nature to fulfill all their reasonable needs.

These beliefs explain why it is that the labor movement has been conscious of itself as representing not a narrow class or sectional interest, but the interests of the broad masses of the population. This remains true even if we recognize, as we must, that sometimes, the prejudices and hatreds of the culture in which labor develops infects its ranks, too; for the life of the labor movement, particularly through the multiple activities of trade union organizations, cooperatives, strikes, relief campaigns, constitutes a great school in which national and racial prejudices, imbibed from other sources, are usually blunted and sometimes shed completely.

By and large the history of the free labor movement in all countries shows it to be a staunch advocate of all progressive measures—by which we mean measures designed to humanize man, to educate him, to enlarge his moral vision as well as his material power. Labor movements have come to maturity slowly in a culture whose classical and feudal traditions regarded the activity of labor as a badge of a menial social estate. The conceptions of work inherited by this culture and reinforced by the early conditions of capitalist accumulation were such that the worker appeared as someone not completely human. The struggles of labor have therefore been part of a still-continuing struggle for the humanization of labor, not only in the obvious sense of making the conditions of labor less onerous, but in the sense of imparting to labor a human significance and social status accorded in the past to the soldier, the priest, the banker, the landowner, the lawyer, and the captain of industry. The philosophy of the labor movement not only glorifies abundant leisure but seeks to transform work from being a means of human enslavement and alienation into an opportunity for creative expression.

The implicit humanism of the labor movement has attracted many individuals from other classes who, although not workers by origin or training, have found their calling or mission in its ranks. They have seen, in the emancipation of labor from inequitable restrictions, the emancipation of society as a whole from a world view that puts things in the saddle, that permits human lives to be moulded and blasted by the blind operations of technology and capital.

The humanism of the labor movement also explains why its history is so intimately tied up with the history of *democracy* in the 19th and 20th centuries. No labor movement can thrive without democracy, and no democracy is safe without a militant, self-conscious, labor movement. Everybody understands why the first casualty of totalitarianism is the free labor movement. The labor movement at its best does not act as a pressure group, one among others, snatching what it can for itself independently of what happens to the rest. Where a labor union does act merely as a pressure group, it has succumbed to capitalist ideology. In the long run it fails to command public confidence and cannot resist the weight of other pressure groups that combine against it.

The conception of the worker as a citizen and of the citizen as a worker, which permeates the social philosophy of the labor movement, comes to life in the actual *participation* of the citizen-worker in the activity of his shop, his trade union, his community. This participation, which is still only at its early beginnings, heightens the sense of effective democracy. It has two major expressions. The workers, through a developed and politically conscious labor movement, think, plan, and agitate for measures bearing on health, housing, education, state of civil liberties, social insurance, for themselves as well as for the community as a whole. And through their respective unions they protect their interests in the trade. Insofar as they are members of healthy trade unions, they participate actively in their affairs. They try to ward off the ossification, and, where it exists, to root out the corruption, of machine control. The labor movement forgets at its peril that democracy begins at home. When it does not forget this, it cleans house itself—without the help of Pegler or the police.

The labor movement naturally favors a society in which no fetters are placed upon expanding production of needed goods and services. Expanding production is necessary as much for public welfare as to create possibilities of full and continuous employment. It is not the case, therefore, that the philosophy of the labor movement is opposed to administrative measures of organization and control that increase efficiency. The considered thought of labor has never been hostile to advances in science, technology, and administration. But it does not make a fetish of efficiency. It subordinates consistently the methods and values of technology, industrial and administrative, to the more basic human values—justice, freedom, personal dignity—which may be called the strategic values of the democratic process. From its point of view, the best methods are not necessarily those that are mechanically the most efficient. There is always the human cost to be considered and provided for. Society cannot shrug away its moral responsibilities for the effects of technological and administrative inventions. *And there are some areas of human experience, notably political activity, in which the argument for managerial efficiency is irrelevant if it involves restrictions upon essential freedoms.*

Sometimes this is overlooked. Sometimes the administrative mind which thinks in terms of organization, units, commodities, rather than in terms of human values, makes its appearance even among those who are close to the labor movement. A striking illustration of the administrative attitude that sacrifices human ends for organizational purposes is found in the position of the Webbs during the British-Boer War. They supported the imperialistic policy on the ground that large national, administrative units are more efficient than small. The same attitude was reflected in their support of the proposal that religious dissenters should be taxed for the upkeep of the established church, on grounds of administrative convenience, and in their much more shocking indifference to the fate of working-class freedom and democracy in the USSR—the most ruthless police state in human history.

By virtue of the historic position of the workers in Western culture and of their long and embittered struggles for emancipation, the philosophy of labor tends not only toward political democracy, but to economic and social *equalitarianism.* This equalitarian faith is not the same thing as a desire for dead uniformity, mechanical equality, or regimented similarity. It is at heart a belief in the moral equality of persons, an insistence that all persons be treated with an equality of care or concern. The treatments may differ, just as children in a happy family may receive different specific treatments, but, provided they are *proportionate* to individual need, guided by knowledge of individual history, and coupled with opportunities for further individual growth, in essence, justice will be done. It is always a disquieting phenomenon when the standards of living of different groups in any community diverge very perceptibly; and it is never tolerable that some groups should enjoy superfluities when others lack bare necessities.

In its humanism, its democracy, its secularism, the philosophy of the labor movement is continuous with the best thought of the Renaissance, the Reformation, the English, American, and French Revolutions. It is also in harmony with the teachings of the soundest prophets and rebels in an illustrious calendar that extends from Babeuf to Debs and Norman Thomas.

INDEX

INDEX

UNIVERSITAS
O. M. L.